WHO'S WHO WHO IN FASHION

FAIRCHILD BOOKS

WHO'S
WHO IN
FASHION

SIXTH EDITION

Holly Price Alford

Anne Stegemeyer

A.A.S., B.A., AND M.F.A.
VIRGINIA COMMONWEALTH
UNIVERSITY

FAIRCHILD BOOKS, AN IMPRINT OF BLOOMSBURY PUBLISHING INC.

Fairchild Books

An imprint of Bloomsbury Publishing Inc

1385 Broadway	50 Bedford Square
New York	London
NY 10018	WC1B 3DP
USA	UK

www.bloomsbury.com

Third edition published 1996

Fourth edition published 2003

Fifth edition published 2010

This edition first published 2014

© Bloomsbury Publishing Inc, 2014

Library of Congress Cataloging-in-Publication Data

Stegemeyer, Anne.
Who's who in fashion / Holly Price Alford, A.A.S., B.A., and M.F.A. Virginia
Commonwealth University, Anne Stegemeyer. — Sixth edition.
pages cm
Includes bibliographical references and index.
ISBN 978-1-60901-969-3 (paperback)
1. Fashion designers--Biography. I. Alford, Holly Price. II. Title.
2. TT505.A1S74 2014 746.9'20922—dc23 2014004666
ISBN: 978-1-60901-969-3

Typeset by Precision Graphics
Text Design by Cara David Design
Cover Design by Eleanor Rose
Printed and bound in China

CONTENTS

The Profiles

EXTENDED TABLE OF CONTENTS

The Profiles

This book is dedicated to my parents, Dr. James and Branda Price, and to all parents who love and support their children who aspire to enter the fabulous world of fashion.

— Holly Price Alford

PREFACE

In this sixth edition of *Who's Who in Fashion*, readers will learn about fashion legends as well as newcomers through profiles that are as current as they can be in the rapidly changing world of fashion. This book was designed to help both students and fashion aficionados understand what is happening now and who got us here. After all, where would fashion be today without pioneers such as CHARLES FREDERICK WORTH, GABRIELLE "COCO" CHANEL, and YVES SAINT LAURENT? How have they inspired contemporary designers such as RAF SIMONS, MARC JACOBS, PHOEBE PHILO, and ALEXANDER WANG?

The lushly detailed profiles presented here trace the development of women, men, and brands that have contributed to fashion. In addition to describing their beginnings and highlights, the text provides important basic information about dates of birth (or founding) and death, nationalities, and major fashion awards. Readers will also learn who has worked with whom and where industry names began their careers, paid their dues, and received critical acclaim. Such information is important in explaining how influences and innovations have worked together in the dynamic field of fashion—and how they persist. Was CHRISTIAN DIOR solely responsible for the post–World War II New Look? Who is reinterpreting those styles today? This sixth edition, like those before it, also covers major fashion contributions and significant life events for the profiled subjects.

NEW TO THIS EDITION

This expanded edition of *Who's Who* in Fashion contains more than 300 updated and 73 new profiles of designers, costume designers, jewelry designers, makeup artists, photographers, and writers, editors, journalists, and stylemakers. The newly added profiles to this edition are: alice + olivia, Altuzzara, Marianne Alvoni, Elizabeth Arden, Colleen Atwood, Band of Outsiders, Michael Bastian, Chadwick Bell, Chris Benz, Blonds, Alexey Brodovitch, Burberry, Cartier, Céline, Richard Chai, Eudon Choi, Grace Coddington, Cushnie et Ochs, Ann Demeulemeester, Garance Doré, Marc Ecko, Max Factor, Nina Garcia, Tim Gunn, Prabal Gurung, Richard Haines, Kevan Hall, John Hardy, Donwan Harrold, Hermès, Paul Iribe, Christopher Kane, Karl Kani, Naeem Khan, Steven Klein, Reed Krakoff, L.A.M.B. (Gwen Stefani), Lana, Byron Lars, Estée Lauder, Dion Lee, Isabel Marant, Pat McGrath, Rebecca Minkoff, Leslie Mobo, Condé Nast, Maki Oh, Duro Olowu, Sandy Powell, Preen (Thorton Bregazzi), Rag & Bone, Judith Ripka, Simone Rocha, Carine Roitfeld, The Row (Mary Kate and Ashley Olsen), Rachel Roy, Helena Rubinstein, Jonathan Saunders, Scott Schuman, Raf Simons, Christian Siriano, Walter Steiger, Brandon Sun, Three Asfour, Riccardo Tisci, Tiffany, Reuben Toldeo, Unconditional (Philip Stevens), Ella Von Unwerth, Harry Winston, Christina Yu (Ipa-Nima), David Yurman, and Izak Zenou.

Because this sixth edition covers a broader scope of profiled subjects than did previous editions, each profile features icons to indicating the its profile category. The profiles are categorizes are as follows:

▲ Fashion Designer

👗 Costume Designer

👜 Accessory Designer

💍 Jewelry Designer

▮▮ Fashion Company

❗ Makeup Artist / Cosmetic Specialist

✐ Illustrator

📷 Photographer

▤ Writer / Editor / Journalist / Creative Director

With over 850 color images, this edition will inspire readers with beautiful illustrations and photographs of profile subjects, designs, and merchandise.

FEATURES

Several elements complement the profiles presented in this book.

Timeline

The timeline for this edition starts in 1820, when haute couture and ready-to-wear began, and ends with information such as the evolution of iconic fashion editor ANNA WINTOUR and the purchase of the VALENTINO brand by the royal family of Qatar. This nearly 200-year span of notable moments in fashion and culture shows how the two are linked. The invention of the sewing machine enabled companies to produce fashion more quickly—such as Brooks Brothers, which began making ready-made suits. World War II and, later, the terrorist attacks of September 11, 2001, led to American designs in patriotic colors of red, white, and blue.

Sometimes just one person can cause a fashion upheaval. After Clark Gable appeared bare-chested in the 1934 film *It Happened One Night*, sales of men's undershirts dropped and never quite recovered. In 1981, Princess Diana

set off a major trend for flounced "meringue"-style wedding and prom dresses when she married Prince Charles. Her son William's wife, Duchess Kate, inspired a trend in maternity wear in 2013 when she was pregnant with her son, George Alexander Louis. The book's timeline puts fashion in sequence and in context and features many of the designers included later in the book as well as many other style makers, icons, and significant historical moments.

Awards

Listings for the Council of Fashion Designers of America (CFDA) Awards, Coty American Fashion Critics' Awards, Neiman Marcus Awards, and Fashion Walk of Fame Awards have been updated to include recipients through the time of publication. The British Fashion Awards have been included as a new appendix.

Instructor Resources

Fairchild Books is pleased to offer a robust ancillary package to instructors for the sixth edition of *Who's Who in Fashion*. An Instructor's Guide with Test Bank includes sample syllabi and units based on the timeline in the book, including objectives, key events, and discussion and test questions. PowerPoint presentations provide slides arranged both chronologically and by category, together with key full-color illustrations from the text.

Profile Subject Selection

Several questions are explored to determine the people and companies profiled in an edition of *Who's Who in Fashion*. How have they affected fashion? What have they contributed to it? Did they leave a lasting imprint on the industry? Did they have an innovative design philosophy that secured them a place in fashion history? These are some of the questions that were asked as the list of profiles was compiled. The book also highlights diverse people from diverse backgrounds, helping to show how fashion is truly global. Readers will have their own opinions about who should or should not be included here—that kind of critical thinking and intense debate about fashion is part of what this book is meant to inspire. It is hoped that this book will be useful to students, professionals, and people everywhere with a passion for fashion.

ACKNOWLEDGMENTS

Writing the sixth edition of this book has required a lot of effort and support from other people. As with previous editions, I am grateful to all the designers, editors, artists, stylemakers, and companies who provided key information and some of the beautiful photographs that appear in this book. I also want to thank Donna Reamy, Interim Chair of the Department of Fashion Design and Merchandising at Virginia Commonwealth University, and my colleagues for their support. From Fairchild Books, I owe thanks to former Executive Editor Olga Kontzias, Publisher Priscilla McGeehon, Acquisitions Editor Amanda Breccia, Development Editor Amy Butler, Art Development Editor Edie Weinberg, and Production Editor Charlotte Frost for their guidance and support. A huge thank you also goes to photo researchers Avital Aronowitz-Krasilovky and Sue Howard; as well as Kiley Kudrna and Susan Seeman, who provided editorial assistance. Special thanks to Anne Stegemeyer, lead author of the third and fourth editions of *Who's Who in Fashion* for laying such a marvelous foundation. On a personal note, I want to thank my husband, Thurmond Alford, Jr., for his patience, guidance, and support, and my parents for their unending support.

Finally, I offer sincere thanks to anyone I have forgotten to acknowledge.

—Holly Price Alford

Introduction

FASHION— ALL ABOUT CHANGE

The challenge—and thrill—of fashion derives from the ever-changing ideas, attitudes, and advocates that influence it. No style lasts forever; no notion is set in stone. In fashion, the only constant is change.

So how did the modern concept of fashion emerge and evolve over the past few centuries? Who led it, how, and when? What events, trends, and changes—both inside and outside the fashion world—have had the most significant effects on how people present themselves through their clothes, accessories, and overall personal styles? In keeping with this book's goal of providing a well-rounded perspective of the moods, modes, models, and masters of modern fashion, this section provides a brief overview of the details that follow.

The Rise of the Designer

Because this book focuses on contributions to fashion, it is important to understand how the role of designers has changed over time. Before designers existed, "fashion" meant that men and women followed the dress conventions of their time, which were often dictated by cultural and religious concepts and by the constraints of social class. For example, a farmer's wife in 18th-century rural England or the American colonies might have worn a corset, but it would hardly have been like the elaborate version worn by royalty. Women were their own dressmakers—it was a basic and necessary skill.

ROSE BERTIN, the first designer known by name, rose to prominence in the French court in the 1700s. A dressmaker and confidante to Marie Antoinette, Bertin created many of the elaborate clothes and hairstyles of that period. But she was exiled during the French

Revolution, and many years passed before the next "name" designer emerged.

CHARLES FREDERICK WORTH was born in England in 1825, but he moved to Paris in 1845 and opened a shop there in 1858—and forever changed approaches to dressmaking and design. Instead of making a few dresses at a time for individual clients, Worth designed entire collections. Instead of displaying his designs on dress forms or miniature dolls, he showed them on live mannequins (in fact, his wife could be considered the first fashion model). Worth was the first *grand couturier*, and his fashions reflected a period of prosperity and conspicuous consumption in Europe. They also influenced other couture houses in Europe that opened in the second half of the 1800s. As a result, the concepts of couture and name designers became well known.

Prosperity continued in Europe through the late nineteenth and early twentieth centuries, then ended with the onset of World War I. New couture houses and name designers continued to emerge—such as PAUL POIRET, who worked for several fashionable couturiers before opening his own house in 1904. Poiret's enormous talent and genius for publicity made him the best-known designer of his era. But he was by no means the only one—JEANNE LANVIN, CALLOT SOEURS, and GABRIELLE "COCO" CHANEL were among the many others who appeared on the scene during this time. A number of English designers (such as Lucile) and tailors (such as Redfern and CREED) also established themselves in Paris.

After World War I, a burst of creativity in the arts was matched by an explosion of fresh design talent in fashion—MADELEINE VIONNET, Chanel, ELSA SCHIAPARELLI, and NINA RICCI were among the most prominent examples. Most had begun working before the war but came fully into their own in the heady days of peace. War rationing of materials ended and designs became more elaborate. The exuberance of the times, reflected in the designs of trendsetters such as Chanel and Vionnet, was a relief after the ravages of war. Fashion designers were still centered in Paris, but their designs became more accessible through copies and patterns available almost everywhere.

Balancing Couture and Common Clothing

Up to this point, many popular styles were dictated from on high (Paris). But they also started to be created in response to recent events and inventions. After the exuberance that followed the end of World War I and persisted throughout the 1920s, the U.S. economy of the 1930s required that fashion adapt. Wealthy women might still have been able to travel to Paris to buy luxury clothes during the global Depression, but regular women had to rely on cheaper knockoffs made with fabrics like cotton and rayon.

In addition, leisure activities such as bicycling and boating—and, later, automobile driving—became more common in the United States and required less restrictive clothing for both women and men. As a result, the demand for ready-to-wear apparel grew during this period, and such clothing had become easier to produce thanks to the recently invented sewing machine and increasingly automated manufacturing—and became a necessity when large numbers of people began working in factories and offices.

The Democratization of Fashion

Fashion was changed by the events of World War II (1939–45), especially the occupation of Paris—the world's fashion capital—and the closure of many of its couture houses by the Nazi regime. The war also led many countries to ration fabrics and other materials. Accordingly, Americans had to find new sources of fashion inspiration. CLAIRE MCCARDELL's designs were informed by American women's need for practical, streamlined clothing suited to active lifestyles. Clare Potter, another seminal figure in American sportswear, also preferred simplicity to the ornamentation of European fashions. Less complicated designs also required less fabric. Moreover, the military's need to mass produce uniforms and other clothing during the war made it possible to do the same for civilian clothing afterward—at lower prices.

But designers also began catering to Hollywood during this period—and many such efforts spread to the masses, influenced by film stars like Gary Cooper and Jane Russell and costume designers such as ADRIAN and TRAVIS BANTON. Couture became popular again after World War II, when European designers such as DIOR, BALENCIAGA, and GIVENCHY reintroduced glamour. Still, the broadening accessibility of quality design did not reverse course. Ready-to-wear collections helped make couture designers more profitable and established a new tradition of designers showing their complete collections at annual shows.

Thus the stage was set for designers to be more responsive to consumer needs, creating new directions for fashion. The timeline and profiles in this edition of *Who's Who in Fashion* trace the path of this democratization of fashion as the twentieth century progressed.

Youthquake: The Shock Worn Around the World

Perhaps no period in modern fashion caused as much social upheaval as the one that began in the early 1960s, when a new generation made its rebellious presence felt around the world. Fashion shifted its focus from mature, elegant clients of couture and refined design to young, irreverent customers who wanted to wear nothing that their parents would consider suitable.

Young British designers such as MARY QUANT and OSSIE CLARK gained attention and customers with their anti-establishment creations. New York's BETSEY JOHNSON introduced playful, punkish designs for a youthful clientele and continues to do so. Designers in Milan became a fashion force. French design did not entirely lose its luster, but adapted to the changing times. Powerhouse YVES SAINT LAURENT, for example, crafted the ladylike dresses worn by Catherine Deneuve in *Belle du Jour*—but also incorporated elements of Pop Art into his designs and even glamorized the hippie look with rich, flowing fabrics.

The aftershocks of the youthquake era eased over time, but several concepts have remained and flourished. Ideas for fashion circulate in all directions—Paris and New York are still central, but innovations also come from Italy, Spain, Belgium, England, Japan, and other parts of the world. The clothes that people wear continue to be heavily influenced by pop culture—especially the music business, from rock and roll to punk to pop to hip hop, and everything in between. Youthful styles might seem less extreme now than they did in the 1960s, but currently, the *idea* of youth has been fully embraced: many people want to dress young even if they aren't, and the notion of "dressing for your age" has shifted dramatically.

Changing Times, Different Customers, and New Designers

Only a few thousand women in the world buy couture, and only a small number of them make regular purchases. So how relevant is couture in today's globalized society? This is hardly the first time that the future of couture has been unclear. In 1965, *The New York Times* asserted that "every 10 years, the doctors assemble at the bedside of French haute couture and announce that death is imminent." But while the House of LACROIX's 2009 filing for bankruptcy protection seemed to be a clear sign of the designers demise, after Sotherby's auctioned everything in 2010, Lacroix made a comeback designing for the House of Scaparelli. An article in a 2009 issue of *Vanity Fair* stated, "At the end of January, reversing the direction of the plummeting stock market,

the two grandest fashion houses in Paris, CHANEL and DIOR, were posting sales increases of 20 and 35 percent. As a Paris insider noted, 'Haute couture is still the best way for a designer to get noticed.'"

Fashion's customers have changed. The wealthy society women who once set the standards have been supplanted by film stars, pop music divas, rapper entrepreneurs, and other celebrities of all kinds. Indeed, it has become almost common for entertainers in other fields to branch out into design—and is yet another way for fashion and the larger cultural milieu to maintain their conversation. Similarly, designers have become celebrities, no longer secluded in their studios but out in the open, appearing as guests and judges on television shows such as *Project Runway*, and *America's Next Top Model*.

Some observers have expressed concern that this wide-open, increasingly global fashion market may be moving too fast and lowering its standards. If someone interested in cutting-edge fashion is ignorant of or uninterested in the finer points of dressmaking, what becomes of quality and creativity?

The Luxury Shift

Fast fashion has helped make trends and designers well-known globally—and quickly. The growth of H&M, Zara, and other fast fashion retailers has enabled shoppers to follow trends at lower prices. Despite concerns and assertions that couture is dead—to say nothing of a slow-moving economy—luxury brands saw their sales increase in 2010 yet stall by 2014. By 2014, there was an increase in prices for luxury goods, begging the question whether consumers would continue to buy. Europeans and Asians have long accounted for the bulk of sales of luxury goods; the number of luxury consumers has increased considerably in countries such as Brazil and China. From Asia to the Middle East and beyond, well-off customers have grown in number, purchasing power, and what they desire to buy. And as the U.S. economy recovers, the desire for luxury brands persists. All of these markets are growing, with consumers who appreciate the social prestige that can come with owning luxury fashions. However, there is evidence that western and wealthier consumers are not concerned with the high price points. This is due to the increase in affordable luxury.

Price points have fallen for brands such as RALPH LAUREN, JIMMY CHOO, BURBERRY, and MICHAEL KORS, giving consumers more—and more affordable—choices. At the same time, brands such as Victoria's Secret and Coach have raised their price points to serve the middle luxury market.

In 2003, ISAAC MIZRAHI took a chance by designing and selling an affordable collection at Target. His collection not only made a profit of $300 million a year, but also made average consumers aware of the high-end designer. Similarly, though KARL LAGERFELD revamped CHANEL in the 1990s but maintained its top-tier prices and reputation, he also designed a limited edition line for H&M. Other couture designers have since partnered with retailers and created signature collections with lower price points. Collaborations have included THAKOON PANICHGUL, ALEXANDER MCQUEEN, and ANNA SUI for Target, VERA WANG AND CATHERINE MALDRIN for Kohl's, and JIL SANDER for Uniqlo. These projects introduced the high-end designers to a larger market and made consumers more likely to buy the designers' pricier products. In addition, some high-end brands, such as BURBERRY, have started selling products at outlet stores, increasing their revenues and the number of outlet malls in the U.S. and Europe.

The middle luxury market is especially strong in the Middle East. Luxury designers sell fashions in Dubai and Qatar to willing and wealthy clients. In 2010, Qatar Holdings—which represents the country's royal family—bought Harrods for more than $2 billion. In 2012, it bought VALENTINO for an estimated $858 million. With a new consumer group emerging, and middle luxury booming, luxury brands are seeing their profits increase.

Eco Is In

The first decade of the new millennium saw an increased emphasis on the importance of sustainability for consumer products. From low-priced goods to luxury brands, sustainability became important to many designers and consumers. For example, some consumers want to know where the materials for their clothes come from and how they are made. Designing sustainable clothes becomes important because of the environment where they are made and their social impact.

Many designers have used eco-conscious materials and methods for many years, including STELLA MCCARTNEY. In 2007, the public started to notice celebrities wearing eco-conscious outfits, including Kate Bosworth, Naomi Watts, and Bono. By 2010, eco fashion had become part of the fashion vocabulary and signified a cultural lifestyle change. As *Vogue* put it, "green is the new black." For example, consumers and designers began asking whether the cotton in fabrics was grown organically or using chemicals, and whether the materials used to make products were recycled. In 2012, the Sustainability Index, also known as the Higg Index, was released to help companies determine their sustainability score. Organizations such as the Sustainable Apparel Coalition can help designers produce more sustainable goods by using new methods and better labor practices.

With all the changes in fashion in just the past hundred years, has the expert couture seamstress from the 20th century become irrelevant in the 21st century? The timeline and profiles in this book suggest that the answer is no: the expert seamstress is now honing her skills at companies like the L.A.-based design firm American Apparel, or in historic fashion houses like CHLOÉ and LOUIS VUITTON. One of today's new stylemakers might be a young actress who designs a line of cruelty-free or vegan shoes, who has launched her own t-shirt line, and is seen wearing a blouse from The Gap with a GUCCI skirt. *Who's Who in Fashion* shows how traditions are adapted and respected for their quality and innovation.

Fashion is driven by our thirst for creativity and need to adapt to changes in society. As designer OSSIE CLARK once said, "Fashion isn't just clothes. It's what's happening in everything." Changes on the fashion scene are obviously not in the same class as changes in government policies, potentially preventable changes in climate or changes in civil rights laws. But fashion can change attitudes, and when talented designers emerge, established ones retire, and the lowly "rag trade" continues to grow into a very big business—and quite possibly a sustainable one—it can affect the lives of untold numbers of people around the world.

TIMELINE

THE DAWN OF THE ROMANTIC PERIOD, 1820–60

1820

Number of U.S. textile workers more than quadruples to 55,000, 1820–30

Missionaries introduce Western-style clothing to Hawaiian islands

Early settlers in western United States adopt Native American moccasins and buckskin clothing

Corsets return with lower, slender waistline

Gored, paneled skirts introduced

1821

Skirts begin to widen

1822

Number of U.S. slaves has tripled since invention of cotton gin

1823

Scottish chemist Charles Macintosh patents method for waterproofing fabric

Metal eyelet holes patented

United States adopts Monroe Doctrine, declaring no further colonization in the Western hemisphere

1824

King George IV of England has corsets made for his 50-inch waist

Female weavers in Pawtucket, Rhode Island, are first women involved in U.S. labor strike

Women's skirts become more bell-shaped

Introduction of the full gigot sleeve

John Quincy Adams elected U.S. president

1825

First public steam trains in operation in England, for the Stockton and Darlington Railway

First women-only strike in New York when tailors strike for better wages

United States begins commercial production of calico cloth

Fashionable English men create slim waistline with stays

1826

Women's dresses feature lower waistlines

Lord & Taylor established as first major store on New York's Fifth Avenue

1827

Invention of glass-pressing machine, leading to larger store window displays

Women walk out in protest of bare-legged ballerina in New York City performance

Fan producer La Maison Duvelleroy opens in Paris

T. S. Whitmarch of Boston advertises "fashionable ready-made garments" for men

1828

The Art of Tying the Cravat is an essential guide for men

Parisian chef Marie-Antoine Carême sets fashion for double-breasted white jackets

Full pleated and gathered skirts

Wide hats and bonnets

Andrew Jackson elected U.S. president

1829

First regular police force established in London

Lydia Maria Child's *The American Frugal Housewife* published

1830

Godey's Lady's Book begins publication in Philadelphia, with articles, poetry, music, illustrations, fashion advice, and patterns

Charles Macintosh expands Mackintosh coat business

First ready-to-wear apparel available in Parisian shops

Wide white Pelerine collars keep women's dresses modest

60 percent of U.S. textile workers are women

Men's slim silhouette goes out of fashion

1831

Women wear down-filled hip pads over layers of petticoats

French Foreign Legion founded, with blue tailcoat uniforms

1832

Omnibus passenger service begins in New York

Parasols increase in popularity

1833

V-shaped points introduced for dress bodices

1834

Wider, shorter skirts show off bright silk slippers

U.S. female shoe binders form union

1835

Beau Brummell lands in debtor's prison

French novelist George Sand (otherwise known as the Baroness Dudevant) scandalizes Parisian society by divorcing her husband and wearing men's clothing in public

Small bonnets replace large hats

1836

Women's sleeves become tighter at the top, fuller at the elbow

Sarah Hale becomes editor of *Godey's Lady's Book* and promotes piety, purity, and domesticity

Martin Van Buren elected U.S. president

1837

Godey's Lady's Book states that fashion choices reflect "moral taste and goodness"

Thierry HERMÈS opens harness workshop in Paris

Jewelry store TIFFANY & Co. opens in New York with revolutionary policy of nonnegotiable prices and distinctive blue box

18-year-old Queen Victoria assumes British throne

Captain of the British ship *HMS Blazer* outfits his men in a short, boxy jacket

Collapsible silk top hat for the opera patented

18,000 women in New England employed in shoe and boot manufacturing

1838

Blazer becomes popular with men for boating and tennis

Dark frock coats worn with colorful waistcoats for men

1839

First successful photographic process, the daguerreotype, introduced

1840

Queen Victoria sets trend for white wedding dresses upon marriage to Prince Albert

World's first postage stamp issued, with Queen Victoria's picture

Seal coats become popular in Europe

Cashmere shawls reintroduced as larger wraps

William Henry Harrison elected U.S. president

1841

U.S. Oberlin College first university to grant degrees to women

William Henry Harrison dies of pneumonia after not being dressed warmly enough for his inauguration; succeeded by John Tyler

1842

Frock coats and top hats for men

English writer James Bulwer-Lytton popularizes the color black for men's formal and day wear

Fashion periodical *Peterson's Magazine* begins publication in United States

Wider skirts demand more petticoats underneath

1843

Flounces and overskirts become more elaborate

Modest dark greens and browns the most popular dress colors for women

1844

First news dispatch via electric telegraph

English Factory Act limits women to 12-hour workday

Dressmaking for Ladies: Universal Pattern Journal published in Dresden, Germany

Women wear an average of 15–20 pounds of clothing

James Polk elected U.S. president

1845

Elias Howe invents sewing machine

Brooks Brothers introduces ready-made suits for men, popular with Gold Rush prospectors

Population of San Francisco skyrockets, from 400 to 50,000, 1845–60

New York City established first police force

Fashion for tight sleeves set in small armholes restricts women's movement

United States annexes Texas from Mexico

Paisley prints popular for men's dressing gowns

Boned bodice elongated for women

1846

First patent for the hoop skirt issued in United States

Buckskin remains a staple of Western pioneer clothing

Sailor suits fashionable for boys after Queen Victoria's son has his portrait painted in one

Henry Poole transforms family's shop on London's Savile Row into high-class bespoke tailoring business

1847

Jeweler Louis-François CARTIER establishes workshop in Paris

British Factory Act reduces women's workday to 10 hours

1848

First women's rights convention held in Seneca Falls, New York

European revolutions engulf France, Austria, the German states, and Italy

United States gains California from Mexico

Zachary Taylor elected U.S. president

1849

Amelia Jenks Bloomer launches the Rational Dress Campaign by wearing full, ankle-length trousers topped with a short dress, dubbed "bloomers"

Abolitionist and slave Harriet Tubman escapes to Philadelphia

London hat maker William Bowler invents the derby hat

Safety pin invented

"49ers" swarm into California for Gold Rush

THE CRINOLINE PERIOD, 1850–69

1850

First department store, Le Bon Marché, opens in Paris

United States population reaches 23 million

2 million slaves work in U.S. cotton fields

Women are less than 8 percent of the population of San Francisco

The average U.S. woman has 5.92 children

Isaac Singer invents sewing machine with foot treadle

Zachary Taylor dies; succeeded by Millard Fillmore

1851

CHARLES FREDERICK WORTH marries his model and muse, Marie Vernet

R.H. Macy opens dry goods store in Haverhill, Massachusetts, serving the whaling community

London specialty grocer Charles Henry Harrod opens small shop in the exclusive Knightsbridge district

Singer sewing machines go on the market

Exhibition in London displays new inventions, including rubber

1852

Franklin Pierce elected U.S. president

1853

Crimean War between European powers and Ottoman Empire, 1853–56

Bavarian immigrant Levi Strauss uses heavy French cotton cloth called "serge de Nimes" to create waist overalls for California Gold Rush prospectors

New York's police force adopts blue frock coats with brass buttons

First foreign merchants permitted in Japan

1854

LOUIS VUITTON founded in Paris as designer of quality luggage

Japan opens for trade with the West

Prince Albert is model for fashionable English men

1855

State visits between France and England result in vogue for English fashions in France

Godey's Lady's Book reaches monthly circulation of 150,000

Knitted waistcoat called the "cardigan" becomes popular after the Earl of Cardigan's successful campaign during the Crimean War

Singer expands operations to Paris

The Panama hat displayed at Paris exhibition

1856

Thomas BURBERRY opens first shop in Basingstoke, England

Punch magazine ridicules the crinoline skirt when it arrives in London

Singer introduces installment-buying plan

Young English chemist William Henry Perkin accidentally creates the first synthetic dye

Nurse Florence Nightingale becomes heroine in England after her service in the Crimean War

James Buchanan elected U.S. president

1857

CHARLES FREDERICK WORTH establishes design house in Paris

New York Omnibus Co. raises fares from 7 to 12 cents for "ladies wearing hoops"

New purple "mauveine" color all the rage for women's clothing

Fringe trimming for women's dresses

Police attack women in New York protesting working conditions

The Louvre in Paris expanded under Napoleon III

1858

Godey's introduces gymnastics costumes for women

Manual washing machine invented

Brooks Brothers expands to new New York location, proclaiming the store to be "the most extensive and magnificent clothing house on either continent"

"Fancy dry goods" store R.H. Macy & Co. opens in New York

1859

New England dressmaker "Madame Demorest" introduces the first paper patterns, which sell millions

Central Park opens in New York City

The hoop skirt travels to western United States with pioneer wagons

Charles Darwin's *On the Origin of Species* published

1860

11-year-old girl writes to U.S. presidential candidate Abraham Lincoln, urging him to grow a beard

Subscriptions to *Godey's Lady's Book* reach 160,000

Men's loose, three-piece sack suit introduced

Luxury fashion house Emile Pingat established in Paris

Gored skirts drape over crinolines wider at the back

Nurses at London's Nightingale School of Nurses wear long dresses with starched white aprons

Invention of the band knife speeds manufacturing by cutting through several layers of cloth at one time

Red-shirted volunteer army in Italy sets trend for leader's "Garibaldi" shirt

Abraham Lincoln elected U.S. president

1861

U.S. Civil War, 1861–65

Former slave ELIZABETH KECKLEY becomes Mary Todd Lincoln's personal dressmaker after designing her gown for the Inauguration Ceremony

Southern cotton production in United States falls dramatically

Due to naval blockades, Southern ladies wait for news of French fashions to reach them via Mexico and Texas

John Wanamaker opens first store in Philadelphia, selling military goods

Loose-fitting Garibaldi blouse with bishop sleeves for women

Death of husband Prince Albert results in Queen Victoria wearing only black for the rest of her life

1862

TIFFANY & Co. supplies the Union Army with swords, flags, and surgical implements

Japanese motifs appear in fabric design after exhibition in London

Northern factories record soldiers' measurements, leading to standardized patterns and ready-to-wear clothing for men

Macy's features the first department store Santa

1863

Ebenezer Butterick begins selling clothing patterns in Massachusetts

Ladies restricted to wearing mourning colors of grey, lilac, or mauve at English royal wedding of Prince Edward to Princess Alexandra of Denmark

J.B. Stetson designs eponymous Western hat

Mount Holyoke College adopts overskirt and Turkish trousers as appropriate dress for women's physical education

Emancipation Proclamation abolishes slavery in United States

1864

WORTH's famous peacock gown and headdress designed for the Princess de Sagan

Quick success results in New York office for Butterick Patterns

Macy's introduces elaborate window displays

Worth declares the crinoline obsolete and introduces the bustle

Lord & Taylor opens "mourning store" to dress Civil War widows

Policemen in London adopt the tall helmet hat

Abraham Lincoln reelected U.S. president

1865

United States receives 33 million immigrants, 1865–1930

Abraham Lincoln wears a custom-made Brooks Brothers coat to his second Inauguration; is assassinated wearing the same coat just over a month later

Andrew Johnson assumes U.S. presidency

Large, colorful, sloppy ties popular for men

The Mad Hatter in Lewis Carroll's *Alice in Wonderland* wears signature top hat

1866

Factory-made suit for men (coat, vest, trousers) costs $9.50

English women copy Princess Alexandra's choker and high neckline look

Margaret Getchell becomes the first woman retail executive when she is promoted to store superintendent at Macy's

1867

Empress Eugenie of France wears a WORTH dress at the Universal Exhibition in Paris

Harper's Bazaar launches as weekly fashion newspaper

Butterick launches first magazine, *Ladies Quarterly of Broadway Fashions*

Russia sells Alaskan territory to the United States

1868

First rubber and canvas shoes for men's sports, later known as "sneakers"

Modernization in Japan popularizes Western-style dress

The Englishwoman's Domestic Magazine cautions against combining more than two bright colors in clothing

Narrower cage crinoline frees women's legs in front

Steam-molding process developed to shape corsets

Ulysses S. Grant elected U.S. president

1869

Transcontinental railroad completed in United States

Modern bicycles invented

Baseball caps worn by first professional baseball team, the Cincinnati Red Stockings

THE BUSTLE PERIOD AND THE 1890s: 1870–1900

1870

Franco–Prussian War, 1870–71

Celluloid patented and used for buttons, washable collars, and cuffs

A sewing machine costs an average of $64

20 percent of U.S. population is illiterate

Small black bow ties for men

Population of England reaches 26 million

1871

TIFFANY introduces the "Audubon" sterling silver flatware design

JOHN REDFERN establishes English couture House of Redfern on the Isle of Wight

Great Chicago Fire

Civil war in France

1872

Mail order begins in United States with Montgomery Ward

Bloomingdale's opens in New York selling a wide variety of European fashions

Wider range of synthetic dyes results in bright, contrasting colors and patterns for women's clothing

Looser "tea gowns" introduced for women to wear at home

Narrower, elbow-length sleeves for dresses

1873

First cable cars in San Francisco

Public kindergartens open in United States

Levi Strauss and Nevada tailor Jacob Davis patent the first denim blue jeans with rivets and pocket stitching

Butterick launches *The Delineator* to market patterns and fashion

Economic depression in United States

Sears, Roebuck, and Co. catalogue offers canvas sport shoes for 60 cents a pair

Rise in popularity of inexpensive men's ready-to-wear apparel

Remington manufactures the first typewriter

1874

Massachusetts passes 10-hour workday law

Chicago sporting goods company Sharp & Smith markets the first jockstrap

Edward Degas' painting *The Dance Class* depicts gauzy white costumes

Lawn tennis becomes popular sport in England and United States

1875

Fabric and clothing emporium Liberty of London opens

Pale complexion fashionable for women

Western cowboys wear leather chaps during cattle drives

1876

Alexander Graham Bell patents the telephone

Butterick has 100 offices in the United States and Canada, and branches in Paris, London, Vienna, and Berlin

Rutherford B. Hayes elected U.S. president

1877

Wanamaker's expands to include both men's and women's clothing and dry goods

House of Doucet transformed into leading couture house by JACQUES DOUCET, grandson of the founders

Phonograph invented

Photography book *Street Life in London* depicts secondhand clothing store

1878

Fitted Princess dresses feature elaborate ruched bodices

1879

HERMÈS expands its business to saddlery

Actress Sarah Bernhardt's dramatic style all the rage upon her arrival in London with the Comédie Française

Soap maker at Proctor & Gamble accidentally invents bubble bath

Wanamaker's becomes first department store with a telephone

Thomas Edison invents the light bulb

1880

Burberry invents waterproof gabardine, which becomes popular for mountain climbers and explorers

Harrods in London boasts over 100 employees

Rise in office employment increases demand for ready-to-wear business attire for men and women

Pair of store-bought cowboy boots costs $7

Magazine *The Queen* depicts illustrations of the latest designs from the House of WORTH

James Garfield elected U.S. president

1881

Marshall Field & Co. opens in Chicago

Boater hats popular for men

James Garfield assassinated; succeeded by Chester A. Arthur

Bulgari jewelry boutique established in Rome

1882

New York City gets electric lights

10,000 workers in New York City participate in the first Labor Day Parade

Writer Oscar Wilde proclaims fashion to be "torture" for women

1883

Brooklyn Bridge opens in New York

Alice Vanderbilt wears diamond-encrusted white satin ball gown and battery-operated hat with lights in honor of Edison's invention

The wide "shelf bustle" becomes fashionable

Walking dresses for women feature adjustable overskirts

1884

Peter Carl Fabergé presents his first jeweled eggs to the Russian court

London clothing store Dr. Jaeger's Sanitary Woollen System opens, featuring "healthful" wovens of fine animal fibers

George Eastman invents the box camera

Maud Watson, winner of first Wimbledon ladies' title, shocks by wearing ankle-length dress for play

The Gentleman's Fashion Magazine dictates white flannels, striped coat, and straw hat for boating

Grover Cleveland elected U.S. president

1885

Oscar Wilde and George Bernard Shaw endorse Jaeger clothing

Marshall Field's department store in Chicago opens "budget floor" in its cellar

Little Lord Fauntleroy sets off fad for boys' black velvet suit with lace collar

Elaborate laced flounces adorn evening gowns

Emile Pingat produces dolman-sleeved jackets to be worn over bustle skirts

Women's bodices feature men's-style lapels and high collars

First sleeveless bathing costumes for women

1886

TIFFANY introduces the diamond solitaire setting, which becomes the standard for engagement rings

Skintight bodywear designated the "leotard" after French acrobat Jules Leotard

Man ejected from a ball at the Tuxedo Club in New York for wearing English-style dinner jacket without long tails

Statue of Liberty erected in New York City

1887

Electric trolleys introduced; operate in more than 200 cities by 1889

Macy's ad declares that the store's wares are "suitable for the millionaire, at prices in reach of the millions"

1888

Sears, Roebuck & Co. issues first mailer for jewelry and watches

Jack the Ripper terrorizes London's East End

Invention of Mum, the first deodorant

Benjamin Harrison elected U.S. president

1889

Eiffel Tower built in Paris

Impressionist painter Claude Monet begins series of paintings of water lilies

Singer introduces the electric sewing machine

1890

Men adopt the belted Norfolk jacket for sports and leisure

Wasp-waisted, spirited, sporty, and feminine Gibson Girl makes her debut

Population of New York increases by 1 million, 1890–1900

Number of U .S. women working outside the home rises from 3.7 million to 5.3 million, 1890–1900

Art Nouveau influences fabrics for evening gowns, 1890–1910

Oscar Wilde declares 19th-century clothing "dreary" and adopts satin knee breeches with silk stockings

Feather boas for evening wear

1891

JEANNE PAQUIN opens couture house in Paris next to the House of WORTH

Creases and cuffs for men's pants become predominant

1892

First form of rayon introduced in France

Vogue magazine begins publication as a weekly New York society gazette

FAIRCHILD Publications formed in New York with men's clothing business newspaper

First zip fastener invented

Grover Cleveland elected for second term as U.S. president

1893

Harper's Weekly praises the "evolution of sensible dress"

Shirtwaist blouse increases in popularity for women

First gas-powered car tested in Springfield, Massachusetts

Sigmund Freud begins publishing on psychoanalysis

Off-the-shoulder line popular for evening gowns

Liberty & Co. in London features flowing, smocked gowns

1894

First motion-picture parlors open in New York City, Chicago, and San Francisco

Cover of Sears catalogue emblazoned with "Book of Bargains: A Money Saver for Everyone"

LUCILE "LADY DUFF" GORDON opens dressmaking shop Maison LUCILE in London

Circular lace machine patented

Wide, puffed gigot sleeves emphasize women's shoulders

1895

Bicycling is a national craze increasing popularity of bloomers for women and knickers for men

Three sisters who are experts in lace establish the House of CALLOT SOEURS in Paris, specializing in intricate eveningwear

CHARLES WORTH dies; succeeded by his sons Gaston and Jean Philippe

CHARLES DANA GIBSON marries Southern belle Irene Langhorne, who becomes his Gibson Girl muse and model

Full "leg of mutton" sleeves adorn women's shirtwaists and dresses

1896

U.S. Postal Service begins Rural Free Delivery, bringing catalogs to rural consumers

Massachusetts Audubon Society condemns feathered plumes on women's hats as "barbarous fashion"

Brooks Brothers introduces the button-down polo collar shirt for men

First modern Olympic Games in Athens

William McKinley elected U.S. president

1897

Tailor-made suits for women increase in popularity

LUCILE GORDON stages first "catwalk" style fashion shows and trains professional models

1898

Spanish-American War begins

United States annexes Hawaii

Trumpet skirt for women

Average Western adult wears 20 pounds of clothing, 1898–1907

Bloused dress front for women

Palmolive hand soap introduced

Creased, cuffed trousers for men

Klondike Gold Rush attracts prospectors to the Yukon Territory

Harrods department store installs the first escalator, offers brandy to nervous customers upon reaching the top

1899

Boer War introduces khaki for uniforms, 1899–1902

Population of New York City nears 3.5 million

Vogue initiates its pattern service

Thorstein Veblen discusses fashion in his book *The Theory of the Leisure Class*

Actress Sarah Bernhardt dons men's hose to play the title role in *Hamlet*

CARTIER moves to the exclusive Rue de la Paix, establishing it as the center of Parisian jewelry

Single-cylinder Oldsmobile introduced

THE EDWARDIAN ERA AND WORLD WAR I, 1900–19

1900

Illiteracy in United States declines to 10.7 percent

U.S. population is 76 million

60 percent of U.S. population still lives on farms

462 shirtwaist factories operating in New York City

Average U.S. work week is 57.3 hours

Couture houses display *belle epoque* designs at the Exposition Universelle in Paris

First electric clothes washers appear

Blocky silhouette for men

S-bend "health corset" shifts women's posture forward

Spaulding makes uniforms for the US Olympic team at the Olympic Games in Paris

Average cost of ready-made women's suit is $10

Japanese art on display at the World's Fair in Paris

William McKinley reelected U.S. president

1901

Jergens hand lotion introduced

Hot summer induces men to wear lighter shirts without jackets

Harper's Bazaar shifts to monthly magazine format

William McKinley assassinated; succeeded by Theodore Roosevelt

Queen Victoria of England dies, ending 63-year reign; Edward VII assumes throne

Ruff necklines popular for women

1902

Women working outside the home rises to 25 percent, 1902–10

Flatiron Building opens in New York

National Women's Trade Union League founded

Tea gowns feature the long bishop sleeve

Lunchbox and thermos invented

First Daughter Alice Roosevelt becomes famous for her outfits and antics

Macy's moves to Herald Square flagship location

1903

Viscose rayon fabric introduced

Actress Lillie Langtry appears in *Vogue*

Wright brothers fly first airplane at Kitty Hawk, North Carolina

The front-button negligee shirt for men worn for sports and casual activities

Butterick building opens in downtown Manhattan

Motoring gear includes duster coats, caps, brimmed hats with veils, goggles, gloves, and boots

Ehrlich Brothers store in New York holds fashion show to attract middle-class customers

The Great Train Robbery is first full-length feature film

1904

Colgate launches first toothpaste

Isadora Duncan makes U.S. debut

Women's sleeves become elbow length and fuller cut

Lane Bryant opens New York boutique specializing in maternity dresses

First permanent wave set at hair salon in London

Shetland sweaters for men by Brooks Brothers

CARTIER designs the first wristwatch, for Brazilian aviator Alberto Santos-Dumont, and the "Santos" style becomes a hit

Theodore Roosevelt reelected U.S. president

1905

Spiegel catalog launched

Vanderbilt Cup Race establishes automobile racing as a society event

Slimmer Princess silhouette for women appears

Rolex Watch Company established in Geneva, Switzerland

The fashionable "Arrow Collar Man" debuts in advertising campaign for detachable collars

Albert Einstein announces the theory of relativity

1906

Great San Francisco earthquake and fire

MARIANO FORTUNY designs his pleated silk "Delphos" gown

Pompadour hair style for women

Filmy, lacy afternoon frocks featured in *The Delineator*

Short jackets and circular skirt suits

Van Cleef & Arpels jewelry business established in Paris

1907

U.S. financial panic

Sears catalog circulation reaches 3.6 million in United States

Loosely cut wraps and kimono coats for women

Swimmer Annette Kellerman arrested for wearing one-piece sleeveless swimsuit on a beach near Boston

Number of movie houses in United States reaches 5,000

44,000 automobiles manufactured in United States

Cincinnati surgeon invents Odo-Ro-No deodorant

Straight-line corsets edge out S-shaped curve

Gored skirts

1908

Ford introduces the Model T, which sells for $850

U.S. unemployment rate at 8 percent

Good Housekeeping features the shirtwaist dress

Filene's department store in Boston opens Automatic Bargain Basement

Maytag patents the first electric washing machine

15,000 women march in New York demanding higher pay, shorter hours, voting rights, and abolition of child labor

William Taft elected U.S. president

1909

Ballets Russes debuts in Paris with exotic costumes

Oriental influence in women's fashion

Vogue publishes first cover featuring a photograph

First newsreel film shown in Paris

HATTIE CARNEGIE opens her first dress and millinery shop in New York

Young publisher CONDÉ NAST buys *Vogue* and shifts its focus to fashion

National Association for the Advancement of Colored People (NAACP) founded by multiracial activists

FORTUNY patents his pleating process

Selfridges department store opens on London's Oxford Street with innovative displays and entertainment

1910

Shift to slimmer and lighter clothing for both men and women, 1910s

High-waisted empire line popular for women

Women's Wear Daily begins publication

Mexican Revolution, 1910–20

George V becomes King of England after death of Edward VII

U.S. colleges and universities enroll 350,000 students

PAUL POIRET becomes first designer to launch a fragrance

LUCILE GORDON introduces the slit skirt

Boy Scouts of America founded, with uniforms based on those of the U.S. Army

Strike by cloakmakers increases union power for U.S. garment workers

Brooks Brothers brings the English polo coat to the United States

1911

POIRET creates the hobble skirt

Women adopt empire styling

Cubist exhibit in Paris

Triangle Shirtwaist Factory fire kills 146 working women and girls in Manhattan; factory owners acquitted

Vogue assesses whether women's trousers are "audacious and sensational" or "demure and coquettish"

Men's silhouette begins to slim

Small dogs become a fashion accessory

1912

Poiret tours Europe and the United States to show his designs, 1912–14

20,000 textile workers strike in Lawrence, Massachusetts, leading to public outcry and Congressional investigation

The *Titanic* sinks

MADELEINE VIONNET establishes Paris couture house

Vernon and Irene Castle's "Castle Walk" is a U.S. dance craze

Dark, pinstriped suits for men's business attire

Film fan magazines proliferate

Lucien Vogel launches French fashion magazine *La Gazette du Bon Ton*, featuring illustrations of couture

Slim line for men's suits featured in *Haberdasher*

Henry Ford introduces the assembly line for mass-producing automobiles

Florence Nightingale Graham introduces European cosmetics to American women through her ELIZABETH ARDEN business, along with the idea of "makeovers" in her salon

Woodrow Wilson elected U.S. president

1913

Income tax begins in United States

Marcel Duchamp's painting "Nude Descending a Staircase" causes furor at the Armory Show in New York

Gideon Sundback invents the slide fastener (later called the zipper)

PRADA founded as a leather goods company in Milan

LUCILE GORDON shows draped tea gowns and evening dresses for the spring season

Orientalism reflected in POIRET's harem and lampshade look

1914

Panama Canal opens

World War I begins in Europe

World War I, 1914–18

Black, white, tan, and blue fashionable due to war-time rationing of dyes

American Mary Phelps Jacobs patents the brassiere; later sells patent to Warners for just $1,500

JEANNE LANVIN designs the *robe de style*

Irene Castle shows off her bobbed hair and short, swirly LUCILE dresses in Broadway ragtime hit *Watch Your Step*

EDNA WOOLMAN CHASE becomes editor of *Vogue*

Russian artist and costume designer ERTÉ creates illustrations for *La Gazette du Bon Ton*

Charlie Chaplin makes film debut in *Making a Living*

BURBERRY designs the trench coat for Britain's War Office

1915

Skirts rise to the ankles

Trench coats and great coats for soldiers on the Western front

Belted pullover sweater for women credited to CHANEL

Explorer Sir Ernest Shackleton wears Jaeger on Arctic expedition

Theda Bara portrays "The Vamp" in *A Fool There Was*

Military influence in women's coats and caps

Maybelline introduces the first cake mascara

First electric clothes dryers in use

Invention of lipstick in round metal tube

Lane Bryant expands, with stores in Brooklyn, Chicago, and Detroit

1916

British *Vogue* begins publication

The brassiere arrives in United States from France

German Army issues body armor to soldiers

Margaret Sanger opens first U.S. birth control clinic

English tailor JOHN REDFERN creates first women's uniform for the Red Cross

First U.S. shopping center opens in Lake Forest, Illinois

Keds canvas sneakers introduced

MAX FACTOR markets first commercial eye shadow and brow pencil

ERTÉ joins *Harper's Bazaar* as fashion illustrator

U.S. Congress allocates $75 million to highway construction

Woodrow Wilson reelected U.S. president

1917

United States enters World War I

Converse launches All-Star athletic shoe

LUCILE GORDON designs ready-to-wear dresses for Sears, Roebuck & Co.

Women join the armed services; uniforms include ankle-length skirts

"Womanalls" popular in homefront factories

Cloche hat debuts in Paris

Exotic dancer Mata Hari executed for treason in France

Metal shortage influences corset designs

Russian Revolution topples monarchy; succeeded by Communists

1918

Compulsory schooling laws become nationwide in United States

Sales of women's cosmetics increase in the U.S.

Wartime production lowers U.S. unemployment rate to 1.3 percent

FENDI established in Rome, specializing in furs, handbags, and luggage

Worldwide influenza epidemic kills more than war; practical fashion for gauze masks

World War I ends in November

Russian royal family executed

Women's Wear Daily depicts safety veil as protection against flu

1919

U.S. Congress approves Prohibition

Bauhaus center for contemporary design established in Germany

Actress Mary Pickford becomes known for frilly, little-girl style

Mass-produced, machine-made lace replaces handmade

General Motors introduces installment buying

High U.S. war casualties put American women into black mourning outfits, followed by a decline in the custom

THE 1920s AND 1930s

1920

U.S. Prohibition, 1920–33

American women granted the right to vote

First commercial radio station begins

Ready-to-wear clothing for women increases in popularity

broadcasting in Pittsburgh, PA

French *Vogue* begins publication

Fictional Arrow Collar Man receives more than 17,000 fan letters a day

CHANEL introduces yachting trousers for women

The dress of the decade makes its film debut in *The Flapper*

First diagonally striped "repp" ties from Brooks Brothers

Warren G. Harding elected U.S. president

1921

Bathing suits part of the first Miss America Pageant

Consumer prices plunge in the United States

Kotex appears in the U.S. market

Converse hires basketball star Chuck Taylor to promote its All-Star shoe

GUCCI company founded in Florence, Italy

Actor Rudolph Valentino stars in *The Sheik*

James Joyce's *Ulysses* banned in the United States as "obscene"

First birth control clinic opens in England

1922

King Tut's tomb discovered, leading to Egyptian fashion craze

POIRET introduces pajamas as leisure wear

Vogue conducts first fashion shoot

Mussolini establishes fascist regime in Italy

MAN RAY begins fashion photography for *Vogue*

1923

Economic upswing begins

Sun tanning becomes fashionable

Purchasing power of the dollar doubles, 1923–27

Tube silhouette for women

HATTIE CARNEGIE opens boutique where VIONNET knockoffs can be had for $50

The Arrow Collar Man inspires the Broadway musical *Helen of Troy, New York*

Dance craze "the Charleston" demands shorter skirts

Warren G. Harding dies of heart attack; succeeded by Calvin Coolidge

Lane Bryant's plus-size clothing outsells maternity wear

Hugo Boss establishes men's wear company in Metzingen, Germany

Chuck Taylor's name added to Converse All-Star logo

1924

Liquor smuggling profits reach $40 million

Height of Harlem Renaissance, 1924–29

Maiden Form popularizes the contour bra

JEAN PATOU designs Wimbledon champion Suzanne Lenglen's tennis clothes

Women adopt the short shingle bob

Fans made of peacock feathers popular

Stretch fabric used for bathing suits

The BURBERRY check print created

Saks Fifth Avenue opens in New York

LILLY DACHÉ opens shop in New York

André Breton founds the Surrealist movement

MAN RAY creates his image *Le Violin d'Ingres*

First Macy's Thanksgiving Day Parade

Calvin Coolidge reelected U.S. president

1925

Josephine Baker dances braless at the Folies Bergère

VIONNET introduces gown with geometric inserts

Jazz thrives with Louis Armstrong's Hot Five

F. Scott Fitzgerald's *The Great Gatsby* published

Acetate fabric introduced

Art Deco exhibit shown in Paris

"Oxford Bags" wide trousers for men

The word "zipper" trademarked by B.F. Goodrich

1926

John Powers modeling agency opens in New York

CHANEL introduces the little black dress

Number of U.S. millionaires reaches 11,000

Raccoon coats popular for men

Buying on credit reaches all-time high in United States

"Plus fours" knickers and Fair Isle sweaters worn by Prince of Wales

Gertrude Ederle becomes first woman to swim the English Channel

Rudolph Valentino dies, causing mass hysteria among female fans

Women's dresses rise above the knee

1927

Charles Lindbergh's nonstop transatlantic flight

The Jazz Singer is first "talkie" film

First Academy Awards presented

Pointed handkerchief hemlines for women's gowns

ELSA SCHIAPARELLI opens Paris boutique and makes her *Vogue* debut with the "trompe l'oeil" sweater

Clara Bow dubbed "It Girl"

Babe Ruth becomes first baseball player to hit 60 home runs in one season

Women rush to copy the Louise Brooks bob

Female tennis stars try men's trousers on the court

1928

Disney introduces Mickey Mouse

Jeans appear as fashion apparel

Men's Wear explains the cummerbund to American men

Billboard magazine launches its first weekly music charts

Dubonnet and gin is cocktail of the moment

Women copy Greta Garbo's slouch hat in *A Woman of Affairs*

Hemlines begin to lower

Penicillin introduced

Speedo introduces the racer-back swimsuit

Women granted the right to vote in England

Over 400,000 Americans travel abroad

Double Bubble bubble gum invented

Herbert Hoover elected U.S. president

1929

U.S. unemployment rate climbs from 8.5 percent to 29.9 percent, 1929–32

U.S. divorce rate climbs past 16 percent

Gang violence results in Saint Valentine's Day massacre in Chicago

Sears catalogs sent to 15 million U.S. homes

Mies van der Rohe designs the Barcelona chair

CHANEL's wool jersey suits promote a "total look"

Foster Grant company sells first sunglasses

PATOU returns women's waistlines to their natural position in his collection

CECIL BEATON photographs heiress Nancy Cunard with her signature stacked bangle bracelets

Virginia Woolf's *A Room of One's Own* published

U.S. stock market crashes in October

1930

Drought and dust storms plague central United States, 1930–39

Over 1,300 U.S. banks have failed due to stock market crash

Preshrunk fabric process patented

CHANEL signs contract with United Artists to design costumes for Hollywood stars

Marlene Dietrich wears a man's suit in *Morocco*

Chrysler building opens in New York

MAX FACTOR invents lip gloss

Philadelphia tailors Marliss and Max Rudolphker produce the first mass-market, ready-to-wear tuxedos

DuPont invents neoprene, a synthetic rubber fabric

1931

Elastic yarn was patented

Empire State Building opens in New York City

U.S. Rubber Company, Dunlop, introduces lastex

Edward G. Robinson displays the gangster look in *Little Caesar*

New and improved Technicolor used in feature film *The Runaround*

VIONNET introduces bias-cut gowns

Vogue depicts women's naval-style, bell-bottom trousers

1932

Joan Crawford's frilly *Letty Lynton* dress (designed by ADRIAN) inspires sales of a half-million knockoffs at Macy's

Stretch cuffs for sportswear featured at the Winter Olympics in Lake Placid, New York

Lord & Taylor begins promoting American designers

Hit song "Brother, Can You Spare a Dime?"

Fashion editor CARMEL SNOW creates fashion world furor when she leaves *Vogue* for *Harper's Bazaar* after just three years

Fashion Originators Guild of America founded to protect designers from copying and piracy

Amelia Earhart is first woman to make solo transatlantic flight; designs flying clothes for female pilots

Pablo Picasso's painting *Girl Before a Mirror*

Bras begin to feature cup sizing and adjustable straps

Franklin Delano Roosevelt elected U.S. president

1933

Platinum blonde Jean Harlow stars in *Bombshell*

Tennis star Alice Marble wears shorts at Wimbledon

French tennis star René Lacoste starts his eponymous company featuring the embroidered crocodile logo

Grant Wood's painting *American Gothic* is a sensation at the Chicago World's Fair

Breck introduces shampoo for different hair types: dry, normal, and oily

Gold Diggers of 1933 provides Depression escapism

Amelia Earhart designs clothing for "the woman who lives actively," sold in Macy's and other department stores

Roosevelt's New Deal legislation announced

Hitler takes power in Germany

Hugo Boss designs uniforms for Nazi troops and Hitler Youth

U.S. Prohibition ends

1934

Increasing acceptance of trousers for women leads to the panty girdle

Clark Gable appears bare-chested in *It Happened One Night*, causing steep drop in sales of men's undershirts

Wider shoulders for women's clothing

Hays Code, adopted in 1930, is finally implemented for films, including a ban on nudity, "suggestive dancing," vulgar language, and illicit sex

Dionne quintuplets born in Canada and set off media frenzy

Esquire lauds the English drape suit for men

Fred Astaire and Ginger Rogers dance away in *The Gay Divorcee*

Jazz singer and bandleader Cab Calloway performs in white tie and top hat at The Cotton Club in Harlem

Introduction of "Lady Levi's," the first jeans for women

National Recovery Act limits work week to 40 hours, sets minimum employment age at 16, specifies minimum wage

1935

Social Security established in United States

SCHIAPARELLI introduces hooded Grecian gowns

Revolution in men's underwear when Jockey shorts are patented

DuPont patents nylon

Katharine Hepburn glamorizes trousers

Child star Shirley Temple sets off copycat fashion craze for girls

U.S. Works Progress Administration opens sewing shops

Germany begins first television broadcasts

Italy invades Ethiopia

1936

Spanish Civil War, 1936–39

Jesse Owens wins four gold medals at the Olympic Games in Berlin

Edward VIII abdicates the throne to marry American divorcee Wallis Simpson

DIANA VREELAND begins fashion editorial career at *Harper's Bazaar* with column "Why Don't You?"

LILLY DACHÉ's glamorous hats popular

Tampax patented

Magli brothers establish Bruno Magli shoe factory in Bologna, Italy

Franklin Roosevelt reelected U.S. president

1937

HERMÈS scarf dubuts

MAINBOCHER designs bias-cut dress for Wallis Simpson's wedding to the Duke of Windsor

Peplum suits are popular

SCHIAPARELLI collaborates with artist Salvador Dali on "lobster" dress

Golden Gate Bridge opens in San Francisco

Cole Porter's "I've Got You Under My Skin" is hit song of the year

Japan invades northern China

JACQUES FATH opens couture house in Paris

First fully automatic washing machine introduced

Esquire calls the zipper fly the "newest tailoring idea for men"

Amelia Earhart disappears during flight over the Pacific

Disney's *Snow White* is first full-length animated film

1938

Nylon stockings introduced

NORMAN HARTNELL becomes official dressmaker to British royal family

Ferragamo introduces the platform shoe

Tourism becomes third largest U.S. industry

Debutante Brenda Frazier appears on the cover of *LIFE* magazine in a white strapless dress

Germany annexes Austria and part of Czechoslovakia

WORLD WAR II, 1939–45

1939

World War II begins in Europe when Germany invades Poland

Nylon fibers displayed at the World's Fair in Flushing, New York

NBC television network broadcasts the opening of the World's Fair, and televisions go on sale to the public

Large sunglasses emulate Hollywood glamour

John Steinbeck's *The Grapes of Wrath* published

Gone With the Wind revives interest in the crinoline and snoods

Marlene Dietrich ignores pleas to return to her native Germany and becomes a U.S. citizen

1940

Nylon bras and girdles marketed

German Army occupies Paris; many couture houses close for the duration of the war

American designers gain prominence due to Parisian fashion shutdown

United States registers 32 million cars on the road

Ernest Hemingway's *For Whom the Bell Tolls* published

Carmen Miranda makes her Hollywood debut in her signature

platform sandals and fruit headdress in *Down Argentine Way*

California's population grows 70 percent in the 1940s

Eleanor Lambert creates the U.S. Best Dressed List

Franklin Delano Roosevelt reelected U.S. president for third term

1941

British chemists invent polyester

Hattie Carnegie protégé Norman Norell forms Traina-Norell with Anthony Traina

Clothing rationed in England, 1941–48

Coach leather goods founded in New York, inspired by the baseball glove

United States enters World War II after Japan bombs Pearl Harbor

Red, white, and blue clothing becomes popular in United States

1942

Claire McCardell's "popover" dress is a hit

Women adopt hairnets, scarves, and the "Victory Roll" hairdo

Humphrey Bogart popularizes trench coat and hat in *Casablanca*

U.S. Navy issues the t-shirt

Rosie the Riveter becomes a fashion icon with "We Can Do It!" poster

Y-front opening added to men's underwear

U.S. clothes rationing forbids pleats, pockets, ruffles, zippers, wide lapels, and trouser cuffs, 1942–46

Elizabeth Arden creates "Montezuma Red" lipstick to match red trim on women's armed forces uniforms

Claire McCardell shows models in black Capezio ballet flats

British designers team up to create the "Utility Collection"

Mainbocher designs uniforms for U.S. Navy WAVES

Betty Grable cheers up servicemen worldwide in her iconic pinup shot

Sales of women's slacks increase

U.S. marriage rate at all-time high

1943

Hawaiian and Polynesian prints popular

Eisenhower jacket for men

The one-piece playsuit

Fashion magazines give tips for drawing "stocking seams" on legs

McCardell makes the leotard fashionable

Film director Howard Hughes uses aircraft cantilever techniques to design Jane Russell's steel underwire push-up bra in *The Outlaw*

Photographer Irving Penn begins working for *Vogue*

First known use of the term "supermodel"

Fashion house of Alix Grès closed in Paris after she defiantly shows first collection in patriotic French colors of red, white, and blue

First Coty American Fashion Critics' Millinery Award given to Lilly Daché

Lena Horne showcases her glamorous style in *Stormy Weather*

Baggy zoot suits flaunt wartime fabric restrictions

American soldiers wear Levi's jeans and jackets overseas

1944

D-Day invasion in Normandy, France

American troops liberate Paris

Traveling exhibit *Théâtre de la Mode* featuring two-foot mannequins wearing French couture helps raise funds for war relief

"Bobby soxers" wear ankle socks and saddle shoes

Bomber jackets inspired by fighter pilots

Maidenform designs pigeon-carrier vests for paratroopers

Seventeen magazine begins publication

Franklin Delano Roosevelt reelected U.S. president for fourth term

1945

Dirndl skirts popular

ELSA SCHIAPARELLI launches her perfume Shocking, coining the term "shocking pink"

French designers JACQUES HEIM and Louis Reard introduce the bikini

PIERRE BALMAIN opens Paris couture house

RICHARD AVEDON becomes staff photographer for *Harper's Bazaar*

Franklin Delano Roosevelt dies; succeeded by Harry S. Truman

United States drops atomic bombs on Hiroshima and Nagasaki, Japan

World War II ends

Car ownership in United States doubles, 1945–55

PIERRE BALMAIN shows bell-shaped skirts with small waists; later claims credit for fashion's postwar "New Look"

Frozen foods become available to consumers in United States

THE NEW LOOK: FASHION CONFORMITY PREVAILS, 1946–59

1946

Postwar explosion in U.S. birth rate, 1946–64

Returning American soldiers bring back duffle coats and cotton t-shirts

Rita Hayworth wears a black strapless satin gown by designer JEAN LOUIS in *Gilda*

Men's pant legs become cuffed again

Minnetonka Moccasin company established

MAINBOCHER designs Girl Scout uniforms

Physician Klaus Martens develops a lace-up boot with an air-padded sole to help him recover from a skiing injury

First edition of Dr. Benjamin Spock's *Common Sense Book of Baby and Child Care* published

1947

CHRISTIAN DIOR's first solo collection is a smash hit with his "New Look"

McCall's declares "the short skirt is out of the running"

Nylon becomes available again after war rationing

First commercial microwave ovens

Princess Elizabeth of England marries Prince Philip wearing a gown by NORMAN HARTNELL

U.S. House Committee on Un-American Activities begins hearings

Planned suburb of Levittown in New York

United Nations approves establishment of Israel

England grants independence to India

Women in New York picket stores selling Dior's New Look

First H&M store opens in Sweden

1948

Polaroid camera invented

Berlin Airlift

Marshall Plan begins in Europe

German shoe mogul brothers Adi and Rudi part ways, resulting in the formation of separate adidas and Puma brands

Copies of New Look dresses sell for $24.95 in New York stores

Velcro invented

JACQUES FATH quadruples sales after U.S. publicity tour

Harry S. Truman elected U.S. president

1949

People's Republic of China founded

Cheongsam banned in China in favor of the unisex Mao suit

Vogue features the Brooks Brothers pink button-down shirt for women

Alaska becomes the 49th U.S. state

Abstract expressionist painter Jackson Pollock featured in *LIFE* magazine

LILLY DACHÉ launches clothing line

DIOR shows strapless evening gowns with full skirts

Russia detonates its first atomic bomb

North Atlantic Treaty Organization (NATO) formed

1950

Korean War, 1950–53

30 percent of global population is urban

U.S. population is 161 million

HARDY AMIES designs Princess Elizabeth's wardrobe for her first royal tour of Canada

DuPont produces acrylic

ALIX GRÈS sculpts Grecian-style pleated gowns directly on live models

HATTIE CARNEGIE designs uniforms for the Women's Army Corps

PIERRE CARDIN opens couture house in Paris

Diner's Club issues the first credit card

IRVING PENN collaborates with fashion model wife Lisa Fonssagrives for photographs of the Paris collections

1951

First collective couture show by Italian designers held in Florence

Television show *I Love Lucy* premieres

Marlon Brando sports the "wife beater" undershirt in *A Streetcar Named Desire*

Chinos popular

J.D. Salinger's *Catcher in the Rye* published

JAMES GALANOS opens his fashion company in California

Teens and young men choose between the crewcut and ducktail haircut

1952

Women's coats with batwing sleeves

The tight "sweater girl" look is in with patterns and embellishments

Dr. Martens and a partner open a factory in Munich to meet the demand for the boots he designed

EDNA WOOLMAN CHASE retires as editor-in-chief of *Vogue* after 56 years there

Queen Elizabeth II assumes the British throne

Dwight D. Eisenhower elected U.S. president

1953

Eisenhower wears homburg to his Inauguration rather than customary top hat

First color television available to the public

Teenage girls popularize felt circle skirts

Soviet Union Premier Joseph Stalin dies

Pregnant Lucille Ball wears maternity fashions on *I Love Lucy*

GUCCI opens its first store in New York City

Queen Elizabeth II wears NORMAN HARTNELL dress to her coronation

Marlon Brando adopts the biker look in *The Wild One*

Discovery of DNA structure

TV Guide and *Playboy* magazines debut

1954

CHANEL reopens her Paris design house

Knee-length Bermuda shorts for women and men

Pedal-pushers popular

First Holiday Inn opens

Interest in Western wear sparked by increasing number of Americans taking car trips

U.S. Supreme Court declares school segregation unconstitutional in landmark case *Brown v. Board of Education*

Americans wear cardboard-framed glasses to view the 3D effects of *The Creature from the Black Lagoon*

Bill Haley and the Comets have a smash hit with "Rock Around the Clock"

First color television broadcast in United States

DIOR adds features of men's suits to women's clothes

Dorothy Dandridge becomes first African-American nominated for an Academy Award for best actress, for her performance in *Carmen Jones*

CHARLES WORTH's great-grandson sells the fashion house to PAQUIN

1955

Rosa Parks inspires a boycott of public buses in Montgomery, Alabama

Sportswear designer CLAIRE MCCARDELL appears on the cover of *TIME* magazine

Disneyland opens in Anaheim, California

MARY QUANT opens youth-oriented Bazaar boutique in London

James Dean sports the t-shirt, jeans, and leather jacket look in *Rebel Without a Cause*

DIOR introduces A-line collection and concept

SALVATORE FERRAGAMO debuts the stiletto heel

LILLY DACHÉ appears as a mystery guest on the popular television show *What's My Line?*

Pat Boone's white buck shoes become famous

Marilyn Monroe's white dress flies up over a subway grate in *The Seven Year Itch*

Grace Kelly embodies cool glamour in *To Catch a Thief*

The first McDonald's opens

Polio vaccine introduced

1956

CRISTÓBAL BALENCIAGA creates the sack dress

Gregory Peck portrays *The Man in the Gray Flannel Suit*

Grace Kelly marries Prince Rainier of Monaco in a dress designed by Hollywood costume designer Helen Rose

PIERRE CARDIN is first European designer to open a business in Japan

Fashion magazines depict models wearing colored eye shadow

Fedora hat for men

Publication of Allen Ginsberg's poem "Howl"

Leotards, ballet flats, and "sloppy joe" sweaters typify the beatnik look for young women

Elvis Presley debuts his rock and roll look on *The Ed Sullivan Show*

PIERRE BALMAIN designs Brigitte Bardot's clothing for *And God Created Woman*

The HERMÈS Kelly bag becomes a classic after the new Princess of Monaco is photographed with one

Dwight D. Eisenhower reelected U.S. president

1957

Jack Kerouac's *On the Road* published

Apprentice YVES SAINT LAURENT, JUST 21, takes over at House of DIOR when its founder dies

American women buy knockoffs of CHANEL's collarless wool suit by the thousands

European Common Market established

French designer Ted Lapidus opens haute couture studio and unisex boutique

Ardee introduces hip-huggers

Doris Day shows off her good-girl style in *The Pajama Game*

Eisenhower sends federal troops to protect black students at newly desegregated schools in Little Rock, Arkansas

Soviet Union launches Sputnik, the first satellite to orbit Earth

The Ed Sullivan Show broadcasts "Elvis the Pelvis" from the waist up only

Audrey Hepburn glamorizes the beatnik look in *Funny Face*

U.S. baby boom peaks, with a birth every seven seconds

1958

Bank of America introduces the Visa card

Jeans displayed as part of the American exhibit at the World's Fair in Brussels

London's "Teddy Boys" adopt drainpipe trousers

American Football League founded

American NORMAN NORELL is first designer elected to the Coty Hall of Fame

First Ebony Fashion Fair visits ten U.S. cities, with proceeds going to charity

Skirts begin to shorten

Elizabeth Taylor wears a white silk slip in *Cat on a Hot Tin Roof*

1.4 million Americans travel abroad

Charles de Gaulle elected French president

1959

Mattel introduces the Barbie doll

Spandex invented

DuPont trademarks Lycra

Hawaii becomes the 50th U.S. state

Revolution brings Fidel Castro to power in Cuba

The Guggenheim Museum, designed by Frank Lloyd Wright, opens in New York City

Sandra Dee stars in the surfer film *Gidget*

S.I. Newhouse purchases controlling interest in CONDÉ NAST publishing business

Pantyhose introduced

1960

U.S. population reaches 176 million

MARC BOHAN takes over at House of DIOR after YVES SAINT LAURENT suffers a nervous breakdown

Birth control pills approved by the U.S. Food and Drug Administration

Optical light laser invented

The Barbie doll gets a boyfriend, Ken

Bryan Hyland's song "Itsy Bitsy Teeny Weeny Yellow Polka Dot Bikini" is a major hit

Italian designer Princess Irene Galitzine introduces palazzo pajamas

NORMAN NORELL introduces the mermaid dress

Levi's opens racially integrated plant in Blackstone, Virginia

Dr. Martens boots arrive in England and become a hit with postal carriers, police officers, and factory workers

Chubby Checker popularizes the song and dance "The Twist"

An estimated 1 million American families have bomb shelters

80 percent of Americans own televisions

Designer Richard Blackwell introduces his "Ten Worst Dressed Women" list; it includes Brigitte Bardot, Shelley Winters, and Lucille Ball

John F. Kennedy elected U.S. president

THE 1960s AND 1970s: STYLE TRIBES EMERGE: 1961–79

1961

Kennedy is first U.S. president sworn in without a hat; hat sales drop and the custom fades

OLEG CASSINI appointed as Jacqueline Kennedy's official dressmaker

Women copy Jacqueline Kennedy's bouffant hair and pillbox hat

Soviet Union erects the Berlin Wall

Bay of Pigs invasion of Cuba

Butterick purchases Vogue Patterns from CONDÉ NAST

Russians put first man in space; Americans follow less than a month later

Jeans and sneakers exemplify gang style in *West Side Story*

HUBERT DE GIVENCHY designs Audrey Hepburn's clothes for *Breakfast at Tiffany's*

Audrey Hepburn inducted into International Best-Dressed List Hall of Fame

Disposable diapers introduced

1962

First U.S. television broadcast from overseas

Yves Saint Laurent launches his own design house

Pop Art exhibit at the New York Museum of Modern Art

Marilyn Monroe sings "Happy Birthday" to U.S. President Kennedy wearing a flesh-toned, skintight rhinestone dress by Jean Louis

Andy Warhol unveil "Campbell's Soup Can" paintings

Fendi hires Karl Lagerfeld to design furs

First Target store opens in Roseville, Minnesota

Bonnie Cashin designs Coach purse inspired by the paper shopping bag

Council of Fashion Designers of America (CFDA) founded

Marilyn Monroe dies

Diana Vreeland becomes editor of Vogue

Ursula Andress wears a white bikini in the James Bond film Dr. No

Cuban Missile Crisis brings United States and Soviet Union to the brink of war

1963

Betty Friedan's The Feminine Mystique published

Weight Watchers founded

Galanos presents the smock dress

Mary Quant launches her Ginger Group line of less expensive separates

Martin Luther King, Jr. delivers his "I Have a Dream" speech during civil rights March on Washington, D.C.

Comfort-oriented ECCO footwear founded in Denmark

Sylvia Plath's autobiographical novel The Bell Jar published; fictionalizes her experience as an intern at Mademoiselle

Ted Lapidus scandalizes couture world by opening mass-market boutique in the Belle Jardiniere department store

John F. Kennedy assassinated; succeeded by Lyndon B. Johnson

1964

Vietnam War, 1964–75

The Beatles arrive in the United States with "mop top" haircuts

André Courrèges shows skirts well above the knee in a futuristic, space-age collection

Rudi Gernreich introduces the monokini

Trendy, inexpensive Biba boutique opens in London

Bell bottoms make first appearance as flamenco pants

First Sports Illustrated swimsuit issue features the bikini

U.S. Congress passes Civil Rights Act

Martin Luther King, Jr., becomes youngest recipient of the Nobel Peace Prize, at age 35

Dr. Strangelove satirizes the atomic bomb scare

Levi's introduces Sta-Prest slacks

Boxer Muhammad Ali defeats Sonny Liston for the World Heavyweight Championship

Yves Saint Laurent introduces first ready-to-wear line and opens first boutique, Rive Gauche

Fashion-forward H&M opens stores in England, Denmark, Norway, Switzerland, and Germany

Lyndon B. Johnson elected U.S. president

1965

Mary Quant raises hemlines, making the miniskirt official

Race riots in Los Angeles spread to other U.S. cities

Vidal Sassoon creates his famous angled bob

The Beach Boys have three number one hits on the music charts by this date

Saint Laurent's geometric "Mondrian" shift dresses bring Pop Art to haute couture

"Swinging" London centered on Carnaby Street

"Mod" clothes for men introduced to the American market

Diana Rigg wears a leather catsuit designed by John Bates on the television show The Avengers

Seamless pantyhose introduced

Levi's expands to Europe and Asia

U.S. Voting Rights Act enacted

Debutante Edie Sedgwick becomes fashion icon and Andy Warhol muse

Seventeen magazine states that teenage girls buy 20 percent of apparel and 23 percent of cosmetics sold in the United States

Bill Blass appears in his own ad, captioned "Who needs Paris when you can steal from yourself?"

Rudi Gernreich patents the "no bra" bra

1966

America's apparel industry is worth $15 billion

The shift dress becomes popular

Nancy Sinatra sings "These Boots Are Made for Walkin'"

Mary Quant launches cosmetics line

National Organization for Women founded in United States

Black Panther Party founded in United States; adopts military-style uniforms and berets

Kevlar patented, later used in bulletproof vests

Paper dress fad

Brigitte Bardot sets off fad for Roger Vivier's patent leather Pilgrim Buckle shoe

SAINT LAURENT creates the "Le Smoking" tuxedo pant suit for women

PACO RABANNE shows dresses made of linked plastic discs

Star Trek debuts on television

Female reporter denied entry to fashionable New York restaurants for wearing a pantsuit

Stick-thin English model Twiggy is dubbed "The Face of '66"

1967

Credit card sales jump from $1 billion to more than $7 billion, 1967–70

Green Bay Packers win the first U.S. Super Bowl

"Summer of Love" in San Francisco

Newsweek declares that "the hippies are antagonizing the squares"

Demonstrations against the Vietnam War

Nehru suit jackets for men

GUCCI expands to London

RALPH LAUREN creates his first Polo tie collection

MISSONI shows his first colorful knitwear collection in Florence

Faye Dunaway makes Depression-era fashion cool in *Bonnie and Clyde*

Dustin Hoffman gets more than a glimpse of Anne Bancroft's stockings in *The Graduate*

YVES SAINT LAURENT creates Catherine Deneuve's ladylike look for *Belle du Jour*

1968

Rock musical *Hair* showcases long locks and love beads

Students riot in Europe and the United States

PUCCI's colorful print collection features a stretch bikini and matching velvet robe

SAINT LAURENT introduces the trapeze dress

SONIA RYKIEL opens her first

Paris boutique, specializing in knitwear

Olympic skier Susie Chaffee competes in a silver unitard

Jimi Hendrix releases the album *Electric Ladyland*

Jacqueline Kennedy wears a Valentino dress for her wedding to Aristotle Onassis

American designer Ken Scott features the "hippie gypsy" look in his collection

The Beatles champion Indian-inspired fashion

Puma introduces the suede basketball shoe

Martin Luther King, Jr. assassinated

Democratic presidential candidate Robert F. Kennedy assassinated

First heart transplant performed

Safari jackets for men and women

Richard Nixon elected U.S. president

1969

Barbra Streisand wears see-through, bell-bottom pajama outfit by ARNOLD SCAASI to Academy Awards

Stonewall Riots in New York launch the gay rights movement

Children's television show *Sesame Street* debuts, with appearances by actors Carol Burnett and James Earl Jones, and singer Grace Slick

Hemlines fall with the maxi skirt

PALOMA PICASSO, daughter of painter Pablo, launches career designing jewelry for YVES SAINT LAURENT collection

The Rolling Stones influence eyeliner choices and popularize dangling earrings with their *Gimme Shelter* tour

The Gap opens its first store in San Francisco, selling Levi's jeans, records, and cassette tapes

Richard Burton buys 69-carat, pear-shaped diamond for wife Elizabeth Taylor

Woodstock music festival held in upstate New York

American astronaut Neil Armstrong becomes first man to walk on the moon

JESSICA MCCLINTOCK invests $5,000 in small California company called Gunne Sax, streamlining and beautifying the granny dress

Men's ties widen to at least 4 inches

Cary Grant inducted into International Best-Dressed List Hall of Fame

1970

Ohio National Guard kills four students at Kent State University

80 percent of shirts manufactured by Arrow are colored or patterned

Women's pant styles include knickers, midis, and gauchos

Women's Wear Daily declares that the midi skirt will replace the mini

First Earth Day celebration

Singer Neil Young brings back the fringed buckskin jacket

FAIRCHILD Publications begins publishing *W*

Rolling Stones singer Mick Jagger wears colorful, flowing GIORGIO SANT'ANGELO trousers

Floppy disks introduced

Twiggy retires from modeling at age 20, saying "you can't be a clothes hanger for your entire life!"

1971

Athletic footwear company Nike founded

Hot pants become a fad

ZANDRA RHODES begins producing her flamboyant, pattern-based designs

Lip gloss debuts

Levi Strauss wins Coty American Fashion Critics award for world fashion influence

Flowing caftans for both women and men

Twin Towers completed at New York's World Trade Center

Sonny and Cher wear matching bell-bottoms on their hit television show

Mick and Bianca Jagger marry in YVES SAINT LAURENT suits

Antiwar march in Washington, D.C. draws more than 200,000 protestors

U.S. constitutional amendment grants 18-year-olds the right to vote

1972

King Tut museum tour inspires Egyptian-themed jewelry

OSSIE CLARK commissions then-unknown MANOLO BLAHNIK to design shoes for his collection

Ms. magazine begins publication

Jacqueline Onassis often seen in her trademark oversized sunglasses

Rosie Casals wears decorated tennis dress at Wimbledon, ending the all-white tradition

David Bowie embraces glam-rock look for his concept album *The Rise and Fall of Ziggy Stardust and the Spiders from Mars*

Israeli team massacred at the Olympic Games in Munich

Video cassette recorders (VCRs) introduced to little success

Democratic National Committee headquarters broken into at the Watergate office complex in Washington, D.C.

Elvis switches to jumpsuits for his fall tour

Richard Nixon reelected U.S. president

1973

Ceasefire agreed in Vietnam

Oil crisis and Yom Kippur War, 1973–74

Yom Kippur War, 1973–74

Benefit fashion show at Versailles widens audience for American designers

Bodysuits become popular as outerwear

Revlon debuts Charlie perfume with ads depicting men's wear look for women

U.S. Supreme Court rules that abortion is legal in *Roe v. Wade* case

David Bowie poses with Twiggy for the cover of his album *Pin Ups*

Blaxploitation spoof *Cleopatra Jones* features outrageous stretch chiffon outfits by GIORGIO SANT'ANGELO

Motorola inventor creates first cell phone

U.S. Endangered Species Act spurs manufacturing of fake fur

L'eggs introduces Sheer Energy pantyhose

1974

Richard Nixon resigns after Watergate scandal; succeeded by Gerald Ford

RALPH LAUREN designs Robert Redford's wardrobe for *The Great Gatsby*

Beverly Johnson is first black model to appear on the cover of *Vogue*

Renowned writer and Nobel Prize winner Aleksandr Solzhenitsyn exiled from Soviet Union

Montgomery Ward catalog features do-it-yourself ear-piercing device

String bikinis are popular

First barcode reader installed in Ohio supermarket

ELIE TAHARI opens Madison Avenue boutique

Pam Grier shows off her afro in *Foxy Brown*

Spanish designer FERNANDO SANCHEZ uses dress construction techniques for lingerie

1975

John T. Molloy's *Dress for Success* published

HALSTON's collection features Ultrasuede separates and slinky disco dresses

CALVIN KLEIN and RALPH LAUREN release separates for women inspired by men's wear

REI KAWAKUBO shows her first collection for Comme des Garçons in Tokyo

Tennis player Arthur Ashe defeats Jimmy Connors, becoming the first African-American to win Wimbledon

Microsoft founded by Bill Gates

Patti Smith exhibits androgynous look on the cover of her debut album *Horses*

The Gap creates its own line of basic clothing

Computer-aided design (CAD) starts to be used for patternmaking

Polyester comes into its own with leisure suits for men

Clogs, platform shoes, and chunky boots are popular

Singer Diana Ross designs the costumes for her role in *Mahogany*

First Zara store opens in Spain, featuring knockoffs of popular fashions

1976

Skimpy Dallas Cowboys cheerleader uniforms attract attention at the Super Bowl

Farrah Fawcett's feathered hair—and braless look—generate high ratings for the television show *Charlie's Angels*

Knee-length t-shirt dresses proliferate

Divorce rates double

Digital watch introduced

Olympic gold medal figure skater Dorothy Hamill sports wedge-cut bob

United States celebrates its bicentennial

LIZ CLAIBORNE establishes ensemble-oriented sportswear line for women

Cover of *Punk* magazine features illustration of band The Ramones wearing Converse All-Stars

GEOFFREY BEENE becomes first American designer to show in Milan

DIANE VON FURSTENBERG's wrap dress makes the cover of *Newsweek*

MARY McFADDEN revives FORTUNY-style pleats in her first collection

Jimmy Carter elected U.S. president

1977

John Travolta struts in a three-piece white suit in *Saturday Night Fever*

VIVIENNE WESTWOOD pioneers the ripped, slashed, and pinned punk look at her SEX shop in London

Punk style includes Dr. Martens boots

Diane Keaton's men's wear look in *Annie Hall* styled by RALPH LAUREN

Television miniseries *Roots* sparks interest in African designs

Queen Elizabeth II celebrates her Silver Jubilee in a pink dress by HARDY AMIES

Bianca Jagger rides a white horse onto the stage in nightclub Studio 54 wearing a red HALSTON DRESS

Elvis Presley dies

Star Wars premieres

The Woman's Dress for Success Book dictates that women wear slim, no-nonsense suits

WILLI SMITH's baggy fatigue pants with high, wrapped waists are a much-copied hit from the designer's first collection

ZANDRA RHODES uses safety pins and chains in her punk-inspired Conceptual Chic collection

ISSEY MIYAKE shows oversized sweaters with narrow leggings

1978

RALPH LAUREN shows his Prairie collection

Gore-Tex patented

Sportswear designer PERRY ELLIS launches a line of loose, oversized clothing

Inflation soars to 10 percent in United States

98 percent of U.S. households own at least one television

United States and China establish diplomatic relations

Italian manufacturer Tecnica trademarks the Moon Boot

World's first test tube baby is born in England

Over 900 cult members die in mass suicide in Jonestown, Guyana

The Complete Book of Running causes sales of running shoes to skyrocket

1979

Sony Walkman introduced in Japan

Arab-Israeli peace treaty signed

Illiteracy rate in United States drops below 1 percent

Margaret Thatcher becomes the first female prime minister of England

Bo Derek wears her hair cornrowed as an object of desire in *10*

Peasant blouses popular

Blondie singer Deborah Harry combines New Wave and disco look

Iranian Revolution overthrows the Shah; Americans taken hostage

Sculptor DAVID YURMAN launches jewelry line with braided gold and silver bracelet

Target stores earn $1 billion in annual sales

Nuclear power plant fails at Three Mile Island in Pennsylvania

DIEGO DELLA VALLE turns his father's cobbler business into luxury loafer brand J.P. Tod's

Heiress Gloria Vanderbilt licenses her name for designer jeans

THE 1980s AND 1990s

1980

Richard Gere wears ARMANI suits in *American Gigolo*

NORMA KAMALI releases skirts and oversized tops made from gray sweatshirt material

Volcano Mount St. Helens erupts in the U.S. state of Washington, killing 57

Italian knitwear company Benetton opens first U.S. store in New York City

American Association of Retired People has 12 million members

The television show *Dallas* and the movie *Urban Cowboy* spark trend for cowboy hats and boots

Brooke Shields, then a 14-year-old model, appears in controversial "nothing comes between me and my Calvins" ad campaign for CALVIN KLEIN jeans

PALOMA PICASSO begins designing for TIFFANY & Co.

VHS defeats Betamax as the VCR format of choice

The Preppy Handbook revives interest in Lacoste polo shirts and madras plaid

Musician John Lennon assassinated

Ronald Reagan elected U.S. president

1981

MTV debuts, and videos quickly become a standard part of music marketing

JAMES GALANOS designs Nancy Reagan's one-shouldered Inauguration gown

LAURA ASHLEY designs are a favorite of Lady Diana Spencer's "Sloane Ranger" set

The television show *Dynasty* debuts, featuring Joan Collins and Linda Evans in glamorous costumes by Nolan Miller

John Hinckley, Jr. claims that an obsession with actress Jodie Foster prompted his attempt to kill President Reagan

Polartec fleece invented

Coach opens flagship store in New York

First factory outlet center opens in Burlington, North Carolina

OSCAR DE LA RENTA updates the Boy Scouts uniform

GIORGIO ARMANI becomes the first designer to launch a lower-priced "diffusion" line, Emporio Armani

Princess Diana's romantic wedding dress designed by husband and wife team David and ELIZABETH EMANUEL

STEPHEN JONES opens his first millinery shop in London and becomes a hit with club-goers

VIVIENNE WESTWOOD's Pirate collection ushers in New Romantic genre

AZZEDINE ALAÏA's first collection earns him the sobriquet "King of Cling"

U.S. Space Shuttle *Columbia* is successfully launched

1982

THIERRY MUGLER shows the wedge dress with exaggerated shoulder pads

Vogue calls Boy George of the band Culture Club a "mover and shaker" of the new club scene

KENNETH COLE kick-starts his business by selling 40,000 pairs of shoes in two and a half days at New York's Market Week

Workout headbands become fashion fad after Olivia Newton-John wears one in her music video for "Physical"

Princess Diana affects the big-shouldered glam look

Photographer BRUCE WEBER shoots his first ad campaign for CALVIN KLEIN underwear, featuring pole vaulter Tom Hintnaus

The Vietnam Veterans Memorial, designed by Yale University student Maya Lin, opens in Washington, D.C.

Compact discs (CDs) start being sold

Grace Kelly dies in car crash

Jane Fonda's workout videos ignite interest in gymwear

Margaret Thatcher becomes famous for her economic policies—and power suits

1983

TIME magazine names the computer its "man of the year"

Swatch wristwatch launched

Flashdance sets off craze for leg warmers and drop-shouldered sweatshirts

Michael Jackson moonwalks while wearing one white glove in his video for "Billie Jean"

President Reagan refers to the Soviet Union as the "evil empire"

First commercial cell phone service available in the United States

The term "yuppie" coined for materialistic young urban professionals

J.Crew catalog launched

Princess Stephanie of Monaco apprentices at DIOR

KARL LAGERFELD becomes design director at CHANEL

VIVIENNE WESTWOOD creates designs using prints by graffiti artist Keith Haring

Elizabeth Taylor appears in Blackglama fur ad with the tagline, "What becomes a legend most?"

Sony begins selling the Discman, the first portable CD player

REI KAWAKUBO's collection for Comme des Garçons is dubbed "post-Holocaust" after its Paris debut

Demand for Ray-Ban sunglasses jumps after Tom Cruise wears them in *Risky Business*

Prince introduces his purple-hued, ruffled, romantic look in his video for "Little Red Corvette"

Gap Inc. buys Banana Republic, a two-store safari and travel clothing company

Dooney & Bourke develop the All-Weather Leather bag

U.S. Embassy bombed in Beirut, Lebanon

1984

Apple introduces the Macintosh computer

Human immunodeficiency virus (HIV)—the precursor to AIDS—identified by French and American researchers

CALVIN KLEIN launches Obsession perfume

Russell Simmons and Rick Rubin launch Def Jam Records

Television show *Lifestyles of the Rich and Famous* debuts

Retailer Uniqlo opens its first store in Japan

Design Industries Foundation Fighting AIDS (DIFFA) established

Jay McInerney's *Bright Lights, Big City* published; is first yuppie coming-of-age novel

MAC Cosmetics founded to create makeup suitable for fashion photography

Men begin wearing t-shirts under suit jackets, inspired by television show *Miami Vice*

Sales of Levi's 501 jeans surge

Nancy Reagan's favored color for her oft-worn ADOLFO suits becomes known as "Reagan red"

Amadeus inspires 18th-century clothing revival in clubwear

Surfer-inspired Reef sandal company founded in California

Ronald Reagan reelected U.S. president

1985

Levi's introduces Dockers khakis

Madonna shows off her street style in *Desperately Seeking Susan*

DONNA KARAN launches her first collection, featuring the jersey body suit and wrap skirts

"High-thigh" one-piece swimsuits for women

Anne White's skintight jumpsuit is banned from future Wimbledon matches for being "not traditional"

WILLI SMITH designs uniforms for workers who help artist Christo wrap the Pont Neuf bridge in Paris

Wreckage of the *Titanic* located

Benetton begins series of multiethnic, socially conscious ads

PRADA issues the black nylon backpack

Spanish chain Zara shortens period between clothing design and distribution to less than two weeks

Rock Hudson dies; was first celebrity to announce that he had AIDS

Automated teller machines (ATMs) widespread

Michael Jackson and other recording stars collaborate on "We Are the World" to raise funds for famine relief in Ethiopia

Madonna channels Marilyn Monroe in her video for "Material Girl"

KARL LAGERFELD's summer collection for CHANEL features a Watteau-inspired suit

Mikhail Gorbachev becomes head of the Soviet Union, proposes reform policies of *glasnost* and *perestroika*

1986

Cher wears black-beaded, midriff-baring BOB MACKIE gown with feather headdress to the Academy Awards

Rap group Run-D.M.C. performs in adidas Superstars

QVC home shopping network founded

Princess Stephanie launches swimwear line

Edwin Schlossberg wears a blue linen suit with silver tie designed by WILLI SMITH for his wedding to Caroline Kennedy; her gown is by CAROLINE HERRERA

Explosion at nuclear power plant in Chernobyl (then part of the Soviet Union; now part of Ukraine) sends radioactive fallout over the Soviet Union and Europe

Reagan administration embroiled in the Iran-Contra Affair

Professional women adopt THIERRY MUGLER's power suit look

Stirrup pants and oversized geometrically patterned sweaters for women

U.S. Space Shuttle *Challenger* explodes after liftoff

1987

New York's Fashion Institute of Technology mounts *Three Women:* KAWAKUBO, VIONNET, McCARDELL exhibit

Michael Douglas, playing Gordon Gekko in *Wall Street,* asserts that "greed is good"

Hugo Boss suits exemplify "power dressing" for men

CHRISTIAN LACROIX introduces the pouf skirt

MARC JACOBS receives the second Perry Ellis Award for New Fashion Talent from the Council of Fashion Designers of America (CFDA), at age 23

George Michael dances in ripped acid-wash jeans in his video for "Faith"

Men spend $1 billion on toiletries and grooming products—twice as much as 10 years earlier

Debit card introduced

Acid-wash jeans and matching jackets for women and men

Musée des Arts de la Mode in Paris holds a major DIOR retrospective

Merger between LOUIS VUITTON AND Moët Hennessy results in LVMH luxury goods conglomerate

U.S. stock market crashes in October

1988

DONNA KARAN introduces less expensive DKNY line

Working Girl depicts the yuppie wannabe style of wearing high-top sneakers and white socks with suits for the commute to work

More than 22 million personal computers sold

Track star Florence Griffith-Joyner competes at the Seoul Olympics wearing a lace bodysuit

Retail giant Walmart posts $20 billion in sales

ANNA WINTOUR becomes editor-in-chief of *Vogue*

South African businessman Johann Rupert establishes Richemont luxury goods group, including part ownership in CARTIER and CHLOÉ

George H.W. Bush elected U.S. president

1989

MIUCCIA PRADA shows her first ready-to-wear collection

Leggings outsell jeans in some parts of the United States

Parsons School of Design honors Lena Horne for her contributions to fashion

First commercial production of microfibers in the United States

J.Crew opens its first store, in New York

Legendary *Vogue* editor DIANA VREELAND dies

United States invades Panama

Berlin Wall falls

Opening of the glass pyramid at the Louvre, designed by I.M. Pei

1990

GIANNI VERSACE launches couture line

U.S. population reaches 248 million

Michelle Pfeiffer wears understated ARMANI dress to the Academy Awards

George Michael's hit video for "Freedom" features lip-synching supermodels

The New York Times runs front-page article titled "The Green Movement in the Fashion World"

RIFAT OZBEK shows all-white collection

JEAN PAUL GAULTIER designs satin corset with cone bra for Madonna's *Blonde Ambition* tour

East and West Germany reunify

Iraq invades Kuwait, leading to the Gulf War

Linda Evangelista, speaking for herself and fellow supermodels, says "We don't wake up for less than $10,000 a day"

Jockey introduces a string bikini for men

MC Hammer sports harem pants in his video for "U Can't Touch This"

VERA WANG establishes her bridal business, featuring sleek, modern gowns

babyGap established

1991

Soviet Union collapses

Recession hits United States

Princess Diana appears on the cover of *Vogue* wearing a plain black sweater

CHRISTIAN LOUBOUTIN opens boutique in Paris featuring his signature red-soled shoes

Seattle grunge scene explodes after Nirvana's hit "Smells Like Teen Spirit"

ANNA SUI shows first collection

Supermodel Christy Turlington signs $800,000 yearly contract with Maybelline

Balkan wars begin in former Yugoslavia, continue through 1998

Gulf War inspires yellow ribbon campaign in support of U.S. troops

Modern art takes a new turn with Damien Hirst's "The Physical Impossibility of Death in the Mind of Someone Living," a work consisting of a shark preserved in formaldehyde in a display case

Douglas Coupland's *Generation X* published, coining a term for marketers worldwide

Elizabeth Taylor wears VALENTINO for her eighth wedding

Environmentally friendly fabric Lyocell developed

1992

Mall of America opens in Bloomington, Minnesota with more than 330 stores, as

well as movie theaters and an amusement park

European Union formed

Vogue's April cover features supermodels in white shirts and jeans from The Gap

Minimalism replaces excesses of the 1980s

Khaki camouflage pattern popular

Belgian deconstructionist ANN DEMEULEMEESTER debuts her first collection in Paris

Sicilian duo DOLCE & GABBANA revive the corset as the "bustier"

Benetton's controversial AIDS campaign depicts dying patient

Daymond John launches FUBU urban gear with a collection of hats produced at his house in Queens, New York

ALEXANDER MCQUEEN discovered by *Vogue* stylist Isabella Blow

Brief fad for men's skirts limited to trendy urban areas

Rap impresario Russell Simmons launches Phat Farm Fashions

Sharon Stone eschews underwear in the interrogation scene in *Basic Instinct*

GALLIANO shows Goth-inspired outfits

DKNY men's wear launched

MARC JACOBS fired from PERRY ELLIS after a critically panned collection inspired by grunge scene

Bill Clinton elected U.S. president

1993

DOLCE & GABBANA design costumes for Madonna's *Girlie Show* world tour

Waifish model Kate Moss featured in *Vogue*'s first grunge fashion shoot

OSCAR DE LA RENTA becomes first American to head a

Paris couture house at Pierre Balmain

People for the Ethical Treatment of Animals (PETA) runs anti-fur campaign featuring supermodels

Prada launches less expensive Miu Miu line

Retro and vintage revival

African kente cloth patterns used in contemporary clothing designs

Bare midriffs emerge

The term "fashionista" is coined

Husband and wife team Suzanne Clements and Ignacio Ribeiro launch line of whimsical separates under the name Clements Ribeiro

Kate Spade introduces her first collection of handbags

First Lady Hillary Clinton wears Donna Karan gown with cut-out shoulder to White House event

Calvin Klein is named both Menswear and Womenswear Designer of the Year by the Council of Fashion Designers of America (CFDA)

New York's World Trade Center hit by major terrorist bombing

Fortune magazine links growing popularity of baseball caps to balding Baby Boomers

Mosaic browser debuts, leading to widespread use of the Internet

1994

Karl Lagerfeld makes the traditional Chanel suit sexier

Levi's introduces first computer-imaged, custom-fit jeans

Economic recovery begins in United States

Rapper Snoop Dogg wears Tommy Hilfiger rugby shirt to host television show *Saturday Night Live*

Gaultier revives punk and body piercing at Paris summer shows

Rock singer Courtney Love popularizes the "kinderwhore" look

Vivienne Westwood pushes bustle dress

Fashion Targets Breast Cancer campaign begins

Issey Miyake shows his colorful, pleated "Flying Saucer" dress

Gucci hires Tom Ford to revamp its image

Nirvana frontman Kurt Cobain commits suicide

Actress Elizabeth Hurley's fame skyrockets after she wears Gianni Versace's safety-pin dress

Supermodel Claudia Schiffer earns a reported $12 million

The year of the Wonderbra

Slip dresses worn over t-shirts

Patent issued for the hair scrunchie

First Old Navy store opens in Colma, California

MAC Cosmetics debuts its first Viva Glam lipstick, with 100 percent of proceeds donated to people with HIV/AIDS

3 million users connected to the Internet worldwide

1995

John Galliano hired by Givenchy, becoming the first British designer to head a French couture house

Ralph Lauren introduces long black halterneck dress

Media dubs use of emaciated models as "heroin chic"

Sheath dress and jacket combination popular

Gucci Group formed with Tom Ford as creative director

Federal buildings in Oklahoma City bombed

Wildly popular television miniseries based on Jane Austen's *Pride and Prejudice* inspires Regency Era touches in women's fashion

Rapper Jay-Z launches Rocawear

Isaac Mizrahi is focus of the documentary *Unzipped*

European Union removes border controls for member countries

Israeli Prime Minister Yitzhak Rabin assassinated

Accessories designer Eric Javits introduces "Squishee" straw hat

Amazon.com opens for online business

Online auction site eBay launched

Vintage Levi's jeans sell for as much as $2,000 in Japan

Red jumpsuit worn by Elvis sells at auction for $107,000

Bloody footprint left by a Bruno Magli shoe featured in O.J. Simpson murder trial

H&M continues to expand, opening stores in France, Finland, Belgium, and Austria

1996

Calvin Klein shows long, lean, clean silhouette

Sharon Stone wears a Gap mock turtleneck to the Oscars

Dries van Noten shows layered textures and colors

Tom Ford collection for Gucci evokes Halston

Slim, structured lines for men's suits

Cargo pants popular

Nokia introduces cell phones with email access

90 percent of U.S. companies have "casual Fridays," allowing workers to dress less formally one day of the workweek

Courtney Love makes herself over with help from Gianni Versace

Platform shoes reemerge for women

Princess Diana granted a divorce from Prince Charles

Narcisco Rodriguez shoots to stardom when he designs Carolyn Bessette Kennedy's dress for her wedding to John F. Kennedy Jr.

Boris Yeltsin becomes Russia's first democratically elected president

Low-rise bootcut pants require thong underwear

10 million users connected to the Internet worldwide

Bill Clinton reelected U.S. president

1997

"Dolly" becomes the first cloned sheep, in Scotland

Alexander McQueen replaces John Galliano at Givenchy when Galliano leaves for Dior

Michael Kors appointed as chief ready-to-wear designer of Céline

Fendi's baguette bag introduced

Stella McCartney, Paul McCartney's daughter, takes the design helm at Chloé, with a contractual clause accepting her decision to use no fur or leather

First DVD players sold in United States

Elie Tahari establishes Theory brand

Height of dot-com boom

Yoga becomes wildly popular

Brighter colors take over from neutrals

Marc Jacobs becomes creative director for Louis Vuitton

Martin Margiela becomes head designer for Hermès

Diane von Furstenberg revives her fashion business with a wrap-dress update

LVMH acquires French beauty chain Sephora and opens its first New York store

China regains control of Hong Kong, ending 156 years of British rule

Princess Diana dies in paparazzi car chase in Paris

Alexander McQueen admits that his first collection for Givenchy is "crap" when panned by critics

Belgian designer Walter Van Beirendonck designs costumes for band U2's *PopMart* tour

Gianni Versace murdered at his Florida mansion; sister Donatella assumes control of his brand

Fashion journalist Carrie Donovan appears in ads for Old Navy

1998

Sex and the City debuts, featuring clothing by Patricia Field

Sales of Manolo Blahnik and Jimmy Choo shoes increase partly because of the love expressed for them by Sarah Jessica Parker's character, Carrie Bradshaw, on *Sex and the City*

Rapper Sean Combs launches Sean John line

Brazilian bikini wax becomes popular

Supermodel Cindy Crawford dons a body-baring slip dress by John Galliano for her second wedding

Human Genome Project announced

Soccer star David Beckham photographed wearing sarong-style skirt by Jean Paul Gaultier

Washington, D.C. intern Monica Lewinsky's stained blue dress becomes evidence during U.S. President Clinton's impeachment trial

Skimpy schoolgirl look shown in teen singer Britney Spears's video for " . . . Baby One More Time"

Actress Gwyneth Paltrow channels Grace Kelly

Hillary Clinton wears Oscar de la Renta on the cover of *Vogue*

Young designers Viktor & Rolf make their debut with "Atomic Bomb" evening dress collection

Fashionable women eschew pantyhose for bare legs

1999

American Express funds $1 million fashion show by Alexander McQueen

Mass shootings at Columbine High School in Colorado

Luggage company Samsonite enters the fashion business with functional jackets

The Matrix renews interest in the long trench coat

Soccer star Brandi Chastain pulls off her jersey at the World Cup finals to reveal a Nike sports bra

Sex and the City fans copy character Carrie Bradshaw's name necklace

Blackberry personal digital assistant invented

Vladimir Putin named acting president of Russia

John F. Kennedy Jr. and Carolyn Bessette Kennedy die in a plane crash

Prada Group acquires Jil Sander

Gucci Group acquires Yves Saint Laurent

Gucci's collection includes a pair of embellished jeans priced at $3,096

Rapper Jay-Z becomes first to reference Jacob the Jeweler in his song "Girl's Best Friend"

Nike Town opens in London, with 70,000 feet of retail space

Target introduces designer line of products by Michael Graves

Netflix launches online DVD rental service

Fairchild Publications becomes part of Condé Nast

National Association for the Advancement of Colored People (NAACP) honors founders of FUBU with Entrepreneurs of the Year Award

Coach launches men's and women's footwear

Y2K panic over feared (but unrealized) global computer shutdown rings in the New Year

A NEW MILLENNIUM, 2000–2014

2000

New York's Guggenheim Museum features an ARMANI retrospective

Dot-com boom slows

Reality television becomes big business with launches of *Big Brother* and *Survivor*

U.S. population is 291.4 million

Latino population in United States reaches 35.5 million

Kmart introduces line of clothing names for Mexican singer Thalia

Speedo invents Fastskin, a new swimsuit material based on sharkskin

HEDI SLIMANE shows streamlined DIOR Homme line

Pashmina shawls popular

Entrepreneur Sara Blakely invents Spanx

U.S. stock market begins to falter

Rapper Lil' Kim becomes spokesperson for Viva Glam lipstick, by MAC Cosmetics

PHILIP TREACY shows first haute couture hat collection in Paris

Supermodel Christy Turlington launches collection of yoga wear

LVMH launches eLuxury.com

Zara chain has expanded into Europe, the United States, South America, and the Middle East

Fashion fans line up overnight for opening of H&M's first U.S. store in New York City

JIL SANDER leaves her fashion house over creative differences with owner PRADA

KENNETH COLE adds a women's clothing line

The Gap introduces a maternity line

Deconstructionist fashion line Imitation of Christ holds first show in an East Village funeral parlor

STELLA MCCARTNEY designs Madonna's dress for her wedding to Guy Ritchie

GEOFFREY BEENE, BILL BLASS, CALVIN KLEIN, RALPH LAUREN, HALSTON, RUDI GERNREICH, CLAIRE MCCARDELL, and NORMAN NORELL become the first designers honored on New York City's Fashion Walk of Fame

CONDÉ NAST launches *Lucky*, a "magazine about shopping"

George W. Bush declared president by U.S. Supreme Court after disputed election

2001

Economic crisis in Japan

Singer Björk performs at the Academy Awards wearing a dress resembling a swan, designed by Macedonian designer Marjan Pejoski

STELLA MCCARTNEY leaves CHLOÉ to launch her own line

CHRISTOPHER BAILEY becomes creative director at BURBERRY

ALEXANDER MCQUEEN featured in *Extreme Fashion* exhibit at New York's Metropolitan Museum of Art

Madonna revives the punk kilt look for her *Drowned World* tour

Young designer ZAC POSEN spurns offers from LVMH and GUCCI Group; opens his own studio in Tribeca, New York

Singer Jennifer Lopez launches fashion line

PRADA opens enormous store designed by Rem Koolhaas in New York's Soho neighborhood

Jaeger hires young designer Bella Freud to jazz up its line of traditional woolens

Court gown designed by CHARLES FREDERICK WORTH and worn by George Washington's great-great-grandniece sells at auction for a record $101,500

Apple releases the first iPod

Former child star twins Mary Kate and Ashley Olsen launch "tween" fashion and product line with Walmart

United States hit by 9/11 terrorist attacks

Americans show their patriotism by wearing red, white, and blue

OSCAR DE LA RENTA, JAMES GALANOS, DONNA KARAN, PAULINE TRIGÈRE, BONNIE CASHIN, GIORGIO SANT'ANGELO, CHARLES JAMES, and ANNE KLEIN are added to the Fashion Walk of Fame

STEPHEN JONES hat featured on British postage stamp

2002

Almost 7 million cosmetic surgery procedures performed in the United States

An ad campaign by The Gap promotes the idea of "everybody in khaki"

Sober black suits are the celebrity outfit of choice at the Academy Awards

Television show *What Not To Wear* debuts in the U.K.

The euro becomes the standard currency for the European Union

YVES SAINT LAURENT retires

Label PROENZA SCHOULER is started by young New Yorkers Lazaro Hernandez and Jack McCollough

United States invades Afghanistan

STEPHEN BURROWS, MARC JACOBS, BETSEY JOHNSON, NORMA KAMALI, LILLY DACHÉ, PERRY ELLIS, MAINBOCHER, and WILLI SMITH are added to the Fashion Walk of Fame

Juicy Couture track suits popular

605 million users connected to the Internet worldwide

2003

Teen consumer market estimated at $70 billion

ISAAC MIZRAHI designs for Target

JEAN PAUL GAULTIER replaces MARTIN MARGIELA at HERMÈS

JIL SANDER returns to designing her line under the PRADA Group

Television show *Queer Eye for the Straight Guy* debuts

Number of people living with AIDS/HIV estimated to be 42 million people worldwide

Lauren Weisberger, a former assistant to ANNA WINTOUR, releases the novel *The Devil Wears Prada*, which becomes a bestseller

T-shirt wholesaler American Apparel enters the retail market

VERSACE glams up the biker look in fall collection

Portuguese designer Fátima Lopes opens her first U.S. store in Los Angeles

Pop star Gwen Stefani launches clothing and accessories line L.A.M.B.

United States invades Iraq; Iraq War begins

Fashion publicist Eleanor Lambert dies at the age of 100

2004

Sarah Jessica Parker becomes spokesperson for The Gap

Final Episode of Sex and the City airs in February.

MICHAEL KORS launches line of high-end career clothes that he calls "carpool couture"

Coach hits $1.3 billion in sales thanks largely to the popularity of "status bags"

Closely cropped facial stubble popular among men

TOM FORD leaves GUCCI Group over business disagreements

NASCAR commissions TIFFANY to design its trophy

French ban on Muslim headscarves in schools causes controversy

CARTIER files trademark infringement suit against Jacob the Jeweler

Tennis star Serena Williams starts clothing line

JIL SANDER leaves PRADA Group for second time

Limited edition collection by KARL LAGERFELD for H&M sells out in an hour

George W. Bush reelected U.S. president

2005

Model Heidi Klum debuts as host of television show *Project Runway*

VIVIENNE WESTWOOD creates a stir with t-shirts declaring "I am not a terrorist, please don't arrest me"

Singer Beyoncé and her mother Tina Knowles launch fashion business House of Deréon

STELLA MCCARTNEY designs collection for H&M

Shopping mall in Dubai offers indoor snow skiing

Portland Fashion Week launched, featuring sustainable designs and apparel

Blonde, tan, and skinny is the look of choice for Hollywood starlets, promoted by stylist Rachel Zoe

Bride and Prejudice sparks interest in Bollywood fashion

Leggings return in capri length, worn under mini skirts

Women's proportion shifts to short-over-long looks

Uniqlo opens first U.S. stores in New Jersey

HELMUT LANG walks away from his label owned by PRADA Group

RAF SIMONS takes over design for JIL SANDER brand

2006

Rachel Zoe blamed for promoting anorexic chic

Fug Girls begin covering fashion week shows for *New York* magazine

VIKTOR & ROLF are H&M's featured designers for fall line

Target launches its Go International guest designer program, starting with LUELLA BARTLEY, Sophie Albou, and BEHNAZ SARAFPOUR

AN INCONVENIENT TRUTH, former Vice President Al Gore's film about global warming, is a hit

The Devil Wears Prada is made into a movie, with Meryl Streep in the title role

Coach launches knitwear collection

Uniqlo establishes global flagship store in New York's Soho neighborhood

Size 0 models banned from Spanish runways after a model collapses and dies from heart failure brought on by fasting

HELMUT LANG brand sold to Japanese group Link Theory

MAC Cosmetics Viva Glam products have raised $70 million for HIV/AIDS support fund

Online clothing sales top computer sales for the first time

2 billion cell phones now in use worldwide

2007

Apple introduces the iPhone

Madonna designs spring collection for H&M

Teen star Miley Cyrus inspires fan Website, dresslikemiley.net

VERA WANG debuts Simply Vera line for Kohl's

ROBERTO CAVALLI's fall collection for H&M flies off the shelves

Stella McCartney introduces entirely organic skin care line

Supermodel Kate Moss designs collection for U.K. chain Topshop

Valentino Fashion Group invests in Proenza Schouler

Target features guest designers Proenza Schouler, Patrick Robinson, Alice Temperley, and Erin Fetherston

Leggings for men shown in Marni (Bluemarine) fall collection

Mary Kate and Ashley Olsen launch high-end line The Row

Converse issues All-Star Ramones high-top shoes

2008

Best Actress winner Marion Cotillard wears a mermaid gown by Jean Paul Gaultier to the Academy Awards

First Dubai Fashion Week held

Controversy over whether purported plus-size winner of television competition *America's Next Top Model* is actually plus-size

Target features guest designers Jovovich-Hawk, Richard Chai, Jonathan Saunders, and Thakoon Panichgul

Anna Wintour bestowed with Order of the British Empire (OBE) by Queen Elizabeth II

Sarah Jessica Parker designs low-priced fashion line Bitten for mall retailer Steve & Barry's

Zac Posen releases capsule collection for Target stores in Australia

Benetton runs Microcredit Africa Works ad campaign

Limited Comme des Garçons collection for H&M creates 14-hour waits in Japan

Supermodel Kate Moss begins second ad campaign for David Yurman jewelry

Fashionistas try to remain stylish as "recessionistas"

Fashion critic Richard Blackwell dies

Jil Sander brand purchased by Japanese company Onward

Barack Obama becomes first African-American to be elected U.S. president

First Lady Michelle Obama wears Narciso Rodriguez dress on election night

2009

U.S. unemployment rate tops 7 percent

Chanel reduces workforce by 200 jobs in Paris

Fashion's Night Out launched during New York Fashion Week to spur local retail economy

Michelle Obama wears Isabel Toledo suit and coat to Inauguration Ceremony and Jason Wu dress to Inaugural Ball

J.Crew kids' wear surges in popularity after Sasha and Malia Obama wear coats from the Crewcuts line to the Inauguration

Matthew Williamson is guest designer for H&M's summer line

Isaac Mizrahi debuts his first collection as designer for Liz Claiborne

Bloggers become increasingly important source of fashion information

The film *September Issue* features behind the scenes drama between *Vogue* editor-in-chief Anna Wintour and her staff

Katie Holmes seen wearing the PRPS "Boyfriend" jean (by Donwan Harrell) which starts a trend

Jason Wu designs Michelle Obama's Inaugural Ball dress

2010

LVMH secretly buys 14.2 percent of the family-owned brand Hermès; the family struggled to ensure that it retained a majority holding

Phoebe Philo makes Céline the "It" brand to wear

Lady Gaga wears a raw meat dress to the MTV Video Music Awards

New York Fashion Week moves from Bryant Park to Lincoln Center

Fashion's Night Out initiative expands to fashion weeks in 16 countries

Alexander McQueen commits suicide; Sarah Burton takes over as the house's creative director

Lanvin creates line for H&M

Christian Siriano designs for Payless ShoeSource

"Don't Ask, Don't Tell" policy banning homosexuals from serving openly in the U.S. military is repealed

Qatar Holdings buys Harrods for $2 billion

Kate Middleton and Prince William get engaged

The Gap redesigns its logo, then brings back the original

American Apparel is $91 million in debt

Burj Khalifa, in Dubai, UAE, becomes the world's tallest skyscraper

2011

Donatella Versace creates collection for H&M

Alexander McQueen retrospective presented at New York's Metropolitan Museum of Art

John Galliano's anti-Semitic rant caught on video and gets designer fired from Dior

Missoni creates collection for Target

Kate Middleton, wearing an Alexander McQueen gown, marries Prince William and becomes Catherine, Duchess of Cambridge

25-year-old Olivier Rousteing named creative director of Balmain

Fashion magazines start selling clothing

Prabal Gurung designs for J.Crew

Elizabeth Taylor's jewelry collection sold at auction for $2.6 million

Christian Louboutin sues Yves Saint Laurent over use of trademarked red soles on shoes

Singer Rihanna designs capsule collection for Armani

Kanye West shows women's wear collection in Paris

Riccardo Tisci places Lea T, a transgender model, on the runway of Givenchy

Hal Vaughan's *Sleeping with the Enemy* claims that Coco Chanel was a Nazi spy

Carine Roitfeld steps down from French *Vogue*

Valentino creates a virtual museum

Miss Piggy, a Muppet, becomes a judge on the television show *Project Runway* and is the face of MAC Cosmetics

Ralph Rucci and Donald Brooks are added to the Fashion Walk of Fame

2012

Diane von Furstenberg begins fourth term as president of the Council of Fashion Designers of America (CFDA)

Raf Simons becomes creative director of Dior

Alexander Wang becomes creative director of Balenciaga

Qatar royal family purchases Valentino for $853 million

Hurricane Sandy slams New York and New Jersey and affects the fashion industry

Target enlists 24 CFDA designers to create a holiday collection

Hedi Slimane becomes creative director of Yves Saint Laurent and shortens the label's name to Saint Laurent

Isabel Marant starts a sneaker craze with the high-top wedge shoe

Jil Sander returns to her namesake label

Stefano Pilati joins Ermenegildo Zegna

Christopher Kane leaves Versus

Michelle Obama wears Tracy Reese to Democratic National Convention

New York Times fashion reporter Cathy Horyn banned from Saint Laurent show for scathing review of Hedi Slimane collection

Kanye West wears leather Givenchy skirt to benefit concert in New York

About 142,000 people employed as sewing machine operators in the United States

Barack Obama reelected U.S. president

2013

Cabiria by Eden Miller is the first plus-size fashion show at New York Fashion Week

Marc Jacobs leaves Louis Vuitton after 16 years to concentrate on his own brand

Rana Plaza Factory collapse in Bangladesh kills more than 1,100 garment workers

Anna Wintour becomes creative director of Condé Nast

Alexander Wang becomes creative director of Balenciaga

Phillip Lim designs collection for Target

Isabel Marant creates collection for H&M

Pinault-Pritemps-Redoute (PPR) changes its name to Kering

Michelle Obama wears Jason Wu to Inaugural Ball a second time

André Leon Talley leaves *Vogue* after 30 years to be editor at Russian magazine *Numéro*

New York Child Labor Law passed to end the exploitation of underage models in New York's fashion industry

Nicolas Ghesquière leaves Balenciaga and becomes creative director of Louis Vuitton

Karl Lagerfeld mounts Chanel Métiers d'Art fashion show in Dallas's Fair Park

Naomi Cambell and Iman call for an end to racism on the runway

2014

New York's Metropolitan Museum of Art changes the name of its Costume Institute to Anna Wintour Costume Center

Actress and singer Zooey Deschanel teams up with Tommy Hilfiger to design a capsule collection of dresses

Lupita Nyong'o becomes the "it girl" for fashion, wearing a blue Prada gown to the Academy Awards, where she wins for Actress in a Supporting Role

"Charles James Beyond Fashion" premiers at the new Anna Wintour Costume Center at the Metropolitan Museum of Art in New York.

Nicholas Ghesquiere showcases first collection for Louis Vuitton at Paris Fashion Week

Kate Moss lands first British *Vogue* cover as fashion editor

French Fashion House Lanvin celebrates their 125th anniversary

Kanye West and Kim Kardashian marry in Italy and make the cover of Vogue

Tom Ford Wins CFDA Lifetime Achievement Award at age 52

Modeling agent Bethany Hardison won a CFDA award for fighting for diversity on the runway. She received the Founders Award in honor of Eleanor Lambert

Yoga Pants become a trend for women in the U.S.

"Clothes and jewellery should be startling, individual. When you see a woman in my clothes, you want to know more about them. To me, that is what distinguishes good designers from bad designers."

– Alexander McQueen

"In order to be irreplaceable one must always be different."

— Coco Chanel

The Profiles

Designer Joseph Abboud.

BORN Boston, May 5, 1950

AWARDS Cutty Sark Men's Fashion Awards *Most Promising Menswear Designer,* 1988 • *Woolmark Award for Distinguished Fashion,* 1989 • Council of Fashion Designers of America (CFDA) *Men's Wear Designer of the Year,* 1989, 1990

Joseph Abboud (Ah-BOOD) brings a fresh viewpoint to the conservative realm of men's clothing, fusing a European aesthetic with American practicality. His clothes are exceptionally well made of beautiful fabrics, classic but with a contemporary attitude, combining colors and textures to give classicism a modern edge.

Of Lebanese descent, Abboud came to designing with a strong retail background—12 years in buying, merchandising, and sales promotion at Louis of Boston. He went to work there part time in 1968 during his freshman year at the University of Massachusetts, and worked full time after graduation. He also studied at the Sorbonne in Paris, where he fell in love with the European sense of style. He left Louis in 1981 for a job as a sales representative at Polo/RALPH LAUREN, joined the design team, and became associate director of

men's wear. Then, after a year at Barry Bricken, Abboud formed his own company in 1986.

In addition to the signature Abboud collection, there are shirts and ties, casual sportswear and golf clothes, loungewear, sleepwear, robes, rainwear, and men's scarves, as well as home products ranging from bedding to bath accessories to flatware. The label was sold at fine specialty stores and in Abboud boutiques around America. Internationally it was distributed in Canada, Great Britain, Japan, and Taiwan.

In 2005, after creative differences with Chief Executive Marty Staff, Abboud left the company to pursue outside interests. In 2012, Russell Simmons asked Abboud to help him relaunch Simmons's line Argyleculture, an "urban graduate" brand. Abboud partnered with Simmons to create two lines for the 2013 collection. In 2013, Abboud was appointed chief creative director of Men's Wearhouse, which also acquired the Joseph Abboud brand.

Spring 2013.

1

AMSALE ABERRA

BORN Addis Ababa, Ethiopia, 1954

Amsale (AHM-sah-lay) Aberra is known for creating elegant, understated, and sophisticated wedding gowns. After immigrating to America to pursue a degree at New York City's Fashion Institute of Technology, Aberra took a position as an assistant designer at Harvé Benard. While planning her 1986 wedding, she encountered a dearth of options for simple, modern wedding gowns—inspiring her to start designing them.

Aberra began her business out of her small New York loft apartment, but it quickly outgrew the space. Aberra's philosophy is to produce gowns that are timeless and elegant. She focuses on updating her gowns with modern bustles, colors, and silhouettes. "People shouldn't be able to look at your pictures and tell what year you got married," she said in a 2001 interview. "When women look at their wedding pictures 50 years from now, I don't want them to say, 'What did I do?'"

Above: Designer Amsale Aberra.
Left: Fall 2013.

Aberra's bridal wear designs became so popular that in 1998 she introduced an evening wear line in 1998, designed with a similar ethos in mind. Her evening wear line has garnered praise from fashion critics and celebrities, including Vanessa Williams, Halle Berry, Julia Roberts, Selma Blair, Salma Hayek, and Lucy Liu.

In 2001, Aberra opened a 5,000 square foot boutique on Madison Avenue. The boutique offers all lines developed by the Amsale group, including Amsale Bridesmaids, Christos, and Kenneth Pool, which is designed by season one *Project Runway* contestant Austin Scarlett. In 2011, Amsale became a reality television star when WE tv aired *Amsale Girls*. The show took the viewer behind the scenes of her Madison Avenue store.

Aberra continues to serve as creative director for the Christos and Amsale lines. With sales reaching upwards of $25 million a year, she is considered the world's top designer of couture wedding dresses.

Designer Reem Acra.

 **REEM ACRA**

sophisticated, meticulously made designs soon gained international recognition.

In 1997, Acra launched her first collection, Reem Acra Bridal, which combined classical elements of design with intricate beadwork and embroidery—resulting in an exotic look with romantic appeal. In 2002, she launched an evening wear line that drew on both European and American styles. In 2008, she launched her first ready-to-wear collection, and in 2012 her first perfume, Reem Acra.

BORN Beirut, Lebanon

A leader in luxury bridal and evening wear, Reem Acra has always had a passion for design. While studying at American University in Beirut, she attended a party wearing a silk embroidered dress that she had made from a tablecloth. The dress attracted the attention of a fashion editor who was so impressed that ten days later she hosted a fashion show featuring Acra's designs.

Acra attended the Fashion Institute of Technology in New York and completed her studies at l'Ecole Supérieure des Arts et Techniques de la Mode (ESMOND) in Paris. She then traveled the world, drawing inspiration from the various cultures to which she was exposed. After working as an interior designer for several years, Acra returned to her first craft—fashion design. She made a splash in the fashion world when a wedding gown she made for a high-society friend grabbed the attention of guests. Her glamorous,

Fall 2014.

ADRIAN

BORN Adrian Adolph Greenburg; Naugatuck,
Connecticut, March 3, 1903
DIED Los Angeles, September 13, 1959

AWARDS *Neiman Marcus Award*, 1943 • Coty
American Fashion Critics' Awards *Winnie*, 1945 •
Parsons *Medal for Distinguished Achievement*, 1956

A top Hollywood studio designer of the 1920s and
1930s, Adrian was also successful at made-to-order
and ready-to-wear. In 1921, he began studying at the
New York School of Fine and Applied Arts, now called
Parsons School of Design. In 1922, he transferred to the
school's Paris campus. After six months in Paris he met
Irving Berlin, who saw a costume Adrian had designed
for a classmate for the annual Bal du Grand Prix. Berlin
offered Adrian a job designing for the *Music Box Revue*.
Adrian then returned to New York, where he continued
to work on stage productions, including the Greenwich
Village *Follies* and George White's *Scandals*. In 1923,
Rudolph Valentino's wife, costume and set designer

Designer Adrian.

Natacha Rambova, invited Adrian to Hollywood to
design costumes for her screen idol husband.

In 1926, Adrian started working for Cecil B. DeMille,
and in 1928 moved with him to MGM. He became the
studio's head designer, creating costumes featured in nearly
200 films for stars such as Greta Garbo, Joan Crawford,
Katharine Hepburn, Rosalind Russell, and Norma Shearer.

Adrian left MGM in 1941 to open his own business,
Adrian Ltd., for couture and high-end ready-to-wear.
He closed his Beverly Hills salon in 1948 but continued
in wholesale until a 1952 heart attack forced his
retirement. Adrian and his wife, actress Janet Gaynor,
then retired to Brazil, where he focused on landscape
painting, a longtime avocation.

Adrian returned to America in 1959 to design the
costumes for Lerner and Loewe's Broadway production
of *Camelot*. While working on the production, he died
of a cerebral hemorrhage.

The Adrian look was sleek and modern, with a
silhouette marked by exaggeratedly wide shoulders
tapering to a small waist. He was a master of the
intricate cut—stripes appeared in opposite directions

Coat of Raymond-Holland satin, 1948.

on shapely, fitted suits, and color patches and bold animal prints were set into sinuous black crepe evening gowns. Diagonal closings, dolman sleeves, and floating tabs were recurring details. Adrian also created draped, swathed late-day dresses and romantic organdy evening gowns such as the widely copied one worn by Joan Crawford in the 1932 film *Letty Lynton*. More than 50,000 versions of the gown were sold at Macy's alone. In addition to women's clothes and stage costumes, Adrian produced several men's wear collections and two perfumes, Saint and Sinner.

Actress Greta Garbo wearing a long satin gown designed by Adrian for the film *Susan Lenox (Her Fall and Rise)*.

AGNÈS B. ▲

BORN Agnès Andrée Marguerite Troublé; Versailles, France, 1941

Agnès B. inspired a generation of laid-back sportswear. After graduating from the École des Beaux-Arts in Versailles, she worked as an editor at *ELLE*, an assistant to Dorothée Bis, and a freelance designer before going into business for herself. The style that she initiated in the early 1970s was a response to the clothing popular in Paris at the time, which she considered overly dressy and trendy. Her unforced, airy, low-key clothes—mainly

Designer Agnès B.

sports separates and accessories for women, men, and children—are primarily sold in her stores around the world, including in New York, Amsterdam, London, and Tokyo.

In 2008, Agnès B. won a national contest to design uniforms for the guards at the Palace of Versailles. Today her line includes accessories, jewelry, watches, perfume, skin care and cosmetics products, and a maternity collection. She tries to keep as much of her production as possible in France.

Spring 2013.

Model Daria Werbowy attends the 2007 Met Costume Institute Gala wearing Azzedine Alaïa.

BORN Tunis, Tunisia, 1940

AWARDS French Government *Chevalier de la Légion d'Honneur (Legion of Honor)*, 2008

Fashion connoisseurs now consider him a genius and one of the last true couturiers. But until Azzedine Alaïa (Uh-LIE-ah) presented his first ready-to-wear collection in 1980, he worked in obscurity, known only to a select group of adventurous customers who also bought from the great couture houses. For the previous 18 years he had worked out of his apartment for clients ranging from PALOMA PICASSO to Dyan Cannon and Raquel Welch.

Raised in Tunis by his grandmother, Alaïa studied sculpture at the École des Beaux-Arts of Tunis. While there, he worked for several dressmakers. In 1957, Alaïa moved to Paris, where he had been promised a job with CHRISTIAN DIOR. Arriving a few months before Dior's death, he did get a job in the Dior cutting room—but it lasted only five days. For the next few years Alaïa worked as an au pair and made clothes for his fashionable young employers and their friends. By 1984, he had become so successful that he was able to buy a townhouse in the Marais section of Paris.

▲ AZZEDINE ALAÏA

Alaïa's clothes, said to be the sexiest in Paris, were seamed, molded, and draped to define and reveal every curve of a woman's body. Alaïa's unique draping, inspired by the work of MADELEINE VIONNET, is the heart of his style—the key to his design is his belief that fashion should be timeless. Translating these techniques from woven cloth to knits is probably his greatest ready-to-wear achievement.

After 1992, Alaïa stopped doing runway shows and essentially dropped off the fashion radar. Although he continued to design for a few customers, his deliveries to retail establishments were so sporadic that few stores were willing or able to cope with them. But he reappeared in the new century as if reborn, both through his influence on younger designers toying with the looks of the 1980s and in his own collections. While unmistakably Alaïa, his recent designs are totally without nostalgia and entirely contemporary.

In 2001, Alaïa sold a minority share of his business to PRADA, and in July of that year staged a showing of just 22 pieces in his home and headquarters for barely 100 people. Only his fourth showing in ten years, it was one of the year's most exhilarating and influential collections—confirming his standing as one of the world's most original designers.

In 2007, Alaïa bought back his ready-to-wear line from PRADA and Richmont bought a percentage of the company. In 2013, the Palais Galliera in the Musée de la Mode in Paris reopened with a retrospective of his work, and a new Alaïa boutique opened in an 18th-century mansion off Avenue Montaigne.

Designer Azzedine Alaïa (left) working on French Revolution 200th anniversary costume.

ALICE + OLIVIA BY STACEY BENDET ◢ ◗

BORN Stacey B. Wiener; Chappaqua, New York, May 17, 1979

alice + olivia, a brand that personifies the personality of its founder Stacey Bendet, began in 2002 and is known for incorporating interesting fabrics, an ultra-flattering fit, and a hip retro vibe. Bendet graduated from the University of Pennsylvania and, instead of pursuing her intended path of law school, began designing websites for other fashion designers. She started wearing boldly striped bell bottoms of her own creation and roller blading around New York City in what many called the "Staceypant." The pants attracted the attention of Barneys New York, where she launched her first collection in 2002. In 2003, Andrew Rosen of Theory became the company's chief financial partner.

alice + olivia's designs reflect the inspiration that Bendet draws from music, art, various cultures, and myriad other

Above: Designer Stacey Bendet for alice + olivia.
Left: Spring 2014.

interests. She is often influenced by what women wear on the street, and her clothes are versatile—suited to the office or the club. In 2008, Bendet launched a children's wear line, which expanded after the birth of her first daughter that same year. In 2011, she launched a line of accessories, including scarves and jewelry. Bendet has collaborated with MAC Cosmetics, jewelry designer Erickson Beamon, The Lake & Stars lingerie, Payless ShoeSource, and on a line for Pretty Polly that included extremely popular printed tights.

Bendet's clients include Gwyneth Paltrow, Jennifer Lopez, Sarah Jessica Parker, and Taylor Swift. alice + olivia is sold at more than 800 retail stores and 12 of the company's boutiques across America. In addition, the brand has expanded globally into Hong Kong, Tokyo, and Dubai. Bendet lives in New York with her husband and two daughters.

Above: Designer Joseph Altuzarra.
Below Right: Spring 2014.

BORN Joseph Altuzarra; Paris, 1983

AWARDS: Council of Fashion Designers of America (CFDA)/Vogue Fashion Fund, 2011; Swarovski Award for Womenswear, 2012; Swarovski Award for Designer of the Year, 2014 • International Woolmark Prize, 2013

Joseph Altuzarra (Al-too-ZAR-uh) is a designer of luxury women's ready-to-wear. His multicultural upbringing—with a Chinese-American mother and French father—has had an enormous influence on his collections. As a child, Altuzarra was obsessed with the glamorous side of fashion, especially TOM FORD for GUCCI and YVES SAINT LAURENT. Altuzarra studied art history at Strathmore College in Strathmore, Pennsylvania and became interested in a career in fashion while working in the school's costume shop.

Altuzarra began his career as an intern at MARC JACOBS, then worked as a freelance designer at PROENZA SCHOULER while it was still a fledgling label. Altuzarra also apprenticed with patternmaker Nicolas Caito to hone his technical knowledge and skills, which he considered weak because he lacked a formal education in fashion design. He ended up back in his birthplace, Paris, after landing a job at GIVENCHY as first assistant to RICCARDO TISCI.

In 2008, Altuzarra returned to New York and launched his own label. In 2010, he collaborated with Swarovski on a jewelry collection. His big break came with his fall 2012

line, which established his signature silhouette and boosted his company's sales by nearly 40 percent—catching the attention of a number of retail stores.

Altuzarra is best known for pairing the masculine with the feminine—the sensual and sexy with the pragmatic and easygoing. The label is renowned for its outerwear, but Altuzarra drives his staff to constantly assess what they do well and what they need to provide to customers. For example, when Altuzarra designed a capsule collection for J.Crew in 2012, he carefully considered the large number and varied characteristics of the women he was targeting.

The year 2013 was pivotal for Altuzarra: he won the first CFDA branding initiative and was among *Crain's New York Business* 40 Under 40 and *Women's Wear Daily's* Ten of Tomorrow. In addition, his label earned more than $10 million, and the designer created outfits for the New York City Ballet. In addition, Altuzarra cohosted the kickoff party for the Emmy Awards and designed the green room for stars backstage. His clothes have been worn by celebrities such as Emma Watson, Rihanna, and Angelina Jolie.

MARIANNE ALVONI ▼

Designer Marianne Alvoni (left) with her designs.

BORN Berne, Switzerland, 1964

One of Switzerland's best-known designers, Marianne Alvoni opened her first atelier in 1985 in Berne. In 1989, she moved to a larger building with a storefront in the old town of Berne. In 2011, Alvoni opened an atelier in Worb, a city near Berne where she lives with her family.

In the 1990s, three of Alvoni's pieces were shown at the Swiss National Museum in an exhibit celebrating the 700th anniversary of the founding of the Swiss confederation, and later became part of the museum's permanent collection. In 2011, she was invited to present her work at a fashion show in Singapore sponsored by V-Zug, the Swiss market leader for household appliances.

Alvoni is known for her elaborate evening wear and intricate wedding dresses, but she has also received acclaim for her ready-to-wear. In addition, she has appeared on numerous television shows such as SF DRS Schweizer Fernsehen in Switzerland and Novosti Modi-Moskwa in Russia, as well as MTV UK.

Designer Sir Hardy Amies (right) photographing models wearing his creations.

BORN Edwin Hardy Amies; Maida Vale, London, July 17, 1909
DIED English Cotswolds, March 5, 2003

AWARDS British Government *Knight Commander of the Royal Victorian Order (KCVO)*, 1989

A dressmaker to Queen Elizabeth II for more than 50 years, Sir Edwin Hardy Amies specialized in tailored suits and coats and in cocktail and evening dresses. The Hardy Amies fashion house also makes breezy, contemporary women's clothes such as pantsuits and casual classics. In addition, men's wear has become a major part of its business.

Amies received no formal training in design. But his mother worked for a London dressmaker, and as a child he sometimes visited her workplace. After graduating secondary school in 1927, Amies spent several years in France and Germany, becoming fluent in both languages. When he was 21 he returned to England to work for a manufacturer of scales.

In 1934, Amies became a designer for Lachasse, a London couture house owned by his mother's former employer, and within a year was managing director. He left Lachasse in 1939 to serve in the British Army Intelligence Corps. During his Army career Amies rose to the rank of lieutenant colonel, and in 1944 was head of the Special Forces Commission to Belgium.

During the war, Amies also worked for the British Board of Trade, designing for the Utility Clothing Scheme. The program continued after the war ended, but at the time only Americans could afford European designer clothing. In 1946, Amies opened his own fashion house, which began with dressmaking and added a boutique line in 1950 and men's wear in 1959. Starting with ties and shirts, the men's wear line expanded to include made-to-measure suits and was soon being sold in America, Canada, and Japan.

In 1984, at 75, Amies announced plans to leave his multimillion-dollar business to his staff but denied any intention of an early departure. Ten years later he was still actively engaged.

In 2001, Amies sold his business to Luxury Brands Group—which also acquired NORMAN HARTNELL, another classic British house that once dressed Queen Elizabeth II. Amies retired at the end of that year, and Jacques Azagury, a Moroccan-born designer with his own label, became head of couture for the House of Amies. A new ready-to-wear line was also planned. In addition, licensing agreements have included jewelry, small leather goods, luggage, and bed linens.

Amies's publications included *Just So Far* (1954), *ABC of Men's Fashion* (1964), and *Still Here* (1984). In 2007, London's Victoria and Albert Museum held an exhibit, *The Golden Age of Couture*, that featured his work.

ANTONIO ✏

BORN Antonio Lopez; Puerto Rico, 1943
DIED Los Angeles, March 17, 1987

Antonio was an illustrator of protean talent, sensitive to every social shift and art movement, and changing his style innumerable times over his 24-year career. His early work was elegant and relatively conventional fashion illustration. But by the mid-1960s, his drawings were inspired by Pop Art, then by Surrealism and the artist Fernand Léger. Antonio later moved to a more fluid style, but every period of his work was flamboyant and dramatic—regardless of whether it was mainly black and white or in color. In addition to women's and men's wear, he applied his unique point of view to children's wear.

Antonio's family moved to New York when he was 9. Even then he was committed to art—as a child he sketched dresses to please his mother, a dressmaker. He attended the High School of Industrial Art (now the High School of Art and Design) and the Fashion Institute of Technology, which he dropped out of at 19 to join *Women's Wear Daily*. Antonio left *WWD* after just four months because he was not allowed to freelance,

Illustration of Yves Saint Laurent design, 1973.

Illustration of model wearing a long, pleated dress, 1973.

and moved to *The New York Times*. During the 1960s, he spent a lot of time in Europe working for *ELLE* and *British Vogue* (among others), and at the end of the decade he moved to Paris. Seven years later, Antonio returned to New York. Other publications he worked for included *Harper's Bazaar*, *Vogue*, and *Interview*.

In 1964, Antonio began what became a five-year project, recording the life work of CHARLES JAMES under the direct supervision of the designer. Antonio was a molder and maker of fashion models, advising them on makeup and hairstyles to fit his ideas for their best looks. He also gave lectures and conducted workshops for students of fashion illustration in America and the Dominican Republic.

In 1988, the Fashion Institute of Technology mounted a retrospective of his career covering 1963 to 1987. In 2012, another retrospective, *Antonio's World*, appeared at the Suzanne Giess Company in Soho. That same year saw the publication of *Antonio: Fashion, Art, Sex, & Disco*, a book by Roger and Mauricio Padilha featuring Antonio's art and photographs.

Designer Elizabeth Arden.

BORN Florence Nightingale Graham; Woodbridge, Ontario, Canada, December 31, 1884
DIED New York City, October 18, 1966

AWARDS French Government *Légion d'Honneur (Legion of Honor)*, 1962

Elizabeth Arden was a pioneer in women's cosmetics. She emphasized the importance of applying makeup properly and taking care of the skin. Her interest in skin care was cultivated while working at E.R. Squibb Pharmaceuticals in Manhattan alongside Eleanor Adair, one of the first beauty culturists.

With a loan from her brother, Arden opened her first Red Door salon in 1910, on New York's Fifth Avenue. She constantly researched beauty treatments for skin health through her extensive travels, including a 1912 trip to France where she learned facial massage. In 1915, she began expanding her business globally.

Arden was a strong advocate for teaching and encouraging woman to hydrate themselves, avoid the sun, and exercise. "To achieve beauty, a woman must first achieve health," she said. Arden was also active in the women's rights movement, once marching past her signature red doors on Fifth Avenue with 15,000 women, all wearing red lipstick as a symbol of strength.

In 1946, Arden became the first woman to appear on the cover of *Time*. She had an intuitive entrepreneurial sense of what would appeal to women—covering everything from the packaging of beauty products to the types of services that women wanted and needed. Among the innovations she introduced to the beauty market were eight-hour beauty cream, the "makeover," travel-size beauty products, eye makeup, and training and sending out her sales teams for demonstrations.

Arden left a legacy of iconic beauty products and sales techniques as well as a company that has received numerous awards around the world. The global chain of Elizabeth Arden Red Door Spas continue to stress the importance of health as well as beauty. In 2001, the company was sold to FFI Fragrances, which subsequently changed its name to Elizabeth Arden.

ARKADIUS ▼

BORN Arkadiusz Weremsczuk; Lublin, Poland, July 5, 1969

AWARDS British Fashion Council *New Generation Award*, 2000 • *ELLE* Style Awards *Polish Designer of the Year*, 2000

From the start Arkadius has amused—and sometimes enraged—fashion observers with wildly creative clothes that are alternately calmly wearable and provocatively out-rageous. His fine tailoring skills and imaginative cutting go hand in hand with a taste for ornate decoration and eccentric presentations. Half-artist, half-businessman, he has been called bizarrely talented and hailed as the next JOHN GALLIANO.

Born into a family of teachers, Arkadius set his sights on London and fashion while attending college in Krakow, Poland, leaving before graduation to pursue his dream. He reached London in 1994—after excursions to Tuscany and Munich—with the goal of attending Central St. Martins College of Art and Design. He first had to learn enough English to walk through its doors, but managed to enroll in September of that year. During his third year there he was invited to work in ALEXANDER MCQUEEN's design studio, and his 1999 graduation collection earned both a job and a sponsor for his debut collection at London Fashion Week that fall.

Appearing to have found a happy medium between commercialism and avant-garde art, Arkadius added ready-to-wear, men's wear, and jeans to his line before it was discontinued in 2006. He also dabbled in costume design. His clothes have been worn by celebrities such as Christina Aguilera, Alicia Keys, and Mary J. Blige.

Designer Arkadius.

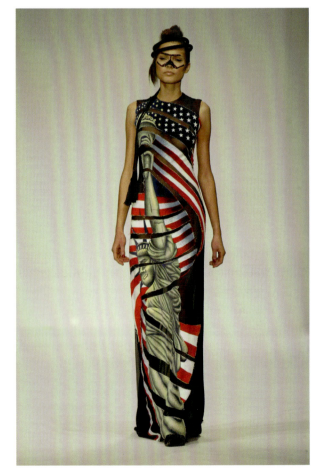

Spring 2004.

Designer Giorgio Armani.

X 👜 GIORGIO ARMANI

uncontrived shapes cut from exquisite Italian fabrics and tailored masterfully. Color and fabric are primary considerations. He prefers neutrals such as taupe, beige, black, and infinite tones of gray. Armani claims to have taught women to dress with the ease of men—but always includes a feminine element in even his most masculine cuts for women. His work is not intended to shock and he is not interested in trends; he aims for a soft, light silhouette, emphasizing femininity and gently disguising imperfections.

Armani is intensely devoted to his work, supervising every aspect of his collections, which are shown in his own theater. He does not use stylists and insists on complete control, down to such details as models' hairstyles and makeup.

Armani's business interests now include fragrances and accessories for men and women sold in high-end retail stores and free-standing shops around the world. The Emporio Armani label and shops were developed for young men and women who could not afford the regular line. A/X Armani Exchange is younger and sportier still.

Armani/Casa premiered in 2000, offering luxury home furnishings, furniture, décor, and fabrics. Armani

(continued)

Giorgio Armani Prive Spring 2009 haute couture.

BORN Emilia-Romagna, Italy, July 11, 1934

AWARDS *Neiman Marcus Award*, 1979 • Council of Fashion Designers of America (CFDA) *International Award*, 1983

After brief attempts at medicine and photography, Giorgio Armani began his fashion career in 1964, first as a window dresser, then as an assistant buyer of men's clothing for La Rinascente, a large Italian department store. During his seven years there he developed his ideas about men's fashion, including a dislike for stiff, formal looks—which, he believed, inhibited individuality.

Armani's next job, as a men's wear designer at the Cerutti Group, expanded his knowledge of the practical and commercial aspects of the clothing business. After that he designed for companies such as Ermenegildo Zegna and EMANUEL UNGARO.

Armani produced his first men's wear collection under his own label in 1974. An unconstructed blazer was his first attention-getter. He moved into women's wear in 1975, bringing to it the same perfectionist tailoring and fashion attitude applied to his men's clothes.

From day into evening, Armani's emphasis is on easy,

has also extended his name and style to Armani/Hotels, beginning in 2007 with 144 private residences and a hotel in Dubai in the world's tallest building, Burj Dubai; and to restaurants and cafés on three continents under the Armani/Ristorante moniker. In 2011, Armani premiered Armani/Roca for bathroom designs and Armani/Dada for kitchen designs. He has also done film work.

Armani's 1,330 stores worldwide comprise Armani Privé, Giorgio Armani, Emporio Armani, EA7, Armani Collezioni, Armani Jeans, Armani Junior, A/X Armani Exchange, Armani/Casa, Armani Beauty, Armani/Fiori, and Armani/Dolci. In 2000, a 25-year Armani retrospective opened at the Guggenheim Museum in New York, moving in 2001 to the museum's outpost in Bilbao, Spain, and in 2003 to Berlin, Germany. According to *Forbes*, Armani has a net worth of $7 billion.

Designer Giorgio Armani with model, 1979.

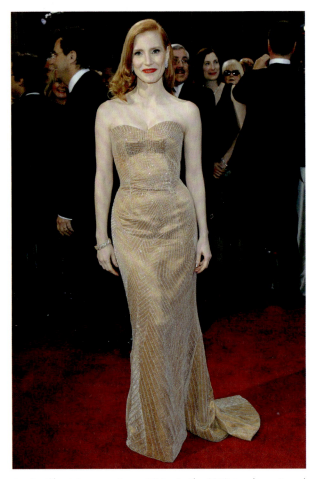

Jessica Chastain wears Armani Prive to the 2013 Academy Awards.

Men's wear, fall 2008, with women's wear, pre-fall 2008.

Flower print dress, 2005.

BORN Merthyr Tydfil, Wales, 1926
DIED Coventry, England, September 17, 1985

Romantic and innocent, the classic Laura Ashley look consists of decorative dresses with long, soft skirts in distinctive small flower prints, sweetly trimmed with lace. Though that template would seem to have little connection with life and fashion in the 21st century, its influence can still be seen on city streets, worn in ways the designer probably would not have imagined—with backpacks and work boots—and in the collections of cutting-edge designers from Italy to America.

In 1953 Ashley and her husband, Bernard, began printing textiles on the kitchen table of their London flat. The couple began with towels, scarves, and placemats that Bernard sold to major London stores—so successfully that the Ashleys formed their first company in 1954. As their business and family grew, they moved to Wales, opening a factory in Carno, Montgomeryshire. In the

early 1980s, the family moved to an 18th-century chateau in northern France, though the business remained centered in Wales.

Laura Ashley died in 1985, but the company has endured. Reaching its apogee in the 1960s, 1970s, and early 1980s, the company went public in 1985. At its height, there were Laura Ashley stores in cities such as New York, Paris, Geneva, and San Francisco, bringing the cozy warmth of an English cottage to harsh urban environments.

In 1989, the company launched its Mother and Child collection of coordinated apparel and home furnishings, which became a great success. In 1993, Sir Bernard Ashley stepped down as chairman to become honorary president, a position he held until 1998. In 2001, the 3 percent of the company still owned by the family and the Ashley trust was sold.

Designer Laura Ashley (left).

COLLEEN ATWOOD

BORN Yakima, Washington, September 25, 1948

AWARDS Academy Awards for Best Costume Design: *Chicago*, 2002; *Memoirs of a Geisha*, 2006; *Alice in Wonderland*, 2010 • British Academy of Film and Television awards for best costume design: *Sleepy Hollow*, 1999; *Memoirs of a Geisha*, 2006; *Alice in Wonderland*, 2010 • Council of Fashion Designers of America (CFDA) *Board of Directors' Tribute*, 2013

Colleen Atwood has been the lead costume designer for more than 50 films. She studied painting at Cornish College for the Arts in Seattle in the early 1970s, then worked at various retail stores, including an YVES SAINT LAURENT boutique. In 1980, she began attending New York University. The mother of an acquaintance was designing sets for the 1981 movie *Ragtime*, and Atwood

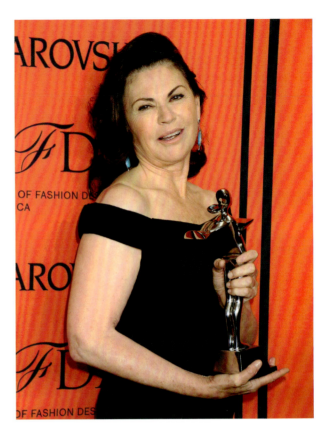

Designer Colleen Atwood.

got a job as a production assistant. Later she was hired to do the costumes for Sting's 1985 *Bring on the Night* world tour, which helped launch her as a costumer.

Atwood's career changed dramatically in the early 1990s, when she met director Tim Burton. Burton and Atwood began collaborating on many of his films, including *Edward Scissorhands, Planet of the Apes, Sweeney Todd,* and *Sleepy Hollow*. In 2005–06, Atwood redesigned all the costumes for the Ringling Bros. and Barnum & Bailey Circus.

Atwood has won the Academy Award for best costume design three times. She was also nominated for her work on *Snow White and the Huntsman* (2012), marking her 10th Oscar nomination in the category.

Atwood's favorite fashion designers are AZZEDINE ALAÏA, YOHJI YAMAMOTO, and ALEXANDER MCQUEEN. She recently expanded her efforts to Broadway, designing the costumes for the 2013 stage adaptation of *Breakfast at Tiffany's*. Although the film is set in the 1960s, with iconic designs from the legendary HERBERT DE GIVENCHY, the book is set in the 1940s. Atwood's designs for the play stay true to the novel; she describes her costumes for lead character Holly Golightly as being a lot "sexier in a less sleek fashion-y way."

Costumes by Colleen Atwood from the movie *Memoirs of a Geisha*.

📷 RICHARD AVEDON

BORN New York City, May 15, 1923
DIED San Antonio, Texas, October 1, 2004

AWARDS Pratt Institute *Citation of Dedication to Fashion Photography*, 1976 • Council of Fashion Designers of America (CFDA) *Lifetime Achievement Award*, 1989

The son of a retail store owner, Richard Avedon (AV-uh-dawn) received his first photographic training in the Merchant Marines. He then took a class in experimental photography at the New School for Social Research taught by ALEXEY BRODOVITCH, art director of *Harper's Bazaar*, and in 1945 joined the staff of the magazine. Thus began Avedon's long, distinguished career in fashion and commercial photography and an association with *Harper's Bazaar* that lasted 20 years. During that time he also did nonfashion assignments for other publications, including *Theatre Arts*. In 1966, he moved to *Vogue*, where he stayed until 1990.

Avedon's fashion photography, notable for its sense of style, freedom, and drama, captured the tone of the 1960s and recorded the sexual revolution. He took the action photography of Martin Munkacsi to a more sophisticated level, working in the studio and, for his simulated photojournalism, on location. He also created photo-collages using the illustrations of Katerina Danzinger, was a visual consultant on the Fred Astaire film *Funny Face*, and directed print and television advertising campaigns for major corporations such as Lincoln Mercury, MAX FACTOR, and CHANEL.

After leaving *Vogue*, Avedon was a staff photographer at *The New Yorker*—its first—providing aggressively unglamorous portraits. Shows of his work have been held at, among other venues, the Museum of Modern Art in 1975, the Metropolitan Museum of Art in 1978 and 2002, and the Whitney Museum in 1994. The latter emphasized his nonfashion work, which he considered more serious. In 2011, Gagosian Gallery announced its worldwide representation of Avedon's work.

Photographer Richard Avedon.

BADGLEY MISCHKA ⬛

BORN Mark Badgley; East St. Louis, Illinois, January 12, 1961

James Mischka; Burlington, Wisconsin, December 23, 1960

AWARDS Mouton Cadet *Young Designer Award,* 1989

Mark Badgley (BADGE-lee) attended the University of Southern California and James Mischka (MEESH-kuh) graduated from Rice University. They met at Parsons School of Design, where both received B.F.A. degrees in fashion design in 1985. After Parsons their paths diverged, though both became design assistants. Badgley worked for Jack Rogers and DONNA KARAN, and Mischka for YVES SAINT LAURENT and WILLI SMITH. The two formed their own company in 1988. In 1992, the firm was acquired by Escada, the large German fashion company, but Badgley and Mischka retained creative control and a financial stake in the business. The designers are best known for their beaded evening wear, worn by celebrities from New York to Hollywood. They describe their clothes as modern and sleek, appropriate for dinner and dancing. They have also broadened their focus to include day wear, separates, and a collection of bridal gowns with the clean, elegant lines and luxurious beading and ornamentation that distinguish their evening wear. In 2004, Iconix Brand Group bought Badgley Mischka from Escada. In 2009, the brand launched a more affordable contemporary line called Mark + James that targets younger customers. Badgley Mischka is sold in some of the world's most prestigious stores, and *Vogue* has called it one of America's top ten design houses. In 2013, Badgley and Mischka got married in a private ceremony in New York.

Resort 2014.

Designers Mark Badgley (left) and James Mischka (right).

Spring 2014.

♛ CHRISTOPHER BAILEY

Designer Christopher Bailey.

BORN Yorkshire, England, 1971

AWARDS British Fashion Awards *Designer of the Year*, 2005, 2009; *Men's Wear Designer of the Year*, 2007, 2008, 2013 • *GQ Designer of the Year*, 2008 • Council of Fashion Designers of America (CFDA) *International Award*, 2010

Though he is one of Britain's most influential young designers, Christopher Bailey (BAY-lee) once wanted to be a veterinarian. But at 18 he won a coveted spot in a two-year fashion course at London's Royal College of Art, setting his career path in motion. DONNA KARAN visited the school and offered Bailey a job after seeing his portfolio. He worked with her design team in New York for more than two years, then joined TOM FORD at GUCCI.

In 2001, Bailey became chief creative director at BURBERRY and was tasked with revamping

Burberry Prorsum Spring 2014.

the image of the venerable label. His runway debut a few months later was a playful, laid-back return to the company's British roots. In 2009, Bailey was promoted to chief creative officer and began overseeing design for all Burberry lines (including Burberry Prorsum, Burberry London, and Burberry Brit), licensed products, advertisements, and store designs. In 2013, he became chief executive officer as well.

Though Bailey's designs for Burberry for both men and women have been fresh and forward-thinking—complemented by ad campaigns feature the likes of Kate Moss—he never forgets that it all began with the trench coat created by Thomas Burberry in 1890. Those coats remain a staple of every Burberry collection, a classic made cool again for the 21st century. In 2013, Bailey received an honorary doctoral degree from his alma mater, the Royal College of Art.

Burberry Prorsum Spring 2014.

GLENDA BAILEY

BORN Derbyshire, England, 1958

AWARDS *Adweek* magazine *Editor of the Year,* 2001; British Government *Officer of the Order of the British Empire (OBE)*, 1989

After earning a degree in fashion design from the University of Kingston, Glenda Bailey (BAY-lee) briefly dabbled in the fashion industry. In 1983, she produced a collection for Guisi Slaverio in Italy. Soon, though, she found her true calling in publishing, launching, and editing a series of successful fashion magazines. The type of magazine that she envisioned—and found missing in English publishing—mixed hard-hitting reporting, chic fashion, and lifestyle features.

Bailey became editor of *Honey* magazine in 1986 and was assigned to launch *Folio* magazine soon after. Her extensive knowledge of fashion and trends, combined with a penchant for bucking convention and trying new ideas, gave her a sort of Midas touch in publishing. In 1988, she was appointed launch editor of British *Marie Claire*, which became the top-selling fashion magazine in the United Kingdom. She moved to New York in 1996 to become editor of American *Marie Claire*. Perhaps her most renowned issue of that magazine focused on "celebrity challenges," where celebrities agreed to perform extraordinary tasks such as living in an igloo or surviving in the desert.

In 2001, Bailey became editor of *Harper's Bazaar*, maintaining her timely and news-tinged perspective on fashion reporting. Sales of the magazine surged 38 percent between 2001 and 2007. Bailey's approach to fashion is atypically populist, and her features in

Editor Glenda Bailey.

Harper's Bazaar often have an instructional angle. "We have these beautiful aspirational images so people can dream," Bailey says, "but at the same time we also know that even the most fashionable, knowledgeable woman wants ideas." In 2012, the book *Harper's Bazaar: Greatest Hits* was published, featuring more than 300 iconic images and highlighting the partnership between creative director Stephen Gan and Bailey during her ten-year tenure at the magazine.

⬛ CRISTÓBAL BALENCIAGA

BORN Guetaria, Spain, January 21, 1895
DIED Valencia, Spain, March 24, 1972

A master tailor and dressmaker, as well as a true original, Cristóbal Balenciaga (Bah-len-see-AH-gah) was possibly the greatest couturier of all time. He was renowned for his ability to do everything—design, cut, fit, and sew an entire garment. He worked alone, using his own ideas and hand-making every piece that appeared in his collections. His beautiful, elegant clothes were also so skillfully designed that women did not have to have perfect figures to wear them. The clothes moved with the body and were both comfortable and fashionable.

The facts of Balenciaga's origins are so obscured by legend that it is hard to distinguish between reality and myth. For example, some have said that his father was the captain of Spain's royal yacht; others have said he was the captain of a fishing boat. It is known that after his father's death, Balenciaga and his mother moved to San Sebastián, where she became a seamstress. Balenciaga followed in her footsteps, becoming a tailor. As the story goes, his career in fashion began when the Marquesa de Casa Torres allowed him to copy a Drécoll suit he had admired on her, and later sent him to Paris to meet its designer. The Marquesa encouraged him to study design and in 1916 helped him set up his own shop in San Sebastián. It was the first of three named

Designer Cristóbal Balenciaga

Eisa; the others were in Madrid and Barcelona.

Balenciaga moved to Paris in 1937 but returned to Spain at the start of World War II. After the war he reopened in Paris on Avenue George V, where he established himself as one of the most imaginative and creative artists of Paris couture.

A great student of art, Balenciaga understood how to interpret his sources rather than merely copy them. The somber blacks and browns used by Spanish old masters (Goya, El Greco, Velázquez) were among his favorite colors. His work also shows the influence of early modernists such as Manet and Monet. His interest in post-Cubists and Abstract Expressionists was reflected in his later designs.

(continued)

Red-skirted evening dress with braided top, 1946.

Black lace dress with pink sash, 1951.

Balenciaga's innovations, especially in the 1950s and 1960s, remain influential: the semi-fitted suit jacket; the middy dress, which evolved into the chemise; the cocoon coat; the balloon skirt; and the flamenco evening gown cut short in front and long in back. To achieve his sculptural designs, he worked with the Swiss fabric house Abraham to develop a loosely woven but stiff silk, called gazar, that is very light but able to hold a shape while floating away from the body.

In 1968, Balenciaga abruptly closed his business and retired to Spain. There has been speculation about his reasons but perhaps he was simply tired—he was 75. He came out of retirement to design a wedding dress for Generalissimo Francisco Franco's granddaughter, whose 1972 marriage occurred just two weeks before Balenciaga's death.

A shy and private man who loathed publicity, Balenciaga was seldom photographed, never appeared in his own salon, and, except for his perfumes, refused to engage in commercial exploitation. Since his death he has been honored by a number of exhibitions: in New York in 1973 at the Metropolitan Museum of Art; in France in 1985 at the Museum of Historic Textiles in Lyon, the center of the country's silk industry; and in New York in 1986 at the Fashion Institute of Technology.

Henri de Toulouse Lautrec inspired designs, 1951.

Red velvet stole over an ivory satin gown, 1952.

In the 1990s, the Balenciaga label was revived for ready-to-wear as Balenciaga Le Dix, with Joseph Thimister as head designer (1992–97), followed by Nicolas Ghesquière. In 2001, the house was bought by Gucci Group, which allotted a nine percent share to Ghesquière as creative director. (The French luxury conglomerate PPR had purchased 42 percent of Gucci in 1999, and in 2003 it acquired a majority stake.) Ghesquière resigned from Balenciaga in 2012, and Alexander Wang was appointed creative director. In 2013, PPR changed its name to Kering and sued Ghesquière for breach of confidentiality.

Despite the changes in leadership, all of the label's creative directors have maintained Balenciaga's sense of proportion and balance, his mastery of cut, and his touches of wit. The architectural quality and essential rightness of his designs still inspire awe and admiration, making Balenciaga one of the giants of 20th-century couture.

Spring/summer 2000.

Designer Pierre Balmain.

BORN Pierre Alexandre Claudius Balmain; St. Jean-de-Maurienne, France, May 18, 1914
DIED Paris, June 29, 1982

AWARDS *Neiman Marcus Award*, 1955 • Drama Desk *Award for Outstanding Costume Design*, 1980

Pierre Balmain (Bal-MAH) claimed credit for creating the New Look, though critics and writers have split that recognition between him, CHRISTIAN DIOR, JACQUES FATH, and CRISTÓBAL BALENCIAGA. Balmain's first collections did accentuate the femininity of the figure with small waists, high busts, rounded hips, and long, full skirts—all New Look characteristics. His clothes always projected quiet elegance, and at his death he had just completed the sketches for his fall 1982 collection.

An only child, Balmain was just seven when his father died. He was raised by his mother, who later worked in his couture salon. In 1934, while studying architecture at l'École des Beaux-Arts in Paris, he began sketching dresses and took his designs to CAPTAIN EDWARD MOLYNEUX. The British-born designer allowed Balmain to work for him in the afternoon while attending school in the morning, but finally advised him to devote himself to dress design. Balmain worked for Molyneux until 1939, when he was drafted into the Army. After the fall of France in 1940, Balmain returned to Paris to work for LUCIEN LELONG, where he stayed until he opened his own house in 1945.

♟ PIERRE BALMAIN

In 1951, Balmain opened a New York ready-to-wear operation for which he designed special collections. He also did theater and film work. In addition, there were perfumes, Vent Vert and Jolie Madame, and more than 60 licenses including men's wear, jewelry, luggage, and accessories. Revlon eventually bought the fragrance business and introduced two new ones: Ivoire in 1981 and Opera in 1994.

Balmain died in 1982, but his business remained intact. Until 1990, Erik Mortensen—Balmain's partner in life and work—was in charge of couture. When the house was sold, Mortensen—who had been there for 42 years—was replaced by Hervé Pierre. Ownership changed again in 1992, and OSCAR DE LA RENTA became artistic director of couture. His first collection was for spring 1993, his last for fall/winter 2002–03. De la Renta was succeeded by Laurent Mercier and Christophe Lebourg. Financial difficulties forced the company to file for bankruptcy in 2004, but in 2005 it returned under the artistic direction of Christophe Decarnin. In 2011, 25-year-old Olivier Rousteing was named creative director of Balmain.

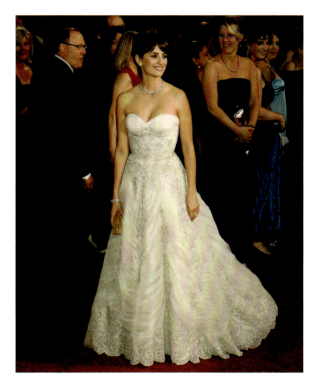

Penelope Cruz wears a vintage dress from Pierre Balmain's collection.

BAND OF OUTSIDERS (SCOTT STERNBERG) ◣ ▮

BORN Dayton, Ohio

AWARDS Council of Fashion Designers of America (CFDA) *Swarovski Award for Menswear*, 2008; *Menswear Designer of the Year*, 2009

Scott Sternberg did not always know that his path in life would lead to fashion. He majored in economics at Washington University in Saint Louis. In 1997, he moved to Los Angeles to work in the media division of Creative Artists Agency (CAA). After a "quarter-life crisis," Sternberg found a new job consulting for a trio of entrepreneurs. One of them, Emily Scott (a cofounder of J.Crew), suggested he start his own company. Band of Outsiders was launched in 2004. Sternberg's line showcased a fun, stylish new generation of men wearing well-tailored, slim-fitted pieces. The brand is often described as "preppy with a twist."

In 2007, Sternberg expanded into women's wear with Boy by Band of Outsiders, which features pieces inspired by men's wear. By 2008, Sternberg was winning numerous awards for his collections, particularly men's wear. In 2010, he introduced a second women's wear collection called Girl, comprising mostly feminine dresses, and a more affordable line for men.

In 2011, Band of Outsiders struck a deal with Sazaby League for distribution in Japan. That same year, Sternberg launched his first resort collection and walked the runway for the first time. In 2013, singer Frank Ocean became the face of the Band of Outsiders spring campaign and Sternberg showed in Paris and opened his first store in Tokyo.

Stenberg has said that his men's wear collections are inspired by the masculine ideal in old cinema— particularly the Nouvelle Vague movement, including the Jean-Luc Godard film from which the label takes its name.

Fall 2010.

Spring 2014.

Designer Jeffrey Banks.

BORN Washington, D.C., November 3, 1955

AWARDS Coty American Fashion Critics' Awards *Special Award (men's furs, for Alixandre)*, 1977; *Menswear Designer of the Year*, 1982 • *Earnshaw* magazine *Earnie Award for Boys' Wear*, 1980 • Cutty Sark Men's Fashion Awards *Designer of the Year*, 1987

Jeffrey Banks began his illustrious career at the age of ten, when he designed an Easter outfit for his mother consisting of a raw silk dress and a side-buttoned wool jersey coat. By 15, he was selling men's wear at Britches of Georgetown, where he was a regular customer. He studied at Pratt Institute in Brooklyn and graduated from Parsons School of Design in 1977. Following stints as an assistant to Ralph Lauren and Calvin Klein, Banks designed for Alixandre, Concorde International, Merona Sport, and Nik. At Merona Sport in the late 1970s, he introduced new colors and innovative fabrics, increasing sales by more than half.

In 1978, Banks opened his own design firm, and in 1980 launched his men's wear and boy's wear labels. In 1988, Japanese investor Tomio Taki bought a one-third interest in a joint venture with Banks, giving him more

◤ JEFFREY BANKS

time to design. He designed for Hartz & Company in 1984 and consulted for Herman Geist in 1990. Licensing agreements were signed with Bloomingdale's for men's wear, Neema Clothing for fine tailored clothing, and Watson Brothers for hosiery and belts. Jeffrey Banks Ltd. and Jeffrey Banks International had sales exceeding $20 million by the late 1990s.

After a hiatus that ended in 1998, Banks became design director of the Johnnie Walker Collection of sportswear and accessories, and creative design director for Bloomingdale's labels The East Island and Metropolitan View. He also designed woven shirts and knits for Haggar Clothing's Haggar Cool 18, increasing sales at department stores.

With a penchant for plaid and classic charm, Banks's designs are handsome and mature even when catering to younger audiences. In stark contrast to his mentors, his boy's wear uses a palette of bright, playful primary and secondary colors. His men's wear is formal yet warm and comfortable. In 2011, Banks and Doria de La Chapelle wrote *Preppy: Cultivating Ivy Style*, a book that references all things tartan and plaid.

Banks has served on the board of trustees at the Fashion Institute of Technology and is an executive board member of the Council of Fashion Designers of America (CFDA). He is also vice chair of the board of the Hetrick-Martin Institute.

Male model (right) wearing a look from Jeffrey Banks, 1981.

TRAVIS BANTON

BORN Waco, Texas, August 18, 1894
DIED Los Angeles, February 2, 1958

Travis Banton worked for Paramount Pictures for 14 years, designing elegant, sophisticated clothes for some of the screen's most legendary actresses—including Claudette Colbert, Marlene Dietrich, Carole Lombard, and Mae West. He favored glow and shimmer over sparkle and shine and was especially partial to the bias cut. With an extraordinarily long career, Banton is most remembered for what became known as "the Paramount look." He produced clothes of the highest quality, with superb fabric, workmanship, and fit. The effect was dreamy, elegant, and understated.

Banton's parents moved to New York City when he was two. He briefly attended Columbia University, then transferred to the Art Students League and the School of Fine and Applied Arts. His apprenticeship to Madame Frances, a New York custom dressmaker, was interrupted by naval service in World War I—but not before Banton had established himself as a designer. On his return he worked for a number of houses, including Lucile, the training ground for Howard Greer and other designers. Banton then opened his own salon, where his designs included elaborate costumes for the *Ziegfeld Follies*.

At the urging of Walter Wanger, Banton went to Hollywood in 1924 to design costumes for Leatrice Joy in Paramount Pictures's *The Dressmaker from Paris*. He stayed at Paramount and in 1927, when Greer left to open his own business, became the studio's head designer. When his Paramount contract expired in 1938, Banton joined Greer as a private couturier. A year later he began working at 20th Century Fox, followed by intermittent projects for Universal Studios. He also ran his own dressmaking business, turning to ready-to-wear in the

Designer Travis Banton (center) with models.

1950s. Banton designed Rosalind Russell's wardrobe for the stage production of *Auntie Mame* and dressed Dinah Shore for her television appearances and private life.

By the end of his career, Banton had designed costumes for more than 122 movies. He is also credited with teaching the craft of costume design to the legendary EDITH HEAD.

Designer/illustrator George Barbier.

BORN Nantes, France, October 10, 1882
DIED Paris, March 16, 1932

GEORGE BARBIER

After World War I, Barbier began designing for the theater. Working with ERTÉ, he designed costumes and sets for the *Follies Bergére* in France and for the *Ziegfield Follies* in America. He also designed costumes for Rudolph Valentino's 1924 film *Monsieur Beaucaire*. The last show that Barbier worked on was *Paris Shakes* at the Casino de Paris, starring Josephine Baker.

Barbier's work has influenced many contemporary designers, including BOB MACKIE and JOHN GALLIANO—both ground-breaking designers in their own right.

George Barbier (Zhorj Bah-BE-yay) began his career as a set and costume designer for the Ballet Russes after graduating from the l'École des Beaux-Arts in Paris. His illustrations gracefully captured the essence of Art Deco, the prevailing art movement of the time. Barbier's first paid job as an illustrator was with the elite fashion journal *de Dames et Des Modes*. Although the publication folded just two years after its inception, Barbier's work there established him in the fashion industry as both a designer and an illustrator. He later illustrated for the *Gazette du Bon Ton*, and his contract continued when *Vogue* took it over. Barbier was commissioned to illustrate for some of the most popular design houses of his generation, including WORTH, LANVIN, and POIRET. The flamboyant, celebratory, and decorative designs in Barbier's illustrations appealed to both cutting-edge designers and adventurous buyers of French fashion.

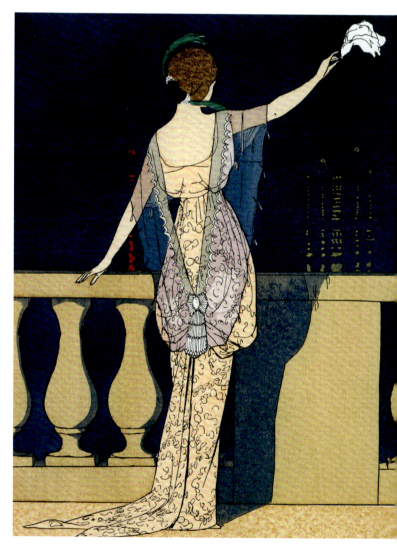
Illustration of woman in a Paquin evening dress, 1913.

JHANE BARNES ♟

BORN Jane Barnes; Maryland, 1954

AWARDS Coty American Fashion Critics' Awards *Menswear,* 1980; *Men's Apparel,* 1981; *Return Award (menswear),* 1984 • Council of Fashion Designers of America (CFDA) *Outstanding Menswear Designer,* 1981 • Chicago Athenaeum Museum of Architecture *Good Design Award,* 2007

Jhane Barnes established her own company in 1977, when she was 23. Though mainly known for men's sportswear, she has also made sportswear for women. Her designs are unconstructed but beautifully tailored in luxurious and original fabrics, many of which she also designs. They are marked by innovative details and carefully developed and produced. Barnes provides an architectural perspective to her clothing, which is now exclusively men's wear—from belts and neckwear to sportswear, suits, and outerwear—and sold at upscale stores and on her website. She also designs products such as textiles, carpets, furniture, upholstery, and drapes.

In 2002, Barnes privatized her textile company, Jhane Barnes Textiles. She draws inspiration from the relationship between technology and environmental sustainability. Barnes created an environmentally friendly line of office furniture for Jofeo, an Indian manufacturer. The line, Tahke, is made from bamboo. Barnes has also furnished offices for companies such as Google, Delta Air Lines, and Sony.

In 2007, Barnes used techniques from her men's wear line to design resin wall panels and tabletops for Lumicar—an undertaking that won her the Good

Designer Jhane Barnes.

Design Award from the Chicago Athenaeum Museum of Architecture four times. She has also designed uniforms for the Orlando Magic basketball team and launched an eyewear line. In 2009, Barnes formed a partnership with A. W. Chang, a necktie and shirt manufacturer that gave her access to its factories, including weaving and printing mills. Fall 2013 marked Barnes's final men's wear collection, as she is shifting her focus to the contract interiors market.

Jhane Barnes men's wear design.

"Mental block" men's wear design.

Designer Neil Barrett.

⬛ NEIL BARRETT

would raid men's stores for his pieces, such as sweaters and motorcycle jackets. Barrett's designs for both women and men are not for extremely fit and thin models, but for regular people with a wide variety of body types. His strengths include the use of innovative fabrics (he has been a consultant to the Italian textile industry) in subtle colors and with clever details, and an ability to make clothes that are both fashionable and wearable.

In 2003, Barrett was named creative director for a series of Puma collections for sport teams, and in 2006 he launched his Indigo Denim Collection for men and women. In 2011–12, he significantly expanded his operations, opening four boutiques in Hong Kong and South Korea that he designed with legendary architect Zara Hadid. Barrett has also created wardrobes for blockbuster movies such as *Spiderman 2* and *3*; *I, Robot*; and *Ghost Rider*.

BORN South Devon, England, 1965

Neil Barrett grew up in southwestern England on the stormy English Channel. He describes himself as having been "a very practical kid who went out dressed for all kinds of rough weather." Many of his family members were master tailors who made uniforms for British naval officers.

In 1989, after graduating from the Royal College of Art, Barrett worked for GUCCI and then PRADA before joining Samsonite, the Belgian luggage company, in 1998. There he designed men's wear geared toward travelers, including a jacket with a built-in watch, a jacket with built-in earplugs and an inflatable neck pillow, and crease-resistant pants with multiple pockets. Intended not as fashion but as practical things for travel, the clothes got an enthusiastic response from the fashion press.

Barrett's first collection under his name, shown in 1999, was also men's wear. Described as haute utilitarian, the spare, durable clothes were designed not just for the runway but also to be worn. Barrett's first capsule collection for women appeared in Milan in 2000, and was shown with his men's collection. Before that, women

Spring 2014.

MICHAEL BASTIAN ▼

BORN Lyons, New York, 1965

AWARDS Council of Fashion Designers of America (CFDA) *Menswear Designer of the Year*, 2011

Michael Bastian (BAS-tee-unh) is an American designer of luxury men's wear. After graduating from Babson College in Wellesley, Massachusetts, he worked as a buyer for Abraham and Strauss. He also worked at Sotheby's, Polo RALPH LAUREN, TIFFANY, and Bergdorf Goodman, where

Above: Designer Michael Bastian.
Left: Fall 2013 men's wear.

he was director of men's fashion for five years. In 2007, Bastian started his own line with the goal of providing "a new American voice, something modern and luxurious, but also a little broken down and familiar."

In 2010, Bastian collaborated with GANT to create GANT by Michael Bastian, a line that includes women's wear, men's wear, eyewear, and watches. This collaboration attracted considerable press coverage, from *GQ* to Forbes.com. The line is sold at more than 35 retail locations in North America, Europe, Asia, and the Middle East, and distributed in over 60 countries through GANT retail stores and specialty boutiques. Bastian has also collaborated on sunglasses with Randolph Engineering, flip-flops with Havaianas, and jewelry with Philip Crangi.

Bastian's spring 2014 collection featured bold pineapple and leopard prints, shoes embroidered with slingshots and balloons, and an overall sense of preppy playfulness—a stark contrast to the dark solids of his fall 2013 collection.

CECIL BEATON

Cecil Beaton.

BORN London, January 14, 1904
DIED Brood Chalke, Wiltshire, England, January 18, 1980

AWARDS Tony Awards for Best Costume Design: *Quadrille,* 1955; *My Fair Lady,* 1957; *Saratoga,* 1960: *Coco,* 1970 • *Neiman Marcus Award,* 1956 • British Government *Commander of the Most Excellent Order of the British Empire (CBE),* 1957 • Academy Awards: *Gigi (costume design),* 1958; *My Fair Lady (art direction and costume design),* 1965 • French Government *Chevalier de la Légion d'Honneur (Legion of Honor),* 1960

Cecil Beaton was a British photographer, artist, writer, and costume and set designer. After attending Cambridge University, in 1927 he began a long affiliation with *Vogue* (British and American), where his first contributions were spidery sketches, caricatures of well-known London actresses, and drawings of clothes worn at society parties; photographs appeared later. In her memoirs, long-time *Vogue* editor EDNA WOOLMAN CHASE described Beaton at their first meeting as "tall, slender, swaying like a reed, blond, and very young," with a demeanor that was "an odd combination of airiness and assurance." Chase also said, "What I like best is his debunking attitude toward life and his

ability for hard work." He did both fashion and portrait photography, and became the favored photographer of the British royal family. During World War II, he took pictures for the Ministry of Information in North Africa, Burma, and China.

In 1935, Beaton began designing sets and costumes for ballets, operas, and plays in London and New York, including *Lady Windermere's Fan, Quadrille, The Grass Harp,* and *The School for Scandal (Comédie Française).* In addition, he created costumes for the New York, London, and film productions of *My Fair Lady* and for the films *Gigi* and *The Doctor's Dilemma.* He also designed hotel lobbies and club interiors.

A prolific writer and diarist, Beaton published many books, illustrating them and those of others with drawings and photographs. He was knighted by Queen Elizabeth II in 1972. In 1974, Beaton suffered a stroke that paralyzed the right side of his body, but he learned to paint and take photos with his left hand. From 1977 until his death, he lived in semi-retirement at his home in Wiltshire.

Audrey Hepburn wearing a costume photographed and designed by Cecil Beaton for *My Fair Lady,* 1963.

GEOFFREY BEENE ⧖

BORN Haynesville, Louisiana, August 30, 1927
DIED New York City, September 28, 2004

AWARDS Coty American Fashion Critics' Awards *Winnie*, 1964; *Return Award*, 1966; *Hall of Fame Award*, 1974; *Hall of Fame Citation*, 1975; *Hall of Fame Citation (contribution to American fashion)*, 1977; *Hall of Fame Citation (contribution to international status of American fashion)*, 1979; *Winnie*, 1981; *Special Award*, 1982 • *Neiman Marcus Award*, 1964, 1965 • Council of Fashion Designers of America (CFDA) *Special Award*, 1985; *Special Award (Designer of the Year)*, 1986; *Special Award (fashion as art)*, 1988; *Geoffrey Beene Lifetime Achievement Award*, 1997 .

Designer Geoffrey Beene.

Mini shirtdress, 1968.

Long considered the most original and creative designer in American fashion, Geoffrey Beene was revered for his subtle cuts, imaginative use of color, and luxurious fabrics. Making clothes that fit the lives of modern women was a major preoccupation—he believed that clothes had to not only look attractive but also move well and be comfortable to wear and easy to pack. Over his career he refined his style, increasing simplicity and emphasizing cut and line using light, unusual fabrics.

The grandson and nephew of doctors, Beene studied medicine for three years at Tulane University in New Orleans. But after deciding that medicine was not for him, he moved to Los Angeles, where he created window displays at I. Magnin. His talent was recognized by an executive who suggested that he pursue a career in fashion.

Beene attended Traphagen School of Fashion in New York for one summer and in 1947 went to Paris to study at l'École de la Chambre Syndicale and Académie Julian. While there, he apprenticed with a tailor who had worked for couturier CAPTAIN EDWARD MOLYNEUX, a master of tailoring and the bias cut. Returning to New York in 1950, Beene designed for several small custom salons and for Samuel Winston and Harmay. In 1958, he joined Teal Traina and for the first time had his name on a label. He opened his own business in 1962.

Beene's first collection, shown in spring 1963, had elements characteristic of his work throughout the 1960s, including loose fits, eased waistlines, bloused tops, and flared skirts. Each collection included at least one tongue-in-cheek style to stir things up, such as a black coat paved with wood buttons and a tutu evening dress with sequined bodice and feather skirt. Beene's memorable designs include long, sequined evening gowns cut like football jerseys—complete with numerals—tweed evening pants paired with jeweled or lamé jackets, a gray sweatshirt bathing suit, and soft evening coats made of striped blankets.

Beene's designs also included furs, swimwear, jewelry, scarves, men's wear, and Lynda Bird Johnson's wedding dress. He had a boutique collection, fragrances for women and men, and licensed his name for shoes, gloves, hosiery, eyewear, loungewear, bedding, and furniture. His clothes were shown in Europe with great success, including in Milan in 1975 and at the U.S. embassies in Rome, Paris, Brussels, and Vienna. In 1989, he opened his first retail shop, in the Sherry Netherland Hotel on Fifth Avenue in New York City.

In 1988, Beene was honored by a retrospective at the National Academy of Design celebrating his first 25 years in business. In 1993, he commissioned a

Linen shirt and wool skirt, 1985.

30-minute film to mark his 30th year in business. And in 1994, the Fashion Institute of Technology mounted *Beene Unbound*, a 30-year retrospective of his work.

Beene ended his wholesale operations in 2001, opting to sell only to private clients. He died in 2004, and the next year a biography titled *Beene by Beene* was published. In 2006, the Geoffrey Beene Cancer Research Center at Manhattan's Memorial Sloan Kettering Cancer Center was established with funds from his estate.

Left and Right: Ready-to-wear, spring/summer 1973.

CHADWICK BELL ⬛

BORN Southern California

Four generations of Chadwick Bell's family were crafts-men, and his family instilled in him a love of art and craftsmanship. In college, Bell studied color theory, design, and form, and developed a passion for fashion. After graduation, he and childhood friend Vanessa Webster moved to New York City with the dream of starting their own business, and in 2007 they founded the Chadwick Bell label. Bell handles the creative side and Webster manages the company.

Bell designs for modern, worldly, chic women. Inspired by how art imitates life, his clothes reflect different fantasies and scenarios that he envisions for every season. For example, his fall 2009 collection was inspired entirely by Catherine Deneuve's character in the French film classic *Belle de Jour*. For fall 2013, Bell explored contrasts between the unstructured and the structured and between East and West, for women who know where they are going and ready for the future. Bell's knowledge of color theory is evident in many of his collections—he places blues with bright oranges, and neutrals with pops of sun-faded yellow.

Designer Chadwick Bell.

Elizabeth Banks wears a design from Chadwick Bell.

Fall 2013.

Photographer Gilles Bensimon.

BORN Paris, 1944

Photographer Gilles Bensimon (Zheal BEN-see-mah) joined the staff of French *ELLE* in 1967. When American *ELLE* was launched in 1985, he moved to America to work as the magazine's creative director. Bensimon soon established a reputation for shooting the best of the best, and at *ELLE* he photographed Christy

GILLES BENSIMON

Turlington, Claudia Schiffer, Lisa Snowdon, Cindy Crawford, Naomi Campbell, Tyra Banks, Rachel Williams, and Elle Macpherson, who Bensimon married in 1985 (and divorced four years later).

Bensimon eventually became international creative director for *ELLE*, thanks in no small part to his meticulous attention to detail. He took his work very seriously, exerting control over models, hair, and clothing in every photo he took for the magazine. Bensimon often shot *ELLE*'s fashion features himself to ensure that they met his high standards.

Bensimon's third marriage, to former model Kelly Killoren—who later became founding editor of *ELLE Accessories* and a fashion and society journalist—ended after ten years. Killoren went on to star in the reality television show *The Real Housewives of New York City*.

In 2003, Bensimon published his first book, *Gilles Bensimon Photography: No Particular Order,* with 200 pages of shots from his 30-year career. In 2009, his photos of country singer Faith Hill (in which she posed as her favorite blonde icons: Grace Kelly, Twiggy, and Brigitte Bardot) appeared on the cover of *Redbook*—marking the first time in 20 years that he shot for a publication other than *ELLE*. In 2013, an exhibit of his work called *Elles* opened at the Sofitel Hotel in Washington, D.C. and later appeared at Sofitel properties in New York, Chicago, and Los Angeles. That same year, Bensimon had an exhibit of photos at London's Hamiltons Gallery, *Watercolour*, that departed from his usual subject matter of beautiful women, instead showing flowers submerged in water.

CHRIS BENZ ▲

BORN Seattle, Washington, 1982

Chris Benz grew up near Seattle on Bainbridge Island, Washington, and left high school early to study at Parsons School of Design. After graduating in 2004, he won the Council of Fashion Designers of America (CFDA) Emerging Designer Award. Benz interned for MARC JACOBS and designed dresses and formal wear for J.Crew before introducing his own collection in 2007 to immediate acclaim. *New York Times* fashion reporter Eric Wilson said that Benz "may be the best example of the heightened level of sophistication that is expected of new designers today."

Benz's designs reflect his Seattle roots, from his color palette to his classic silhouettes, combined with elements of surprise. His clothes are intended for an "elegant tomboy" who loves to dance, with a little bohemian

Designer Chris Benz.

Spring 2013.

flavor. The designer calls her "a carefree, artsy girl who likes to have fun and forgets to pay her cellphone bill."

In 2008, Benz won the first Fur Information Council of America (FICA) award for Emerging Designer of the Year and developed frames for Moscot eyewear. In 2010, he created Chris & Tell lipstick for Lancôme. Benz has also been a columnist for Fashionista.com, and in 2012 he created clothes for Mattel's Presidential Barbie line. During the global recession, Benz lowered the prices of his clothes and was among one of the few designers whose line prospered.

Benz's designs are regularly worn by Eva Amurri Martino (daughter of Susan Sarandon) and Lola Montes Schnabel (daughter of Julian Schnabel). He got a huge media boost in 2012 when Sasha Obama wore his emerald green skirt on election night. For spring 2013, Benz created CB Denim, a jeans label, and that fall he skipped New York Fashion Week to focus on developing and rebranding his line.

Artist Christian Bérard (right).

BORN Paris, 1902
DIED Paris, 1949

CHRISTIAN BÉRARD

Mode, a touring exhibition of mannequins wearing designs from Paris's top couturiers. In addition, Bérard designed for Comédie Française and collaborated with actor-producer Louis Jouvet.

The fashion reputation of Christian Bérard (BAY-rarh) is largely based on his illustrations for *Vogue* in the 1930s. But as an artist, decorator, and costume designer, his life was intertwined with the creative lives of Paris in his time, and his influence was enormous. In great demand for his comments, suggestions, and technical advice, Bérard (also known as Bébé) was a familiar figure in creative circles, with a rumpled and disheveled appearance that was a marked contrast to the refinement and beauty of his work.

One of the great designers in French theater, Bérard designed scenery and costumes for many productions by his friend Jean Cocteau, from *La Voix Humaine* (1930) to *La Folle de Chaillot* (1949). After World War II, Bérard also worked with Cocteau on Théâtre de la

Illustration, 1935.

ROSE BERTIN 👗 👜

BORN Marie-Jeanne Rose Bertin; near Abbeville, France, July 2, 1747

DIED Épinay-sur-Seine, France, September 22, 1813

At 16, Rose Bertin became an apprentice in the Paris millinery shop of a Mademoiselle Pagelle. When sent to deliver hats to the royal princesses at the Conti Palace, she was noticed by Princesse de Conti, who became her sponsor. In 1772, Bertin was appointed court milliner. She was introduced to Marie Antoinette and became her confidante.

Such connections helped make Bertin's shop, Le Grand Mogol, extremely successful with the French court and the diplomatic corps. She was commissioned to create dresses and hats for foreign courts, making her one of the first exporters of French fashion. She also produced fantastic headdresses that reflected current events—enormously costly and symbolic of the excesses that led to the French Revolution.

Bertin is sometimes considered the first "name" designer. Despite her reputation for pride, arrogance, and ambition, she was widely celebrated and dubbed the "Minister of Fashion." At the onset of the French Revolution, Bertin fled to England but remained loyal to the Queen. After returning to France in 1800, she transferred her business to her nephews.

Hat designed for Easter, 1943.

Easter bonnet decorated with a bird, 1943.

Designer Laura Biagiotti (right).

BORN Rome, 1943

Laura Biagiotti (BEE-uh-jot-tee) graduated from Rome University with a degree in literature, then worked at her parents' dressmaking business, where she produced clothes for other designers. Her first collection under her own label appeared in Florence in 1972. Soon afterward, she bought a cashmere firm and discovered her true calling.

Biagiotti became known as the "Queen of Cashmere," producing beautiful sweaters from the fiber for both men and women. Of exceptional coloring and quality, the sweaters were sold under the MacPherson label. For her label, Laura Biagiotti Roma, Biagiotti has collaborated with her daughter, Lavinia Biagiotti Cigna, to produce women's clothes that are feminine

✕ LAURA BIAGIOTTI

and wearable, interestingly detailed, and of excellent workmanship, reflecting a mastery of knitwear. Baigiotti's first fragrance, Fiori Bianchi, was introduced in 1982 and followed by numerous others for women and men. In fall 2001, Biagiotti launched a new fragrance line, Laura Biagiotti Roma. By 2013, her lines also included eyewear, handbags, lingerie, children's wear, and home goods.

The Italian government has honored Biagiotti for her consistent support of Italian culture and trade both domestically and abroad. In 2011, she became the first woman to receive the Leonardo Award, presented by the president of the Italian Republic to celebrate Italian excellence worldwide.

Spring/Summer 2014.

DIRK BIKKEMBERGS ▲

Designer Dirk Bikkembergs.

BORN Cologne, Germany, January 2, 1959

AWARDS Golden Spindle Award *Best Young Designer in Fashion*, 1985 • Moët & Chandon *Esprit du Siècle*, 2000

Autumn/winter 1995.

Fall 2013.   Fall 2013.

A 1982 graduate of the Royal Academy of Fine Arts in Antwerp, Belgium, Dirk Bikkembergs is one of the "Antwerp Six" group of avant-garde fashion designers. He first worked at various Belgian fashion firms, but his 1985 Golden Spindle Award led to a collaboration with a Belgian shoe manufacturer and his first collection of men's shoes in 1986. Men's wear followed, and in 1988 he presented his first full collection in Paris.

Bikkembergs's first women's wear collection in 1993 shared the runway with the men's—essentially the same garments but fitted for a woman's body. The collection now ranges from outerwear to evening wear. In 2000, he launched Bikkembergs Sport and a diffusion line for both men and women. Bikkembergs sees the same person wearing pieces from each collection.

Bikkembergs aims to make clothes and shoes that are beyond fashion and will endure for years. His creative vision is driven by the proverb, "A healthy mind resides in a healthy body," and his work fuses the strength of sport with the artistry of fashion design. In 2010, Zeis Excelsa SpA acquired the Bikkembergs brand, and in 2012 Harnish Marrow became its new creative director. Dirk Bikkembergs stores can be found throughout Asia.

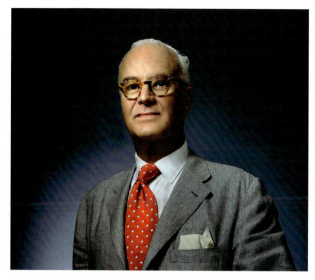

Designer Manolo Blahnik.

BORN Santa Cruz de la Palma, Canary Islands, November 27, 1942

AWARDS Council of Fashion Designers of America (CFDA) *Special Award (accessory design),* 1987, 1989; *Stiletto Award,* 1997 • British Fashion Awards *Outstanding Achievement,* 2012

One of the world's most creative and influential shoe designers, Manolo Blahnik (BLON-ik) is based in London, where every year he produces four collections of his fantastical, elegant shoes. His designs are sold at top specialty stores and his own boutiques—including to celebrities such as Bianca Jagger, Cher, Madonna, Paloma Picasso, and Sarah Jessica Parker—and have been used in runway shows by designers as different as Zandra Rhodes and Bill Blass. He has done collections for Perry Ellis, Calvin Klein, and Anne Klein, and men's shoes for Yves Saint Laurent.

Blahnik's father was Czech and his mother was Spanish, an elegant woman who shopped for clothes in Paris, Monte Carlo, and Madrid. She exposed Blahnik to the great designers of the day, including Dior, Balenciaga, and Spain's famous cobbler, Rius. He first attended the University of Geneva, then moved to Paris to study art at l'École du Louvre. Around 1968, he moved to London.

In 1971, Blahnik went to New York, where his friend Paloma Picasso arranged for him to show his sketches to *Vogue* editor Diana Vreeland. She was so impressed that she urged him to go into shoe design and helped connect him with an Italian manufacturer. Today Blahnik uses four Italian factories to translate his ideas into reality, spending nearly three months a year in Milan supervising their work. He works without assistants, drawing as many as 300 designs a year. Blahnik's shoes are quite expensive, with each pair made by hand from the costliest fabrics and finest leathers; a few rare designs are studded with diamonds and other precious gems. Though he makes a few low-heeled designs, Blahnik is mainly identified with extremely high, spiky heels.

A man of prodigious energy, Blahnik personally cuts 80 or more samples each season—a skill that took him seven years to acquire. He also draws and paints, but mainly he thinks about shoes. He has filled two floors and the attic of his weekend house in Bath, England, with his collections: one shoe of every pair he has made. He is constantly traveling between London, Milan, America, and Asia.

In 2003, the Design Museum of London opened a major Blahnik exhibit; a book of his drawings was published in conjunction. In 2005, Eric Boman published *Blahnik by Boman,* a photographic celebration of the designer's shoes. In 2006, Blahnik designed the footwear for Sofia Coppola's film *Marie Antoinette,* which won the Academy Award for best costume design. Blahnik is also known for designs worn by Sarah Jessica Parker in the television series and films *Sex and the City.*

In 2012, Blahnik celebrated 40 years in business, and in 2013 he provided imagery for the fall/winter London Fashion Week inspired by his career.

Blue pump and original sketch from the movie *Sex and the City,* 2008.

BILL BLASS

BORN Fort Wayne, Indiana, June 22, 1922
DIED New Preston, Connecticut, June 12, 2002

AWARDS Coty American Fashion Critics' Awards *Winnie,* 1961; *Return Award,* 1963; *Men's Wear,* 1968; *Hall of Fame,* 1970; *Hall of Fame Citation,* 1971, 1982, 1983; *Special Award (furs for Revillon America),* 1975 • *Neiman Marcus Award,* 1969 • Council of Fashion Designers of America (CFDA) *Lifetime Achievement Award,* 1986; *Dom Pérignon Award,* 1995; *Special Award (Dean of American Fashion),* 2000

Designer Bill Blass.

When Bill Blass announced his retirement and the sale of his business in 1999, anguished cries went up from New York City's social establishment, of which he was a member. For more than 30 years he had produced high-priced, high-quality clothes for the women in that circle and their peers around the world—first for other labels and then under his own name.

Blass considered himself a quintessential American designer, and his work—from simple but elegant day wear to glamorous evening wear—reflected that attitude. Evening clothes, for example, could resemble dressy sportswear, with skirts of crisp taffeta or sheer chiffon topped by cashmere twin sets. Interesting mixtures of patterns and textures were expertly coordinated to create a polished, worldly look for women with active social lives.

Blass graduated high school in 1939, then studied fashion in New York for six months. His first fashion job was in 1940 as a sketch artist for David Crystal, but he resigned to enlist in the Army for World War II, where he engaged in counterintelligence. After the war he worked briefly for ANNE KLEIN (who told him that he had good manners but lacked talent), and in 1946 became a designer at Anna Miller & Co. When the company merged with Maurice Rentner, Blass quickly rose to head designer; his name went on the label when

Zebra print wrap pajama, 1974.

Blass gave time and support to his industry and was an early vice president of the CFDA. He was also a perceptive and generous supporter of design talent in others, and in 1994 he donated $10 million to the New York Public Library.

Blass died shortly after finishing his memoir, *Bare Blass*. The label continues to produce new collections with the help of designers PETER SOM and MICHAEL BASTIAN.

Blazer, skirt, vest, and scarf, 1972.

Rentner died in 1960. Ten years later Blass bought the company and renamed it Bill Blass Ltd.

In addition to his designer clothes for women, Blass's design projects have included women's sportswear, rainwear, *Vogue* patterns, loungewear, and scarves, as well as men's wear. His name has also been licensed for automobiles, uniforms for American Airlines flight attendants, and even chocolates. The first Bill Blass perfume was introduced in 1978.

Actress Candice Bergen wearing kimono dress, 1970.

KENNETH PAUL BLOCK ✐

BORN Larchmont, New York, July 26, 1924
DIED New York City, April 23, 2009

Illustrator Kenneth Paul Block.

Even after fashion magazines started using photographers instead of illustrators, Kenneth Paul Block remained in demand. Indeed, Block was an illustrator—and, for a time, chief features artist—for *Women's Wear Daily* for nearly 40 years. He later worked for *W* as well.

Block graduated from Parsons School of Design. His first job was in 1945 as a sketch artist for McCall's Patterns. In the mid-1950s, he joined *WWD*, where he became known for his sketches of designer clothes as well as celebrities and socialites such as Babe Paley, Gloria Vanderbilt, Catherine Deneuve, and Sophia Lauren. Block's illustrations coincided with *WWD*'s growing popularity, and he became famous for capturing intricate details that made his glamorous subjects look even more alluring. His penchant for capturing small gestures—say, in the way his subjects sat or held objects—gave him an edge above other illustrators. Block's style was so influential that he was the subject of a 2008 book, *Drawing Fashion: The Art of Kenneth Paul Block*.

Despite the prevalence of photography, Block was so widely respected that he was perhaps single-handedly responsible for keeping illustration in fashion publications. He sketched the previews and runway shows of all the major designers from the time of CoCo Chanel through the psychedelic designs of the 1960s and 1970s, though he was famous for never changing his personal style—an ascot, brightly colored jacket, and white buck shoes.

Susan Mulcahy's book *Drawing Fashion: The Art of Kenneth Paul Block* was published in 2008. Before his death, Block donated 1,844 of his illustrations to Boston's Museum of Fine Arts, ensuring that his work will always be available to the public.

Illustration of black dress from Ungaro, 1973.

Illustration of Italian coats from Ferragamo, Genny, Ver-sace, and Krizia, 1990s.

Designers David Blond and Phillipe Blond.

BORN Phillipe Rollano; Puerto Rico
David Trujillo; Key West, Florida

AWARDS *Ecco Domani Fashion Foundation Award*, 2010

The Blonds are a design duo comprising Phillipe Rollano and David Trujillo. Raised in New York City,

Spring 2014.

Rollano had a passion for fashion and attended the Fashion Institute of Technology. After graduating, he became a freelance illustrator and makeup artist for MAC Cosmetics. Trujillo studied fashion merchandising and design at the International Fine Arts College in Miami. After that, he created window displays for Saks Fifth Avenue in Bal Harbor, Florida, and Macy's in New York City, where he met Rollano and the two realized they shared similar views and goals. They launched their first collection in 2004 and gained fame in 2007 when Beyoncé wore one of their diamond-crusted corsets in the music video for "Upgrade U."

Both men are Latino and are partners creatively and romantically. Both colored their hair platinum blond and changed their names to Phillipe and David Blond for the stage. "It's a state of mind, you don't have to be blond to be 'blond.'" They aim to test the boundaries of art and fashion, and are known for their handmade corsetry. Some call them "The "Kings of Bling."

The Blonds have dressed many female pop stars, including Beyoncé, Rihanna, Britney Spears, Katy Perry, Fergie, Jennifer Lopez, and Pink. "They are redefining couture," says PATRICIA FIELD, who has been one of their biggest supporters and helped launched their careers when she started selling some of their pieces at her Eighth Street store in New York. But the biggest muse for the Blonds is Phillipe himself, who walks the runway in drag at all of their shows—always elaborate, entertaining events infused with glamor.

In 2012, the Blonds started designing custom bridal gowns, including one for a Romanian client that was inspired by an outfit in a Kylie Minogue video and cost between $100,000 and $150,000.

Spring 2014.

B MICHAEL ▼

Above: Designer b Michael.
Right: Spring 2009.

BORN Durham, Connecticut

b Michael's career began not on Fashion Avenue but on Wall Street, where the University of Connecticut graduate was an account executive. He left finance to work for OSCAR DE LA RENTA, and later launched a successful line of women's hats that expanded to accessories and clothing. In 1998, Michael was inducted into the Council of Fashion Designers of America (CFDA). He unveiled his first couture collection in 1999, and today offers extensive collections for both women and men, all made entirely in America.

Michael has been a fashion critic and frequent guest lecturer at New York's Fashion Institute of Technology. His celebrity clients include Cicely Tyson, Halle Berry, Cate Blanchett, and Lynn Whitfield. His gowns are colorful and elegant but usually simple. One notable exception was a "kaleidoscope" dress made from 50 pieces of fabric.

Michael is one of the only male African-American designers who shows at New York Fashion Week. He has said that for black designers to make headway in fashion, they must disregard their minority status. "The most important point for me," he says, "is that the industry sees us as American designers that dress a diverse mainstream market." In 2003, Michael formed Dm Fashion Group with Wayne Demar to market the b Michael brand. In 2012, Michael designed the clothes for the movie *Sparkle* and launched a ready-to-wear collection, b michael America Red, for Macy's.

Designer Ozwald Boateng.

BORN London, November 28, 1968

AWARDS Trophees de la Mode *Best Male Designer*, 1996 • British Fashion Awards *Top Men's Wear Designer*, 2000 • Cologne Fashion Awards *Best Male Designer*, 2002 • British Government *Order of the British Empire* (OBE, for services to the clothing industry), 2006 • Mayfair Times Awards *Fashion Personality of the Year*, 2008

✠ OZWALD BOATENG

year and by Daniel Day-Lewis in 2003. Boateng was interviewed in *Live Forever*, a 2003 film highlighting the conception of Cool Britannia and Britpop. He also introduced his fragrance Parfum Bespoke in 2003.

Boateng was appointed creative director of GIVENCHY Homme in 2003, bringing his unique blend of Savile Row tradition and contemporary design to the French men's wear brand. His first collection there, shown in 2004 in Paris, was hugely successful. Boateng left Givenchy in 2006.

Boateng's bespoke suits have been described as a perfect hybrid of tradition and modernity. Credited with revolutionizing the world's most famous street for men's tailoring, he redefined the cut of the traditional suit and added bold colors, slim silhouettes, and luxurious fabrics—drawing younger customers to Savile Row.

In addition to suits, Boateng produces two ready-to-wear collections a year. In 2009, he dressed Barack Obama for his trip to Ghana, and between 1998 and 2010 Boateng was filmed for the documentary *A Man's Story*, an examination of his evolution as the youngest and first black designer to own a business on Savile Row. He has also written and directed more than ten short films.

Born in London to Ghanaian parents, Ozwald Boateng (BO-tang) learned to sew at an early age. He studied computing at Southwark College, where his girlfriend asked him to help design clothes for her college fashion show. At 23, he quit his job in information technology to sell his designs along Portobello Road.

Boateng opened his own store near Seville Row in 1995. By 1996, he was winning awards, and in 1997 he showed his first men's wear line—the first men's wear show ever presented at London Fashion Week. In 1999, Boateng was included in *The New Alchemists* by Charles Handy, profiled as one of 12 people predicted to have a huge impact on society. In 2002, Ozwald Boateng headquarters opened at 12A Savile Row, and his suits were worn to the Academy Awards by Will Smith that

Left: Spring 2013 men's wear.

Right: Spring/summer 1998.

MARC BOHAN

Designer Marc Bohan.

BORN Roger Maurice Louis Bohan; Paris, August 22, 1926

As chief designer and artistic director of CHRISTIAN DIOR from 1960 to 1989, Marc Bohan was responsible for the brand's couture and ready-to-wear collections as well as accessories, men's wear, and bed linens. Refined and romantic, his clothes there were also very wearable, and notable for their beautiful fabrics and exquisite workmanship. He has always believed that elegance requires adapting clothes to the place, atmosphere, and circumstance.

The son of a milliner who encouraged his early interest in sketching and fashion, Bohan had a solid background when he took over design direction at Dior. He was an assistant to Robert Piguet from 1945 to 1953, worked with CAPTAIN EDWARD MOLYNEUX and Madeleine de Rauch, and had his own couture salon that closed because of insufficient funding. Bohan became head designer at JEAN PATOU in 1954, then left after a few years to freelance, working briefly for Originala in New York.

Bohan began at Dior in 1958, designing the London, New York, and South American collections. When YVES SAINT LAURENT was drafted into the Army in 1960, Bohan was chosen to design the January collection and replaced Laurent as chief designer. In 1989, after 29 years as chief designer, Bohan left Dior and became fashion director for NORMAN HARTNELL, the British fashion house. His first collections there were couture, followed by ready-to-wear in fall 1991. He left Hartnell when the house closed in 1992 and has since designed under his own name.

Short overcoat, 1974.

Little black evening dress, 1984.

BORN Brooklyn, New York

Monica Botkier (BOUGHT-key-air) began her career as a fashion photographer for magazines such as *Surface* and *Mademoiselle.* An aficionado of accessories, she began making leather bags that she took to photo shoots, where they attracted interest from editors and models. In 2003, Barneys began selling items from her first collection. In 2007, Botkier was inducted into the Council of Fashion Designers of America (CFDA).

Botkier's handbags are luxurious and decorated yet highly functional. The image of an elephant—a good luck symbol in India, where Botkier traveled in her youth—recurs subtly in her handbags. In 2008, she released her first shoe collection, which she said was influenced by Miu Miu and CHRISTIAN LOUBOUTIN. That same year, Botkier designed a line of bags for

Limited edition Bianca bag, 2008.

Target, followed by a collaboration with Nine West in 2012. Botkier's shoes and handbags both use leather and hardware to provide a postured, urban edge.

In 2011, the CFDA and Luxottica chose Botkier to design for Vogue Eyewear, and in 2012 she created a limited edition handbag for the CFDA and eBay. Botkier continues to take photographs for her ad campaigns, and her accessories (including mini handbags and wallets) have been worn by celebrities such as Angelina Jolie, Beyoncé, and Halle Berry.

Designer Monica Botkier with pieces from her luxury collection.

VERONIQUE BRANQUINHO ▼

BORN Vilvoorde, Belgium, June 6, 1973

AWARDS VH1 *Fashion Award for Best New Designer*,
1998 • Moët & Chandon *Fashion Award*, 2000

One of the many fresh talents nurtured and based in
Belgium, Veronique Branquinho (Vaigh-raw-NEEK
BRAWN-key-no) first studied painting at the Saint
Lucas School of Art in Brussels before switching to
fashion studies at the Royal Academy of Fine Arts
in Antwerp. After graduating in 1995, she worked
for several commercial labels before opening her
own business in 1997. That year, she showed her first
collection at the trendy Paris store Colette, attracting
favorable press notice and orders. Branquinho has since
designed two collections for the Italian leather firm
Ruffo Research, which often hires young designers for
brief stints. In addition, she has participated in fashion

Designer Veronique Branquinho.

events in Italy (at the Venice Biannale), New York (at
the Fashion Institute of Technology), Japan, and South
Korea. She also designs shoes.

Branquinho works with a light touch, very aware of
current trends while going her own way. Even her most
tailored pieces—jackets, pants, coats, and leathers—have
a relaxed, easy assurance, while dresses, blouses, and
knits are fluid and feminine with a mysterious elegance.
Branquinho is happy to see women personalize her
clothes by mixing them with things they already own.

In 2003, Bransquinho launched a men's wear line
in Paris and opened a flagship store in Antwerp. In
2007, she celebrated her brand's tenth anniversary
and presided over the Arts of Fashion Foundation's
International Symposium and Fashion Student
Competition. In 2008, the Mode Museum (MoMu) in
Antwerp presented *Moi, Veronique Branquinho TOuTe
NUe*, a showcase of her designs from 1998 to 2008.

In 2009, Branquinho announced that her label was
closing due to declining in sales, and she began working
as creative director for Delvaux, a Belgian maker of
leather goods. But Branquinho made a comeback with
her eponymous spring 2013 line, which critics considered
very elegant while still exhibiting her signature hints of
masculinity. Branquinho says that she has always "been
attracted to everything that is ambiguous, the tension
between femininity and masculinity."

Spring 2014.

BORN Alexey Cheslavovich Brodovitch; Ogolithchi, Russia, 1898
DIED Le Thor, France, April 15, 1971

AWARDS American Institute of Graphic Arts (AIGA) *Special Medal (excellence in design; posthumous),* 1987

Alexey Brodovitch was art director at *Harper's Bazaar* between 1934 and 1958, creating dazzling graphics for its covers and pages. When he was young, Brodovitch's family moved to Moscow, where he had hoped to eventually enroll in the Imperial Art Academy. But when he was 16, he ran away to join the Russian Army—only to be returned home soon afterward to finish school. In 1918, Brodovitch was badly wounded in the Russian Civil War and forced into exile through the Caucasus and Turkey, where he met his future wife Nina.

After the war, the family was reunited and moved to Paris. There Brodovitch worked as a painter, which began his transition into graphic arts. In 1925, he received five awards for his design work at the Paris International Exhibit of the Decorative Arts. In 1928, Brodovitch was hired by Athélia, the design studio of the Aux Trois Quartiers department store, to design its catalogs and advertisements. While employed there he started freelancing and eventually was able to open his own studio, L'Atelier A.B. Brodovitch expanded his design work to jewelry, textiles, and china.

In 1930, Brodovitch moved to Philadelphia to head the new Advertising and Design Department at the Pennsylvania Museum School of Industrial Art. In 1934, the Directors Club of New York asked Brodovitch to design its 13th Annual Art Directors Exhibition. Carmel Snow, the new editor of *Harper's Bazaar,* saw his work and offered him a provisional appointment as the magazine's art director. To make the offer a permanent position, Brodovitch enlisted

Harper's Bazaar Art Director Alexey Brodovitch.

his students to help create two dummy issues of the magazine that contained an element of shock value on each page. That impressed owner William Randolph Hearst, who agreed to let Brodovitch stay on.

In 1949, Brodovitch helped create *Portfolio,* widely recognized as the definitive graphic design magazine of the 20th century. Throughout his career, his Design Laboratory—which borrowed beliefs from the Bauhaus movement and focused on illustration, graphic design, and photography—provided rigorous critiques for advanced students who aspired to careers in magazine work. Photographer IRVING PENN believed that all designers, photographers, and art directors are students of Brodovitch—whether they knew it or not.

After Brodovitch's wife died in 1970, he spent time in and out of hospitals for severe depression. His son eventually took him to Paris, where he died.

DONALD BROOKS ▟

Designer Donald Brooks.

BORN Donald Marc Blumberg; New Haven, Connecticut, January 9, 1928
DIED Long Island, New York, August 1, 2005

AWARDS International Silk Association Award, 1954 • National Cotton Council Award, 1962 • Coty American Fashion Critics' Awards *Special Award (influence on evening wear)*, 1958; *Winnie*, 1962; *Return Award*, 1967; *Special Award (lingerie design)*, 1974 • New York Drama Critics' Award: *No Strings (costume design)*, 1963 • Parsons *Medal for Distinguished Achievement*, 1974 • Emmy Award: *The Letter (costume design for a special)*, 1982

Noted for romantic evening wear and uncluttered day wear, Donald Brooks also designed extensively for theater and film. He is known for his use of clear colors in unexpected combinations, careful detailing, and dramatic prints of his own design.

Brooks attended the School of Fine Arts at Syracuse University and Parsons School of Design, where he graduated in 1950. He had his own company from 1964 to 1973 and freelanced extensively, specializing in dresses. He designed for Albert Nipon, Lord & Taylor department stores, and casts of Broadway musicals—including Diahann Carroll in *No Strings* and Liza Minnelli for *Flora the Red Menace*.

Draped jersey evening gowns, 1972.

Brooks's ten film credits include costumes for Julie Andrews in *Star* and *Darling Lili*. He won an Emmy for his designs for the 1982 television movie *The Letter*. He also designed furs, bathing suits, men's wear, shoes, costume jewelry, wigs, and bed linens.

Purple-print seraglio pajamas, 1967.

⬛ THOM BROWNE

BORN Allentown, Pennsylvania, 1965

AWARDS Council of Fashion Designers of America (CFDA) *Menswear Designer of the Year*, 2006, 2013 • *GQ Designer of the Year*, 2008 • Cooper-Hewitt *National Design Award (fashion)*, 2012

In 2006, Thom Browne produced a high-end unisex collection for the Brooks Brothers line Black Fleece line. The deal was the culmination of a rags-to-riches narrative that started in 1997, when Browne moved to New York City with the proceeds from the sale of his car. A job at a GIORGIO ARMANI showroom led to a high-profile position at Club Monaco, owned by Polo RALPH LAUREN. Browne left Club Monaco in 2001 to start his own label. So, the legend goes, Browne

Designer Thom Browne (front) and models.

sewed up five narrow suits and declared war on casual Fridays—which, at the end of the dot-com boom, had become standard on Wall Street.

Whatever its origins, the Thom Browne suit quickly caught the attention of the fashion press. Its muted, flannel-square silhouette cut an instantly recognizable shape on catwalks, with a narrow waist and high-pegged trousers topped by a proportionately slender jacket. The suits are either celebrated as an outré riff on 1950s corporate America or derided as a sly, if too pricey, wink at it. Indeed, at nearly $6,000, the creations are an expensive statement.

Browne toned down some of his outrageous impulses with a sportswear line and renewed his contract with Brooks Brothers through 2011. He launched a women's ready-to-wear collection in 2011, and in 2012 Michelle Obama wore a Browne silk coat to her husband's second inauguration. The coat's navy blue checked fabric was inspired by a men's tie.

Spring 2014.

BARBARA BUI

In addition to a boutique and a café in Paris, Bui has shops in Milan and New York City. In 2004, she launched her first fragrance, Barbara Bui Le Parfum. In 2007, she collaborated with legendary rock and roll photographer David Bailey for a print ad campaign in America. In 2013, she partnered with Frends—an electronics company based in southern California—on a limited edition accessories line, Barbara Bui × Frends. The line, sold in select Barbara Bui stores, aims to "change the relationship between women and electronics" and consists of two styles of headphones that incorporate Bui's signature leather and metal. All profits from the line go to charity.

Designer Barbara Bui.

BORN Paris, 1957

Barbara Bui (BOO-ee) came to fashion self-taught and by a route as diverse as her French-Vietnamese origins—first having studied literature and theater. In her theater classes she met her future partner, William Halimi. When they tired of theater in the 1980s, the pair opened a boutique to sell her designs and called it Kabuki, later renaming it Barbara Bui.

After successful shows in Paris, Bui withdrew from runway presentations until the mid-1990s, when she showed in New York. Her collections include suits, dresses, furs, evening wear, separates, bags, and shoes. Bui sees her clothes as balancing the masculine and feminine, the delicate and the assertive, for women with strong points of view who consider themselves citizens of the world.

Spring 2014.

Burberry Prorsum Fall 2013.

FOUNDED Basingstoke, United Kingdom, 1856

Known for its distinguished tartan pattern and trench coat, the British luxury brand Burberry was founded in 1856 by 21-year-old Thomas Burberry. For most of its existence, the brand focused on developing outerwear. In 1880, Burberry added gabardine—a tightly woven, non-breathable, water-resistant fabric that he invented—to his collections. In 1891, the brand expanded to Haymarket, London, which for many decades was home to its national headquarters. Today its global headquarters are at Horseferry House in Westminster, London.

The Burberry Equestrian Knight logo was established in 1901, and when Roald Amundsen wore Burberry in 1911 while leading the first expedition to reach the South Pole, it elevated the brand in the public eye. In 1914, Britain's War Department commissioned Burberry to create an officer's coat suited to wartime conditions. That effort resulted in the iconic Burberry trench coat, which was adopted by civilians after World War I. In the 1920's, the famous tartan print was created and used in the linings of the coat.

After Thomas Burberry died in 1926, the brand began sponsoring famous aviators and maintained its focus on outerwear. In 1955, Great Universal Stores bought the brand, and in the 1970s soccer fans began wearing it. Burberry continued to expand in the 1990s, and in 2001 CHRISTOPHER BAILEY became its chief creative director. He has been credited with transforming the brand into its modern iteration.

In 2006, Angela Ahrendts became Burberry's chief executive officer. The company's finances improved strongly under her lead, and in 2012 Ahrendts became the highest-paid executive in the United Kingdom—the first woman ever to do so. In 2013, Ahrendts left the company and was replaced by Bailey, who will continue to be chief creative officer. Burberry has stores all over the world and three main lines: Burberry Prorsum, Burberry London, and Burberry Brit.

Burberry Prorsum Spring 2014 men's wear.

TORY BURCH ⧗

BORN Tory Robinson; Valley Forge, Pennsylvania, June 15, 1966

AWARDS Accessories Council of Excellence *Accessory Brand Launch of the Year*, 2007 • Council of Fashion Designers of America (CFDA) *Accessory Designer of the Year*, 2008

Drawing from the same tradition as RALPH LAUREN, Tory Burch is one of the most successful examples of how to market a stylized version of oneself as a ready-to-wear lifestyle. Her breezy, early 1960s Palm Beach meets Upper East Side style has won her a niche among a cross-section of women. The Tory Burch brand was launched in 2004 and includes ready-to-wear, handbags, shoes, and jewelry. Buoyed by a 2005 endorsement from Oprah Winfrey, it has achieved widespread popularity.

Burch is a well-known New York socialite and mother. Her sophisticated American aesthetic drives the design of her accessories, which are popular among upper-middle-class professional women. Celebrity fans include Cameron Diaz, Jennifer Lopez, Uma Thurman, and Hilary Swank.

Burch studied art history at the University of Pennsylvania and worked in public relations at RALPH LAUREN and VERA WANG. Her mid-priced off-the-rack collections are usually centered on a classic silhouette—such as a slit-necked tunic—that is updated with embroidery and detail. Burch has said that her mother, Reva Robinson—a 1960s socialite—is the muse for these updates of iconic 1960s designs. The Tory Burch Reva line, which features shoes and handbags, is named after her. The Tory Burch brand has also entered into eyewear (in partnership with Luxottica, in 2009), fragrance and beauty (with ESTÉE LAUDER, in 2013), and watches (with Fossil, slated for 2014). There are 49 Tory Burch boutiques in America and 24 abroad, and more than 1,000 department and specialty stores worldwide carry the company's merchandise.

In 2009, the Tory Burch Foundation was created to help economically empower American women through small business loans, mentoring, and entrepreneurial education. In 2013, *Forbes* estimated Burch's net wealth to be $2 billion.

Designer Tory Burch (left) with model.

Tory Burch's jewelry design, 2013.

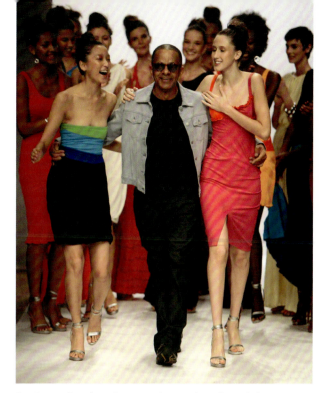

Designer Stephen Burrows (center) and models.

BORN Newark, New Jersey, September 15, 1943

AWARDS Coty American Fashion Critics' Awards *Special Award (lingerie)*, 1974; *Winnie,* 1977 • Council of Fashion Designers of America (CFDA) *Board of Directors' Tribute,* 2006

Stephen Burrows has always gone his own way in fashion, favoring soft, clinging fabrics such as chiffon and matte jersey, and with an affection for the asymmetrical. In the early 1960s, he used patches of color for a mosaic effect, top-stitched seams in contrasting thread, and finished edges in a widely copied, fluted effect known as "lettuce hems."

The first African-American designer to gain international acclaim, Burrows started making clothes as a boy under the tutelage of his grandmother. He honed his design skills at the Philadelphia Museum College of Art and the Fashion Institute of Technology in New York City. In 1968, he and a FIT classmate, Roz Rubenstein, opened a boutique. The next year both went to work for Henri Bendel—Burrows as a designer in residence, Rubenstein as an accessories buyer. In 1973, Burrows and Rubenstein opened a store on Seventh Avenue in New York. That same year, Burrows was one of five American designers to show in France at a benefit for the Versailles Palace—an event that was a smash success for the Americans. A few years later

⬥ STEPHEN BURROWS

KARL LAGERFELD called Burrows "the most original American talent since CLAIRE MCCARDELL."

Burrows and Rubenstein returned to Bendel's in 1977, remaining until 1981. Since then, Burrows has been in and out of business, ascribing his lack of commercial success at least partly to weak business skills. He has supported himself by designing costumes for the theater, the licensing divisions of other designers, and the occasional private client. He has also done furs.

In 2002, Burrows was back at Bendel's as a designer, with an in-store studio and staff; the small collection that resulted was only sold at the Fifth Avenue store. In 2006, the 40th anniversary of his clothing line, Burrows was awarded the CFDA Board of Directors' Tribute. In 2010, Burrows opened new studios in the New York Garment Center and developed a new following after Michelle Obama wore his fashions. In 2013, the Museum of the City of New York held an exhibit of his work, *Stephen Burrows: When Fashion Danced.* Burrows's clothing is sold at upscale stores in America, Europe, and the Middle East.

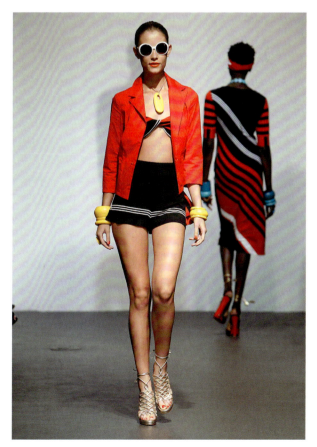

Spring 2012.

CALLOT SOEURS ◼

FOUNDED 1895
CLOSED 1937

Founded by four sisters—Marie Callot Gerber, Martha Callot Bertrand, Regina Callot Tennyson-Chantrell, and Joséphine Callot Crimont—the couture house of Callot (KAH-low) Soeurs (Soor) was best known for formal evening wear featuring intricate cuts and rich colors. It was famous for its delicate lace blouses, use of gold and silver lamé, embroidery in flowers, and floating fabrics such as chiffon, georgette, and organdy. The house's high standards built its reputation, and the world's most fashionable women went there to be dressed. Among them was Spanish-American beauty Rita de Acosta Lydig, who was rumored to be a financial backer.

The sisters were daughters of an antiques dealer who specialized in fabrics and lace. He was also said to be a painter. All were talented, but Marie Callot Gerber, the eldest, was the genius. Tall and gaunt, her hair dyed a brilliant red, she was usually dressed in baglike outfits draped with Oriental jewelry and ropes of freshwater pearls. Gerber possessed great technical skill and was an artist of impeccable taste. Her sisters eventually retired, leaving her sole proprietor of the house, which at one time had branches in London and New York.

Henri Bendel was a great admirer of Gerber, calling her the backbone of Europe's fashion world. She was an early influence on MADELEINE VIONNET, who worked for some time at Callot Soeurs. During the 1920s, the house produced every up-to-the-minute look—yet with such taste, subtlety, and workmanship that the clothes had the timelessness and elegance of classics. Gerber's son, Pierre Gerber, took over the business in 1928; it was absorbed by Calvet in 1937.

Evening dress, 1910–1914.

Designer Ennio Capasa.

BORN Lecce, Italy, 1960

Ennio Capasa's parents owned upscale boutiques in Lecce, a city on the heel of the Italian boot. While growing up he hated fashion, which he considered to be for "tired rich people." But after graduating from the Milan Academy of Fine Arts in 1982 and wanting to avoid Italy's mandatory military service, Capasa looked for work in industrial design in Japan, and instead found a job in fashion design with YOHJI YAMAMOTO. There he learned to drape, cut, and sew.

In 1987, Capasa left Yamamoto at the older designer's suggestion that he start his own label. Rather than use his own name, Capasa chose CoSTUME NATIONAL, from the title of an antique book on French uniforms. Capasa felt that it was time for a new, more relaxed silhouette closer to the body—more style than fashion. His first women's wear collection was based on the skimpy proportions of Charlie Chaplin and was greeted with disdain by the Italian fashion press. Since then he has gained success without the press hype usually considered necessary to gain recognition. Capasa's first

men's collection debuted in 1993 and now includes bags, belts, and leather goods.

In 2001, CoSTUME NATIONAL produced the first live online fashion show, revealing new collections to the public with an unprecedented immediacy. In 2004, Capasa launched C'N'C, a streetwear line produced by Itierre SpA.

Capasa's cool, hip clothes for women and men have found a receptive audience worldwide, sold by forward-thinking retailers such as Barneys New York and in his own boutiques in Milan, Rome, Tokyo, and New York. Fully embracing technological minimalism, Capasa's designs are often executed with laser-cut fabrics, Pantone colors, and futuristic silhouettes. In 2009, CoSTUME NATIONAL released a solar-powered bag that can charge mobile phones and other portable electronics. The bag won the Chi è Chi Award (Who's Who Award, given for journalism and fashion in Italy) for best eco-friendly fashion product of the year.

Costume National Spring 2014.

ROBERTO CAPUCCI ⏳

Designer Roberto Capucci.

BORN Rome, December 2, 1930

Scion of a wealthy Roman family, Roberto Capucci (Kuh-POO-chay) studied art at the Accademia di Belle Arti in Rome. In 1950, at the age of 21, he opened a small fashion house in Rome and showed successfully in Florence the following year. He opened a house in Paris in 1962 and moved back to Rome seven years later.

Considered a genius at the level of CRISTÓBAL BALENCIAGA and CHARLES JAMES, Capucci has made daring experiments with cut and fabric to achieve dramatic sculptural and architectural effects. Fittingly, because he has raised dressmaking to the level of art, his clothes are shown in silence. He does not use design assistants.

In 2003, while still doing couture on a limited basis, Capucci agreed to produce a ready-to-wear collection

Pleated cocktail dress.

under his name. The collection was designed by Spain's Sybilla, Germany's Bernhard Willhelm, and America's Tara Subkoff, working individually and drawing on Capucci's archives for inspiration.

In 2001, the Philadelphia Museum of Art staged *Roberto Capucci: Art into Fashion*, which was the first U.S. retrospective of his work and featured more than 80 of his pieces as well as original drawings and sketches.

Designer Pierre Cardin surrounded by models.

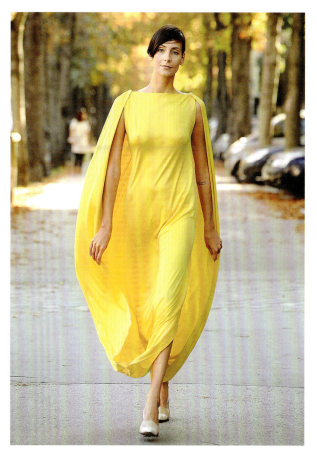

Spring 2011.

BORN San Biago di Callalta, Italy, 1922

AWARDS Golden Thimble Award *French Haute Couture*, 1979, 1982 • Council of Fashion Designers of America (CFDA) *International Award*, 2007

Pierre Cardin (CAR-donh) is one of the world's most creative, intellectual, and avant-garde couturiers. The son of Italian immigrants, he grew up in St. Etienne, France, and moved to Vichy at the age of 17. Cardin was a tailor in Vichy, then went to Paris at the end of World War II and worked at PAQUIN. There he made costumes based on sketches by CHRISTIAN BÉRARD for Jean Cocteau's film *La Belle et la Bête*, and Cocteau introduced him to CHRISTIAN DIOR. Cardin worked briefly for ELSA SCHIAPARELLI, then as an assistant to Dior, where in 1947 he headed the coat and suit workroom. He left Dior to form his own business, and in 1950 showed his first collection.

Boutiques followed for women and men, with men's ready-to-wear appearing in 1958 and children's wear ten years later. Cardin was the first couturier to make fashion accessible to the masses by licensing his brand's name, starting in 1960. He eventually issued more than 600 licenses for products carrying the Cardin name—from wines to bicycles, jewelry to bed sheets, and swimwear to toiletries—covering the world. In 1966, Cardin showed the first nude look,

Twiggy in short, pleated silk dress, 1967.

followed by metal body jewelry, unisex astronaut suits, helmets, batwing jumpsuits, and other clothing then considered suitable for space travel.

Cardin was also a leader in expanding his company's global operations—most notably in Japan, China, and the Soviet Union. In 1970, he established his own Paris theater, l'Espace Pierre Cardin, and later that decade purchased the famous Paris restaurant, Maxim's, which he expanded to multiple locations in China and Japan. In 1979, Cardin entered a trade agreement with China to manufacture clothes there.

In 1987, Cardin named his long-time collaborator, Andre Oliver, artistic director of his couture house, but continued to share design duties. After Oliver's death, Cardin reassumed artistic direction of the house.

In 1982, the Sogetsu Kaikan Museum in Tokyo held a retrospective of Cardin's work. In 1991, he was named a peace ambassador to the United Nations Educational, Scientific, and Cultural Organization (UNESCO). Cardin celebrated his 60th year in fashion in 2010.

HATTIE CARNEGIE 🏷️ 👜

BORN Henrietta Kanengeiser; Vienna, Austria, 1889
DIED New York City, February 22, 1956

Hattie Carnegie began as a milliner, opening her first shop when she was just 20. By the end of her life she had a multimillion-dollar business, including resort shops, made-to-order workrooms, ready-to-wear factories, millinery, jewelry, and perfumes. She is said to have been the first American custom designer to go into ready-to-wear. Her knack for discovering design talent was legendary—JAMES GALANOS, NORMAN NORELL, PAULINE TRIGÈRE, and CLAIRE MCCARDELL all worked for her.

Carnegie's designs were youthful and sophisticated, never faddish or extreme. Less than 5 feet tall, she was noted for suits with nipped waists and rounded hips that were especially flattering to smaller women, as well as embroidered, beaded evening suits, theater suits, pajamas, and long wool dinner dresses. Beautiful fabrics and excellent workmanship were her hallmarks, and she abhorred anything but the best.

Carnegie arrived in America when she was 11 and started working in her early teens—first as a messenger at Macy's, then in a millinery workroom, and later as

Designer Hattie Carnegie.

a millinery model. In her spare time she designed hats for neighborhood women. She changed her name to Carnegie in emulation of Andrew Carnegie, at one time the world's richest man. She opened her own hat shop in 1909, and in 1915 a custom dressmaking salon on New York City's West 86th Street, near fashionable Riverside Drive. Her partner, Rose Roth, made dresses; Carnegie made hats and waited on customers. Carnegie did not know how to cut or sketch, and never learned. But she had great fashion flair and acute business intelligence, and bought out Roth in 1917.

Carnegie's first buying trip to Europe was in 1919. She then went four times a year, bringing back Parisian designs that she adapted. She dressed society beauties, movie celebrities, and stage stars such as Constance Bennett, Tallulah Bankhead, and Joan Crawford. In the early 1930s, recognizing the hard facts of the Great Depression, Carnegie opened a ready-to-wear department in her shop where a good copy of a VIONNET design could be had for as little as $50.

Carnegie was married briefly in 1918 and 1922. In 1928, she married John Zanft, who survived her. Her clothing business continued for some years after her death.

Black dress and white hat, 1953.

A 18-karat gold, diamond, emerald, and onyx ring from Cartier.

FOUNDED Paris, 1847

Louis-François Cartier (CAR-tea-a) founded luxury jeweler Cartier in Paris when he took over his master's shop. In 1874, the company passed to his son Alfred, who later turned it over to his sons Louis, Jacques, and Pierre, who established the brand worldwide. The brand owes Louis for some of its most creative and popular designs—including the "Mystery," a clock with mechanisms hidden in a transparent dial; the first men's wrist watch, dubbed "Santos" after his friend Albert Santos Dumont, who complained that pocket watches were difficult for aviators to use; and the beloved jewels on the faces of the company's watches. By the early 20th century, Cartier was extremely successful and offered several watches still popular today, including the Baignoire, Tortue, and Tank.

In the 1920s, Edmond Jaeger was hired to produce timepieces solely for Cartier. During that period the company also began stamping watches with four-digit codes, Jacques took over the London office and moved it to its current Bond Street location, and Pierre established the New York City branch on Fifth Avenue.

Jeanne Toussaint became Cartier's director of fine jewelry in 1933 and added the brand's iconic "panther" motif to its jewelry collection as well as feminine touches such as floral designs. Between 1904 and 1939, Cartier received 15 royal patents, making it the official jeweler of kings and queens around the world—including the maharaja of India and the British royal family. Cartier also created jewelry made popular by celebrities, such as the "love" bracelet worn by Sophia Loren and Elizabeth Taylor. Cartier thrived until Pierre's death in

1964. The children of the three Cartier brothers, who were heading the company's affiliates in London, Paris, and New York, sold the businesses.

In 1972, Cartier was bought by a group of investors led by Joseph Kanoui. Robert Hocq, the company's president at the time, coined the slogan "Les Must de Cartier" meaning "Cartier, It's a Must"—something one simply must have. Cartier had many turnovers until 1981, when Cartier SAA and Cartier International merged under new Chairman Alain Perrin. New lines and updated classics soon reestablished Cartier as an innovative, fashionable watchmaker.

In 1996, more than 150 Cartier pieces were featured in a major exhibition in Switzerland titled *Splendours of Jewelry*. In 2013, *Cartier: Style and History* opened at the Grand Palais in Paris, showcasing the brand's rich history. Cartier is sold in more than 200 stores and 125 countries.

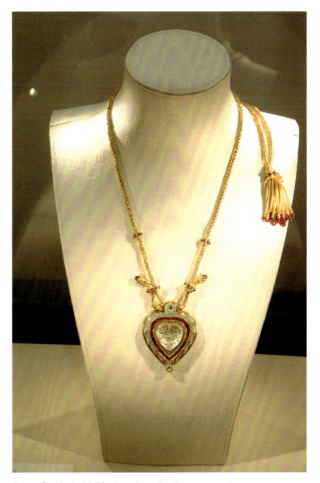

From Cartier's 100th American Anniversary party.

BONNIE CASHIN ▲ 👜

Designer Bonnie Cashin.

BORN Oakland, California, September 28, 1908
DIED New York City, February 3, 2000

AWARDS Coty American Fashion Critics' Award *Winnie,* 1950; *Special Award (leather and fabric design),* 1961; *Return Award,* 1968; *Hall of Fame Award,* 1972 • *Neiman Marcus Award,* 1950

Bonnie Cashin was always guided by her own vision, uninfluenced by Paris. She especially believed in functional layers of clothing and showed this way of dressing long before it became an international fashion cliché. From the beginning she specialized in comfortable clothes for country and travel, using wool jersey, knits, canvas, leather, and tweeds in subtle, misty colors.

Dominant Cashin themes included the toga cape, the kimono coat and the shell coat, a sleeveless leather jerkin, the poncho, the bubble top, the hooded jersey dress, and a long, fringed, plaid mohair at-home skirt. Signature details included leather bindings and the use of toggles and similar hardware for closings. Clothes were coordinated with hoods, bags, boots, and belts,

all of her own design. Her clothes are included in the costume collections of museums, colleges, and design schools around the country.

A third generation Californian, Cashin was raised in San Francisco, where her father was an artist, photographer, and inventor; her mother was a custom dressmaker. She played with fabrics from an early age, was taught to sew, and her ideas were encouraged. She studied at the Art Students League of New York before returning to California, where she designed costumes for the theater, ballet, and motion pictures—*Anna and the King of Siam* and *Laura* are among her 60 film credits. She moved back to New York in 1949.

In 1953, Cashin started freelancing, designing collections for sportswear houses Adler and Adler and Philip Sills, and bags for Coach Leatherware. In 1967, she founded The Knittery, which produced limited edition collections of hand knits and cashmeres from Scotland, as well as coats and raincoats.

In the early 1980s, Cashin established The Innovative Design Fund, a public foundation, with herself as president. Its purpose was to nurture uncommon, directional ideas in design—clothing, textiles, home furnishings, or other utilitarian objects—with awards to be used solely for producing prototypes. Another fund, The James Michelin Distinguished Lecturer Program, at the California Institute of Technology at Pasadena, started in 1992 to bring together the arts and sciences.

Shopping bag tote for Coach, 1964.

Designer Oleg Cassini.

BORN Paris, April 11, 1913
DIED Long Island, New York, March 17, 2006

AWARDS Council of Fashion Designers of America (CFDA) *Board of Directors' Tribute,* 2003

Perhaps best known as the designer to Jacqueline Kennedy and other glamor icons of the 20th century, Oleg Cassini's origins are in Western Europe, where he was born to parents stripped of their nobility in the Russian Revolution. When he was young, his parents moved to Italy, where he helped his mother in her dressmaking shop. He later studied fine art at the Academia di Belle Arte in Florence.

In 1936, Cassini moved to New York and worked as a junior designer. He soon relocated to Hollywood, where he worked at Paramount Studios designing costumes for B movies. By the 1950s, Cassini found himself back in mainstream fashion, designing glamorous ready-to-wear sheath dresses, cocktail dresses, and knit suits. His high-profile clients included Joan Crawford, Joan Fontaine, Grace Kelly, Marilyn Monroe, and Gene Tierney—whom he later married.

In 1960, he became Jacqueline Kennedy's official dressmaker. As her iconic style garnered international acclaim, so did Cassini. Many of the outfits he created—including a high-necked silk ottoman evening dress and Kennedy's one-shoulder strapless gowns—became some

⚫ OLEG CASSINI

Jacqueline Kennedy in apricot silk ziberline dress, 1962.

of the most imitated pieces in American fashion history.

Among Cassini's other fashion innovations were the sheath evening dress, A-line dress, little white collar dress, and women's military look. In the 1990s, he partnered with David's Bridal to create a line of Oleg Cassini bridal dresses. In 2001, Cassini's designs were showcased in the Metropolitan Museum of Art's exhibition *Jacqueline Kennedy: The White House Years.*

Jacqueline Kennedy in a red wool suit and beret, 1961.

CONSUELO CASTIGLIONI ⟰

BORN Lugano, Italy/Switzerland, circa 1959

Consuelo Castiglioni (Cass-TIG-lee-oh-knee) became a fashion designer more by chance than by design, driven by difficulties at her husband's family firm. As Italy's foremost supplier of top-quality fur pelts to houses such as FENDI and PRADA, the firm was suffering from the anti-fur movement of the early 1990s. Although she had never been involved in fashion, in 1993 Castiglioni designed a small fur collection, called Marni, for the Milan ready-to-wear shows. But her initial efforts attracted little or no attention. Not until 1999—when she showed a colorful "deluxe hippie" collection of patchwork coats, tie-dyed crushed velvet dresses, and multicolored fur jackets—did her firm take off. A men's wear line was launched in 2002, followed by eyewear in 2005.

Designer Consuelo Castiglioni.

Using luxurious materials such as cashmere, silk, and fur, Castiglioni creates pretty clothes with a modern edge sold in upscale retail stores and, increasingly, the company's boutiques. There are nearly 100 Marni stores worldwide, and Castiglioni oversees their interior designs—giving each its own authentic character. In 2012, RENZO ROSSO, owner of Diesel, bought a majority stake in Marni. Castiglioni still maintains creative control, and in 2013 created its first evening wear collection.

Marni Spring 2013.

Marni Spring 2013.

 # EDMUNDO CASTILLO

Designer Edmundo Castillo.

BORN San Juan, Puerto Rico, April 13, 1967

AWARDS Council of Fashion Designers of America (CFDA) *Perry Ellis Award for Accessories*, 2001

Even as a teenager, Edmundo Castillo (Cass-TEA-yo) was a shoe addict, obsessed with having the newest and best sneakers. He began his design studies at the Altos de Chavon School of Design in the Dominican Republic, then moved to the Fashion Institute of Technology and Parsons School of Design in New York. He began his real training in shoemaking in 1989 at DONNA KARAN, who he credits for "half of what I know." He stayed there eight years as a shoe designer, moved to Polo RALPH LAUREN for a year as senior design director, and returned to

Karan to design Donna Karan and DKNY men's shoes. In 1999 he began his own line of women's shoes.

Castillo's focus is on feminine, sexy shoes designed along classic lines with a modern edge and made of only the finest materials—shoes that women want to both wear and collect. He views them as more makeup for the feet than mere foot-coverings. According to him, "The beauty of a shoe is in how it transforms and takes life when it makes contact with the foot."

Castillo designed the Edmundo Castillo brand for Sergio Rossi from 2004 to 2008, though he maintained his own line of designer shoes. In 2011, he became the creative director of Via Spiga, and in 2013 he received the *Travel + Leisure* Design Award for Best Travel Shoes.

Fall 2011.

ROBERTO CAVALLI 👗

BORN Florence, Italy, November 14, 1940

Born into a family richly endowed with artistic capability, Roberto Cavalli's fierce individualism and creativity were forged early in life. His grandfather, Giuseppe Rossi, was a prolific impressionist painter, and his mother was a tailor. Cavalli enrolled at the local art institute, where he created a series of flower prints on knit that immediately caught the attention of major Italian hosiery factories, opening the door to a long, innovative career. Cavalli's experimentation soon led to the development of a unique process of printing on lightweight leather. After patenting the process, he started piecing together scraps of leather to create what would become his signature patchwork pieces, commissioned by HERMÈS and PIERRE CARDIN.

Designer Roberto Cavalli.

Spring 2013.

Cavalli showcased his first namesake collection at the Salon du Prêt-à-Porter in Paris and the White Room of Palazzo Pitti in Florence in 1970. The collection showcased his delicate, unique creations, including jeans made of printed denim (formerly a fabric exclusively of the Italian working class), intarsia leathers, and exotic prints. In 1980, Cavalli married Eva Duringer, who has become his lifelong companion and business partner. After a respite from the fashion world to focus on raising a family and breeding horses, Cavalli relaunched his look in Milan in the 1990s.

Cavalli is known for his sensual rock-and-roll influenced couture, glamorous animal prints, and well-cut sensual pieces that flatter the figure, as well as partnerships with musicians and celebrities ranging from Christina Aguilera to Victoria Beckham. Cavalli aroused controversy when he announced that Kate Moss would be the face of his spring 2006 collection immediately after her drug scandal.

In 2007, Cavalli created a special collection for H&M, including women's wear, men's wear, lingerie, and accessories. In 2012, he created a high-street capsule collection for Target Australia. The Cavalli brand is distributed in more than 50 countries. When asked about retirement, the designer says that "fashion is a part of my DNA. I could never live without it."

Spring 2014.

FOUNDED Paris, 1945

Céline Vipiana founded Céline as a made-to-measure children's shoe business with the help of her husband Richard. By the late 1960s, the business has grown to include women's shoes, handbags, and ready-to-wear. The concept behind Céline's women's wear was that it was designed for every woman, by a woman. Vipiana was the house's creative director for more than 40 years, and during her tenure Céline became one of the first luxury brands to expand into Japan. Céline enjoyed continued international success with stores not only in Asia, but also throughout America and Europe.

■▌ CÉLINE

In 1987, Bernard Arnault bought the brand, and in 1994 it became part of the LVMH empire. In 1997, MICHAEL KORS became Céline's creative director, reinvigorating and bringing a lot of attention back to the label. When Kors left in 2007, the label passed hands many times before LVMH hired British designer Phoebe Philo, best known for her work at Chloé. Philo is credited with bringing Céline back to international acclaim.

Céline is sold in America, Europe, Asia, and the Middle East. The brand has also expanded to include accessories. The Céline aesthetic is described as chic yet sophisticated—luxury sportswear with couture finishes.

In 2010, Philo was named Designer of the Year by the British Fashion Council, and in 2011 the Council of Fashion Designer of America (CFDA) made her its International Designer of the Year.

Spring 2014.

NINO CERRUTI ▲

BORN Biella, Italy, 1930

Nino Cerruti (Chay-ROO-tee) was forced to quit his philosophy studies and take over his family's textile business when he was 20, after his father's death. Inspired to take the company in a more modern direction, he began designing men's wear and took an innovative approach to the trade. Cerruti is known for deboning the formerly structured Italian men's jacket—resulting in supple, light, body-conscious suits. GIORGIO ARMANI worked for him from 1964 to 1970, and often shares credit for taking the stuffiness out of Italian clothing.

In 1967, Cerruti opened a boutique in Paris called Cerruti 1881. It was known for its classic wool suits and for furnishing costumes for more than 150 movies. Among the best-known characters dressed by Cerruti are Richard Gere's in *Pretty Woman* and Clint Eastwood's in *In the Line of Fire*.

In an effort to secure global expansion of his company and the succession of his son, Cerruti sold 51 percent of his brand to the Italian corporation Fin. part in 2000. A year later, Fin.part took over the entire company, and Cerruti was forced to bow out. Still, he continues to control the fabrication end of his family

Designer Nino Cerruti.

textile business. Since 2012, the House of Cerruti has been under the creative direction of Aldo Maria Camillo, who previously worked at Ermenegildo Zegna and VALENTINO.

Richard Gere wearing a classic wool suit in the movie *Pretty Woman*, 1990.

♛ RICHARD CHAI

Designer Richard Chai.

BORN Westchester County, New York, 1974

AWARDS Council of Fashion Designers of American (CFDA) *Swarovski Menswear Designer of the Year*, 2010

Richard Chai began his career at the age of 13, taking night classes in graphic design at Parsons School of Design—though he quickly switched his emphasis to fashion illustration. Chai had a prestigious internship at GEOFFREY BEENE while at Parsons, and after graduation relocated to Paris to continue his studies at the Lissa School. While in Paris, Chai worked as a sketcher at LANVIN. After returning to New York, he was a designer at ARMANI Exchange and DONNA KARAN. Between 1998 and 2001, Chai was design director for MARC JACOBS men's and women's wear.

In 2001, Chai was appointed creative design director for TSE Brand, which was notable because it was the first time that one person oversaw all of the brand's lines. These experiences gave Chai the knowledge and confidence to create his own brand, and in 2004 he launched his eponymous label for women. In 2009, Chai launched a contemporary women's line entitled Richard Chai LOVE. Both lines offer affordable, inspired classics with a whimsical touch.

In 2008, Chai launched his first men's wear collection, which featured arched seams, eclectic color palettes, and unique fabrics and textures. His men's wear collections have received many accolades, including nominations for *GQ* Best Men's Wear Designer and the CFDA/*Vogue* Fashion Fund.

Richard Chai Love Spring 2014

HUSSEIN CHALAYAN

Designer Hussein Chalayan.

BORN Hüseyin Çağlayan; Nicosia, Cyprus, 1970.

AWARDS British Fashion Awards *Designer of the Year*, 1999, 2000

Hussein Chalayan (Shuh-LAY-anh) attended Central St. Martin's College of Art and Design in London, and while there apprenticed with a Savile Row tailor. His eccentric 1993 graduation collection was featured in the window of one of London's most adventurous boutiques, immediately establishing him as a hot new talent.

Subsequent collections have included unrippable paper clothes and sharply tailored suits printed with illuminated flight patterns, reflecting Chalayan's interest in technology-inspired fabrics. Despite financial ups and downs, he has managed to get new backing and continue producing collections.

Chalayan has shown the dedication and self-belief needed to survive in fashion. His work, with its clearly defined, minimalist silhouettes, has ranged from the wildly conceptual to the highly wearable designs he produced for Tse, the New York-based cashmere

Autumn/winter 2000/2001.

house. In 2001, he was included in the exhibition *London Fashion* at New York City's Fashion Institute of Technology. He is admired by such unconventional fashion thinkers as Rei Kawakubo and Alexander McQueen and has been mentioned as a possible designer for several major European houses.

In 2008, Chalayan's pieces were shown in *Gothic: Dark Glamour* at the Museum at FIT and *Superheroes: Fashion and Fantasy* at the Costume Institute of the Metropolitan Museum of Art. His work has also been exhibited at museums in London, Paris, and elsewhere. In addition, Chalayan has been creative director of Puma, released a fragrance called Airborne, and signed a licensing agreement to produce and distribute women's wear with Italian manufacturer Pier SpA. In 2013, he received the *Fashion Visionary Award* at Singapore's Audi Fashion Festival for 20 years of design excellence.

Spring 2014.

⏳ GABRIELLE "COCO" CHANEL

BORN Gabrielle Bonheur Chanel; Saumur, France, August 19, 1883
DIED Paris, January 10, 1971

AWARDS *Neiman Marcus Award*, 1957

Some evaluations of Gabrielle "Coco" Chanel place her alongside such giants as MADELEINE VIONNET and CRISTÓBAL BALENCIAGA, while others see her as more personality than creator, with a knack for knowing what women would want just before they knew it themselves. Either way, her early designs were liberating—and even her evening wear had a youthful quality all its own.

Chanel obscured the details of her early life, but it is believed that she was one of five children to an unmarried mother. By the time she was 12, her mother was dead, her father had deserted his family, and she had been sent to an orphanage run by nuns where she spent six years and learned to sew. Chanel started in fashion making hats—first in a Paris apartment in 1910, later in a shop in Deauville. In 1914, she opened a shop in Paris,

Designer Coco Chanel.

making her first dresses of wool jersey, a material not considered suitable for fashionable clothes at the time.

Chanel's business was interrupted by World War I, but she reopened in 1919—by which time she was famous among the fashionable. Slender and vital, with a low, warm voice, she was a superb saleswoman—and her personality and private life undoubtedly contributed to her success. Her friend Misia Sert, wife of Spanish painter Jose Maria Sert, introduced her to such leading figures of the 1920s art world as Sergei Diaghilev, Pablo Picasso, Jean Cocteau, Serge Lifar, and Leon Bakst. She was famous for feuds with other designers, notably ELSA SCHIAPARELLI. Although Chanel never married, she had many love affairs. Grand Duke Dmitri, grandson of Czar Alexander II, was a frequent escort, and a three-year liaison with the Duke of Westminster might have contributed to her longstanding use and appreciation of Scottish tweeds.

Chanel closed her couture house in 1939 at the outset of World War II. During and after the Occupation she shared her life with a German officer, for which many refused to forgive her. She left Paris for Switzerland in 1945, remaining there in exile for eight years.

At the age of 70, Chanel went back into business, presenting her first postwar collection in 1954. A continuation of her original themes of simplicity and

Spaghetti-strapped sheer-lace dress, 1928.

(continued)

wearability, it received a brutal reception from both the French and English press. But by the end of the year, it was clear that Chanel had once again seized the moment when women were ready for change; the dresses from the reviled collection sold very well, especially in America and France. Her success continued into the 1960s, when her refusal to change her basic style or raise hemlines led to a decline in her influence. But the pendulum swung back, and in 1969 Chanel's life was the basis for *Coco*, a Broadway musical starring Katharine Hepburn.

Chanel's daytime palette was neutral—black, white, beige, red—with pastels introduced at night. Trademark looks included the little boy look, wool jersey dresses with white collars and cuffs, pea jackets, bell-bottom trousers, and touches of suntanned skin, bobbed hair, and magnificent jewelry worn with sportswear.

Chanel's post-World War II period is best remembered for her suits made of jersey or the finest, softest Scottish tweeds. Jackets were usually collarless and trimmed with braid, blouses soft and tied at the neckline, skirts at or just below the knee. Suits were shown with multiple strands of pearls and gold chains set with enormous fake stones. Other widely copied signatures included quilted handbags with shoulder chains, beige sling-back pumps with black tips, flat black hair-bows, and single gardenias.

In addition to couture, Chanel's empire encompassed perfumes, a costume jewelry workshop, and a textile house. Chanel No. 5 was created in 1922, and in 1924 Parfums

Beige tweed skirt and plaid grey coat, 1970.

Chanel was established to market the perfumes, which have continued to proliferate. A line of cosmetics was introduced after her death.

The House of Chanel has also continued, directed by a succession of designers. Ready-to-wear was added in 1977, with Philippe Guibourgé as designer. KARL LAGERFELD then took over design duties for both couture and ready-to-wear, and is credited with bringing the house into the modern era.

Chanel remains a legend for her taste, wit, style, and unfaltering dedication to perfection. Her luxury style was based on the most refined simplicity of cut, superb materials, and workmanship of the highest order.

Left: Fall 2013.
Right: Fall 2013.

EDNA WOOLMAN CHASE

BORN Asbury Park, New Jersey, March 14, 1877
DIED Locust Valley, New York, March 20, 1957

AWARDS French Government *Légion d'Honneur*
(Legion of Honor), 1935 • *Neiman Marcus Award*, 1940

The child of divorced parents, Edna Woolman Chase was raised by her Quaker grandparents, whose principles and plain style of dress were a lasting influence. When she was 18, she went to work in the Circulation Department of *Vogue*, then just two years old, for $10 a week. She spent 56 years at *Vogue*, 37 of them as editor.

Chase fell in love with the magazine immediately. Because she was enthusiastic, hardworking, and willing to take on any task, she acquired more and more responsibility. By 1911, she was the equivalent of managing editor. Her name first appeared on the masthead as editor in 1914. British and French *Vogue* were introduced in 1916 and 1920; Chase was editor-in-chief of all three editions. During World War I she began to feature American designers in *Vogue's* pages and is credited with originating the modern fashion show in 1914, when *Vogue* produced a "Fashion Fête" benefit sponsored by prominent society women.

During Chase's tenure, *Vogue* survived two world wars, a depression, and tremendous social changes. With CONDÉ NAST, who bought it in 1909, she helped shape the magazine according to her strong sense of propriety and high standards of professionalism. She refused to suffer second-rate efforts and respected talent and industriousness. Taste, business ability, and hard work put her at the top of her profession and kept her there for an amazingly long time. She retired as

Vogue editor Edna Woolman Chase (right) with Condé Nast (center).

Vogue's editor-in-chief in 1952 and became chair of its editorial board. Chase's requirements for success are still worth considering by those thinking of a career in fashion: taste, sound judgment, and experience—the training and knowledge gained from actually working in a business, which she considered more valuable than taking formal courses.

She married and divorced Francis Dane Chase, with whom she had one child, writer and actress Ilka Chase. A second marriage in 1921 to Richard Newton ended with his death in 1950. Chase released her autobiography *Always in Vogue* in 1954.

MADELEINE CHÉRUIT ▼

BORN France, 1880s
DIED 1935

Madeline Chéruit (Share-WHEE) was the first woman to head a major French design house. She began her business in 1906 after working for a Paris couturier. She was known for her heavily embroidered and beaded evening gowns and her use of rich fabrics such as taffeta, lamé, and silvery gauze. She was fascinated by how natural and artificial light hit fabrics, which helped her choose fabrics that complemented dresses.

In 1913, Chéruit and Lucien Vogel launched *La Gazzette du Bon Ton.* Six other designers, including PAUL POIRET and JACQUES DOUCET, joined the project thinking that theirs would be the only designs published in the magazine. That assumption proved to be incorrect.

In 1914, Chéruit became known for her walking suits and afternoon dresses, and in 1925 she became fascinated with Cubist art. This fascination led her to hand-paint dresses in designs influenced by the art form. The House of Chéruit closed in 1935, when ELSA SCHIAPARELLI took over its location for her business.

Black-net-and-sequin dress, 1927.

Cape of gossamer-gold tissue over a dress, 1921.

Designer Gaby Aghion (left).

FOUNDED Paris, 1952

Chloé was founded by Gaby Aghion, a fashion-forward Egyptian-born Parisienne who rejected the stiff formality of 1950s fashion and partnered with Jacques Lenoir to create the first luxury prêt-a-porter design house. Aghion favored soft silhouettes that clung to the body and emphasized the feminine form. She named the house after a close friend, and believed that the word Chloé evoked a warm, flowing femininity. Aghion and Lenoir defined the house by hiring young, innovative designers whose collections reflected the youthful, modern attitude of Paris's denizens. They launched their first collection in 1956.

This first group of Chloé's designers defined the Paris ready-to-wear movement "Le Style." KARL LAGERFELD became head designer in 1966 and made Chloé one of the most iconic fashion brands of the 1970s, attracting celebrities such as Jacqueline Kennedy, Brigitte Bardot, Maria Callas, and Grace Kelly with elegant daywear, flowing skirts, and romantic, airy blouses.

◼ CHLOÉ

Chloé established the careers of MARTINE SITBON in the 1980s (when it was acquired by the luxury conglomerate Richemont Group), STELLA McCARTNEY in the late 1990s (who provided a mix of vintage lingerie and custom tailoring), and PHOEBE PHILO (who was the designer at the fashion house from 1997 to 2008). In 2008, Hannah MacGibbon, a former assistant to Philo, was credited with reenergizing the brand and bringing out Chloé's signature "girl naiveté." Appointed in 2011, Clare Waight Keller was the former creative director of Scotland's *Pringle*, and in 2012 *Vogue* called her the "embodiment of the brand."

Spring 2014.

EUDON CHOI ▼

BORN South Korea

Eudon Choi started his career in Seoul, South Korea, where he was trained as a men's wear designer. He moved to London to attend the master's program at the Royal College of Art, where he immediately became a rising star. Choi's collection was sold at London's Dover Street Market, and before graduation he was hired as the senior men's wear designer for All Saints. In 2008, Choi was hired as senior designer for Twenty8Twelve. The following year he launched an eponymous label.

In 2010, Choi was among the "Ones to Watch" selected by Vauxhall Fashion Scouts. That was followed by a Vauxhall Fashion Scouts Merit Award, which served as a springboard for Choi to launch his first catwalk show at London Fashion Week. In 2011, ANNA WINTOUR and Franca Sozzani asked Choi to present

Designer Eudon Choi.

in honor of the *Vogue* Fashion Fund in Milan. Choi has received numerous prestigious awards, including the Samsung Fashion and Design Fund Award and the Lycra Style Emerging Talent Award at the WGSN Global Fashion Awards.

Choi is known for his masculine cuts and sartorial techniques, yet his designs maintain a feminine side. He conducts meticulous research and often uses vintage garments and historical photographs for inspiration. He pays close attention to detail and has a futuristic sensibility. In 2013, Choi created a capsule collection for the U.K. high-street label River Island. His clothes are sold in London, Hong Kong, and South Korea.

Fall 2014.

 JIMMY CHOO

Designer Jimmy Choo.

BORN Jimmy Choo Yeang Keat; Penang, Malaysia, 1961

AWARDS British Fashion Council *British Accessory Designer of the Year*, 2000 • Hong Kong Design Center *World's Outstanding Chinese Designer Award*, 2011

Jimmy Choo was raised the son of a shoemaker in Malaysia, and he reportedly made his first pair of shoes when he was 11 years old. In the early 1980s, he studied fashion at Cordwainers College in London. Choo sold his first label, Lucky Shoes, out of a stall on the city's South Bank in 1986.

A few years later he was discovered by Princess Diana, who as a member of the royal family was obliged to use a British designer. Choo was suddenly cast in the fashion spotlight, and began creating shoe collections for twice-yearly runway shows in Great Britain. To contend with the ballooning workload, he hired his niece, Sandra Choi, to help with shoe production.

In England the pair lacked the materials readily available to shoe designers in fashion centers like Paris and Milan. So they would improvise their way to interesting toe shapes, "using the filler you'd use to fix your car," as Choi told *The New York Times*. Choo and Choi were soon approached by Tamara Mellon, a fashion enthusiast working for British *Vogue*, who convinced them to start a shoe label. Mellon came to

work for them, and they opened the first Jimmy Choo store in London in 1997.

Mellon handled the business end of the operation while Choo strained to expand beyond his accustomed role of made-to-order shoe cobbler. Mellon made deals with Italian factories so that the company could increase production, and soon it was producing shoes for major Hollywood stars.

But Mellon and Choo found themselves increasingly at odds over the management of the Jimmy Choo line, over which Mellon appeared to be exerting more and more control. In 2001, Choo was bought out of the company by Equinox Luxury Holdings, part of a billion-dollar venture capital firm. Mellon and Choi now control Jimmy Choo, Ltd. Choo maintains a line of Jimmy Choo couture footwear, for which he licenses his own name from the larger company. These shoes are available by appointment only from a storefront off Oxford Street in London.

In 2009, Choo collaborated on a collection for H&M. In 2011, he launched a men's collection, Mellon left the company, and Choi and Simon Holloway were named co-directors of the Choo brand. In 2013, Holloway left and Choi became sole creative director.

Spring 2013.

DOO-RI CHUNG ▲

BORN South Korea, 1973

AWARDS Council of Fashion Designers of America (CFDA) *Swarovski Perry Ellis Award for Emerging Talent in Womenswear*, 2006 • CFDA/*Vogue* Fashion Fund, 2006

Korean-American Doo-Ri Chung was raised in New Jersey, where her parents ran a dry-cleaning shop. Perhaps it was this early exposure to fabrics that led to her appreciation and skill with jersey knit. After graduating from Parsons School of Design in 1995, she joined the design team at GEOFFREY BEENE, where she spent six years and eventually became head designer.

Chung began producing her own line of draped jersey dresses in 2001, working from the basement below her parents' business. She made her runway debut in 2003 and quickly gained a loyal following among the younger fashion set. In 2006, she received two major awards that netted her $200,000. She has since collaborated on capsule collections for J.Crew and The Gap, and sells her line to exclusive stores such as Barneys New York and Bergdorf Goodman. In addition to expanding her

Designer Doo-Ri Chung.

collection to accessories and resort wear, she launched a lower-priced line, Under.Ligne, in 2009.

In 2011, Michelle Obama wore a purple Chung gown to the state dinner for South Korean President Lee Myung-bak. Though it received rave reviews, in 2012 Chung announced she was leaving her brand. Six months later, she became creative director of Vince.

Fall 2012.

Fall 2012.

⚊ ◧ LIZ CLAIBORNE

Designer Liz Claiborne.

BORN Anne Elisabeth Jane Claiborne; Brussels, Belgium, March 31, 1929
DIED New York City, June 26, 2007

AWARDS Council of Fashion Designers of America (CFDA) *Special Award*, 1985; *Humanitarian Award (Liz Claiborne and Art Ortenberg Foundation)*, 2000 • *Dallas Fashion Award*, 1985

Liz Claiborne made her name in sportswear, where her strength lay in translating new trends into simple, uncomplicated, moderately priced clothes. She was known for her use of color and knowledge of fabric. As her company expanded into other areas—such as dresses, men's wear, and children's wear—she largely became an editor of other designers.

Claiborne spent her childhood in New Orleans and went on to study painting in Belgium and France. Her career in fashion began in 1949, when she won a trip to Europe in a *Harper's Bazaar* design contest. After her return to America, she worked as a model sketcher and assistant to Tina Leser, Omar Kiam, and others. In 1976, she formed Liz Claiborne, Inc., with her husband Arthur Ortenberg as business manager.

Claiborne served as a critic at the Fashion Institute of Technology and received numerous awards from retailers and industry associations. In 1989, she and her husband retired from the company to devote themselves to environmental issues. The company has since grown enormously through acquisitions, including Kenneth Cole and Ellen Tracy. Isaac Mizrahi became creative director for the Liz Claiborne label in 2008.

Knee length pleated skirt, 1972.

OSSIE CLARK ♟

BORN Raymond Oswald Clark; Lancashire, England, June 9, 1942

DIED London, August 6, 1996

In his heyday in the 1960s, Ossie Clark was the top designer for English film and rock stars, in touch with everything in music, art, politics, film, and photography. He dressed Julie Christie and Brigitte Bardot, was painted by David Hockney, vacationed with the Rolling Stones, and put the Beatles in the front row of his shows, setting precedents that other designers still try to follow. The difference was that those celebrities were actually Clark's friends—not just invited for their publicity value.

Clark entered Manchester Regional Art College at 16, immediately becoming part of a circle that included actors Ben Kingsley and Celia Birtwell. Birtwell was a textiles student who created brightly colored, naïve prints that Clark used in his designs; she later became his wife. In 1962, Clark won a scholarship to London's Royal College of Art, where he met Hockney.

Designer Ossie Clark.

Model wearing a crepe playsuit from Ossie Clark's "Quorum" fashion show in London, 1973.

In 1965, Clark and Birtwell, along with fellow designer Alice Pollock, opened a shop called Quorum just off King's Road in the heart of swinging London. By the early 1970s, drugs, numerous affairs with women and men, and erratic work habits had undermined Clark's life. Birtwell took the couple's two sons and left him in 1973; Quorum closed two years later. By the end of the decade, Clark was broke and living in a tiny public housing flat.

By the late 1980s, Clark had converted to Buddhism, started to rebuild his life, and was once again being recognized. CHRISTIAN LACROIX went to London to meet him, and RIFAT OZBEK and JOHN GALLIANO greatly admired him and invited him to their shows. In 1995, several of Clark's pieces were included in an exhibition of street fashion at the Victoria and Albert Museum. But in 1996, Clark was murdered by a drug addict with whom he had lived for nearly a year, then kicked out.

Clark's success was based on two things: he loved women's bodies and made clothes for them that were sexy but not too obvious, and his designs were based on his genius as a master cutter. He studied the masters—VIONNET, CHANEL, POIRET—and picked up ideas such as bias-cut bodices or Peter Pan collars that he translated into creations entirely his own.

In 2003, the Victoria and Albert Museum featured Clark's work in a retrospective exhibition. London fashion tycoons Marc and Julian Worth relaunched the Ossie Clark label in 2008 but announced plans to close it a year later.

⏳ CLEMENTS RIBEIRO

Designers Suzanne Clements (left) and Inacio Ribeiro (right).

BORN Suzanne Clements; England, 1969
Inacio Ribeiro; Brazil, 1963

Suzanne Clements and Inacio Ribeiro trained at
Central St. Martins College of Art and Design, and both
graduated in 1991 with top honors. They married a year
later. Before moving to London to get formal training,
Ribeiro had worked as a designer for several years;
Clements had a fledgling knitwear line that was sold at
Harrods and Liberty. After graduation the two went to
Brazil, where they worked as design consultants. They
returned to London in 1993.

Their first collection under the Clements Ribeiro label
was shown in 1993 and featured crisp separates in cotton
pique, hand-painted silk chiffon, and textured linen. The
label quickly became known for uncluttered, exuberant
designs with bold stripes of color and for luxurious
cashmeres. A shoe collection was added in 1996. In 2001,
the couple was hired by the French firm Cacharel, though
they continued to design for their own label. In 2009,
they launched their limited edition Projects, which are
up-cycled, hand-crafted designs sold at net-a-porter.com
as well as select stores around the world.

Fall 2013.

GRACE CODDINGTON

BORN Isle of Anglesey, Wales, United Kingdom, 1941

Known for styling some of the most stunning pages of *Vogue* for more than four decades, Grace Coddington propelled into fame after the documentary *The September Issue* was released in 2009. Coddington started her career as a model and worked with London designers MARY QUANT and Vidal Sassoon. Even ANNA WINTOUR has acknowledged that Coddington was a unique beauty that the camera simply adored. In 1961, Coddington was in a major car accident that required many reconstructive surgeries, but she continued to model until 1968. At that time it was suggested that Coddington transition into editorial work, and she became the junior fashion editor for British *Vogue*.

Coddington's life changed again in 1971 when she visited the Seychelles, inspiring the fantasy travelogues for which she is known. In 1979, Coddington was promoted to senior fashion editor of British *Vogue*. In 1987, she became fashion director at CALVIN KLEIN. The following year, Wintour was hired as editor-in-chief at American *Vogue* and Coddington as fashion director.

Coddington has been at American *Vogue* ever since, creating some of its most iconic images. For Coddington, being a fashion editor means "choosing the clothes to shoot . . . but it's also much more than that. It's playing with everyone's personalities and making sure that everything is jelling. When I'm on top of a mountain with a photographer who doesn't want to shoot something because it doesn't look sexy, and the magazine wants it in the issue—at that point, I'm the one who has to keep everyone motivated."

Grace Coddington at the 2012 CFDA Fashion Awards.

Much to the delight of its audiences, *The September Issue* showed Coddington's multifaceted, quarter-century-plus working relationship with Wintour—and the approaches that she uses to get her way at *Vogue*. Certain scenes were especially interesting because of Coddington's tendency to be blunt. In 2012, she published *Grace: A Memoir*. She is one of the world's best-known stylists and has no plans of stepping down.

Anne Cole (center) with models.

BORN Los Angeles, circa 1930

AWARDS *Dallas Fashion Award*, 1987 • Otis College of Art and Design *Fashion Achievement Award*, 1993, 2001

Anne Cole is the daughter of Fred Cole, one of swimwear's great innovators. She studied at the University of California, Los Angeles (UCLA) and Holy Names College before joining her family's firm, West Coast Knitting Mills, in 1951. She had to work her way up in the company, from sorting deliveries in the mailroom to posting orders to taking trunk shows on the road.

Working in the family business was a Cole tradition: Fred Cole starred in silent movies until his mother made him join the firm. It made drop-seat underwear until Fred started having it knit the first fashionable swimsuits for women—transforming what had been a drab and shapeless garment by lowering the back, defining the bust and waistline, and introducing brilliant colors. He continued to innovate, working with Margit Fellegi, a Hollywood costume designer. They introduced a cotton swimsuit puckered with rubber thread and, when rubber supplies were limited during World War II, created the two-piece "swoon suit," which laced up the sides of the trunks and had a tie bra. In 1941, the company's name was changed to Cole of California, and after the war came plunging necklines, cut-outs, bare

midriffs, and suits made of sequins, gold lamé jersey, and water-resistant velvets.

When her father sold Cole of California to Kayser-Roth in 1960, Anne Cole left the company but later returned to establish its New York office and become stylist and company spokesperson. The firm has since had several owners—most recently Los Angeles–based Authentic Fitness, which also owns Speedo and Catalina.

The Anne Cole Collection, launched in 1982, expresses her most advanced fashion ideas. She considers swimsuits to be objects between fashion and beauty aids, reflecting current trends but with the primary function of enhancing the appearance of the wearer. She is credited for creating the tankini, the popular two-piece suit with a tank top and bikini bottom.

In 2001, Anne received an award from L.A.'s Otis College of Art and Design in recognition of her innovations in swimwear design and efforts to mentor its students. At the time she was still actively engaged in swimsuit design—making her, as she put it, "the oldest living swimwear designer in the world." In 2012, the Anne Cole Collection celebrated 30 years in business.

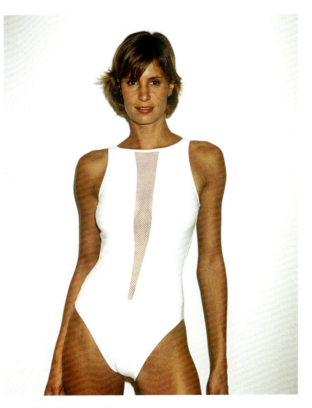

Anne Cole Collection Swimwear.

KENNETH COLE

BORN Long Island, New York, March 23, 1954

AWARDS Council of Fashion Designers of America (CFDA) *Dom Pérignon Award for Humanitarian Excellence*, 1996 • Fashion Footwear Association of New York (FFANY) *Fashion Medal of Honor Award*, 1997

Kenneth Cole exhibits both creative entrepreneurship and downright chutzpah—valuable qualities in his chosen field. He grew up on Long Island, working in his spare time as a stock boy at the local shoe store. After graduating from Emory University in 1976, he worked for his family's shoe business in Brooklyn before striking out on his own.

In 1982, with limited money, he launched Kenneth Cole Productions from a 40-foot trailer parked across the street from a hotel where a shoe show was taking place. He claimed to be filming a movie, but he was actually showing his shoes—and sold out his production quota in two and a half days. Since then the company has

Designer Kenneth Cole.

expanded beyond shoes for men and women to clothes for men, women, and children as well as luggage, accessories, and fragrances sold worldwide in upscale stores and his own shops. He has also designed uniforms for the W hotel chain.

Cole is nearly as well-known for his provocative, socially conscious advertising and participation in causes—from AIDS awareness to homelessness to abortion rights—as for his cool, hip fashions. His fashion and humanitarian work has been recognized by organizations ranging from *New York* magazine to Amnesty International, and he has received honorary degrees from Manhattanville College and the University of Illinois School of Public Health. After taking a seven-year hiatus and buying back his company from investors in 2012, Cole returned to New York Fashion Week in February 2013.

WE ALL WALK IN DIFFERENT SHOES.

SONNY CABERWAL, PRACTICING SIKH AND ENTREPRENEUR SPEAKING OUT AGAINST RACIAL PROFILING.

KENNETHCOLE.COM 25 YEARS OF NON-UNIFORM THINKING.

Advertisement, 2008.

Spring 2013.

ESTEBAN CORTÁZAR

BORN Bogotá, Colombia, May 17, 1984

One of the youngest designers to emerge in fashion, Esteban Cortázar (Core-ta-CZAR) presented his first collection at 15. He credits his early family life for inspiring his interest in design. Born to jazz singer Dominique Vaughan and artist Valentino Cortázar, Esteban was immersed in the creative process early, both in his native Colombia and in Miami, Florida, where his family moved when he was 11. Cortázar flourished in Miami's cultural landscape, becoming a local style icon and dressing the windows of vintage shops.

When TODD OLDHAM opened a boutique in Miami in 1997, Cortázar approached the designer with a book of his sketches. Oldham was so impressed that he invited Cortázar to attend his upcoming Fashion Week show in New York. The experience further cemented Cortázar's love and passion for fashion.

Cortázar's inspired 30-piece collection unofficially debuted at Miami International Fashion Week in 1999 as part of a group show, alongside fashion luminaries such as CAROLINA HERRERA. In 2002, he launched his eponymous label with a 14-piece evening wear collection that caught the eye of Kalman Ruttenstein from Bloomingdale's—earning Cortázar a highly coveted window display at the flagship Bloomingdale's store in New York.

Cortázar asked retired supermodel and longtime supporter Cindy Crawford to open and close the show for his spring/summer 2004 collection, adorning her in a dazzling floor-length gown constructed entirely of Swarovski crystal mesh, much to the surprise and delight of his audience. The collection was so well-received that 7th on Sixth's Fern Mallis invited Cortázar to open Los Angeles Fashion Week. In 2007, he was appointed designer of EMANUAL UNGARO, but left the company in 2009.

Cortázar has attracted a large celebrity following, and his designs have been worn by Beyoncé, Eva Longoria, and Paris Hilton. His pieces have also been used by designer PATRICIA FIELD in her role as stylist for the television show *Sex and the City*. Cortázar's work is now available exclusively on net-a-porter.com.

Designer Esteban Cortazar (left) with model.

Spring/summer 2013.

FRANCISCO COSTA

BORN Guarani, Brazil, 1961

AWARDS Council of Fashion Designers of America Award (CFDA) *Women's Wear Designer of the Year,* 2006, 2008 • Fashion Group International *Star Honoree in Fashion,* 2008 • Cooper-Hewitt *National Design Award (fashion),* 2009

Francisco Costa grew up outside Rio, Brazil, watching his parents run their successful apparel business. Determined to carve his own niche in fashion by designing for a large fashion house, Costa moved to New York City when he was 21. He first studied English as a second language at Hunter College, then enrolled in night classes at the Fashion Institute of Technology, where his talent and vision were soon recognized with the Idea Como/Young Designers of America Award. After graduating, Costa worked for Susan Bennett Studio and BILL BLASS, then spent five years collaborating with OSCAR DE LA RENTA on his signature line and PIERRE BALMAIN haute couture, and colaunching the Oscar de la Renta Pink label. Costa

Designer Francisco Costa.

then moved to TOM FORD for GUCCI, where he was a senior designer focused on evening wear and custom client designs.

In 2002, CALVIN KLEIN chose Costa to be his successor as creative director of the Calvin Klein Collection for women, just months before Klein sold his company to Phillips-Van Heusen for $730 million. Hired to breathe complexity into the minimalist aesthetic of Klein's structured designs, Costa's airy, feminine collections received some of the best reviews in the company's history. Costa says that his collections are for women who are "sexy, independent, and confident; and each piece represents effortless, sensual, timeless style." In 2013, Costa received the Savannah College of Art and Design (SCAD) André Leon Talley Lifetime Achievement Award, which included an exhibition at the SCAD Museum of Art of his spring 2013 collection for Calvin Klein.

Sequined jersey dress, 2004.

Calvin Klein Collection, fall/winter 2009.

▼ ANDRÉ COURRÈGES

Designer André Courrèges (center) with models.

BORN Pau, France, March 9, 1923

André Courrèges (Koo-REJ) emerged on the fashion scene in 1962 as a brilliant tailor. Using fabrics with considerable body, he cut his coats and suits with a triangular flare that disguised many defects of women's figures, creating balanced silhouettes defined by crisp welt seaming. Courrèges sought to make functional, modern clothes for active women. His successes—many of them widely copied—included all-white collections inspired by his Basque heritage and tunics worn over narrow pants with flared bottoms that slanted from front to back. There were also squared-off dresses ending above the knee, short white "baby" boots, industrial zippers, and unusual accessories such as sunglasses with slit "tennis ball" lenses. He was called "The Couturier of the Space Age."

Courrèges studied civil engineering before switching to textiles and fashion design. His first job was with Jeanne Lafaurie. From 1952 to 1960 Courrèges was a cutter for CRISTÓBAL BALENCIAGA, whose influence was evident in his early designs. In 1961, with Balenciaga's blessing, Courrèges and his wife Coqueline—who became his close collaborator—opened their own business. Together they designed, cut, sewed, and presented their first collection in a small apartment on Avenue Kléber in Paris.

White jumpsuits and sunglasses.

Courrèges was so widely plagiarized that the couple sold the business in 1965, then spent two years working for private clients and setting up their own manufacturing and production. They returned in 1967 with the Couture Future ready-to-wear collection, which featured a distinctive logo on the outside of the clothes—another fashion first. There were see-through dresses, cosmonaut suits, knitted catsuits with flowers appliquéd on the body, and knee socks. The Courrèges name also extended to

White dress and sunglasses.

accessories, luggage, perfumes, men's wear, and boutiques in America and other countries. The stores carried everything from sports separates to accessories to Couture Future. The name continued to appear through the years on ready-to-wear lines designed by Courrèges in collaboration with other designers.

In 1996, Courrèges and his wife bought back their company, which has remained in business under the active control of Madame Courrèges. Her husband retired in 1995 to devote himself to painting and sculpture. The line is still made in their factory using the original patterns and fabrics, and sold in their shops and fine specialty stores. Madame Courrèges has said that the couple was always designing for 2000, and in 2001 the label's influence was noted in numerous collections by other designers.

Short, black sequin dress.

Designer Patrick Cox (right) with Ingle-Finch.

BORN Edmonton, Canada, March 19, 1963

AWARDS British Fashion Council *Accessory Designer of the Year,* 1994, 1995 • Footwear Association of New York *Fashion Medal of Honor,* 1996

Patrick Cox's shoe designs are known for their distinctive and often eccentric details—such as a chainmail skirt over the heel of a black pump or a Union Jack symbol on a pair of loafers. "I am a magpie," Cox has said. "My eye collects details."

Born in Canada, Cox moved to London at 19 to study footwear design at Cordwainers Technical College. In the early 1980s, he created shoes for maverick designers such as John Galliano and Vivienne Westwood. Cox became known for his attention to detail, and by 1985 had enough name recognition to start his own company.

In 1991, Cox opened the first of several boutiques in London. But he did not achieve widespread fame until his 1993 Wannabe line, which began with a pair of loafers inspired by entertainer Pee Wee Herman. Cox's shoe designs are colorful and innovative showpieces that demand attention. In 2001, he presented the Light Boot, a disco boot that lit up using fiber-optic technology.

In 2003, Cox became creative director of the French shoe company Charles Jourdan, though he continued to design for his own label. In 2005, he decided to expand his business and refurbished his London boutique. He launched a line of luxury accessories in 2006. Cox's work can be seen at the Victoria and Albert Museum in London, the Museum at the Fashion Institute of Technology in New York, and the Bata Shoe Museum in Toronto, Canada.

In 2008, Cox was forced to sell his business for $3.5 million, but he maintained his position on its board of designers.

Handbag from luxury accessories line, 2006.

A pair of Geox SpA shoes designed by Patrick Cox.

HOUSE OF CREED 👜 ▮

FOUNDED London, 1760

One of the world's oldest family businesses, the House of Creed has been producing fragrances for the world's elite for 239 years. Established in London by saddle maker James Henry Creed, the house quickly achieved premier status when Queen Victoria made it an official supplier to her court. Known for its high-quality natural ingredients and exacting production methods, the House of Creed's fragrances were soon used by aristocrats across continental Europe.

In the 1850s, Henry Creed (James Henry's grandson) expanded the business to include tailoring. The House of Creed moved to Paris in 1854. Henry's son (also Henry) joined the house in the early 1900s and produced riding habits for European royalty. Fashionable women of leisure were drawn to his shapely Basque jackets (which feminized lines from men's wear), full skirts, and fitted tweeds. Devotees of Creed's tailoring included glamorous accused German spy Mata

Designer Henry Creed.

Designer Charles Creed (right) with model.

Hari (who reportedly faced the firing squad in a Creed suit) and Alice Roosevelt, the trend-setting daughter of U.S. President Theodore Roosevelt.

Henry Creed passed the family business to his son Charles in the 1930s. Having first opened his own house in London, Charles continued the family's tradition of tailoring by producing elegant women's suits and coats, sheer wool blouses, and evening dresses. Forced to close the Paris business with the advent of World War II, Charles later designed wholesale lines for firms in London and America. The clothing design arm of the House of Creed ended with Charles's death in 1966.

Today the company today is overseen by sixth-generation Olivier Creed, a perfectionist credited with reestablishing the House of Creed as masters of exclusive fragrances. Creed fragrances are worn by royalty, celebrities, and world leaders seeking unmistakably luxurious scents. In the spring of 2009, Creed introduced Acqua Fiorentina for women—the house's first new fragrance in years—and in the fall released a limited edition of Windsor, originally created for the Duke of Windsor in 1936. In keeping with family tradition, Olivier is grooming his son Erwin to shepherd the House of Creed into its seventh generation.

The House of Creed has created more than 64 fragrances worn by British royalty and American presidents and first ladies, including John F. Kennedy, Laura Bush, and Michelle Obama. In 2010, the House of Creed celebrated its 250th year by opening its first U.S. store on Madison Avenue in New York.

Brown suede coat, 1948.

BILL CUNNINGHAM 📷

BORN Boston, circa 1929

AWARDS Council of Fashion Designers of America (CFDA) *Media Award in Honor of Eugenia Sheppard*, 1993 • French Ministry of Culture *Officier dans l'Ordre des Arts et des Lettres*, 2008

A familiar New York figure in his beret, corduroys, and parka, camera unobtrusively at the ready, Bill Cunningham observes and records fashion not as it is worn on the runway, but as it appears in the real world. In fair weather or foul, from one of his favorite posts at 57th Street and Fifth Avenue, in SoHo, or at the GreenMarket or flea market, he catches passersby for his *On the Street* column in the Sunday *New York Times*. His second feature, *Evening Hours*, chronicles benefits, art openings, and other social events.

Cunningham's early attraction to fashion was totally alien to his conservative New England background. In Boston he worked after school at Bonwit Teller department store. After graduation, he worked for Nona Park and Sophie Shonnard in their Chez Ninon boutique at the Bonwit's in New York City. There he first saw the fashionable women who later became his photographic subjects. On his own time, Cunningham made masks and headdresses for women attending then-popular masked balls, and later opened a hat shop called William J. with backing from Rebecca Harkness, the noted ballet patron. Drafted into the Army during the Korean War, he was stationed in the south of France and able to see his former employers, Park and Shonnard, when they were in Paris shopping for clients.

Once out of the Army, Cunningham was hired by *Women's Wear Daily's* JOHN B. FAIRCHILD to write a twice-weekly column, but left after nine months to write about fashion for the *Chicago Tribune*. A friend,

Photographer Bill Cunningham.

illustrator ANTONIO, suggested that Cunningham use a camera to take notes—a move that opened his world and was the beginning of a new career. In the mid-1970s, he began freelancing at *The New York Times,* and in 1993 became a staff member. To attract Cunningham's photographic attention, a subject must be more than perfect, which he finds uninteresting. For him, a person with style must have something extra: "something so personal—flawless but with a dash." In 2011, filmmaker Richard Press and Philip Gefter of *The Times* produced *Bill Cunningham New York*, a documentary that received massive critical acclaim.

Designers Michelle Ochs (left) and Carly Cushnie (right).

BORN Carly Cushnie; London, 1984
Michelle Ochs; Calgary, Canada, 1984

The design team of Cushnie et Ochs have become a new force in the fashion industry. Carly Cushnie grew up in London, Michelle Ochs in Maryland. Ochs attended Parsons School of Art and Design in Paris before transferring to its New York campus. She and Cushnie met during their junior year at Parsons and bonded over their stand-out talents. Cushnie and Ochs have interned at some of the most prestigious New York design houses, including Marc Jacobs, Proenza Schouler, and Donna Karan. Their senior year collections were featured in a *Women's Wear Daily* cover story. When the designers graduated in 2007, Ochs was named Student Designer of the Year; Cushnie came in second. In 2008,

♦ CUSHNIE ET OCHS

the team launched their first collection, which was inspired by the movie *American Psycho*. Bergdorf Goodman was so impressed that it asked for exclusive rights to the collection.

Cushnie et Ochs clothing is luxurious, edgy, and bold, yet sensual and feminine. The extremely sexy clothes showcase the designers' knowledge of form and women's bodies, and are designed for modern women who are aware of their individuality. In 2009, Cushnie et Ochs won the Ecco Domani Fashion Foundation Award, and in 2011 was nominated for the Council of Fashion Designers of America (CFDA)/*Vogue* Fashion Fund. In 2013, Cushnie et Ochs was a finalist for a CFDA Swarovski Award. Rihanna, Reese Witherspoon, and Michelle Obama have all been seen wearing the brand.

Spring 2014.

Cushnie et Ochs' silk georgette and tulle dress.

LILLY DACHÉ 👜

BORN Beigles, France, October 10, 1898
DIED Louvecienne, France, December 31, 1989

AWARDS *Neiman Marcus Award*, 1940 • Coty American Fashion Critics' Awards *Special Award (millinery)*, 1943

Vivacious and feminine, Lilly Daché (Da-SHAY) brought an inimitable French flair to American fashion at a time when no woman was considered fully dressed without a hat. She left school at 14 to apprentice with a milliner aunt, at 15 was an apprentice in the workrooms of the famous Paris milliner Reboux, and later worked at Maison Talbot. She moved to New York City in 1924, spent a week behind the millinery counter at Macy's, then opened a millinery shop with a partner. When her partner left, Daché moved to the same neighborhood as HATTIE CARNEGIE.

Designer Lilly Daché.

Eventually Daché moved to her own nine-story building on East 57th Street. It contained showrooms, workrooms, and an apartment where she lived with her husband Jean Després, executive vice president of Coty. By 1949, Daché was designing dresses to go with her hats. She also produced lingerie, loungewear, gloves, hosiery, men's shirts and ties, and even a wired strapless bra.

Her major design contributions were draped turbans, brimmed hats molded to the head, half hats, colored snoods, romantic massed flower shapes, and visored caps for war workers. She was America's foremost milliner and influenced many American designers, including HALSTON. She closed her business in 1969 upon her husband's retirement.

Floral hats, 1945.

BORN San Francisco, November 19, 1895
DIED Allendale, New Jersey, December 13, 1989

Accomplished in both fashion and portrait photography, Louise Dahl-Wolfe attended the California School of Design (now San Francisco Institute of Design). Before buying her first camera in 1923, she worked at everything from designing electric signs to decorating. After travels to Europe and Africa—during which she met her future husband, artist Mike Wolfe—she moved to San Francisco, then the Great Smoky Mountains of Tennessee. Her first published photographs were of her Tennessee neighbors and appeared in *Vanity Fair* in 1933.

Dahl-Wolfe's first black-and-white fashion photography appeared in *Harper's Bazaar* in 1936, and her first color in 1937; her elegant photographs graced the magazine until 1958. With dramatic lighting and backgrounds ranging from intricate Chinese screens to seamless paper, she caught the essence of individual fashions as simple as a CLAIRE MCCARDELL linen sundress and as structured as a pair of satin ball gowns by CHARLES JAMES.

Dahl-Wolfe was the first to use color effectively in fashion photography, driving color separators and *Bazaar's* Art Director ALEXEY BRODOVITCH to distraction with her insistence on perfection. Unlike many of her peers, she never considered photography as art but rather as a commercial medium. She left *Harper's Bazaar* after CARMEL SNOW and Brodovitch resigned, worked for a few months at *Vogue*, then retired to Frenchtown, New Jersey, with her husband.

Photographer Louise Dahl-Wolfe (right) shooting a model for *Harper's Bazaar*, 1947.

Photograph for *Vogue*, 1959.

SANDY DALAL

BORN Sandy Agashiwala; Bronx, New York, 1977

AWARDS Council of Fashion Designers of America (CFDA) *Perry Ellis Award for Men's Wear,* 1997

Sandy Dalal first became interested in making clothes when he was ten and traveled with his mother on a trip to the Far East, where she was assessing factories to make clothing for designers. He started sewing at 14 and by his senior year in high school had made more than 30 pieces, mostly shirts and pants—any jacket designs were sent to a tailor to execute. By 18 he felt ready to begin a design career, but at his family's insistence enrolled at the University of Pennsylvania, where he majored in international trade and marketing. He was also on the fencing team, but always continued to sew.

Designer Sandy Dalal.

In 1996, Dalal made his first tailored suit by himself. The next year, he established his own business, Sandy Dalal Ltd., financed with a few thousand dollars from summer jobs and backing from family and friends. The clothes were cut with clean, simple lines, and made of beautiful fabrics—a mix of 1960s Swinging London and colonial India, appealing to men with a sense of adventure and a taste for luxury.

Dalal's clothes have been well received by stores such as Barneys New York and Fred Segal of Los Angeles. He has also worked for Italian and Japanese firms, including Onward Kashiyama and its International Concept Brand (ICB) label, while continuing to design for his own label. In addition, Dalal cofounded Teleport, a company that connects design entrepreneurs with communication tools online.

Spring/Summer 2001.

Above: Designer Daryl K.
Below: Resort 2012.

BORN Daryl Kerrigan; Dublin, Ireland, 1964

AWARDS Council of Fashion Designers of America (CFDA) *Perry Ellis Award for Women's Wear*, 1996

Daryl Kerrigan studied fashion at Dublin's National College of Art and Design, and moved to New York City in 1986. Starting out working in thrift shops and as a wardrobe consultant on films, she developed a hip, "downtown" aesthetic that she soon put to good use in her own designs. Kerrigan established her own salon in the East Village in 1991. Her low-slung leather pants and lean t-shirts, produced under her Daryl K line, quickly earned her a cult following and made her a critic's darling.

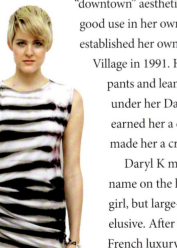

Daryl K may have been the name on the lips of every cool girl, but large-scale success proved elusive. After being courted by French luxury line Céline and consulting for Tommy Hilfiger, in 2000 Kerrigan sold her company to an investment firm that promised to fund its expansion. When the deal collapsed, she was out of business and struggled to come up with the financing needed to produce new work.

Kerrigan's indie credibility has held up, however, and seems to support her best work. After a collaboration with Barneys New York for an in-store boutique in 2005, which increased the exposure of her line, she regained her financial footing. She then sold her collections to other exclusive stores and reopened her original space on New York's Bond Street, where she sold both her Daryl K and lower-priced Kerrigan lines.

In 2010, Kerrigan closed the Bond Street store to sell her clothes online. Her spring 2012 ready-to-wear collection debuted the jump-dress, a cross between a dress and jumpsuit that was the sole new silhouette on the runway. More recently, Kerrigan collaborated with Steven Alan on his resort 2013 collection, which featured tailored silk blazers, leather leggings, and Chelsea boots.

Spring 2012.

JESSICA DAVES

Vogue editor Jessica Daves.

BORN Cartersville, Georgia, February 20, 1898
DIED New York City, 1974

Jessica Daves (Dayvz) arrived in New York City in 1921. She worked in the advertising departments of various stores, including Saks Fifth Avenue, writing fashion copy and learning about fashion merchandising. In 1933, she started at *Vogue* as a fashion merchandising editor, where her ability was recognized by editor-in-chief EDNA WOOLMAN CHASE.

In 1936, Daves was made managing editor, and in 1946 became editor. Upon Chase's retirement in 1952, Daves became editor-in-chief. She was also a director of CONDÉ NAST Publications from 1946 until she retired in 1963, served as an editorial consultant for a year, and worked on specialized books until 1966.

An accomplished writer and editor, Daves could fix a piece of ailing copy in minutes. She was known for clearheadedness and sound judgment, and was astute at business. The years of her editorship coincided with phenomenal growth in America's ready-to-wear industry. Daves recognized its increasing importance and broadened *Vogue's* coverage of domestic ready-to-wear, including more moderately priced clothes. Under her direction, *Vogue* took a more serious tone and ran more articles of intellectual interest.

⚀ JEAN-CHARLES DE CASTELBAJAC

BORN Casablanca, Morocco, November 28, 1949

Part of the ready-to-wear movement that burgeoned in France in the 1960s and came into full flower in the 1970s, Jean-Charles de Castelbajac (CASSEL-buy-jack) is best known for the flair he gives to survival looks—blanket plaids, canvas, quilting, rugged coats—and sportswear for both men and women. He has been called "the space age BONNIE CASHIN."

Castelbajac's parents moved to France when he was five. His mother started a small clothes factory, and he

Fashion designer Jean-Charles de Castelbajac (left) and model.

went to work for her when he was 18. He designed for Pierre d'Alby, joined a group of young designers in 1974, then opened his first retail shop. He has collaborated with COURRÈGES on ready-to-wear, designed for a number of manufacturers (including some in Italy), and done costumes for the theater.

In 2011, Castelbajac collaborated with Coca-Cola to create the 125th anniversary JC/DC collection, which was sold at select boutiques worldwide. In 2013, Castelbajac was chosen as honorary chair of the Fashion + Design Festival in Montreal, Canada.

Spring 2014.

Ready-to-wear, spring/summer 2009.

OSCAR DE LA RENTA ⬧

BORN Santo Domingo, Dominican Republic, July 22, 1932

AWARDS Coty American Fashion Critics' Awards *Winnie*, 1967; *Return Award*, 1968; *Hall of Fame*, 1973 • *Neiman Marcus Award*, 1968 • Council of Fashion Designers of America (CFDA) *Women's Wear Designer of the Year*, 2000; *Founders Award*, 2013

Oscar de la Renta is known for sexy, extravagantly romantic evening clothes in opulent materials. His daytime clothes, sometimes overshadowed by his more spectacular

Designer Oscar de la Renta (right) and model.

Fall 2009.

evening designs, have a European flavor—sophisticated, feminine, and eminently wearable.

Educated in Santo Domingo and Madrid, de la Renta remained in Madrid after graduation to study art, intending to become a painter. His fashion career began when sketches he made for his own amusement were seen by the wife of the American ambassador to Spain, who asked him to design a gown for her daughter's debut. His first professional job was with Balenciaga's Madrid couture house, Eisa. In 1961 he went to Paris as an assistant to Antonio de Castillo at Lanvin-Castillo, and in 1963 went with Castillo to New York to design at Elizabeth Arden. He joined Jane Derby in 1965 and was soon operating as Oscar de la Renta, Ltd., producing luxury ready-to-wear.

Dress, 2004.

A signature perfume introduced in 1977 has been enormously successful. A second fragrance, Ruffles, appeared in 1983. De la Renta has also done boutique lines, bathing suits, wedding dresses, furs, jewelry, bed linens, and loungewear. In 1992 he took over the design of BALMAIN couture, remaining until his retirement in 2002. He continues to design his own New York collection.

De la Renta is considered the poster child of the Dominican Republic. In 1982, he built La Casa de Niño, an orphanage and school for children of La Romana. Over 1,200 kids occupy the orphanage each year. Today, de la Renta represents a home line, eyewear, and bridal wear collection. Though his family now runs the business, de la Renta remains at the helm. His son-in-law Alex Bolen is chief executive officer, his stepdaughter Eliza Bolen is creative director, and his son Moises de la Renta works in the design studio.

De la Renta's clothes have been worn by U.S. first ladies from Jacqueline Kennedy to Hillary Clinton and Laura Bush. His clothes have also been worn by celebrities such as Gisele Bündchen and Anne Hathaway. In an unprecedented move, in 2013 Oscar de la Renta showed its fall 2013 collection exclusively on Instagram.

Spring 2014.

BARON ADOLF DE MEYER 📷

BORN Adolf Meyer-Watson; September 1, 1868
DIED Los Angeles, 1946

Baron Adolf de Meyer is considered the first true fashion photographer, the one who transformed fashion photography into a major artistic expression. He dropped Watson from his last name, took a Saxon title, and in 1899 married Olga Alberta Caracciolo, the godchild of Edward VII of England. The marriage opened society to de Meyer, and the couple devoted themselves to the pleasures and pursuits of the English upper crust.

Upon the king's death in 1910, it became necessary for de Meyer to earn some money. He soon established

Photographer Baron Adolf de Meyer.

a reputation as a photographer in Paris and London; his early pictures of Diaghilev's Ballets Russes captured the dazzling splendor and drama that so captivated the European avant-garde. In 1913, the onset of World War I persuaded de Meyer and his wife to leave for New York City, where he worked for *Vogue* and *Vanity Fair*. In 1923, he was given the opportunity to work in Paris.

De Meyer's primary interest was in creating an ideal of feminine beauty and softness based on luxury and romance. His photographs relied on glamorous backgrounds and elaborate settings, reflecting a life of opulent ease and aristocratic idleness. With their emphasis on glowing light and romantic atmosphere, they embodied the painterly traditions of 19th-century art.

De Meyer employed soft focus—using a lens that was sharp in the center, soft at the edges—and sometimes stretched silk gauze over the lens. He made extensive use of backlighting, his most famous and influential technique. Many other photographers imitated his approach but failed to achieve the same extravagantly flattering and glamorous results.

De Meyer's influence declined with women's liberation. A new age had begun, and he could not evolve with the times.

Photograph for Elizabeth Arden, 1940.

Designer Giles Deacon and models.

Deacon was part of a high-profile class at St. Martins that included Luella Bartley, ALEXANDER MCQUEEN, STELLA MCCARTNEY, and Katie Grand.

Deacon graduated in 1992 and for several years worked for a diverse range of design teams at brands such as JEAN-CHARLES DE CASTELBAJAC, LOUIS VUITTON, MARC JACOBS, and French Connection. After a brief but high-profile stint as head designer for BOTTEGA VENETA in 2000, he returned to fashion freelancing in London.

Deacon debuted his own line, Giles, at London Fashion Week in 2004, and received raves for his sexy yet grown-up designs. Recent collections have included beautifully constructed dresses with edgy embellishments such as bold prints, ripped suede, mohair, and safety pins. In addition to couture, Deacon has a more affordable mid-range line and has produced inexpensive capsule collections of skirts and t-shirts for New Look. In 2010, Deacon was appointed creative director of EMANUEL UNGARO, but in 2011 they decided to part ways.

BORN Darlington, England

AWARDS British Designer of the Year, 2006

Giles Deacon (Jeels DEE-kin) was raised in a remote area of the Lakes District in England. He went to Central St. Martins College of Art and Design in London to study art, but quickly gravitated to fashion.

Fall 2012.

Fall 2012.

LOUIS DELL'OLIO ▼

BORN New York City, July 23, 1948

AWARDS Coty American Fashion Critics' Awards
Winnie *(with Donna Karan)*, 1977; *Hall of Fame (with
Donna Karan)*, 1982; *Special Award (women's wear, with
Donna Karan)*, 1984

Louis Dell'Olio is best known for his years at ANNE
KLEIN, first as codesigner with DONNA KARAN and then
as sole designer after Karan left to open her own house.
After her departure he continued in the direction they
had begun—a modern, sophisticated interpretation of
classic Anne Klein sportswear, marked by clean, sharp
shapes in beautiful fabrics. His other design projects
included furs for Michael Forrest.

In 1967, Dell'Olio received the Norman Norell
Scholarship to Parsons School of Design, from which

Designer Louis Dell'Olio (right).

Beaded crochet dress from Louis Dell'Olio for Anne Klein, 1993.

he graduated in 1969, winning the Gold Thimble Award
for coats and suits. He assisted Dominic Rompollo
at Teal Traina and was designer at the Giorgini and
Ginori divisions of Originala. In 1974, he joined Karan,
a friend from Parsons, as codesigner at Anne Klein.
Spring 1985 was their last joint collection. Dell'Olio
continued as sole designer for Klein until 1993, when he
was replaced by RICHARD TYLER. He has continued to
design for Klein on a freelance basis.

Dell'Olio's design philosophy has always been "to
make women look and feel beautiful." In 2000, he
agreed to sell sportswear on the television network
QVC under the label Linea by Louis Dell'Olio. The line
won QVC's product star award during its first year, but
was discontinued just shy of its ten-year anniversary.
Linea fans were outraged and threatened to boycott
QVC—leading it to restore the line.

♦ DIEGO DELLA VALLE

BORN San Elpidio a Mare, Italy; December 30, 1953

Designer Diego Della Valle.

Diego Della Valle (VAW-lay) was the grandson of Filippo Della Valle, a cobbler who began a modest business in 1924. His son, Diego's father, developed the leather goods company to large-scale industrial production—but it was Diego who gave it glamour.

Diego attended law school in Bologna, then spent a year in America before returning to Italy to enter the family business. With an excellent design sense and a flair for promotion, he expanded the business and brought the company international recognition, linking up with such prominent designers as GIANFRANCO FERRÉ, FENDI, CHRISTIAN LACROIX, and AZZEDINE ALAÏA.

Under the Diego Della Valle label the firm continues to make exquisite, one-of-a-kind shoes on special order, as well as fine, traditional, ready-to-wear footwear. But it is best known for J.P. Tod's, the leather driving shoe with an American-sounding name introduced in 1987. It is a moccasin with 133 leather pebbles, or *gommini*, set in the sole and running up the heel. Available in countless materials and colors, it's the casual shoe of choice for celebrities worldwide. In 1999, the company's name was formally shortened to Tod's.

The company is family-owned, with Valle as president and chief executive officer. Valle's brother is vice president, and his son Emmanuelle is creative director. Tod's produces boots, loafers, handbags, and a less expensive collection of casual shoes called Hogan.

PATRICK DEMARCHELIER 📷

Photographer Patrick Demarchelier.

BORN Le Havre, France, August 21, 1943

AWARDS Council of Fashion Designers of America (CFDA) *Eleanor Lambert Award*, 2007 • French Ministry of Culture *Officier dans l'Ordre des Arts et des Lettres*, 2007

Photographs by Patrick Demarchelier (DAY-ma-chay-lee-a) have graced the covers of hundreds of international beauty and fashion magazines. Knowing that he wanted to make his living as a photographer, Demarchelier asked for a camera for his 17th birthday. He began working for a freelance photographer who taught him about fashion photography, and his work drew the attention of *ELLE* and *Marie Claire* in France, Italy, and Germany.

Demarchelier moved to New York City in 1975 and learned to speak English by watching television and listening to people on the street. He worked for international magazines such as *Glamour, Mademoiselle, Vogue,* and *Harper's Bazaar*. In 1989, he photographed Princess Diana, and soon became the first non-British photographer to the U.K. royal family.

Demarchelier believes that society is too obsessed with perfection, and is credited with bringing out his subjects' natural beauty in his photographs. He does so by creating an environment of spontaneity during his shoots and forming a bond of trust with his subjects. Many of his famous photographs are nudes, which he says capture the timidity and nakedness of the subject. His celebrity subjects have included Ronald Reagan, Bill Clinton, Elton John, Madonna, Nicole Kidman, Paul Newman, and Britney Spears.

In 2007, the CFDA gave Demarchelier the Eleanor Lambert Award to honor his contributions to fashion. That same year, the French Ministry of Culture named him an Officier dans l'Ordre des Arts et des Lettres on the 50th anniversary of the prestigious award. In 2008, Le Petit Palais, Musée des Beaux Arts de la Ville de Paris, presented 400 of his photographs. Demarchelier's fashion photography is so well known that he is often referenced in popular culture, including in the movies *The Devil Wears Prada* and *The September Issue*.

In 2014, Demarchelier shot a black and white campaign for Chanel watches. The campaign was unveiled at the Baselworld Watch Fair in Switzerland. He shot photos of the Chanel Première, J12, and Mademoiselle Privé watch collections.

Above: Designer Ann Demeulemeester (right) and Patti Smith.
Below: Spring 2014.

BORN Waregem, Belgium, 1959

Ann Demeulemeester (Day-moo-la-MEEST-er) started studying fashion in 1978 at Antwerp's Royal Academy. After graduation, she received the annual *Golden Spoel* (Golden Spool) prize. She graduated with DRIES VAN NOTEN, Dirk Van Saene, Marina Ye, Walter Van Beirendoncke, and DIRK

⬛ ANN DEMEULEMEESTER

BIKKEMBERGS, who later became known as the "Antwerp Six" after taking the London fashion world by storm in the 1980s with their avant-garde clothing. The Antwerp Six were recognized by the Belgian government for bringing the country's fashion to the world stage.

In 1985, Demeulemeester released her first collection as a freelance designer with her husband Patrick Robyn. Her clothes were well received in cities such as Milan, London, and New York, helping expand her fashion brand BVBA 32. In 1992, she premiered her woman's wear collection in Paris, and in 1995 she introduced men's wear. She opened her namesake shop in 1999.

Demeulemeester is a deconstructionist: her clothes are modern and uniquely elegant, yet mix fabrics such as wool and leather, avoid color, and focus on details. There is not much ornamentation, but a coat will mix a frayed look with a hard edge. Demeulemeester's coats and long dresses have become her signature pieces, and she is a master of cobweb knitwear and oversized masculine slouch suits.

Demeulemeester's collections include a range of shoes and accessories. Her brand is sold in more than 30 countries and is worn by celebrities such as Jennifer Aniston, Nicole Richie, and Jennifer Lopez. In 2013, Demeulemeester surprised the fashion world by announcing that she was retiring from fashion.

Spring 2014.

PAMELA DENNIS ▼

BORN Newark, New Jersey, August 24, 1960

Pamela Dennis has carved a distinctive niche in designer evening wear. She entered design by chance when she was invited to a wedding and, despite having no formal training in design, took a few yards of silk to a tailor and had him make a columnar dress. Another wedding guest, a photostylist, asked to use the dress in a diamond commercial, which led to three more and inspired Dennis to design her first collection.

Designer Pamela Dennis.

Spring 2001.

Her clothes are distinguished by simple shapes in luxurious fabrics—silk crepe, chiffon, georgette, charmeuse, wool bouclé, stretch crepe—enhanced with crystals or hand-beaded lace. They have been sold by fine stores around the world and worn by celebrities.

In 2000, with the aim of making her signature styles more affordable, Dennis sold her company to a newly formed luxury conglomerate. The move proved disastrous, and in 2001 there was an acrimonious parting of ways. By 2002, though not yet able to use her own name, Dennis was back in business on a limited basis with plans for expansion. The Pamela Dennis Private Client Group sportswear line is sold on the QVC television network, and a namesake boutique is part of Bergdorf Goodman in New York City.

Designer Jean Dessès.

 JEAN DESSÈS

called Jean Dessès Diffusion. This move is seen as marking the beginning of French couture's expansion into ready-to-wear.

A gentleman of refined and luxurious tastes, Dessès was inspired by native costumes he saw in museums on his travels, especially in Greece and Egypt. His customers included Princess Margaret, the Duchess of Kent, and the Queen of Greece. Other designers worked for him, including VALENTINO in the 1950s and GUY LAROCHE. Dessès gave up couture in 1960 because of poor health but continued ready-to-wear until 1965, when he retired to Greece. With the recent renewed interest in vintage couture, his classic gowns have had a second coming on celebrities such as Renée Zellweger.

White dress with black lace trim, 1951.

BORN Alexandria, Egypt, August 6, 1904
DIED Athens, August 2, 1970

Jean Dessès (DAY-say) is remembered primarily for draped evening gowns of chiffon and mousseline in beautiful colors, and for the subtlety with which he handled fur. Of Greek ancestry, as a child he was interested in beautiful clothes and designed a dress for his mother when he was just nine. He attended school in Alexandria, Egypt, studied law in Paris, and in 1925 switched to fashion design. He opened his own shop in 1937.

Dessès visited America in 1949, and in 1950 designed a lower-priced line for American women

Actress Renée Zellweger wearing a Jean Dessès design at the Academy Awards, 2001.

COLLETTE DINNIGAN ▼

BORN South Africa, September 24, 1965

AWARDS Australian Designer of the Year, 1996

Collette Dinnigan is one of Australia's top designers, known for her use of luxurious fabrics, beads, and lace. She began studying fashion by accident, after enrolling in a fashion course instead of a graphic design one. After graduation, she moved to Australia and worked at the Costume Department of the Australian Broadcasting Commission in Sydney for several years. Dinnigan started her business in 1990, and her clothes are sold in stores such as Barneys New York, Neiman Marcus, and Joyce in Hong Kong. In 1995, Dinnigan became the first Australian to mount a full-scale ready-to-wear show in Paris—having been the first to be invited by the Chambre Syndicale du Prêt à Porter des Couturiers et des Crèateurs de Mode. She has received widespread recognition for her business practices, including the Leading Women Entrepreneurs of the World Award and induction into the Australian Business Women's Hall of Fame.

In 2001, Dinnigan teamed up with London retailer Marks & Spencer to launch a lingerie line called Wild Hearts. She was the subject of a postage stamp in 2005, and in 2006 became the first Australian featured in television and print ads for American Express. In 2012, Dinnigan collaborated with luxury jewelry chain

Spring 2014.

Designer Collette Dinnigan.

Lovisa, and in 2013 became the first Australian designer invited to show at the Audi Fashion Festival in Singapore. Her clothes have been worn by celebrities such as Halle Berry, Naomi Watts, and Elle Macpherson.

Spring 2013.

BORN Granville, France, January 21, 1905
DIED Montecatini, Italy, October 24, 1957

AWARDS *Neiman Marcus Award*, 1947 • Parsons *Medal for Distinguished Achievement*, 1956

The name Christian Dior is most associated with the New Look. This silhouette was, in essence, a polished continuation of the rounded line seen in the first postwar collections, appearing at the same time at a number of design houses. Dior's designs had rounded shoulders, feminine busts, tiny waists, and enormous spreading skirts. Everything was exquisitely made of the best materials available.

Designer Christian Dior (center) with models.

Dress, fall/winter 1949–1950.

Dior was the son of a well-off manufacturer of fertilizers and chemicals. Though Dior wanted to become an architect, his family wanted him to enter the diplomatic service. He studied political science at l'École des Sciences Politiques, performed his obligatory military service, and in 1928 opened a small art gallery with a friend. The gallery was soon wiped out by the Great Depression, which also ruined Dior's family. In 1931, he traveled to Russia, returned disillusioned by communism, and for the next few years lived from hand to mouth, eating little and sleeping on the floors of friends' apartments.

Dior became seriously ill in 1934 and had to leave Paris. During a forced rest in Spain and the south of France, he learned tapestry weaving and developed a desire to create. He returned to Paris in 1935, 30 years old and without means of support. Unable to find any kind of job, he started making design sketches and did fashion illustrations for *Le Figaro*.

Dior's early hat designs were successful, his dresses less so. In 1937, after a two-year struggle to improve his dresses, he sold several sketches to Robert Piguet and was asked to make a number of dresses for an upcoming collection. He was hired by Piguet in 1938 but in 1939 went into the Army. The fall of Paris in June 1940 found him stationed in the south of France. Piguet asked Dior

(continued)

to come back to work, but Dior delayed his return until the end of 1941, by which time another designer had been hired. Dior then went to work for Lucien Lelong, a much larger establishment. At the end of 1946, Dior left Lelong to open his own house.

Dior was backed in his new project by Marcel Boussac, a French financier, race horse owner, and textile manufacture who was originally looking for someone to take over an ailing couture house he owned. Instead, Dior persuaded Boussac to back him, and in spring 1947 he presented his wildly successful first New Look collection. Dior continued to produce beautiful clothes in collection after collection, continually refining and expanding his talent. In 1955, he collaborated with Roger Vivier, and together they introduced the first ready-to-wear designer label shoes, Christian Dior created by Roger Vivier.

Actress Natalie Portman wearing vintage Dior haute couture at the 84th annual Academy Awards.

Dior described himself as silent, shy, and reticent, but strongly attached to his friends. Since his death, the House of Dior has been led by Yves Saint Laurent, Marc Bohan, Gianfranco Ferré, John Galliano, and Raf Simons. Christian Dior, Inc., has become a vast international merchandising operation, with licensing agreements for jewelry, scarves, men's ties, furs, stockings, gloves, ready-to-wear, and perfumes.

2014 haute couture.

Designers Stefano Gabbana (left) and Domenico Dolce (right).

BORN Domenico Dolce; Polizzi Generosa, Palermo, Italy, September 13, 1958 Stefano Gabbana; Venice, November 14, 1962

♟ DOLCE & GABBANA

chose the line as one of three young Italian talents to give formal presentations. Their first knitwear collection appeared in 1987; they have since added men's wear and, in 1994, a lower-priced collection called D&G.

Dolce & Gabbana continues to evolve along a highly individual path. The brand's look mixes the modern with romantic historical references, and the pieces are designed to be worn in different ways. In men's wear, a Sicilian-influenced combination of strict, structured tailoring and avant-garde shirts and accessories appeals to men who are not afraid of attention. In 2005, the two designers split as romantic partners, but maintained their thriving business. By 2013, they were estimated to be worth $2 billion apiece, but that same year the Italian government accused them of tax evasion—a charge they are appealing.

Members of the avant-garde of Italian fashion, Dolce (DOLE-chay) and Gabbana (Guh-BAH-nah) came to their craft by disparate routes. Dolce, whose father had a small clothing factory in Sicily, attended fashion school. But Gabbana lacked a fashion background, having studied graphics and worked in advertising. The two met in Milan in 1980, and in 1982 formed their own business, working as consultants to other companies while creating their own line. Dolce & Gabbana's first international recognition came in 1985, when Milano Collezioni

Spring 2013.

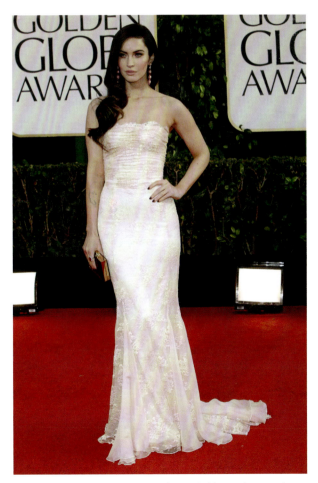

Actress Megan Fox wearing a Dolce & Gabbana dress at the 70th annual Golden Globe Awards.

CARRIE DONOVAN 📄

BORN Carolyn Gertrude Amelia Donovan; Lake Placid, New York, March 22, 1928
DIED November 12, 2001

Fashion writer and the *New York Times* editor Carrie Donovan.

The last in a line of fashion editors with larger-than-life personalities, including DIANA VREELAND and CARMEL SNOW, Carrie Donovan had a varied career that lasted nearly 50 years. Her first ambition was to be a designer, and she studied dressmaking at Parsons School of Design, where she graduated in 1950. She turned to fashion journalism in 1955, working at *The New York Times* before moving to *Vogue* under Vreeland. When Vreeland was fired in 1972, Donovan moved to *Harper's Bazaar* as fashion editor, then became vice president of communications at Bloomingdale's in 1976.

Donovan returned to *The Times* in 1977 as style editor for *The New York Times Magazine*, where she stayed until 1995. She wrote a column for *Allure* before undertaking a new career in 1997 as spokesperson for Old Navy—which made her a celebrity in the world beyond fashion.

Donovan actively promoted new talent, introducing designers such as DONNA KARAN and PALOMA PICASSO to her readers and acting as matchmaker between designers and prospective employers. She was instrumental in bringing ELSA PERETTI's modern jewelry to TIFFANY, a bastion of tradition.

With her enthusiasm and outgoing personality, Donovan had a wide circle of friends in the fashion community, and even those who knew her only slightly found the world a little less colorful after her death in 2001.

BORN Corsica, France

AWARDS Council of Fashion Designers of America (CFDA) *Media Award in Honor of Eugenia Sheppard*, 2012

Garance Doré (DOOR-a) is one of the world's hottest fashion bloggers, but is also known for her illustrations, videos, photography, and interviews. Born to an Algerian mother and Italian father, her parents did not think the arts were the right path for her, so she initially studied communications and began her career as an assistant programmer. But Doré knew that she wanted something more, and quit her job to study illustration for two years.

Doré started her blog in 2006 to communicate with and meet other illustrators. With the help of SCOTT SCHUMAN from *The Sartorialist*, whom she met in 2008, she started taking photos and posting them on her blog. Doré and Schuman began dating and have been together ever since.

Doré's blog is recognized for its honesty and optimism. She elicits passionate feedback, and the blog is a multidisciplinary platform for her creative output—with photos, illustrations, and videos. In 2013, Doré introduced a video series called *Trending* in which she addresses the camera directly.

To finance the blog, Doré works on promotional campaigns, creates illustrations for brands, and develops advertising concepts. In 2012, Doré created a capsule collection of prints for KATE SPADE based on her

Garancé Dore (left) and Scott Schuman.

popular "spidery" illustrations. In 2013, she teamed up with Schuman to work on the Superga shoe campaign, designed by MARY KATE AND ASHLEY OLSON. Schuman shot the photography and Doré shot the video.

JACQUES DOUCET ⬧

BORN Paris, 1853
DIED Paris, 1929

With its beginnings in the silk trade around 1820, the House of Doucet (Due-SAY) is the oldest Paris couture house. Jacques Doucet joined the family business in 1870, and began with a focus on custom-made women's apparel. He was just 18 when he opened his first boutique. Doucet was known for his love of iridescent silk and abundant use of lace. His tea gowns and tailored suits were among his most popular ensembles. Doucet designed for several of the most popular actresses of the time, including Gabrielle Réjane and Sarah Bernhart. Many designers apprenticed with Doucet, including PAUL POIRET.

By the 1920s, Doucet's designs had fallen behind the times. In 1929, after his death, the company merged with Doeuillet, but soon folded in 1932.

Wool, silk, and glass dress, 1920–1923.

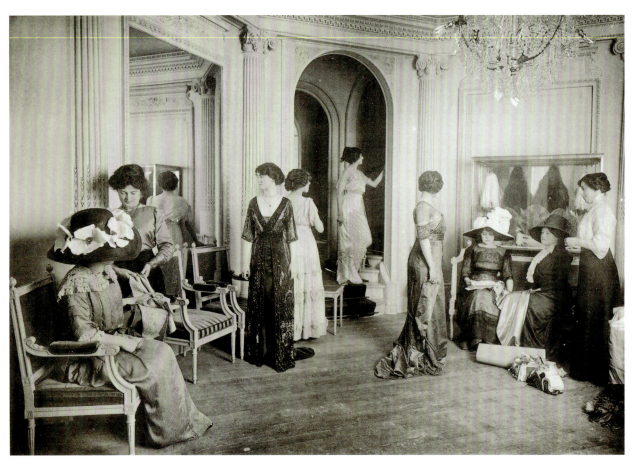

Salon de vente (sale room) at the House of Doucet, 1910.

Designers Dean Calen (left) and Dan Calen (right).

the movie character Mad Max. Using reams of leather and denim, their creations are witty, steamy, ironic, and not for the faint of heart. Their staples include lean tailored jackets and outerwear, tight t-shirts, and low-cut jeans, mixed and matched with a subtext of sex.

The Dsquared2 flagship store opened in Milan in 2007. In 2008, the pair signed an eyewear deal with Marcolin, one of Italy's top sunglass and spectacle manufacturers. The brothers have also opened stores in Capri, Kiev, Istanbul, Hong Kong, Dubai, and Cannes. Their celebrity clients include Justin Timberlake, Lenny Kravitz, Ricky Martin, Nicolas Cage, and Madonna. Dsquared2 are known for opening their runway shows with celebrities, and have featured Christina Aguilera, Rihanna, and Bill Kaulitz.

BORN Dean and Dan Calen; Ontario, Canada, 1965

AWARDS La Core *Most Original Designers Award*, 2003 • *Aquja de Oro (Golden Needle Award)*, 2006

Dean and Dan Caten are identical twins behind the label Dsquared2. The two brought their rugged American dreams to Milan in 1991 and forged them with Italian craftsmanship and fine tailoring. Since 1994, their collections have been building a steady audience around the world.

Their influences are clear: cowboys, truckers, military men, motocross riders, matadors, the residents of trailer parks, and

Spring 2014.

Spring 2014.

GILLES DUFOUR ▲

BORN Lyon, France

AWARDS French Ministry of Culture *Officier dans l'Ordre des Arts et des Lettres*, 2008

Gilles Dufour (DOO-for) established his own prêt-à-porter label in 2001 after an already extensive career, including collaborations with KARL LAGERFELD at CHLOÉ and FENDI and 15 years as Lagerfeld's second in command at CHANEL. He has freelanced in New York and Paris for ready-to-wear, leathers, and furs, and put in three seasons as prêt-à-porter stylist at BALMAIN. He graduated from l'École Supérieure des Arts Décoratifs in Paris and studied at the School of Visual Arts in New York, after which he worked at CARDIN on both ready-to-wear and couture.

Extremely versatile, Dufour has designed just about everything a woman could wear, from accessories to bridal wear to furs to sportswear—as well as sportswear for men. He has also created sets and costumes for ballet, opera, and film. His assured designs show a light touch—witty trompe l'oeil knits, sexy sweaters, little black dresses, and trademark t-shirts bearing naughty phrases that vary with each collection.

In 2008, Dufour collaborated with London-based Browns on a capsule collection of fine knitwear. In 2009, he became creative director for Erdos, which runs more than 2,000 boutiques in China. He is currently designing for Gripoix.

Designer Gilles Dufour (center) with Karl Lagerfeld and models.

8th Chocolate Fair in Paris, 2002.

Prêt-à-porter, autumn/winter 2002.

Designer Randolph Duke (center) with models.

BORN Las Vegas, January 14, 1958

Randolph Duke studied at the University of Southern California and at the Fashion Institute of Design and Merchandising in Los Angeles, from which he graduated in 1978 with the Bob Mackie and Peacock awards. He began his career immediately as a swimwear designer, working for various West Coast companies—Jantzen, Cole of California, the Anne Cole Collection—and until 1987 for Gottex.

To establish his label, Duke moved to New York. For a time he had a shop on the Upper West Side of Manhattan and a wholesale business, but they closed in 1992. He then joined a private label producing exclusive collections for retail stores.

In 1996, Duke became creative director for the newly resuscitated Halston label, where over several seasons he oversaw its revival with clothes of an American smartness consistent with the Halston name—glamorous and luxurious. He then launched Randolph Duke, a couture evening wear collection.

Duke has sold his clothes on the QVC shopping channel and created collections of apparel and accessories for the Home Shopping Network, meanwhile selling his signature collection through select specialty stores such as Neiman Marcus, Saks Fifth Avenue, and Barneys. In 2006, he released *The Look: A Guide to Dressing from the Inside Out* to help women of various shapes and sizes find their style. Numerous actresses—including Jennifer Aniston, Minnie Driver, Angelina Jolie, and Hilary Swank—have worn Duke's attention-getting evening dresses to award shows. Duke has appeared as a fashion commentator on *Entertainment Tonight*, *The Oprah Winfrey Show*, *Good Morning America*, *The View*, *E!*, *Extra*, and *Access Hollywood*.

Right: Actress Amber Tamblyn wearing Randolph Duke at the 56th annual Primetime Emmy Awards.

Left: Actress Edie Falco wearing Randolph Duke at the 56th annual Primetime Emmy Awards.

STEPHEN DWECK Ŏ

Designer Stephen Dweck.

Lapis and turquoise rings, 2007.

BORN Brooklyn, New York, August 10, 1960

After graduating from New York's School of Visual Arts in 1980 with a gold medal in sculpture, Stephen Dweck went into business as a jewelry designer. Working with sterling silver, vermeil, and bronze, he combines the metals with natural minerals and semiprecious stones for jewelry that is modern with overtones of fantasy and hints of ancient cultures. He uses natural forms such as beetles, butterflies, leaves, and vines for his jewelry as well as his home collections, which have included china for Sasaki and sterling silver gifts and accessories for Lunt Silversmiths. He has also designed a belt collection.

Dweck has worked with some of the biggest designers in the country, including GEOFFREY BEENE, DONNA KARAN, and OSCAR DE LA RENTA. His designs can be viewed at the Smithsonian Institute Fashion Archives in Washington, D.C., the Metropolitan Museum of Art in New York, and the Dallas Museum of Art. His one-of-a-kind pieces are easily recognized by their use of "Adam," a beetle that is one of his signatures.

Free-form pyrite and bronze ring, 2008.

Designer Marc Eckō.

BORN Marc Milecofsky; Lakewood, New Jersey, 1972

Marc Eckō is an American fashion designer, entrepreneur, investor, artist, and philanthropist who grew up inspired by hip hop and skateboarding. He has always loved graffiti, and in eighth grade started airbrushing letters on his classmates' denim jackets and producing custom t-shirts. He studied pharmacology at Rutgers University in the early 1990s but continued to design clothes. In 1993, he dropped out of school to form his company, Eckō Unltd., based on six t-shirt designs and with funding from his twin sister Marci Tapper and friend Seth Gerszberg, who are still with him.

In 1996, Eckō designed clothes for the film *Jurassic Park 2: The Lost World*. By 1997, he was one of fashion's youngest and hottest entrepreneurs, and in 1999 he launched a footwear collection. In 2000, director Spike Lee produced a short film and runway show for Eckō for *7th on Sixth*, an event sponsored by the Council of Fashion Designers of America (CFDA). At one point, Eckō was about $6.5 million in debt, but he has said that going back to basics—illustrations, t-shirts, and sweatshirts—helped him get back on track.

In 2001, Eckō bought the action sport brand Zoo York and launched a watch collection. In 2002, he started a men's style magazine, *Complex*, that has expanded into Complex Media. He also created G-Unit Clothing with 50 Cent, who later purchased the line. In 2004, he created

Eckō Cut & Sew (men's wear), Eckō footwear for women, and Eckō Red (children's wear). In 2005, Eckō became the youngest member of the CFDA, and in 2007 he launched a partnership with Lucasfilm on a series of Cut & Sew collections featuring characters and imagery from *Star Wars*. He has also launched Eckō MFG (denim for women), Eckō Function (sportswear and outerwear), Marc Eckō Scopes (eyewear), Eckō Storage, and many other lines.

Eckō is a strong advocate of social issues and philanthropic activity, and in 2004 he founded Sweat Equity Education, a nonprofit that provides underserved urban students with real-world design and business opportunities. Although Iconix Brand Group acquired the Eckō portfolio in 2013, the designer still has creative control over Marc Eckō Enterprises, is on the board of Complex Media, and is estimated to be worth more than $100 million. His 2013 book, *Unlabel: Selling You Without Selling Out*, focuses on how authenticity can produce a strong brand.

Spring 2001.

FLORENCE EISEMAN ▼

BORN Minneapolis, Minnesota, September 27, 1899
DIED Milwaukee, Wisconsin, January 8, 1988

AWARDS *Neiman Marcus Award* (first recipient for children's wear), 1955 • Swiss Fabrics Award, 1956 • Dallas Fashion Award, 1980

Florence Eiseman raised the standards of fashion and quality for children's clothes, guided by her beliefs that "children have bellies, not waists" and should not be dressed in small versions of adult clothing. Her simple styles were distinguished by fine fabrics and excellent workmanship—with prices to match. The clothes were so classic and well made that they were often handed down from one generation to another.

Eiseman started sewing after the birth of her second son, then began creating quilts and clothing for her children and her neighbors' children. In 1945, when family finances were pinched, her husband Laurence took samples of her organdy pinafores to Marshall Field & Company in Chicago. The $3,000 order he landed put them in business, with her as designer and him as business manager and salesman.

Florence initially worked out of her home, employing other women to sew. Then, with two sewing machines, she took over part of her husband's toy factory. Within a few years, Laurence Eiseman gave up his toy business to devote himself to the clothing firm, which quickly grew into a large operation with sales across America and abroad.

Florence became known as the "NORMAN NORELL of children's clothes," making dresses and separates, swimsuits, playclothes, sleepwear, and boys' suits. In 1969, she added less expensive knits, brother-sister outfits, and a limited collection of women's wear. In 1984, Neiman Marcus asked the company to create a luxury collection of dress-up clothes for children at

Designer Florence Eiseman, left.

Display at Denver Art Museum's 1984 retrospective of Eiseman's designs.

prices starting where the regular collection left off. The result was Florence Eiseman Couture, not custom-made but using rich fabrics and featuring many hand touches. Its introduction coincided with Eiseman's 85th birthday, and she was still actively involved in the company she founded. The same year, the Denver Art Museum presented a retrospective of her work.

Lanvin, Fall 2013.

BORN Morocco, 1961

AWARDS Council of Fashion Designers of America (CFDA) *International Award*, 2005 • French Government *Légion d'Honneur (Legion of Honor)*, 2007 • *TIME* magazine's *100 Most Influential People in the World*, 2007

Alber Elbaz (Al-BEAR El-BAHZ) grew up in Tel Aviv, where he graduated from the Shenkar College School of Fashion and Textiles. He served three years in the Israeli Army, then at 25 moved to New York City. He started working on Seventh Avenue, designing inexpensive evening dresses, and a few years later met GEOFFREY BEENE, who immediately hired him. Elbaz was a design assistant at Beene for seven years, then moved to Paris in 1996 for the top job at GUY LAROCHE.

After two years invigorating Laroche, Elbaz became head designer of women's wear for YVES SAINT LAURENT Rive Gauche. In 1999, when GUCCI bought Saint Laurent, Elbaz was supplanted by TOM FORD.

Designer Alber Elbaz.

He then worked for Krizia before becoming creative director for LANVIN in 2001.

Elbaz's style is based on classic shapes, flattering colors, and a few feminine details such as beading or ribbons. Without losing sight of wearability, he is fascinated by new ways of cutting fabric and placing seams, visualizing clients who want clothes that are both beautiful and comfortable. For evening wear he strives for glamour but never extravagance, saying that "when a woman walks into a room [wearing his clothes], no one will faint, but she will be noticed." In 2010, Elbaz designed the Lanvin Hearts collection for H&M, and fans waited outside stores all night for a chance to buy pieces from the line. In 2012, Elbaz released a limited edition book of 3,000 photographs documenting Lanvin's work, in celebration of his ten-year anniversary with the design house. In 2013, he launched a limited edition makeup line for Lancôme featuring his whimsical illustrations.

Lanvin, fall 2013.

PERRY ELLIS

BORN Portsmouth, Virginia, March 3, 1940
DIED New York City, May 30, 1986

AWARDS *Neiman Marcus Award*, 1979 • Coty American Fashion Critics' Awards *Winnie*, 1979; *Return Award*, 1980; *Hall of Fame*, 1981; *Special Award (men's wear)*, 1981; *Hall of Fame Citation (women's wear)*, 1983; *Return Award (men's wear)*, 1983; *Hall of Fame (men's wear)*, 1984; *Hall of Fame Citation (women's wear)*, 1984 • Council of Fashion Designers of America (CFDA) *Outstanding Designer in Women's Fashion*, 1981; *Outstanding Designer in Men's Fashion*, 1982, 1983 • Cutty Sark Men's Fashion Awards *Outstanding Men's Wear Designer*, 1983, 1984 • *Fashion Walk of Fame*, 2002

Designer Perry Ellis.

Design by Perry Ellis.

Perry Ellis started in fashion design relatively late, having previously worked in retailing and merchandising. He received a B.A. in business from William and Mary College and an M.A. in retailing from New York University. He was a sportswear buyer for Miller & Rhoads in Richmond, Virginia, before leaving in 1967 to work as a merchandiser for John Meyer of Norwich, a conservative sportswear firm. There Ellis acquired three important design skills—sketching, patternmaking, and fabric selection. In 1974, he joined Vera Companies as a merchandiser, and the next year became a designer for its Portfolio division.

Perry Ellis Sportswear was established in 1978 with Ellis as designer and president; men's wear followed in 1980. Then came furs, shearling coats for both women and men, cloth coats, and, for Japan, a complete sportswear line. There were shoes, legwear, scarves,

Vogue patterns, sheets, towels, and blankets. A fragrance collection was launched in 1985.

From the beginning, Ellis's clothes exhibited a young, adventurous spirit and used natural fibers such as cotton, silk, linen, and wool. Hand-knitted sweaters became a trademark. The use of fine fabrics and handwork soon drove the line into a higher price bracket, so in 1984 the Portfolio name was revived for a moderately priced collection with much the same relaxed, classic look.

Ellis was active in the CFDA and served two terms as its president—and was elected to a third a week before his death in 1986. The organization then established the Perry Ellis Award (now known as the Swarovski Emerging Talent Award), to be given annually for the greatest impact on fashion by a new talent.

Perry Ellis International has continued under the direction of a number of designers. MARC JACOBS took over in 1989 but left in 1993, when the designer and bridge sportswear collections were discontinued. John Crocco was creative director between 2003 and 2011. For spring 2013, the brand teamed up with Steven Cox and Daniel Silver for the Perry Ellis by Duckie Brown collection. The Perry Ellis name continues to be licensed in America and Europe.

Design by Perry Ellis.

ELIZABETH EMANUEL

BORN Elizabeth Florence Weiner; London, July 5, 1953

Elizabeth and David Emanuel (Eh-MAN-you-awl) created ball gowns and wedding dresses afloat in lace, taffeta, organza, and tulle, evoking a romantic fantasy era. They attended London's Harrow School of Art, got married in 1976, and together earned master's degrees in fashion from the Royal College of Art. The couple opened a ready-to-wear firm in 1977, switched to couture in 1979, and in 1981 gained international attention for the wedding gown they designed for Princess Diana. In 1990, they closed the business and announced their divorce. The company's licenses included bed linens, sunglasses, and fragrances.

During the 1990s, Elizabeth focused on designing costumes for films. She also designed uniforms for Virgin Airlines and Britannia Airways. In 1999, she launched a new venture with backer Richard Thompson consisting of bridal wear, couture, and ready-to-wear—all with the same attention to detail and exquisite fabrics that have become her hallmark. In 2001–02, Emanuel was a designer for the Luxury Brand Group, focusing on its NORMAN HARTNELL

Designers David Emanuel (left) and Elizabeth Emanuel (right).

brand. In 2005, she acquired a studio in Little Venice and launched her Art of Being label.

In 2006, Emanuel and her former husband released the book *A Dress for Diana*. In 2007, it was reissued as a limited edition with framed swatches of fabric from the same bolt used to make the princess's wedding dress. That same year, Emanuel released a DVD, *Metamorphosis*, featuring her fall/winter collection. After ten years of absence, Emanuel returned to the runway in fall 2010, showing her Little Black Dress collection at London Fashion Week.

A sketch of Lady Diana's wedding dress by Emanuel.

Designer Elizabeth Emanuel (left) and model wearing Emanuel's design.

BORN Carl Erickson; Joliet, Illinois, 1891
DIED New York City, 1958

The son of Swedish immigrants, Eric studied at the Art Institute of Chicago before moving to Paris to become a painter. After he married a fashion artist on the staff of French *Vogue*, his seemingly off-hand fashion sketches began appearing in the magazine. During the 1930s and 1940s, Eric influenced fashion with his elegant watercolors of chic, thin women, often shown from the back and against backgrounds of elegant restaurants, exclusive resorts, and other haunts of the rich and famous. In her book *In My Fashion*, fashion editor Bettina Ballard wrote, "His drawings over the years evoked a promise of beauty that photographs could never equal." Eric's sketches are still coveted by collectors.

Illustration of Vionnet design in Vogue, 1937.

Illustration of Christian Dior design.

ERTÉ

BORN Romain de Tirtoff; St. Petersburg, Russia, November 23, 1892
DIED Paris, April 21, 1990

The son of an admiral in the Russian Imperial Navy, Erté (Air-TAY) studied painting in Russia before moving to Paris in 1912 to study at Académie Julian. He took his name from the French pronunciation of his initials, R. T. Erté did sketches for PAUL POIRET and designed for opera and theater, creating costumes for luminaries such as soprano Mary Garden.

From 1914 into the 1930s, Erté produced illustrations and covers for various magazines—including *Harper's Bazaar*, for which he created more than 250 covers. He designed for the Folies Bergère, moved to America in the 1920s to work for Ziegfeld and other impresarios, and created beautiful, esoteric costumes for several silent films—including *The Mystic*, *Ben Hur*, and *La Boheme*—before financial restrictions forced him to return to Paris.

In 1967, Erté attracted the attention of art dealer Eric Estorich. To celebrate his 80th birthday, Erté selected more than a hundred of his clothing, jewelry, and accessory designs for shows in London and New York. The exhibition contained some of the most elegant and unique designs from the Art Deco period. The entire New York exhibition was bought by the Metropolitan Museum of Art. Erté also produced three large format books: *Erté at Ninety*, *Erté at Ninety-Five*, and *Erté Sculpture*. After his death, Erté was hailed as "a mirror of fashion for 75 years."

Designer Erté.

Designer Erté (left) with actress wearing his costume design.

Designer Veronica Etro.

FOUNDED Milan, 1968

Established by Gimmo Etro as a family business, the Italian fashion house Etro made its debut with colorful, luxurious textiles for couture and ready-to-wear. In 1981, it introduced a paisley collection, and the brightly patterned designs—combined with impeccable classic tailoring—became the company's signature look. By the time Etro's flagship store opened in Milan in 1983, its accessories included luxury ties and scarves, followed by handbags, luggage, home accessories, shoes, and eyewear. The Etro fragrance collection, launched in 1989, now consists of more than 25 scents.

The company made its foray into ready-to-wear in 1994. Today both its women's wear (designed by Veronica Etro) and men's wear

(designed by Kean Etro) are known for their sharp tailoring, contrasted with printed and bright patterns. Continuing the family legacy are Jacopo and Ippolito, who run Etro's textiles, accessories, and home divisions. Available at boutiques in Europe and Asia, as well as upscale department stores such as Harrods and Bergdorf Goodman, Etro remains a distinctive family business that combines tradition with innovation. In 2009, Michelle Obama wore Etro on a state visit to France.

Above: Men's wear, spring 2010.

Left: Ready-to-wear, fall 2009.

MAX FACTOR ▮

BORN Maksymillian Faktorowicz; Lodz, Poland, 1872
DIED Beverly Hills, August, 30, 1938

Max Factor is considered the father of modern makeup. One of ten children, he started working as a pharmacist's assistant at the age of eight. He then became an apprentice to the premier wigmaker and cosmetician in his hometown of Lodz. Factor joined the Russian Army at 18 and, after being discharged, opened a shop selling creams, rouges, and wigs. He became extremely popular with the Russian royal court and aristocrats, and concealed his identity as a Jew as well as his marriage and children. But in 1903, Czar Nicholas II turned a blind eye to mounting mob violence against Jews. With help from a friend, Factor was able to arrange passage to America for himself and his family.

In 1904, Factor sold his rouges and creams at the St. Louis World's Fair. After his first wife died and he divorced his second, he married Jennie Cook and moved to Hollywood in 1908. In 1914, Factor created a makeup for movie actors and actresses that did not crack or cake. Hollywood's brightest stars were soon inundating Factor for the "flexible greasepaint" and his wigs made of human hair. In 1918, Factor launched a range of face powders based on individual skin tones. That breakthrough paved the way for other inventions such as false eyelashes, lip gloss, pancake makeup, the eyebrow pencil, and waterproof mascara.

Factor is credited with inventing the word makeup, and in the 1920s began selling it to the general public. His advertising campaigns claimed that his products could make every woman look like a movie star, and his clients included Jean Harlow and Bette Davis. After Factor died, his son Frank changed his name to Max Jr. and, with his brothers, continued to run the business. It supplied the makeup for *The Wizard of Oz* and invented Tru-Color, the first nondrying, indelible lipstick. Max Jr. also launched many cosmetic products for men, including shampoo and aftershave. The company released its first fragrance in 1955.

Max Jr. worked for the company until the 1970s, when it was handed down to members of the next generation. But they wanted to focus on their own interests, and the company was sold. Today Procter & Gamble

Make-up designer Max Factor.

Lipstick from Max Factor's cosmetic line.

owns Max Factor, which still creates innovative products. In 2012, the company introduced Colour Effect Flipstick, a double-ended design that enables wearers to mix shades and create their own lip color.

📰 JOHN B. FAIRCHILD

BORN Newark, New Jersey, 1927

John B. Fairchild began his career as a reporter for *Women's Wear Daily* in 1951, two years after graduating from Princeton University. Three years later he moved to Paris to take over the French bureaus of the newspaper—part of Fairchild Publications, a company founded by his grandfather.

In Paris, Fairchild shook up the world of haute couture by mixing gossip with traditional stories and printing sketches of clothes when he wanted, as opposed to when fashion houses approved their release. When Fairchild arrived, reporters for *WWD* were often seated in the back rows of fashion shows. Feeling slighted, Fairchild worked to raise the paper's visibility, turning it into "the Bible of fashion" and ensuring his reporters the access and respect he felt they deserved.

In 1960, Fairchild was named publisher of *WWD* and returned to New York City. He brought his innovations with him, and the paper soon began including society and event coverage in addition to trade stories. Five years later, Fairchild became chief executive officer of Fairchild Publications, steering the company to launch the *WWD* offshoots *W* and *M*.

Also in 1965, Fairchild penned *The Fashionable Savages*, a series of candid looks at the designers who ruled the fashion world and the women who kept them in business. In 1989, Fairchild wrote another book, *Chic Savages*, a biting memoir that took on fashion industry giants like OSCAR DE LA RENTA, MARY MCFADDEN, and ANNA WINTOUR. It cemented his reputation as a

Women's Wear Daily editor John B. Fairchild.

provocateur—albeit a well-liked one.

Fairchild retired in 1997 but is still contributing editor at large for *W* and *WWD*. He also writes a column for *W* under the name Louise J. Esterhazy.

JACQUES FATH

Designer Jacques Fath (right) with model.

BORN Lafitte, France, September 6, 1912
DIED Paris, November 13, 1954

AWARDS *Neiman Marcus Award*, 1949

Jacques Fath's clothes were flattering, feminine, and sexy without slipping into vulgarity. They followed the lines of the body with hourglass shapes and swathed hips, and often had full, pleated skirts and plunging necklines. He did not sew or sketch, instead draping material while his assistants made sketches.

The son of an Alsatian businessman, grandson of a painter, and great-grandson of a dressmaker, Fath attended business school and drama school, acting briefly in films. He showed his design talent early on in costumes for theater and films, and opened his first couture house in Paris in 1937 with a collection of 20 pieces. Fath joined the Army in 1940, was captured, and on his release reopened his house, which he managed to keep open during World War II. After liberation he became enormously successful, eventually expanding his salon from a single wartime workroom with one

fitter to an establishment with 600 employees. In 1948, he signed with a U.S. manufacturer to produce two collections a year, one of the first French couturiers to venture into ready-to-wear. The Fath brand also included perfumes, scarves, stockings, and millinery.

Handsome and personable, Fath had a flair for publicity and showmanship and became one of the most popular designers of his time. He loved parties, and he and his actress wife Geneviève de Bruyère hosted elaborate affairs at their chateau in Corbeville. He was also an excellent businessman. After Fath died in 1954, de Bruyère continued the business until 1957.

In 2002, the Fath brand was bought by a new conglomerate, France Luxury Group, and Lizzy Disney was hired as its head designer. In 2007, Daniel Chocu became its chief executive officer. Despite having no creative director, in 2008 the company showed a well-received collection designed by an in-house team.

Polka dot strapless dress, 1951.

Designer Silvia Fendi (left) with Karl Lagerfeld (right).

FOUNDED Rome, 1918

Autumn/winter 1998/1999.

In 1918, Adele and Edoardo Fendi opened an eponymously named shop that specialized in furs, handbags, luggage, and sportswear. After her husband died in 1954, Signora Fendi asked her five daughters for help running the business. The sisters and their husbands have expanded Fendi, continuing to explore new areas. Their daughters have also come into the firm. Adele Fendi died in 1978. In 1965, Fendi hired KARL LAGERFELD to design its furs, supporting his innovative techniques and use of a dazzling array of new, unusual, and neglected pelts. Adele Fendi had made coats out of squirrel fashionable; the company still uses squirrel—as well

Fall 2013.

as badger, Persian lamb, fox, and sundry unpedigreed furs, often combining several in one garment. The designs are noted for innovations such as furs woven in strips and coats left unlined for lightness. Fendi styles are glamorous, but their success is based on an understanding of what women need and want. The company's double F logo, designed by Lagerfeld, has become an international status symbol.

In addition to furs, Fendi produces accessories and ready-to-wear for women and men. Lagerfeld is responsible for the women's ready-to-wear, while Silvia Fendi designs accessories and leather goods for the avant-garde men's collection. Once a family business, the firm is now part of the LVMH empire. In 2012, Pietro Beccari replaced Michael Burk as chief executive officer and the brand celebrated the 15-year anniversary of the Baguette, one of its most famous bags.

LOUIS FÉRAUD ▼

Designer Louis Féraud.

BORN Arles, France, February 13, 1921
DIED Paris, December 28, 1999

AWARDS French Government *Légion d'Honneur*
(Legion of Honor), 1995

In 1950, Louis Féraud founded a couture house in Cannes,
France, that was visited by many movie stars attending
the city's famous film festival. In 1957, he opened a shop
in Paris and designed for the city's elite and his close
friend Brigitte Bardot. In the early 1960s, Féraud started
a ready-to-wear line, hiring Jean-Louis Sherrer. By 1962,
the line was being sold at Saks Fifth Avenue and Harrods.
Inspired by the colors of South America, Féraud was an
accomplished painter and used that art in his designs.
Throughout his life, exhibitions of his work were presented
at some of the world's most prestigious venues.

In 1965, Féraud introduced
his first perfume, Justine. Later
in the decade, he introduced
the first Russian model to
Paris, Tamara. In the 1980s,
he designed perfume
for Avon and founded
the Louis Féraud Golf
Tournament in Cannes.
In the 1990s, he opened
a boutique in New York
City, and in France he
was elected *Prince de
L'art de Vivre* and named
an *Officier de la Légion
d'Honneur*.

After Féraud died in
1999, his company chose
Yvan Mispelaere as artistic
director in 2000. Two years
later, the German company
Escada bought 90 percent
of the company and made
Jean-Paul Knot its artistic
director. He stayed at Féraud
for three years, leaving when
the company joined the
Alliance Designers Group.
The current artistic director
is Jean-Pierre Marty.

Autumn/winter
1997–1998.

Designer Salvatore Ferragamo (left).

Couture shoe design.

BORN Bonito, Italy, June 5, 1898
DIED Fiumetto, Italy, August 7, 1960

AWARDS *Neiman Marcus Award*, 1947

Salvatore Ferragamo (Fair-a-GAH-moe) began working as a shoemaker in Bonito when he was 13, then immigrated to America in 1923. He studied mass shoemaking before opening a shop in Hollywood, where he designed and made shoes by hand for film stars such as Dolores Del Rio, Pola Negri, and Gloria Swanson. He also maintained a successful ready-made shoe business.

Ferragamo returned to Italy and in 1936 opened a shop in Florence. By the time of his death, he had ten factories in Italy and Great Britain. The business was carried on by his wife, two daughters, and son.

Early Ferragamo designs are fantasies of shape, color, and fabric. He is said to have originated the wedge heel and the platform sole, also called the Lucite heel. Though still elegant, for many years the house focused on conservative styles and comfortable fits—but in the age of the stiletto, it has shown more extreme styles and proved itself in step with the times. In addition to shoes, the Ferragamo name appears on handbags, scarves, and luxury ready-to-wear sold at freestanding boutiques and major specialty stores. Massimiliano Giometti is the creative director of the Ferragamo Group.

Autumn/winter 1993/1994.

GIANFRANCO FERRÉ

BORN Legnano, Italy, August 15, 1944
DIED Milan, June 17, 2007

Gianfranco Ferré (Fair-A) designed day clothes with a strong sculptural quality, yet fluid, clean-lined, and comfortable. A fine tailor and advocate of architectural design, Ferré originally intended to be an architect. After working for a furniture maker and traveling, he began designing jewelry, and by 1970 had made a name for himself as an accessories designer. He sold his shoes, scarves, and handbags to other designers, including KARL LAGERFELD, and designed striped t-shirts for Fiorucci. As a freelancer, Ferré began designing sportswear and raincoats, and by 1974 was showing under his own name.

In 1989, he replaced MARC BOHAN as design director at CHRISTIAN DIOR. There his clothes were marked by lush extravagance in the traditional couture mode. He was replaced by JOHN GALLIANO in 1996. Ferré produced his signature ready-to-wear collection until his death in what is considered the most accomplished workroom in Milan.

Designer Gianfranco Ferré.

Above: Spring 2005.
Left: Spring 2007.

Designer Alberta Ferretti.

♛ ALBERTA FERRETTI

and a Japanese operation with boutiques in Tokyo, Osaka, and Yokohama. She is owner and managing director of Aeffe, which produces and distributes her clothes. It also produces Moschino Cheap & Chic, Ultra Ozbek, Narciso Rodriguez, and Jean-Paul Gaultier.

Ferretti's approach is feminine and elegant—soft, traditional shapes tweaked to make them contemporary, and interpreted in the finest Italian fabrics. The look is both witty and sexy. Her other projects have included glassware, ceramics, and a perfume, Femina. Her youthful line, Philosophy di Alberta Ferretti, appointed a new creative director in 2012: Natalie Ratabesi, who has worked at many prestigious global design houses, including John Galliano for Christian Dior, Oscar de la Renta, Valentino, and Gucci.

BORN Gradara, Italy, May 2, 1950

Born into the business, Alberta Ferretti (Fee-REE-tee) began at an early age to collaborate with her mother, who owned an atelier. By 18, she had her own boutique, and her first collection appeared in 1974. Since 1981, when she presented her first ready-to-wear collection, her business has grown to include couture, sportswear,

Spring 2014.

Spring 2014.

141

PATRICIA FIELD

BORN New York City, February 12, 1942

AWARDS Emmy Awards (costume design) *Mother Goose Rock 'n' Rhyme*, 1990; *Sex and the City*, 2002 • Costume Designers Guild Awards *Sex and the City*, 2000, 2001, 2004, 2005; *Ugly Betty*, 2009

Patricia Field is a costume designer, stylist, and fashion designer who established her own boutique with a downtown style in New York City's Bowery neighborhood in 1966. Her eclectic sensibility was a hit with cutting-edge urban fashion fans, club kids, drag queens—and Hollywood. She helped create the looks for television shows such as *Crime Story*, *L.A. Takedown*, and

Stylist and designer Patricia Field.

Actress Sarah Jessica Parker wearing flower dress in *Sex and the City*, 2008, styled by Patricia Field.

Wiseguy. In 1995, on the set of the film *Miami Rhapsody*, she met Sarah Jessica Parker; when Parker was slated to star in HBO's *Sex and the City* (1998–2004), her fashion-obsessed character Carrie Bradshaw became a fashion icon in Field's hands. Field combined pricey designer duds with whimsical accessories (including MANOLO BLAHNIK shoes) and almost single-handedly banished the idea of severe, all-black professional outfits.

Though Field has a brand, House of Field, that she designs with David Dalrymple, her costuming skills and ability to create entire looks earn her the most acclaim. In addition to her Emmys and Costume Designers Guild Awards, she received BAFTA (British Academy of Film and Television Arts) and Academy Award nominations for her work on the 2006 film *The Devil Wears Prada*. She also worked on the television series *Ugly Betty*, for which she received an Emmy nomination (2009) and Costume Designers Guild Award (2009). Field continues to design for movies, such as *Confessions of a Shopaholic*.

Designer Eileen Fisher.

BORN Des Plaines, Illinois, 1950

Eileen Fisher's fashion ideal—simple, loose, yet flattering outfits—was imprinted on her at a young age, when she attended parochial schools in Chicago. After graduating from the University of Illinois at Urbana-Champaign, Fisher moved to New York City. The daily routine of getting dressed for work became overwhelming to her, and she longed for the ease and simplicity of her school uniforms.

In 1984, with $350 in startup money, Fisher began designing tops, vests, and pants. She presented four of her designs at the Boutique Show in New York and subsequently received clothing orders worth about $3,000. Her eponymous company now earns more than

$250 million a year and is sold by at least 37 stores. The company has been praised by Social Accountability International for its labor and safety standards, and in 2007 it was named one of the 50 best companies to work for by the Society for Human Resource Management.

Fisher is known for using natural fibers like silk crepe and Irish linens to create spare, comfortable garments, including kimono jackets, sleeveless shells, loose tunics, and elastic-waist skirts and slacks. She designs for working women who do not have time to deal with complex outfits. "What we do is keep what's good about the school uniform, but not that limited," she has said. "It's a simplified system, like a Lego system, where its simple pieces [are] used in different ways."

Fisher is an outspoken advocate of environmental conservation and a champion for women's rights. In 2013, she presented a collection of films that took "a deeper look at our clothes, our employees, and our social responsibility practices."

Spring 2008.

ANNE FOGARTY

Anne Fogarty is best known for her "paper doll" silhouette and crinoline petticoats under full-skirted shirtdresses with tiny waists, a chemise gathered onto a high yoke, and lounging coveralls. In the early 1970s, she showed a peasant look with ruffled shirts and hot pants under long quilted skirts. She also designed lingerie, jewelry, shoes, hats, coats, and suits.

After studying at the Carnegie Institute of Technology, Fogarty moved to New York City, where she worked as a model and stylist. Between 1948 and 1957, she designed junior-size dresses for the Youth Guild and Margot, Inc., then spent five years at Saks Fifth Avenue. She established Anne Fogarty Inc. in 1962 and closed it 12 years later. At the time of her death, she had just completed a collection of spring/summer dresses and sportswear for a Seventh Avenue firm, Shariella Fashion.

Silver sequined dress, 1966.

BORN Pittsburgh, Pennsylvania, February 2, 1919
DIED New York City, January 15, 1981

AWARDS Coty American Fashion Critics' Awards *Special Award (dresses)*, 1951 • *Neiman Marcus Award*, 1952 • *International Silk Association Award*, 1955 • *National Cotton Council Award*, 1957

Voile dress, 1970.

Designer Tom Ford.

BORN Austin, Texas, August 27, 1961

AWARDS Council of Fashion Designers of America (CFDA) *International Award (for GUCCI)*, 1995; *Women's Wear Designer of the Year*, 2001; *Accessories Designer of the Year (for YVES SAINT LAURENT)*, 2002; *Board of Directors' Tribute*, 2004; *Men's Wear Designer of the Year*, 2008; *Geoffrey Beene Lifetime Achievement Award*, 2014 • VH1/*Vogue* Fashion Awards *Fashion's Future Award*, 1995; *Men's Wear and Women's Wear Designer of the Year*, 1996; *Women's Wear Designer of the Year*, 1999; *Designer of the Year*, 2002 • ELLE Style Awards *Style Icon (U.K.)*, 1999 • Fashion Editors Club of Japan, 2000 • *British GQ International Man of the Year Award*, 2000 • Fashion Group International *Superstar Award*, 2000 • *TIME* magazine's *Best Fashion Designer*, 2001 • *GQ Designer of the Year*, 2001 • *U.S. Accessories Council Award*, 2001, 2006 • Cooper-Hewitt *National Design Award (fashion)*, 2003 • *Rodeo Drive Walk of Style Award*, 2004 • *André Leon Talley Lifetime Achievement Award*, 2005 • GLAAD *Vito Russo Award*, 2007

Tom Ford studied art history at New York University, then architecture at Parsons School of Design in New York and Paris. In 1990, he moved to Milan to be a women's wear designer at Gucci. In 1992, he became design director, and in 1994 he was appointed creative director, responsible for the design of all of the firm's product lines, advertising campaigns, and store designs.

In 2000, after the Gucci Group acquired Yves Saint Laurent and YSL Beauté, Ford became creative director of Yves Saint Laurent Rive Gauche and YSL Beauté in addition to his duties at Gucci. He was also creative director of the Gucci Group, and in 2002 became vice chairman of the board. In 2004, Ford resigned from Gucci Group after it was bought by Pinault-Printemps-Redoute (now known as Kering).

In 2005, Ford announced the creation of his eponymous brand. He partnered with the Marcolin Group to produce and distribute eyewear under his name, and in 2006 joined with ESTÉE LAUDER to launch a fragrance and beauty collection under the Tom Ford Beauty label. Its signature fragrance, Tom Ford Black Orchid, was followed by Tom Ford Black Orchid Voile De Fleur and Tom Ford for Men. In 2006, Ford also announced a licensing agreement with the Ermenegildo Zegna Group for the production and worldwide distribution of luxury men's ready-to-wear and made-to-measure clothing, footwear, and accessories under the Tom Ford label.

In 2007, Ford opened a flagship store on Madison Avenue in New York, and Tom Ford International announced a global expansion. Exclusive, limited distribution of Tom Ford men's wear began in 2008.

In 2009, Ford directed and produced his first film, *A Single Man*, with his production company Fade to Black. In 2010, Ford returned to women's wear with a runway show at his flagship store that ANDRÉ LEON TALLEY described as "beyond dazzling." In 2011, Michelle Obama wore one of Ford's gowns to a state dinner at Buckingham Palace.

Spring 2014.

MARIANO FORTUNY 👗 👗

BORN Granada, Spain, May 11, 1871
DIED Venice, May 3, 1949

Mariano Fortuny's father was a well-known painter who died when his son was just three. After studying painting, drawing, and sculpture, Fortuny studied chemistry and dyes, which he studied in Germany. At the turn of the 20th century he moved to Venice, where he experimented with every aspect of design—from dyeing and printing silks using methods and patterns of his own creation to designing clothes in line with his aesthetic standards.

Fortuny's rich and subtly colored silk tea gowns have been widely collected by museums and by women who treasure the rare and beautiful. His most famous design is the Delphos gown, which first appeared in 1907 and was patented. A simple column of many narrow, irregular, vertical pleats set in silk using a secret process, it clings to the figure and spills over the feet. It can have

Evening cape, early 1930s.

sleeves or be sleeveless. There is also a two-piece version called Peplos, with a hip-length overblouse or longer, unpleated tunic.

Both dresses are beautiful and amazingly practical. For storage, each is simply twisted into a rope and coiled into a figure eight, then slipped into a small box. Status symbols when they were made, the dresses have become so once again, bringing such high prices at auction that they are almost too costly to wear. Fortuny also designed tunics, capes, scarves, and kimono-shaped wraps to be worn over the Delphos.

Fortuny invented a process for printing color and metals on fabric to achieve an effect of brocade or tapestry. Velvets were dyed in many layers and sometimes printed with gold or silver. The fabrics, manufactured in Venice, are still used in interior design.

Also a painter, photographer, set and lighting designer, and inventor, Fortuny has recently been recognized again for his originality and creativity. An exhibition with more than 100 examples of his work—including dresses, robes, textiles, and clocks—opened in Lyon, France, in 1980. From there it traveled to the Fashion Institute of Technology in New York and the Art Institute of Chicago. Fortuny's designs are regularly included in costume exhibitions at museums and design schools.

Natalia Vodianova wearing Fortuny at the MET's 2009 Costume Institute Gala.

146

📷 TONI FRISSELL

BORN Antoinette Frissell Bacon; New York City, March 10, 1907
DIED Saint James, New York, May 17, 1988

Before taking up photography, Toni Frissell worked for a painter and trained as an actress; she also worked in the advertising department of Stern Brothers, and in 1929 began writing captions for *Vogue*. She dabbled in photography but did not take it seriously until the death of her brother, a documentary filmmaker. At *Vogue* she took her first fashion photographs in the informal style described by the magazine as "sunlit, windblown records of action outdoors." Frissell is also known for her work at *Harper's Bazaar*, with outdoor work being her specialty. She would tilt her camera to achieve dramatic diagonals, and often shot from below with a short-focus lens to elongate the bodies of models.

During World War II, Frissell was a volunteer photographer for the American Red Cross, Women's Army Corps, and Eighth Army Air Force. She produced

Photographer Toni Frissell (left) with daughter.

The Duchess of Windsor, photographed by Toni Frissell.

thousands of images of nurses, soldiers, orphans, and African-American airmen. That work led her to abandon fashion and focus more on hard news stories and, later, portraits.

In the 1950s, Frissell photographed famous and powerful subjects in America and Europe, including Winston Churchill, Eleanor Roosevelt, John F. Kennedy, and Jacqueline Kennedy. In 1953, she became the first female staff member at *Sports Illustrated* and worked there during its first four years. She also did assignments for *LIFE* and *LOOK* magazines and some documentary projects. In her later years, Frissell concentrated on photographing women from all walks of life.

JAMES GALANOS ⬛

Designer James Galanos.

BORN Philadelphia, September 20, 1925

AWARDS *Neiman Marcus Award*, 1954 • Coty American Fashion Critics' Awards *Winnie*, 1954; *Return Award*, 1956; *Hall of Fame Award*, 1959 • *National Cotton Council Award*, 1958 • Council of Fashion Designers of America (CFDA) *Lifetime Achievement Award*, 1984 • *Fashion Walk of Fame*, 2001

One of the greatest, most independent designers working in America in the second half of the 20th century, James Galanos is widely considered the equal of the great European couturiers. His ready-to-wear became a symbol of luxury for both its extraordinary quality and stratospheric prices—comparable to those of couture.

The son of Greek immigrants, Galanos studied at Traphagen School of Fashion in New York City and after just a few months began selling sketches to manufacturers. He worked for HATTIE CARNEGIE in 1944, and for ROBERT PIGUET in Paris in 1947–48. He returned to New York and designed for Davidow, then moved to Los Angeles and worked at Columbia Pictures as an assistant to JEAN LOUIS. In 1951, with two assistants and a $500 loan from Louis, he started his own business; he gave his first New York showing in 1952 in a private apartment.

In an age when hems were left unfinished, linings banished, and seams worn inside-out, Galanos still believed that clothes should be as luxurious inside as out and insisted on lining his creations. Intricate construction, flawless workmanship, and magnificent imported fabrics were his hallmarks, as well as detailing—rare in ready-to-wear. Impeccably precise matching of plaids and delicate cross-pleating of chiffons are just two examples. Long admired by connoisseurs of fashion, he achieved wider recognition as one of Nancy Reagan's favorite designers. She wore Galanos to both of her husband's Inaugural Balls: a white satin gown in 1981 and a slim, jeweled dress with a bolero top in 1985.

Because he likes its climate and relaxed living style, Galanos lived and worked in Los Angeles. He did not give large public showings, preferring to exhibit his clothes to the press and retailers in the more intimate settings of hotel suites. In 1976, New York's Fashion Institute of Technology presented *Galanos—25 Years*, an exhibition celebrating his 25th year in business. He retired and closed his business in 1998.

Printed silk dress, 1965.

Designer John Galliano (left) with actress Charlize Theron.

BORN Gibraltar, November 28, 1960

AWARDS British Fashion Council *Designer of the Year*, 1987 • Council of Fashion Designers of America (CFDA) *International Award*, 1997 • French Government *Légion d'Honneur (Legion of Honor)*, 2009

The son of a Spanish mother and English father, John Galliano (Gal-lee-AH-no) was not allowed to study art until college. At London's Central St. Martins College of Art and Design, he studied textiles, learning about fabrics, colors, and draping before switching to design. He called his 1984 graduation collection *Les Incroyables*, after the young French dandies of the Directoire period (1795–99) who went by the name.

Galliano started his career as part of the wildly uninhibited avant-garde London design scene. His designs were twisted and artfully torn, weird but also beautiful. By the end of the 1980s, his style had become smoother and more sophisticated, based on flawless technique and complete command of craft—a synthesis of the original and the salable. In 1990, he joined the Paris ready-to-wear showings; he has also shown in New York. His worldly and assured work is at the forefront of fashion.

In 1993, Galliano met Portuguese socialite and fashion patron Sao Schlumberger and investment bankers from Paine Webber International. The partnership he formed with them provided the funds and high-society seal of approval he needed to gain credibility in Paris, and the resulting collection was an important development for Galliano's fashion house.

⯆ JOHN GALLIANO

In 1995, Galliano succeeded HUBERT DE GIVENCHY as designer of Givenchy couture and ready-to-wear. In 1996, he moved to CHRISTIAN DIOR, another LVMH holding. Galliano's first couture show for Dior, in 2007, coincided with the label's 50th anniversary. In collection after collection, Galliano deconstructed Dior's bourgeois image—sometimes to critical outrage—and helped return the house to profitability. Between his own label and Dior, Galliano produced six couture and ready-to-wear collections a year, as well as a mid-season line called G Galliano.

In 2011, after a breakup with his boyfriend, Galliano publicly made anti-Semitic comments in Paris. He was soon dismissed from Dior and told that he could no longer wear the French Legion of Honor medal. With the help of ANNA WINTOUR, he was invited to work on the fall 2013 ready-to-wear collection for OSCAR DE LA RENTA. Galliano has apologized for his comments and hopes that the world can forgive him.

Fall 2012.

NINA GARCIA

BORN Ninotchka Garcia; Barranquilla, Colombia, May 3, 1967

As a child, Nina Garcia's parents took her out of school for a couple months every winter to travel the world. Garcia began studying at Dana Hall School in Massachusetts after her father decided that Colombia was too dangerous for her. She then earned a liberal arts degree from Boston University. Garcia had a keen interest in fashion and later studied at l'École Supérieure de la Mode in Paris and the Fashion Institute of Technology in New York City.

Garcia's first job in fashion was at PERRY ELLIS, working in public relations under MARC JACOBS. She later worked as an assistant stylist and marketing editor for *Mirabella* magazine. In 1995, Garcia started at *ELLE*, where she rose to fashion director and then to editor-at-large.

In 2004, Garcia became a judge on the television show *Project Runway*, which helped promote *ELLE* and increased its popularity. The position also established Garcia as a reference for anything related to fashion. *Project Runway* received nine Emmy Award nominations for outstanding reality competition program.

In 2008, Garcia left *ELLE* and became fashion director at *Marie Claire*, where she covers the markets in New York, Paris, and Milan. She has also written several books: *The Little Black Book of Style*; *The One Hundred: A Guide to the Pieces Every Stylish Woman Must Own*; *The Style Strategy: A Less-Is-More Approach to Staying Chic and Shopping Smart*; and *Nina Garcia's Look Book: What to Wear for Every Occasion*. In 2013, Garcia was asked to represent the Platinum Jewelry Guild and promote her favorite jewelry and bridal pieces. She believes that her job as a fashion writer is to transform women's style choices, giving them the confidence they need to transform their lives.

Marie Claire fashion director Nina Garcia.

Designer Jean-Paul Gaultier.

BORN Paris, April 24, 1952

AWARDS Council of Fashion Designers of America (CFDA) *International Designer of the Year*, 2000

By 14, Jean-Paul Gaultier (GO-tee-a) was presenting mini-collections of clothes to his mother and grand-mother, and at 15 he invented a coat with bookbag closures, an idea he later used in a collection. When he was 17, he sent some sketches to Pierre Cardin, then worked for him as a design assistant for two years. Other stints

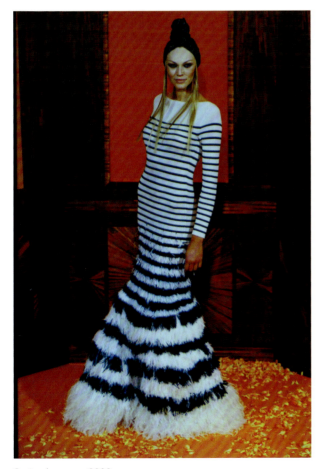

Spring/summer 2000.

♔ JEAN PAUL GAULTIER

followed at Esterel and PATOU, after which he turned to freelancing in 1976.

Once on his own, Gaultier rejected the attitudes of his couture training, focusing more on the spirit of London street dressing. He became the bad boy of Parisian fashion, using his considerable dressmaking and tailoring skills to produce irreverent sendups of the fashion establishment. His juxtapositions of fabrics, scale, and shapes are unexpected and often witty, such as gray lace layered over voluminous gray wool knits, and oversized coats over tiny vests cropped above the waist. Madonna has worn his designs—such as the notorious cone bra—and modeled in his showings. His first fragrance, a perfume in a bottle shaped like a woman in a corset and packaged in a beverage can, was introduced in 1993.

HERMÈS acquired a 35 percent share of Gaultier's company in 1997, enabling him to open shops internationally and enter couture. The fashion world has since watched, astonished, as its one-time *enfant terrible* has applied his considerable creativity and technical ability to French classicism. In 2003, Gaultier replaced MARTIN MARGIELA at Hermès; his first collection was for fall/winter 2004. He left in 2010.

In 2006, he renamed his men's wear line Gaultier 2 and presented his first show for the label. Gaultier launched a cologne, Fleur du Mâle (Flowers of Evil), in 2007. The newest in his family of fragrances are Ma Dame and La Gaîté Lyrique. Gaultier's designs are still wowing audiences—in 2012, he showed a collection inspired by iconic pop stars such as Madonna and Boy George. In 2013, New York's Brooklyn Museum hosted *The Fashion World of John Paul Gautier: From the Sidewalk to the Catwalk*, a retrospective of his work. It was hailed as one of the most exciting fashion exhibits in New York since Alexander McQueen's *Savage Beauty* at the Metropolitan Museum of Art in 2011.

Fall 2013.

RUDI GERNREICH ♟

BORN Vienna, Austria, August 8, 1922
DIED Los Angeles, April 21, 1985

AWARDS Coty American Fashion Critics' Awards *Special Award (innovative body clothes)*, 1960; *Winnie*, 1963; *Return Award*, 1966; *Hall of Fame Award*, 1967 • Knitted Textile Association *Crystal Ball Award*, 1975 • Council of Fashion Designers of America (CFDA) *Special Tribute*, 1985 • *Fashion Walk of Fame*, 2000

Designer Rudi Gernreich (left) with models.

Perhaps the most original and prophetic American designer of the 1950s and 1960s, Rudi Gernreich (GURN-rike) was the only child of an Austrian hosiery manufacturer who died when his son was eight. Gernreich was first exposed to fashion in his aunt's couture salon, where he made sketches and learned about fabrics and dressmaking. In 1938, he left Austria with his mother and settled in Los Angeles, where he attended Los Angeles City College and Art Center School. In 1942, Gernreich joined the Lester Horton Modern Dance Theater as a dancer and costume designer. He became a U.S. citizen in 1943.

Gernreich left Horton after five years, having decided that he was not a sufficiently talented dancer. For the next few years he sold fabrics. A series of dresses that he designed to demonstrate his wares attracted so much interest that in 1951, Gernreich formed a partnership with William Bass, a young Los Angeles garment

manufacturer, and began developing his view of fashion. He established his own firm in 1959, and, during this time, designed a collection for Harmon Knitwear, a Wisconsin manufacturer.

Gernreich specialized in dramatic sports clothes of stark cut, enriched by bold, graphic patterns and striking color combinations. Always interested in liberating the body, he introduced a knit maillot without an inner bra in 1954, the era of constructed bathing suits. He favored halter necklines and cut-back shoulders to allow free movement and designed the soft "no bra" bra in skin-toned nylon net. Gernreich also created "Swiss cheese" swimsuits with multiple cutouts, see-through blouses, and knee-high hosiery patterned to match tunic tops and tights. His shifts kept getting shorter until they were little more than tunics, which he showed over tights in bright colors or strong patterns.

Gernreich's innovations often caused a commotion, as with the see-through blouse and the topless bathing suit he showed in 1964. Gernreich was never interested in looking back, disdaining revivals of past eras. In 1968, at the height of his career, he announced that he was taking a sabbatical from fashion. He never again worked at it full time, though he did return in 1971 with predictions for a future of bald heads, bare bosoms with pasties, and unisex caftans. He also freelanced, creating furniture, ballet costumes, and professional dance and exercise clothes.

High-waisted dress, 1967.

Topless swimsuit, 1964.

♟ NICOLAS GHESQUIÈRE

Designer Nicolas Ghesquière.

BORN Comines, France, 1971

AWARDS Council of Fashion Designers of America (CFDA) *International Designer of the Year*, 2001

Unlike many of his designer contemporaries, Nicolas Ghesquière (NEE-co-la Guess-KEY-air) never formally studied dress design. Instead he learned from part-time internships, starting at 14 with designers such as Agnès B. and Corinne Cobson. He grew up in central France to a Belgian father who managed golf courses and a French mother with a fondness for fashion. As a child, Ghesquière loved the *Star Wars* films and sports, particularly riding, swimming, and fencing.

After completing school, Ghesquière worked from 1990 to 1992 with JEAN PAUL GAULTIER, designing knits and working on Gaultier's junior line, a period he considers his true fashion education. He was at BALENCIAGA designing uniforms and funeral clothes for a Japanese licensee when head designer Joseph Thimister left, and in 1997 Ghesquière took the top job. He was so unknown that no one attended his first show, but is now considered one who must be watched, a leader of avant-garde fashion. His clothes range from elaborate patchwork minis to rugged leather jackets, and he has developed a devoted following of young fashionables, particularly for his fitted trousers.

Ghesquière has switched the emphasis at Balenciaga Le Dix from evening wear to day clothes, in which some viewers find subtle references to Balenciaga styles of the 1940s and 1950s. In 2001, when the GUCCI Group bought Balenciaga, Ghesquière was given a nine percent share in the house and, as creative director, extensive responsibility for its creative direction and image. Ghesquière left Balenciaga in 2012, and in 2013 it sued him for breach of confidentiality. Ghesquière had said in an interview that he was being "sucked dry" by the brand and that it lacked direction and did not provide enough support on the business end.

In 2013, LOUIS VUITTON made Ghesquière its artistic director of women's wear, taking over from MARC JACOBS, and his first collection for the house was Autumn/Winter 2014 in Paris.

Look from Balenciaga, fall 2007.

CHARLES DANA GIBSON ✏

BORN Roxbury, Massachusetts, September 14, 1867
DIED Maine, December 23, 1944

Charles Dana Gibson learned to draw at an early age from his father, an amateur artist who nurtured his son's talent. By the time Gibson was a young adult, his family had saved enough money to send him to the Art League in Manhattan—but after two years, financial hardships forced him to leave. In 1886, Gibson sold four drawings to *LIFE* magazine, which featured his drawings weekly for the next three decades. In 1889, Gibson studied in London and Paris, working with his idol, the admired English illustrator and intellect George du Maurier, who introduced Gibson to drawing high-society women. By 1890, Gibson was illustrating for *Harper's Monthly, The Century, Harper's Bazaar,* and *Scribner's Magazine.*

Illustrator Charles Dana Gibson.

Illustration of "Gibson Girl" wearing gown with corset, 1890s.

Inspired by his wife, Virginia aristocrat Irene Longhorne, Gibson created the "Gibson Girl," a spunky, down-to-earth, turn-of-the-century American society girl. The Gibson Girl was an iconic figure for more than two decades, arguably setting the first American standard for feminine beauty. Gibson capitalized on merchandising opportunities created by this incredible popularity, including Gibson Girl wallpaper, ashtrays, china, souvenir spoons, pillows, and umbrellas. To complement the Gibson Girl, he created the handsome, courteous, and witty "Gibson Man." In 1918, after firmly establishing his reputation as an illustrator and accumulating his wealth (earning a reported $75,000 a year by 1910), Gibson became owner and editor of *LIFE.* The Gibson Girl's popularity did not fade until after World War I.

In 1932, Gordon sold *LIFE* and retired as one of the most respected illustrators of the late 19th and early 20th centuries. He drew and painted with oils until his death.

Designer Romeo Gigli.

▲ ROMEO GIGLI

In 1989, Gigli made a controversial move, taking his style presentations from Milan to Paris, where he showed under tents outside the Louvre. In 1991, Gigli separated from his two partners and restructured his business, creating the line Romeo World.

In 1999, IT Holding acquired majority control of the brand, which in 2004 led Gigli to sever all connections with the house that bore his name. In 2005, his successor Anna Cuimo presented the fall/winter Romeo Gigli collection in Milan. Romeo Gigli clothes are now sold in more than 200 boutiques in Europe and America. In 2013, the designer made a comeback with a special collection for *Joyce*, a luxury retailer based in Hong Kong.

BORN Italy, 1950

Romeo Gigli's (ZHEE-lee's) father and grandfather were antiquarian booksellers, and he grew up in an aura of antiquity. This background is in some contrast to the simplicity and modernity of his clothing designs, which nevertheless have something romantically rich and strange about them. Trained as an architect, Gigli began designing in 1979 and launched his own company in 1983.

Since then, his style has become more pronounced—with a close, gentle fit, soft draping, and fondness for asymmetry—and an overall sense of fluidity and graceful movement. His pieces may not seem like much on a clothes hanger, but they take shape on the body. Using rich and luxurious fabrics in sundry colors, he achieves a kind of throwaway chic. Were it not for their romanticism, his designs could be considered minimalist.

Fall 2003.

MARITHÉ & FRANÇOIS GIRBAUD ⧖

BORN Marithé Girbaud; Lyon, France, 1942
François Girbaud; Mazamet, France, 1945

Champions of relaxed sportswear, brothers Marithé and François Girbaud established their business in 1964. Their clothes, for men and women, seem unconstructed but are more complex than they appear, and entirely functional. Jackets are often double, with a layer that

Designers François Girbaud (left) and Marithé Girbaud (right).

buttons on for warmth; sweaters may be wool on the outside and cotton on the inside. This same thinking goes into their children's wear. In America, Girbaud is best known for jeans and soft, stonewashed denim pants. In 2001, the brothers were commissioned to design uniforms for Air France.

Affected by the global recession that started in 2008, the Marithé & François Girbaud label filed for bankruptcy in 2012. But Indian manufacturer Fibers & Fabrics International recently provided backing for the label, allowing the Girbaud family to maintain creative and marketing control.

Spring 2011 men's wear.

Designer Hubert de Givenchy.

⏦ HUBERT DE GIVENCHY

In 1988, Givenchy sold his business to LVMH under a seven-year contract that kept him as head designer. He retired in 1995 after presenting his final haute couture collections. JOHN GALLIANO replaced him, followed by ALEXANDER MCQUEEN in 1996. McQueen

(continued)

BORN Beauvais, France, February 20, 1927

Hubert de Givenchy (You-BEAR Do Zhee-vahn-SHE) studied at l'École des Beaux Arts in Paris, and at 17 went to work in couture at Lelong. He later worked at Piguet and Fath, and spent four years designing at SCHIAPARELLI. In 1952, Givenchy opened his own shop near BALENCIAGA, who he greatly admired and influenced his work.

Givenchy's youthful separates brought early recognition—especially the Bettina blouse, a peasant shape named for the famous French model who worked with him when he first opened. When Balenciaga closed his house, Givenchy hired many of its workroom staff— helping him earn a reputation for super-refined couture much like that of the older designer, with clothes noted for their masterly cut, exceptional workmanship, and beautiful fabrics. Day clothes were quietly elegant, while late-day and evening wear lines were more glamorous—in line with the lives of Givenchy's conservative clients, who included the Duchess of Windsor, Jacqueline Kennedy, and Mercedes Kellogg. Givenchy's friendship with Audrey Hepburn inspired some of his most recognizable work. A devoted fan, Hepburn asked Givenchy to design costumes for her films *Breakfast at Tiffany's* and *Funny Face*.

Audrey Hepburn wearing lamé dress, 1966..

157

left in 2001 and was replaced by JULIEN MACDONALD. In 2003, OZWALD BOATENG became creative director for Givenchy Homme, and in 2005 RICCARDO TISCI was appointed creative director for Givenchy's haute couture and ready-to-wear lines for women.

In addition to couture, Givenchy's interests include Nouvelle Boutique ready-to-wear, perfumes, and men's toiletries. Licensing commitments have extended from men's and women's sportswear and shirts to small leather goods, hosiery, furs, eyewear, and home furnishings.

Transparent pleated lapel, 1969.

Quilted jacket and printed ballet length skirt, 1953.

BORN Detroit, Michigan, 1965

AWARDS Pulitzer Prize, 2006 • Council of Fashion Designers of American (CFDA) *Media Award in Honor of Eugenia Sheppard*, 2007

Valedictorian of her high school class and a graduate of Princeton University with a bachelor's degree in English, Robin Givhan (GIVE-hahn) earned a master's degree in journalism from the University of Michigan in 1988. Starting out at the *Detroit Free Press* as an entertainment reporter, Givhan worked her way up to features writer and eventually became the paper's fashion reporter. In 1995, she left for a brief stint as a features writer at the *San Francisco Chronicle*, but later that year moved to *The Washington Post* to cover fashion. Givhan soon left *The Post* to work as an associate editor at *Vogue*, but after six months she returned to *The Post* and stayed until 2010.

Givhan has developed a devoted following thanks to her acerbic wit and no-holds-barred writing style, taking on the sartorial choices of celebrities and political figures with uncommon candor. In 2006, Givhan received the Pulitzer Prize for criticism—the first ever awarded to a fashion critic—and in 2007 the CFDA Media Award in Honor of Eugenia Sheppard. Givhan appeared on the television show *The Colbert Report* in 2006 and has become a closely watched fashion insider.

In 2009, Givhan, who had been based in New York, returned to Washington, D.C. for *The Post* in a new role covering Michelle Obama and the first family as well as penning a weekly fashion column. In 2010, Givhan left *The Post* for *Newsweek* and the *Daily Beast*, but in a shocking decision was let go in 2013. Rumors began swirling that Givhan had again been hired by *The Post*,

Writer Robin Givhan.

but she quickly put them to rest after making it clear that she was freelancing and concentrating on her book about the 1973 Versailles fashion show.

Givhan has also written for the magazines *Harper's Bazaar*, *Vogue Italia*, *Marie Claire*, and *Essence*, and contributed to the books *Runway Madness*; *No Sweat: Fashion, Free Trade, and the Rights of Garment Workers*; and *Thirty Ways of Looking at Hillary: Reflections by Women Writers*.

ANDREW GN

BORN 1966, Singapore

Andrew Gn (Gin) grew up amid rich textiles. His father would bring home exotic fabrics from his travels, and Andrew soon developed a strong interest in learning about fabric. He graduated from Central St. Martins College of Art and Design in London in 1989 and received a master's degree from Domus Academy in Italy in 1992. Also in 1992, he took a position as assistant designer to EMANUEL UNGARO. In 1996, he started his eponymous line, using manufacturing facilities in Italy and France.

In 1997, Gn became artistic director of ready-to-wear and accessories at BALMAIN. But after his debut collection received negative reviews, Gn left to focus on his solo collection, which has been critically successful. Gn's clothes feature lots of bows, floral appliques, and cashmere. His exquisite handiwork is often comparable to that of haute couture.

Designer Andrew Gn.

In 2008, Gn debuted his made-to-measure atelier line: 18 limited edition outfits boasting lavish couture-grade handwork. Gn continues to make red carpet gowns for stars including Jessica Chastain, Emma Stone, and Leslie Mann.

Spring 2014.

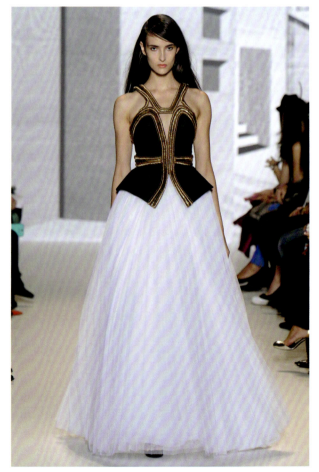
Spring 2014.

Designer Alix Grès.

BORN Germaine Emilie Krebs; Paris, November 30, 1903
DIED South of France, November 24, 1993

AWARDS French Government *Légion d'Honneur* (*Legion of Honor*), 1947 • Chambre Syndicale de la Couture Parisienne *Golden Thimble Award*, 1976

Considered one of couture's most talented, imaginative, and independent designers, Alix Grès (Al-LEAKS Gray) is ranked by many with MADELEINE VIONNET, though Grès was very different. Later known as Madame Grès, she first wanted to be a sculptor, but family disapproval and lack of money led her to dressmaking. Under the name Germaine Barton, she apprenticed at the House of Premet and in the early 1930s began making and selling muslin toiles copied from couture.

In 1933, with anonymous financial backing, she opened Alix, a salon where she was not a principal but a salaried employee. She obtained a half-interest in the house in 1938. Because Grès refused to take German clients and tended to defy Nazi edicts, the house closed in 1940. A few years later, having lost the rights to the name Alix, she reopened as Grès—but was forced to close after just six months. After World II, she reopened under the same name.

Her background as a sculptor showed in her mastery of draping, especially in evening dresses of chiffon or the fine silk jersey (called Alix after her use of it) she encouraged textile mills to make. Working with fabric directly on live models, Grès molded it to their figures, often baring part of the midriff; a gown could take two

or three months to complete. These dresses, so fluid in feeling, were intricate marvels of construction. Other recurring themes were jersey day dresses with cowl necklines, deep-cut or dolman sleeves, kimono-shaped coats, and asymmetrical draping. Grès traveled widely, and returned with ideas that inspired her work.

Grès avoided publicity, and details of her private life are scarce. Her husband was a painter and sculptor who left Paris for Tahiti soon after the birth of their daughter in 1939. Professionally, she went her own way; she resisted doing ready-to-wear until 1980, the last of the couture designers to make the move.

Grès was elected chairman of the Chambre Syndicale de la Couture Parisienne in 1973 and continued as honorary president throughout the 1980s. Grès sold her house to a French industrialist in 1984; it was resold in 1986, then went bankrupt and closed in 1987. In 1988, the Grès name was sold to a Japanese company and the business continued, primarily in Japan in ready-to-wear and with numerous licenses in France and elsewhere.

In 1994, the fashion world was shocked to learn in French newspaper *Le Monde* that Grès was dead—and had died more than a year earlier in the Var region of France.

Evening dress, 1958.

JACQUES GRIFFE

BORN Carcassonne, France, 1910
DIED Villesiscle, France, 1994

As a boy, Jacques Griffe (Guh-REEF-uh) learned tailoring by watching his mother make and repair clothes. At 16, he interned with a tailor and apprenticed with a couturier. After his family moved to Paris in 1936, Griffe obtained an internship at the House of VIONNET from 1936 to 1939. There he learned how to apply and maneuver fabric on mannequin and human bodies.

While serving France in World War II, he was captured and spent 18 months as a prisoner of war.
In 1951, Griffe started his own line, Jacques Griffe Revolution. Through his internship at Vionnet, he had become a master of cut in its relationship to fabric. Griffe could drape with ease and was bold in his use of stiffer fabrics such as taffeta and dupioni. His designs were innovative and of high quality. In 1958, he was credited with creating the sack dress. Griffe retired from fashion in 1974.

Wedding gown, 1955.

Evening dress, 1955.

FOUNDED Florence, 1921

The son of a struggling Italian merchant, Guccio Gucci (GOO-chee) was the founder of one of the world's most successful luxury brands. Gucci, who grew up in Florence, Italy, developed the Gucci clothing company out of his family's leather saddlery shop. His strong work ethic and appreciation for fine craftsmanship revived his family's ailing business, helping it become a powerful leather company. In 1938, the company expanded to Rome, and in 1953 opened a shop in New York City.

Gucci made his mark by capitalizing on the strength of the company's equestrian-inspired collections. During the 1940s, shortages of traditional materials led the company to innovate with new ones. Those efforts led to Gucci's iconic "Bamboo" bag and helped cement the company's status as a luxury leader.

After Guccio's death in 1953, the Gucci brand continued to grow—thanks in part to a large following of celebrity admirers, including Elizabeth Taylor, Jacqueline Kennedy, and Peter Sellers, all of whom loved the company's unisex "Hobo" bag. But though Gucci expanded into a global brand, it remained a family business; Guccio's four sons and grandson Maurizio all worked for it. In the early 1980s, the company hired Domenico De Sole to head Gucci's American division, with Maurizio as chief executive officer.

Under Maurizio's leadership, however, the company floundered, and the Gucci brand was sold to multinational conglomerate Investcorp in 1993. Two years later, Tom Ford took the helm and helped revitalize the brand; De Sole became chief executive officer. De Sole pushed the company to become a multibrand conglomerate, and under his leadership the Gucci Group acquired Yves Saint Laurent, Stella McCartney, and Alexander McQueen. Ford and De Sole left in 2004, but the company continues to flourish—in part because of Guccio's legacy of high-quality luxury goods.

In 2005, Frida Giannini was named creative director of Gucci women's wear, in addition to her responsibility for all accessories. In 2006, she took over men's wear, thus becoming the label's sole creative director. Giannini's clothes have been a huge critical

Designer Roberto Gucci.

Designer Frida Giannini.

(continued)

and commercial success, and in 2013 she showcased a line inspired by the women's power suit. She culls inspiration from the Gucci archives, combining the label's heritage with her unique vision.

In 2009, Patriziodi Marco replaced Mark Lee as chief executive of Gucci's fashion and leather goods. In 2010, Gucci launched children's wear, featuring Jennifer Lopez and her twins in its advertising campaigns. In 2012, Marco became chief executive officer of the Gucci Group under Kering (formally PPR).

Spring 2014.

Model holding Gucci bag, 1956.

Tim Gunn (right) and Heidi Klum at the 65th annual Primetime Emmy Awards.

BORN Washington D.C., July 29, 1953

Tim Gunn grew up with one parent in the Central Intelligence Agency (CIA) and the other in the Federal Bureau of Investigation (FBI). While young, Gunn faced constant pressure to conform to the image that his father envisioned for him, resulting in social anxiety that caused him to switch schools frequently. He majored in sculpture at the Corcoran College of Art and Design, then worked in its Admissions Department. In 1983, Gunn became assistant director of admissions at Parsons School of Design, where he rose to dean. In 2000, he noticed that the school's Fashion Design Department was floundering—its once cutting-edge curriculum had become stale. Gunn decided to chair the department for a year, which became seven.

In 2003, the Bravo television network approached Gunn about appearing on the reality show *Project Runway*. Initially, Gunn was not interested and did not believe the fashion industry needed a reality show. But Bravo convinced him to do it, and *Project Runway* premiered in 2004. In 2005, Bravo launched *Tim Gunn's Guide to Style*, a spinoff based on Gunn's immediate popularity.

Known for his quirky statements such as "make it work" or "it's a little costumey," Gunn followed his television success by writing *Tim Gunn: A Guide to Quality, Taste, and Style*. In 2007, Gunn left Parsons to become the creative director at LIZ CLAIBORNE.

Gunn's television success has led to appearances on shows such as *Late Night with Jimmy Fallon*, *The Daily Show*, and *Larry King Now*. During those appearances in the early 2010s, Gunn revealed that he had never told his parents he is gay, though he suspects his mother knew, and had been celibate for almost 30 years. In the fashion world, Gunn has been an advocate for designers exploring the petite and plus size markets, which are both underserved. Gunn has quipped that when it comes to fashion and judging what others are wearing, "we're all entitled to present ourselves as we choose to as long as we accept responsibility for it."

PRABAL GURUNG ⬛

BORN Singapore, March 31, 1979

AWARDS Ecco Domani Fashion Fund Award, 2010
• Council of Fashion Designers of America (CFDA)
Swarovski Award for Womenswear, 2011

Prabal Gurung (PRAW-bul Goo-ROONGH) was born
in Singapore but grew up in Kathmandu, Nepal. Gurung
began his fashion education in Nepal but earned his
degree in fashion design from Parsons New School
of Design in 2001. He then worked on the design and
production team at CYNTHIA ROWLEY. Two years later,
Gurung was appointed design director at BILL BLASS.
He stayed there for five years, then launched his own
label in 2009.

Gurung's designs are a hot commodity in American
fashion—he completed a collaboration with Target

Designer Prabal Gurung.

in 2013 and with J.Crew in 2010. He is methodical in
terms of what inspires him, whether it be a color, a
muse, or even a feeling. For his 2014 collection, Gurung
scented the showing room and used mood lighting to
invoke the right ambiance for the audience to connect
with his pieces.

Gurung has dressed Michelle Obama and the
Duchess of Cambridge. In 2103, he collaborated with
OLIVIER THEYSKENS on costumes for the New York City
Ballet's fall gala at the request of Sarah Jessica Parker,
who sits on the board. Parker attended the gala in a
one-of-a-kind creation by Gurung and Theyskens.

Spring 2014.

BORN Panama, October 21

Richard Haines is one of the most revered and exciting fashion illustrators working today, but he did not go to school for fashion illustration. Although Haines had been sketching dresses since he was little, he decided to study painting and graphic design. He admits that his background in art helped him with color and composition. But all the other technical and theoretical aspects of fashion design, like patternmaking, he learned on his own.

Haines moved to New York City in 1975 and worked as a designer for some of the biggest brands, such as Calvin Klein, Sean Jean, and Bill Blass. At these labels, he learned how to critically look at fabrics, colors, and shapes, which helped inform his illustrations. Haines loves New York and calls it "an endless runway."

After working in design for years, Haines felt that the industry had become stale, and in 2008 started his blog, *What I Saw Today*. The blog showcases what he sees around him, his inspirations, and, most important, his illustrations. Haines is among an exclusive group of illustrators found in the front row at top runway shows, trying to complete detailed sketches in 30 seconds. He also sketches for patrons. Haines feels that illustrations engage viewers in a way that photographs do not—allowing for additions, cuts, and reinterpretations. He uses paper, pencil, and sometimes charcoal in his illustrations. Although Haines is an avid fan of technology, he prefers to hand draw all of his illustrations by hand and limits his use of technology to Twitter, Facebook, and his blog.

Haines's work has been featured in publications such as *The New York Times*, *London Times*, and *GQ,* as

Illustrator Richard Haines.

well as for brands such as Coach and Calvin Klein. He is currently under contract with *InStyle* magazine and J.Crew. For its fall 2012 collection, Prada hired Haines to create illustrations that resulted in limited edition t-shirts, a book, and an iPad app called Il Palazzo. Haines attributes the resurgence in demand for hand-drawn illustration to the fact that people want a break from intense technology.

H

KEVAN HALL

BORN Detroit, Michigan

AWARDS National Association for the Advancement of Colored People (NAACP) *Great American Designer Award*, 1990

One of the top African-American designers in America, Kevan Hall's creations have graced the red carpet for over two decades. Performers who have worn his gowns include Salma Hayek, Celine Dion, Sharon Stone, and Charlize Theron. Hall has known that he wanted to design since he was seven. He attended the Cass Technical High School in Detroit, then the Fashion Institute of Design and Merchandising (FIDM) in California. While studying there, he toured Europe and visited the houses of DIOR, CARDIN, and GIVENCHY. The trip validated his dream of working in haute couture. At graduation, Hall received the prestigious Peacock Award for Outstanding Fashion Design.

In 1988, Hall started his business in partnership with his wife Deborah. He began selling his collections to retailers such as Bergdorf Goodman and Neiman Marcus. In 1989, Fairchild included him in its *Soul of Seventh Avenue* show. The following year he received the NAACP's Great American Designer Award, and in 1992 the Center for the Performing Arts in Southern California produced a ten-year retrospective of his work. Hall also worked as a costume consultant for the films *Gridlock* and *Eve's Bayou*.

In 1998, Hall was tapped as design and creative director for HALSTON. There he brought the brand back to life and gained the respect of New Yorkers who did not think a designer from California could revive the stagnating New York–based brand. In 2001, Absolut vodka honored Hall by including his work in its exhibit, *A Tribute to African Designers*. In 2002, he won the 47th Annual Gold Coast Award for Designer of the Year and

Designer Kevan Hall (right) with model.

launched the Kevan Hall Signature Collection. In 2010, after getting rave reviews for Tia Mowry's wedding gown, he formally launched Kevan Hall White Label, his wedding collection.

Hall has always been drawn to vintage and iconic styles. His designs buck trends, and his signature style is a hallmark of glamour infused with a modern sensibility. His advice to fashion design students: "You must study at a school or study as an apprentice so that you really get your hands into the design process. You should immerse yourself in books, magazines, and museums, and go to the stores to shop and look at all kinds of clothing. And pick something that really speaks to you, and follow that dream."

BORN Roy Halston Frowick; Des Moines, Iowa, April 23, 1932
DIED San Francisco, March 26, 1990

AWARDS Coty American Fashion Critics' Awards *Special Award (millinery)*: 1962, 1969; *Winnie*, 1971; *Return Award*, 1972; *Hall of Fame Award*, 1974 • *Fashion Walk of Fame*, 2000

Halston grew up in Indiana and attended Indiana University and the Chicago Art Institute. While still in school, he designed and sold hats. He moved to New York City in 1957, worked for LILLY DACHÉ, and in 1959 joined Bergdorf Goodman as a milliner. There he gained a name and a fashionable clientele. He originated the scarf hat and designed the pillbox hat Jacqueline Kennedy wore for her husband's inauguration.

Designer Halston.

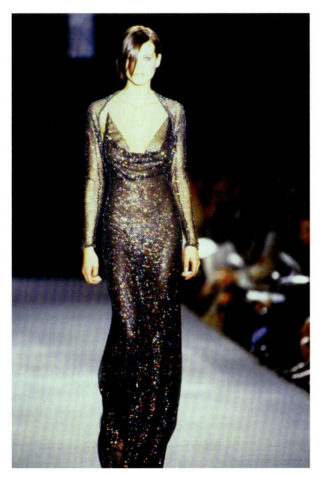

Ready-to-wear 1997/1998.

In 1968, Halston opened his own firm for private clients and immediately established himself with a pure, all-American look. His clothes were elegant and well-made, with the casual appeal of sportswear. His formula of luxurious fabrics in extremely simple, classic shapes made him one of the top designers of the 1970s. Among his successes were the long cashmere dress with a sweater tied over the shoulders; the combination of a wrap skirt and turtleneck; evening caftans; and long, slinky, haltered jerseys. He was also a pioneer in the use of Ultrasuede. Halston worked closely with ELSA PERETTI, who designed the packaging for his successful signature fragrance, Halston.

He expanded into knitwear and accessories in 1970, then into ready-to-wear. In 1973, Halston sold his business to a conglomerate, becoming the first American designer to franchise his name. In 1983, when he signed with JC Penney for a cheaper line, a number of his accounts dropped his regular line. He tried to regain ownership in 1984 but was unable to do so, and went out of business.

After his death in 1990, the Halston label had eight separate owners and six designers, from John David Ridge to Bradley Bayou, including RANDOLPH DUKE in 1997 and KEVAN HALL in 1998—who ANDRÉ LEON TALLEY says "channeled Halston" during his tenure. In 2007, the label was acquired by Hilco Consumer Capital and The Weinstein Company, and in 2008, Harvey

(continued)

169

Weinstein, JIMMY CHOO's Tamara Mellon, and stylist Rachel Zoe sought to revive the name. The owners installed as creative chief former VERSACE designer Marco Zanini, who showed his first collection in February 2008. Net-a-porter.com signed on to sell his pieces immediately, but Zanini was dismissed in July 2008.

Halston's spring 2009 collection was created by an unnamed design team. In July 2009, Marios Schwab was appointed creative director and resurrected the brand's once-thriving fragrance line. That year also marked the launch of Halston Heritage, a collection of iconic pieces with lower prices than the ready-to-wear, handbag, and shoe collections. In 2012, sportswear, accessories, and dresses were added to the line.

In 2011, Ben Malka was appointed chairman and chief executive officer, and Marie Mazelis as creative director. Both came from BCBG.

Black jumpsuit for Halston Limited, 1971.

Designer Katharine Hamnett (left) and Naomi Campbell (right).

BORN Katharine Eleanor Appleton; Kent, England, August 16, 1947

AWARDS *National Cotton Council Award*, 1982 • British Fashion Awards *British Designer of the Year*, 1984 • British Government *Commander of the Order of the British Empire (CBE)*, 2011

As both a feminist and a supporter of the peace movement, Katharine Hamnett's work often reflects her political concerns. Her 1983 Choose Life t-shirt collection, for example, displayed slogans such as "Worldwide Nuclear Ban Now," "Stop Acid Rain," and "Preserve the Rainforests."

Born into a diplomatic family, Hamnett was educated at Cheltenham Ladies College and studied art in Stockholm before enrolling at Central St. Martins College of Art and Design in London to study fashion. While still in school, she worked as a freelance designer. After graduation in 1969, she opened a sportswear firm, Tuttabankem, with a school friend. After its demise, she designed for a number of firms in England, France, Italy, and Hong Kong before establishing Katharine Hamnett Ltd. in 1979.

Her clothes are relaxed and easygoing classics with a witty attitude and are often based on work clothes. Men's wear—with the same feeling as her women's wear—appeared in 1982. The clothes have been sold through high-end specialty stores and in her own shops; she has also had her own accessory, shoe, tie, and eyewear lines.

⏳ KATHARINE HAMNETT

True to Hamnett's beliefs, her company emphasizes environmentally sound practices, making minimum use of packaging and maximum use of natural fibers such as cotton and wool—plus those, like Tencel, considered environmentally friendly. In 2001, financial problems forced her to close part of her business, shrinking it "back to the core." As a result of the Iraq War and environmental problems, her political designs regained popularity in 2003. In 2008, she criticized designers at London's Fashion Week for what she deemed an increasing exclusion of women of color on the runway.

In 2011, Hamnett was appointed Commander of the Order of the British Empire (CBE). In 2013, she designed t-shirts for the Campaign for Nuclear Disarmament, National Health System, and Education Not Trident (the British nuclear weapons system).

Design by Katharine Hamnett.

JOHN HARDY Ŏ

BORN Canada, 1949

John Hardy's love for Indonesian artistry began in 1975 when he moved to Bali, where he studied jewelry-making under descendants of the artisans of the Royal Court. In 1989, Hardy started his company by combining this artistry, quality, and techniques with modern design. In 1994, with his wife Carol, he started building an eponymous jewelry house in Bali, making sure that the company relied on green business practices.

In 1998, Hardy hired Guy Bedarida as the company's head designer and creative director. Bedarida brought vast knowledge of and experience with haute couture jewelry from both America and Europe. He designed exquisite modern jewelry, and Balinese artisans brought his visions to life. In 2003, Damien Dernoncourt became the company's president and expanded it internationally to Hong Kong, Russia, Japan, and Dubai. The company aims to be the leader in luxury handmade jewelry inspired by the essence of the Earth.

In 2007, Hardy retired and sold the company to Bedarida and Dernoncourt. The John Hardy brand debuted at Le Bon Marche Rive Gauche in Paris in 2008, followed by expansion to Harrods in the United Kingdom in 2010. The company continues to follow the same artisanal practices and traditions used by Hardy.

Model Cecilia Wang wearing John Hardy Jewelry at a promotional event in Hong Kong.

◭ DONWAN HARRELL

Designer Donwan Harrell.

BORN Mufreesboro, North Carolina, November 3, 1970

Donwan Harrell is the owner and designer of the luxury denim line PRPS, and his upbringing instilled a work ethic that has helped him throughout his career and inspired many of his collections. Harrell was raised in Virginia by his mother, a seamstress, and his father, a carpenter from a long line of hunters and loggers. Harrell's love for fashion blossomed at Virginia Commonwealth University, and at the Air France Competition he won the top prize—to study at Chambre Syndicale de la Couture Parisienne in Paris for two years.

After graduating, Harrell worked for designer Robert Stock, then Donna Karan. His next job was at Nike, where he was quickly promoted and sent to Hong Kong to design activewear. While there, Harrell made friends with investors and came up with the idea of creating his own company. After five years at Nike, he and his brother Emmett created Akademiks, an urban sportswear brand. The brand catered to the hip hop community and was guided by the idea that minority kids wear what everyone else wears, just larger. Within a year, Harrell had paid off his investors, and in 2002 he launched PRPS Jeans, which is shorthand for product with a purpose.

In 2009, Nike named Harrell one of its top designers of all time. He sold Akademiks to focus on PRPS. The brand's jeans are made of high-quality African cotton on 1960 looms in Japan, which is where the business first began to thrive. The brand now includes PRPS Goods and Company and PRPS Noir, a high-end line that charges up to $1,200 for individual pieces. PRPS jeans are for "someone who appreciates certain details they can't find elsewhere, and that the average consumer wouldn't necessarily wear." They are sold to athletes, actors, and rock stars—including David Beckham, Brad Pitt, Tom Cruise, and Jay-Z—and in upscale stores such as Nordstrom and Bergdorf Goodman.

Harrell's studio, office, and showrooms display the inspirations for his designs. The idea behind his products is that no two denim pants are the same. Harrell prides himself for collections inspired by the American working class, but many believe he is revolutionizing denim. The reason for his popularity, Harrell says, is that PRPS is "functional, very American, and very wearable."

PRPS Spring 2009.

NORMAN HARTNELL ⬥

BORN London, June 12, 1901
DIED Windsor, England, June 8, 1979

AWARDS *Neiman Marcus Award*, 1947

Educated at Cambridge University, where he designed costumes and performed in undergraduate plays, Norman Hartnell was expected to become an architect but instead turned to dress design. After working briefly for a court designer and selling sketches to Lucile, he opened a business with his sister in 1923. At the time a French name or reputation was indispensable to success in London, so in 1927 he took his collection to Paris. In 1930, he showed there again, resulting in many orders—particularly from American and Canadian buyers. The Hartnell couture house became the largest in London. He was a dressmaker to Queen Elizabeth II, whose 1953 coronation gown he designed. He was knighted in 1977.

Hartnell is most closely identified with elaborate evening gowns, lavishly embroidered and sprinkled with sequins, particularly the bouffant gowns he designed for the Queen Mother and Queen Elizabeth II. He also

Top: Designer Norman Hartnell (center) with models.
Bottom: Queen Elizabeth II wearing Norman Hartnell design, 1957.

Autumn/winter 1991/1992.

made well-tailored suits and coats in British and French woolens and tweeds. By the 1970s, Hartnell was making clothes in leather and fur and designing men's wear.

Hartnell died in 1979, but the house was revived in 1990 with MARC BOHAN as fashion director. The first collections were couture; ready-to-wear followed in 1991. The firm has since gone out of business.

Top: Designer Edith Head (right).

Bottom: Actress Marlene Dietrich wearing an Edith Head costume in the film *Desire*, 1936.

BORN San Bernardino, California, October 28, 1897
DIED Los Angeles, October 24, 1981

AWARDS Academy Awards for Best Costume Design
The Heiress, 1949; *Samson and Delilah*, 1950; *All About*

Eve, 1950; *A Place in the Sun*, 1951; *Roman Holiday*, 1953; *Sabrina*, 1954; *The Facts of Life*, 1969; *The Sting*, 1973

Edith Head's illustrious career ran more than 50 years—starting at Paramount Pictures, where she was head designer for 29 years. Hired as a junior designer by Howard Greer in the 1920s, she became the studio's top designer in 1938 when TRAVIS BANTON left for Universal Studios.

Head graduated from the University of California at Berkeley, where she majored in languages, and went to Stanford University for a master's degree in French. She then taught French at private schools for girls and studied at Otis and Chouinard art institutes before answering a help wanted ad that led to her first job at Paramount. When Greer left Paramount to open his own salon, he was succeeded by Banton, who made Head his assistant.

As Banton's assistant and later as head designer, she designed for stars as diverse as Mae West, Dorothy Lamour, Barbara Stanwyck, and Audrey Hepburn. Head created designs for all types of films, including Westerns, drawing room comedies, musical comedies, and monster movies. Given the variety of movies and sheer quantity of her production, it is not surprising that she did not establish an "Edith Head look." After Paramount was acquired by Gulf+Western in 1966, Head moved to Universal to become resident costume designer. She also freelanced at MGM, Warner Brothers, Columbia, and Fox. Head was nominated for 35 Academy Awards for best costume design and won eight—a record in the category.

In addition to her film work, Head designed opera costumes, women's uniforms for the Coast Guard and Pan American Airlines, and printed fabrics. She also taught at the University of California at Los Angeles, wrote articles and books, appeared on television and radio talk shows, and lectured to clubs around the country. Unlike many of her colleagues, she did not do custom work and was not interested in dressing women for the world outside of movies.

STAN HERMAN ⧖

BORN New York City, September 17, 1930

AWARDS Coty American Fashion Critics' Awards *Special Award (Designers of Young Fashion)*, 1965; *Winnie*, 1969; *Special Award (loungewear)*, 1975 • Store awards: Burdine's, 1965; Hess, 1967; Joseph Horne, 1968 • Council of Fashion Designers of America (CFDA) *Geoffrey Beene Lifetime Achievement Award*, 2006

Hard working and versatile, Stan Herman has designed hats, dresses, sportswear, lingerie, loungewear, and uniforms. He has also worked as a nightclub entertainer. After earning a B.A. from the University of Cincinnati, he worked in the New York garment industry while attending Traphagen School of Fashion. By 1954, he was designing hats at John Frederics. Herman worked at a number of firms before arriving at Mr. Mort in 1961, leaving in 1971. He has since designed for many other companies, often concurrently, including Henri Bendel, Youthcraft-Charmfit, Slumbertogs, and multiple

Designer Stan Herman.

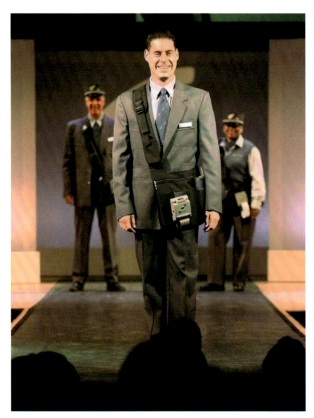

Amtrak employee uniform, 1999.

uniform houses. His designs are always affordable and have sold well on the television network QVC.

Herman believes that fashion is one of life's nourishments—which, like good food, must be grown each season to remain fresh. That is why he prefers to freelance. He recharges his creative energies through painting, singing, sailing, tennis, opera, and community activism. A member of the CFDA since 1967, he served as vice president from 1982–91, then as president from 1991–2006. As president, he played a key role in developing the highly successful fashion industry AIDS fundraiser *Seventh on Sale*.

In 2008, Herman celebrated his tenth year on QVC, where he has expanded his collection to include accessories and housewares. He has also designed uniforms for FedEx, McDonald's, Amtrak, TWA, United Airlines, and JetBlue Airways.

Hermès silk scarves.

FOUNDED Paris, 1837

Thierry Hermès (TARE-ee Air-MEZZ) was born in Germany, but his family moved to Paris in 1827. When he started Hermès in 1837, it specialized in custom luxury bridles for horses, which is why the logo for the brand remains a horse and carriage. The brand served nobility at first, but when son Charles-Émile Hermès took over in 1880, Hermès began retail sales of saddles. With help from his sons, Adolphe and Émile-Maurice, Charles-Émile sold worldwide. In 1900, a major breakthrough occurred when the company introduced a handbag for riders to carry their saddles.

Charles-Émile retired in 1914, but his sons continued introducing new products, such as leather bags with zippers and an accessories collection that debuted in 1920. In 1922, Hermès produced its first leather handbag for women, and in 1937 its signature scarves as well as the iconic Sac à Dépêches bag (which was rebranded the Kelly bag in 1956 after Grace Kelly was photographed shielding herself from the paparazzi with it).

In 1951, Thierry Hermès's great-great-grandson, Jean-Louis Dumas, became head of the company. He maintained the traditional artistry used to craft the bags, many of which take 18 hours to complete. In 1980, the brand's most popular bag, the Birkin, was born—named after British actress Jane Birkin, who had complained to Dumas on a flight they shared that her Kelly bag could not fit all that she needed.

Jean-Louis stepped down in 2006, and his son Pierre-Alexis Dumas took over as creative director. In 2008, he launched Hermès Editeur, a collaboration with famous artists to create limited edition Hermès scarves. From that collaboration the arts initiative Fondation d'Enterprise Hermès was born. Pierre-Alexis has led the company to record sales and design success. In 2012, Pierre-Alexis's cousin, Axel Dumas, was named chief executive officer of the company.

Hermès craftsmanship remains legendary. A colorist for their scarves can chose from over 75,000 hues, and leather ateliers have access to more than 600,000 skins for their bags. Some bags retail for more than $200,000, and many require putting together several dozen pieces of leather. In 2013, Hermès created a $13,000 basketball to celebrate the renovation of its Beverly Hills store.

Spring 2014.

CAROLINA HERRERA

Designer Carolina Herrera.

BORN Maria Caroline Josefina Pacanias y Niño; Caracas, Venezuela, January 8, 1939

AWARDS Dallas Fashion Awards *Fashion Excellence Award* • Council of Fashion Designers of America (CFDA) *Women's Wear Designer of the Year*, 2004 • *Geoffrey Beene Lifetime Achievement Award*, 2008 • Style Network Style Awards *Designer of the Year*, 2012

Bridal, spring 2010.

Carolina Herrera (Hair-AIR-uh) came to fashion from a background where couture clothes and private dressmakers were the norm—she grew up among women who appreciated and wore beautiful clothes. In 1980, she moved to New York City with her husband and family and, encouraged by DIANA VREELAND and others, established her own firm in 1981 with the backing of a South American publisher. Going into the dress business seemed a natural step, as Herrera had worked closely with couturiers, often designing her clothes herself. She quickly established her name and developed a following.

Best known for her designer ready-to-wear—elegant clothes with a couture feeling and feminine details—Herrera also makes clothes to order for private clients, many of whom are her friends.

Her clothes have been worn by ESTÉE LAUDER, Jacqueline Kennedy, and Nancy Reagan. She is also known for making Caroline Kennedy's wedding dress. In 2000, Herrera opened her flagship store on New York's Madison Avenue. In 2001, she launched CH Carolina Herrera, expanding the brand to accessories, handbags, shoes, and eyewear. She has also had licensing agreements in Japan and designed furs for Revillon. In 2003, she launched the perfume Carolina and has since created numerous other fragrances, including 212 Sexy and 212 Sexy Men.

Herrera calls BALENCIAGA her greatest influence. His example can be seen in her emphasis on clear, dramatic lines and her insistence that women can be feminine, chic, and elegant while also being comfortable.

In 2009, Herrera became a U.S. citizen, and in 2011 she received praise for designing the wedding dress of the character Bella in the film *Twilight: Breaking Dawn*. Her daughters Carolina Adriana and Patricia Cristina are now involved in the creative direction and design of Herrera's brand.

Ruffled satin dress, 2008.

♔ TOMMY HILFIGER

Hilfiger has proved himself a gifted marketer and astute businessman. In addition to his core men's business, he has introduced sportswear and intimate apparel for women and juniors, clothes for children, and plus sizes. There are also multiple accessories and fragrances for both men and women, as well as home furnishings.

In 2006, Hilfiger sold the company for $1.6 billion to Apax Partners, which sold it to Phillips-Van Heusen in 2010. The company continues to sell the "classic American cool" aesthetic, and by 2013 had more than 1,200 stores and was distributed in 90 countries. Further branching out in 2013, Hilfiger created a limited edition surfing collection.

Actively involved in a number of charities, Hilfiger serves on the board of directors for the Fresh Air Fund and the Race to Erase MS (Multiple Sclerosis).

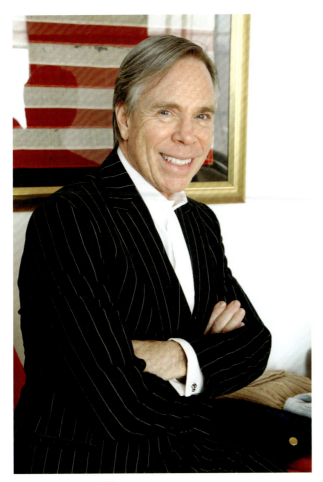

Designer Tommy Hilfiger.

BORN Elmira, New York, March 24, 1951

AWARDS Council of Fashion Designers of America (CFDA) *Menswear Designer of the Year*, 1995; *Geoffrey Beene Lifetime Achievement Award*, 2012 • Parsons *Designer of the Year Award*, 1998

Tommy Hilfiger was something of a fashion boy wonder, starting out by selling hippie chic to New York college kids, and had ten specialty stores in upstate New York by the time he was 26. He moved to New York City and into designing in 1979; his first collection under his own label appeared in 1984, preceded by an advertising campaign that pronounced him the new leader in men's fashion.

His first customers were predominantly middle-class white men. But in the early 1990s, after rapper Snoop Dogg wore one of his shirts on the television show *Saturday Night Live*, sales took off and he immediately began to exploit the urban market. Designs moved toward the street, with baggier pants and more casual styles.

Spring 2014.

HORST P. HORST 📷

BORN Horst Paul Albert Bohrmann; Weissenfels-an-der-Saale, Germany, August 14, 1906
DIED Palm Beach Gardens, Florida, November 18, 1999

Horst P. Horst studied furniture design with Walter Gropius at the School for Applied Arts in Hamburg and went to Paris in 1930 to study architecture with Le Corbusier. In Paris he met and modeled for GEORGE HOYNINGEN-HUENE, who became a lifelong friend, and took up photography. He shot for French *Vogue*, then moved to New York City to work for American *Vogue*. He joined the Army during World War II, working as a photographer. Because his birth name, Bohrmann, was too close to that of a close associate Hitler's, he had it legally changed.

When Horst went to work for *Vogue*, publisher CONDÉ NAST exerted rigid control over photography, demanding that all work be done on large-format studio cameras. Sets were elaborate and every detail was

Model wearing an Emme design, photographed by Horst, 1961.

expected to be perfect, resulting in refined but static images. Despite these limitations, Horst introduced energy into his photographs through dramatic lighting and camera angles, and managed to take risks, giving an edge to the required elegance. With the magazine's acceptance of smaller cameras, he moved outdoors and brought action into his shots. His influences include both Hoyningen-Huene and EDWARD STEICHEN, though he considered Steichen better at portraits than fashion. In addition to fashion, Horst photographed interiors for *Vogue*. His last fashion commission for the magazine was in 1992.

Model Jean Patchett in a bathing suit, photographed by Horst, 1951.

BORN Coshocton, Ohio, September 11, 1956

AWARDS Council of Fashion Designers of America (CFDA) *Media Award in Honor of Eugenia Sheppard*, 2001

Best known as the widely read fashion critic for *The New York Times*, Cathy Horyn is a powerful force in the fashion world. An Ohio native, she went into journalism after learning that a local reporter was sent to New York City twice a year to cover fashion shows. Horyn graduated from Barnard College in 1978 and earned a master's degree in journalism from Northwestern University's Medill School of Journalism. Her first job, from 1986 to 1990, was as a fashion reporter for the *Detroit News*—a post she got by answering a help wanted ad. She then worked as a fashion reporter at *The Washington Post*, and in 1994 became a contributing editor to *Vanity Fair*. She joined *The New York Times* in 1998 and was soon promoted to fashion critic.

Horyn is known for her sharp tongue and has been barred from high-profile fashion shows like those of GIORGIO ARMANI, who uninvited her from his fall 2008 show because he disliked her previous coverage. More recently, Horyn was barred from the SAINT LAURENT Paris shows after writing: "One of the first things the new designer, HEDI SLIMANE, did was to remove 'Yves' from the label, thereby severing a symbolic connection to the founder and everything he stood for, like good taste and feminine power." Horyn has taken on the biggest names in fashion, covering designers, their collections, and media figures with the same intense scrutiny.

Journalist Cathy Horyn.

Horyn has contributed to a number of books, including biographies of fashion titans BILL BLASS and NARCISO RODRIGUEZ. In addition to serving as its fashion critic, Horyn helmed the blog *On the Runway* for *The New York Times*, until her retirement in 2014.

GEORGE HOYNINGEN-HUENE 📷

Photographer George Hoyningen-Huene (left).

BORN Baron George Hoyningen-Huene; St. Petersburg, Russia, September 4, 1900
DIED Los Angeles, September 12, 1968

George Hoyningen-Huene was the son of chief equerry to the tsar; his mother was the daughter of a former American ambassador to Russia. His family fled the Russian Revolution, ending up in London. During World War I, Hoyningen-Huene served with the British; after the war he moved to Paris, where he worked odd jobs, including as an extra in the burgeoning movie industry. There he was able to observe and learn lighting techniques that formed the basis for his later photography. He worked as a sketch artist in his sister's dressmaking firm, and in 1925 was designing and preparing backgrounds in the photo studios of French *Vogue*; by 1926, he was taking photographs.

Hoyningen-Huene was discovered by MAINBOCHER, then *Vogue's* editor, and became chief photographer. In 1935, he moved to New York City and went to work for *Harper's Bazaar*. He lost interest in fashion during the 1940s, moved to Los Angeles in 1946, and taught photography at the Art Center School. He was also a color consultant to Director George Cukor. He traveled widely, taking what he called "archeological photographs" in Greece, Egypt, and Mexico, and subsequently published them in books.

At the start of his career, Hoyningen-Huene was influenced by EDWARD STEICHEN, but soon developed his own style. His fashion photographs have an aristocratic assurance and innate, unforced elegance that seem to come from within. His later, nonfash-

Divers, 1930.

ion photographs have this same quality of confident communication.

BORN Paul Iribarnegaray; Angouleme, France, June 18, 1883

DIED Roquebrune-Cap-Martin, France, September 21, 1935

Paul Iribe (E-reeb) was an illustrator, designer, cartoonist, decorator, and art director. He began his career at 17 in France working for newspapers such as *Le Rire*. Iribe attended l'École des Beaux-Arts in Paris with such famous illustrators as GEORGE BARBIER and eventually worked for illustrated journals *Le Sourire* and *L'Assiette au Beurre*. Iribe found fame in 1908, when fashion designer PAUL POIRET asked him to create promotional illustrations for his designs. The resulting brochure, *Les Robes de Paul Poiret*, escalated both the designer and the illustrator into the fashion spotlight.

Illustrator Paul Iribe.

Les Robes de Paul Poiret, 1908, by Paul Iribe.

Iribe became known for his unique illustrative style, which focused on the details of the garments portrayed. He contributed to French *Vogue* and had a business in Paris that catered to design houses such as CALLOT SOEURS and PAQUIN—providing illustration and advertising services as well as furniture, fabric, and fashion designs.

In 1914, Iribe moved to Hollywood, where he worked for Paramount Studios and Cecil B. DeMille. In 1920, he returned to Paris and became a contributor to the *Gazette du Bon Ton*, which merged with French *Vogue* in 1925. Iribe produced stunning fashion illustrations and worked with legends such as Barbier and Lepape.

Iribe first married in 1911, then again in 1919. But he separated from his second wife in 1928 due to an affair with COCO CHANEL. Iribe was initially hired to design jewelry for her collection, and eventually she became his muse. In 1935, he died while playing tennis at her villa in southeastern France.

There are two books of Iribe's work: *Les Robes de Paul Poiret* and *Paul Iribe: Precurseur de l'art deco,* published in 1983.

MARC JACOBS ▲

BORN New York City, April 9, 1963

AWARDS Council of Fashion Designers of America (CFDA) *Perry Ellis Award for New Fashion Talent*, 1987; *Womenswear Designer of the Year*, 1992, 1997, 2010; *Accessories Designer of the Year, 1998–1999; Lifetime Achievement Award*, 2011 • *Fashion Walk of Fame*, 2002

While still a student at Parsons School of Design, Marc Jacobs was designing sweaters and working as a stock boy at one of New York's Charivari stores. He was hailed as a hot talent on his graduation and built a reputation as an original designer of young fashion with a flair for lighthearted, individualistic clothes when the firm he was working for, Reuban Thomas—the parent company of Sketchbook—went out of business in 1985.

Jacobs and his business partner and creative collaborator Robert Duffy then formed Jacob Duffy Designs Inc. In 1986, they showed the first line of clothing under the Marc Jacobs label. In 1988, Jacobs became vice president and Duffy became president of women's wear at PERRY ELLIS International. Though often well-received by retailers and the press, the collection was never profitable and was dropped in 1993. After freelancing as a design consultant, Jacobs showed a small collection under his name for fall 1994, partly backed by Perry Ellis. The spirited clothes were favorably received.

In 1997, Jacobs sold the company to LVMH and became artistic director at LOUIS VUITTON, creating its first lines for both women and men. He moved to Paris but has continued to show in New York—a men's collection and two women's lines, Marc Jacobs and the

Spring 2009.

lower-priced Marc by Marc Jacobs, launched in 2001. In 2007, he launched a children's wear line, Little Marc Jacobs.

Jacobs has a lot of muses, from Lil' Kim to Victoria Beckham. In 2009, he designed a dress for Miss Piggy, the porcine prima donna puppet from *The Muppets*. In 2013, he became creative director for Diet Coke and was featured in its advertising. Jacobs's spring 2014 ready-to-wear collection for Louis Vuitton was his last for the design house, as he departed to focus on his own label as it moves toward an initial public offering (IPO).

Designer Marc Jacobs.

Fall 2012.

Designer Charles James (center).

BORN Sandhurst, England, July 18, 1906
DIED New York City, September 23, 1978

AWARDS Coty American Fashion Critics' Awards *Winnie,* 1950; *Special Award (innovative cut),* 1954 • *Neiman Marcus Award,* 1953 • *Fashion Walk of Fame,* 2001

Stormy, unpredictable, and fiercely independent, Charles James is considered a genius by many students of fashion, one of the greatest designers and on par with Balenciaga. His father was a colonel in the British Army, his mother an American from a prominent Chicago family; James was educated in both England and America. After studying briefly at the University of Bordeaux, he moved to Chicago and began making hats. He moved to New York City in 1928, then to London, where he produced a small dress collection that he took back to New York. He continued to travel between the two cities before moving to Paris around 1934 to open a couture business.

In Paris, James formed close friendships with many legendary couture figures, including Paul Poiret and Christian Dior. His exceptional ability was recognized by his design peers. Though James admired Elsa Schiaparelli in her unadorned period, Alix Grès was his favorite designer because she thought as he did in terms of shape and sculptural movement.

James returned to New York around 1939 and established his custom house, Charles James, Inc. He worked exclusively for Elizabeth Arden until 1945, and continued to operate in New York and sometimes London until 1958, when he retired from couture to devote himself to painting and sculpture.

⏳ CHARLES JAMES

During the 1960s, James conducted seminars and lectured at the Rhode Island School of Design and Pratt Institute. He also designed a mass-produced line for E.J. Korvette in 1962, invented new techniques for dress patterns, created a dress form, jewelry designs, and even furniture, and occupied himself with preparing his archives. For five years he worked with the illustrator Antonio, who made drawings of all his work to establish a permanent record.

James was a daring innovator, a sculptor with cloth. Every design began with a certain shape, and hours could be spent on the exact placement of a seam. Bold and imaginative, his designs depended on intricate cut and precise seaming rather than trim. He was noted for his handling of heavy silks and fine cloths, and for his batwing, oval cape coat, bouffant ball gowns, dolman wraps, and asymmetrical shapes.

James considered his designs works of art, so it is appropriate that they are in the costume collections of many museums, including the Metropolitan Museum of Art, Brooklyn Museum, Smithsonian Institution, Fashion Institute of Technology, and Victoria and Albert Museum. His ideas remain influential. In 2014, the exhibit Charles James: Beyond Fashion opened at the Metropolitan Museum of Art to critical acclaim.

Gowns, 1948.

ERIC JAVITS 👜

BORN New York City, May 24, 1956

Eric Javits came to hat design through a combination of genes and childhood influences—his grandmother, Lily Javits, was a milliner in the 1920s and later became a painter. As a child, Javits loved to watch her work in her studio. After graduating from the Rhode Island School of Design, where he studied painting, sculpture, drawing, and photography, he became fascinated with how hats could transform the face, creating balance and harmony.

Javits launched his women's hat business in 1985, and within a few years was the hat designer of choice for a large and diverse international clientele. His hats are romantic and flattering and have been worn in films, used in advertising promotions, shown in designers' runway presentations, and featured on the covers and editorial pages of *Vogue, W, Harper's Bazaar, Vanity Fair, Town & Country,* and *ELLE.* Javits's creativity and use of advanced fibers have made wearing hats a more common element of fashion in the 21st century.

In 1995, Javits launched the Squishee, a design he developed in response to a need for hats that could be

Designer Eric Javits.

rolled up for travel without being damaged and protect wearers from the sun's harmful rays. The Squishee concept evolved into an extensive collection of packageable accessories; handbags were added in 1997 and coordinating footwear in 2001.

Javits promotes his business with television appearances and is active in professional organizations; he is a member of the Council of Fashion Designers of America (CFDA) and Millinery Institute of America. Outside business, he pursues his interest in painting and is involved in community service and charitable activities. His work can be found in the archives of the Metropolitan Museum of Art's Costume Institute.

A hat and bag by Eric Javits.

actress Sissy Spacek to disgraced figure skater Tonya Harding. Jensen is celebrated for adding a postmodern twist to buttoned-up, traditional styles. Nicole Kidman is among the London-based designer's many fans.

In 2010, Jenson received rave reviews for his collaboration with American artist Laurie Simmons. Her photographs helped drive his spring/summer women's wear collection.

Designer Peter Jensen.

BORN Logstor, Denmark, 1969

After graduating from London's Central St. Martins College of Art and Design in 1999, Peter Jensen immediately created his first men's wear collection. Within two years he had achieved cult-like status for his playful take on conventional clothing. At first glance his collections for men and women seem quite traditional, with tailored pants, floral print frocks, and Oxford shirts. But a closer viewing might reveal a hemline a bit too high or a trouser fit a bit too tight by mainstream standards.

Jensen's subversive style is also reflected in the women who inspire his collections, from acclaimed

Fall 2012.

J. MENDEL

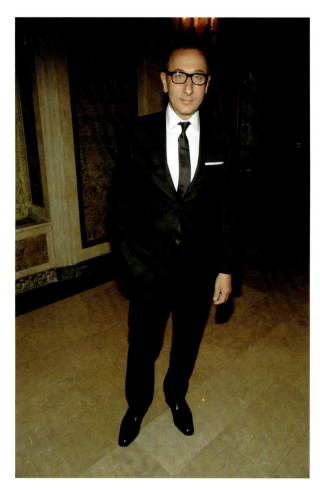

Gilles Mendel for J. Mendel.

FOUNDED Paris, 1870

Established in 1870 by furrier Joseph Breitman, J. Mendel gained a reputation for luxury by keeping the Russian aristocracy in well-designed sable furs. The company has remained family-owned since its inception and today—five generations later—Gilles Mendel has both maintained and expanded that tradition.

Based in New York City since the 1990s, J. Mendel ventured into women's ready-to-wear more or less accidentally. Facing protests from the animal rights group People for the Ethical Treatment of Animals

(PETA), Mendel displayed simple yet elegant sheath dresses in the windows of its flagship store as a distraction. Gilles Mendel debuted his first women's wear collection at New York's Fashion Week in fall 2004. His designs combine skillful, clean tailoring with luxurious details such as fur trim and piping, and have been described as "old world meets new." The collection now includes women's suits and jackets.

Though J. Mendel is undeniably aimed at high-end customers—the spring 2009 collection included colorful fur vests as thin as fabric over floating, draped chiffon dresses—Gilles Mendel has also reinvented the concept of fur in fashion for a new generation. In 2011, he launched the brand's handbag collection and received the National Design Award for Fashion Design from the Smithsonian's Cooper-Hewitt National Design Museum.

Spring 2014.

 # MR. JOHN

BORN John Pico Harberge; Munich, March 14, 1902
DIED New York City, June 25, 1993

AWARDS Coty Fashion Critics' Awards *Special Award (millinery)*, 1943

Gloria Swanson, the Duchess of Windsor, Rosalind Russell, Greta Garbo, Marlene Dietrich, and Marilyn Monroe were just a few who wore hats created by Mr. John. An original and prolific designer, he made every style from close-fitting cloches to picture hats, relying on shape when other milliners were loading hats with flowers and plumes. Wearable and flattering, his creations included such touches of wit as a face-hugging veil studded with a single rhinestone as a beauty mark.

Born in Germany to Rose and Henry Harberger, Mr. John moved to America with his parents. He worked briefly in his mother's Manhattan millinery shop, then in 1928 formed a partnership with Frederic Hirst to

Dotted dress with wide collar, 1972.

make hats under the name John-Frederics. He legally changed his name to John-Frederics but in 1948, after splitting with Hirst, opened the Mr. John salon on East 57th Street and changed his name again, this time to John P. John. He designed accessories, women's clothing, and furs, but hats were his main claim to fame. The business closed in 1970, though he continued to design for private clients until a year or so before his death.

Designer Mr. John (right) with model.

BETSEY JOHNSON

BORN Wethersfield, Connecticut, August 10, 1942

AWARDS Coty American Fashion Critics' Awards *Winnie*, 1971 • Council of Fashion Designers of America (CFDA) *Special Award (timeless talent)*, 1998–1999 • *Fashion Walk of Fame*, 2002

Betsey Johnson attended Pratt Institute for a year, then went to Syracuse University, graduating cum laude and a member of Phi Beta Kappa. In her senior year she was guest editor at *Mademoiselle*, where the sweaters she made for editors earned her a job designing for Paraphernalia boutiques. Her original and irreverent collections there established her, at age 22, as a leader of the youth-oriented, anti–Seventh Avenue design movement of the 1960s. She also became part of Andy Warhol's Factory scene. Edie Sedgwick was her house model, and she designed for the Velvet Underground's John Cale, who she married in 1968.

In 1969, Johnson and two friends started the boutique Betsey Bunky Nini; she has designed for Alley Cat, Michael Milea, and Butterick Patterns. In 1978, with partner Chantal Bacon, she formed Betsey Johnson, Inc., to manufacture sportswear, bodywear, and dresses. She also operates Betsey Johnson retail stores. In addition to apparel, her line includes handbags, fragrances, eyewear, watches, jewelry, hosiery, and swimwear.

Johnson has always designed to please herself. Over the years her ideas have included the "Basic Betsey," a clinging t-shirt dress in mini, midi, or maxi lengths; a clear vinyl slip-dress complete with a kit of paste-on stars, fishes, and numbers; and the "Noise Dress," with loose grommets at the hem. There have been tutu skirts, bubble minis and microminis, pretty suits that managed to be both cheeky and wearable, and dresses that balance the cute and risqué. She has worked in a variety of fabrics, from cotton-and-spandex knits to rayon challis to

Designer Betsey Johnson.

heavyweight spandex in vibrant colors, and designed her own fabrics and knits.

Imaginative and uninhibited, Johnson designs for spirited nonconformists like herself—enough of whom exist to have kept her in business for more than 30 years. She has consistently kept her clothes affordable for younger customers, only adding a more expensive Ultra line in the late 1990s, which she says was necessary to expand the business.

Johnson is a survivor of breast cancer, and in 2003 the CFDA invited her to be an honorary chair of its *Fashion Targets Breast Cancer* initiative. In 2004, the

National Breast Cancer Coalition awarded her another honor for her continued fight against the disease. Johnson, often viewed as fashion's "wild child," has even used her designers and staff members as models, shocking—and delighting—the fashion world with her rebellious streak. Her most signature quirk is the cartwheel with which she graces audiences at the end of her shows.

In 2012, Johnson celebrated 40 years of her brand, but was forced to file for bankruptcy. In 2013, she and her daughter Lulu debuted a reality television show on the Style Network, *XOX Betsey Johnson*, documenting the struggles in their relationship while planning for their future careers and rebuilding after bankruptcy.

Spring 2014.

Spring 2014.

STEPHEN JONES 👜

Designer Stephen Jones (center).

BORN West Kirby, England, May 31, 1957

AWARDS British Government *Order of the British Empire (OBE)*, 2010

In 1984, Stephen Jones became the first British milliner to work in Paris, designing hats for JEAN PAUL GAULTIER, THIERRY MUGLER, and REI KAWAKUBO of Comme des Garçons. He has worked with ZANDRA RHODES, JOHN GALLIANO, and VIVIENNE WESTWOOD, among other English designers. Combining fantasy with confident style, his hats have been described as witty, outrageous, and daring; he continues to collaborate with designers around the world.

Educated at Liverpool College, Jones went on to study at Central St. Martins College of Art and Design, graduating in 1979. He immediately began making hats for his friends in pop music, including Steve Strange, Boy George, and members of Duran Duran. In 1980, he opened his first salon in a store called PX in Covent Garden, and soon established a burgeoning custom clientele. Jones has represented Great Britain in fashion shows in New York, Montreal, Helsinki, and Tokyo, and his hats are in the permanent collections of the Victoria and Albert Museum in London, Brooklyn Museum, and Australian National Gallery in Canberra. They can also be seen in the Louvre, Kyoto Museum, Australian National Gallery, and Museum at the Fashion Institute of Technology.

Other design projects have run the gamut from scarfs, handkerchiefs, and gloves to interior design and television commercials. Jones has also curated exhibitions—his largest, in 2009 at the Victoria and Albert Museum, was called *Hats: An Anthology by Stephen Jones*. It received more than 100,000 viewers and traveled the world for the next four years. Jones's designs are favorites of members of the Royal British Court such as Catherine, Duchess of Cambridge, and celebrities such as Sarah Jessica Parker.

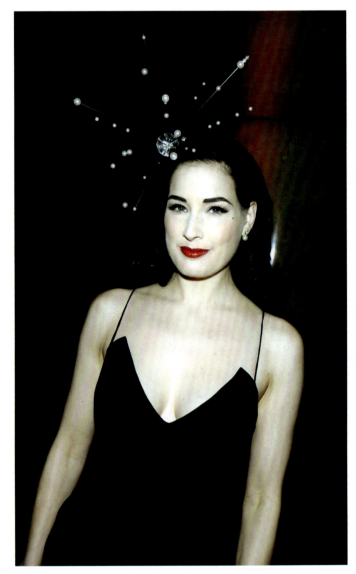

Dita Von Teese in a Stephen Jones design.

Designer Woolfgang Joop.

BORN Potsdam, Germany, November 18, 1944

AWARDS *Fil d'Or*, 1983

Wolfgang Joop (Yoop) is one of Germany's most celebrated designers. Born near the Sanssouci Palace—the palace of Frederick the Great—he grew up surrounded by inspiration. He studied advertising, psychology, and art education at the University of Braunschweig but dropped out before completing his degree. He then went to work as an art professor at the University of Fine Arts in Berlin and as a freelance designer for design houses in France, Italy, and Germany.

In 1970, with the help of his former wife Karin Benatzky, Joop entered a fashion design competition and won the top three prizes. He presented his first collection in 1979, and in 1981 launched the JOOP! label. He showed his first ready-to-wear line in 1982 and began designing

Spring/summer 1996.

◢ WOLFGANG JOOP

a fur collection in 1987. He later added eyewear, knitwear, shoes, accessories, and perfume to the label's roster. In 1998, Joop sold 95 percent of his company, and in 2001 completely divested of it.

Three years later Joop returned with Wunderkind, a line for contemporary, sophisticated, independent women. The clothes are soft and fluid but retain structural and masculine elements. Wunderkind was shown in 2004 at New York's Fashion Week and made its Paris premiere in fall 2006 with the spring/summer 2007 collection. Wunderkind was sold in more than 100 stores, but in 2011 there were rumors that it was being restructured. More than a year of inactivity followed. Wunderkind returned in 2012.

A well-known illustrator, Joop now draws professionally. His illustrations have been exhibited and are part of several museums' permanent collections. He has also written editorials for several magazines and newspapers, including *Zurichen* and *Der Spiegel*.

Joop is also known for his charitable works. He is involved in Dunkeziffer e.V., which helps children who have been sexually and physically abused. He has also worked with Hamburg Leuchtfeuer, which supports HIV-positive people.

Spring 2010.

NORMA KAMALI ▼

BORN Norma Arraes; New York City, June 27, 1945

AWARDS Coty American Fashion Critics' Awards *Winnie,* 1981; *Return Award,* 1982; *Hall of Fame Award,* 1983 • Council of Fashion Designers of America (CFDA) *Outstanding Women's Fashions,* 1982; *Innovative Use of Video in Presentation and Promotion of Fashion,* 1985; *Board of Directors' Tribute,* 2005 • Fashion Institute of Design & Merchandising (Los Angeles) *FIDM Award,* 1984 • Fashion Group International *Night of Stars Award,* 1986 • *Fashion Walk of Fame,* 2002

Of Basque and Lebanese descent, Norma Kamali grew up on New York's Upper East Side. Her mother made most of her daughter's clothes as well as costumes for neighborhood plays, dollhouse furniture—"anything and everything." Kamali studied fashion illustration at

Designer Norma Kamali.

the Fashion Institute of Technology, graduating in 1964. Unable to find work in the field, she took an office job with an airline, using the travel opportunities to spend weekends in London.

In 1968, she married Eddie Kamali, an Iranian student. They opened a tiny shop in New York where they sold European imports, largely from England, as well as Kamali's designs. In 1974, they moved to a larger, second floor space on Madison Avenue and Kamali began making suits, lace dresses, and delicates. Divorced in 1977, she established a retail boutique and wholesale firm the next year on West 56th Street, naming it OMO Norma Kamali (OMO stands for On My Own). In 1983, she moved her thriving business across the street into a multilevel structure finished in concrete. Monitors there show films of everything she designs, from accessories to couture.

Kamali was first recognized for adventurous, body-conscious clothes with large, removable shoulder pads. Definitely not for the timid, her clothes were collected by members of the fashion avant-garde such as Donna Summer, Diana Ross, and Barbra Streisand.

Subsequent collections have included swimsuits cut daringly high on the hip, children's wear, lingerie, and a moderately priced line for the Jones Apparel Group. She has since added fragrance and beauty products, as well

Spring 2013.

Dancers at the Metropolitan Opera House perform "Rabbit and Rogue" in costumes by Kamali, 2008.

of commerce in making a living. The same year, the school inducted her into its Hall of Fame, which honors alumni who have contributed to the arts.

By 2006, Kamali was collaborating with several companies. She partnered with Everlast on a sportswear collection, and with Spiegel to create Norma Kamali Timeless. In 2007, she created a collection for Walmart, normakamali, that was released in fall 2008. In 2010, Kamali was named to the CFDA Board of Directors, and in 2011 she donated the iconic swimsuit that graced Farrah Fawcett to the Smithsonian Institution.

as eyewear and innovative activewear. In 1976, Farrah Fawcett wore a red swimsuit by Kamali in what became the top-selling poster in American history. In 1978, Kamali's draped and shirred jumpsuits, using parachute fabric and drawstrings, were included in the *Vanity Fair* show at the Costume Institute of the Metropolitan Museum of Art, where they are now part of the permanent collection. She has continued to include parachute materials in her work.

Starting with her *Fall Fantasy* video in 1984, Kamali began using technology and direct mail to sell her designs. Her fall 1996 collection was presented online, and since 1998 it has been possible to shop her website for anything Norma Kamali—from shoes to swimwear to wedding gowns.

In 1997, Kamali started helping art students at New York's Washington Irving High School (her alma mater) form businesses so that they could learn the importance

Spring 2013.

CHRISTOPHER KANE ▼

BORN North Lanarkshire, Scotland, 1982

Christopher Kane is known for his classic yet innovative designs, and *Vogue* has hailed him as the "Mad Hatter of British Fashion." He was first noticed at Central St. Martins College of Art and Design, where he won the prestigious Harrods Design Award while in graduate school. The following year, in 2006, he started his label with the help of his sister and business partner Tammy. Kane's debut runway show in 2006 at London Fashion Week was highly anticipated by fashion designers and editors, and helped establish his reputation. In 2007, DONATELLA VERSACE called him her favorite designer, saying that his work reminded her of work she had done with her brother GIANNI VERSACE. That year, Kane created limited edition jewelry for Swarovski as well as a capsule collection for Topshop.

Designer Christopher Kane.

Spring 2014.

In 2009, he launched a second collection for Topshop and showed a spring/summer collection for Donatella Versace's Versus line in Milan. Featured on net-a-porter.com, the collection sold out in 24 hours. Kane then launched a line of t-shirts based on the monkey-print dress from the collection, which catapulted the piece into universally high demand. In 2010, Kane launched his first men's wear line and resort collection. In 2011, he collaborated with J Brand, creating a line of funky colored jeans. But Kane knew that his brand needed help, so he and Tammy brought in their older sister, Sandra.

After designing eight collections, Kane left Versus in 2012. He said that he was indebted to Donatella Versace but needed to concentrate on his own business. In 2013, Kering (formerly PPR) bought 51% of the Christopher Kane brand, adding to its collection of luxury brands such as ALEXANDER McQUEEN and BALENCIAGA. Kane's first store opened on Mount Street in London at the end of 2013. Chief Executive Officer Alexandre de Brettes called it "the first step in a new chapter for the Christopher Kane brand." The brand is also sold at retailers such as Harvey Nichols, Barneys, and Browns. In 2014, Kane launched his first handbag collection at London Fashion Week.

Designer Karl Kani.

BORN Carl Williams; Brooklyn, New York, 1968

Called the "Godfather of Urban Sportswear," Karl Kani grew up in a tough Brooklyn neighborhood where he saw violence kill many of his friends. He decided that he would take a different path and focused on his flair for dressing. Kani moved to California, where he helped a friend open Season's Sportswear in Crenshaw in 1989. There he changed his last name to Kani—a twist on "Can I"—and changed his first name from Carl to Karl.

During that time, Kani met Carl Jones, owner of Threads 4 Life Corporation. Jones hired Kani for the company's Afro-centric Cross Colours line, and Kani soon found his niche when a style of jeans he designed raised the line's profits from $15 million to $89 million in one year. Kani expanded the colors available and made the jeans larger because, he said, "black men do not like tight jeans; we buy them two to three sizes bigger"—creating the first comfortable baggy pants.

In 1994, dissatisfied with Threads 4 Life, Kani took $500,000 in profits and created the Kani brand. Kani wanted to stay true to his roots and create looks from the streets, but he also wanted to appeal to more mature customers. Many rappers have worn his clothing, including Tupac, Biggie Smalls, Sean Combs, and Snoop Dogg.

The brand became so popular that counterfeiters proliferated, so Kani added a message to patches on his clothes that reads: "Inspired by the vitality of the streets of Brooklyn, New York. Karl Kani, the young African-American designer of Karl Kani Jeans, encourages you to follow your dreams and accomplish your goals. Wear the clothing that represents the knowledge of African-American creativity and determination. Recognize the signature that symbolizes African-American unity and pride . . . Peace, Karl Kani."

Kani has created many sub-brands—including Kani Ladies, Karl Kani for Life, Karl Kani Black Label, and Karl Kani Boys—and sold many of his collections in Europe and Japan. In 2008, he created Kani Kouture Exclusively for Saks and showed at L.A. Fashion Week. The Kani brand still reflects the street culture of America's urban hubs while maintaining its high-fashion appeal. After a brief hiatus, the Kani brand relaunched its American collection in 2013.

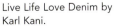

Live Life Love Denim by Karl Kani.

DONNA KARAN ▲

BORN Donna Ivy Faske; Forest Hills, New York, October 4, 1948

AWARDS Coty American Fashion Critics' Awards "*Winnie*" *(with* Louis Dell'olio*)*, 1977; *Hall of Fame Award (with Louis Dell'Olio)*, 1982; *Special Award (Women's Wear)* • Fashion Group International *Night of Stars Award*, 1986; *Superstar Award* (first American), 2003 • Council of Fashion Designers of America (CFDA) *Special Award*, 1985; *Special Award*, 1986; *Women's Wear Designer of the Year*, 1992, 1996; *Lifetime Achievement Award*, 2004 • Parsons *Fashion Critics Award for Influence in Head-to-Toe Dressing*, 1996 • *Fashion Walk of Fame*, 2001

Designer Donna Karan.

Resort 2013.

Daughter of a fashion model and a haberdasher, Donna Karan was in fashion from childhood. After her second year at Parsons School of Design, she took a summer job with Anne Klein and never returned to school. She was fired by Klein after nine months and went to work for another sportswear house, returning to Klein in 1968 and becoming associate designer in 1971. When Klein became ill in 1973, Karan became head designer and asked Louis Dell'olio, a school friend, to join her as co-designer. While it is impossible to separate her designs at Anne Klein from Dell'Olio's, their hallmark was always wearability—terrific blazers, well-cut pants, strong coats, sarong skirts, easy dresses, and classic sportswear looks with a stylish edge and element of tough chic.

In 1984, Karan and her late husband, sculptor Stephan Weiss, founded Donna Karan New York with the backing of Takihyo Corporation of Japan, Anne Klein's parent company. Karan's first collection under her own label immediately established her as a fashion star. It was based on a bodysuit worn under long or short skirts, blouses, or pants, making a complete, integrated wardrobe. These pieces were combined with

Karan is on the board of directors of the CFDA, Design Industries Foundation Fighting AIDS (DIFFA), and Parsons School of Design, where she also lectures and is a critic. She has also been involved in numerous activities linked to social causes, including her Urban Zen Initiative founded in 2007. In 2010, Karan launched a denim line, and in 2012 she received the Clinton Global Citizen Award for her work in Haiti through Urban Zen, which uses philanthropy and commerce to create change by helping develop, market, and present the work of Haitian artisans to the Western world.

Right: Spring 2009.
Left: Fall 2007.

well-tailored coats and bold accessories, everything made of luxurious materials. Because the clothes followed the body closely without excess detail or overt sexiness, the effect was both spare and sensuous. Karan only designed clothes and accessories that she would wear—the best of everything for a woman who could be a mother, a traveler, and perhaps a business owner, someone who does not have time to shop.

Karan's company has grown into a giant with myriad divisions, including the hugely successful DKNY brand launched in 1989 and its numerous offshoots. Donna Karan Men was founded in 1991, followed in 1992 by DKNY Men. Home furnishings, eyewear, accessories, and underwear are all part of the mix; fragrances and cosmetics were licensed to ESTÉE LAUDER in 1997. There are also retail stores worldwide, both company-owned and licensed. The firm went public in 1996, and in 2001 was acquired by LVMH. Karan still has creative control of the company's fashion lines.

Pre-fall 2012.

REI KAWAKUBO ♟

Designer Rei Kawakubo.

BORN Tokyo, October 11, 1942

AWARDS Mainichi Fashion Awards, 1983 • Fashion Group International *Night of Stars Award*, 1986 • Veuve Cliquot *Business Woman of the Year*, 1991 • French Ministry of Culture *Chevalier de l'Ordre des Arts et des Lettres*, 1993 • Council of Fashion Designers of America (CFDA) *International Award*, 2012

The most avant of Tokyo's avant-garde, Rei Kawakubo (Ray KUH-wah-coo-bo) was a literature major at Keio University in Tokyo, graduating in 1965. She started designing women's clothes in 1969 under the label Comme des Garçons after working in the advertising department of a textile firm and as a freelance stylist. Comme des Garçons Co., Ltd. was established in 1973. Kawakubo is president of the company, which has since expanded to men's wear, knits, fragrances, home furnishings, and freestanding stores worldwide. Her collections are shown in Tokyo and Paris.

Kawakubo originally designed almost exclusively in gray and black; she has since added subtle touches of color. She plays with asymmetrical shapes, and drapes and wraps the body with cotton, canvas, and linen, often torn and slashed. In her early Paris showings, she emphasized the violence of her designs by making up her models with an extreme pallor and painted bruises and cuts.

Kawakubo has been successful in America with in-store boutiques and freestanding shops so minimalist

Commes des Garçons Fall 2009.

that there is often nothing on display. In spring 1987, the Fashion Institute of Technology included her clothes in an exhibition, *Three Women: Kawakubo, VIONNET, McCARDELL*.

Kawakubo created the 2008 fall guest designer collection for H&M, designing men's, women's, and children's clothing. Wearers can still infuse her clothes with their own spirit and individuality—showing how fashion can become art.

Comme des Garçons Spring 2014.

⬛ ELIZABETH KECKLEY

BORN Virginia, circa 1818
DIED Washington, D.C., 1907

Born into slavery, Elizabeth Keckley's perseverance and skills as a seamstress secured her a place in fashion history. Her early life was one of hardship: fathered by a white plantation owner, she was separated from her family in Virginia and sent to work for her master's son in North Carolina, where she endured physical and sexual abuse. At the age of 14 she gave birth to an illegitimate son. She was later sent to St. Louis with her master's daughter and her husband and, in her words, soon "acquired something of a reputation as a seamstress and dressmaker." She supported the entire family with her earnings. Eventually one of her St. Louis patrons, impressed with her talents and her integrity, loaned her the funds needed to secure freedom for herself and her son.

After her emancipation, Keckley moved to Washington, D.C. in 1860 and established her own dressmaking business. Her reputation in the city grew, and one of her clients recommended her to First Lady Mary Todd Lincoln.

Mary Todd Lincoln wearing an Elizabeth Keckley dress for the inauguration of Abraham Lincoln, 1861.

Keckley designed several gowns for Lincoln—many of which received glowing praise in newspapers—and her business thrived.

Keckley also became the troubled Lincoln's closest confidante—a relationship that later soured when Keckley wrote *Behind the Scenes*, a memoir that included details of her time in the White House. In 1892, Keckley joined the faculty of Wilberforce University in Ohio (the first private university for African-Americans), teaching in the Department of Sewing and Domestic Science Arts. She returned to Washington, D.C. six years later and lived the rest of her life at the Home for Destitute Women and Children.

Designer Elizabeth Keckley.

PATRICK KELLY ▲

Designer Patrick Kelly (front center) and models.

BORN Vicksburg, Mississippi, September 24, 1954
DIED January 1, 1990

Patrick Kelly was an African-American designer whose work was characterized by energy, exuberance, and an envelope-pushing critique of staid fashion culture. Kelly studied art history and African-American history at Jackson State University in Mississippi, and after graduation, moved to Atlanta, Georgia, to work as a window dresser for YVES SAINT LAURENT's Rive Gauche boutique. In the early 1980s, an anonymous admirer bought Kelly a one-way ticket to Paris; he moved there immediately and began selling his flamboyant garments at street fairs and flea markets. In 1984, his designs caught the attention of the Parisian boutique Victoire, which furnished him with a workshop and showroom. Within three years, his work had been purchased by the Warnoac fashion conglomerate for millions. The deal put Kelly's designs into Henri Bendel, Bergdorf Goodman, and Bloomingdale's.

Kelly was known for his attention to detail: he used whimsical mismatched buttons, fringe, patterns, and prints. He also gained recognition for his savvy critique of racial politics. Kelly's designs often challenged traditional conceptions of African-Americans by presenting darkly comic interpretations of racial themes. Kelly claimed to be as equally inspired by the couture work of ALIX GRÈS and YVES SAINT LAURENT as by the fashion in a church on Sunday.

Like many designers, Kelly struggled to fund his elaborate designs, but with the help of high-profile

Top: Spring/summer 1989.
Bottom: Spring/summer 1989.

patrons such as Grace Jones and Bette Davis, his clothes were known nationally and internationally. His immense skill was also recognized by others in his field. In 1988, Kelly became the first American to be accepted into the Chambre Syndicale de la Couture Parisienne, an organization of prestigious French designers. Two years later, Kelly died of complications from AIDS.

Designer Kenzo.

BORN Kyoto, Japan, February 28, 1940

The son of hotel keepers, Kenzo won top prizes in art school and began his fashion career in Tokyo designing patterns for a magazine. He arrived in Paris in 1964, one of the first of his compatriots to make the move, and found work with a style bureau. He sold sketches to FÉRAUD and freelanced for several lines, including Rodier.

Spring 2014.

In 1970, Kenzo opened his own boutique, decorating every inch with jungle patterns, and named it Jungle Jap. The clothes were an immediate success with fashion models and individualists.

Money was scarce for his first ready-to-wear collection, so although designed for fall/winter, it was made entirely of cotton—much of it quilted. He showed it to the sound of rock music and used mannequins instead of live models.

Spring 2009.

These innovations, like many other Kenzo ideas, started a trend.

Kenzo was always a prolific originator of fresh ideas, known for spirited combinations of textures and patterns in young, wearable clothes that were often copied. His designs have been widely distributed in America in both his own shops and in-store boutiques. A renowned party-lover, he celebrated his 1999 retirement with a two-hour extravaganza, presenting his final collection and a retrospective of his 30-year career to 4,000 guests. The Kenzo brand has continued with Gilles Rosier as designer of women's wear and a succession of designers for men. It is now part of the LVMH fashion empire. In 2005, Kenzo reemerged as a home fashions designer with his Gokan Kobo line of tableware, furniture, and home accessories. Carol Lim and Humberto Leon are the current creative directors at Kenzo.

KENZO

NAEEM KHAN ⬛

BORN Mumbai, India, May 21, 1958

Naeem Khan grew up with a grandfather and father who made intricate clothes for Indian royalty. Khan was so intrigued by the fashion industry that when he was a teenager he moved to America and, with the help of his father, secured a position at HALSTON. There he learned about draping and clean, elegant styles. Khan also learned to merge the worlds of clean and intricate, creating his own aesthetic. Before launching his own business, Khan befriended and learned from such great artists as Andy Warhol and YVES SAINT LAURENT. Khan honed his skills in the industry for decades before starting his company in 2003.

Khan's clothing has been described as reflecting the influences of India, but internationally appealing. Khan began selling to Bergdorf Goodman's, Neiman Marcus,

Spring 2014.

Designer Naeem Khan.

and Harrods. His lines feature exquisite gowns and chic separates. Khan's collections soon became sought after by stars such as Penélope Cruz, Beyoncé, and Eva Longoria. In 2009 and 2011, Michelle Obama wore his gowns to two state dinners—one for Indian Prime Minister Manmohan Singh and the other for German Chancellor Angela Merkel.

In 2008, Khan was inducted as a member of the Council of Fashion Designers of America (CFDA). In 2009, he premiered a collection for HSN that included cocktail dresses and separates. It sold out in minutes. He has also designed for movies such as *Sex and the City* and *Dreamgirls*, and today is one of the most sought-after designers in the industry.

Khan is married to jewelry designer Ranjana Khan, and together they work for charities and support nonprofit organizations such as Wishwas, which empowers low-income immigrant women and assimilates them in society by training them in vocational skills to make them financially self-sufficient.

Designer Emmanuelle Khanh.

BORN Plain, France, September 7, 1937

AWARDS French Ministry of Culture *Chevalier de l'Ordre des Arts et des Lettres*, 1989

Emmanuelle Khanh started designing in 1959 with a job at Cacherel. Although she began her fashion career as a fitting model for BALENCIAGA and GIVENCHY, she

▲ EMMANUELLE KHANH

rebelled against couture in her work and is credited with starting the youth fashion movement in France. She was a revolutionary who once said, "This is the century of sex. I want to make the sexiest clothes."

She first became known for "The Droop," a slim, soft, close-to-the-body dress, contrasting sharply with the structured couture clothes of the time. Her clothes had a lanky 1930s feeling with signature details such as dog ear collars, droopy lapels on long, fitted jackets, dangling cufflink fastenings, and half-moon moneybag pockets. Her work reflected an individual approach symbolic of the 1960s. Khanh survived the era and continued to produce soft, imaginative fashions. In 2002, her company was acquired by France Luxury Group, a new conglomerate that at the same time bought the JACQUES FATH and Jean-Louis Scherrer brands.

She is married to Vietnamese engineer and furniture designer, Nyuen Manh (Quasar) Khanh, also prominent in avant-garde fashion circles of the 1960s.

Knit poncho, 1970.

Spring/summer 1976.

BARRY KIESELSTEIN-CORD Ŏ

Designer Barry Kieselstein-Cord.

A selection of Kieselstein-Cord fine jewelry pieces.

BORN New York City, November 6, 1943

AWARDS Art Directors Club of New York, 1967 • Society of Illustrators New York, 1969 • Coty American Fashion Critics' Awards *Outstanding Jewelry Design*, 1979; *Excellence in Women's Wear Design*, 1984 • Council of Fashion Designers of America (CFDA) *Excellence in Design*, 1981

Barry Kieselstein-Cord comes from a family of designers and architects, including his mother, father, and both grandfathers. His formal education included study at Parsons School of Design, New York University, and the American Craft League. He first attracted the attention of the fashion world with his jewelry, which was introduced at Georg Jensen around 1972. By the end of the decade, his designs included handbags and other accessories sold across America and abroad.

Working mainly in gold and platinum, Kieselstein-Cord starts with a sketch, moving from there directly into metal or wax depending on whether the design will be reproduced by hand or from a mold. Each piece is finished by hand. His jewelry has been praised for its elegance, beauty, and superb craftsmanship, which is also true of his handbags and other accessories. While he aims at timeless design not tied to fashion, pieces such as the Winchester buckle and palm cuffs have been collected by fashion designers and celebrities everywhere. In 2010, the company took a hiatus, but it reemerged in 2012 with a book titled *Awarded* and an exhibition at the Eckert Fine Art Gallery in Millerton, New York.

In addition to his designing career, Kieselstein-Cord has been an art director and producer of films at an advertising agency. He has also served as vice president of the CFDA.

⬙ CHARLES KLEIBACKER

Designer Charles Kleibacker.

BORN Cullman, Alabama, November 20, 1921
DIED Columbus, Ohio, January 3, 2010

Charles Kleibacker was exposed to fashion at an early age, having grown up in the ready-to-wear department of his parent's department store in Cullman, Alabama. After graduating from the University of Notre Dame, he

White dress.

worked as a reporter in his home state and then moved to New York City to work as an advertising copywriter. He later took a job for the singer Hildegarde, who took him to Paris and exposed him to haute couture. Kleibacker then worked as an assistant designer to Antonio Castillo of the house of LANVIN in Paris for three years. He returned to New York in 1958 to design for Nettie Rosenstein.

Inspired in part by MADELINE VIONNET's delicate and meticulously made creations, Kleibacker opened his own studio in Manhattan in 1960. His designs were known for their traditional couture look and produced in limited numbers. Diahann Caroll and Irving Berlin are among the celebrities who wore his garments.

From 1984 to 1995, Kleibacker was director and curator of the Department of Consumer and Textile Sciences at Ohio State University. In 2001, the Kent State University Museum held an exhibition titled *Charles Kleibacker: Master of Bias*. In 2008, the Ohio Arts Council's Riffe Gallery presented *Kleibacker: New York Designer to Ohio Curator*, a retrospective of his work.

Design cut on the bias.

ANNE KLEIN ▼

Designer Anne Klein.

BORN Brooklyn, New York, August 3, 1923
DIED New York City, March 19, 1974

AWARDS Coty American Fashion Critics' Awards *Winnie,* 1955; *Return Award,* 1969; *Hall of Fame Award,* 1971 • *Neiman Marcus Award,* 1959, 1969 • *Fashion Walk of Fame,* 2001

Anne Klein was just 15 when she got her first job, as a sketch artist on New York's Seventh Avenue. The next year she joined Varden Petites as a designer, and in 1948 she and her first husband Ben Klein formed Junior Sophisticates. She designed for Mallory Leathers in 1965, operated Anne Klein Studio on West 57th Street in New York, and in 1968, with Sanford Smith and her second husband, Chip Rubenstein, formed Anne Klein & Co., wholly owned by Takihyo Corporation of Japan.

Early in her career, Klein became known for her pioneering work in shifting junior-size clothes from little-girl cuteness to adult sophistication. At Junior Sophisticates there was the skimmer dress with its own

jacket, long, pleated plaid skirts with blazers, and gray flannel used with white satin. At Anne Klein & Co. the emphasis was on investment sportswear, an interrelated wardrobe of blazers, skirts, pants, and sweaters, with slinky jersey dresses for evening. Klein was also a pioneer in recognizing the value of sportswear as a way of dressing uniquely suited to the American woman's way of life. In 1973, she was among five American and five French designers invited to show at the *Grand Divertissement* at the Palace of Versailles. The other Americans were BILL BLASS, STEPHEN BURROWS, HALSTON, and OSCAR DE LA RENTA.

After Klein's death, the firm continued with DONNA KARAN and LOUIS DELL'OLIO as co-designers. When Karan left in 1984 to establish her own label, Dell'Olio became sole designer. Struggling to redefine its identity, the Klein company ran through a dizzying succession

Spring/summer 1994.

of designers, including RICHARD TYLER. In 1999, it was acquired by Kasper ASL, Ltd., which in 2001 changed designers once more, naming Charles Nolan. Nolan, formerly with Ellen Tracy, left in 2003.

Meanwhile, after many label changes, Anne Klein became Anne Klein New York while Anne Klein 2 was rechristened AK Anne Klein. Furs, coats, swimwear, sleepwear, and accessories were added to existing licenses. The label was purchased by The Jones Group, Inc. in 2003. Designer ISABEL TOLEDO was hired in 2007 to design a top-tier collection, but the line was shut down after two seasons. From 2008 to 2012, Ted Kim, who had previously designed for DONNA KARAN and MICHAEL KORS, was vice president of design.

Actress Candice Bergen wearing a look from Anne Klein for Mallory Leathers, 1967.

CALVIN KLEIN ♜

Designer Calvin Klein.

BORN New York City, November 19, 1942

AWARDS Coty American Fashion Critics' Awards *Winnie,* 1973; *Return Award, 1974; Hall of Fame Award,* 1975; *Special Award (fur design for Alixandre),* 1975; *Special Award (contribution to international status of American fashion),* 1979; *Women's Apparel,* 1981 • Council of Fashion Designers of America (CFDA) *Best American Collection*: 1981, 1983, 1987; *Womenswear Designer of the Year,* 1993; *Menswear Designer of the Year,* 1993 • *Fashion Walk of Fame,* 2000

Calvin Klein attended New York's School of Industrial Art (now the High School of Art and Design) and Fashion Institute of Technology, where he graduated in 1962. He spent five years at three large firms as apprentice and designer; his first recognition came for his coats.

In 1968, with long-time friend Barry Schwartz, he formed Calvin Klein Ltd., which has developed into an extensive design empire. Besides women's ready-to-wear, sportswear, and men's wear, it has produced everything from jeans to furs to shoes to women's undergarments. He has also created bed linens, cosmetics, skin care, and fragrances. Calvin Klein Home, a luxury home furnishings collection, was introduced in 1995. Klein has promoted his products with provocative, sexy, often controversial advertising, notably for his jeans and for Obsession, the first of his women's fragrances. He created the boxer brief and helped escalate the trend of "sagging" pants.

Considered the foremost exponent of spare, intrinsically American style, Klein has maintained a

Spring 2014.

consistent vision while remaining completely in touch with the times. He has said, "It's important not to confuse simplicity with uninteresting," and executes his refined, sportswear-based shapes in luxurious natural fibers such as cashmere, linen, and silk, as well as leather and suede. His color preferences are earth tones and neutrals—his hallmark is a lean, supple elegance and an offhand, understated luxury.

In 1993, as part of a benefit at the Hollywood Bowl for AIDS Project Los Angeles, Klein presented a 20-minute showing of his collection that also marked his 25th anniversary in business. In 2002, he hired FRANCISCO COSTA as creative director of his women's wear line. Later that year, the company was sold to Phillips-Van Heusen, at which point Klein retired. The company's current creative director for men's wear is Italo Zucchelli and the creative director for Calvin Klein, ck Calvin Klein, and Calvin Klein Jeans is Kevin Carrigan.

Spring 2014.

1992 advertisement featuring Mark Wahlberg and Kate Moss.

LLOYD KLEIN

BORN Montreal, Canada, February 15, 1967

Lloyd Klein was a student of architecture, but his interest turned to fashion after attending a GIVENCHY show. He began studying the works of YVES SAINT LAURENT, HALSTON, and JACQUES FATH to educate himself on couture. In 1994, he presented his first collection in Paris, and that fall he was appointed head designer at ALIX GRÉS. He was quickly recognized by many critics as a master of drapery, technical cutting, and fit. Klein remained with Grés for five seasons, then left to establish his own label. He set up headquarters in America in 1998 and began showing at New York Fashion Week in 1999. Klein presented his first men's wear collection in his fifth show at New York Fashion Week. He designs in Paris, but his parent company, Groupe Klein Vendome, is based in

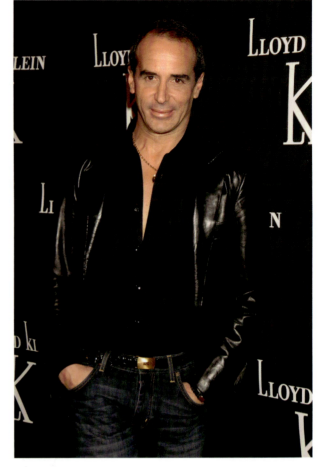

Designer Lloyd Klein.

West Hollywood, California. In 2012, he created LKLA, a sportswear collection for men and women.

Klein has shown collections around the world, and his designs have been worn by celebrities such as Jessica Simpson, Halle Berry, and Eva Longoria, and are sold at Ultimo, Tootsies, Martha's, and Red Velvet. Klein is also the spokesman for Unicorn Children's Foundation, which is "dedicated to education, awareness, and research on behalf of children and young adults with developmental, communication, and learning disorders."

Spring 2005.

STEVEN KLEIN

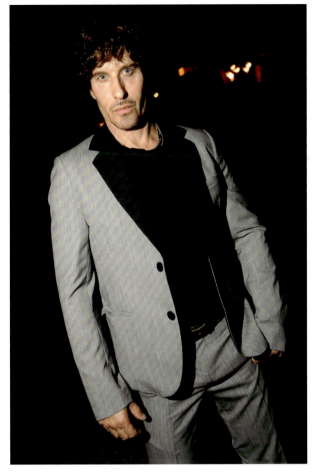

Photographer Steven Klein.

BORN Cranston, Rhode Island, April 30, 1965

AWARDS International Center of Photography *Infinity Award for Fashion*, 2014

Steven Klein became obsessed with American and French *Vogue* when he was a child. He attended Rhode Island School of Design, where he received a degree in painting. Klein got his first major break photographing an ad campaign for CHRISTIAN DIOR Mascara in Paris. By 1994, he was shooting his first *Vogue* portfolio for GRACE CODDINGTON, and in 1997 he had a solo exhibit in New York at Staley-Wise Gallery. In 2002, Klein shot one of ALEXANDER MCQUEEN's first ad campaigns, and in 2003 he teamed up with Madonna to create *X-STaTIC PRO=CeSS*, an exhibition in Soho.

Klein was one of five photographers featured in the 2007 exhibit *Face of Fashion* at London's National Portrait Gallery. Klein often works with singers, actors, and designers to create unusual photography, but it is his ongoing relationship with CONDÉ NAST that is truly rare—Klein contributes to all editions of *Vogue, L'Uomo Vogue,* and *W.* He has been hailed as more of an artist than a fashion photographer, and his work often asks viewers to examine things that "we tend not to want to focus on." ANNA WINTOUR calls Klein's photographs "clever, conceptual, and ultimately lyrical," and he strongly believes in the personal relationship between subject and photographer.

In 2013, Klein showed his work in film—once again, in collaboration with Madonna—with a 17-minute piece at the Gagosian Gallery in New York.

KOOS ♟

Designer Koos.

BORN Koos van den Akker; Holland, circa 1932

AWARDS American Printed Fabrics Council *Tommy Award (unique use of prints)*, 1983

Koos started making dresses when he was just eleven. He studied at the Netherlands Royal Academy of Art, worked at department stores in The Hague and Paris, and whizzed through a two-year fashion program at l'École Guerre Lavigne in Paris in seven months. After an apprenticeship at CHRISTIAN DIOR, he returned to The Hague and spent six years selling custom-made dresses at his own boutique.

In 1968, with a portable sewing machine and little money, Koos moved to New York City. He first set up an "office" by the fountain at Lincoln Center, taking commissions from passersby. After that he designed lingerie for Eve Stillman and eventually opened his own boutique. Koos has survived the death of a partner and severe financial problems and been reborn with a new partner, a new boutique, and a monthly show on the television network QVC. There he has, with great success, sold his secondary line—Chinese-made

versions of his signature collages of colorful prints and lace, but translated into printed fabrics. The boutique sells the collage originals and one-of-a-kind furniture. Past projects have included men's wear, furs, home furnishings, and theater designs.

For his women's clothes, Koos has always specialized in simple shapes in beautiful fabrics enriched with his collages. They are considered collectors' items and have displayed at New York's Museum of Contemporary Crafts. His clients have included Cher, Madeleine Kahn, Elizabeth Taylor, and Gloria Vanderbilt.

Recently, references to Koos's patchwork collages have shown up in the work of several younger designers, including MARC JACOBS and NICOLAS GHESQUIÈRE. In 2008, the famous Koos van den Akker sweaters worn by Bill Cosby on *The Cosby Show* were auctioned for charity. In 2013, Koos served as the summer artist-in-residence at the Academy of Art University's School of Fashion in San Francisco. Koos still works in his Madison Avenue studio in New York.

Inspiration for designs.

Designer Michael Kors.

BORN Long Island, New York, August 9, 1959

AWARDS Council of Fashion Designers of America (CFDA) *Women's Wear Designer of the Year,* 1998/1999; *Men's Wear Designer of the Year,* 2003

Michael Kors attended the Fashion Institute of Technology for one semester in 1977. He then worked for three years as designer, buyer, and display director for a New York boutique before starting his own

Spring 2014.

⬧ MICHAEL KORS

business in 1981. His first collection of 16 pieces, entirely in brown and black, sold to eight accounts. By 1986, his list of clients had grown to over 75 specialty stores. He has also designed a secondary collection, Kors by Michael Kors, that sells for about half the price of his regular collection, created cashmere knits for the Scottish firm Lyle & Scott, and had licensing agreements for shoes and swimwear.

In 1997, Kors signed an agreement with CÉLINE, a division of LVMH, to be its design director for ready-to-wear; his first collection there was for fall 1998. That made him part of the group of younger American and British designers hired to reenergize aging French houses—including JOHN GALLIANO, TOM FORD, MARC JACOBS, ALEXANDER McQUEEN, and JULIEN MACDONALD. When objections were raised that he was really an American sportswear designer, he pointed out that both CHANEL and YVES SAINT LAURENT, quintessentially French designers, had strong sportswear orientations. He has continued to present his Michael Kors and Kors by Michael Kors collections in New York.

Kors designs individual pieces, then combines them into outfits. His goal is to provide a flexible, versatile way of dressing that allows women to put pieces together in different ways to achieve any desired effect, from the most casual to the dressiest. The clothes are clean and understated in cut and executed in the most luxurious fibers and fabrics—cashmere, silk, leathers, fur. They fit securely into the deluxe sportswear category and are meant for sophisticated, modern women of means who dress to please themselves.

In 2004, Kors became a judge on the Emmy-nominated television reality show *Project Runway.* That same year, he launched the Michael Kors line, which includes ready-to-wear, swimwear, and accessories. His dresses have been worn by Michelle Obama and Alicia Keys. Kors left *Project Runway* in 2012 to focus on his label.

Spring 2014.

REED KRAKOFF ▲

BORN Westport, Connecticut

AWARDS Council of Fashion Designers of America
(CFDA) *Accessories Designer of the Year*, 2001, 2004, 2012

Reed Krakoff started his design career at Parsons New
School of Design. After graduation, he worked briefly at
ANNE KLEIN and RALPH LAUREN. In 1997, Krakoff became
executive creative director and president of Coach. While
there, his vision transformed the brand's handbag designs,
store concepts, and marketing initiatives, making Coach a
chic label sought by fashion insiders.

Krakoff is also a photographer whose work been displayed in New York and Tokyo. His books on photography include *Claude & Francois-Xavier Lalanne*, *Mattia
Bonetti*, and *Fighter: The Ultimate Fighters of the UFC*.
Krakoff is also a patron of the arts and is involved in the

Spring 2014.

Designer Reed Krakoff.

Smithsonian's Cooper-Hewitt National Design Museum
and the Whitney Museum of American Art.

From 2006 to 2010, Krakoff was vice president of the
CFDA, and he continues to mentor young designers participating in the CFDA/*Vogue* Fashion Fund. But he is
best known for his work with Coach, which earned him
three CFDA Accessories Designer of the Year awards. In
2010, Coach helped Krakoff fund his own label.

Krakoff has redefined traditional sportswear for his
clients—strong, sensual woman who love luxury. The label
is managed by Valarie Hermann, who has worked at DIOR
and SAINT LAURENT. In 2013, Krakoff announced that he
was leaving Coach to focus on his label, which is sold at
Saks Fifth Avenue, Neiman Marcus, and net-a-porter.com.

Designer Albert Kriemler.

▲ ALBERT KRIEMLER

remains the only Swiss brand to be granted membership to the Chambre du Prêt-à-porter in Paris and to present two collections a year in the city of fashion.

Because the Akris studio is still in its original remote location, Kriemler relies on the town's expensive tailors and technicians. Many of the brand's textiles are made for a specific dress design, and all of its pieces are constructed in the company's studios. Kriemler also has a somewhat less expensive, younger-looking line called Akris Punto. All of his collections give the impression that time has stood still while also moving forward into contemporary fashion. Kriemler continuously strives to combine sophisticated fabrics of the highest quality with his keen eye for trends.

Akris is now sold by 600 outlets around the world. The brand's flagship stores are on Avenue Montaigne in Paris, Bond Street in London, and Madison Avenue in New York. Akris is one of the top-selling luxury labels at American department stores such as Neiman Marcus and Bergdorf Goodman. Kriemler's client list includes Princess Caroline of Monaco, Condoleezza Rice, and Diane Sawyer.

BORN Speicher, Switzerland, 1960

Albert Kriemler, with the help of his brother Peter—who handles the business end—has expanded his grandmother's apron business into a dynasty. His company's name, Akris, is derived from his grandmother's name, Alice Kriemler Schoch. Kriemler had planned to attend fashion school in Paris and intern with GIVENCHY. But he joined the family business in 1980, when his father's key aide died. Much to the fashion world's surprise, a family company from provincial St. Gallen, Switzerland, has come to be a ready-to-wear brand of international standing. Founded just over 20 years ago, and equally represented in Asian, American, and European markets, Akris

Fall 2013.

In 2008, Kriemler designed modern, sculptural costumes for the Hamburg Ballet's production of *The Legend of Joseph*, by Richard Strauss. Kriemler was approached for the project by fellow creative John Neumeier, who was in charge of the set and choreography. The duo had previously worked together on the ballet's New Year's 2006 concert. In 2010, Fashion Group International named Kriemler a star honoree for fashion design. He says that "when a woman walks into a room, I want people to notice her personality first and her clothing second."

Spring 2014.

CHRISTIAN LACROIX ♟

Designer Christian Lacroix.

Fall 2009.

BORN Arles, France, May 16, 1951

AWARDS French Government *Légion d'Honneur (Legion of Honor)*, 2002

Christian Lacroix (La-KWA) is given credit by some critics for revitalizing Paris couture at a time when it had grown stale and, with his irreverent wit, returning an element of adventure to fashion.

A native of Provence in the south of France, Lacroix grew up surrounded by women and developed an early interest in fashion and accessories. After studying art history and classic Greek and Latin at the University of Montpellier, he went to Paris in 1972 to attend l'École du Louvre. A stint as a museum curator followed, then in 1978 Lacroix turned to fashion—first as a design assistant at HERMÈS, next for two years at Guy Paulin. He worked in Japan for a year as an assistant to a Japanese designer, then returned to Paris and joined JEAN PATOU in 1982 as chief designer of haute couture.

At Patou, he produced collection after idea-filled collection of theatrical, witty clothes and fantastic accessories. Imaginative and elegant, not all were wearable by any but the most daring, but many appealed to adventurous women with flair and confidence in their own style. After five years with Patou, Lacroix left in 1987 to establish his own couture house backed by LVMH, the French conglomerate that also owns DIOR. The arrangement also includes ready-to-wear. Under his own name, Lacroix has shown the same irrepressible taste for drama, with the ready-to-wear somewhat less extreme than the couture. In 2002, he was also named creative director of PUCCI, another LVMH holding, and stayed with the house until 2005.

In 2004, Lacroix signed a five-year contract to create a lingerie line for Société Internationale de Lingerie (SIL), and in 2007 he partnered with Avon to market two fragrances: Christian Lacroix Rouge for women and Christian Lacroix Noir for Men. In 2009, Lacroix exhibited a 20-year collection of costumes at the National Museum of Singapore. That same year, he filed for bankruptcy and lost the right to design under his own name—leading him to retire. But retirement was short-lived: in 2011, under the name Monsieur C. Lacroix, he collaborated with Spanish retail giant Desigual. In 2013, DIEGO DELLA VALLE, who revived the SCHIAPARELLI line, asked Lacroix to create a capsule collection.

Fall 2013.

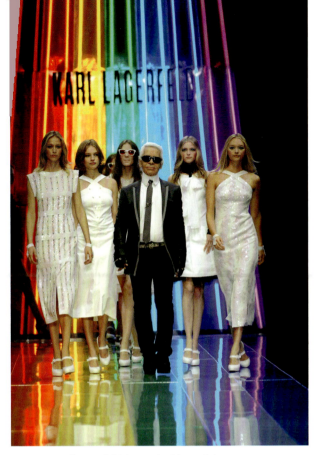

Designer Karl Lagerfeld (center) with models.

▲ KARL LAGERFELD

working exclusively for Chanel and showed his first collection under his own label. Extremely hard-working and prolific, Lagerfeld has had a sportswear collection under his own name designed specifically for America, designed gloves and shoes for Mario Valentino and Charles Jourdan, and created sweaters for Ballantyne. He does furs and sportswear for FENDI, and resumed designing for Chloé, where he was succeeded in 1997 by STELLA McCARTNEY. He has a number of successful fragrances for women and men.

In 2004, Lagerfeld designed some outfits for Madonna's *Re-Invention* world tour and recently designed outfits for Kylie Minogue's *Showgirl* tour. Lagerfeld has also collaborated with H&M, offering a limited line for men and women in select stores. In 2006, he launched a new collection for men and women, K Karl Lagerfeld, that included fitted t-shirts and a wide range of jeans. He has also signed a deal with Dubai Infinity Holdings, an investment firm, to design limited edition homes on Isla

(continued)

BORN Hamburg, Germany, September 10, 1939

AWARDS *Neiman Marcus Award*, 1980; *Distinguished Service in the Field of Fashion Award*, 2013 • Council of Fashion Designers of America (CFDA) *Special Award*, 1982; *Special Award (for* CHANEL*)*, 1988; *Accessories Designer of the Year (for Chanel)*, 1991; Geoffrey Beene Lifetime Achievement Award, 2002

Karl Lagerfeld arrived in Paris in 1953 at 14, already determined to be a clothes designer. That year he won an award for best coat in the same International Wool Secretariat design competition at which YVES SAINT LAURENT won for best dress. In 1954, Lagerfeld began working for BALMAIN, and three and a half years later went to work for PATOU.

Lagerfeld left Patou and returned to school, and after two years began freelancing. In 1963, he went to work for the upscale ready-to-wear house CHLOÉ as one of four designers. The team of four became two, Lagerfeld and Graziella Fontana. They designed the collection together until 1972, when Lagerfeld became sole designer.

In 1982, he became design director for Chanel and continued with Chloé until 1984, when he began

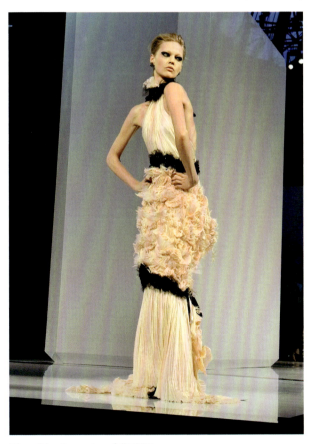

Chanel haute couture fall 2009.

Moda—the world's first island dedicated to fashion—set in the iconic development, The World.

Lagerfeld is an unpredictable, original designer, highly professional and a master of his craft. At his best, he mixes inventiveness and wearability, spicing the blend with a dash of wit. He likes to remove clothes from their usual contexts—he has used elaborate embroidery on cotton instead of the usual silk, made dresses that could be worn upside down, and showed *crepe de chine* dresses with tennis shoes long before it was a styling cliché. He has modernized Chanel while retaining its distinctive character—though the house has become more Karl than Coco. Much like Chanel, Lagerfeld has what many call "Karlisms," unique and interesting sayings such as "I design like I breathe. You don't ask to breathe—it just happens" and "I love to be creative all the time . . . if I weren't, I would be bored—and boredom is a crime."

In 2014, Pier Paolo Righi, president of the Karl Lagerfeld brand, announced that it had sold a minority stake to Phillips-Van Heusen to foster its growth in North America. This means that PVH will control the franchise.

Chanel haute couture spring 2014.

Freida Pinto in Chanel and Karl Lagerfeld, 2009.

Designer Derek Lam.

BORN San Francisco, 1966

AWARDS Ecco Domani Fashion Foundation *Award for New Designers*, 2004 • Council of Fashion Designers of America (CFDA) *Swarovski Perry Ellis Award for Womenswear*, 2005

When Derek Lam was a child, his Chinese-American parents ran a garment manufacturing business in San Francisco that specialized in wedding dresses, and he spent a lot of time with the seamstresses in the factory. Later he attended Parsons School of Design in New York. After graduating, he went to work for MICHAEL KORS and eventually became head designer at KORS by Michael Kors. Lam spent 12 years at Kors, leaving briefly once to work for a major Asian retail brand in Hong Kong.

Lam ventured out on his own in 2002, when he debuted his women's clothing line at Olympus Fashion Week. Buyers from Barneys and Bergdorf Goodman were quick to place orders. In 2006, he was appointed creative director of Tod's accessory company.

Fall 2013.

Fall 2013.

While formfitting dresses are not anomalous in Lam's collections, he leans toward fabrics that hold their shape rather than mold to the woman's body. "I like to take fabrics and not make costumes, but very modern silhouettes," Lam says.

Concerned with the restrictiveness of genre, Lam eschews Eastern influences in his work. His style is influenced by Kors in that it seeks to reinvent American sportswear in a way that is modest yet highly adaptable. His collections include fall/winter and spring/summer ready-to-wear as well as colorful, feminine resort wear.

In 2011, Lam debuted a diffusion line, 10 Crosby, and presented a signature dress collection designed for eBay at Fashion Week in New York. In 2013, he created a capsule collection for Kohl's DesigNation that was so popular with celebrities, it could be seen on stars before it was available in stores.

L.A.M.B. (GWEN STEFANI) 👜 📊

FOUNDED 2003

Gwen Stefani is best known as the lead singer of No Doubt, but she came from a long line of seamstresses—starting with her great-grandmother. Stefani was used to making her own clothes after she grew up, having had them made for her as a child by her mother and grandmother. Andrea Lieberman introduced Stefani to haute couture and helped define her aesthetic. In 2003, Stefani launched L.A.M.B. with LeSportsac. L.A.M.B. stands for Love. Angel. Music. Beauty., which are the things most dear to Stefani. She began the label by producing punk wristbands and hobo bags made from guitar straps. In 2006, L.A.M.B. became independent.

South American and Asian trends often influence L.A.M.B. collections, and many fashion critics see a strong aesthetic link to punk fashion. When Stefani purchased

L.A.M.B. Fall 2012.

Designer Gwen Stefani for L.A.M.B.

her first couture corset for a music video, it was from the queen of punk fashion, VIVIENNE WESTWOOD.

L.A.M.B. collections mix classic Hollywood glamour and modern street style—the old and the new, the masculine and the feminine. Stefani has said that she started the business because she cannot sing forever and loves fashion, so it seemed like a logical path to take. Stefani feels the same passion for designing that she does for songwriting.

L.A.M.B. now includes clothing, handbags, shoes, and a fragrance called L. Stefani has three lines: L.A.M.B., Harajuku Lovers, and Harajuku Mini, a collection for children and babies sold exclusively at Target. In 2011, Stefani pared down her design duties at L.A.M.B. by hiring Paula Bradley as design director. L.A.M.B. has been worn by Lucy Liu, Kelly Osbourne, and Penélope Cruz.

○ LANA

BORN Moscow

Lana Bramlette is known in the fashion world as the "Queen of Hoops" for her sleek, modern jewelry of fine gold. Her family moved from Russia to Chicago in 1981, when she was seven. Encouraged to do anything she wanted, in 2003 Lana decided to start a jewelry business. Her father agreed to be her partner, and the business now has offices in Chicago, Dallas, and New York.

The idea for the jewelry line was born when a woman approached Bramlette in a shopping mall while she was wearing her "Rob" 14-karat gold nameplate necklace in honor of her (now) husband. The woman asked if Bramlette could replicate the necklace with the same name, and gave her cash to do so. That helped spark the creation of more pieces. Bramlette's husband felt that she should sell her collection in a more trendy setting such as Los Angeles, so she signed a deal to sell the collection at Fred Segal. Soon after, Cameron Diaz was dazzled and bought the entire collection, wearing Lana earrings to the premiere of the film *Charlie's Angels*.

The resulting buzz made it easy for Bramlette to get other retailers to carry her designs. High-profile stars such as Halle Berry, Angelina Jolie, and Sandra Bullock have worn Lana jewelry. Her signature pieces include three-tier earrings, sunrise hoops, and the eternity necklace. Bramlette has a policy of not gifting to celebrities—meaning that they pay for the jewelry just like everyone else.

Lana jewelry is known for making yellow gold popular again. The collections are sexy and strong but can be worn every day. Bramlette is the founder of the Chicago

Designer Lana Marks.

Fashion Foundation, which raises awareness of and promotes the city's fashion industry and raises money for scholarships. Bramlette lives in Chicago with her husband and daughter.

KENNETH JAY LANE Ŏ

BORN Detroit, Michigan, April 22, 1932

AWARDS Coty American Fashion Critics' Awards *Special Award (outstanding contribution to fashion)*, 1966 • *Neiman Marcus Award*, 1968

Kenneth Jay Lane attended the University of Michigan for two years, then went to the Rhode Island School of Design, where he graduated in 1954 with a degree in advertising. He worked on the promotion art staff at *Vogue* and there met French shoe designer ROGER VIVIER. Through him, Lane became an assistant designer for Delman Shoes, then associate designer of CHRISTIAN DIOR Shoes, spending part of each year in Paris working with Vivier.

In 1963, still designing shoes, Lane made a few pieces of jewelry that were photographed for fashion magazines and sold by a few stores. Working nights and weekends,

Above: Designer Kenneth Jay Lane (left) and Nan Kempner (right).

Below: Couture bangles.

he continued to design jewelry under the name K.J.L., his initials. By 1964, Lane was able to make jewelry design a full-time career.

Lane first makes his designs in wax or by carving or twisting metal. He has said that he wants "to make real jewelry with not-real materials," and sees plastic as the modern medium—lightweight, available in every color, and perfect for simulating real gems. He likes to see his jewelry mixed with the real gems worn by his international roster of celebrity customers. The list is long and has included Jacqueline Kennedy and the Duchess of Windsor and, more recently, Nancy Reagan, Barbara Bush, Hillary Clinton, and Laura Bush.

Lane's jewelry is sold in fine department and specialty stores around the world, and he has promoted it with great success on the television network QVC in America and Japan. Lane has been recognized worldwide with awards from magazines, design schools, and his industry. His book, *Kenneth Jay Lane: Faking It*, was published in 1996. In 2010, Lane teamed up with Via Spiga to create a limited edition capsule collection. His designs can also be purchased at J.C. Penney and his watches at worldofwatches.com.

Necklace and earrings by Kenneth Jay Lane.

Designer Helmut Lang.

BORN Vienna, Austria, March 10, 1956

AWARDS Council of Fashion Designers of America (CFDA) *International Award*, 1996; *Menswear Designer of the Year*, 2000

Helmut Lang was raised in the Austrian Alps, and at 18 moved to Vienna to study business. He worked at a bar, became involved with artists and "night people," and was encouraged by his friends to do something creative. He got into fashion when he met someone who could create the things he envisioned, because at the time he had no idea how to put them together himself. His vision of fashion developed gradually, and in 1984 he opened a shop in Vienna. By 1987, Lang had a contract with a textile firm in Italy and a licensing agreement with Mitsubishi in Japan, where he now has numerous boutiques. Lang lived in Vienna and showed in Paris until 1999, when he sold 50 percent of his company to PRADA, moved to New York City, and began showing in the 7th on Sixth shows there.

Variously dubbed a deconstructionist, a minimalist, and a follower of the Japanese avant-garde, Lang is really none of those things—he is very much his own man. An anomaly simply by being Austrian, he exhibited his distinctive view of fashion and clothes fully formed with his first Paris showing in 1986, when he sent out waiflike models with scrubbed faces in simple silhouettes and somber colors. His signature stamps—experimentation with fabric technology (including PVC, nylon, Lurex, and stretch synthetics),

shiny cellophane-like effects, and rumpled looks and subtle layers—were there from the beginning and have been enormously influential.

One wing of fashion sees Lang as a prophet; the other as the antithesis of fashion. Regardless, it cannot be denied that he helped define luxe minimalism in the 1990s. He believes that fashion involves attitude, appearance, and character, and that it defines the spirit of the time. His clothes express his view of how modern men and women want to dress: without affectation and with the understanding that perfect cut, comfort, and ease of movement are among fashion's great luxuries.

In 2005, Lang resigned from his label, and in 2006 Prada sold it to Link Theory Holdings. The company then revived the Helmut Lang label at a more affordable price point by hiring new creative directors, Nicole and Michael Colovos.

Meanwhile, Lang began exploring other artistic endeavors, and in 2008 had his first solo art exhibition, in Hanover, Germany. He plans to open a new boutique on Prince Street in New York in spring 2014.

Spring 2014.

JEANNE LANVIN

BORN Brittany, France, January 1, 1867
DIED Paris, July 6, 1946

AWARDS French Government *Légion d'Honneur*
(Legion of Honor), 1938

Designer Jeanne Lanvin.

The eldest of a journalist's ten children, Jeanne Lanvin (Lon-VAH) was apprenticed to a dressmaker at the age of 13, and became a milliner when she was 23. The dresses she designed for her daughter were admired and bought by her hat customers, and her children's wear business evolved into the couture house of Lanvin, located in Paris on rue du Faubourg St. Honoré.

Lanvin's designs had a youthful quality, often reflecting the styles of her native Brittany. She collected costume books, daguerreotypes, and historical plates, and drew inspiration from them—notably for the *robes de style* for which she was famous, and for her wedding gowns. She took plain fabrics and decorated them in her workrooms, maintaining a department for machine embroidery under the direction of her brother. The house also produced women's sportswear, furs, and lingerie as well as children's wear. In 1926, Lanvin opened a men's wear boutique, the first in couture, directed by her nephew, Maurice Lanvin.

Lanvin was famous for her use of quilting and stitching, her embroidery, and her discreet use of sequins. Fantasy evening gowns in metallic embroideries were a signature; she introduced the chemise during World War I. She was also one of the first couturiers to establish a perfume business, with Arpège and My Sin among the most notable fragrances.

Lanvin was an accomplished businesswoman and was elected President of the Haute Couture Committee of the Paris International Exhibition in 1937. She represented France and couture at the 1939 New York

World's Fair. After her death the House of Lanvin continued under the direction of her daughter, the Comtesse de Polignac.

Lanvin couture was designed by Antonio del Castillo from 1950 to 1963, and by Jules-François Crahay from 1963 to 1984. Control of the firm passed from the Lanvin family in 1989. Maryll Lanvin, who had taken over design direction of ready-to-wear and, after Crahay's retirement, of couture, was replaced by CLAUDE MONTANA for couture and Eric Bergère for ready-to-wear. Couture was discontinued in 1992. Since 1989, women's ready-to-wear has been overseen by a succession of designers, including Dominque Morlotti, Ocimar Versolato, and Cristina Ortiz.

The firm, which had been owned by l'Oréal, was sold in 2001 to a Taiwanese investment group. ALBER ELBAZ was named designer for women's wear, and his first collection was for fall/winter 2002. He was also appointed creative director of couture. Lanvin Paris has subsidiaries in Asia, the Middle East, America, and Europe.

⧗ GUY LAROCHE

conservative when I started. I gave it color . . . youth, suppleness, and informality." His evening pants were worn by the most fashionable women in Paris.

At the time of Laroche's death, he presided over an extensive company producing both couture and ready-to-wear, with boutiques around the world. Other licensed ready-to-wear labels in the group included Christian Aujard, Lolita Lempicka, Angelo Tarlazzi, and a lower-priced collection by THIERRY MUGLER. The Laroche name has been on products ranging from intimate apparel, furs, luggage, sportswear, rainwear, dresses, and blouses to sunglasses, accessories, footwear, and fragrances. Marcel Marongiu is the creative director of Laroche.

Designer Guy Laroche.

BORN La Rochelle (near Bordeaux), France, circa 1923
DIED Paris, February 16, 1989

Guy Laroche (La-ROASH) arrived in Paris at 25 with no immediate goals and no interest in clothes. Through a cousin working at JEAN PATOU, he toured several couture houses and fell in love with the business. He got a job as assistant to JEAN DESSÈS and stayed with him five years. From 1950 to 1955 he freelanced in New York City, then returned to Paris and opened a couture establishment in his apartment. Laroche's first collection was for fall 1957. In 1961, he expanded and moved to Avenue Montaigne, where the house is still located.

Influenced by BALENCIAGA, in the beginning Laroche developed a livelier look. "It was very, very

Autumn collections, 1971–1972.

BYRON LARS

Designer Byron Lars (front center) with models.

BORN Oakland, California, 1965

Byron Lars knew that he wanted to go into fashion design by the time he was 15. Lars designed a prom dress for a high school friend and delighted in the feeling that it gave him to make her excited and happy. He attended the Fashion Institute of Technology in New York and represented America at the International Concours des Jeunes Createurs de Mode in Paris in 1986. Lars also won the first annual Texitalian contest for fashion design students, held by the Fashion Institute of Technology and Italian Trade Commission in 1987.

Lars showed his first collection on Seventh Avenue in 1991, and received rave reviews. His second collection led *Women's Wear Daily* to hail Lars as "Rookie of the Year" and was sold at Neiman Marcus, Bloomingdale's, Saks Fifth Avenue, and Bergdorf Goodman. His runway shows featured accessories that helped him win licenses for handbags, furs, and hats.

In 1996, Mattel contracted Lars to design a collectible Barbie, a collaboration that continued every year through 2011. The dolls that Lars created helped increase the number of African-American Barbies and were featured in *Vogue* in 2009.

Once licensing agreements had expired for his couture lines, Lars decided to concentrate on a more affordable and contemporary line. In 2002, Byron Lars Beauty Mark was born. The line started with shirts and shirtdresses, and has grown to include sportswear, dresses, and knitwear, and has been very popular with Michelle Obama. She has worn Lars dresses in the White House family official portrait in 2011, to the White House's Christmas in Washington event in 2011, and on several other high-profile occasions.

Lars excels at fit. In 2009, he announced plans to release a plus-size collection, wanting plus-size women to have the same quality and styling that he brings to the mainstream market. Lars is also fiercely loyal and supportive of his friends, and is sometimes seen backstage helping designer TRACY REESE with her shows. Angela Bassett and Zoe Bell are among the fans of Byron Lars Beauty Mark.

Left: Fall 2013.
Right: Fall 2013.

Estée Lauder.

FOUNDED New York City, 1946

Josephine Esther Mentzer was raised in Queens, where her family nicknamed her Esty. She was always fascinated with beauty and admired her uncle and mentor, chemist John Schotz. He created skin and beauty products that she sold to beauty salons and beach clubs while living above her father's garage. In 1946, she established the Estée Lauder brand with the help of her husband, Joseph Lauder.

Lauder got her first business when the owner of a salon in Florida asked her what she put on her skin. She took her products to the salon and started showing woman how to apply them. The owner was so impressed that he allowed her to sell her products in the salon. In 1948, Lauder took her products to retail stores and convinced managers to give her counter space at Saks Fifth Avenue, providing one-on-one contact with customers to show the products' benefits.

ESTÉE LAUDER

Lauder fostered several innovations—the most important being the power of touch. She believed that clients must see and touch products and be taught how to apply them. Lauder personally trained her beauty advisers. The company's advertisements emphasized that every woman is beautiful and that beauty is attainable and approachable. That approach gained her loyalty from celebrities such as Princess Grace Kelly of Monaco.

In 1953, Lauder created her first fragrance, Youth Dew, a bath oil that doubled as a perfume. In its first year on the market, it sold 50,000 bottles—and by 1984 it had sold 150 million. Lauder died in 2004, with her age remaining a mystery even to her family (some say she was 95; some say 97). Her children and grandchildren now run the company, known as Estée Lauder Companies, which owns and licenses makeup and fragrances for more than 25 companies, including MAC Cosmetics, Bobbi Brown, Clinique, Origins, Aveda, Coach, and Michael Kors. In 2013, Estée Lauder had net sales of more than $10 billion.

Makeup collection by Estée Lauder.

RALPH LAUREN ▾

BORN Ralph Lifshitz; New York City, October 14, 1939

AWARDS Coty American Fashion Critics' Awards *Menswear Award*, 1970; *Return Award (menswear)*, 1973; *Winnie*, 1974; *Return Award*, 1976; *Hall of Fame Award (menswear)*, 1976; *Hall of Fame Award (womenswear)*, 1977; *Men's Apparel*, 1981; *Special Award (womenswear)*, 1984 • Council of Fashion Designers of America (CFDA) *Special Award*, 1981; *Retailer of the Year*, 1986; *Geoffrey Beene Lifetime Achievement Award*, 1991; *Womenswear Designer of the Year Award*, 1995; *Menswear Designer of the Year*, 1996, 2007; *Dom Pérignon Award*, 1997; *American Fashion Legend Award*, 2007 • *Fashion Walk of Fame*, 2000

Designer Ralph Lauren.

A gifted stylist, Ralph Lauren has taken his dream of a mythical American past of athletic grace and discreet elegance, and transformed it into a fashion empire. He chose the name Polo as a symbol of men who wear expensive, classic clothes, and wear them with style. He extends the same blend of classic silhouettes, superb fabrics, and fine workmanship to his women's apparel. For both women and men, the attitude is well-bred and confident, with an offhand luxury. He has projected his romantic view in his advertising, featuring a large cast of

Above: Spring/summer 1989.
Right: Fall 2008.

Spring 2014.

models in upper-crust situations, and through his flagship New York stores. Definitely investment caliber, the clothes are known for their excellent quality and high prices.

The son of an artist, Lauren arrived in the fashion world without formal design training. He took night courses in business while working days as a department store stock boy. After college he was a salesman at Brooks Brothers, an assistant buyer at Allied Stores, a glove company salesman, and New York representative for a Boston necktie manufacturer. He started designing neckties, and in 1967 persuaded Beau Brummel, a men's wear firm, to form the Polo neckwear division. The ties were unique—exceptionally wide, and made by hand of opulent silks. They quickly attracted attention, resulting in a contract to design the Polo line of men's clothing for Norman Hilton, with whom Lauren established Polo in 1968 as a separate company producing a complete wardrobe for men. In 1971, Lauren introduced finely tailored shirts for women and the next year a complete ready-to-wear collection.

Lauren has also done film work, designing for the leading men in *The Great Gatsby* in 1973, and in 1977 the clothing for *Annie Hall*. His myriad brands include Polo Ralph Lauren, Polo Sport, and the Ralph Lauren Collection, as well as home furnishings, accessories, and fragrances for men and women. In 2002, Lauren showed his top-of-the-line Purple Label men's collection in Milan, where it was very well received.

Some collections are only distributed outside America, in countries such as Canada and Japan, and licensing has expanded worldwide. In 1997, Lauren took his company public on the New York Stock Exchange.

Lauren recently launched the Rugby line, which is targeted to 16- to 25-year-olds. Polo Ralph Lauren was an official outfitter of the U.S. Open through 2009, and of Wimbledon through 2010. Lauren also designed the uniforms worn by the U.S. team at the opening of the 2008 Olympics in Beijing, though he received some criticism because they were made in China. In 2013, *Forbes* estimated Lauren's net worth at $7.5 billion, making him one of the wealthiest people in fashion.

Spring 2014.

DION LEE ▼

BORN Sydney, Australia

Hailed as the future of Australian fashion in 2010, Dion Lee made a rapid leap into the international world of fashion. He is a graduate of the Sydney Institute of Technology and in 2010, at 24, won the l'Oréal Fashion Festival Design Award, and in 2012 the International Woolmark Prize. Lee debuted his fall 2012 collection in London, where it received rave reviews.

Lee's elegant collections display his knowledge of architecture and patternmaking. His well-tailored collections feature signature elements of intricate folding and sharp geometric shapes. Lee's garments display hard edges with soft pleats, which can sometimes seem unwearable—but the garments are in fact flattering and extremely popular. Many critics agree that Lee has mastered the art of design.

Designer Dion Lee.

In 2011, Audi asked Lee to be its brand ambassador. He says that customizing the interior and exterior of a car parallels the construction and design of his brand, which is why he took the job. Lee believes that collaboration with big companies whose design values align with his own is good for business.

Lee's clothing is extremely popular in Australia, and is sold overseas through net-a-porter.com. Famous Australian women who wear the brand include Miranda Kerr, Megan Gale, and Lara Bingle. Outside Australia, Charlize Theron has worn Lee's designs. In 2013, the Cue Clothing Company acquired an undisclosed percentage of the Dion Lee brand, and that September he showed at New York Fashion Week for the first time, featuring his spring/summer 2014 collection.

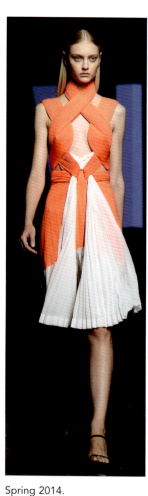

Spring 2014.

Spring 2014.

Designer Judith Leiber.

👜 JUDITH LEIBER

Minaudière clutch purse in the shape of a sitting Buddha, 2009.

BORN Judith Peto; Budapest, Hungary, January 11, 1921

AWARDS Coty American Fashion Critics' Awards *Special Award (handbags)*, 1973 • *Neiman Marcus Award*, 1980 • Council of Fashion Designers of America (CFDA) *Lifetime Achievement Award*, 1994 • Accessories Council *Hall of Fame Award*, 2001

Renowned for her fantastic jeweled evening bags, Judith Leiber learned her craft in Budapest, starting as an apprentice at 19—the only woman in what was considered a man's trade. There she met her future husband, an American, at the end of World War II; they married and

moved to the United States in 1946. She worked in the handbag industry until 1963, gaining experience with every type of bag and every price range. She and her husband then went into business for themselves. The company was sold to a British conglomerate in 1993, resulting in its expansion—including the addition of a retail presence.

Leiber designed everything for the brand, from evening bags with small animal shapes encrusted with thousands of jewels to daytime bags in rare leathers, softened with pleats, braids, coins, charms, and stones. She was influenced by pieces from the 1920s and 1930s and by Oriental art, and wanted her bags to be great to hold, beautiful to look at, and practical. Leiber also made accessories such as wallets, key chains, and belts, but is best known for her crystal-adorned minaudières, which appeared in 1967. Each was handmade and took up to two weeks to complete. The bags have become collectors' items for women who wear real jewelry and designer clothes.

Leiber has received numerous awards from trade groups, colleges and universities, and charitable organizations. In 1994, New York's Fashion Institute of Technology marked her 30th year in business with an exhibition of her work. Leiber announced her retirement in 1998.

In 2000, the company was sold again, this time to a consortium of investors known as the Pegasus Group, subsequently renamed the Leiber Group for its most productive division. Leiber handbags are displayed at the Metropolitan Museum of Art, Victoria and Albert Museum, and Smithsonian Institution.

Judith Leiber's Spring 2011 Bridal collection.

ANNIE LEIBOVITZ 📷

BORN Waterbury, Connecticut, 1949

AWARDS Clio Award, 1987 • Barnard College *Medal of Distinction*, 2000 • French Ministry of Culture *Commandeur dans l'Ordre des Artes et des Lettres*, 1991 • International Center of Photography *Infinity Award for Lifetime Achievement,* 2009 • Smithsonian Magazine *Innovators of Our Time Award*, 2005 • Library of Congress *Living Legend,* 2000 • Georgia O'Keeffe Museum *Women of Distinction Award*, 2009

Photographer Annie Leibovitz.

Known for close collaboration with her subjects, Annie Leibovitz has created some of the most iconographic portraits of the 20th and early 21st centuries. She studied painting at the San Francisco Art Institute in the late 1960s, but discovered a passion for photography after visiting Japan and the Philippines. When she returned to America in 1970, she was hired as a staff photographer for the fledgling magazine *Rolling Stone.* She was named its chief photographer in 1973, and in 1975 was official tour photographer for the band the Rolling Stones. Leibovitz worked for *Rolling Stone* until 1983, and her celebrity portraits shaped the look of the magazine.

In 1980, she took a photo for *Rolling Stone* of the nude John Lennon curled up next to a clothed Yoko Ono in bed. Five hours later, Lennon was murdered outside his apartment in New York City, making Leibovitz's photograph the last professional picture of the musician.

She published her first book, *Annie Leibovitz: Photographs*, in 1983, and started working for *Vanity Fair* that same year. Notable photographs for the magazine include cover shots of actress Demi Moore pregnant and nude (1991) and actresses Keira Knightley and Scarlett Johansson nude with clothed designer TOM FORD (2006). Controversy erupted in 2008 when Leibovitz shot the 15-year-old singer Miley Cyrus clad in a sheet, leading the teen to apologize for participating in the photo shoot.

Leibovitz has also taken photographs to support social and political causes. In 1989, she photographed author Susan Sontag for her book *AIDS and Its Metaphors*, sparking a romantic relationship that Leibovitz has said profoundly influenced her work and lasted until Sontag's death in 2004. Encouraged by Sontag, Leibovitz documented her trip to war-torn Sarajevo in 1993, and in 1999 she published *Women*, juxtaposing photographs of famous women with those of miners, soldiers, and showgirls.

A major retrospective featuring more than 200 of her photographs opened at the Brooklyn Museum in 2006 and later traveled to major venues in Washington, D.C., San Francisco, and Berlin. That same year, Leibovitz had some bad financial dealings that nearly caused her to lose all the rights to her work. She resolved her financial woes in 2013. In 2007, she began a partnership with Disney, taking pictures of celebrities dressed in Disney Fantasy scenes for a campaign that continues today.

BORN Paris, October 11, 1889
DIED Anglet (near Biarritz), France, May 1, 1958

Lucien Lelong made his first designs at the age of 14 for his father, a successful dressmaker. He decided on a career in couture and designed his first collection; two days before its presentation in 1914, he was called into the Army. He was wounded in World War I, discharged after a year in the hospital, and received the French government's *Croix de Guerre*.

In 1918, Lelong entered his father's business and took control soon after. By 1926, the year he established Parfums Lelong, the house was flourishing and continued to do so until World War II. A farsighted businessman, in 1934 he was one of the first to establish a ready-to-wear line. Lelong was elected president of the Chambre Syndicale de la Couture Parisienne in 1937. He held the post for ten years—including throughout the Occupation period, when Germany wanted to move France's dressmaking industry to Berlin and Vienna. Lelong blocked the plan and guided couture safely through the war years. He reopened his own house in 1941 with CHRISTIAN DIOR and PIERRE BALMAIN as designers. In 1947, a serious illness caused Lelong to close his couture house, but he continued to direct his perfume business.

Lelong was considered a director of designers rather than a creator. In addition to Dior and Balmain, HUBERT DE GIVENCHY worked for him, and Dior particularly praised him as a good friend and generous employer. From 1919 to 1948, the House of Lelong produced distinguished collections of beautiful, feminine clothes for a conservative clientele. Lelong strongly believed in honest workmanship and good needlework, and it was his credo that a Lelong creation would hold together until its fabric wore out. He was also an accomplished painter, sculptor, composer, and sportsman.

Designer Lucien Lelong (left) and Lady Mendl (right).

NANETTE LEPORE

BORN Youngstown, Ohio, 1958

The child of an art professor and an abstract painter, Nanette Lepore was from a family that placed a high value on art. Inspired by the myth and romance of gypsy wanderlust, Lepore's creative spirit blossomed during family road trips across historic U.S. Route 66. She exhibited an early inclination for fashion when, at age nine, she designed an outfit for the child of a neighbor. After graduating from Youngstown University with a bachelor's degree, she moved to New York City to attend the Fashion Institute of Technology, earning a degree in design. After graduation she worked for several shops in New York's Garment District and married painter Robert Savage before opening her own business in 1992.

With her husband serving as president of her corporation, Lepore markets her collections to stores

Designer Nanette Lepore.

such as Saks Fifth Avenue, Neiman Marcus, and Macy's. She launched a shoe collection in 2006, adding to her already popular lines of dresses and handbags. She has also produced two perfumes, Shanghai Butterfly and Nanette Lepore, available at her nine boutiques worldwide. Lepore's colorfully patterned clothes are often described as gypsy-like and free-spirited.

Lepore is a strong advocate for clothing made in America and worked on the Save the Garment Center campaign. She documented the making of her Absolute Wonder Wedge shoe on film to showcase the shoe's origins at the LaLaLand factory in Los Angeles. Lepore has a strong following among editors, stylemakers, and celebrities such as Eva Longoria, Kerry Washington, and America Ferrera.

Spring 2014.

BORN Hervé Peugnet; Bapaume (Pas de Calais), France, May 30, 1957

In his previous design incarnation as Hervé Léger (Er-VAY LAY-zhay), Hervé Leroux (Luh-ROO) was known for his instantly recognizable, body-enhancing banded dresses. He was forced from his own design house by investors in 1999, but reemerged in 2000 with a small fall/winter collection and a new name suggested by KARL LAGERFELD, Hervé L. Leroux, which in English means Hervé the Red.

The designer's preparation for a fashion career was an education in art history and theater. In 1975, he began designing hats and accessories for designers such as Tan Giudicelli, and two years later he became an assistant first to Giudicelli, then to Lagerfeld at

Designer Hervé L. Leroux.

FENDI and CHANEL. He spent two years designing for the Italian firm Cadette, then in 1985 joined LANVIN, working with Maryll Lanvin on its ready-to-wear and couture collections. That same year, Lanvin gave Léger a boutique under his name and he collaborated with DIANE VON FURSTENBERG. He has designed furs for CHLOÉ, ready-to-wear for Charles Jourdan, and costumes for theater and advertising campaigns.

His first collection under the Léger label appeared in 1992, with both couture and deluxe ready-to-wear. The sensuous clothes wrapped the body closely with bands and tucks, at their best both seductive and beautiful. Later he replaced bands with draping and brash, bright colors with subtler, deeper tones, resulting in clothes that were beautiful, glamorous, and elegant. He has said that at the time, he was looking for a new way to wrap and follow the female form. Leroux calls CHARLES JAMES his main influence, followed by Lagerfeld.

In 1999, the couture house Hervé Léger was acquired by L.A.-based fashion giant BCBGMAXAZRIA Group. In 2000, Léger made a comeback and opened a boutique in Paris under the name Hervé L. Leroux, and briefly designed for GUY LAROCHE from 2004–2006. He rejoined Paris couture week in 2012, showing stunning made-to-measure draped dresses.

Guy Laroche.

Spring 2013.

MONIQUE LHUILLIER ⬛

BORN Cebu City, Philippines, 1971

AWARDS *Wedding Dresses* magazine *Glamorous Bridal Designer Award*, 2001; *Avant Garde Bridal Designer Award*, 2002; *Designer of the Year Award*, 2003, 2005–2006 • Philippines Government *Presidential Medal of Merit*, 2006

Designer Monique Lhuillier.

Spring 2014.

Raised in a prominent society family in the Philippines, Monique Lhuillier (LOO-lee-a) was interested in fashion at an early age. After attending boarding school in Switzerland, she moved to Los Angeles to enroll at the Fashion Institute of Design and Merchandising, where she later received a scholarship in the advanced studies program. As a young bride-to-be in the early 1990s, she designed dresses for herself and her wedding party when she could not find any to her liking. Thus her business was born. With her husband, Tom Bugbee, she launched her upscale bridal company in 1996, and success among celebrities and the fashion-savvy quickly followed.

Spring 2014.

Lhuillier's designs distinguish themselves from much of the bridal market for their glamour and sophistication—designs that are dramatic but soft, often with a textural interplay of fabrics. This sensibility

has translated well to her expansion into eveningwear, launched in 2001, and ready-to-wear, introduced in 2003. Her spring 2009 ready-to-wear collection reached even further by pairing floaty evening fabrics with sportier skirts for a chic contrast. Her wedding and evening wear dresses have been worn by Avril Lavigne, Ashley Greene, and Michelle Obama.

Spring 2014.

ALEXANDER LIBERMAN

BORN Kiev, Ukraine, September 12, 1912
DIED Miami, November 19, 1999

AWARDS Paris Exposition Internazionale *Gold Medal for Design*, 1937

As editorial director at CONDÉ NAST for 34 years, Alexander Liberman nurtured his love of painting, sculpture, and photography while fulfilling vast professional responsibilities. While he is a legend in the fashion publication business, it is impossible to overlook his accomplishments in public sculpture or his influence on intellectual and artistic life in the 20th century.

Born to a prosperous timber merchant, Liberman was so disturbed by the 1917 Russian Revolution that his father took him to London in 1921 at the age of nine. He attended boarding schools, learning the language and manners of the English gentry, then moved again in 1924 with his mother to Paris. There he studied painting and architecture at l'École des Beaux-Arts and worked for graphic designer Adolphe Cassandre.

In 1931, Liberman became art director and later managing editor of *Vu* magazine, an early precursor to *LIFE*. He fled occupied France in 1941 and made his way to New York City, where he took a position at *Vogue*, eventually becoming its artistic director. In 1960, Liberman became art director of all Condé Nast publications, and in 1962 editorial director, continuing in that position until he retired in 1994. Such longevity is rare in an industry known for short editorial tenures.

Liberman was responsible for Condé Nast's avant-garde vision throughout the 1960s and 1970s, forever altering the look and philosophy of fashion magazines.

Art Director Alexander Liberman.

His adaptive style and eye for social change kept the publications under his watch fresh, hip, and attuned to the zeitgeist.

Liberman also exhibited his own work while at Condé Nast. He produced several books, including *The Artist in His Studio; Marlene: An Intimate Photographic Memoir* (a tribute to Marlene Dietrich); and *Then,* a collection of black and white photos of celebrities ranging from Truman Capote to COCO CHANEL. His highly regarded metal sculptures are found in parks, campuses, and private grounds around the world.

Designer Phillip Lim.

a runner-up in 2007. In 2007, he was also a finalist for the Fashion Design Award presented by the Cooper-Hewitt Museum of Design and opened his first store in Soho, New York. In 2008, Lim created a limited edition line for The Gap and opened new boutiques in Tokyo and Los Angeles.

Lim's mission is to design "clothes people wear," and his collections have been described as "pretty but cool" and "super-chic without the sky-high prices." His collections include shoes, belts, handbags, men's wear, and a children's wear line called kid by phillip lim. They have been worn by stars such as Keira Knightley, Kate Bosworth, and Amanda Peet.

In 2013, Target hired Lim to design a fall capsule collection that was highly sought-after. Lim told *The Wall Street Journal* that Target had been eying him for years, but he had previously not been ready to design for the masses.

BORN Thailand, 1973

AWARDS Fashion Group International *Women's Designer Rising Star*, 2006
• Council of Fashion Designers of America (CFDA) *Swarovski Award for Emerging Talent in Womenswear*, 2007; *Swarovski Award for Menswear*, 2012; *Accessories Designer of the Year*, 2013

Phillip Lim is one of America's most popular young sportswear designers. After graduating from California State University, Long Beach in 1997, Lim was a design assistant to Katayone Adeli for a year and a half before becoming cofounder and head designer for the L.A.-based label Development. In 2005, Lim moved to New York and, with the help of his friend and business partner Wen Khou, established his label, 3.1 Phillip Lim. In 2006, less than a year after launching his company, Lim was a finalist for the prestigious CFDA/*Vogue* Fashion Fund, and was

Spring 2009.

Spring 2014.

CHRISTIAN LOUBOUTIN 👜

BORN Paris, January 7, 1964

AWARDS Fashion Group International *Fashion Footwear Association of New York Award*, 1996 • Footwear News Achievement Awards *Person of the Year*, 2010

Christian Louboutin (LOO-boo-tawn), whose father was an architect-designer of train interiors, fell in love with shoes at an early age when he was taken to a museum with a magnificent parquet floor. At the entrance there was a large sign with the silhouette of a high-heeled pump in a red circle sliced through with a red line, and inside women were walking around shoeless. He started sketching the design on school books, homework, and notebooks. At 16, he was given a book on shoe designer ROGER VIVIER, and his dedication to shoes became total.

His education continued backstage at the Folies Bergère, where he learned the importance of function— shoes had to be sturdy enough to take the grind of dancing, jumping, and kicking, and not cause injuries. At 18, he landed a job with CHRISTIAN DIOR's shoe designer, Charles Jourdan, where he learned technique. He

Designer Christian Louboutin.

freelanced for CHANEL, SAINT LAURENT, and Maud Frizon, then worked with his idol Vivier on his retrospective at the Louvre. Watching and studying, Louboutin developed his characteristic silhouette—slim and pointy-toed, reminiscent of the 1950s—and signature red soles.

The first Louboutin boutique opened in Paris in 1992, followed by London, New York, and Los Angeles. His shoes also are sold in luxury stores from Tokyo to São Paulo. He has continued to collaborate with designers as varied as Saint Laurent, GAULTIER, RODARTE, and SCOTT.

In 2011, Louboutin celebrated his 20th anniversary with the release of a book, *Louboutin*. In 2012, he entered the beauty market, created a *Cinderella*-inspired slipper to complement the Blu-ray release of the film, and created a Barbie doll for Mattel. In 2013, his first men's wear store opened in New York City. Though many have tried to copy his shoes, in 2012 a court ruled that only Louboutin could sell his trademarked red soles.

Left: Red-soled peep-toe, 2009.
Right: Blue sequin heel, 2010.

BORN Jean Louis Berthault; Paris, October 5, 1907
DIED Palm Springs, California, April 20, 1997

AWARDS Academy Award for Best Costume Design
The Solid Gold Cadillac, 1956

First at Columbia, where JAMES GALANOS worked as his assistant, and later at Universal, Jean Louis was head designer for major Hollywood movie studios. His 60 film credits include *Pal Joey*, *Ship of Fools*, *Born Yesterday*, *A Star is Born*, and *From Here to Eternity*.

Designer Jean Louis (left) and Nina Foch (right).

He made costumes for the films and fashions for many of Hollywood's brightest stars, including Lana Turner, Vivien Leigh, Joan Crawford, Rosalind Russell, Greta Garbo, Katharine Hepburn, and Judy Garland. He also designed gowns for Loretta Young's entrances on the *Loretta Young Show*, an eight-year fixture on NBC.

Louis trained in Paris, moved to America in 1936, and went to work at HATTIE CARNEGIE, where he designed the prototype of the little Carnegie suit. With its closely fitted jacket and straight skirt, it became the uniform of ladies who lunch. His tenure there coincided with those of CLAIRE MCCARDELL and NORMAN NORELL.

In 1943, Louis left New York and private customers for Hollywood, working for the studios until the early 1960s. He then opened a salon in Beverly Hills, continuing film work on a freelance basis. Louis retired in 1988 and in 1993 married Loretta Young.

Actress Marilyn Monroe wearing dress by Jean Louis.

ANNE COLE LOWE

BORN Clayton, Alabama, 1898
DIED Queens, New York, 1981

AWARDS New York Fashion Society *Couturier of the Year*, 1961

Anne Cole Lowe is one of many talented African-American designers that time has forgotten. Her mother was a competent seamstress who sewed for some of Alabama's top figures. When Lowe was a child, she and her mother moved to New York City; shortly after, her mother died, and Lowe took over her seamstress work. At 14, she married; that same year, she began attending S.T. Taylor School, pursuing a degree in fashion design—the first African-American to do so.

After graduating, she moved with her husband to Tampa, Florida, and opened a small salon. A few years later, she and her husband divorced and she returned to New York. In 1951, she had a chance meeting with Jacqueline Bouvier, who requested several dresses from her. After her engagement to then-Massachusetts Senator John F. Kennedy, Bouvier asked Lowe to design her wedding dress, as well as ten others for members of her wedding party. The dress was called the most photographed wedding dress in American history. Though few acknowledged her contribution at the time, Lowe's relationship with Jacqueline Kennedy led to other high-profile positions designing for New York and D.C. elites, such as the Rockefellers.

In 1960, Lowe closed her shop and became a featured designer in the Adam Room at Saks Fifth Avenue

Jacqueline Kennedy in her wedding gown designed by Anne Cole Lowe, 1953.

in New York, where she was known for using the trapunto—whole-cloth quilting—technique in sewing. In 1964, she reopened her salon. In 1964, on the *Mike Douglas Show*, Lowe said that her desire was not fame and fortune, but "to prove that a Negro could become a major dress designer."

In her later years she was stricken with glaucoma and became blind in one eye. By her retirement in 1970, Lowe was penniless. She died in 1981.

Designer Julien Macdonald.

Above: Fall 2013.
Right: Spring 2014.

♛ JULIEN MACDONALD

BORN Wales, March 19, 1971

When LVMH chose Julien Macdonald to replace ALEXANDER MCQUEEN at GIVENCHY in 2001, he was not well known beyond fashion's inner circles but had a solid background designing knitwear for CHANEL couture. His success at knits seems natural, as he grew up in a family of gifted knitters steeped in an age-old Welsh tradition.

After some dance training, Macdonald studied for a year at Cardiff Art College, where he discovered a passion for textile design. He moved on to the University of Brighton, began experimenting with knitwear techniques, and earned a B.A. in fashion textiles. He then obtained an M.A. from the Royal College of Art in London. His 1996 graduate collection of finely spun knit dresses and cobwebby crochets caught the attention of KARL LAGERFELD, who brought him to Chanel as a knitwear designer.

Macdonald launched his own company in 1997 with a spectacularly experimental collection. Subsequent showings—a combination of ethereal, gossamer knits and glitzy, sequined dresses featuring serious slits—have attracted a considerable celebrity following. The London fashion press has dubbed him "the Welsh GIANNI VERSACE."

Macdonald stayed with Givenchy for three years, and in 2004 announced he was leaving a day after showing his spring 2004 haute couture collection. Since 2003, Macdonald has also designed the lower-priced Star label for Britain's Debenhams department store.

Macdonald appeared on the television show *Britain & Ireland's Next Top Model* from 2010 to 2013 as a host and judge, and in 2013 he collaborated with the English National Ballet and Swarovski to create ten costumes for the Queen's Coronation Festival that were shown at Buckingham Palace.

BOB MACKIE 👗 👗

Designer Bob Mackie.

BORN Los Angeles, March 24, 1940

AWARDS Council of Fashion Designers of America
(CFDA) *Special Award (fashion exuberance)*, 2001

Bob Mackie grew up in Los Angeles, where he studied art
and theater design. While still in art school, he worked
as a sketcher for designers JEAN LOUIS and EDITH
HEAD, and for Ray Aghayan, whose partner he became.
The spectacular costume designs that he and Aghayan
have designed, together and separately, for nightclub
performers and television and movie stars have put
them at the top of their field.
Among the celebrities
they have dressed are
Marlene Dietrich,
Carol Burnett, Mitzi
Gaynor, Barbra Streisand, Raquel
Welch, Carol Channing,
and—most notably—Cher.

Mackie's talents extend well beyond
costumes. He has been successful in
both couture and ready-to-wear and has also
ventured into swimwear and loungewear. His
work was the subject of a major show at New
York's Fashion Institute of Technology in fall
1999. It covered every aspect of his work, from
his designs for *The Carol Burnett Show* and
costumes for Cher to his couture and ready-to-
wear lines. There were even costumes for Barbie

Fall 2002.

that presented the doll as various historical figures.
Mackie's technical mastery, allied with his ebullient wit
and sense of fun, was evident in every element of the
exhibit. In 2008, Cher signed a three-year contract to
perform at Caesars Palace in Las Vegas, and Mackie
designed her costumes for the engagement. He also
designed singer Pink's wardrobe for her 2009 *Funhouse*
tour, including the costume she wore during her
performance at the 52nd Grammy Awards.

Mackie has done other memorable designs
for Barbie, including the
Went with the Wind! doll
honoring Carol Burnett in
2009. The doll and its dress
were featured at the National
Museum of American History as
part of the Kennedy Center Honors
Collection.

In 2011, Mackie received the Design
Legend Award from Otis College of Art and
Design in Los Angeles. Mackie now has a home
classics collection and has developed a devoted
following from his 20-year-old *Wearable Art*
program on the QVC television network.

Fall 2002.

♦ ⚫ TOMAS MAIER (BOTTEGA VENETA)

Designer Tomas Maier.

BORN Phorzheim, Germany, 1957

Tomas Maier grew up watching his architect father working at his drafting table, and may have inherited his love of precision and clean lines. After training in Paris with Sonia Rykiel, Revillon, and Hermès (where he spent ten years), Maier launched his own label in 1997. His line of elegant resort wear and accessories is sold in boutiques in Florida and elsewhere.

Maier went high-profile in 2001, when the Gucci Group purchased the ailing Italian luxury leather goods brand Bottega Veneta and hired him as creative director. The company's original advertising slogan from the 1970s, "When Your Own Initials Are Enough," along with its famous woven *intrecciato* pattern, was a perfect fit for Maier's concept of timeless luxury. Maier has claimed that the company will never produce a short-lived "It" bag. Expansion proved to be the key to success: today Maier oversees Bottega Veneta's handbags, luggage, shoes, eyewear, jewelry, and home collection, along with ready-to-wear lines for men and women. His designs are sleek, classic, and super-luxe, both upholding and updating the company's profile

In 2011, Maier introduced Bottega Veneta's first fragrance for women, and in 2013 its first for men. In 2012, the company released an eponymous coffee table book to rave reviews. Maier said that "the book is a kind of declaration about the tight relationship between designers and artisans. We don't work that well without each other."

Bottega Veneta, fall 2009.

Bottega Veneta men's wear, spring 2010.

MAINBOCHER ⧖

BORN Main Rousseau Bocher; Chicago, October 24, 1890
DIED Munich, Germany, December 26, 1976

Noted for a nearly infallible sense of fashion, Mainbocher (Man-bo-SHAY) created high-priced clothes of quiet good taste, simplicity, and understatement. He was the first American designer to succeed in Paris and before that had a distinguished career as a fashion journalist.

Encouraged by his mother, Mainbocher studied art at the Chicago Academy of Fine Arts and in New York, Paris, and Munich. During World War I, he went to France with an American ambulance unit and stayed in Paris afterward to study singing. To support himself, he worked as an illustrator for *Harper's Bazaar* and French *Vogue*. In 1922, he became a full-time fashion journalist, eventually becoming the editor of French *Vogue*. During his journalism career, Mainbocher created the *Vogue's Eye View* column and discovered artist ERIC and photographer GEORGE HOYNINGEN-HUENE. He left publishing in 1929 to open his own Paris salon.

Designer Mainbocher.

With his many influential contacts and sure fashion sense, Mainbocher was an immediate success. The Duchess of Windsor, whose wedding dress he made, and Lady Mendl were among his clients. It is said that in his first year in business, he introduced the strapless evening gown and persuaded French textile manufacturers to once again set up double looms and weave the wide widths not produced since before World War I.

Mainbocher left Paris at the outbreak of World War II and in 1939 opened a couture house in New York City. He designed elegant and expensive clothes for elegant and expensive women, screening clients based on his stringent standards. He also designed uniforms for the American Red Cross, the Navy WAVES, the Coast Guard SPARS, and the Girl Scouts.

Mainbocher's work was greatly influenced by MADELEINE VIONNET, and he made masterful use of the bias cut. Elegant evening clothes were his forte, from long ball gowns of lace or transparent fabrics to short dresses and beaded sweaters with jeweled buttons. He made dinner suits of tweed, combining them with blouses of delicate fabrics. Pastel gingham was a signature, accessorized with pearl chokers, short white kid gloves, and plain pumps. Mainbocher knew his worth and insisted that fashion magazines show his designs on facing pages—never mixed with those of other designers, no matter how great.

Also a skilled editor of others' work, Mainbocher has been ranked with MOLYNEUX, SCHIAPARELLI, and LELONG. His oft-quoted design philosophy was: "The responsibility and challenge . . . is to consider the design and the woman at the same time. Women should look beautiful, rather than just trendful."

The Duke and Duchess of Windsor (in Mainbocher) on their wedding day, 1937.

Models backstage at Catherine Malandrino's spring 2007 runway show.

BORN Grenoble, France, April 22, 1963

A graduate of l'Ecole Supérieure des Arts et Techniques de la Mode (Esmod) in France, Catherine Malandrino began her career with the houses of Dorothée Bis, Louis Féraud, Emanuel Ungaro, and Et Vous. In 1998, she moved to New York City to help relaunch the Diane von Furstenberg label as head designer and presented her first Collage collection. In 2000, her Flag collection debuted to critical acclaim and was worn by several celebrities, including Halle Berry and Madonna. Malandrino also created a collection with Mary J. Blige in 2001 and a collection worn by Sarah Jessica Parker on the television show *Sex and the City* in 2002.

Malandrino opened her flagship store in 2004 in New York's Meatpacking district, and a boutique in Paris the following year. In 2006, she debuted her couture line, Malandrino, to supplement her contemporary line, Catherine Malandrino. In 2008, she presented her first costume jewelry line and opened a boutique in Istanbul, Turkey. She has also opened boutiques in Kuwait and the United Arab Emirates. Two additional boutiques opened in America in 2008, including Catherine Malandrino Maison—a concept store that includes a café, library, and outdoor terrace.

Designer Catherine Malandrino.

Malandrino uses knitwear, silks, and playful accents to showcase a rock-and-roll attitude. She has said that she wants to "design irresistible clothes that make a woman desirable." Her spring/summer 2010 collection inspired a new BMW 5 Series Gran Turismo, and Malandrino starred in advertising for the car, which presented it as her ultimate companion. In 2011, Elie Tahari and Arthur Levine invested in the Malandrino brand as "equal partners" to help expand sales. In 2013, Malandrino released a collection for Kohl's inspired by her love for Paris. She lives in New York with her husband and son.

Flag dress, Spring 2001.

MAN RAY 📷

BORN Emmanuel Radnitzky; Philadelphia, Pennsylvania, August 27, 1890
DIED Paris, November 18, 1976

Man Ray was the eldest child of Jewish Russian immigrants. In 1912, his family changed its surname from Radnitzky to Ray—a reaction to the ethnic discrimination and anti-Semitism prevalent at the time. He shortened his first name Emmanuel to Man, and gradually began using Man Ray as his combined single name.

More interested in art than commercial photography, Man Ray was nevertheless one of the fashion world's most innovative photographers, introducing elements of Surrealism into his fashion work. He started working for PAUL POIRET around 1921, using glass plates and operating out of Poiret's darkroom. He photographed

Photographer Man Ray.

the couture section of the 1925 Decorative Arts Exposition in Paris. After working in New York City, he returned to Paris with American models, who brought an American accent to his work. He photographed the Paris collections from 1938 to 1940, sometimes during air raid warnings, before returning to America. After World War II, he abandoned fashion to devote himself to art and experimental photography.

Rrose Sélavy (alter-ego of Marcel Duchamp) photographed by Man Ray.

Designer Isabel Marant.

BORN Paris, 1967

AWARDS *British Glamour* Women of the Year Awards *Female Designer of the Year*, 2010

Known for her bohemian aesthetic and chic tomboy looks, as well as for creating the wedge sneaker, Isabel Marant was a tomboy while growing up. But while she enjoyed dressing in her father's clothing, she often refashioned it into dresses. Her parents divorced when she was a child, and she spent a lot of time traveling abroad to destinations such as Asia and Africa. Her father remarried a refined, chic West Indian woman who—along with Marant's eccentric nanny, who wore unconventional outfits—inspired the young Marant. In 1982, her father gave her a sewing machine, and she began creating designs using refurbished clothes and fabrics and selling them to her friends. Marant soon realized that she wanted to study fashion, so in 1985 she enrolled in Studio Bercot Fashion School in Paris.

After graduation, Marant interned with Michael Klein and worked with Bridget Yorke. In 1989, she began working on her own collections. She first launched a jewelry line and in 1990, a knitwear line with her mother that became the namesake Isabel Marant label in 1994, when she set up her own studio in the trendy Marais district of Paris. In 1997, Marant received the Award de la Mode and in 1998, the Whirlpool Award for best female designer. In 1998, she also created a collection for French mail catalog La Redoute, launched I*M in Japan, and opened her first store on the rue de Charonne.

◤ ISABEL MARANT

In 1999, she debuted a diffusion line, Etoile by Isabel Marant, featuring jeans, t-shirts, and lingerie. In 2004, she launched a children's wear line, and in 2006 she collaborated with Anthropologie. In 2010, Marant opened her first store in New York City and premiered her Otway studded biker bootie featuring a triangular heel. *The Wall Street Journal* reported on the buying frenzy for the shoe, which sparked an international waiting list.

In 2012, Marant opened a London store and expanded her Paris headquarters. That same year, she launched her iconic wedge sneaker, which instantly became a cult favorite and was quickly copied. In 2013, Marant collaborated with H&M to create women's, men's, and children's wear collections. She also recently collaborated with Heritage Paris to create two skateboards, inspired by the opening of her store in Los Angeles. Marant is a major force in fashion and is building her business "step by step, in order to maintain full freedom and honesty in my work."

Spring 2014.

MARTIN MARGIELA ▼

BORN Belgium, April 9, 1957

Martin Margiela burst onto the Paris fashion scene in the late 1980s, one of a group of fashion iconoclasts from unexpected venues—Belgium for Margiela and DRIES VAN NOTEN, and Austria for HELMUT LANG. Well-trained in classic techniques, they have used their considerable skills to turn accepted ideas about clothes inside-out and upside-down, dismantling conventional approaches to beauty and fashion.

From 1976 to 1980, Margiela studied at the Academy of Fine Arts in Antwerp, and in 1984 moved to Paris to work as an assistant to JEAN PAUL GAULTIER. In 1988, he presented his first collection, for spring/summer 1989. Reflecting his view of the times we live in, Margiela has made clothes of recycled materials—turning used linings into dresses, making subway posters or broken china into waistcoats, and constructing shirts from torn-apart socks and hosiery. He thinks "it is beautiful to make new things out of rejects or worn stuff," and when he slashes down old or new clothes, it is not to destroy them but rather to bring them back to life in a different form. For his fifth anniversary in 1993, he recreated his favorite pieces from the previous five years.

Margiela's unconventional clothes have been matched by offbeat show locations: a children's playground, a parking lot, an abandoned subway station, a Salvation Army flea market, and the cellar of the Pont Alexandre III—perhaps the most beautiful bridge in Paris. One of fashion's true originals, he became known through his press-attracting ploys but is personally reclusive and refuses to be photographed; he

Spring 2014.

Haute couture, spring 2014.

would not even bow at the end of his shows. He is a master of classic tailoring, on which his best work rests.

In addition to his own collection, Maison Martin Margiela, he has been a consultant to two Italian sportswear houses and, from 1997 to 2003, was head designer for HERMÈS, a French bastion of tradition. At the end of his contract there, he was replaced by Gaultier. In 2002, his company was sold to Renzo Rosso, the owner of the Italian company Diesel Group. The company celebrated its 20th anniversary in 2008 with a special exhibition at the MoMu Fashion Museum in Antwerp.

In 2009, Margiela left the business he created. In 2012, the former creative director of CÉLINE, Ivana Omazic, was hired by Maison Martin Margiela, but her position was not formally announced due to the company's collaborative and often secretive nature. This brought about much curiosity from the press. In 2013, Maison Martin Margiela outfitted Kanye West for his *Yeezus* tour.

Designer Vera Maxwell.

 VERA MAXWELL

BORN Vera Huppe; New York City, April 22, 1901
DIED Rincón, Puerto Rico, January 14, 1995

AWARDS Coty American Fashion Critics' Awards
Special Award (coats and suits), 1951 • Neiman Marcus Award, 1955

Vera Maxwell was one of a small group of American designers of the 1930s and 1940s, including true originals such as BONNIE CASHIN and CLAIRE MCCARDELL, who worked independently of Europe. She was also among an even smaller group of women who successfully ran their own businesses.

Maxwell was the daughter of Viennese parents with whom she traveled to Europe and whose values provided the core of her early education. She went to high school in Leonia, New Jersey, studied ballet, and danced with the Metropolitan Opera Ballet from 1919 until 1924.

Maxwell specialized in simple, timeless clothes marked by the effortless good looks and ease of movement highly valued by active American women. They were largely go-together separates in fine Scottish tweeds, wool jersey, raw silk, Indian embroideries, and Ultrasuede. Among her numerous innovations were the weekend wardrobe of 1935, consisting of a collarless jacket in tweed and gray flannel, a short pleated flannel tennis skirt, a longer pleated tweed skirt, and cuffed flannel trousers. There was also a cotton coverall for war workers that could be considered the precursor of the jumpsuit, print dresses with coats lined in matching print, and the "Speed Dress" consisting of a stretch-nylon top, full skirt of polyester knit, and print stole—no zippers, buttons, or hooks.

Maxwell was honored in 1970 with a retrospective at the Smithsonian Institution in Washington, D.C. In 1978, a party and show were given at the Museum of the City of New York to celebrate her 75th birthday and 50th year as a designer. She continued to work until 1985, when she abruptly closed her business. In 1986, at 83, she went back to work with a fall collection of sportswear, dresses, and coats but soon retired again to spend most of her time working on her memoirs, which were never published.

CLAIRE McCARDELL ⧗

BORN Frederick, Maryland, May 24, 1905
DIED New York City, March 23, 1958

AWARDS Coty American Fashion Critics' Awards *Winnie*, 1944; *Hall of Fame Award (posthumous)*, 1958 • *Neiman Marcus Award*, 1948 • National Women's Press Club *Certificate of Achievement*, 1950 • Parsons *Medal for Distinguished Achievement*, 1956 • *Fashion Walk of Fame*, 2000

Claire McCardell is credited with originating the "American Look," easy and unforced, and a striking contrast to structured, European-inspired fashion. She fully understood the needs of the modern American woman, with her full schedule of work and play, and designed specifically for her. Her philosophy was simple: clothes should be clean-lined, functional, comfortable, and appropriate to the occasion. They should fit well, flow naturally with the body, and, of course, be attractive.

Designer Claire McCardell.

Model wearing Claire McCardell design.

Buttons had to button, and sashes had to be long enough not only to tie, but also to wrap around.

Her father was a banker and state senator, and McCardell grew up in comfortable circumstances. As a child she showed an interest in clothes with outfits for paper dolls, and as a teenager she designed her own clothes. She attended Hood College for Women in Maryland and studied fashion illustration at Parsons School of Design in New York City and for a year in Paris. Returning to New York, she painted lampshades for B. Altman & Co. and modeled briefly, joining Robert Turk, Inc. in 1929 as a model and assistant designer. When Turk moved to Townley Frocks, Inc., McCardell moved with him, taking over as designer after his death. She stayed with Townley until 1938, when she moved to Hattie Carnegie, returning to Townley in 1940, first as designer, then as designer-partner. She remained there until her death in 1958.

McCardell picked up details from men's clothing and work clothes, such as large pockets, blue-jeans topstitching, trouser pleats, rivets, and gripper fastenings. Her favorite fabrics were sturdy cotton denim, ticking, gingham, and wool jersey. She used colored zippers in an ornamental way, spaghetti ties, and surprise color

Model wearing bare-back sundress.

American designers whose work might be considered in the McCardell tradition: DONNA KARAN, ISAAC MIZRAHI, ANNA SUI, Adri, and MICHAEL KORS.

Interest in McCardell was also strong in 1998. Her designs were included in the show *American Ingenuity* at the Costume Institute of the Metropolitan Museum of Art, she was honored by a show at the Maryland Historical Society, and the Fashion Institute of Technology mounted an exhibition, *Claire McCardell and the American Look*. Stanley Marcus, a major retailer of the era, called her "the master of the line, never the slave of the sequin. She is one of the few creative designers this country has ever produced."

juxtapositions. The result was sophisticated, wearable clothes, often with witty touches.

Among her many innovations were the diaper bathing suit, the monastic dress—waistless, bias-cut, dartless—the "Popover," the kitchen dinner dress, and ballet slippers worn with day clothes. She also designed sunglasses, infant and children's wear, children's shoes, and costume jewelry. Her designs were totally contemporary; the proof of her genius is that they still look contemporary. Parsons honored her in 1994 with an exhibition, *Claire McCardell: Redefining Modernism*, one of the events celebrating the school's 100th anniversary. The show also included clothes from contemporary

Model wearing pink dinner shirt tucked into light, full skirt in sheer cotton chambray.

PATRICK MCCARTHY

BORN June 15, 1951

AWARDS Council of Fashion Designers of America (CFDA) *Media Award in Honor of Eugenia Sheppard*, 1994

Patrick McCarthy has spent his entire career in journalism with Fairchild Publications since taking a job as a reporter at its Washington, D.C. bureau in 1977. He has held many positions, including London bureau chief, Paris bureau chief, European editor, and editor and executive editor of *W* and *Women's Wear Daily*. He was also executive vice president of editorial for the company and in 1993 oversaw the transformation of *W* from a biweekly broadsheet newspaper to a monthly glossy magazine, broadening its focus beyond traditional couture houses to include stories on new luxury brands and popular retail operations as well as celebrities, lifestyles, and business. Since 1997, he has been chairman and editorial director, succeeding John B. Fairchild, and in 2006 McCarthy was named chairman and editorial director of *W* and Fairchild Fashion Group, which includes *WWD* and *Footwear News*.

McCarthy studied at Boston and Stanford universities before joining Fairchild, where he became known early on for his biting interview technique. Having sat down with famous designers from KARL LAGERFELD to GIORGIO ARMANI, he often gets his subjects to divulge more than they had intended. During his tenure, *W* received 13 National Magazine Award nominations, winning for photo portfolio/

Journalist and editor Patrick McCarthy.

photo essay in 2004 and photography in 1998 and 2006. In 2010, McCarthy stepped down from his role at *W*. Many reporters and designers considered his departure the end of an era.

Designer Stella McCartney (center) with models wearing her Resort 2014 collection.

▲ STELLA MCCARTNEY

one-off collection Stella McCartney for H&M sold out worldwide in record time. Her fragrance Stella in Two was introduced in 2006.

She unveiled CARE by Stella McCartney, the first luxury 100 percent organic skincare line, in collaboration with YSL Beaute in 2007. That was followed by a lingerie line and limited edition travel collection with LeSportsac in 2008. In 2009, McCartney debuted a children's wear collection for Gapkids and BabyGap, and in 2010 she collaborated with Disney to create an *Alice in Wonderland* jewelry collection. In 2012, she made history by being appointed creative director for Adidas Team Great Britain, the first time a designer has been hired to create apparel for both the Olympic and Paralympic Games.

McCartney operates 23 stores worldwide and her collections are distributed in more than 50 countries, including through specialty shops and department stores.

BORN London, September 13, 1971

AWARDS VH1/*Vogue* Fashion and Music *Designer of the Year Award*, 2000 • *Glamour Designer of the Year Award*, 2004; *Woman of the Year Award*, 2009 • Fashion Group International *Star Honoree*, 2004 • *Organic Style Woman of the Year Award*, 2005 • *ELLE Style Designer of the Year Award*, 2007 • British Style Awards *Designer of the Year*, 2007 • Spanish *ELLE Designer of the Year Award*, 2008 • ACE Awards *Green Designer of the Year*, 2008 • *TIME Magazine 100*, 2009 • British Fashion Council *Designer and Brand of the Year, 2012* • British Government *Officer of the Order of the British Empire (OBE)*, 2013

Stella McCartney graduated from Central Saint Martins College of Arts and Design in 1995. Her signature style of sharp tailoring, natural confidence, and sexy femininity was immediately apparent in her first collection. After just two collections, in 1997 she was appointed creative director of CHLOÉ in Paris and enjoyed great success during her tenure.

In 2001, McCartney launched her own fashion house in a joint venture with GUCCI Group. She understands the needs of those in her age group and designs clothes to fit their lives, combining sensuality with a contemporary edge. She does not use any leather or fur in her designs. McCartney's collections include women's ready-to-wear, accessories, eyewear, fragrance, and organic skincare. Her perfume, Stella, launched successfully in 2003.

McCartney also entered into a long-term partnership with adidas in 2004. The acclaimed sports performance collection, adidas by Stella McCartney, has since grown to include several sports categories. In 2005, the

Spring 2014.

JESSICA MCCLINTOCK ▼

Designer Jessica McClintock (center) with models.

BORN Presque Isle, Maine, June 19, 1930

AWARDS American Printed Fabrics Council *Tommy Award*, 1968 • Dallas Fashion Awards, 1987, 1988, 1990, 1993

Jessica McClintock was raised in Maine by her mother, and as a child made patterns and designed her own clothes. Her training came from her grandmother, who was a patternmaker and seamstress. McClintock married at 19, moved to California, and after her husband's death in 1963, remarried, divorced, and taught school. In 1969, she invested $5,000 in a tiny California company called Gunne Sax. From this small beginning, she has built a multifaceted company operating internationally and carved a niche with her highly personal blend of prettiness and old-fashioned allure.

A formidable businesswoman, McClintock has added divisions over time, extending her romantic viewpoint to bridal fashion and children's wear, plus licensing for accessories, china, and home furnishings. There are numerous fragrances and company-owned boutiques. She has received awards from a wide range of business, charitable, and educational organizations and is a member of the Council of Fashion Designers of America (CFDA).

Model wearing Jessica McClintock design.

Designer Mary McFadden.

BORN New York City, October 1, 1938

AWARDS Coty American Fashion Critics' Awards *Winnie*, 1976; *Return Award*, 1978; *Hall of Fame Award*, 1979 • American Printed Fabrics Council *Tommy Award*, 1984, 1991

Until she was ten, Mary McFadden lived on a plantation near Memphis, Tennessee, where her father was a cotton broker. After his death, she returned north with her mother. She attended Foxcroft School in Virginia, Traphagen School of Fashion in New York City, and École Lubec in Paris; she also studied sociology at Columbia University and the New School for Social Research.

From 1962 to 1964, McFadden was director of public relations for CHRISTIAN DIOR New York. She married an executive of the DeBeers diamond firm and moved to Africa in 1964. There she became editor of *Vogue* South Africa; when it closed, she contributed to the French and American editions. She also wrote weekly columns on social and political life for *The Rand Daily Mail*. She divorced, remarried in 1968, and moved to Rhodesia, where she founded Vokutu, a sculpture workshop for native artists.

⬥ MARY MCFADDEN

McFadden returned to New York in 1970 and went to work for *Vogue* as a special projects editor. While there she designed three tunics using unusual Chinese and African silks she had collected on her travels; they were shown in the magazine and bought by Henri Bendel, New York. The silks were hand painted using various resist techniques, with colors that had an Oriental feel, and used the calligraphy and negative spacing that became hallmarks of her style. Mary McFadden Inc. was established in 1976.

Exotic colorings, extensive use of fine pleating and quilting, and ropes wrapping the figure have all been recurring themes. McFadden's poetic evening designs are her best-known work, but all of it shares a refined and sophisticated perspective. In addition to the high-priced luxury collection, her design projects have ranged from lingerie and at-home wear to furs, bed and bath, and upholstery fabrics. She is a past president of the Council of Fashion Designers of America (CFDA).

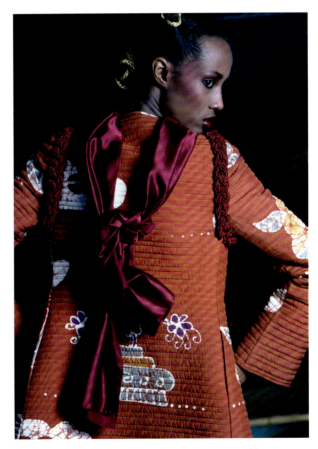
Model wearing hand-quilted jacket by Mary McFadden.

ARTHUR MCGEE

BORN Detroit, Michigan, 1933

Arthur McGee grew up in Detroit watching his mother sew for a living. In 1951, he noticed an ad for a design competition at the prestigious Traphagen School of Design in New York City. He won the contest and was awarded a scholarship to attend the school, but was disappointed with its curriculum and transferred to the Fashion Institute of Technology.

In 1957, McGee produced designs for Bobby Brooks, becoming the first African-American to design on Seventh Avenue. He later opened his famous shop on St. Mark's Place in New York. His shop produced outfits for a variety of professional clientele that included many celebrities, such as Cicely Tyson, Mrs. Harry Belafonte, Stevie Wonder, and Arthur Mitchell—founder of the Dance Theater of Harlem. His designs were influenced by African and Asian cultures. He loved ethnic prints and simple shapes.

Designer Arthur McGee.

McGee takes great pains to be viewed not as an African-American designer but simply as an American designer. In a 1992 interview with *Newsweek* he said, "We are not 'black' designers but American designers, the way BILL BLASS is an American designer. As soon as you categorize us, you can erase us." Still, in 2009 the Costume Institute of the Metropolitan Museum of Art honored McGee and his legacy, calling him the dean of African-American designers. Interviews with McGee appear in the documentary *Defining Style: The Untold Story of Fashion Designers of Color: Circa 1960s–1990s.*

Design by Arthur McGee.

Makeup artist Pat McGrath.

BORN East Midlands, England, 1970

AWARDS British Government *Member of the Order of the British Empire (MBE), 2014*

Vogue considers Pat McGrath the world's most influential makeup artist. Born to a single mother of Jamaican descent, McGrath's upbringing was quite strict and religious. Her mother was a devoted Jehovah's Witness, but she was very knowledgeable about fashion and color. She would quiz Pat about different shades of eye color and was always mixing her own colors due to the lack of flattering shades available for black skin. Pat McGrath became fascinated by musicians such as Boy George and the members of Spandau Ballet, who used makeup to create theatrical stage identities.

McGrath went to Northampton College and completed her art foundation courses toward her fashion degree. During her second year, she met stylist Kim Bowen, who invited her to work at the magazines *I-D* and *The Face*. Between working there and clubbing, she never finished school. But she eventually became beauty director for *I-D*.

McGrath is known for her innovative uses of makeup and the techniques she uses in applying it. She loves to use her hands and creates fantastical and adventurous looks. McGrath has said that her work is influenced by fabrics and textures, which help determine the look she will create for models' faces. But as ANNA SUI has reported, McGrath likes to hear the story behind every collection as well, then conduct more research on her own. When McGrath arrives at a shoot or show she is usually armed with at least 20 cases, "from standard-issue mascara to sequins, dollies, and art books." The world's leading fashion houses ask McGrath to do the makeup for their shows, and she collaborates on major advertising campaigns for brands such as LOUIS VUITTON, PRADA, and BALENCIAGA. As a beauty editor, she regularly shoots for Italian and American *Vogue*.

In 1999, McGrath developed makeup for GIORGIO ARMANI and in 2009, for DOLCE & GABBANA. In 2004, she was chosen to be global creative director for Procter & Gamble and in 2010, she collaborated with LeSportSac on a series of cosmetic bags. That same year, she styled more than 200 models for the Fashion's Night Out show at Lincoln Center. Her influence and artistry have made her a trendsetter, and her celebrity clientele includes Oprah Winfrey, Sarah Jessica Parker, and Madonna. McGrath hopes to launch her own line of makeup in the near future.

Pat McGrath (right) working on model Gisele Bundchen.

ALEXANDER MCQUEEN ▲ ▮▮

BORN London, March 17, 1969
DIED London, February 11, 2010

AWARDS British Fashion Awards *Designer of the Year*, 1996, 1997 (shared with JOHN GALLIANO), 2001, 2003 • Council of Fashion Designers of America (CFDA) *Designer of the Year*, 2007; *Board of Directors' Tribute*, 2010 • British Government *Commander of the Most Excellent Order of the British Empire* (OBE), 2003

Alexander McQueen cultivated his image as a bad boy of fashion with outrageous presentations and designs—such as his low-cut "bumsters"—that attracted headlines and disguised their exquisite craftsmanship. The son of a taxi driver, he graduated from Central Saint Martins College of Arts and Design and was immediately awarded an apprenticeship with a prestigious Savile Row firm of

Designer Alexander McQueen.

Sarah Burton for Alexander McQueen, Spring 2013.

tailors. He then worked for ROMEO GIGLI and Koji Tatsuo before opening his own East London studio.

In 1996, citing his "creative brilliance and technical mastery," LVMH named McQueen to succeed Galliano as chief designer at GIVENCHY. He produced four collections at the house before making an arrangement with LVMH's rival, GUCCI, to back him in his own business. He was replaced at Givenchy by JULIEN MACDONALD.

In 2001, McQueen was among the designers featured in the *London Fashion* exhibit at New York's Fashion Institute of Technology and the *Extreme Fashion* exhibit at the Metropolitan Museum of Art.

In 2005, McQueen collaborated with Puma on two lines of footwear for men and women. A casual denim ready-to-wear collection called McQ followed in 2006. Then in 2007, he partnered with luggage giant Samsonite to create the Black Label by Alexander McQueen collection. His 2009 line for Target, McQ Alexander McQueen, was inspired by youth subcultures, music, rebellion, and style revolution.

In 2010, McQueen was found dead at his home. He was memorialized in song by Lady Gaga and Bjork, and models Naomi Campbell and Kate Moss wore his famous "manta" dresses. In 2011, the Metropolitan Museum of Art in New York held a retrospective of

Fall 2008.

Sarah Burton for Alexander McQueen, Spring 2014.

McQueen's work, *Savage Beauty*. Though it only ran three months, the exhibit was among the most popular in the museum's history.

Sarah Burton, who had worked under McQueen for 14 years, took over as creative director of the label following his death. She has proven herself an innovator who pays homage to McQueen's dramatic aesthetic but added her own, more feminine take. Burton designed Catherine Middleton's wedding dress for her 2011 wedding to Prince William.

STEVEN MEISEL 📷

Photographer Steven Meisel.

BORN New York City, 1954

Steven Meisel studied photography at Parsons School of Design. He was working as a fashion illustrator for *Women's Wear Daily* and as an art teacher at his alma mater when photographs he had taken of actress Phoebe Cates caught the attention of the fashion community. He went on to work on advertising campaigns for PRADA, DOLCE & GABBANA, VALENTINO, and GIANNI VERSACE.

Meisel later moved to the editorial side of publishing, and in 1988 he became the premier photographer for both the Italian and American editions of *Vogue*. In 2005, he designed a controversial issue of Italian *Vogue* called "Makeover Madness," a glossy, glamorous photo-narrative of dramatic plastic surgery operations.

One of Meisel's most famous works is *Sex*, published in 1992. The book was replete with gritty, erotic photographs of Meisel's friend Madonna and her androgynous young playmates. In 2004, Meisel's work was featured in an exhibition titled *Fashioning Fiction in Photography since 1990* at the Museum of Modern Art in New York. He has also exhibited work at the Moderna Museet in Stockholm and at the National Museum of Photography, Film, and Television in Bradford, England. In 2008, Meisel released a 1,000-piece jigsaw puzzle of the model Meghan Collision that retailed for $750.

"I hate the technical stuff," Meisel has said. "I'm an artist. The camera and lights get in my way. They distract me. I would like to just blink my eyes and have the picture." Meisel continues to photograph campaigns for the top international design houses such as PRADA, Mulberry, LANVIN, LOUIS VUITTON, BALENCIAGA, and DOLCE & GABBANA. In fall 2014, a retrospective exhibition, the first for Meisel, will appear in Milan.

Editor Suzy Menkes.

BORN England, December 24, 1943

AWARDS British Government *Order of the British Empire* • French Government *Légion d'Honneur (Legion of Honor)*

The famed fashion editor of the *International Herald Tribune,* Suzy Menkes is known for both her signature pompadour hairstyle (which has earned her the nickname Samurai Suzy) and for attending hundreds of fashion shows a year—writing nearly two million words on fashion as a result.

After graduating high school in East Sussex, England, Menkes moved to Paris to study dressmaking for a year and attended her first fashion show, by NINA RICCI, where she immediately fell in love with couture. She then left to attend Cambridge University on a scholarship, studying history and English literature. There she began honing her journalism skills as a fashion columnist for the school newspaper, *Varsity,* and became its first female editor in her senior year.

Menkes was later hired by *The Times of London* as a junior fashion reporter and in 1978 became its fashion editor. Ten years later the *Tribune* hired Menkes away, making her the third fashion editor in the paper's history—following in the footsteps of Hebe Dorsey and Eugenia Sheppard, for whom the annual media (fashion journalism) award from the Council of Fashion Designers of America (CFDA) is named.

Menkes is known for her detailed reviews of runway shows and evenhanded opinions, though she is not afraid to share an occasional biting putdown. Menkes makes it a point not to accept gifts from fashion houses or wear designer clothes often, but has set herself apart with a miniature pompadour set loosely above her forehead.

Menkes has contributed to several books on fashion and on British royalty, including *The Royal Jewels* and *Queen and Country.* In 2013, Menkes sold a vast array of her designer wardrobe through a single owner auction at Christie's. She said that she had not cleaned out her clothing collection since 1964 and that the garments needed to "live again." In March 2014, she left *The New York Times* to become international fashion editor for *Vogue,* calling it the "perfect time to embrace a new challenge in the digital age."

NICOLE MILLER ▟

BORN Lenox, Massachusetts, 1952

AWARDS Fashion Group International *Lifetime Achievement Award, 2012*

Nicole Miller was raised in Lenox, Massachusetts, the child of an American father and French mother. She attended the Rhode Island School of Design, where she took a year off to study dress-cutting in Paris. She was designing coats at Rain Cheetahs in 1975 when she was hired as head dress designer at P. J. Walsh; in 1982, the company was renamed Nicole Miller.

She first gained attention for the prints she designed for scarves, which became an immediate hit when transferred to men's ties. The prints—featuring images of everything from comic book characters to magazine covers to wine labels to brand logos—are in bold graphics and brilliant colors. Boxer shorts followed, along with men's wear that used her inimitable prints as linings. The Miller brand also includes mid-priced ready-to-wear that is young and sexy.

Miller is also known for her festive special occasion clothes, including a sophisticated bridesmaid collection that she says is "for brides who want to keep their friends." She has an extensive list of licenses, including for handbags, shoes, eyewear, fragrance, cosmetics, and skincare. A collection of fine and costume jewelry was launched in 2002 on the television network QVC.

In 2003, Miller launched a contemporary sportswear line, millergirl, as well as a new line of shoes. In 2007, she launched a line

Fall 2009.

Top: Designer Nicole Miller.
Bottom: Spring 2014.

of cold weather accessories. In 2012, she received the lifetime achievement award from Fashion Group International and was awarded the key to the city of Miami Beach.

![dress icon] ![bag icon] REBECCA MINKOFF

After four years of designing handbags, Minkoff launched her first ready-to-wear collection in 2009. In 2011, Minkoff received the Breakthrough Designer Award from the Accessories Council. Her company is run and supported by her brother Uri Minkoff, its chief executive officer and cofounder. He also leads the company's social media efforts.

Minkoff has used Tumblr and other media sources to advertise and hype her upcoming shows and collections. Her brand had become extremely popular with celebrities and is distributed in over 900 stores worldwide. Her shows are highly anticipated; in 2013, her New York Fashion Week show featured Janelle Monae singing in the background and, due to incredible demand, too many tickets were accidentally sold.

In 2012, Minkoff opened her first standalone store. Celebrities seen with her bags include Jessica Szohr, Michelle Trachtenberg, and Vanessa Hudgens.

Above: Designer Rebecca Minkoff.
Left: Spring 2014.

BORN San Diego, California

Known for her luxury handbags, accessories, footwear, and apparel, Rebecca Minkoff is an industry leader in America. Minkoff knew from a young age that she wanted to go into design and made sure that she participated in the costume department in high school. After graduating from high school, she moved to New York City and rose to fame after designing an "I Love New York" t-shirt as part of a capsule collection that appeared on *The Tonight Show Featuring Johnny Carson* and became a huge success.

In 2005, Minkoff created a handbag that she called the "morning after bag" or "M.A.B." It became incredibly popular with the style set. Her handbags feature creative studs, leather, and interesting and edgy hardware.

MISSONI

FOUNDED Gallarate, Italy, 1953

AWARDS *Neiman Marcus Award*, 1973 • Fashion Group International *Design Award*, 1991

There's no mistaking a colorful Missoni knit—and this family-owned company has produced its innovative designs for over 50 years. Founded in a small town north of Milan in 1953 by newlyweds Ottavio and Rosita, the company first produced knitwear for Italian department stores and for other designers. The Missoni label was

Margherita Missoni (left), Rosita Missoni (center), and Angela Missoni (right).

Spring 2014.

introduced five years later. Stripes and zig-zags adorned Missoni dresses, tunics, sweaters, and pants. Though the line took a few years to catch on, it received its first big boost in 1965, when Italian fashion editor Anna Piaggi praised the collection. In 1966, the line took a radical shift when French stylist Emmanuelle Khanh was hired to collaborate on design. At that point Rosita took over designing the clothes, while Ottavio created the knits.

At the Florence fashion shows in 1967, Rosita had the models remove their bras when the lines interfered with those of the light knit dresses they were wearing. The stage lighting turned the clothes transparent—and Missoni made fashion headlines. The controversy resulted in Missoni being disinvited to show at Florence the following year, so the company took its collection to Milan—contributing to the city's rise as Italy's fashion capital. By then, Missoni designs were being featured in Italian *Vogue*.

Missoni was at its height as a status symbol in the 1970s. Keeping the clothing shapes simple and production limited, Missoni designs were often considered a form of art. This philosophy was embraced by the company, which believes that current trends should not overrule timeless style.

Missoni branched out from women's clothing to create men's and children's wear, along with fragrances, textiles, and home decor. The Missoni children joined the company in the 1990s—Vittorio as marketing director, Luca as creative director, and Angela (who originally went into business for herself) at the helm of design. Licensing deals have been expanded, and a bridge line, M Missoni, was introduced in 1999. The third generation is now also involved, with Angela's daughter Margherita launching the fragrance Missoni Profumi in 2006. She is also a model and the face of the perfume and officially joined the company to begin designing in 2009.

Though established as a fashion classic, Missoni continues to draw attention by keeping its look both classic and energetic. The spring 2010 collection was praised for its light layers, slender silhouettes, and exceptional handiwork. Sadly, in early 2013, the plane carrying Vittorio Missoni and his wife crashed in Venezuela, killing all passengers. Ottavio Missoni passed away in early May of 2013.

Missoni sketch.

ISSEY MIYAKE

Designer Issey Miyake.

BORN Hiroshima, Japan, April 22, 1938

AWARDS *Mainichi Newspaper Fashion Award*, 1976, 1984 • Council of Fashion Designers of America (CFDA) *Special Award*, 1983 • *Neiman Marcus Award*, 1984

From his first collection in 1971, Issey Miyake has been one of the most innovative and influential designers of his time. His imagination ranges far beyond the business of fashion to a fascination with the human body, the space that surrounds it, and the movement that reveals it. He prefers to be considered simply as a designer and maker of clothes, rather than as a fashion designer per se. His clothes have long been favorites of women with a strong sense of fashion and of their own style.

A 1964 graduate of Tama Art University in Tokyo, Miyake moved to Paris in 1965 to study at l'École de la Chambre Syndicale. Starting in 1966, he spent two years as an assistant designer at GUY LAROCHE, worked at GIVENCHY in the same capacity, and in 1969–70 was in New York City with GEOFFREY BEENE. In 1970, he returned to Tokyo and formed Miyake Design Studio, showing his first collection in 1971 in Tokyo and New York.

One of the earliest Japanese designers to move to Europe, Miyake has shown regularly at the Paris prêt-à-porter collections since 1973. Previously the 1968 Paris student revolution shook up his thinking, leading him to question traditional views of fashion as applied to the modern woman. At that time he began to use wrapping and layering, combining Japanese attitudes toward clothes with exotic fabrics of his own design.

Spring 2014.

Miyake is known for his innovative fabrics, brilliant use of textures, and mastery of proportion. He created a garment dubbed A-POC (A Piece of Cloth), a tube-shaped ready-to-wear garment that consumers could cut into different shapes. Licenses have ranged from home furnishings and hosiery to bicycles and luggage; a fragrance, L'eau d'Issey, appeared in 1994. Miyake's Pleats collection was introduced in 1989, and in 1993 it was launched as the standalone line Pleats Please by Issey Miyake for the spring/summer collection.

Issey Miyake Making Things, a retrospective of the designer's work, opened in Paris at the Cartier Foundation for Contemporary Art in 1998 and was restaged at the Ace Gallery in New York in 1999. The exhibition, an exhilarating mating of architecture, space, and movement—clothes floated up in the air and descended, appeared as flat abstractions that turned into three-dimensional dresses, and generally explored the outer possibilities of clothing the human form—illustrated the designer's radical approach to clothing, combining respect for tradition with the most unfettered technological experimentation. Miyake turned over design of men's and women's wear to Naoki Takizawa in 1999.

Since spring 2006, designer Dai Fujiwara has run the House of Miyake. Miyake continues to oversee his lines and is co-director of 21 21 Design Sight, Japan's first dedicated design museum.

Designer Isaac Mizrahi.

BORN New York City, October 14, 1961

AWARDS Council of Fashion Designers of America (CFDA) *Perry Ellis Award*, 1988; *Womenswear Designer of the Year Award*, 1989, 1991; *Special Award (with Douglas Keeve, for* Unzipped*)*, 1995 • Fashion Footwear Association *Best* Designer, 1990 • Dallas Fashion Awards *Fashion Excellence Award*

When Isaac Mizrahi opened his own company, he was 26, but had already worked on Seventh Avenue for six years. He grew up in Brooklyn, the son of a children's wear manufacturer and of a fashionable mother who wore clothes from BALENCIAGA and NORELL. Mizrahi attended the Yeshiva of Flatbush, the High School of Performing Arts, and Parsons School of Design. At Parsons he received the Chester Weinberg Golden Thimble Award and a CLAIRE MCCARDELL scholarship. Starting in 1981, his last year at Parsons, Mizrahi worked at PERRY ELLIS Sportswear, staying there until 1983, when he went to JEFFREY BANKS, and from there to CALVIN KLEIN. In 1987, he left Klein to form his own business. Ten years later he lost his financial backing and closed his company. He has continued with collections of shoes, coats, and fine jewelry, but has moved on to other pursuits.

Mizrahi's chosen category was luxury sportswear, running the gamut from raincoats to evening wear. His work was notable for a constant flow of new ideas and for audacity—playing it safe was not his way. The clothes were young and inventive in the CLAIRE MCCARDELL idiom—using unexpected colors and fabrics, but with an ease and pared-down glamour that appealed to sophisticates with a sense of adventure and an appreciation of quality.

Mizrahi has designed costumes for movies, theater, dance, and opera in collaboration with Mark Morris, Twyla Tharp, Bill T. Jones, and Mikhail Baryshnikov. The documentary *Unzipped*, which recorded the travails of producing his 1994 collection, was made with his friend Douglas Keeve for an AIDS benefit, then shown at the 1995 Sundance Film Festival—where it won the audience award for a documentary. It was later released commercially. Mizrahi has also written a series of comic books, *The Adventures of Sandee the Supermodel*.

In addition, Mizrahi has indulged his theater ambitions with an off-Broadway show and cabaret act, *Les Mizrahi*, plus a television talk show. His numerous design projects have included sets and costumes for theater and dance, as well as interiors.

In 2004, Mizrahi returned to his fashion design origins with the launch of two ventures aimed at very different members of the buying public: an affordable line for Target and Isaac Mizrahi to Order, a company creating high-end custom clothing.

Mizrahi served as creative director at LIZ CLAIBORNE for a year before launching *Isaac Mizrahi Live!* on the television network QVC in 2010. In 2011, he sold his brand to Xcel Brand Inc., which has helped him venture into denim, footwear, and his first fragrance, *Fabulous*. Those lines can now be found at Bloomingdale's and Nordstrom.

Mizrahi has participated in a variety of entertainment ventures, from hosting duties on Bravo's reality competition *The Fashion Show* and a radio show on Sirius XM called *Tell Me Everything* to serving as head judge on the premiere of *Project Runway: All-Stars*.

A bridal look from Isaac Mizrahi for Kleinfeld, spring 2013.

LESLEY MOBO ▼

BORN Kalibo, Aklan, the Philippines, November 7, 1981

Lesley Mobo grew up in the Philippines under modest means. He had to use his creativity to create toys, and those early imaginative projects helped him when he got older. Mobo attended school thousands of miles away from home at Central Saint Martins College of Arts and Design in London. During his senior year, he showed his designs at London Fashion Week's Central Saint Martins showcase. His collection was well received and he was offered a position at JOHN GALLIANO, but he turned it down to attend graduate school. Mobo was determined to get a master's degree from Central Saint Martins because its graduate program director had a reputation for producing the "new generation" of designers. While completing his master's, Mobo worked with CLEMENTS RIBERIO and Cacharel. He also presented a design product for CHLOÉ under PHOEBE PHILO. After Mobo was

Designer Lesley Mobo.

included in the *Fashion and Motion* exhibition at the Victoria and Albert Museum, he was wooed by Harrods and started working there part-time.

Mobo graduated with distinction and started working for Harrods full-time, and served as chief designer of its in-house brand Jasmine Di Milo from 2003 to 2012, when the brand was sold. In 2009, he launched the Mobo brand, a women's ready-to-wear line, with his business partner Michael Bowden. In 2012, after leaving Harrods, Mobo was named head designer of the British brand Ghost. He is proud of his Filipino heritage and has appeared on the television show *Project Runway Philippines*.

Mobo's high-end designs are sold to European socialites, celebrities, and international royalty. In 2012, Mobo showed his designs at the Philippine Fashion Showcase London 2013, sponsored by Ayala Foundation and Prospero World. Princess Marie Chantel and Prince Pavlos of Greece were in attendance and fell in love with Mobo's lace tulle ball gowns and layering effects for evening wear.

Autumn/Winter '12–'13.

Designer Anna Molinari.

BORN Capri, Italy, June 25, 1950s

AWARDS *Isimbardi Fashion Award*, 2001 • La Kore *Fashion Oscar*, 2003

In 1977, with the help of her husband, Gianpaolo Tarabini, and urged by designer FRANCO MOSCHINO, Anna Molinari established Blumarine, a line "for that

Bluemarine, spring 2014.

brand of Italian miss for whom no dress is too small nor any diamond too big." In 1981, Molinari debuted her collection in front of an international audience at the Modit in Milan. Less than a decade later, she and Tarabini had expanded the Blumarine brand into a worldwide conglomerate. In 1988, the company was set up as a stock holding company called Blufin.

Besides Bluemarine, the company has more than 700 stores worldwide and boasts lines for girls and teens, Miss Bluemarine and Blugirl. Molinari also introduced an eponymous division aimed at high-end customers, Anna Molinari, founded by her daughter Rosella Tarabini. In 2004, the company added a men's division, and in 2007 further expanded with a denim line, Blugirl Folies.

Molinari's husband died in 2006 and her son, Gianguido Tarabini, took over as chief executive officer. In 2007, her daughter, Rosella Tarabini, resigned as creative director artistic director of the Blufin labels and Blumarine advertising campaigns. The collections are now under the direction of Rosella Tarabini's former team and is produced by Italian manufacturer Sinv SpA. In 2008, the company entered a licensing agreement with Vicini to develop a shoe collection. In 2011, the company's collections were presented at the Brandery Fashion show in Barcelona.

Bluemarine, spring 2014.

CAPTAIN EDWARD MOLYNEUX ▼

See-thru jersey evening dress, 1965.

BORN Hampstead, England, September 5, 1891
DIED Monte Carlo, March 23, 1974

Captain Edward Molyneux is remembered for fluid, elegant clothes with a pure, uncluttered line—well-bred and timeless. These included printed silk suits with pleated skirts and softly tailored navy-blue suits, coats, and capes with accents of bright Gauguin pink and *bois de rose*. Molyneux used zippers to mold the figure and was partial to handkerchief-point skirts and ostrich trims. His distinguished clientele included Princess Marina of Greece, whose wedding dress he made when she married the Duke of Kent; the Duchess of Windsor; and stage and film personalities such as Lynn Fontanne, Gertrude Lawrence, and Merle Oberon.

Of French descent and Anglo-Irish birth, Molyneux got his start in fashion in 1911 when he won a competition sponsored by the London couturiere Lucile, and was engaged to sketch for her. When she opened branches in New York City and Chicago, he went to America with her, remaining until the outbreak of World War I. He joined the British Army in 1914, earned the rank of captain, and was wounded three times, resulting in the loss of an eye. He was twice awarded the Military Cross for Bravery.

In 1919, Molyneux opened his own couture house in Paris, eventually adding branches in Monte Carlo, Cannes, and London. He enjoyed a flamboyant social life, assembled a fine collection of 18th century and Impressionist paintings, opened two successful nightclubs, and was a friend of many of his clients. At the outbreak of World War II, he escaped from France by fishing boat from Bordeaux and during the war worked out of his London home, turning over the profits to national defense. He established international canteens in London and was one of the original members of the Incorporated Society of London Fashion Designers.

In 1946, Molyneux returned to Paris and reopened his couture house, adding furs, lingerie, millinery, and perfumes. Because of ill health and threatened blindness in his remaining eye, he closed his London house in 1949, and in 1950 turned over the Paris operation to JACQUES GRIFFE. He retired to Montego Bay in Jamaica, devoting himself to painting and travel. Persuaded by the financial interests behind his perfumes to reopen in Paris as Studio Molyneux, he brought his first ready-to-wear collection to America in 1965. The project was not a success: Molyneux's elegant, ladylike designs were out of step with the youth-obsessed 1960s. He soon retired again, this time to Biot, near Antibes, France.

Designer Claude Montana (center) and models.

BORN Paris, 1949

Claude Montana began designing in 1971 on a trip to London. To make money, he concocted papier-mâché jewelry encrusted with rhinestones that was featured in fashion magazines and earned him enough to stay for a year. On his return to Paris, he went to work for Mac Douglas, a French leather firm. Montana has also designed knitwear for the Spanish firm Ferrer y Sentis and collections for various Italian companies, including Complice. His reputation grew throughout the 1970s and 1980s, and in 1989 he joined Lanvin to design its couture collection, while continuing his own ready-to-wear business. His couture designs were well received by the press and praised for their elegance and modernity, but he and Lanvin parted ways in 1992 and Lanvin discontinued its couture operations.

Beyond the biker's leathers that made his name, Montana developed into one of the more interesting contemporary French designers, with an eye for proportion, cut, and detail. He is a perfectionist, with the finesse of a true couturier and a leaning toward operatic fantasy. His clothes feature strong, uncompromising silhouettes and a well-defined sense of drama. They have been sold in fine stores in America, Italy, Germany, and England, and under license in Japan.

In 1999, Montana designed Montana Blu, a more affordable collection for women. He also has several perfumes, including Montana en Turquoise, which

launched in 2008. After retiring in 2010, Montana made what many called a comeback, releasing a book called *Claude Montana: Fashion Radical* in 2011 and then designing three looks for Erie Tibushi's fall 2013 collection during Paris Fashion Week. When asked if he was returning to the runway, Montana was vague—simply stating, "watch this space."

Spring 2003.

HANAE MORI ▲

BORN Tokyo, January 8, 1926

AWARDS *Neiman Marcus Award*, 1973

Designer Hanae Mori.

Actively engaged in fashion for more than 40 years, Hanae Mori was a quiet phenomenon—a working wife and mother who became the first Japanese woman to show on the runways of both New York and Paris. She graduated from Tokyo Christian Women's College with a degree in Japanese literature, and after marrying Ken Mori, heir to a textile firm, went back to school to study sewing, sketching, and design. In 1955, she opened a small boutique in the Shinjuku district of Tokyo, where her clothes attracted the attention of the burgeoning Japanese movie industry. After designing costumes for innumerable films, she opened a shop on the Ginza, Tokyo's famous shopping street.

With her husband, Mori developed a multimillion-dollar business with approximately 20 affiliated companies. Her ready-to-wear was sold at fine stores worldwide and in her own boutiques in Japan, Paris, and America, along with accessories, sportswear, and children's wear. Fabric designs were licensed for bed and bath linens. There were hair salons, television shows, and a publishing division headed by Akira Mori, the elder of her two sons, who edited the Japanese edition of *Women's Wear Daily*, among other titles. Her younger son, Kei, directed the firm's European operations.

In 1977, Mori took her couture collection to Paris and continued to show there each season. She was the first Japanese designer to be admitted to the Chambre Syndicale de la Haute Couture Parisienne. In 1978, Mori consolidated her business offices, couture operation, and boutiques in a glass and steel headquarters building designed by noted Japanese architect Kenzo Tange.

While her design approach was the most international of her compatriots, Mori made extensive use of her Japanese background in her fabrics, which were woven, printed, and dyed especially for her. She used the vivid colors and bold linear patterns of Hiroshige prints, while butterflies and flowers—the Japanese symbols of femininity—showed up frequently in her prints, which she used to great advantage in cocktail and evening dresses, meticulously executed in Eastern-flavored patterns with Western styling and fit. Her clients included film celebrities and the wives of affluent Japanese politicians; she designed the ivory satin gown for Masako Owada's 1993 wedding to Japan's Crown Prince Naruhito.

In 2001, the company sold most of its ready-to-wear, licensed apparel business, and directly owned shops to a Japanese-British investment group. Mori was expected to continue with couture. But a few months later, buffeted by the long-term Japanese recession, the company filed for bankruptcy.

The Hanae Mori brand remains a force to be reckoned with in fragrances. In 2012, the brand announced the launch of Eco-Chic No. 6, an eco-friendly perfume, and continues to have success with the Hanae Mori Parfums line—particularly Butterfly, the centerpiece fragrance that refers to Mori's nickname "Madame Butterfly."

Fall 2004.

Princess Diana in a Moschino suit, 1991.

BORN Abbiategrasse, Italy, February 27, 1950
DIED Lake Annone, Italy, September 18, 1994

Franco Moschino's father, the owner of an iron foundry, died when his son was four. As a child, Moschino amused himself by drawing; at 18, he went to Milan to study at the Accademia di Belle Arti, supporting himself by work as a waiter and a model. In the early 1970s, the fashion drawings he was making for various magazines attracted the attention of GIANNI VERSACE, who used his work in a publicity campaign. He worked as a sketcher for GIORGIO ARMANI on collections for Beged-Or and Genny, and for 11 years designed for Cadette. In 1983, he launched his own company.

Moschino became known, if not universally admired, for his irreverent sendups of conventional fashion thinking. He sent pairs of models out on the runway in the same outfit, one wearing it as it would appear in a serious fashion presentation, the other as it might be worn on the street. He distributed fresh tomatoes to the audience so they could toss them at styles they disliked. He incorporated statements such as "Ready to Where?" and "Waist of Money" into jackets, shirts, and belts. These and similar pieces became bestsellers not only because of the gags but also because the clothes were carefully tailored and of fine quality.

Moschino believed that fashion should be fun and that people should wear clothes with their own style.

⬛ FRANCO MOSCHINO

His motto was "Who is to say what is good taste?" The paradox was that as much as he made fun of the fashion establishment, he was so successful that in the end he became part of the very thing that he was ridiculing.

At the time of Moschino's death in 1994 there was, in addition to the signature collection, a secondary line called Cheap & Chic, men's wear, children's wear, jeans, accessories, perfumes, and two Milan shops. His last collection was shown after he died and well received. Moschino's creative director, Rossella Jardini, took over the company in 1994, and in 1999 the label became part of the Aeffe Fashion Group SpA.

With a design staff of about a dozen and licenses ranging from swimwear and lingerie to perfumes and sunglasses, the firm has remained in business, celebrating its 20th year in 2003. The brand has also expanded its Moschino Love stores (featuring a women's and men's diffusion line once called Moschino Jeans) into China and Saudi Arabia.

Autumn/winter 2000/2001.

ROLAND MOURET

BORN Lourdes, France, 1962

AWARDS *ELLE* Style Awards *British Designer of the Year*, 2002

The London-based French designer Roland Mouret (MOO-ray) is a former stylist and art director who has little formal training in fashion—just a few months at a Paris fashion college in the late 1970s. When he debuted his own designs in 1998, he became known for his draping and folding skills, which allowed him to create "cut without pattern." Financial backers purchased his line and Mouret moved to New York City, where he had his first sellout hit with his "Galaxy" dress in 2005. Just months later, he split from his backers, citing creative differences, but they retained the rights to the Roland Mouret brand.

Designer Roland Mouret.

Spring 2014.

For two years Mouret produced in limited quantities: a limited edition run of dresses for Bergdorf Goodman, each individually signed, and a capsule collection for The Gap. He relaunched his own line in 2007 after securing new financial support. RM by Roland Mouret was a highly anticipated collection, and Mouret did not disappoint. His "Moon" dress sold out within days. The rest of the collection was sold online and also went quickly.

For his 2009 collections, Mouret expanded into knitwear and applied his figure-hugging style to a wider range of daytime dresses appropriate for stylish working women who still want to be fashion-forward. In 2010, Mouret bought back the rights to his name, and in 2011 presented a collection under it. He is credited with mentoring Victoria Beckham when she launched her collections.

Designer Thierry Mugler.

THIERRY MUGLER

Fall 2012.

BORN Strasbourg, France, 1948

The son of a doctor, Thierry Mugler started making clothes while in his teens. He was part of a Strasbourg ballet company, dressed windows for a Paris boutique, and moved to London in 1968. After two years he moved on to Amsterdam, then back to Paris. His first collection appeared in 1971 under the label Café de Paris; by 1973 he was making clothes under his own name. Inventive and individual, Mugler came into prominence in the late 1970s with high-priced separates and dresses marked by broad-shouldered, defined-waistline silhouettes. Though he claimed to admire ALIX GRÈS, his clothing appeared to be descended more from the structured chic of JACQUES FATH. His tendency toward histrionic, often outrageous presentations tended to obscure what he was trying to say, but he cut a sexy, saucy suit as well as or better than anyone, and his collections were known for a sunny

Spring/summer 1997.

freshness and gaiety. As shown, Mugler's clothes were apt to appear aggressive and tough. Close up, they proved to be simple, well-cut, body-fitted, and not overly detailed, with the ready-to-wear more accessible than the couture.

Mugler retired from fashion in 1999 to concentrate on perfume. His firm, owned by Clarins, closed in 2002, with the perfume business continuing—his latest being Angel Sunessence, introduced in 2009. Angel, the original perfume launched in 1992, is still one of his most popular perfumes.

In 2009, Mugler was an adviser and costume designer for Beyoncé's *I Am . . .* world tour. In 2010, Nicola Formichetti became creative director of Thierry Mugler, which was rebranded as Mugler. In 2013, Formichetti left for Diesel, and Mugler was named creative adviser to Joel Palix, president of Clarins Fragrance Group and director general of Thierry Mugler SAS.

JEAN MUIR ▼

Designer Jean Muir

BORN London, July 17, 1928
DIED London, May 28, 1995

AWARDS Maison Blanche *Rex Award*, 1967, 1968, 1974, 1976 • Fellow of the Royal Society of Arts, 1973 • *Neiman Marcus Award*, 1973 • British Government *Commander of the British Empire*, 1983 • British Fashion Council *Hall of Fame Award*, 1994

Of Scottish descent, Jean Muir began her career in 1950 in the stockroom at Liberty. She then sold lingerie, became a sketcher in Liberty's made-to-measure department, and in 1956 joined Jaeger and soon became responsible for designing its main dress and knitwear collections. Starting in 1961, Muir designed under her own label, which she established with her husband, Harry Leuckert, but they did not own. In 1966, the two founded their own company, Jean Muir, Inc.

Muir was among the anti-couture, anti-establishment designers who came on the scene in the late 1950s and early 1960s. While others disappeared, she not only survived but flourished; her clothes are treasured by women looking for a low-profile way of dressing and quality of a very high order. Muir created a signature look of gentle, pretty clothes in the luxury investment category, flattering and elegant, usually in the finest English and Scottish wools, cashmeres, and suedes. She was especially admired for her leathers, which she treated like jersey, and for her jerseys in tailored shapes that are soft and feminine, distinguished by the most

Model wearing design by Jean Muir.

Autumn/winter 1997.

refined details—the slight bell cut of a cuff, the subtle flare of a jacket.

Hardworking and demanding, Muir believed in technical training as the only serious foundation for a designer. She encouraged and worked with British art students, urging more emphasis on craft, less on art. Since her death, the company has continued with a design team that worked with Muir.

BORN Edward Nardoza; New York, October 29, 1953

AWARDS Council of Fashion Designers of America (CFDA) *Media Award in Honor of Eugenia Sheppard,* 2009

Ed Nardoza has been editor-in-chief of *Women's Wear Daily (WWD)* since 1991. He is also associate editorial director of Fairchild Fashion Media, with editorial responsibility for the company's business publications. Before *WWD*, Nardoza was editor of *Daily News Record*, the former business and fashion publication for the men's wear industry. He joined Fairchild in 1978 as a general assignment reporter for *Footwear News*.

At *WWD*, Nardoza has expanded international, marketing, media, financial, and technology coverage. His work is considered top notch—in no small part because he considers all aspects of a fashion story. Covering clothing is not just about trends for him, but also about breaking stories on fascinating people, places, and businesses.

During Nardoza's tenure, *WWD* has started covering many new industries and launched new publications and special editions, including *WWD Collections*, a quarterly consumer/business hybrid covering international collections of women's and men's wear; *WWD Scoop*, a magazine covering international fashion and culture; *WWD Accessories*, a twice-yearly magazine on trends; *WWD 100 Years,* a one-time magazine on the paper's history; and *BeautyBiz,* a magazine about business strategies for cosmetics and fragrances.

Editor Ed Nardoza.

In 2008, *WWD* relaunched its website, wwd.com, based on a paid circulation, 24/7 news model. In 2009, the site won *Media Industry Newsletter*'s 2009 Best of the Web Award for design.

CONDÉ NAST ▪️ ▤

BORN New York City, 1873
DIED New York City, 1942

Condé Nast built a publication empire based on readers' lifestyles, interests, and class. Nast grew up in New York City and graduated from Georgetown University in Washington, D.C., then from law school at Washington University in St. Louis. Though he had a legal background, he opted to work in publishing. Nast's first job in the field was as advertising manager for *Collier's Weekly*, where he transformed the magazine—for example, by introducing editorials on single topics. His next position was as vice president of the Home Pattern Company, where he learned about what women wanted from fashion.

In 1909, Nast bought *Vogue*, which had been created in 1892 as a society magazine. He turned it into a bimonthly publication and marketed it as essential reading for the elite and affluent. Nast hired the best illustrators and photographers available—and within a year, *Vogue* had tripled its sales and had 44 percent more advertising revenue than its competitors. In 1911, Nast purchased *House and Garden*; in 1913, *Vanity Fair*; in 1924, *Golf Magazine*; and in 1939, *Glamour*. He created British *Vogue* in 1916, Condé Nast's first international magazine, followed in 1920 by French *Vogue*. In 1924, Nast took over operations at Arbor Press in Greenwich, Connecticut, where he developed the "bleed" printing method, which allows ink to go to the edge of a page after trimming. In 1932, Nast produced the first full-color cover.

Nast died in 1942, and in 1959 the Newhouse family purchased Condé Nast. The company continued to grow under the Newhouse family, hiring illustrator PAUL IRIBE, photographers IRVING PENN and RICHARD AVEDON, editorial director ALEXANDER LIBERMAN, groundbreaking editor ANNA WINTOUR, and Keija Minor, the first African-American editor-in-chief at a Condé Nast publication, *Brides* magazine, in 2012. Condé Nast now owns more than 18 magazines, 27 websites, and 50 apps.

Above: Designer Josie Natori.
Right: Spring 2014.

BORN Josefina Almeda Cruz; Manila, Philippines, May 9, 1947

AWARDS Corazon Aquino *Galleon Award*, 1998 • *LaKandula Award (highest civilian award in the Philippines)*, 2007 • Statue of Liberty Ellis Island Foundation *Peopling of America Award*, 2007

Before she became known for sophisticated, sensuous lingerie, Josie Natori had established herself in the world of finance as the first female vice president at Merrill Lynch. As a child she studied music in Manila, but with business genes in her blood (both her mother and grandmother were successful businesswomen), she moved to New York City at 17 to study economics at Manhattanville College. After her marriage and the birth of her son, Natori began looking for something more creative to do, her own business. "I was really looking for something that would allow me to take advantage of being Filipino and a woman," she has said. She found her niche when a friend back home sent her some hand-embroidered blouses and a Bloomingdale's buyer suggested that she lengthen them into nightshirts.

Natori designs rely on simple, sexy shapes in luxurious fabrics, usually with signature Philippine embroideries and appliqués, lace, and feminine

detailing. In addition to sleepwear, made in the Philippines at her own factory, there are robes, bras, panties, and accessories such as shawls of piña fabric (derived from pineapple) and evening handbags of exotic skins or antique silks. There is also a hipper, more affordable Josie line, Natori Home, and Natorious, a ready-to-wear line launched in 2008. In 2009, Natori launched her first perfume, a towel line, and an eyewear collection. She collaborated with Target and released a lingerie and loungewear line there in 2011 and 2012.

Natori has received much recognition for her achievements. She is a member of many business groups, including the Council of Fashion Designers of America (CFDA) and Fashion Group International, and is involved in a number of cultural institutions—the Asia Society, for one. She is also active in the Philippines on behalf of women and fashion.

HELMUT NEWTON 📷

BORN Helmut Neustädter; Berlin, October 31, 1920
DIED Los Angeles, January 23, 2004

AWARDS French Ministry of Culture *Grand Prix National de la Photographie*, 1990; *Commandeur de l'Ordre des Arts et des Lettres*, 1996 • German Government *Das Grosse Verdienstkeruz*, 1992

Photographer Helmut Newton (center) and models.

Helmut Newton achieved enormous fame in the late 20th century as a provocative, controversial photographer. His subject of choice was nude women, and he seemed to never run out of creative ways to capture their images. He grew up in Berlin and attended the American school there, followed by another school in Berlin—Grunewald. Between 1936 and 1938, Newton apprenticed with fashion photographer Yva (Elsa Neulander Simon). But the Nazi occupation prompted him to flee Berlin in 1938. Newton first went to Singapore, where he worked as a reporter and portrait photographer at *The Straits Times*. He then made his way to Australia and became a citizen in 1946.

Newton's photographs gained a reputation for their bold color, lighting, and style. He preferred to shoot on the streets; if he shot indoors, he would manipulate the setting to gain every advantage. These methods intrigued *Vogue*, and in 1956 he acquired a contract with its British edition. Newton left after less than a year to work for Australian *Vogue*. By 1961, he had advanced to a full-time position with French *Vogue*. In addition, he oversaw editorial photography at French *ELLE* from 1964 to 1966. He established a trademark of erotic, stylized scenes, often with sadomasochistic and fetishistic touches.

After a severe heart attack in 1970, Newton's wife, actress June Brunell, took over some of the photography. By 1975, he had recovered and had his first one-man show, at the Nikon Gallery in Paris. He published more than 35 books of his work and received numerous awards; in 1992, Newton was appointed Officier des Arts, Lettres et Sciences by S.A.S. Princess Caroline of Monaco, and in 1996 he was honored as Commandeur de l'Ordre des Arts et des Lettres by the French Ministry of Culture. For his 80th birthday in 2000, there was an exhibition in his honor at the New National Gallery in Berlin.

In 2011, the first major U.S. exhibition of Newton's work premiered at the Houston Museum of Fine Arts, titled *Helmut Newton: White Women, Sleepless Nights, Big Nudes*. The exhibition featured photographs from three of his major books and received rave reviews in Houston and again in 2013 at the Annendale Space in Los Angeles.

BORN Norman David Levinson; Noblesville, Indiana, April 20, 1900
DIED New York City, October 25, 1972

AWARDS Coty American Fashion Critics' Awards *Winnie*, 1943; *Return Award*, 1951; *Hall of Fame Award*, 1958 (the first recipient for all three) • *Neiman Marcus Award*, 1942 • Parsons *Medal for Distinguished Achievement*, 1956 • City of New York *Bronze Medallion*, 1972 • Pratt Institute, Brooklyn, Honorary Degree of Doctor of Fine Arts, 1962

Norman Norell and HATTIE CARNEGIE could be said to be the parents of American high fashion, setting

Designer Norman Norell (center) and model.

standards of taste, knowledge, and talent, and opening the way for the creators of today.

As a child, Norell moved with his family to Indianapolis, where his father opened a haberdashery. From early boyhood, Norell's ambition was to be an artist, and in 1919 he moved to New York City to study painting at Parsons School of Design. He switched to costume design, and in 1921 graduated from Pratt Institute. His first costume assignment was for *A Sainted Devil*, a Rudolph Valentino film. He created Gloria Swanson's costumes for *Zaza*, then joined the Brooks Costume Company.

In 1924, Norell switched to dress design, working for manufacturer Charles Armour until 1928, when he joined Carnegie. He stayed with Carnegie until 1940, not only absorbing her knowledge and sense of fashion, but traveling with her to Europe, where he was exposed to the best design of the day. In 1941, Norell teamed with manufacturer Anthony Traina to form Traina-Norell.

Above: A yellow wool jersey double-breasted belted coat, 1967.
Right: Model in Norell brown dress, 1962.

(continued)

The association lasted 19 years, at which point Norell left to head his own firm, Norman Norell, Inc. Its first collection was presented in 1960.

From his first collection under the Traina-Norell label, the designer established himself as a major talent, quickly becoming known for lithe, cleanly proportioned silhouettes, audacious use of rich fabrics, faultless workmanship, precise tailoring, and purity of line. Norell created numerous trends that have become part of the fashion vocabulary and are now taken for granted. He was the first to show long evening skirts topped with sweaters and introduced cloth coats lined with fur for day and evening, spangled with sequins. He revived the chemise, initiated the smoking robe, and

Above: Sketch of Norell design, 1941.

Left: Flamenco dancer wearing a pailletted-jersey top with black organza overskirt, 1964.

perfected jumpers and pantsuits. His long, shimmering, sequined dresses were so simple they never went out of date, worn as long as their owners could fit into them and treasured even longer. The perfume Norell, made in America, was a major success.

Norell was a founder and president of the Council of Fashion Designers of America (CFDA). In 1972, on the eve of a retrospective at the Metropolitan Museum of Art, Norell suffered a stroke; he died ten days later. His company continued briefly with Gustave Tassell as designer.

▲ MAKI OH (AMAKA OSAKWE)

FOUNDED Nigeria, 2010

Maki Oh's owner and designer, Amaka Osakwe, says of her label, "We are colorful and flamboyant—true Africans." She hates to see her African heritage and culture disappear from design. A graduate of the Arts University College at Bournemouth in the United Kingdom, Osakwe started Maki Oh with the goal of embracing cultural heritage, sustainability, and ethical practices in her collections. The label, which began in 2010, is based in Nigeria but has gained an international following. Osakwe's pieces are graphically textured and bright, reflecting Nigerian culture, but her collections have a modern twist and represent what it means to be a contemporary woman—one who understands her body and explores her sensuality.

In 2012 *Arise* magazine named Osakwe its designer of the year. In 2013, she showed Maki Oh at New York Fashion Week for the first time, in the fall. Her collection told of the story of the "woman"—each piece a progression of the story. The line is extremely popular in Nigeria and has been seen on celebrities such as Oroma Elewa and Solange Knowles. Also in 2013, Michelle Obama attended the event *Connecting Continents: A Conversation with U.S. First Lady Michelle Obama*, in Johannesburg, South Africa, wearing a Maki Oh dress. The publicity helped propel Osakwe into the design spotlight.

Maki Oh Spring 2014.

TODD OLDHAM ▲

Above: Designer Todd Oldham.
Right: Model wearing silk striped dress by Oldham.

BORN Corpus Christi, Texas, October 22, 1961

AWARDS Council of Fashion Designers of America (CFDA) *Perry Ellis Award*, 1991 • Dallas Fashion Awards *Rising Star Award*, 1992; *Fashion Excellence Award*, 1993

Todd Oldham first appeared as a "designer as showman." His desire to be a film director was evident in the bravura of his showings, attended by celebrity friends and with such features as rap music and drag performers on the runway. Oldham barely graduated high school, never went to design school, and taught himself patternmaking. His first fashion experience was in the alterations department of a Polo RALPH LAUREN boutique.

Oldham started his business in Dallas in 1985 and two years later moved to New York City. There he started Times Seven, making women's shirts in basic styles fastened with the uninhibited buttons that

became a trademark: some were antique, and many were designed by his brother, Brad. In 1989, Oldham designed a collection for a Japanese company; his first formal presentation, for fall 1990, attracted considerable attention from the press and orders from stores. Oldham has been a design consultant for the German firm Escada and appeared regularly on MTV. His final runway collection was in fall 1998, and he has since sold his trademark to Jones Apparel group, which produces and markets Todd Oldham Jeans.

Spring/summer 1998.

Using simple shapes, Oldham added unconventional prints or beading and embroidery done in India, sometimes quirky and whimsical, sometimes lavish. A mix of the commercial and the offbeat, the clothes were very well made and sold in such bastions of the establishment as Bergdorf Goodman and Saks Fifth Avenue.

Oldham has also designed for, among others, La-Z-Boy and FTD Florists. In 2007, Oldham began hosting the reality television show *Top Design*. The same year, he was named creative director of Old Navy, but his collection for 2008 was never released. He was subsequently let go and sued the company for breach of contract. In 2010, the lawsuit was dismissed, but when the amount sought was reduced to $20 million on appeal, a judge reallowed the suit in 2011.

Oldham is considered a designer of all trades—from clothes to products to industrial and interiors, he does it all. In 2013, the Sundance Institute asked Oldham to create an exclusive line of products for the Sundance Film Festival that included apparel, accessories, and recycled bags and wallets.

Aside from the Times Seven line, sold only in Japan, Oldham has concentrated on his varied other interests. He has designed hotel interiors, worked as a photographer, and designed home furnishings for Target. He has also been active in a wide range of social causes, from AIDS to environmental conservation, to child abuse to the humane treatment of animals.

DURO OLOWU ⧖

BORN Lagos, Nigeria

AWARDS British Fashion Awards *New Designer of the Year*, 2005 • African Fashion Awards *Best Designer Award*, 2010

Duro Olowu has always loved fashion. As a child, he enjoyed watching the women around him in their rich fabrics and bright colors. Born to a Jamaican mother and Nigerian father, his parents encouraged him to embrace everything around him, especially different genres of music. Olowu grew up in a London boarding school and followed in his father's footsteps, becoming a lawyer. Not until he married his first wife, a shoe designer, did he realize that he wanted to go into fashion. After helping with design duties at his wife's boutique, Olowu started his own business and came on the fashion scene in 2004.

Designer Duro Olowu.

His first collection, Love and Joy, was a huge success. Olowu's garments display the shades, prints, and bold colors of his African heritage but are not defined by his ethnicity. His first collection featured his signature "Duro Dress," which features an empire waist and billowing sleeves in different silk prints. American and British *Vogue* both called it the dress of the year.

Olowu's work was featured in the *Global Africa Project* exhibition at the Museum of Art and Design in New York City in 2010, and in *New African Fashion*, a book by Helen Jennings, in 2011. Olowu's clothes are sold at his boutique in London as well as at fine shops in the United Kingdom and America. In 2013, he designed a collection for J.C. Penney with an ad campaign featuring top Nigerian model Oluchi. He said that he did so because of the lack of diversity on runways—a widely discussed topic in the fashion industry. But Olowu's clothes are worn by a diverse group of women, including Uma Thurman, Linda Evangelista, and Michelle Obama. He created another line for JC Penny for spring/summer 2014. Olowu is married to Thelma Golden, chief curator of the Studio Museum in Harlem and a renowned art A-lister.

Designs from Duro Olowu's spring 2012 collection.

Designer Rick Owens.

BORN California, 1962

AWARDS Council of Fashion Designers of America (CFDA) *Perry Ellis Award* 2002 • Cooper-Hewitt *National Design Award (fashion)*, 2007 • Fashion Group International *Rule Breakers Award*, 2007

Rick Owens is from southern California, where he studied art at Parsons in Los Angeles, and now works out of Paris. In 1994, after dropping out of school, he began his career as an indie designer with inspirations collected from the eccentric, broken world of Hollywood Boulevard. As the number of his dissidents grew, so did the attention of the New York fashion world. His first runway show in New York was in 2001 and sponsored by *Vogue*, which led to his winning the CFDA PERRY ELLIS Award (for emerging talent) in 2002. Moving to Paris in 2003, Owens became artistic director of the centuries-old furrier Revillon.

Inspired by furniture designer Eileen Grey and Romanian sculptor Constantin Brâncuşi, in 2005 Owens introduced a furniture collection using raw plywood, resin, fiberglass, cashmere, and marble. He opened

⚜ RICK OWENS

his own boutique in Paris in 2006, and in 2007 started designing his own fur collection, Jardins du Palais Royal. That same year, Owens received the Cooper-Hewitt National Design Award for fashion and Fashion Group International's Rule Breakers Award, and released a photo book titled *L'Ai-Je Bien Descendu?* The Rick Owens store opened in Tribeca, New York City, in 2008. In 2009, Owens opened stores in Tokyo and London.

Owens's style invokes a postapocalyptic period, if not simply postadolescent. He creates from his personal journey, from wreckage to recovery in dusty gray asymmetry. His fitted jackets and draped knits cater to rock stars, but there are many wearable separates for those looking for function over form. Most recently introduced is Rick Owens Lilies, a collection of simple yet sterling basics, the perfect introduction to Owens's aesthetic. Also hot on the scene is Drkshdw, a reinterpretation of his design ideology in denim.

Still working with a small design team, Owens presents some of the most spectacular runway shows in the industry. For his spring/summer 2014 show, Owens did not use fashion models and instead recruited step dancers from multiple American sororities to show how well his clothes move on the body. Public opinion was divided—and the fashion media both praised Owens for including women of color with diverse body types and criticized him for cultural appropriation.

Spring 2013.

RIFAT ÖZBEK ▼

Designer Rifat Ozbek.

BORN Turkey, 1953

AWARDS British Fashion Council *Designer of the Year*, 1988

Rifat Özbek (UZZ-beck) arrived in England in 1970. He studied architecture for two years at the University of Liverpool then switched to fashion, studying at Saint

Rifat Ozbek for Pollini, fall 2007.

Autumn/winter 1999/2000.

Martins School of Art in London. After graduation in 1977, he worked in Italy for Walter Albini and an Italian manufacturer before returning to London and a stint designing for Monsoon, a line made in India. Özbek presented his first collection under his own label in 1984, showing out of his apartment; by his third collection he had a stylish new studio off Bond Street. In 1991, he moved his business to Milan, where he showed his collections until 1994, when he began showing in Paris.

The influence of London street fashion was evident in Özbek's early work but translated with refinement and understatement. He has also been inspired by the way Africans mix traditional and Western elements in their dress and by the Italian and French movies he saw while growing up. He admires the fashion greats: BALENCIAGA for cut, SCHIAPARELLI for humor, CHANEL for timelessness, and SAINT LAURENT for classicism. From his first collections and whatever the inspiration, Özbek's clothes have been sophisticated and controlled, without the rough-edged wackiness associated with much of London fashion.

In 2005, Özbek began designing cushions using unique textiles and patterns, and by 2010 he had left fashion and started a luxury cushion business. His brand Yastik—the Turkish word for cushion—has shops in London, Istanbul, and Alacati.

Designer Thakoon Panichgul (right) and model.

BORN Chiang Rai, Thailand, September 25, 1974

AWARDS Ecco Domani Fashion Foundation *New Talent Award*, 2005

Thakoon Panichgul (Tah-KOON PEHN-each-ghoul) came to America when he was 11, but did not begin his fashion career until almost 20 years later. After earning a degree in business from Boston University, Panichgul worked as a merchandiser for J.Crew. He then held an editorial position at *Harper's Bazaar* and, while there, took tailoring classes at Parsons School of Design in his spare time. In 2004, at the age of 29, he started his eponymous label Thakoon, characterized by a sophisticated and minimal style. His

Spring 2009.

⏳ THAKOON PANICHGUL

designs are at once ethereal and urban—and heavily influenced by his Eastern heritage.

In 2006, Panichgul was asked to create a capsule collection for Nine West, and a year later developed a limited edition line of t-shirts for The Gap. That same year, he was a runner-up for the Council of Fashion Designers of America (CDFA)/Vogue Fashion Fund Award. In 2008, Panichgul debuted his collection for the Hogan brand—an accessory and shoe brand owned by Tod's—and was catapulted into the spotlight when Michelle Obama wore one of his floral print dresses on the last day of the Democratic National Convention. In 2010, he premiered Carbon Copy, a youth-oriented line. In 2012, Michelle Obama sported another Thakoon creation at church on Easter Sunday.

Panichgul's chic, simple, restrained designs are a favorite of celebrities such as Natalie Portman, Demi Moore, and America Ferrera.

Fall 2013.

PAQUIN ⬛ ▮

FOUNDED Paris, 1891
CLOSED 1956

One of couture's great artists, Jeanne Paquin (Pah-KWAHN) trained at Maison Rouff and opened her couture house with backing from her husband Isidore, a banker and businessman. The House of Paquin developed into a major couture force, becoming synonymous with elegance during the 1910s.

The Paquin reputation for beautiful designs was enhanced by the decor of the establishment and the lavishness of its showings, as well as by the Paquins' extensive social life. Management of the house and its relations with its employees were excellent, with some workers remaining for more than 40 years and women as department heads. Paquin's standards were so high that there was always demand from other couture houses for any employees who left.

Jeanne Paquin was the first woman to achieve importance in haute couture. She was chair of the fashion section of the 1900 Paris Exposition and

Light coat with a Lynx fur trim over a sleeveless, two-piece crêpe dress, 1928.

president of the Chambre Syndicale from 1917 to 1919. Hers was the first couture house to open foreign branches—in London, Madrid, and Buenos Aires. She was the first to take mannequins to the opera and the races, with as many as ten wearing the same outfit. The house was the first to make fur garments that were soft and supple.

Jeanne Paquin was a gifted colorist, a talent especially evident in her glamorous and romantic evening dresses. Other specialties were fur-trimmed tailored suits and coats, furs, lingerie, and blue serge suits with gold braid and buttons; accessories were made in-house. She claimed not to make any two dresses exactly alike, individualizing each to the woman for whom it was made. Her customers included the queens of Belgium, Portugal, and Spain as well as actresses and courtesans of the era. Paquin retired and sold the house to an English firm in 1920.

The House of Paquin had a number of successors and merged with the House of Worth in 1953. The company closed a few years later.

Robe featuring high-waisted, polonaise style tunic and narrow-trained skirt, 1913.

Designer Jean Patou.

BORN Normandy, France, 1887
DIED Paris, March 8, 1936

Known as the father of sportswear, Jean Patou's first couture venture was a small house called Parry. It opened in 1914—just in time for World War I, which forced him to cancel his first major show. After four years in the Army, he reopened under his own name in 1919. The house was an immediate success; the clothes were simple but elegant and looked as if they were intended to be worn by real women, not just by mannequins (models).

 JEAN PATOU

An admirer of American business methods, Patou introduced daily staff meetings, a profit-sharing plan for executives, and a bonus system for mannequins. He was also an excellent showman: in 1925, he brought six American mannequins to Paris and used them alongside his French ones; he also instituted gala evening openings, had a cocktail bar in his shop, and chose exquisite bottles for his perfumes. These included Moment Suprême and Joy, promoted as the world's most expensive perfume. He was among the first couturiers to have colors and fabrics produced especially for him, and is credited with being the first to return the waistline to its normal position and to lengthen skirts, which he dropped dramatically to the ankle in 1929, and the first to put his initials on clothing.

After Patou's death, the house remained open under the direction of his brother-in-law, Raymond Barbas, with a series of resident designers including MARC BOHAN (1953–57), KARL LAGERFELD (1958–63), Michel Goma (1963–72), Angelo Tarlazzi (1972–76), Roy Gonzalez (1976–81), and CHRISTIAN LACROIX (1981–87).

Evening dress, 1925.

IRVING PENN

BORN Plainfield, New Jersey, June 16, 1917
DIED New York City, October 7, 2009

A major figure in fashion photography, Irving Penn attended the Philadelphia Museum School of Industrial Art and studied design from 1934 to 1938 with *Harper's Bazaar's* renowned artistic director and developer of talent, ALEXEY BRODOVITCH. Penn also freelanced as an artist for *Harper's Bazaar* from 1937 to 1939. In 1941, he spent a year painting in Mexico. His first *Vogue* photographs appeared in 1943, the beginning of a long and fruitful relationship that resulted in more than 150 *Vogue* covers over 50 years.

After war service in the American Field Service in Italy and India, Penn's career blossomed, resulting in a wide variety of photographs of fashion, personalities, and travel. In addition to CONDÉ NAST publications, his client roster included international advertising agencies. In 1950, he married model Lisa Fonssagrives, with whom he had first worked in 1947 for photographs of the Paris collections; these were unadorned but rich in feeling. Their later location trip to Morocco foreshadowed his future interests and so-called anthropological pictures.

At a time when fashion photography was marked by elaborately artificial lighting, Penn used his lights to simulate daylight, an important and influential move. Posing his models against the plainest backgrounds, he achieved a monumental simplicity and clarity, as well as an elegant femininity. On his location trips he used the same economy of means for portraits of native people. In the style of 19th-century photographers, he used a

Photographer Irving Penn.

portable studio that he had built to ensure his desired working conditions in Cameroon, Peru, and other places where no studios existed.

Penn's work has been exhibited in one-man shows at the Museum of Modern Art and the Metropolitan Museum of Art in New York City, and is in the permanent collections of both. His works were also shown in 2005 at the National Gallery of Art in Washington, D.C. at an exhibition titled *Irving Penn: Platinum Prints*, which later traveled to the Morgan Library in 2007 and the J. Paul Getty Museum. He produced numerous books of photography, from *Moments Preserved* (1960) to *Passage* (1991).

Ŏ ELSA PERETTI

Designer Elsa Peretti.

BORN Florence, Italy, May 1, 1940

AWARDS Coty American Fashion Critics' Awards *Special Award (jewelry)*, 1971 • Cultured Pearl Industry of America and Japan *Outstanding Contribution Award*, 1978 • Fashion Group International *Night of the Stars Award*, 1986 • Council of Fashion Designers of America (CFDA) *Accessories Designer of the Year*, 2000

The daughter of a well-off Roman family, Elsa Peretti earned a diploma in interior design and worked briefly for a Milanese architect. In 1961, she went to Switzerland, then moved to London and started modeling. She was seen by models' agent Wilhelmina, who suggested that Peretti go to New York City. There she worked for several top houses, including HALSTON and DE LA RENTA.

In 1969, Peretti designed a few pieces of silver jewelry that Halston and GIORGIO SANT'ANGELO showed with their collections. These witty objects—heart-shaped buckles, pendants shaped like small vases, silver urn pendants that held fresh flowers—were soon joined by horseshoe-shaped buckles on long leather belts and other designs in horn, ebony, and ivory. Peretti also designed the bottles for Halston's fragrance and cosmetic lines. In 1974, she began working with TIFFANY & Co., the first time in 25 years the company had carried silver jewelry. Among her much-copied designs there are necklaces with small, open, slightly lopsided heart pendants and Diamonds by the Yard—diamonds spaced at intervals on a fine gold chain. She has also designed desk and table accessories for Tiffany.

Peretti is inspired by her love of nature and Japanese designs. She works in Spain and New York, and has traveled to Asia to study semiprecious stones. Prototypes for her silver and ivory designs are made by artisans in Barcelona; crystal pieces are produced in Germany. As a celebration of her 50th birthday and 15-year association with Tiffany, Peretti was honored by the Fashion Institute of Technology in 1990 with a retrospective of her work called *Fifteen of My Fifty with Tiffany*. In 2012, Peretti signed a 20-year, $50 million agreement with Tiffany to exclusively license her designs. Jodie Foster, Gwyneth Paltrow, and Jennifer Aniston are just a few of her devoted fans.

PHOEBE PHILO ⧗

BORN Paris, 1973

AWARDS British Fashion Council *British Designer of the Year*, 2010 • Council of Fashion Designers of America (CFDA) *International Award*, 2011 • British Government *Officer of the Order of the British Empire* (OBE), 2014

Designer Phoebe Philo.

Phoebe Philo grew up in a London suburb and entered Central Saint Martins College of Arts and Design in 1993, graduating three years later. In 1997 she joined the French ready-to-wear firm CHLOÉ as an assistant to her friend STELLA McCARTNEY, who had just been made creative director. When McCartney left Chloé in 2001 to form her own business, Philo moved into her position.

Philo's first collection immediately established her style—cool and sexy, yet romantic and luxurious, with a modern edge appealing to the younger customers attracted to the label under McCartney. Philo was named creative director of CÉLINE (a fashion division of LVMH) in 2008, replacing Ivana Omazic, and returned to her fashion roots after a sabbatical from the industry that had started in 2005. Her first collection for Céline was presented in March 2009 for the fall/winter season. In 2011, Céline saw record sales under Philo. The label opted not to show at the fall 2012 fashion shows because of Philo's third pregnancy.

Céline, spring 2014.

Céline, spring 2010.

Designer Paloma Picasso.

BORN Paris, April 19, 1949

AWARDS Hispanic Designers Council *MODA Award,* 1988 • Council of Fashion Designers of America (CFDA) *Accessories Designer of the Year,* 1989 • National Museum of Women in the Arts *Award for Achievement in the Arts,* 2011

Paloma Picasso is the daughter of two artists—one a monumental figure in 20th-century art—and a successful designer in her own right. She is at the center of a business involved in everything from jewelry to perfume and cosmetics to home design. Her first jewelry collection was in 1971 for the Greek firm Zolotas. In 1972, she met Rafael Lopez-Cambil, an Argentine playwright who she married in 1978. She designed sets and costumes for him and, after their marriage, her husband devised a strategy aimed at establishing her name in the world of design. They later divorced.

In 1980, Picasso joined TIFFANY & Co. with a collection of gold jewelry set with precious and semiprecious stones. She continues to design for Tiffany; her style is marked by bold, sensuous shapes, sometimes inspired by urban graffiti, sometimes by Renaissance opulence. In addition to cosmetics and perfume, her other U.S. design projects have included high-end handbags and less expensive, more casual accessories, as well as eyewear, table wear, fabrics, and wall coverings.

In 2010, Picasso celebrated her 30th year with Tiffany with a Moroccan-inspired collection called Marrakesh. Her next collection, Olive Leaf, was inspired by the beauty of nature and released in 2013.

STEFANO PILATI ⧖

BORN Milan, 1955

Stefano Pilati took over creative control of YVES SAINT LAURENT couture (along with its ready-to-wear line, Rive Gauche) in 2004 from GUCCI Group's marketing head, TOM FORD. French fashion pundits considered Ford a cultural vandal, not least because he had moved the brand heavily into accessories—focusing on his chunky, YSL-emblazoned handbag.

Not yet 40, Pilati had moved to Saint Laurent in 2000 from the PRADA imprint Miu Miu. He was charged with restoring Saint Laurent to its chic glory with clothes geared toward the "bohemian jet set." That aesthetic was epitomized by the "Le Smoking" pantsuit, created by Saint Laurent in the 1960s and popularized by the Nouvelle Vague (French New Wave). Saint Laurent died in 2008, creating a window of publicity that the company capitalized on.

By then, Pilati—who had a rocky first couple years as creative director—was finding his footing and

Designer Stefano Pilati.

influencing high-end prêt-a-porter lines like Max Mara. He began to be seen as a steady hand guiding the brand back to its cosmopolitan roots. For example, his spring 2009 collection expanded earlier elements of androgyny, with geometric shapes and soft, luxurious fabrics. He remained as creative director until 2012, when he became head of design at Ermenegildo Zegna and creative director at Agnona. His fall 2013 debut show for Zegna received rave reviews; he showed women's wear for Agnona in the fall of 2014.

Ermenegildo Zegna, spring 2014.

Yves Saint Laurent Fall 2010.

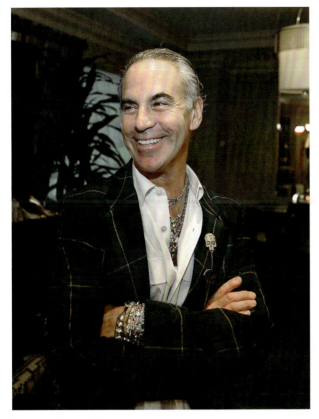

Designer Donald Pliner.

BORN Chicago, 1943

Donald Pliner was destined to make shoes. His family owned a shoe business and, after learning how the business was run, he opened his own store in Beverly Hills in 1967. The company turned a profit of $1 million in its first year. In 1971, Pliner opened The Right Bank Clothing Company, renamed The Right Bank Shoe Company three years later. It was the first American outlet for European designers such as THIERRY MUGLER and Castlebajac. The store had a celebrity following selling clothes, shoes, and accessories.

In 1984, Pliner became head of a new line of Spanish footwear called Glacé, and within two years the line was sold internationally. In 1989, he reintroduced his own

line of footwear and accessories. In 1994, Pliner created an all-elastic shoe that was so successful he introduced a line of men's shoes in 1998. Pliner's shoes are known for their comfortable fit. His motto is to "live the luxury of comfortable fashion."

In 2002, Pliner relaunched his handbag collections. The Couture handbag line is produced in Italy, and the Donald Pliner line in China. In 2004, Pliner launched Friends of Babydoll Pliner, a line for dogs offering accessories, outerwear, collars, and carriers.

Pliner and his wife cofounded the Peace for the Children Foundation, created to fund projects that advance peace, care, and welfare for children in need. They are also partners in the Lisa for Donald J. Pliner collection of luxury shoes.

Shoe designs by Donald Pliner.

WALTER PLUNKETT

BORN Oakland, California, June 2, 1902
DIED Santa Monica, California, March 8, 1982

Walter Plunkett was best known for period costumes, particularly for the film *Gone with the Wind*. In the mid-1920s, after studying law and attempting an acting career, he took a job in the wardrobe department of FBO Studios, then specializing in Westerns. The studio soon changed its name to RKO, and Plunkett—despite his lack of formal training—became its costume

Designer Walter Plunkett.

Vivian Leigh in *Gone with the Wind*, wearing a Walter Plunkett design, 1939.

designer and tasked with creating a design department. In 1931, he got his first important assignment, *Cimarron*, starring Irene Dunne. In 1933, he did *Flying Down to Rio*, the first film in which Fred Astaire danced with Ginger Rogers, and in 1935 he dressed Katharine Hepburn in *Alice Adams*, the beginning of a long collaboration with the actress.

Underpaid and overworked, Plunkett quit RKO in 1935, though at Hepburn's request he returned the next year to dress her for *Mary of Scotland*. From then until his retirement in 1966, Plunkett worked as a freelance designer, dressing some of the greatest stars in some of Hollywood's most ambitious productions, sometimes working with other designers such as TRAVIS BANTON and IRENE SHARAFF.

✗ PAUL POIRET

Designer Paul Poiret.

BORN Paris, April 20, 1879
DIED Paris, April 28, 1944

Paul Poiret's extraordinary imagination and achievements flowered in the brilliant epoch of Sergei Diaghilev and Léon Bakst, influencing international taste throughout the early 20th century. Fascinated by the theater and the arts, Poiret was a flamboyant figure who spent fortunes decorating his homes and throwing parties, pageants, and costume balls. He designed costumes for actresses such as Réjane and Sarah Bernhardt; his friends included Diaghilev, Bakst, Raoul Dufy, ERTÉ, and PAUL IRIBE.

When Poiret was young, while apprenticed to an umbrella maker, he taught himself costume sketching. He sold his first sketches to MADELEINE CHÉRUIT at Raudnitz Soeurs, joined JACQUES DOUCET in 1896, and spent four years at WORTH before opening his own house in 1904.

Considered by many to be one of the greatest originators of feminine fashion, Poiret was enormously talented, with a penchant for the bizarre and dramatic. Though costume was his forte, the modern silhouette was to a great extent his invention. He freed women from corsets and petticoats, and introduced the first modern, straight-line dress. Yet he also invented the harem and hobble skirts, so narrow at the hem that walking in them was almost impossible. His minaret skirt, inspired by and named after a play he costumed, spread worldwide.

Inspired by Diaghilev's Ballets Russes, Poiret designed a Russian tunic coat, straight in line and belted, made from sumptuous materials. His Oriental influences were reflected in little turbans and tall aigrettes (headdresses) he put on his models, and in 1911 he created a scandal by taking mannequins to the Auteuil races dressed in *jupes culottes*, also called Turkish trousers.

Poiret also established a crafts school, where Dufy designed textiles for a while, and was the first couturier to release a perfume. In 1912, he was the first to present

(continued)

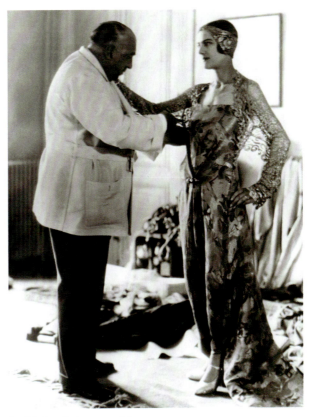

Paul Poiret fitting a model.

a collection in other countries, taking along 12 models. In 1914, along with Worth, Paquin, Chéruit, and Callot Soeurs, he founded the Protective Association of French Dressmakers and became its first president.

Unable to adjust his style to changes brought about by World War I, Poiret went out of business in 1924. Bankrupt, he was divorced by his wife in 1929. Four

An overskirt wired to give a "lampshade effect" also known as a "sorbet," 1912.

years later he was offered a job designing ready-to-wear, but his attitude toward money was so irresponsible that the venture failed. He took bit parts in movies, wrote his autobiography, and moved to the south of France. He spent his last years in poverty and died of Parkinson's disease in a charity hospital.

Metal, silk, and cotton dress, 1911.

VIRGINIA POPE

BORN Chicago, June 29, 1885
DIED New York City, January 16, 1978

As fashion editor at *The New York Times* from 1933 to 1955, Virginia Pope is credited with practically inventing fashion reporting. One of the first to look for news in the wholesale market, she reported on the people who made clothes at a time when only Paris fashion was considered newsworthy. She encouraged the American fashion industry in its early years, originating the Fashions of The Times fashion show in 1942 as a showcase for American designers and staging the show each fall for the next nine years. In 1952, the show became a twice-yearly fashion supplement of the same name still published by the *Times*.

After Pope's father died when she was five, her mother took her to Europe, which they toured for the next 15 years. She became fluent in French, German, and Italian, and familiar with the best European art and music. They returned to Chicago in 1905. Pope served in the Red Cross during World War I, then tried various careers in Chicago and New York, including social work, the theater, book translation, and writing.

Though a late starter in journalism, Pope had a long run. Her first published pieces, in *The New York Times*, were interviews with a visiting German theater group and articles about an Italian neighborhood—results of her facility in languages. She joined the Sunday staff of the *Times* in 1925 and eight years later became fashion editor, a position she held and developed for 22 years. Afterward, Pope became fashion editor of *Parade* magazine; her name stayed on its masthead until her death.

In addition, she held the Edwin Goodman Chair established by Bergdorf Goodman at the Fashion Institute of Technology, teaching a course on fashion in contemporary living. She could often be seen on Seventh Avenue with her students, escorting them to fashion shows and behind the scenes to see how the business worked. She also believed that exposure to culture was essential to a designer's development and regularly took her students to performances at the Metropolitan Opera. While her personal style was of the establishment, she understood innovation and could look at clothes objectively. Referring to her conservative appearance and "grande dame" reputation, a fellow editor once said, "she could play the Queen of England without rehearsal."

ZAC POSEN ▟

BORN New York City, October 24, 1980

AWARDS Ecco Domani *Fashion Foundation Award* (one of five young designers), 2002 • Council of Fashion Designers of America (CFDA) *Swarovski's Perry Ellis Award for Menswear*, 2004

A precocious talent whose designs first appeared on celebrities who happened to be friends or schoolmates, Zac Posen was born into the art world, his father a successful painter. From 1996 to 1998—after school and on weekends and holidays—he interned with Richard Martin at the Costume Institute of the Metropolitan Museum of Art. There he developed a passion for the work of MADELEINE VIONNET and was able to study her bias-cut designs up close. While at London's Central Saint Martins College of Arts and Design, he was one of ten students chosen to submit designs to the *Curvaceous* exhibit of Victorian underwear at the Victoria and Albert

Designer Zac Posen.

Museum (2001–02). He contributed a fitted, six-foot column constructed from vertical strips of glossy brown leather held together by hundreds of hooks and eyes. It won the V & A Prize and became part of the museum's permanent collection.

Posen's designs—dresses, blouses, coats—rely to a great extent on his favored bias cut and possess both disciplined construction and refined workmanship. They have a modern femininity—sexy but not vulgar—and have been worn by actresses and models such as Natalie Portman and Coco Rocha. They have also been sold at Henri Bendel in New York.

In 2004, SEAN JOHN owner Sean Combs acquired half of Posen's company, establishing a business partnership and plans to expand the Posen brand. In 2005, Posen debuted a denim line for the label 7 For All Mankind. In 2010, he created a line for Target that was sold in its stores in Australia, and in 2014 he introduced Truly Zac Posen, a collection of bridal and evening dresses for David's Bridal.

Fall 2004.

Costume designer Sandy Powell.

SANDY POWELL

"who care about the visuals," and has worked with Mike Figgis, Neil Jordan, Todd Haynes, and Martin Scorsese.

Powell's process is to first allow a film's script to inspire her costumes, then meet with its actors to determine fit and fabrics before drawing designs. She prefers to do period films to contemporary, but she does not think about the historical accuracy of a film. Instead she focuses on whether the film feels and looks right. That strategy has helped Powell earn nominations for more than 32 awards and win 14—including three Academy Awards for best costume design and two from the British Academy of Film and Television Arts (BAFTA).

Powell's latest project is designing the costumes for *Cinderella*, directed by Kenneth Branagh, which she loves because "it's a film about girls for girls . . . the antithesis of a Scorsese."

BORN London, April 7, 1960

AWARDS Academy Awards for Best Costume Design *Shakespeare in Love,* 1998; *The Aviator,* 2004; *The Young Victoria,* 2009 • British Academy of Film and Television Arts Awards for Best Costume Design *Velvet Goldmine,* 1998; *The Young Victoria,* 2009

A major force in the film world for her costumes, Sandy Powell did not grow up in an artistic family. But her mother taught Powell how to sew at a young age, and her talent started to emerge as she began making clothes for her Barbie dolls. When she was 16, she saw Lindsey Kemp perform and decided that she wanted a career in the performing arts. Powell attended Saint Martins School of Art in London, majoring in theater design. She considered focusing on fashion but felt that costume design was more interesting.

After graduation, Powell worked for fringe theater companies. A friend got her an interview with director Derek Jarman, who hired her to design outfits for his music videos. He then asked her to design the costumes for his film *Caravaggio* (1986). She worked on four films with Jarman and credits him for inspiring her and helping launch her career. Powell gravitates toward directors

Costume design by Sandy Powell from the film "Gangs of New York."

MIUCCIA PRADA ⍓

BORN Maria Bianchi, Italy, May 10, 1949

AWARDS Council of Fashion Designers of America (CFDA) *International Award*, 1993 • British Fashion Awards *International Designer of the Year*, 2013

Designer Miuccia Prada.

Miuccia Prada (Me-OOH-cha PRAH-duh) entered design through her family's firm, Fratelli Prada, a maker of high-quality leather goods since 1915. A committed member of the Communist Party during and immediately after her university years, she resisted joining the family business until 1978, when she took over from her mother. Her first success was a black nylon backpack; later ones were handheld bags of the same fabric—washable, flexible, tough, and soft.

Prada's first ready-to-wear collection was for fall 1989, and in 1994 she showed in New York City. Her clothes, highly coveted by the more forward-thinking fashion press, are described as supremely comfortable—showing almost nothing on the hanger but coming to life on the body. There is a younger, less expensive Miu Miu collection as well as men's wear and accessories.

Under the leadership of her husband, Patrizio Bertelli, the Prada firm has become one of fashion's foremost conglomerates. Its interests include leading international design houses, fine shoemakers, and major Italian production facilities. Prada also operates about 250 stores worldwide.

Prada is a designer of many talents. For example, in 2010, she created the costumes for the New York Metropolitan Opera's rendition of Giuseppe Verdi's *Attila.* In 2012, the fashion house was celebrated in an exhibit at the Metropolitan Museum of Art's Costume Institute, *Schiaparelli and Prada: Impossible Conversations.*

In 2014, Miuccia Prada became joint chief executive officer of the Prada company with her husband.

Pre-fall, 2009.

Pre-fall, 2009.

Designers Justin Thornton (left) and Thea Bregazzi (right).

Preen clothes merge the design perspectives of two distinct visions. The brand's style has been called a "paradoxical blend of feminine, vintage echoes, and a futuristic, clinical minimalism." The two designers acknowledge that over time their collections have moved from a younger to more grown-up aesthetic. Their clothes are very flattering to the female form and make women look elegant and glamorous.

In 2003, Preen launched a men's wear line and created the first of many collections for TopShop. In 2006, the book *Decade* was published, cataloguing the work of Bregazzi and Thorton over the previous ten years. Preen also premiered the "Power Dress," a bandage mini that became a signature piece. In 2008, Preen showed a moderately priced line at Copenhagen Fashion Week, and in 2009 it debuted a resort collection. Preen is sold in New York, Hong Kong, and London, and has been worn by celebrities such as Beyoncé, Rihanna, Amy Winehouse, Kate Moss, and Cate Blanchett.

FOUNDED Thea Bregazzi and Justin Thorton, 1996

Preen is the brainchild of designers Thea Bregazzi and Justin Thorton, who have risen to fame without much publicity or sponsorship. Both grew up on the Isle of Man, on opposite sides of the island, and both attended the Isle of Man College in Douglas, where they met at 18. Bregazzi majored in fashion and business at the University of Central Lancashire, and Thorton in fashion and textiles at the Winchester School of Art. They were designing for different companies when they were reunited on a project for Helen Story.

In 1996, Bregazzi and Thorton developed the concept for Preen—which they say is what dressing up is all about. The couple set up shop in West London's Portobello Green and debuted their first collection at London Fashion Week in 2001. They moved their twice-yearly runway shows to New York Fashion Week in 2008, but returned to London for 2013.

Preen, spring 2003.

CANDY PRATTS PRICE 🗋

BORN Candida Rosa Theresa Pratts; New York City, February 18, 1950

AWARDS Council of Fashion Designers of America (CFDA) *Media Award in Honor of Eugenia Sheppard*, 2008

Best known as the former executive fashion director at style.com—once the online home of *Vogue* and *W*—Candy Pratts Price credited the site's success to her experience at *Vogue*. She called the site an online magazine, breaking stories and running original content and photos instead of simply aggregating material from other sources—though it did feature news from *Vogue* and *W*. Under Pratts Price, style.com became a go-to spot for fashion insiders. The site was lauded for its coverage of both major and up-and-coming designers.

Pratts Price joined *Vogue* as accessories editor in the 1980s and was soon promoted to fashion director of accessories. A graduate of the Fashion Institute of Technology, she has a strong fashion resume, having worked as fashion director at *Harper's Bazaar*, creative director at RALPH LAUREN, and under famed merchandiser Marvin Traub as a designer of store windows and displays for Bloomingdale's. Pratts Price also worked as an executive producer on an E! Networks documentary about a Jacqueline Kennedy exhibit at the Metropolitan Museum of Art and as creative director of the VH1/*Vogue* Fashion Awards. In addition, she appears as a trend and fashion expert on television programs such as *Today* and *Good Morning America*, and in 2008 published her first book, *American Fashion Accessories*. Pratts Price says she returned to CONDÉ NAST because of *Vogue* editor ANNA WINTOUR, who was her mentor. Known for her

Fashion director Candy Pratts Price.

sharp eye and keen fashion instinct, Pratts Price has credited her success to journalistic curiosity and a love for fashion.

In 2009, to everyone's surprise, Pratts Price was laid off from style.com. But in 2010, after *Vogue* launched its own site, Condé Nast rehired her as creative director of vogue.com. Pratts Price has also been recognized for her philanthropy: in 2012, she received the Hero Award from AID for AIDS, an organization that donates HIV/AIDS medications to Latin American communities.

Above: Spring 2014.

Below: Proenza Schouler designers Lazaro Hernandez (left) and Jack McCollough (right).

FOUNDED Lazaro Hernandez and Jack McCollough, 2002

AWARDS Council of Fashion Designers of America (CFDA) *Swarovski Perry Ellis Award for Ready-to-Wear*, 2003; *Womenswear Designer of the Year*, 2007, 2011, 2013; *Accessories Designer of the Year*, 2009

Lazaro Hernandez and Jack McCollough met in 1999 at Parsons School of Design, where they arrived after starting out on other career paths—Hernandez in medicine, McCollough in glass blowing. During his sophomore year at Parsons, Hernandez interned at MICHAEL KORS, a position he obtained in storybook fashion through *Vogue* editor ANNA WINTOUR. After

◼◻ PROENZA SCHOULER

discovering that she was on his plane from Miami, he sent her a note midflight, describing himself, his love of fashion, and his admiration for her; she told Kors that he should hire Hernandez. McCollough interned at MARC JACOBS. McCollough and Hernandez freelanced together at another company during their senior year and were allowed to do their senior thesis as a collaboration, producing a 15-piece collection using fabric donated by Kors. The collection was so impressive that the judges recommended the designers to Barneys' vice president for merchandising, who bought it for the store.

Hernandez and McCollough create clothes "for women, not kids," giving a sophisticated twist to classics. Their emphasis is on spare silhouettes in fresh proportions and subdued colors, mostly black and gray, in deluxe fabrics such as cashmere, angora, and silk. The clothes have received an enthusiastic response from celebrities and been embraced by the press and retailers.

The duo founded Proenza Schouler (PRO-en-zuh SCHOOL-er)—the name combines the maiden names of the designers' mothers—in 2002. For spring 2007, they created an affordable collection of clothing and accessories for Target. In 2008, Proenza Schouler collaborated with Giuseppi Zanotti for a line of shoes that in spring 2009 expanded to 100 styles. Available in New York, Milan, and Paris, the styles include ballet slippers, loafers, lace-up sandals, and heels. In 2012, a Proenza Schouler store opened in New York on Madison Avenue. In 2014, a retrospective of their collections was exhibited at Le Bon Marche Department Store in Paris.

EMILIO PUCCI ▼

BORN Marchese di Barsento; Naples, Italy, 1914
DIED Florence, Italy, November 29, 1992

AWARDS *Neiman Marcus Award*, 1954 • Council of Fashion Designers of America (CFDA) *Special Award,* 1990

A descendant of Russian nobility and Italian aristocracy, Emilio Pucci was educated in Italy and America. He was on Italy's Olympics Ski Team in 1933–34 and an officer in the Italian Air Force during World War II, remaining in the service after the war. Even after he became involved with fashion, he retained an interest in politics and in the 1950s served two terms in the Italian Chamber of Deputies.

Pucci got into fashion by accident when the ski clothes he was wearing in Switzerland caught the attention of photographer TONI FRISSELL. Snug and close-fitting, they were among the first made of stretch fabrics. When Frissel's photographs were published and attracted attention, Pucci decided to market the clothes. But it was his simple chemises of thin silk jersey that made him a favorite of the international jet set in the 1960s. These dresses, wrinkle-resistant and packable in little space, were beloved by fashion professionals everywhere, and their brilliant signature prints—in designs

Above: Designer Emilio Pucci.
Left: Slit-prints skirt and thin-strapped top, 1966.

inspired by heraldic banners—were copied in every price range. In 1990, there was a worldwide renewal of interest in the prints. Pucci's design projects also included accessories, sportswear, underwear, fragrances for women and men, porcelain, sheets, bath linens, rugs, and airline uniforms. The business has continued since his death in 1992.

In the 1990s, Pucci's daughter, Laudomia Pucci, took over the family business, and in 2000 the Pucci family formed an alliance with the LVMH luxury brand, which now controls 67 percent of the company. Laudomia serves as image director. CHRISTIAN LACROIX was appointed creative director in 2003, followed by MATTHEW WILLIAMSON in 2006 and Peter Dundas in 2008. Pucci celebrated its 60th anniversary in 2007, and a book showcasing the brand's iconic prints was published in 2009 and republished by Taschen in 2013 with four different collector's edition covers.

Designer Gareth Pugh.

BORN August 31, 1981

At the 2013 MTV Europe Awards, Beyoncé's stylists replaced her usual glittery frocks with an edgy black and white mini dress by Gareth Pugh (PYOO). The dress's strikingly architectural silhouette created a media buzz

for Pugh in America. But the designer had been the darling of London catwalks since 2003, his final year at Central Saint Martins School of Arts and Design, when his balloon-inflected collection caught the eye of the senior fashion editor at *Dazed & Confused* magazine.

Since then Pugh has been cast as the *enfant terrible* of the British fashion industry, in the vein of ALEXANDER MCQUEEN. Pugh's couture collections—which rely heavily on fetish materials like latex and chain mail—make almost no concessions to established modes of dress. In 2007, after *Vogue*'s ANNA WINTOUR called him a genius, Pugh told *Icon* magazine that he had yet to sell a single dress. Pugh's wearable sculptures are often menacing or distorting, refiguring the bodies of models beyond even the most stylized conception of the human body.

A clear line runs from VIVIENNE WESTWOOD's do-it-yourself, groundbreaking Sex collection—which influenced music-tinged British fashion from punk through the New Romantic London club scene—to Pugh's creations. He shares more than just an aesthetic with those youth cultures; his posture is avowedly working class. When Pugh was asked why he appeared on the BBC reality show *The Fashion House* (which raised his profile considerably), he replied, "My only other option was the dole." Pugh's 2013 collection surprised both fans and detractors, indicating a shift to a more wearable line.

Spring 2012.

Spring 2014.

LILLY PULITZER ▼

BORN Lilly McKim; Roslyn, NY, 1931
DIED Palm Beach, Florida, April 7, 2013

Lilly Pulitzer started out as a New York socialite, having attended the Chapin School in Manhattan with the Bouvier sisters Jacqueline and Lee, as well as other private academies. In 1950, she married Peter Pulitzer, grandson of the legendary publisher Joseph Pulitzer. In addition to being known for their bohemian lifestyle, the couple ran several citrus groves that Peter had inherited. Lilly decided to open a juice stand right off trendy Worth Avenue, partly because she thought it would be fun and partly because she wanted to use all the fruit from their groves. She soon discovered that working at the juice stand put vibrant stains all over her clothing.

So, Lilly asked her dressmaker to create cotton shifts in bright, flowered patterns that would hide the discoloration. The dresses were striking, and within a short period, Pulitzer's clothing became more

Above: Designer Lilly Pulitzer.
Left: Models wearing Lilly Pulitzer designs, 2002.

famous than her juice. She wore summery shift dresses, capri pants, and simple sheaths, all made from brightly patterned fabrics that became her signature. Her outfits gained early acclaim when Jacqueline Kennedy was photographed wearing one in *LIFE* magazine.

Pulitzer's bright colors came to exemplify the Palm Beach lifestyle, and her signature shades of bright pink and green were considered the color scheme of the affluent at play. The designs were often worn by vacationers in the Hamptons, Cape Cod, and tony resorts. Popular patterns included turtle prints, flowers, and sea life, all in bright summer colors. In 1980, *The Preppy Handbook* called the Lilly Pulitzer dress an essential piece for preppy women. The label thrived well into the 1970s. In 1984, Pulitzer retired and closed the company.

The Pulitzer label experienced a revival in 1993, eventually expanding to over 75 freestanding stores. The brand is also sold in leading department stores and, in addition to women's wear, produces bedding, men's wear, a maternity line, children's wear, shoes, and accessories.

In 2008, Pulitzer celebrated 50 years in the business. To mark the occasion, Parsons School of Design in New York launched a retrospective featuring Pulitzer dresses from 1959 to the present. James Bradbeer, Jr., the president of Lilly Pulitzer, said that it was hard to date some of the pieces because Pulitzer threw out many of the archives when she retired. Some dresses were dated by identifying whether they had metal, painted metal, or plastic zippers, as well as by the prints of the fabrics. In 2010, the Museum of Lifestyle & Fashion History in Boynton Beach, Florida, staged an exhibit of Pulitzer's designs.

Designer Mary Quant.

BORN Blackheath, Kent, England, February 11, 1934

AWARDS British Government *Order of the British Empire* (OBE), 1966

Mary Quant was a leading figure in the youth revolution of the 1950s and 1960s—her awareness of social changes and understanding of young customers made her a celebrity and helped put London on the fashion map. She studied at Goldsmiths College of Art in London, where she met Alexander Plunket-Greene, whom she later married. In 1955, with a partner, she and her husband opened a small boutique called Bazaar, the first on King's Road in London's Chelsea district. At the start they sold clothes from outside designers, but soon became frustrated by the difficulty of getting the kind of clothes they wanted. Quant then began making her own designs, which were spirited, unconventional, and instant hits with young women—probably because

they were unlike anything their mothers had ever worn or would wear.

Quant began on a small scale, creating designs in her own flat, but her fame grew along with that of "swinging London." By 1963, she had opened a second Bazaar, moved into mass production with her less expensive Ginger Group, and was exporting to America—making her a full-scale designer and manufacturer. She designed for J.C. Penney in America and for Puritan's Youthquake promotion. Her autobiography, *Quant by Quant*, was published in 1966. In the 1970s, while no longer a fashion innovator, she added to her business with licenses for jewelry, carpets, household linens, men's ties, and eyewear. In 1973–74, the London Museum presented the exhibit *Mary Quant's London*.

Around 1964, Quant became interested in makeup, and in 1966 she launched a cosmetics line. With Japanese partners, she developed a complete body and skincare collection, as well as makeup, sold in freestanding shops in Japan. There is a flagship store in London and shops in New York and the Far East, Australia, and New Zealand.

Quant is credited with starting the Chelsea or Mod look of the mid-1950s and the miniskirts of the late 1960s. Whether or not she actually originated the mini, she certainly popularized it in England and America. She initiated ideas that are now common, using denim, colored flannel, and vinyl in clothes that only the young could wear. For her innovative shows, Quant used photographic mannequins (models) rather than regular runway models and had them dance down the runway. Quant was a pivotal figure in a fashion upheaval that reflected major social changes around the world. The Mod look has since returned in the work of designers in both Europe and America. Quant's mini slipdress in bold prints reappeared under her own label in 2003.

In 2001, New York's Fashion Institute of Technology mounted an exhibit, *London Fashion*, that traced the history of the city's style contributions—from Quant's miniskirt to more recent designs. It included, among others, JOHN GALLIANO, ALEXANDER MCQUEEN, HUSSEIN CHALAYAN, and VIVIENNE WESTWOOD.

PACO RABANNE ▲

Three models wearing brightly patterned dresses by Rabanne, 1966.

Above: Designer Paco Rabanne.

Below: Model wearing mini dress made of lacquered-aluminum discs, designed by Paco Rabanne, 1968.

BORN Francisco Rabaneda y Cuervo; San Sebastian, Spain, February 18, 1934

AWARDS French Government *Officier de la Légion d'Honneur (Legion of Honor),* 2010

Paco Rabanne's family fled to France in 1939 to escape the Spanish Civil War. At the time, his mother was head seamstress at Balenciaga in San Sebastian. In Paris, Rabanne studied architecture at the École Supérieure des Beaux-Arts and began designing on a freelance basis—handbags, shoes, plastic accessories, and embroideries.

In his first show in 1966, called "12 Unwearable Dresses," the dresses in question were made of plastic discs linked with metal chains, accessorized with plastic jewelry and sun goggles in primary colors. He continued the linked-disc theme in coats of fur patches and dresses of leather patches, and also used buttons and strips of aluminum laced with wire. In 1970, Rabanne was one of the first to use fake suede for dresses. He combines unlikely materials—for example, he has designed coats of knit and fur as well as dresses made of ribbons, feathers, or tassels, linked for suppleness. His experiments have had considerable influence on other designers. Rabanne also has a wide range of fragrances for men and women.

A mystic by nature, Rabanne lives monastically, unencumbered by possessions, and gives the bulk of his money to charity. Although still actively engaged in his firm, he turned over creative direction to Rosemary Rodriguez in 2000. Patrick Robinson replaced Rodriguez in 2005. The brand has had a series of design turnovers in recent years. In 2011, Manish Arora became creative director, but in 2012 was replaced by Lydia Maurer—who announced in 2013 that she was leaving the brand. The company is owned by the Spanish firm Puig, which also owns Nina Ricci.

Above: Rag & Bone designers Marcus Wainwright (left) and David Neville (right).

Right: Spring 2014.

FOUNDED Marcus Wainwright and David Neville, 2002

AWARDS Ecco Domani Fashion Foundation Award, 2005 • Council of Fashion Designers of America (CFDA) *Swarovski Award for Menswear*, 2007; *Menswear Designer of the Year*, 2010

Rag & Bone is the British term for 19th-century scavengers who collected scraps, metal, rags, and bones. It is also the name of the label created by the dynamic pair David Neville and Marcus Wainwright. The two attended the same boarding school in Berkshire, England, when they were young, but were not friends. Neville went to college in Durham and studied molecular biology, while Wainwright—who is a year older—went to Newcastle.

Years later, they reconnected at a local pub, where they got to know each other and cemented their friendship. Their lives had taken them in different directions, with Wainwright forming a telecommunications firm and Neville becoming an investment banker. After several years, Wainwright moved to Mexico, where he met his wife. He followed her to New York City, where he launched Rag & Bone in 2002. He asked Neville to handle the financial side of the business, beginning their partnership.

RAG & BONE

Rag & Bone set out to make the perfect pair of men's dark jeans, which neither Wainwright nor Neville could find on the market. Their partnership has succeeded because they are a good team with very different skills. Wainwright is obsessed with the artistic and creative side of the company, Neville with the commercial and branding aspects.

Rag & Bone clothes are distinctly British but exhibit elements of modern design, American work wear, and classic tailoring. The clothes have the understated feel of the New York aesthetic. Though neither partner received formal design training, craftsmanship and attention to detail are core to the Rag & Bone philosophy. The brand offers men's wear, women's wear, shoes and accessories, all "clothes for people to enjoy their lives in." There are six boutiques in New York, one in Tokyo, and flagship stores in London, Seoul, and Los Angeles. Rag & Bone is sold in more than 39 countries. Celebrity fans of the label include Julianne Moore, Gisele Bündchen, and Drew Barrymore. In 2014, they received their third nomination for the CFDA Menswear Designer of the Year award, having won twice before.

JOHN RAWLINGS 📷

BORN Ohio, 1912
DIED 1970

Photographer John Rawlings began his illustrious career in 1936, when he became a studio assistant at *Vogue*. Rawlings helped transform editorial fashion photography. He worked closely with *Vogue* editor EDNA WOOLMAN CHASE to create photos that, as she put it, contained more information and less art—photos that truly celebrated the clothes.

After attending Wesleyan University in the early 1930s, Rawlings moved to New York City and worked as a window dresser. He soon bought a camera to take pictures of his work and discovered a passion for photography. He began shooting photos of his clients with their animals, and one landed on the desk of legendary publisher CONDÉ NAST. Nast hired Rawlings at *Vogue*, where he built props and assisted several well-known photographers, including

Photographer John Rawlings.

CECIL BEATON and HORST P. HORST. Rawlings was quickly promoted to first assistant and then sent to British *Vogue*, where he worked until the 1940s.

Always criticizing the master photographers, Rawlings was one of the first to craft a truly all-American look— one that CHRISTIAN DIOR called the "look sportif." Rawlings consciously moved away from dark imagery and metaphors and focused instead on literal portrayals of clothes.

Rawlings was also one of the first fashion photographers to associate couture with Hollywood celebrities. His photographs graced the covers of over 200 issues of *Vogue* and *Glamour*, and he left an archive of more than 30,000 photos. In addition to his editorial work, he produced two books of nudes, and was considered one of the few photographers who could shoot strong images in both black and white and in color.

Photograph by John Rawlings, 1943.

Designer Tracy Reese.

BORN Detroit, Michigan, February 12, 1964

Tracy Reese specializes in young designer sportswear—knits, separates, and dresses for women with careers and busy, varied lives. The clothes combine a playful spirit with shape and structure.

After spending her childhood weekends in art classes, Reese took a fashion design class at Cass Technical High School in Detroit. She attended New York's Parsons School of Design on scholarship, graduating in 1984, and the same year went to work as a design assistant to MARTINE SITBON. In 1987, Reese

 TRACY REESE

opened her own company, which two years later fell victim to the recession, then worked at PERRY ELLIS as designer for the Portfolio division until it closed the following year. She freelanced briefly with Gordon Henderson, and from 1990 to 1995 was design director at Magaschoni for a bridge collection, Tracy Reese for Magaschoni. Reese then designed a line for The Limited and started her own company, Tracy Reese Meridian.

Reese's designs are sold at upscale stores in America, Europe, and Asia. The company has two lines: the ultra-feminine Tracy Reese and the free-spirited Plenty by Tracy Reese. The collections are inspired by vintage apparel and bohemian style as well as Reese's extensive travels. Her trademarks include a vibrant, playful use of color and a curvy cut that emphasizes the beauty of the female figure. Reese also oversees a home collection and accessory line. In 2006, she opened a flagship boutique in New York's West Village, and in 2011 a boutique in Tokyo.

The designer became even better known after Michelle Obama wore Reese's custom-designed blue and pink brocade dress to give her speech at the 2012 Democratic National Convention.

First Lady Michelle Obama wears a pink silk jaquard dress designed by Tracy Reese at the 2012 Democratic National Convention.

Spring 2014.

ZANDRA RHODES

Above: Designer Zandra Rhodes.
Right: Spring/Summer 2014 collection.

BORN Chatham, England, 1942

AWARDS British Clothing Institute *Designer of the Year*, 1972 • British Government *Commander of the British Empire (CBE)*, 1998

Zandra Rhodes came into view in the late 1960s when she established her dress firm. She had planned to be a textile designer and set up her own print works and a shop to sell dresses made of her fabrics, then decided she was better at interpreting them than anyone else. She was undoubtedly right—her designs and fabrics are of a piece, unmistakably hers, as eccentric and original as she is.

Rhodes's father was a truck driver; her mother was head fitter at WORTH in Paris before her marriage and afterward a senior lecturer in fashion at Medway College of Art. Rhodes studied textile design and lithography at Medway, then went to the Royal College of Art, graduating in 1966. By 1969, she was producing imaginative clothing, for the most part working in very soft fabrics that float and drift—chiffon, tulle, silk—hand-screened in her own prints. The prints included Art Deco motifs, lipsticks, squiggles, teddy bears, stars, teardrops, and big splashy patterns.

Rhodes always made news, alternately criticized and applauded. She finished edges with pinking shears and made glamorized punk designs with torn holes or edges fastened with jeweled safety pins, sleeves held on by pins or chains. She received acclaim for her champagne bubble dresses drawn in at the knee with elastic, and flounced hems finished with uneven scallops and adorned with pearls, pompoms, or braids became a signature. The clothes were beautiful and romantic, a

fantasy of entirely distinctive and personal dressing. Rhodes designed for Princess Diana, and in 1997 was made a Commander of the British Empire.

Rhodes has often been as imaginative with her appearance as with her clothing, with hair dyed in a rainbow of colors—such as magenta and bright green—and makeup effects such as eyebrows drawn in one continuous arc. Many consider her one of the creative geniuses of "Swinging London," and she has continued to thrive and take risks long after many of her contemporaries have faded from the scene. Her designs appeared in the 2001 *London Fashion* exhibit at New York's Fashion Institute of Technology.

In 2003, Rhodes experienced a resurgence in her career when she opened a small museum dedicated to modern fashion and textiles. In 2010, the book *Zandra Rhodes: Textile Revolution: Medals, Wiggles and Pop 1961–1971* was published. Rhodes designed the Lady Godiva puppet for the 2012 Olympic Games in London and was one of the punk designers shown at the Metropolitan Museum of Art's Costume Institute Gala in 2013.

Model and actress Natalie Wood wearing a hand-printed, chrome-yellow felt fabric with swirling scarlet pattern dress designed by Zandra Rhodes in 1970.

NINA RICCI ▼

Enid Boulting wearing a 1960s design by Nina Ricci.

BORN Marie Nielli; Turin, Italy, 1883
DIED Paris, November 29, 1970

Nina Ricci moved to Paris with her family when she was 12. As a child she made hats and dresses for her dolls, and at 13 became an apprentice to a couturier. By 18 she was the head of an atelier, and by 21 a premier stylist. In 1932, encouraged by her jeweler husband, Louis, she opened her own couture house at the age of 49.

Ricci was a skilled technician who usually designed by draping fabrics onto mannequins, but she was not an originator of fashion ideas. The House of Ricci created graceful clothes for elegant women who preferred to be in fashion rather than ahead of it; trousseaux were a specialty. Typical of her attention to elegance and detail is the Ricci perfume, L'air du Temps, presented in a Lalique flacon with a frosted glass bird on the stopper. Ricci was one of the first in couture to show lower-priced models in a boutique. After 1945, the house was managed by her son Robert. In 1951, Jules-Francois Crahay became Ricci's collaborator on the collections; he took over complete design responsibility in 1959. He was succeeded in 1963 by Gérard Pipart, who

Resort 2014.

Spring 2014.

was one of the label's defining talents, known for his bright and avant-garde creations.

Since 1998, when it was sold to the Spanish beauty and fashion conglomerate Puig Group, the House of Ricci has had a changing cast of designers—including OLIVIER THEYSKENS, who left in 2009. Peter Copping left LOUIS VUITTON to replace Theyskens and created a ten-piece capsule collection for Neiman Marcus in 2011.

Anne Larsen wearing a Nina Ricci design, 1962.

JUDITH RIPKA ⍉

Judith Ripka 2009 collection.

Designer Judith Ripka.

BORN Bronx, New York City, August 18, 1942

Judith Ripka knew what she wanted to do at an early age; her mother was a couturier and taught her to appreciate art. Ripka loved to experiment with accessories—for example, she would weave necklaces through her belts. After attending Hunter College in New York City, she studied at Parsons School of Design. Ripka's first job was as a jewelry buyer for the May Company, but she left to concentrate on making her own jewelry. Married with children, Ripka relied on loans and support from friends. But she persevered through financial difficulties and started selling her designs out of a concession store on Long Island. After 15 years, she opened her first store in Manhattan.

Ripka's work began in 1977 with a humble collection made of 18-karat gold. Today her jewelry collections are considered the ultimate in luxury and include materials such as14-karat gold, sterling silver, and precious stones. Ripka's designs have been worn by Jessica Simpson, Kate Hudson, and Miley Cyrus. She also sells a popular collection of jewelry on the QVC television network.

In her spare time, Ripka donates to charitable organizations and sits on several boards and steering committees. In 2007, she created a custom bracelet to benefit autism research for Autism Speaks, followed in 2009 by a pendant. All the profits from these efforts fund research. Judith Ripka jewelry is sold in over 150 department stores and 15 freestanding stores across America. She has been chief executive officer of her company for nearly 40 years.

BORN Los Angeles, August 13, 1952
DIED Los Angeles, December 26, 2002

AWARDS MTV Music Video Awards: *Best Female Video (Janet Jackson)*, 1991; *Best Male Video (Chris Isaak)*, 1991

Herb Ritts is an internationally acclaimed fashion and celebrity photographer and filmmaker. He became legendary in the 1980s and 1990s for his striking, clean lines and black and white editorial fashion portraits for *Vogue*, *Vanity Fair*, *Interview*, and *Rolling Stone*. Ritts is also renowned for his successful advertising campaigns for CALVIN KLEIN, CHANEL, DONNA KARAN, The Gap, GIANNI VERSACE, GIORGIO ARMANI, Levi's, Polo RALPH LAUREN, and VALENTINO.

Ritts's first passions were economics and art history, which he studied at Bard College in New York. After graduating, he took pictures of Ricky Schroeder and Jon Voight on the set of the 1979 movie *The Champ*; the photos were then featured in *Newsweek*. Soon afterward, Ritts photographed aspiring actor Richard Gere in an impromptu photo session at a desert gas station.

Ritts was credited with capturing with his camera what the Greek masters carved into marble—the human form as a classical study. His images not only captured human beauty but also challenged notions of race and gender. Ritts's striking and memorable portraits featured noted individuals from film, fashion, music, politics, and society. He also directed two award-winning music videos.

Photographer Herb Ritts.

On a personal and philanthropic level, Ritts was strongly committed to HIV/AIDS awareness and contributed to many related charities, including the Elton John AIDS Foundation and Focus on AIDS. Ritts died at 50 from pneumonia-related complications.

SIMONE ROCHAS ⧖

BORN Dublin, Ireland, 1986

Simone Rochas was born into fashion royalty. Her father, John Rochas, is a famous fashion designer in London and Ireland, and Simone grew up surrounded by musicians and artists representing the rich diversity of her Irish and Chinese heritage. In her father's studio, Rochas learned how to do everything from knitting to draping. She attended the National College of Art and Design in Dublin, and in 2010 received a master's degree in fashion from Central Saint Martins College of Arts and Design in London. In 2011, Rochas collaborated on a collection for TopShop and created a display for Selfridges Bright Young Things showcase. Her first solo show, also in 2011, was at London Fashion Week and helped her land TopShop's NEWGEN sponsorship for her next three collections.

Rochas's partner in her company is her mother, Odette. When designing, Rochas is attracted to the

Designer Simone Rochas.

overtly feminine, but what makes her talent unusual is that she decontextualizes those feminine qualities. She also uses her knitting skills and craft knowledge in her collections—attributes that give her collections a modern but distinctive twist. Stars that love her clothes include Chloe Moretz, Lady Gaga, and Alexa Chung.

Fall 2013.

Spring 2014.

Rodarte fashion designers Kate Mulleavy (top) and Laura Mulleavy (bottom).

FOUNDED Kate Mulleavy and Laura Mulleavy, Pasadena, California

AWARDS Ecco Domani Fashion Foundation Award, 2005 • Council of Fashion Designers of America (CFDA) *Swarovski Award for Womenswear*, 2008; *Womenswear Designer of the Year*, 2009 • Swiss Textile Federation *Swiss Textiles Award*, 2008 • Cooper-Hewitt *National Design Award (fashion)*, 2010

Sisters Kate and Laura Mulleavy were fashion outsiders when they graduated from the University of California at Berkeley in 2001, where neither majored in fashion or design. But in 2005, they took the fashion world by storm when they made the cover of *Women's Wear Daily* within days of their arrival in New York City. The magazine showed designs from their 10-piece, hand-sewn sample collection, and the debut of Rodarte (Ro-dar-TAY) was a smash hit. The line, named after their mother's maiden name, was soon being sold by exclusive retailers such as Barneys, Neiman Marcus, and Bergdorf Goodman.

Rodarte is known for its meticulously detailed romantic dresses. Hand-crafted pleats, netting, cobwebbing, stripes, draping, and other trim lend an almost otherworldly look to the designs. They have become a favorite with fashion editors and devotees who crave a singular statement look that is also intensely feminine. For some, the Mulleavys' creations

Spring 2013.

are almost too ethereal and delicate to wear, but the designers have proven themselves capable of more down-to-earth looks, such as the 2009 collection of white shirts and dresses they produced for The Gap.

For fall 2009, Rodarte showed experimental knits and leathers with the innovative detailing that they are known for—proving that wearable art may have staying power for a wider audience. That same year, Rodarte designed a collection for Target. In 2010, the sisters created costumes for the Het National Ballet in Amsterdam, and in 2012 for the New York City Ballet Spring Gala

Spring 2009.

NARCISO RODRIGUEZ ▟

BORN New Jersey, January 27, 1961

AWARDS Council of Fashion Designers of America (CFDA) *Perry Ellis Award for Womenswear,* 1997; *Womenswear Designer of the Year,* 2002, 2003

Narciso Rodriguez, the son of Cuban-American parents, studied at New York's Parsons School of Design and first became widely known in 1996 for the bias-cut wedding dress he designed for the late Carolyn Bessette-Kennedy. But he was hardly a beginner, having worked under DONNA KARAN at ANNE KLEIN immediately after graduating from Parsons. He later worked at CALVIN KLEIN.

Rodriguez was soon recognized for his excellent tailoring and feminine, wearable designs and was hired by CERRUTI to update the label; he then moved on to Madrid-based Loewe (owned by LVMH). Rodriguez

Designer Narciso Rodriguez.

turned Loewe, previously a little-known leather firm, into a major luxury goods label.

In contrast to the eccentricity of his British design peers, Rodriguez has focused on a less assertive look that emphasizes the woman rather than the clothes. His skillful tailoring, simple and elegant shapes in beautiful fabrics, and merchandising savvy have built his considerable reputation. His own collection, established in 1998 and shown in Milan and New York, has been an outlet for the more extreme elements of his imagination. In 2001, Rodriguez left Loewe to concentrate on his own company, which also produces shoes and handbags.

Rodriguez says that his Latin roots give his designs "distinctive curve and flair." Today his label is known worldwide. In 2008, Michelle Obama wore a dress from the spring 2009 collection when she joined her husband in their first television appearance after he became president-elect. The dress received mixed reviews from the fashion press and public, though it had fared well at the fall 2008 New York Fashion Week.

In 2010, a retrospective of Rodriguez's work was shown in San Juan, Puerto Rico to benefit Alas a la Mujer, a nonprofit that supports women's education. That same year, his designs were featured in the exhibit *American Beauty: Aesthetics and Innovation in Fashion* at the Museum at New York's Fashion Institute of Technology. In 2013, Rodriguez launched three fragrances: For Him, For Her, and Essence.

Spring 2013.

Editor Carine Roitfeld.

BORN France, September 19, 1954

Carine Roitfeld became interested in fashion when she was 15. When she was 18, she was asked to model for a photographer who saw her on the streets of Paris. While still young, Roitfeld became a stylist and writer for French *ELLE*, then started freelancing as a stylist. In 1990, she met photographer MARIO TESTINO at a shoot for *Vogue Bambini* and forged a friendship and collaboration that has lasted throughout her career. Roitfeld also forged a strong bond and working relationship with TOM FORD while he was creative director of GUCCI. After Ford left the fashion house, Roitfeld was recruited by MISSONI.

In 2001, Roitfeld became editor-in-chief of French *Vogue*. While there, she pushed for controversial covers and allowed all aspects of the magazine to be experimental. One cover featured two models in blonde wigs and spiked heels, carrying leather bags and wearing no clothing. Many critics said that Roitfeld pushed the envelope too far with nude shots and created a magazine that exuded sex—an approach that made French *Vogue* much edgier than its American counterpart. Roitfeld's personality also differed from that of her American counterpart, ANNA WINTOUR, as she had a reputation for being friendly and approachable.

Under Roitfeld, advertising revenue at French *Vogue* rose ten percent and circulation increased 27 percent. In 2011, after ten years as editor-in-chief, Roitfeld left the magazine to focus on other projects. In 2012, she announced the launch of her magazine, *CR Fashion Book*. In 2013, *Mademoiselle C* premiered, a documentary about Roitfeld's creative process. It contains footage highlighting her friendship with KARL LAGERFELD and shows how she has always put her family first. Though her children are grown and have attained fame of their own (her daughter was the face of Tom Ford's Black Orchid perfume in 2006), they have been an important part of her life, and she looks forward to her newest role—as a grandmother.

LELA ROSE

BORN Dallas, Texas, 1968

Lela Rose moved from Texas to New York City to study fashion at Parsons School of Design, graduating in 1993. She then worked with designer Christian Francis Roth, and then for three years with RICHARD TYLER, before debuting her own line in 1998. Her fame grew considerably when she designed gowns for Jenna and Barbara Bush to wear to their father's presidential inauguration in 2001.

"Casual luxury" is Rose's signature style: classic silhouettes with embellished fabric and trim, often with a light, whimsical touch. After securing a following for her dresses, separates, and jackets, Rose launched a bridal collection in 2006; her gowns pair clean, elegant lines with hand-crafted details and sometimes unusual fabrics. She brought a glamorous touch to the discount chain Payless ShoeSource in 2007, launching a line of shoes and accessories. Her flagship store opened in 2011 in her hometown of Dallas, and features ready-to-wear, accessories, and home decor.

Designer Lela Rose.

Left: Spring 2013. Right: Resort 2014.

 RENZO ROSSO

partners and took full creative control of Diesel. The company experienced remarkable growth in the 1980s and 1990s thanks to Rosso's vision of dynamic, cosmopolitan ready-to-wear clothing—centered on its trademarked faded and distressed denim—combined with innovative marketing campaigns rivaling those of mega industry players CALVIN KLEIN and United Colors of Benetton.

Under Rosso's leadership, Diesel partnered with Fossil to produce watches. In 2008, his holding company, Only the Brave, acquired a majority stake in VIKTOR & ROLF, expanding Rosso's collection of inventive labels geared toward young, edgy consumers. That same year, Rosso entered into a business arrangement to produce men's wear collections for MARC JACOBS beginning in 2010. The company has also acquired Maison MARTIN MARGIELA, Marni, and Staff International. And Rosso launched a premium line, Diesel Black Gold, which applies fine tailoring techniques to denim and casual wear.

Rosso's company continues to expand, making him a major power in the fashion industry, and Diesel has become one of the most profitable brands in the clothing business.

Top: Designer Renzo Rosso.
Bottom: Diesel, fall 2013.

BORN Padua, Italy, September 15, 1955

AWARDS Bocconi Institute of Milan and Bain & Company *Premio Risultati Award*, 1996 • Ernst & Young *Entrepreneur of the Year*, 1997

Renzo Rosso and his partners at the Genius manufacturing group launched Diesel as a designer jeans label in 1978. Rosso had graduated from textile manufacturing school just a few years earlier and was determined to carve a niche for himself in the still malleable high-end denim industry. In 1985, Rosso bought out his remaining

Diesel, spring 2014.

MAGGY ROUFF

BORN Maggie Besançon de Wagner; Paris, 1896
DIED Paris, August 7, 1971

Maggy Rouff's fate as a fashion designer was decided almost from birth. Her parents were directors of the great couture house Drècoll in Paris, and though she initially pursued medicine, Rouff eventually followed her parents into fashion design. In 1928, she took over as director of Drècoll and, when the house merged with Beer, she created her own line, Maggy Rouff. As the line's head designer, she created sporty, highly tailored outfits with collars made of scarves and shawls. During the 1920s, 1930s, and 1940s, she was just as well known for her refined casual coats, jersey plus-fours, and beach skirts.

Rouff had a knack for designing not only sportswear but also evening wear. Her evening dresses often included girlish flourishes like ruffles, puffed sleeves, and bows. She used a variety of fabrics, including organdy, crepe, jersey, and silk. Her designs were known for their feminine style and light, airy feel.

Rouff was also an accomplished author. She published *America Seen through a Microscope*, a book

Designer Maggy Rouff.

about her study trip of the United States, and *Philosophy of Elegance*, a polemic on the need for style and grace. She retired in 1948, and her daughter Anne-Marie Besançon de Wagner took over the business. The House of Drècoll closed in 1965 after failing to capture the interest of young, modern customers.

A model wearing a taffeta evening coat from Maggy Rouff, 1955.

A model wearing a woolen design by Maggie Rouff, 1957.

Designers Mary Kate and Ashley Olsen for The Row.

FOUNDED Mary Kate and Ashley Olsen, 2004

AWARDS Council of Fashion Designers of America (CFDA) *Womenswear Designer of the Year*, 2012; Accessory Designer of the Year, 2014

Twins Mary Kate and Ashley Olsen first gained fame on the hit television series *Full House*. Afterward, the Olsens began making videos for tweens, leading to a billion-dollar business called Dualstar that included dolls, accessories, and clothing. The two have been immersed in couture their entire lives, wearing clothing such as MARC JACOBS and CHANEL—cut to their size—since they were six. When the twins turned 18, they began attending New York University. During their freshman year they became owners of Dualstar, but juggling fashion, television, and school proved to be too much, so they left school after their first year.

Their idea of how to make the perfect t-shirt led to The Row. The brand's first collection came out in 2004, and its New York Fashion Week debut followed in 2010. Over the years, the fabrics used have become more

luxurious. The Row caters to an older customer who is well-educated and, as Ashley Olsen says, wants luxury basic fashion pieces.

The twins have also expanded their fashion empire beyond The Row. In 2007, they launched a contemporary brand called Elizabeth and James, named after their siblings; and in 2009 they launched a line exclusively for J.C. Penney called Olsenboye, after their true Norwegian last name. In 2011, the twins became creative directors of the Superga footwear label, and in 2013 they became minority owners in the e-commerce company BeachMint.

In 2013, the Olsens also collaborated with TOMS on a shoe collection called TOMS + The Row that sold over 13,000 pairs. The twins were able to go to Honduras and give free shoes to children in need. Mary Kate and Ashley Olsen are estimated to have a net worth of $300 million.

The Row, spring 2014.

CYNTHIA ROWLEY ▼

BORN Highland Park, Illinois, July 29, 1958

AWARDS Council of Fashion Designers of America (CFDA) *Perry Ellis Award for New Fashion Talent* (a tie with Victor Alfaro), 1994

Cynthia Rowley was just seven when she made her first dress. She was also precocious in business, selling her first eight-piece collection, a senior design project, while still at the Art Institute of Chicago. After a few seasons in Chicago, Rowley moved to New York City in 1983; five years later she incorporated her business with herself as sole owner. Though truly interested in the financial side of the business, she retains a creative insouciance that shows in fresh and fanciful ready-to-wear, where her greatest strength lies in dresses.

Designer Cynthia Rowley.

Fall 2013.

Rowley has expanded her scope in many directions, including shoes, men's wear, handbags and myriad accessories, intimate apparel, and tableware. She introduced cosmetics in 2002 and has her own boutiques in America and Japan. In 1999, Rowley collaborated with *New York Times* editor Ilene Rosenzweig on *Swell: A Girl's Guide to the Good Life*. The book was a sensation among smart, stylish women. The pair continued in what became the Swellco partnership, with sequels *Home Swell Home* in 2002, *Swell-Dressed Party* in 2005, and *Slim: A Fantasy Memoir* in 2007. The two friends also created a line of home accessories called Swell, which debuted at Target in 2003.

In 2013, Rowley's newest retail store opened at 78th and Madison Avenue in New York City. The two- story townhouse sells apparel, art, accessories, and Curious Candy, a collection of candies and party accessories. Rowley also received a lot of press for her stainless steel flask bangle, launched in summer 2013.

Designer Rachel Roy.

BORN Monterey, California, January 15, 1974

AWARDS Accessories Council ACE Awards *Brand Launch of the Year*, 2010

Born to an Indian Asian father and Dutch mother, Rachel Roy has become a leading force in American fashion. She has always been fascinated with fashion, collecting copies of *Vogue* when she was young. Roy went to college in Washington, D.C., then moved to New York City to style photo shoots for magazines and music videos. She interned at Jay-Z's streetwear brand, Rocawear, which was cofounded by her former husband, Damon Dash. Roy learned a lot there, and in 2004 was ready to debut her own fashion line, Rachel Roy. In 2006, she received a Bollywood industry award for her contributions to American fashion.

Roy's clothing lines are exotic yet elegant, and she has an excellent eye for mixing prints and patterns. She creates staples of a woman's wardrobe such as the trench, the blouse, and the dress. In 2007, Roy

was inducted into the Council of Fashion Designers of America (CFDA). In 2009, she introduced a more affordable line called the Rachel Roy collection, collaborated with Grammy Award winner Estelle to create a jewelry line, and worked with the Jones Apparel Group to create an exclusive line for Macy's.

In 2013, Roy created a digital magazine called *The Life* that features articles about fashion, food, beauty, and travel. There she gives insider tips about business and showcases young female entrepreneurs. Roy passionately believes in giving back and participates in charities Orphan Africa, Water Haiti, and Kindness is Always Fashionable. She has said that "through giving back you gain clarity, peacefulness, happiness, and balance in your own life."

Rachel Roy clothing and jewelry is sold in retail stores and boutiques across America. Celebrities who have worn her clothes include Lucy Liu, Gabrielle Union, and Penélope Cruz. In 2014, the Jones Group announced that it was dropping the Rachel Roy label, which closed its doors in March.

Pre-fall 2013.

HELENA RUBINSTEIN █

BORN Krakow, Poland, December 25, 1870
DIED New York City, April 1, 1965

Helena Rubenstein's mother encouraged her to gain influence and power through beauty and love. Fascinated by chemistry, Rubenstein went to school to study medical science, but the chemicals and odors made her sick. At the age of 18, after refusing to marry the man her father had chosen for her, Rubenstein moved to Australia to live with her uncle. There she began selling a face cream, Valaze, created by a prominent European skin specialist.

Rubenstein was selling so much beauty cream that she decided to open her own shop. A patron whose complexion had benefited from the cream provided the startup money. The Helena Rubinstein salon received wonderful press, helping it grow.

Within just over a decade, Rubenstein had become a millionaire and expanded her business to London, Paris, and New York, where she moved during World War I. In 1908, she married her husband, American newspaperman Edward William Titus, and in 1909 their first child was born. By 1928, Rubenstein offered over 62 creams, 78 powders, and 46 fragrances. She sold the business to Lehman Brothers that year, but after serious mismanagement during the Great Depression, she bought back the company and led it to new heights.

Rubenstein produced the first waterproof mascara and the first skin creams to counter sun damage and the effects of aging. She insisted on being called Madame and lived an opulent life, filling countless rooms with paintings by famous artists. In 1953, the Helena Rubinstein Foundation was formed to provide scholarships and support community-based organizations. When she died in 1965, Rubenstein was one of the world's richest women. But her fame and wealth came at a price: in her later years, she admitted that she had always been torn between satisfying her ambition and being a true presence in the lives of the people she loved.

L'Oreal bought Helena Rubinstein Inc. in 1988. The brand has continued to create innovate cosmetics, including the first skin treatment containing vitamin C (1995), the first pure retinol anti-aging cream (1999), and the first instant-effect anti-aging cream (2008).

A perfume from Helena Rubinstein's collection.

Designer Ralph Rucci.

BORN Philadelphia, 1957

AWARDS Cooper-Hewitt *National Design Award (fashion)*, 2008

Ralph Rucci's fashion career began when he moved from Philadelphia to New York City to attend the Fashion Institute of Technology in the late 1970s. After graduating, he began his own line and opened a showroom on New York's famed Seventh Avenue. In 1994, Rucci launched

Spring 2013.

Chado, named for the Japanese tea ceremony symbolizing respect, grace, and tranquility. Chado embraces an Eastern sensibility, elements of which can be seen in every drape, cut, and seam of the line's clothes.

Using the finest European mills, Rucci creates gowns in the spirit of master couturiers VALENTINO and BALENCIAGA. His garments are one-of-a-kind artistic designs—architecturally clean, innovative in construction and cut, and made from the most luxurious fabrics available. Fine art provides much of Rucci's inspiration. In 2002, he became the first American designer since MAINBOCHER to be invited by the Paris Chambre Syndicale to show his collection.

Rucci's work has appeared in numerous exhibits, including at the Cooper-Hewitt National Design Museum, Museum of the Fashion Institute of Technology, Costume Institute of Kent State University, and Phoenix Art Museum. In 2011, *Autobiography of a Fashion Designer: Ralph Rucci with Photographs by Baldmero Fernandez* was published, and in 2012 Rucci received the ANDRÉ LEON TALLEY Lifetime Achievement Award from the Savannah College of Art and Design.

Resort 2013.

SONIA RYKIEL ⬛

BORN Paris, May 25, 1930

AWARDS Fashion Group International *Night of the Stars Award,* 1986 • French Government *Commandeur de l'Ordre des Arts et des Lettres,* 2012; *Grande Médaille de Vermeil de la Ville de Paris,* 2012

Sonia Rykiel (REE-key-el) began in fashion by making her own maternity dresses, then designed for friends and for her husband's boutique, Laura. The first Sonia Rykiel boutique opened in 1968 in the Paris department store Galeries Lafayette, followed by her own shop on the Left Bank.

Called the "Queen of Knitwear" by *Women's Wear Daily* in 1970, Rykiel has made her name with sweaters and sweater looks in seemingly endless variations, usually cut seductively close to the body but softened with detail near the face. She is known for creating

Designer Sonia Rykiel.

the poor-boy sweater, inventing the inside-out stitch, placing seams on the exterior of garments, and occasionally doing away with both hems and lining.

After her daughter, Nathalie, became pregnant, Rykiel showed pregnant-looking models in oversized sweaters, and later added a line of children's wear. She also introduced a men's wear line noted for its color, wit, and joie de vivre. Her daughter designs for the brand, which now encompasses lingerie and the fitness-minded Sonia Rykiel Karma: Body and Soul. In 2008, the redesigned flagship boutique reopened on Boulevard St. Germain in Paris.

In 2011, April Crichton became creative director for the brand, but in 2012 was succeeded by Geraldo da Conceicao. In 2013, Rykiel produced a footwear line for shoemaker Robert Clergerie. The latter two events occurred because in 2012, Fung Brands Ltd. acquired an 80 percent stake in the House of Rykiel; Fung also owns Clergerie. In recent years, Rykiel's health has deteriorated because she has Parkinson's disease.

Spring 2009.

Fall 2007.

Designer Elie Saab.

BORN Damour, Lebanon, July 4, 1964

In the Middle East, Elie Saab's florid, conspicuous dresses decorate a parade of female royalty. The American cadre of royalty—red-carpet celebrities—caught on to his distinctive style when it saw Halle Berry accept her 2002 Academy Award wearing a Saab purple taffeta skirt and burgundy tulle top, liberally embroidered with silk flowers and vines.

Saab grew up in a suburb of Beirut, once considered the Paris of the East. A self-taught designer, the young Saab was perpetually cutting up dress designs and decorating his little sister with odds and ends he found in his mother's bedroom. When civil war broke out in Lebanon, Saab's family began to shuttle between Paris, Cyprus, and their homeland. After a brief stint at a Paris

design school, Saab returned to Lebanon to open his first atelier at the age of 18. A year later, he showed his first collection at the Casino du Liban in Beirut.

In 1997, Saab became the first non-Italian invited to show at the Camera Nazionale della Moda Italiana. This success sparked the launch of his ready-to-wear collection the following year. He opened a salon and showroom in Paris in 2000. In 2003, Saab was invited by the Chambre Syndicale to show his first haute couture collection in Paris. He has boutiques in Paris, Beirut, and at Harrods in London.

Saab captured the imaginations of Western fashionistas by applying the adornments of the Orient to the design cuts of the West. His unabashedly sexy dresses cut close to the body and accent their wearer with elaborate handiwork—beads and sequins,

(continued)

Spring 2014.

embroidery and jewels. One such dress, slinky and glittering with fat emeralds and diamonds, was purchased by a Persian Gulf princess for $2.4 million.

"There is a certain kind of look—big minks, big hair, big lips—that migrates to certain kinds of shows," the *Times of London* wrote in reference to a Saab fashion show. "When you see it, you know you're about to witness a collection where the glamour is turned on full beam."

In 2011, Saab debuted his first fragrance, Le Parfum, which sold extremely well.

Spring 2014 haute couture.

Fall 2013 haute couture.

Designer Yves Saint Laurent.

BORN Oran, Algeria, August 1, 1936
DIED Paris, June 2008

AWARDS *Neiman Marcus Award*, 1958 • Council of Fashion Designers of America (CFDA) *Special Award*, 1981

When Yves Saint Laurent (Sahn LORE-ahn) announced his retirement in 2002, the story made headlines on the front pages of the world's leading newspapers—reflecting his position as a fashion giant. In an extraordinary career spanning more than 40 years, he changed how women dressed as profoundly as CHANEL had before him. Like her, he seemed to sense a woman's needs almost before she was aware of them, introducing looks that have become so accepted that it is hard to remember they were once considered revolutionary or even scandalous.

The son of a well-off French colonial family, Saint Laurent left Algeria when he was 17 to study art in Paris. In 1954, he shared first prize with KARL LAGERFELD in an International Wool Secretariat design competition, and a year later CHRISTIAN DIOR hired him as a design assistant. When Dior died suddenly in 1957, Saint Laurent succeeded him as head designer for the house, remaining until 1960 when he was called

⏳ YVES SAINT LAURENT

for military service. In the Army he suffered a nervous breakdown and was discharged after just three months.

In 1961, with Pierre Bergé—his then lover and subsequent partner in business and, on and off, in life—Saint Laurent opened his own couture house, showing the first collection in 1962. Rive Gauche prêt-à-porter appeared in 1966, and men's wear in 1974. He also designed for film, notably for Catherine Deneuve in *Belle de Jour*, and for opera and ballet. Over the years the YSL initials were licensed for nearly 170 products—everything from bed and bath linens to eyewear to children's wear—and there were numerous fragrances, including Y, Rive Gauche, Opium, and Paris.

It took just 20 years for Saint Laurent to establish himself as the king of fashion, alternately taking inspiration from the street and influencing it. Above all, he understood the life of the modern woman. For day, he designed simple, wearable clothes with a slightly masculine quality in beautiful fabrics—and for evening, clothes of unabashed luxury and sensuousness, enriched with fantasy and drama.

In 1983, the Costume Institute of the Metropolitan Museum of Art mounted a 25-year retrospective of Saint

(continued)

Model wearing suit designed by YSL, 1967.

Laurent's work, the first time a living designer had been so honored. The exhibit contained many of the highlights of his career, from the trapeze dress shown at his first Dior collection to classics such as the pea coat, safari jacket, and smoking jacket. It was possible to track his increasing mastery and polish, and the blending of creative vision and rigorous dedication that led to his preeminence.

In 1993, YSL was sold for $650 million to Sanofi, which in 1999 was acquired by GUCCI Group. TOM FORD—already in charge of Gucci's fashion operations—was made creative director for both the women's and men's YSL Rive Gauche collections. Saint Laurent continued to create the couture line until he retired, remaining dedicated to the ideal of haute couture and the art of dressing women sensibly yet with a feeling of poetry. In his parting statement he said, "In many ways I feel that I have created the wardrobe of the modern woman . . . I am extremely proud that women [all over] the world today wear pantsuits, smoking suits, pea coats, and trench coats."

Saint Laurent died of brain cancer in 2008. In 2010,

Look from 1967 at YSL haute couture retrospective show, 2002.

a documentary titled *L'Amour Fou* on Saint Laurent and his partner Bergé was released. In 2012, the Gucci Group announced that HEDI SLIMANE was replacing STEFANO PILATI as creative director, and that the brand was formally changing its name to Saint Laurent.

Haute couture fashion show, 2002.

Designer Jil Sander.

BORN Wesselburen, Germany, November 27, 1943

Before becoming a major international fashion force, Jil Sander studied textile design, spent two years in America, and worked as a fashion journalist. She started designing in 1968, opened a boutique in Hamburg-Poseldorf, and was a fashion designer for a major fabric manufacturer. Her first collection under her own label appeared in 1973. Cosmetics were added in 1979 and leathers and eyewear in 1984; the flagship store opened in Paris in 1993. Boutiques were also established in Europe, Japan, Hong Kong, and America.

When Sander began, the only German with an international design reputation was KARL LAGERFELD, and he was working in Paris. From the start, her objective was clear—design without decoration, proportions refined to perfection, with lines and cuts that were out of the ordinary. Sander brought a subtle fluidity to the most severe tailoring: her suits were extraordinary for their combination of authority and sensuality, and her dresses had a purity and sexy

austerity. Her demands for the highest-quality materials and craftsmanship were matched by her prices.

In 1999, Sander's business was acquired by PRADA; less than a year later she left abruptly after a disagreement with Patrizio Bertelli, Prada's head. Design of the collection was taken over by Milan Virkmirovic, formerly the buyer for the Paris boutique Colette. Under the terms of the sale, Sander could not design for anyone else until 2003. That year, she and Bertelli made peace and she rejoined the company she founded, only to leave again in 2005. In 2006, Change Capital Partners bought the company from Prada, only to sell it to Onward Holdings Co. in 2008.

In 2012, Sander returned to the label, replacing RAF SIMONS. Simons had been fired because the brand mistakenly thought he was going to take a job with SAINT LAURENT. Simons later became creative director for DIOR.

Spring 2014.

GIORGIO SANT'ANGELO ▼

Designer Giorgio Sant'Angelo (right).

BORN Count Giorgio Impiriale di Sant'Angelo; Florence, Italy, May 5, 1936
DIED New York City, August 29, 1989

AWARDS Coty American Fashion Critics' Awards *Special Award (fantasy accessories and ethnic fashions)*, 1968; *Winnie*, 1970 • Council of Fashion Designers of America (CFDA) *Special Award (contribution to evolution of stretch clothing)*, 1987 • *Fashion Walk of Fame*, 2001

Giorgio Sant'Angelo spent much of his childhood in Argentina and Brazil, where his family owned property. He trained as an architect and industrial designer before going to France to study art. His art influences ran the gamut from studies with Picasso to work with Walt Disney. He arrived in America in 1962 and moved to New York City in 1963, where he freelanced as a textile designer and stylist and was a design consultant for various environmental projects. For DuPont, his experiments with Lucite as a material for fashion accessories were a sensation and received extensive press coverage.

Though Sant'Angelo's early success was with accessories, his first clothing collection of gypsy dresses and patchwork clothes was highly influential. He went on to break more ground with ethnic-inspired clothing, especially a collection dedicated to Native Americans. Very much an individualist, Sant'Angelo was always interested in new uses for materials, such as stretch fabrics incorporating spandex. His designs were for people who liked their clothes a bit out of the ordinary, and he maintained a couture operation for celebrity customers. He also did costumes for films. The black exploitation vehicle *Cleopatra Jones* is among the many projects on which he's worked.

Sant'Angelo's many businesses included ready-to-wear, separates, and extensive licenses—from swimwear and active sportswear to furs to men's wear to environmental fragrances and home furnishings. The business went on for several years after his death, and the licensing operation continues.

Designs by Sant' Angelo suspended in the Metropolitan Museum of Art, 2009.

⬛ BEHNAZ SARAFPOUR

Designer Behnaz Sarafpour.

BORN Tehran, Iran, 1969

AWARDS Parsons School of Design *Golden Thimble Award* • Cooper-Hewitt *National Design Award (fashion)*, 2013

Behnaz Sarafpour (Suh-RAFF-poor) went to New York to study at Parsons School of Design in 1989. Her design career began even before she graduated, interning at ANNE KLEIN under the guidance of NARCISO RODRIGUEZ and RICHARD TYLER. Soon after Parsons, she worked for the designer she considers her mentor, ISAAC MIZRAHI. While working with Mizrahi, she began developing her signature look, involving meticulous design and an appreciation for fabrics not often used in fashion.

Sarafpour was championed by Julie Gilhart, fashion director at Barneys New York, and became head designer of its private collection. In 2002, she produced her first runway show, sponsored by style.com. That same year, she received her first of three award nominations for the Council of Fashion Designers of America (CFDA). Since then her collections have been sponsored by style.com as well as Moët & Chandon, Hewlett-Packard, Van Cleef & Arpels, and TIFFANY & Co.

Sarafpour's aesthetic ranges from the elegant to the playful. Her preferred colors are black and white, cool and warm grays, an array of tertiaries, and occasional bold metallics. In 2004, *Vogue* editor-in-chief ANNA

WINTOUR recognized Sarafpour's achievements, and she was inducted into the CFDA. Sarafpour then created limited edition lines for Earnest Sewn with Behnaz Sarafpour Jeans and for Lancôme with a dramatic red lipstick titled simply, Behnaz.

In 2006, Sarafpour was the first American designer to be featured in Target's Go International campaign. Her work appeared in the *New York Fashion Now* exhibit at the Victoria and Albert Museum in London in 2007. Committed to the environment, she created a line of organic high-end sportswear in 2008, the success of which inspired her to continue using sustainable fabrics in her collections. In 2011, Sarafpour celebrated her tenth anniversary in business, and in 2013 she received the Cooper-Hewitt National Design Award for fashion.

Fall 2012.   Fall 2012.

JONATHAN SAUNDERS

BORN Glasgow, Scotland, 1977

AWARDS British Fashion Council *Fashion Enterprise Award*, 2006 • British Fashion Council/*Vogue Designer Fashion Fund*, 2012

Jonathan Saunders is known for his use of colors and graphics in silk prints, and his beautiful, simple clothes have become a favorite of fashion editors. Saunders was raised in a very religious household, and his family wanted him to be a carpenter. But he had other plans, and attended the Glasgow School of Art and the Central Saint Martins College of Arts and Design, where he received a master's degree in printed textiles. Saunders won the prestigious Lancôme Colour Design Award and was immediately hired by ALEXANDER McQUEEN. His prints have caught the eye of design houses such as

Designer Jonathan Saunders.

PUCCI and CHLOÉ, and he has consulted for them and others. In high demand, Saunders started his solo collection in 2003, just a year after graduating from Central Saint Martins.

Saunders began receiving awards in 2005, such as the Scottish Designer of the Year at the Scottish Style Awards and the British Fashion Council Fashion Enterprise Award. In 2008, Saunders became creative director for Pollini and presented in Milan. That same year, he created a capsule collection for Target and the first of four collections for TopShop. In 2012, he teamed up with motilo.com, a shopping website, and created *Vogue*'s t-shirt for Fashion Night Out.

Saunders's prints are timeless, and he has been hailed for his skill in mixing prints and colors. One of his runway collections featured over 20 prints. He also loves using knits, which he considers essential.

Spring 2014.

Spring 2014.

346

Designer Arnold Scaasi.

BORN Arnold Isaacs; Montreal, Canada, May 8, 1931

AWARDS Coty American Fashion Critics' Awards *Winnie,* 1958 • *Neiman Marcus Award,* 1959 • Council of Fashion Designers of America (CFDA) *Special Award (extravagant evening dress),* 1987; *Geoffrey Beene Lifetime Achievement Award,* 1996 • Dallas International Apparel *Fashion Excellence Award,* 1992

Best known for spectacular evening wear in luxurious fabrics, Arnold Scaasi is one of the last true custom designers in America. The son of a furrier, he finished high school in his native Canada, then took off for Melbourne, Australia, to live with his stylish aunt, who dressed in CHANEL and SCHIAPARELLI. With her disciplined approach to dress and living, she was an important influence on Scaasi. He began studying art in Australia and returned to Montreal to study couture. There he designed clothes for private clients and saved enough money to go to Paris to continue his fashion studies at l'École de la Chambre Syndicale de la Couture Parisienne. He then traveled around Europe for a year, returning to Paris to work as an apprentice to PAQUIN.

 ARNOLD SCAASI

After moving to New York City in 1955, Scaasi worked as a sketcher for CHARLES JAMES, designed coats and suits for a Seventh Avenue manufacturer, and in 1957 opened his own wholesale business on a shoestring budget. In 1960, he bought and renovated a Manhattan townhouse for his ready-to-wear presentations, but in 1963 changed his focus to couture. It was 20 years before he returned to ready-to-wear with the Arnold Scaasi Boutique, for cocktail and evening dresses.

With the mood of fashion moving away from flamboyance and toward minimalism, Scaasi closed the ready-to-wear business in 1994, focusing on a handful of licenses and on made-to-order dresses for women who still cherished his entrance-making designs. Licenses have included costume jewelry, furs, men's ties, loungewear, bridal apparel, sportswear, and knits. Scaasi's clients have included socialites and celebrities such as Barbara Walters and Elizabeth Taylor. He has also designed for Barbara Bush and her daughter-in-law, Laura Bush.

In 2010, Scaasi announced that he was retiring aside from his jewelry business. In 2011, Scaasi married his partner of 50 years, Parker Ladd.

Model Veruschka in striped evening pajamas, 1966.

ELSA SCHIAPARELLI ⏳

BORN Rome, September 10, 1890
DIED Paris, November 13, 1973

AWARDS *Neiman Marcus Award*, 1940

The daughter of a language professor, Elsa Schiaparelli (Ski-APP-uh-rell-e) studied philosophy and wrote poetry and articles on music. She married and moved to America, where she lived until the end of World War I. When her husband left her in 1920, she returned to Paris with her daughter and no money.

Her involvement in fashion began when a sweater she designed for herself was seen and ordered by a store

Designer Elsa Schiaparelli.

buyer. By 1929, Schiaparelli had established Pour le Sport on the Rue de la Paix; by 1930, she was producing clothes from 26 workrooms and had 2,000 employees. In 1935, she opened a boutique on the Place Vendôme for sportswear, later adding dresses and evening clothes.

Like her great rival, CHANEL, Schiaparelli was not only a dressmaker but also part of the brilliant artistic life of Paris in the 1920s and 1930s. She was close friends with many artists, among them Jean Schlumberger, who also designed jewelry for her; Salvador Dalí, with whom she designed prints and embroideries; Jean Cocteau; Kees van Dongen; and MAN RAY. Highly creative and unconventional, she shocked the couture establishment by using rough "working class" materials for evening, colored plastic zippers as decorative features, and huge ceramic buttons in the shape of hands, butterflies, or whatever else caught her fancy. She also created wildly imaginative accessories.

Schiaparelli showed little "doll hats" shaped like, for example, lamb chops or pink-heeled shoes, and gloves that extended to the shoulders and turned into puffed sleeves. She fastened clothing with padlocks, clips, and dog leashes. She showed amusing novelties such as glowing phosphorescent brooches and handbags that lit up or played tunes when opened. And she was

Silk organza "lobster" dress, 1937.

spectacularly successful with avant-garde sweaters and worked with tattoo and skeleton motifs.

Schiaparelli changed the shape of the figure with broad, padded shoulders inspired by the uniform of the guardsmen at Buckingham Palace, a silhouette that lasted until the advent of the New Look. Both a genius at publicity and a trailblazer, she commissioned a fabric patterned with her press clippings, then used it in scarves, blouses, and beachwear. She also pioneered the use of synthetic fabrics. Her signature color was the brilliant pink she called "shocking"—the same name she gave to her famous fragrance in its dressmaker dummy bottle.

After the fall of France, Schiaparelli returned to America, where she waited out World War II. She reopened in Paris in 1945. Though she remained in business until 1954, she never regained her prewar position. She served as a consultant to companies licensed to produce hosiery, perfume, and scarves under her name, and lived out her retirement in Tunisia

Rayon tulle and glass bead veil, 1938.

and Paris. Schiaparelli's irreverence and energy could result in vulgarity, but she also produced extremely chic clothes of great elegance. Her main contribution was her vitality, and her sense of mischief was a reminder not to take things too seriously.

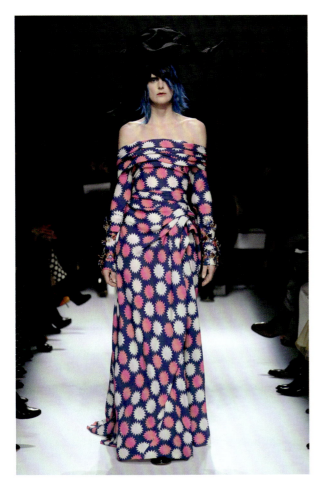

Spring 2014 haute couture.

SCOTT SCHUMAN 📷 📄

BORN Indianapolis, Indiana, October 15, 1968

AWARDS Council of Fashion Designers of America (CFDA) *Media Award in Honor of Eugenia Sheppard*, 2012

Photographer and blogger Scott Schuman's site The Sartorialist (www.thesartorialist.com) is one of the most respected and widely visited online destinations for fashion. Schuman majored in apparel merchandising and minored in costume construction at Indiana University. After graduation, he worked in marketing for high-end designers in New York City—including JEAN PAUL GAUTIER, VALENTINO, and HELMUT LANG—before becoming director of men's fashion at Bergdorf Goodman. That same year, he opened a showroom that helped up and coming designers manage sales and press and establish their brands.

After the terrorist attacks of September 11, 2001, Schuman decided to focus on photography. In 2005, he started a website to display his photographs, which focused on real people on the street. The Sartorialist became so popular that the following year Vogue hired him to shoot collections in Milan, Paris, and London. He also began writing a monthly column for GQ. In 2007, *TIME* named The Sartorialist one of the top 100 influences in fashion, and in 2008 Schuman's pictures were exhibited at Danziger Projects Gallery in New York. In 2009, Penguin published an anthology of his images that sold over 100,000 copies. Several of Schuman's photographs are part of the permanent collections of the Victoria and Albert Museum and the Tokyo Metropolitan Museum of Art.

Schuman's popularity skyrocketed when he collaborated with his partner in life and business, blogger and photographer Garance Doré. The pair have collaborated

Photographer and writer Scott Schuman.

on projects for TIFFANY AND CO., BURBERRY, and MOSCHINO. In 2013, they collaborated with Mary Kate and Ashley Olsen (of THE ROW) on Superga footwear.

Questions have been raised about whether street style is still significant and cutting edge enough to blog about. But one thing is clear: Schuman will be there with his camera to discover what fashion trend is hot, no matter what the setting.

 JEREMY SCOTT

Designer Jeremy Scott.

BORN Kansas City, Missouri, 1976

AWARDS Venus de la Mode Fashion Awards *Designer of the Year, 1996–97*

Spring 2014.

A fashion nonconformist, Jeremy Scott studied at New York City's Pratt Institute, then went to Paris in 1995 "because in Paris you can show whatever you want." After a visit to California, he moved to Paris in 2001.

In Paris he earned headlines and awards, starting in 1996 with a collection inspired by car crash victims, Band-Aids, and hospital gowns. Later shows featured cloven-toed stilettos, one-legged trousers, dresses made from trash bags, and white dresses with pleated angel wings. Other shows dazzled with everything gold—leather dresses, ruched lamé skirts, asymmetrical mink boleros.

Scott spent the 1998–99 season as artistic director for Trussardi's secondary lines, at the same time moving away from trash bag couture and closer to the mainstream. While showing both imagination and skill, his work can veer wildly between the cute-and-wearable and the kitschy.

Scott teamed up with Kazuki and Alyasha Owerka-Moore to create a line for adidas called Originals by Originals, which launched in 2009. The apparel features materials such as leathers, cashmere, and silk, while the footwear builds on iconic adidas styles.

Scott is no stranger to controversy. In 2012, his JS Roundhouse Mids for adidas were criticized for their resemblance to shackles, resulting in low sales. In 2013, he was accused of plagiarizing Jimbo Phillips, who does artwork for Santa Cruz skateboards, but no legal action was taken. Also in 2013, Scott was named creative director of MOSCHINO.

Spring 2014 men's wear.

SEAN JOHN 👗

FOUNDED Sean Combs, 1998

AWARDS Council of Fashion Designers of America (CFDA) *Menswear Designer of the Year*, 2004

Sean John is a fashion lifestyle company founded by rap star Sean Combs. Combs created the brand because he felt that there was a void in men's wear—a lack of well-made, sophisticated, fashion-forward clothing that maintained an urban sensibility. Starting as an eponymous urban sportswear label, Sean John became an international brand, including Sean John, Bad Boy Sportswear, Sean John Tailored, and Sean John accessories. Product categories have expanded to include leather accessories, eyewear, fragrances, and hats.

Since 2000, Sean John has been nominated five times for excellence in design, sharing that distinction with

Designer Sean Combs.

designers such as MARC JACOBS and HELMUT LANG. In 2001, Sean John produced the first nationally televised runway show on E! Television and The Style Network. In 2002, *The New York Times* ran a front page story about the company's success. And in 2004 Sean Combs received the CFDA's *Menswear Designer of the Year* award and opened its first boutique, on Fifth Avenue and 41st Street in New York. Combs also invested in young ZAC POSEN's company, becoming an equal partner.

Sean John has been credited with making the men's suit popular again and bringing excitement back into fashion. Combs says that his goal is to be the "future of fashion." He is also an advocate of young people participating in politics, and through his nonprofit Citizen Change launched a registration campaign to increase the youth vote in the 2004 and 2008 elections. Combs is also an advocate for increasing the number of African-American models on runways.

In 2010, Combs signed a deal making Macy's the exclusive American department store for his men's sportswear, and in 2013 he and Macy's teamed up with the National Basketball Association (NBA) to create events and activities that will allow them to showcase the Sean John brand. Combs also made social media history in 2013 by having the first fashion show on Instagram. That year, Combs had an estimated net worth of $550 million.

Fall 2011.

Designer Ronaldus Shamask.

BORN Amsterdam, the Netherlands, November 24, 1945

AWARDS Coty American Fashion Critics' Awards *Winnie*, 1981 • Council of Fashion Designers of America (CFDA) *Menswear Designer of the Year*, 1988

⬛ RONALDUS SHAMASK

One of a small group of designers with a strong architectural bent, Ronaldus Shamask arrived in New York City in 1971 by a circuitous route that led him to Australia, London, and Buffalo, New York. Essentially self-taught, he moved with his family to Australia when he was 14, worked in the display department of a large Melbourne department store, and in 1967 moved to London, where he became a fashion illustrator and began to paint. He then went to Buffalo and spent three years designing sets and costumes for ballet, theater, and opera. Next he moved to New York and worked on commissioned designs from private clients for interiors and clothing.

Later, Shamask created a 20-piece collection in muslin, cut from patterns that were life-sized blueprints. In 1978, he and a friend, Murray Moss, formed a company called Moss and opened a pristine, all-white shop and "laboratory" on Madison Avenue. The first presentation, in 1979, consisted of the original muslin collection executed in three weights of linen. The clothes, which combined strong architectural shapes with beautiful fabrics, were cut with the utmost precision and exquisitely made. They were praised for their purity of design and exceptional workmanship.

Starting in the mid-1980s, Shamask moved in and out of women's and men's wear, designed costumes for dancer Lucinda Childs, and returned to women's wear. The clothes, primarily high-end sportswear, were sold at a select group of fine stores, including Bergdorf Goodman and Neiman Marcus. A 10-year absence from the runway followed, but in 2011 Shamask made a comeback—and in 2012, the Philadelphia Museum of Art premiered the exhibit *Ronaldus Shamask: Form, Fashion, Reflection.*

Spring/summer 1990.

Spring 2012.

IRENE SHARAFF

BORN Boston, January 23, 1910
DIED New York City, August 16, 1993

AWARDS Academy Awards for Best Costume Design
An American in Paris, 1952; *The King and I*, 1957; *West Side Story*, 1962; *Cleopatra*, 1964; *Who's Afraid of Virginia Woolf?*, 1967; Tony Award for Best Costumes *The King and I*, 1952; Theatre Development Fund/Irene Sharaff *Lifetime Achievement Award*, 1993

In a remarkable career spanning more than 60 years, Irene Sharaff designed costumes for 60 stage productions and 40 films, in addition to ballet and television work and even fashion illustration. Her first project occurred while she was still in art school, in 1928 for Eva Le Gallienne's Civic Repertory Theatre in New York; her last film costumes were for *Mommie Dearest* in 1981 and her last for the stage were for *Jerome Robbins' Broadway* in 1989. Sometimes she designed sets as well. She won a variety of awards, including five Academy Awards for best costume design, and was nominated often. In addition, the Theatre Development Fund created the TDF/Irene Sharaff Award in 1993 to honor the art of costume design, and she was its first recipient.

Sharaff studied at the New York School of Fine and Applied Arts and the Art Students League while

Costume designer Irene Sharaff with Elizabeth Taylor, 1963.

working part time. By 1931, she had saved enough to spend a year in Paris and attend l'Académie de la Grande Chaumière. School was important, but she learned more from her exposure to the theatrical designs of painters CHRISTIAN BÉRARD, Pavel Tchelitchew, and André Derain, along with her discovery of French couture, with its emphasis on perfection in both design and execution. Sharaff's experiences in France greatly influenced her later work. For ten years after her return to America, she was extremely successful designing for the New York stage, then in 1942 moved to Hollywood to work on musicals at MGM. Her design projects ranged from *Meet Me in St. Louis* to *Who's Afraid of Virginia Woolf?*, from *Madame Curie* to *Hello Dolly* and *The Taming of the Shrew*. Most of her work was at MGM, but she also designed for other studios.

Sharaff was highly versatile and had a solid understanding of theater, dance, and film, was adept at both modern and period settings, and felt comfortable with both realism and fantasy. Her meticulous research ensured authenticity as well as functionality, with exquisitely made costumes that were never overpowering.

West Side Story, 1961.

Above: Design Raf Simons.

Right: Spring 2014 men's wear.

BORN Belgium, 1968

AWARDS Council of Fashion Designers of America (CFDA) International Award, 2014

Raf Simons (Rauph SEE-mon) grew up in a small Belgian village and attended college in Genk, where he earned a degree in industrial and furniture design. He started working in that field, but his interest turned to fashion after designer Walter Van Beirendonck took him to a Maison MARTIN MARGIELA runway show while he was an intern.

At the urging of Linda Loppa, head of the fashion department at the Antwerp Royal Academy, Simons launched a men's wear label, presenting his first collection in Paris in 1997. In 1998, he was tapped—along with VERONIQUE BRANQUINHO—to create two collections for Ruffo Research, an Italian leather company. In 2000, Simons became a professor of fashion at the University of Applied Arts in Vienna, a position he held until 2005. That year, he became creative director of JIL SANDER, released a book celebrating ten years of his brand titled Raf Simons

Redux, and launched Raf by Raf Simons. CATHY HORYN of The New York Times said that Simons was probably "the most influential designer of the last decade."

His designs for Sander were futuristic and seductive, focusing on the female form. Simons believes that, whether at Sander or his own brand, everyone at a company should share the same goals in order for things to proceed smoothly. In 2010, he showed his first haute couture collection, which was extremely feminine.

In 2011, JOHN GALLIANO left DIOR, and in 2012 the house confirmed that Simons was the new creative director. His first collection for Dior received rave reviews, with critics commenting on how he had kept the historic Dior aesthetic, but added a modern twist. In 2013, the book *Raf Simons* was published by Taschen. Edited by Terry Jones, a founder of i-D magazine, the book contains interviews about and photographs of Simons's work—from his namesake men's wear line, to Sander, to Dior.

CHRISTIAN SIRIANO ▟

Above: Designer Christian Siriano.

Right: Actress Selma Blair attends the Christian Siriano Spring 2014 presentation.

BORN Annapolis, Maryland, November 18, 1985

Widely known as the winner of the fourth season (2008) of the reality television design competition *Project Runway*, Christian Siriano has gone on to much bigger and brighter things. A graduate of the Baltimore School of the Arts and the American Intercontinental University in London, Siriano has worked with some of the world's most prestigious designers. He interned with VIVIENNE WESTWOOD and ALEXANDER MCQUEEN before returning to America.

After he won Project Runway, Siriano's collections started being sold at Neiman Marcus and Saks Fifth Avenue. Since his label's debut in 2006, he has shown every year at New York Fashion Week. His designs are fantastical and whimsical, and his evening and cocktail dresses are especially popular. Siriano has said that his clothes are for "women who want to shop and buy clothes," not for downtown women. His collections have also included tailored sportswear, shoes, eyewear, and home decor.

A 2009 collaboration with Payless ShoeSource was so successful that Siriano now designs four collections of shoes a year for the discount retailer. Other collaborations have included wedding dresses for Nordstrom, a makeup line for Victoria's Secret, and clothing lines

for HSN and Spiegel. Siriano also cofounded the online accessories retailer Send the Trend, which the QVC television network purchased in 2012.

Siriano has a large celebrity clientele, including Sarah Jessica Parker, Rihanna, Nicki Minaj, and Lady Gaga. Oprah Winfrey has called his designs "works of art," and TIM GUNN has called him a "prodigy" and "the next great American fashion designer." Siriano's clothing is sold at retail stores and specialty boutiques around the world. In 2012, his first standalone store opened in New York City, and his first fragrance was released in 2014. Siriano was inducted into the Council of Fashion Designers of America (CFDA) in 2013.

In summer 2013, Siriano announced his engagement to his boyfriend, musician Brad Walsh. The couple collaborates on Siriano's runway shows, with Walsh creating the music.

Designer Martine Sitbon.

BORN Casablanca, Morocco, circa 1952

After graduating from the Studio Berçot, Paris, in 1974, Martine Sitbon was a freelancer and fashion consultant before starting her own line in 1984. Her first show was in 1985 in Paris, and was followed in 1986 by shows at the Louvre and at the Palladium in New York City. Within three years of starting her line, Sitbon

⧖ MARTINE SITBON

was appointed creative director of CHLOÉ. She stayed for nine seasons before opening a boutique in Paris in 1995. In 1998, she signed a licensing deal with Giba, launching Martine Sitbon Tricot.

In 1998, Sitbon surprised her audience by launching men's wear designs during her women's wear show. In 2001, she became director for women's wear at Byblos and introduced MS Martine Sitbon handbags. Before her spring/summer 2003 show, she was a major force in Paris and Tokyo, but she wanted to create a new label that could showcase her independent spirit and Parisian elegance. So, after challenges with financing and reacquiring the rights to her name, she launched Rue de Mail in 2004. It was named after the street where her showroom is located. The company's first show was in 2007 at the Couvent des Cordeliers for the fall/winter 2008 ready-to-wear collection.

Sitbon rocks the Rue de Mail with her 1970s-inspired rock and roll designs, while at the same time exhibiting a mastery of luxurious fabrics and exotic textiles. Urban hues are predominant in her winter collections, but touches of red accentuate. Her spring collections celebrate the rebirth of color; a field of psychedelics. Sitbon is known for her collaborations with photographer Javier Vallhonrat, art director Marc Ascoli, and graphic designers Michael Amzalag and Mathias Augustyniak, who help market her clothing.

Fall 2013.

Spring 2009.

HEDI SLIMANE ▼

BORN July 5, 1968

With his international heritage—Tunisian father, Italian mother, and Brazilian grandmother—Hedi Slimane could be considered the epitome of the modern, multicultural man. He studied at l'École du Louvre and worked for José Levy before starting at YVES SAINT LAURENT.

When the house was sold to Gucci in 1999 and TOM FORD became creative director for the company, Slimane left as creative director for men's wear, moving to CHRISTIAN DIOR as designer for Dior Homme. His first show there, in 2001, was a highly successful blend of classic French style and a younger, edgier attitude. Silhouettes were narrow and precisely cut, epitomizing Slimane's personal blend of classicism and modernism. Subsequent collections have confirmed his reputation as an assured tailor whose proportions are just right— mean and lean, with no allowance for extra pounds.

Designer Hedi Slimane.

In 2012, Slimane was appointed creative director of Yves Saint Laurent, which officially rebranded itself Saint Laurent. In 2013, his duties expanded to include photographing advertising campaigns and managing all strategic projects for the brand.

Dior Homme, spring 2010.

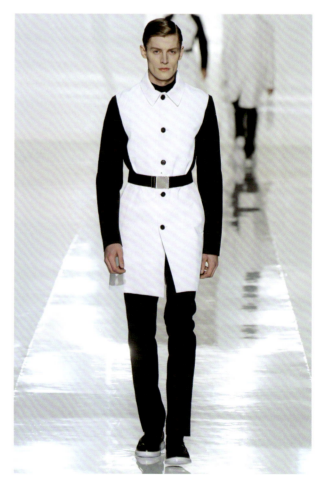

Dior Homme, fall 2013.

Designer Paul Smith.

BORN Nottingham, England, July 5, 1946

AWARDS British Government *Commander of the British Empire (CBE)*, 1994, 2000; Queen's Award for Export, 1995; Queen's Award for Enterprise, 2009 • British Fashion Awards *Outstanding Achievement in Fashion,* 2011

Paul Smith worked his way up in fashion from the bottom, starting at 18 as a gofer in a clothing warehouse. He opened his first tiny shop for men in 1970, using his own savings, open only on Fridays and Saturdays, and carrying designers such as KENZO not then available outside London. Smith studied tailoring at night and gradually added his own designs so successfully that by 1974 the shop had moved to larger quarters and was open full time. Developing his own cool, smart style, he had his first Paris showing by 1976 and was a consultant to an Italian shirt manufacturer and to the International Wool Secretariat.

Smith's clothes, now for both men and women, rely on simplicity of style with a twist of wit. They are notable for their unusual, luxurious

Spring 2014.

Spring 2013 men's wear.

fabrics and attention to detail—hand stitching, embroidery, vivid linings—and include tailored suits, separates, and knits, plus luggage, accessories, and swimwear. Though the Paul Smith enterprise has grown into a global concern, Smith still guides each division, maintaining a personal character for both merchandise and presentation. In 1995, London's Design Museum celebrated Smith's 25th anniversary in fashion with an exhibit called PAUL SMITH TRUE BRIT. His book, YOU CAN FIND INSPIRATION IN EVERYTHING, was published in 2002.

The Paul Smith brand now encompasses 14 collections and is sold in more than 66 countries. Smith says, "We're a leading and uniquely British brand. We mix one-off antiques with high-quality tailoring: the chair you sit on when you buy a suit is for sale and we can wrap the suit and have the chair waiting for you when you get home." In 2010, Smith opened his first standalone store in Mayfair, London.

WILLI SMITH

BORN Philadelphia, February 29, 1948
DIED New York City, April 17, 1987

AWARDS Coty American Fashion Critics' Awards *Special Award*, 1983 • *Fashion Walk of Fame*, 2002

One of several African-American designers who rose to prominence in the late 1960s, Willi Smith was the son of an iron-worker and a housewife. He originally intended to be a painter, studied fashion illustration at the Philadelphia Museum College of Art, and in 1965, at the age of 17, arrived in New York City with two scholarships to Parsons School of Design. He got a summer job with ARNOLD SCAASI and spent two years at Parsons, during which he freelanced as a sketcher. He then worked for several manufacturers, including Bobbie Brooks, Talbott, and Digits.

Designer Willi Smith and model, 1987.

After several failed startup attempts, WilliWear Ltd. was established in 1976 with Laurie Mallet as president and Smith as designer and vice president. His innovative, spirited clothes—described as classics with a sense of humor—were fun to wear as well as functional, and brought fashion verve to the moderate price range. Collections were consistent in feeling from one year to the next, so new pieces mixed comfortably with older ones. Preferring natural fibers for their comfort and utility, Smith designed his own textiles and went to India several times a year to supervise the production of his collections. His sister, Toukie, was his primary model.

Men's wear was introduced in 1978 to "bridge the gap between jeans and suits." Smith also designed for Butterick Patterns, did lingerie and loungewear textiles for Bedford Stuyvesant Design Works, and furniture for Knoll International. In 1986, Smith caused a stir when he dressed Caroline Kennedy's groomsmen in blue linen suits with silver ties.

Fall 1987.

Editor Carmel Snow (center) with Diana Vreeland (left), 1952.

BORN Carmel Whilte; Dublin, Ireland, August 27, 1887
DIED New York City, May 9, 1961

Carmel Snow was raised in the fashion business—her mother visited America to promote Irish industries at the 1893 Chicago World's Fair and stayed, founding a dressmaking business, Fox & Co. One of the exhibitors at *Vogue's* first "Fashion Fête" in 1914, the firm made the dress worn on that occasion by *Vogue's* editor, EDNA WOOLMAN CHASE. A friendship developed, and in 1921 Chase offered Snow a job in the magazine's fashion department. In 1929 she became editor of American *Vogue*.

In 1932, in a move that sent shock waves through the fashion world, Snow left *Vogue* to become fashion editor at *Harper's Bazaar*. She then became editor and, in 1957, chair of the editorial board. Her successor was Nancy White, her niece and godchild.

Tiny in stature but a major fashion presence and forceful personality, Snow was a woman of wit and intelligence, of strong views expressed frankly and with passion. She dressed in great style in clothes from Paris couture and, like a high priestess of fashion, championed each change as it appeared. She recognized BALENCIAGA's genius and promoted him indefatigably long before most of the fashion press; CHRISTIAN DIOR spoke of her "marvelous feeling for what is fashion today and what will be fashion tomorrow." A loyal and powerful champion of the talented, Snow demanded their best and received their finest efforts. After World War II, she took a leading role in helping the French and Italian textile and fashion industries get back on their feet. She was considered legendary. It is said that Dior would delay openings until she arrived. Even after Snow no longer had official connections and despite precarious health, she continued to go to Paris twice a year for the collections.

She married George Palen Snow in 1926 and had three children. Her memoirs were published in 1962 in Ireland and New York, written with the help of Mary Louise, a fiction editor at *Harper's Bazaar*.

PETER SOM

BORN San Francisco, 1970

The son of architects, Chinese-American designer Peter Som grew up in San Francisco and attended Connecticut College, where he majored in art. He continued his studies at the Parsons School of Design in New York, where he was an intern for MICHAEL KORS and CALVIN KLEIN. In 1997, Som was recognized by the Council of Fashion Designers of America (CFDA) as a rising young talent. In 2004, he was one of ten semifinalists in the CFDA/*Vogue* Fashion Fund initiative, and was nominated for the CFDA *Swarovski Perry Ellis Award* in 2002 and 2005.

Som showed his collection in New York City's Bryant Park in 2001. Described by critics as a new leader in American sportswear, his clothes are noted for their clean lines, luxurious fabrics, and comfortable fit. Som

Designer Peter Som.

has found fans among a new generation of celebrities; his designs have been worn by the likes of Scarlett Johansson, Maggie Gyllenhaal, and Natalie Portman.

In 2007, Som became creative director of BILL BLASS Limited, overseeing the company's women's wear until 2008. He is widely credited with returning the Bill Blass brand to the fore of the fashion world. In 2003, Cathy Horyn of *The New York Times* called Som "one of the best young designers working today."

From 2009 to 2012, Som designed women's runway collections for TOMMY HILFIGER, then left to focus on his business. In 2013, he debuted an 11-piece capsule collection for Anthropologie as part of the Made in Kind Initiative, which markets to a wide range of customers. He did not show at New York Fashion Week that fall, opting to show his work digitally instead—a growing trend in the industry. In 2014, he designed a line for Kohl's.

Spring 2013.

Designer Kate Spade.

Accessories at Kate Spade's fall 2012 presentation.

BORN Katherine Noel Brosnahan; Kansas City, Missouri, December 24, 1962

AWARDS Council of Fashion Designers of America (CFDA) *Perry Ellis Award for Accessories*, 1995; *Accessories Designer of the Year*, 1997

Kate Spade has spent most of her professional life with accessories. After her 1986 graduation from Arizona State University, where she majored in journalism, she moved to New York City for a job at *Mademoiselle*. When she left the magazine in 1991, she was senior fashion editor and head of accessories.

Feeling that the market lacked stylish, practical handbags, she decided to create her own. In 1993, with her husband Andy Spade, she launched kate spade new york—handbags with six designs, simple shapes in satin-finished nylon, emphasizing utility, color, and fabric. These are still the label's signature styles. Spade believes that accessories should bring color and texture to a wardrobe, expressing the wearer's sense of style and adding personality to her dress. The criterion for new additions is always the same—if it will be out of style tomorrow, it won't be in the line today.

In 2007, LIZ CLAIBORNE, Inc. acquired the brand and Deborah Lloyd took the helm as creative director. The Kate Spade design universe has expanded to include leather bags and accessories, evening bags, luggage, eyewear, shoes, home accessories, paper, and beauty products. In 2013, the brand expanded into the digital world. The Kate Spade Saturday digital window shops opened in the summer

as a touchscreen storefront. In partnership with eBay, the brand's four interactive window shops in downtown Manhattan are open and operable 24 hours a day.

A model wears Kate Spade's holiday 2012 dress with spring 2010 necklace.

EDWARD STEICHEN 📷

BORN Luxembourg, March 27, 1879
DIED West Redding, Connecticut, May 25, 1973

Brought to the United States as an infant, Edward
Steichen grew up in the Midwest and studied art at the
Milwaukee Art Students League from 1894 to 1898,
during which time he was a lithography apprentice and
began teaching himself photography. He became a U.S.
citizen in 1900, but lived in Paris painting and doing
photography from 1900 to 1902 and again from 1906 to
1914. During World War I, Steichen served in the U.S.
Army Expeditionary Forces (1917–19) as commander
of a photo division. Around 1922, he committed himself
entirely to photography.

Above: Photographer Edward Steichen.
Right: Photograph of Gloria Swanson by Edward Steichen, 1924.

Steichen's first fashion photographs were made in 1911
for PAUL POIRET; it was not until after he was hired by
Condé Nast in 1923 as photographic editor-in-chief that
he developed his mature style, deeply influenced by his
involvement with modern art. He replaced the pictorialism
of his predecessor, Adolfo, with a modernism based on
strong, clean lines, plain backgrounds, and an all-new
model, the "flapper." He also worked for the advertising
agency, J. Walter Thompson.

Steichen essentially abandoned his own photography
in 1947 when he became director of the Department of
Photography at New York's Museum of Modern Art, a
post he held until his retirement in 1962. His best-known
show from that era was "The Family of Man," which
traveled to a number of other museums across America.
During his long and distinguished career, Steichen
accumulated a staggering list of honors and affiliations.

 # WALTER STEIGER

present his first collection, which became extremely popular in America.

Steiger began designing for UNGARO and, by the mid-1970s, KARL LAGERFELD, KENZO, and CHLOÉ. Steiger also opened his first boutique in Paris on the Rue du Tournon. In 1982, he opened a store in New York City, where he started designing shoes for CALVIN KLEIN, BILL BLASS, and OSCAR DE LA RENTA. In 1986, he moved his family to his design studio in Ferrera, Italy.

Steiger's designs are diverse—from simple pumps to blinged-out flats and heels. He enjoys using wild patterns and colors on his shoes, as well as creating unusual heel styles.

Steiger's company is thriving, and his sons Paul and Giulo are now involved in the company in New York and Paris, respectively. In 2013, Natascia Rendell became general manager for the U.S.-based arm of the business.

Designer Walter Steiger.

BORN Geneva, 1942

Walter Steiger's father was a successful shoemaker with a business that he started in Geneva in 1932. At the age of 15, Steiger completed his own training at the prestigious studio Molnar Bottier in Zurich. He moved to Paris in 1962, where he joined the Capucine studio, then moved to London in 1963 and started designing for MARY QUANT. Steiger's shoe designs were noticed by Lady Rendlesham and photographed by *Vogue* and *Harper's Bazaar*. In 1967, Steiger returned to Paris to

Spring 2013.

JILL STUART

BORN New York City, January 5, 1965

Jill Stuart, a New York-based designer known for her youthful, vintage-inspired clothing, grew up in the Garment District (her parents owned the popular Seventh Avenue boutique Mister Pants) and entered the fashion industry while still in high school. At the age of 15 her collection of handbags and jewelry was displayed in Bloomingdale's windows.

After studying art and design at the Rhode Island School of Design, Stuart returned to New York, where she met and married Ron Curtis, now chief executive officer of her company. She opened her first boutique in 1988, and in 1993 launched her first full women's collection, Skinclothes, a sexy line of leather slip dresses, skirts, jackets, and jeans. Stuart's designs were worn by Alicia Silverstone in the 1995 movie *Clueless*, resulting in nationwide recognition. Recent collections have featured romantic tiered and layered

Designer Jill Stuart.

frocks highlighting the use of silk and organza—sensual clothing with a modern edge and a soft color palette.

In addition to clothing, Stuart offers watches, handbags, eyewear, perfume, and makeup. In spring 2007, she surprised the fashion community by launching her first men's wear line, called Stuart Curtis, created with her husband. Her lines are enormously successful in Japan, where she has flagship stores in Tokyo, Osaka, and Kobe. In 2010, she launched a lower-priced collection, Jill Jill Stuart.

Fall 2013.

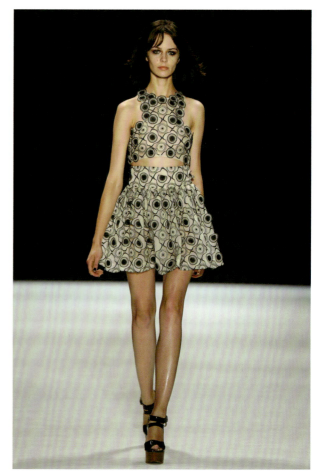

Spring 2014.

Above: Designer Anna Sui.
Right: Autumn/winter 1999/2000.

BORN Dearborn Heights, Michigan, August 4, 1964

AWARDS Council of Fashion Designers of America (CFDA) *Perry Ellis Award for New Fashion Talent*, 1992; *Geoffrey Beene Lifetime Achievement Award*, 2009

Anna Sui (Swee) has a restless curiosity and eclectic, unconventional approach to dress that was apparent early in her work. While still in junior high, she sewed many of her own clothes, even appliquéing some of the dress fabrics onto her shoes. In her teens she began saving clippings from fashion magazines in what she calls her "genius files" (she still uses them). Sui enrolled at Parsons School of Design in New York, where she became close friends with STEVEN MEISEL, who soon became a top fashion photographer.

Sui left Parsons in her second year to work for a junior sportswear company, designing everything from swimsuits to knits and moonlighting as a stylist for Meisel's fashion shoots. Torn between styling and designing, she continued to design, and after selling six of her pieces to Macy's, opened her own business. Her first runway show was in 1991. By 1993, Sui had moved

(continued)

her business from her apartment to a space on Seventh Avenue and opened two boutiques, one in New York's SoHo district and the other in Los Angeles.

In addition to clothing, the Anna Sui label produces seven fragrances and has designed a mobile phone and a limited edition Anna Sui Boho Barbie doll. The designer's products are sold in more than 300 stores in 30 countries. In 2009, Sui created a line for Target

Above: Fall 2013.
Left: Spring 2014.

inspired by the television show *Gossip Girl*, and in 2012 she collaborated on a line for Coach. In addition, a book exploring her 20 years in the business, titled *ANNA SUI* and written by Alexander Bolton, was released in 2010.

Designer Brandon Sun.

as Saks Fifth Avenue and Bergdorf Goodman. In 2012, Sun presented his first ready-to-wear collection at New York Fashion Week. The collection was inspired by classic Kung Fu films and was titled "Silent Assassins." His 2013 collection was inspired by the "Onna Bugeisha," feudal Japanese samurai women, and the architectural elements of Katsura, the imperial villa of Kyoto, Japan.

Sun continues to incorporate fur and leather in his collections. When asked by *PAPER* magazine how he feels about People for the Ethical Treatment of Animals (PETA), he said, "I don't mind when people have opinions. I just don't like it when they act like zealots."

BORN New York

A new talent in fashion, Brandon Sun was the star pupil at Parsons School of Design when he attended in his mid-20s. He started out in 2002 designing websites, but quickly realized that he loved fashion and making beautiful clothes. While at Parsons, he won the Designer of the Year and Gold Thimble awards. Sun was an intern at CALVIN KLEIN and Jeffrey Chow. He also won national scholarships from the Council of Fashion Designers of America (CFDA) and the Young Menswear Association (YMA) Fashion Scholarship Fund.

After graduating in 2006, Sun began working at OSCAR DE LA RENTA and J. MENDEL. At J. Mendel he rose to the position of designer within five years, specializing in fur. At de la Renta he became director of the fur division. In 2010 and 2011, he collaborated with the Blackgama fur company on its campaign "What Becomes a Legend Most?" The campaign features Pavarotti, Frank Sinatra, and the company's new spokeswoman, Janet Jackson.

In 2011, Sun introduced his own collection of fur accessories, which were sold at high-end stores such

Spring 2014.

Fall 2013.

ELIE TAHARI ▼

BORN Israel, 1952

Tahari—an Israeli of Iranian Jewish descent—has no formal training in fashion. When he arrived in New York City in 1971, he slept in Central Park and eventually found work replacing light bulbs by day and selling women's clothes at night. In the late 1970s, he got a job cutting fabric for disco-themed apparel. In 1997, he cofounded Icon with Andrew Rosen, but has since bought him out.

The fine lines and subtle embellishments that are the hallmarks of Elie Tahari's eponymous luxury women's wear line seem to contradict his famous tough-talking persona. But his style is actually a perfect extension of a maven's expertise. Because of the slow-moving silhouette of Tahari's women's business suit—a well-known item in America—he is usually not considered a high-end designer. He has stuck by his refusal to do runway shows and, despite having been in the industry for three decades, has met *Vogue* editor-in-chief ANNA WINTOUR just once. These facts can only be assessed properly when one

Designer Elie Tahari.

considers that Tahari takes in an estimated $500 million a year. Most of the revenue comes from his robust share of the massive global market for affordable luxury goods.

Tahari has said that his aesthetic and his approach to business come from his gut—from street smarts that tell him what type of products will make sense and sell well. In recent years the Elie Tahari brand has expanded to include licenses for shirts, ties, leather goods, and men's suits.

Tahari most decidedly does not allow sentimentality or excess analysis to guide his business decisions. For many years the creative director of the Elie Tahari brand was his wife Rory, whom he married in 2000. By 2011, their marriage was over, so Tahari hired Kobi Halperin to replace her. In 2012, Tahari hired former KENNETH COLE creative director Ingo Wilts as its new design head, while Cole named Halperin as creative director of its women's sportswear.

Fall 2011.

Spring 2012.

ANDRÉ LEON TALLEY

Editor André Leon Talley.

BORN Durham, North Carolina, October 16, 1949

AWARDS Council of Fashion Designers of America (CFDA) *Media Award in Honor of Eugenia Sheppard*, 2003

An icon in the fashion world, editor and writer André Leon Talley is one of the most prominent African-American voices in the industry. Though his various positions at *Vogue*, Talley was often in the front row of top fashion shows in New York, Milan, Paris, and London.

In 1977, after graduating from Brown University with a master's degree in French literature, Talley moved to New York and started working as a reporter for *Women's Wear Daily*. Talley stood out—partly because of his imposing six-foot, seven-inch frame—and quickly ingratiated himself in the New York social scene, becoming friends with Andy Warhol, KARL LAGERFELD, and Bianca Jagger. His work for *WWD* led to jobs at *Interview* and *The New York Times*, and in 1983 a position as fashion news director of *Vogue*. By 1989, he was the magazine's creative director. He used his personality, knowledge, and position at *Vogue* to promote new designers, and was especially committed to helping African-American designers and models.

In 1995, Talley left *Vogue* to become editor-in-chief of *W*. Three years later he returned to *Vogue* as editor-at-large. He became contributing editor in 2010 but continued writing his *Life with André* column, a popular commentary on global fashion events. In 2013, he was named artistic Director of Zappos Couture. That same year, he left *Vogue* to be editor-at-large of *Numéro* magazine's Russian edition. But Talley still maintains a relationship with *Vogue*, where he has helped propel the careers of several African-American luminaries, including Mariah Carey, Beyoncé, and Jennifer Hudson, and raised the profile of several designers, including BYRON LARS and TRACY REESE.

From 2009 to 2011, Talley was a judge on the reality television competition *America's Next Top Model*, and was wildly popular with audiences. In 2011, the Savannah College of Art and Design honored him by creating the André Leon Talley Gallery.

VIVIENNE TAM

Designer Vivienne Tam.

BORN Guangzhou, China, November 28, 1957

Vivienne Tam grew up in Hong Kong when it was a British crown colony—a bicultural background fundamental to her East-meets-West design philosophy. After graduating from Hong Kong Polytechnic University, she moved to New York City, where her first collection appeared in 1982 under the East Wind Code label. She first showed under her own name in 1993. Her spring 1995 collection created considerable controversy, with prints on t-shirts, jackets, and dresses of Chairman Mao Tse-tung wearing a pigtail or looking cross-eyed at a bee on the end of his nose.

Spring/Summer 1995.

Tam's stretch mesh prints—featuring images such as dragons, peonies, and Buddhas—are well known, but she is committed to creating fashionable clothes for modern women that are well designed, of superior quality, and affordable. Since she is a dedicated traveler, they must also be wearable and travel well. Tam's clothes are sold in fine stores in America and abroad, and her work is part of the collections of the Metropolitan Museum of Art and Fashion Institute of Technology in New York, and the Andy Warhol Museum in Pittsburgh. A book she wrote, *China Chic*, was published in 2000.

Tam ventured into evening and special occasion dresses in 2003, and launched a secondary sportswear and denim line called Red Dragon. Her flagship store on New York's Mercer Street opened in 2007, and she designed the first "virtual digital clutch" for

Hewlett-Packard in 2008. In 2013, during her spring fashion show, Tam debuted her Chinese jewelry brand TSL. Her celebrity clients include Julia Roberts, Drew Barrymore, and Reese Witherspoon.

Spring 2013.

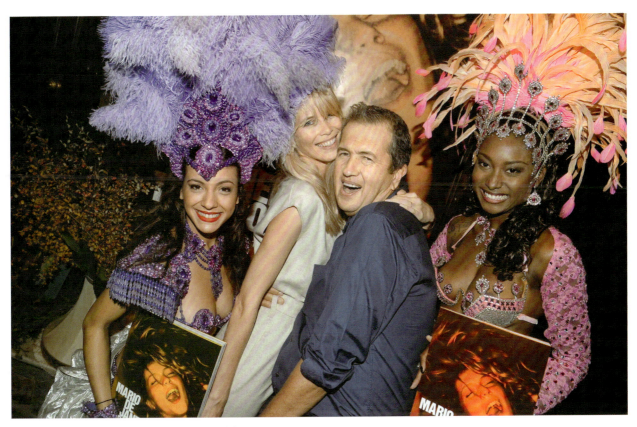

Photographer Mario Testino, center, with models.

BORN Lima, Peru, October 30, 1954

World-renowned fashion photographer Mario Testino began his career by selling portfolios to models trying to jumpstart their careers. His work with models propelled him to the international stage and made him one of the most sought-after photographers in fashion.

Considered by many to be a "luxury photographer," Testino has produced glamorous work for dozens of companies and appeared on the editorial pages of nearly every high-profile fashion magazine. He is a major editorial voice at *Vogue* and has produced ad campaigns for Tom Ford, Burberry, and Michael Kors, to name a few. One of the highest-paid photographers in the industry, he is hailed for his ability to take shots that sell clothes. He is also credited with helping end the reign of the supermodel. Testino refused to pay the fees demanded by many high-profile models in the 1990s and instead introduced new faces to the scene, including Kate Moss—his favorite—and Stella Tennant. It should be noted that Kate Moss has

been an expensive, high-profile model for the past couple decades.

Testino became famous for his portraits of Madonna, Gwyneth Paltrow, and Angelina Jolie. In 1997, he photographed Princess Diana for *Vanity Fair*. In 2002, the National Portrait Gallery in London staged the landmark exhibit *Mario Testino: Portraits*, which over the next four years was shown in Milan, Amsterdam, Edinburgh, Tokyo, and Mexico City. In 2005, his exhibit *Diana: Princess of Wales*, opened at Kensington Palace. In 2010, Testino took the engagement photo of Prince William and Kate Middleton.

Testino has released several books of his photography, including *Any Objections?*, *Alive*, *Let Me In!*, and *Private View*. His 2009 book, *Mario de Janeiro Testino,* featured provocative shots of Brazilian model Gisele Bündchen. In 2011, *Kate Moss by Mario Testino* was released, showcasing the supermodel. In 2012, Testino created MATE (Asociación Mario *Testino*), a nonprofit arts organization in Lima, Peru, to raise cultural awareness and promote arts programs for both local and international audiences.

OLIVIER THEYSKENS ♟

BORN Brussels, Belgium, January 4, 1977

AWARDS Council of Fashion Designers of America
(CFDA) *International Award*, 2006

The son of a Belgian father and French mother, Olivier
Theyskens is among the fresh talents from Belgium who
have shown in Paris and shined on the international
fashion scene. He entered Brussels's l'École Nationale
Supérieure des Arts Visuels de la Cambre in 1995, but
left in early 1997 to work on his first collection. It was
shown later that year in Amsterdam and Knokke, Belgium. His first Paris showing was the following March.

Above: Designer Olivier Theyskens.
Left: Theyskens' Theory, spring 2014.

In what he calls "semi-couture," Theyskens creates brilliant dresses, coats, and suits notable for their
assured cut, adventurous and experimental shapes,
and sophisticated color palette—clothes for confident
women with a sense of drama. His customers include
Madonna, Nicole Kidman, and Queen Rania of Jordan.
In 2002 he joined Marcel Rochas as creative director,
but in 2006 Procter & Gamble discontinued the company's fashion division. Theyskens became artistic director
of Nina Ricci later that year, and stayed until 2009. In
2010, the chief executive officer of the global brand Theory, Andrew Rosen, asked Theyskens to create a capsule
collection. They worked together to create the brand
Theyskens' Theory, where he is head designer, in addition to being creative director of Theory.

ThreeASFOUR designers Gabi Asfour, Adi Gil, and Angela Donhauser.

FOUNDED Gabi Asfour and Angela Donhauser, 1996

AWARDS *Ecco Domani Fashion Foundation Grant*, 2002

ThreeASFOUR is a team of three fashion designers known for their avant-garde and 3-D works. The group started in 1996 as a four-member collective called ASFOUR and became known for their runway antics—for example, showing their first collection on miniature hula dolls instead of real models. In 2005, after Kai Kuhne left to pursue his own label, the remaining members renamed the collective threeASFOUR. They participate in all aspects of their brand, from design to styling to advertising, to make the best use of their unique skills.

In 2005, threeASFOUR created Five Four Denim, launched three fragrances for the Parisian boutique Colette, and collaborated with Kate Spade on an

accessories collection, Four Kate Spade. In 2007, the collective created a capsule collection for The Gap.

ThreeASFOUR's collections define a fresh market in fashion. The clothes reflect a new quality of avant-garde architecture, craftsmanship, construction, texture, and technologies, such as computer-generated laser cutting for 3-D looks and complex origami pleats. The brand's designers come from diverse cultural backgrounds, but together they seek to create wearable art and "encourage cross-cultural harmony through fashion." In 2013, threeASFOUR exhibited its spring and summer 2014 collection, MER KA BA, at the Jewish Museum of New York. MER KA BA "embraces many spiritual concepts: Merkaba is a mystical form of Judaism; ka ba alludes to the Kaaba, one of the holiest sites in Islam and the focal point of the Mecca pilgrimage; Muraqaba is a Sufi meditation practice." Celebrities who wear threeASFOUR include Björk and Yoko Ono.

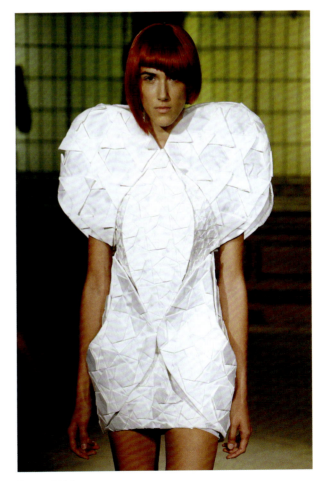

Spring 2014.

TIFFANY Ŏ ▪️

FOUNDED Charles Lewis Tiffany; New York City, 1837

AWARDS Paris Exposition Universelle *Award of Merit*, 1867

Charles Lewis Tiffany and John B. Young founded Tiffany & Young in 1837. At first they sold stationary and "fancy goods," but soon expanded into jewelry and silverware. In 1841, J.L. Ellis joined the company and it was renamed Tiffany, Young & Ellis. In 1848, Tiffany took a chance and bought a lot of diamonds, and the company started manufacturing jewelry. It was the first time the American market had seen major gemstones, and Tiffany was called "The King of Diamonds." Two years later, the company opened a store in Paris.

Tiffany became known for finding rare, large, and unique jewelry items, and became popular with the well-to-do and elite. In 1851, he used new standards for English silver in his company's products, and the term *sterling* was adopted in America. In 1853, Tiffany bought out his partners and shortened the company's name to Tiffany & Co. When the Civil War approached, realizing that jewelry might not be a hot commodity, he started selling swords, medals, and lightweight armor.

In 1867, Tiffany became the first American company to win an Award of Merit (for silver) at the Paris Exposition Universelle. In 1868, Tiffany & Co was incorporated and expanded to Geneva, London, and Paris. Tiffany & Co. was influencing trends in jewelry and setting standards that everyone wanted to follow. It was also winning awards, particularly at the Paris Expositions, and became the royal and imperial jeweler for heads of Europe, the Middle East, and Russia. In 1877, the company purchased what is now known as the Tiffany Diamond, a 287-carat yellow South African diamond, for $18,000. It took over a year to cut it down to

The Tiffany®-Setting engagement ring.

128.54 carats and for the diamond to be put on display at the Smithsonian Institution for an extended period. In 1961, Audrey Hepburn wore the diamond for publicity stills for the movie *Breakfast at Tiffany's*.

Tiffany & Co. introduced other innovations such as the first catalog and the first six-prong tableware setting. Charles Tiffany believed that "good design is good business," and he passed that philosophy to his son, Louis Comfort Tiffany. Louis Tiffany became equally successful after his father's death in 1902 by working in glass and lamps.

Today, Tiffany hires prominent designers such as PALOMA PICASSO and ELSA PERETTI to maintain its legendary quality and style. In 2013, Tiffany appointed Francesca Amfitheatrof as its design director and launched tiffany.com. The company is worth an estimated $8 billion.

BORN Elizabeth Jane Kelly; Shirehampton, England, 1949
DIED New York City, April 21, 1999

AWARDS Society of Publication Designers *Gold Medal for Overall Redesign*, 1993 • Council of Fashion Designers of America (CFDA) *Special Award*, 1993; *Humanitarian Award*, 1998

Liz Tilberis achieved celebrity status in America when she became editor-in-chief of *Harper's Bazaar*. She began her career in 1970 at British *Vogue*, where she started as an intern but eventually became executive fashion editor, then editor-in-chief. By 1991, she was director of CONDÉ NAST Publications in the United Kingdom. In 1992, during the 125th anniversary of Hearst Corporation's *Harper's Bazaar*, Tilberis was offered a position as its editor-in-chief. She accepted and moved her family to New York City. While she was at *Harper's Bazaar*, the magazine received the National Magazine Award for photography and for design. But just one year into her new position, Tilberis was diagnosed with ovarian cancer.

Despite her illness, Tilberis introduced many changes to revitalize the magazine. She experimented with new designers, innovative layouts, and playful typography. She also broke ground with photographers; in particular, the well-established PATRICK DEMARCHELIER and Peter Limbergh both came to work for her. While Tilberis underwent extensive chemotherapy and surgery, the magazine underwent a makeover. Hearst President and Chief Executive Officer Frank Bennack, Jr., said that Tilberis aimed "for *Harper's Bazaar* to set the agenda for modern elegance." In fact, the cover story of the September 1992 issue, her first, invited readers to "enter the age of elegance."

Editor Liz Tilberis.

Tilberis made no effort to hide her personal story from the public. She spoke out against the fertility drugs that she believed had caused her disease, and in 1997 became president of the Ovarian Cancer Research Fund. She also penned her memoirs, *No Time to Die*. During the course of her work, Tilberis befriended Princess Diana, who graced the cover of *Harper's Bazaar* twice under Tilberis's mantle.

RICCARDO TISCI ♟

BORN Taranto, Italy, 1974

AWARDS Council of Fashion Designers of America
(CFDA) *International Award, 2013*

Riccardo Tisci (TEA-she) is creative director of GIVEN-
CHY, one of the most respected design houses in Paris.
Tisci's father died when he was four, and he was raised
by a single mother. He attended Central Saint Martins
College of Arts and Design in London on a scholarship; after graduating in 1999, he worked for Antonio
Berardi, Puma, and Ruffo Research back in Italy. In
2004, he established his own label, and his first collection was for fall/winter 2005.

Tisci was appointed creative director for Givenchy
in 2005. His designs are sexy and seductive—assum-
ing confidence in the wearer. They have helped bring
Givenchy back to life and turned around its fortunes.

Riccardo Tisci (left) and Rooney Mara attend the Metropolitan
Museum of Art's 2013 Costume Institute Gala featuring the
opening of the exhibit Punk: Chaos to Couture.

Tisci also added men's wear to the brand, and it now
accounts for 30 percent of sales and has made Givenchy
a label of choice for many male celebrities.

In 2010, Tisci made waves when he used transsexual
model Lea T in a runway show and ad campaigns. Lea T
(born Leandro Cerezo) worked as a fit model and assistant for Givenchy, but Tisci recognized her je ne sais
quoi and made her the face of the brand. Tisci served
as art director for Kanye West's and Jay-Z's *Watch
the Throne* tour in 2011, and convinced West to wear
a leather skirt on stage—making fashion headlines.
In 2012, Tisci designed Madonna's costumes for the
12-minute Super Bowl halftime show.

In 2013, for the second time since starting at Givenchy,
Tisci did not show at Haute Couture Fashion Week. His
schedule was too busy, and the label was enlarging its atelier. Tisci did manage to design several costumes for the
Paris Opera Ballet's production of *Bolero*.

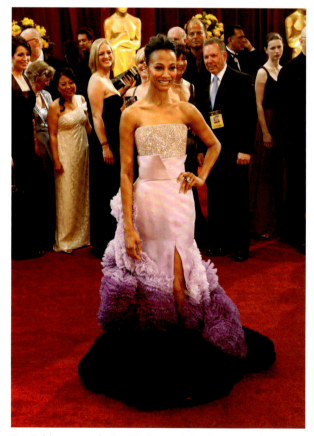

Zoe Saldana attends the 82nd annual Academy Awards at
the Kodak Theatre. Saldana in Givenchy Haute Couture by
Riccardo Tisci.

♟ ✏ ISABEL AND RUBEN TOLEDO

has a floor—one for her fashions, the other for his art and illustrations.

Isabel Toledo is among the designers working in a very personal way somewhat outside the mainstream. She learned to sew as a child and started making her own clothes because manufactured clothing was too big for her. After immigrating to America with her family, she attended the Fashion Institute of Technology and Parsons School of Design in New York City, and studied painting and ceramics before switching to design. She worked with DIANA VREELAND at the Costume Institute of the Metropolitan Museum of Art, restoring clothes from the museum's collection.

Ruben Toledo started his career by selling work to Fiorucci while still in high school. He has designed a wide range of items, including mannequins, store

(continued)

Above: Isabel and Ruben Toledo.

Right: Illustration by Ruben Toledo.

BORN Isabel Toledo; Havana, Cuba, April 9, 1961; Ruben Toledo; Havana, Cuba, 1961

AWARDS Coty American Fashion Critics' Awards *Winnie*, 2005 • Cooper-Hewitt *National Design Award (fashion)*, 2005 • Museum at the Fashion Institute of Technology Couture Council *Award for Artistry of Fashion*, 2008 • American Apparel & Footwear Association *Fashion Maverick Award*, 2011

Isabel and Ruben Toledo have what has been called a creative love affair. They met in Cuba when they were 13, and Isabel admits that she fell in love with Ruben's art before falling in love with him. In their studio, each

window displays, fabrics, patterns, and album covers. He also works as a freelance illustrator for *The New Yorker*, *Harper's Bazaar*, and *Vogue*.

Isabel's fashion career began in 1985 when, at Ruben's urging, she made a few pieces that he then took to stores. Patricia Field and Henri Bendel were her first customers—followed by Bergdorf Goodman, which displayed clothes from her first full collection in its windows on 57th Street.

Line and shape are paramount for Isabel, who starts with a shape such as a circle and experiments to see how far she can take it. She believes in arriving at simplicity through innovation, and insists that design must not be contrived but evolve naturally. Ruben then illustrates her creations or listens to Isabel and her assistants to document their thought processes. Her clothes, which she calls classic, range from sportswear to evening wear, from simple to flamboyant. They derive their uniqueness from the strength of their shapes and from her eye for detail.

Ruben has published several books, including *Style Dictionary*, *Louis Vuitton City Guide*, and *Roots of Style: Weaving Together Life, Love and Fashion*. In 1998, the book *Toledo/Toledo: A Marriage of Art and Fashion* was published to accompany an exhibit of the same name at the Fashion Institute of Technology. In 2009, FIT unveiled an exhibition titled, *Holy Toledo! Isabel Toledo and the Art of Fashion*.

Also in 2009, Michelle Obama chose a green wool lace coat, dress, and cardigan set designed by Toledo to wear to the inauguration of her husband. It was not the first

President Obama and First Lady Michelle Obama in Isabel Toledo, 2009.

time Obama had worn a Toledo design, but it gave Isabel huge international recognition. Soon after, she designed collections for Payless ShoeSource and Target. Meanwhile, Ruben collaborated with Nina Garcia on several books and with Nordstrom to create *Fashion Almanac*, marking his ten-year relationship with the chain.

In 2011, the Toledos appeared on PBS's *The Artist's Toolbox*. In 2013, they made history by being the first high-end designers to collaborate with plus-size brand Lane Bryant, producing a capsule collection of t-shirts and bags based on Ruben's sketches.

Above: Designer Philip Treacy.
Below right: Spring 2013.

BORN County Galway, Ireland, May 26, 1967

AWARDS British Fashion Awards *Accessories Designer of the Year*, 1991, 1992, 1996, 1997 • British Government *Honorary Officer of the Most Excellent Order of the British Empire*, 2007

After studying at Dublin's National College of Art and Design, Philip Treacy moved to London in 1988 to attend the Royal College of Art on a scholarship. While still in school, he worked for RIFAT ÖZBEK and JOHN GALLIANO, among others, and soon after graduating was house milliner at HARTNELL. An interview at Chanel led to a collaboration with KARL LAGERFELD for the spring/summer 1991 couture show, and since then Treacy has provided hats to Chanel for both couture and ready-to-wear collections. His creations have also appeared in the collections of VALENTINO and THIERRY MUGLER. They are sold in some of the world's finest stores—Bergdorf Goodman and Saks Fifth Avenue in America, Harrods and Harvey Nichols in England, and in his own London boutique.

Treacy is fascinated with Surrealist themes—animal shapes, insects, hands, a crown of thorns—and gives them form using stripped feathers and distressed materials in unlikely juxtapositions. Still, he believes that hats should be worn with "simple" outfits to avoid looking frightening. GIANNI VERSACE is reported to have said of Treacy, "Give him a pin, he makes a sculpture; give him a rose, he makes a poem." In 2000, Treacy took his creations to Paris for the first showing of haute couture hats there in 70 years.

In 2005, he created hats for the wedding of Prince Charles and Camila Parker Bowles, and in 2011 for the wedding of Prince William and Kate Middleton—though his creation for Princess Beatrice was considered by some to resemble a toilet seat. In 2007, Treacy was appointed Honorary Officer of the Most Excellent Order of the British Empire in recognition of his services to the British fashion industry.

Treacy made news in 2010 when he designed a headpiece for Lady Gaga shaped like a telephone—including a removable handset—for the television show *Saturday Night Live*. He has also designed for films, including the *Harry Potter* series, and television shows such as *Sex and the City*.

PAULINE TRIGÈRE ◢

BORN Paris, November 4, 1908
DIED New York City, February 13, 2002

AWARDS Coty American Fashion Critics' Awards *Winnie*, 1949; *Return Award*, 1951; *Hall of Fame Award*, 1959 • *Neiman Marcus Award*, 1950 • City of Paris *Medaille de Vermeil*, 1972, 1982 • Council of Fashion Designers of America (CFDA) *Lifetime Achievement Award*, 1993 • *Fashion Walk of Fame*, 2001 • French Government *Légion d'Honneur (Legion of Honor)*, 2001

The daughter of Russian émigrés, her father a tailor, her mother a dressmaker, Pauline Trigère's first career choice was to be a surgeon. When her father opposed the idea, she got a job making muslins at a Paris couture house. In 1929, she married Lazar Radley, another Russian-Jewish tailor. Her husband became alarmed at the rising Nazi tide, and in 1936 the family—Trigère, her husband, and their two sons, as well as her brother and mother—left France for Chile. (Her father had already died.) But their first stop was New York City, and there they stayed.

Designer Pauline Trigère.

After a business partnership with her brother and husband fell apart, her husband disappeared and Trigère found work with manufacturer Ben Gershel and then HATTIE CARNEGIE as an assistant to TRAVIS BANTON. Fired by Carnegie at the outbreak of World War II, in 1942 Trigère scraped together enough fabric for her first collection—just 11 dresses. Her brother took the samples in a suitcase and, traveling by bus, sold them to specialty shops from Los Angeles to Minneapolis to Chicago to Philadelphia.

Trigère cut and draped directly from the bolt, creating coats, capes, suits, and dresses of near-couture quality in luxurious fabrics and unusual tweeds and prints. The deceptive simplicity of the clothes was based on artistic, intricate cut, especially flattering to mature figures. She took care of designing for her firm, Trigère Inc., while her elder son, Jean-Pierre Radley, oversaw the business end. The Trigère name has appeared on scarves, jewelry, furs, men's ties, sunglasses, bedroom fashions, paper, servingware, and a fragrance.

Trigère closed her business in 1993. In 2001, she was inducted into the Fashion Walk of Fame, on the Seventh Avenue sidewalk between 35th and 41st Streets. Trigère, whose tailoring and draping skills were legendary, chose tailoring shears as her symbol rather than a sketch. In her acceptance speech, she quipped that it was the first time she had ever allowed anyone to walk on her.

Evening sheath of silk lace ca. 1953.

Designer Trina Turk.

AWARDS Los Angeles Fashion Awards *Fashion Achievement Award*, 2005 • California Mart *California Designer of the Year Award*, 1998

Trina Turk designs.

Trina Turk always knew she wanted to go into fashion, but she did not expect to be so successful at it. A California native, her Japanese mother taught her how to sew at age 11, and her love of designing clothes was born. After attending the University of Washington, Turk landed her first job with the Seattle-based sportswear manufacturer Britannia Jeans. She then returned to California to design prints for Ocean Pacific. Tired of working for others, in 1995—with the help of her husband, photographer Jonathan Skow—she opened Trina Turk Company. The collection was so successful that it sold at Barneys, Saks Fifth Avenue, and Fred Segal that same year.

Turk's vision for the company is shaped by her memories of growing up in California in the late 1960s and the 1970s. She is also inspired by the multicultural mix and architecture of Los Angeles. Her philosophy is to create wearable, optimistic fashion that incorporates the best aspects of classic American sportswear. In 2002, she opened her first freestanding boutique in Palm Springs, and four years later followed with a boutique in New York's Meatpacking district. In 2009, she launched a hosiery "guest designer" line with Hue and printed fabrics for home furnishings manufacturer Schumacher. In 2012, she collaborated with Banana Republic on its summer line. Her simple, modern designs are popular with many celebrities, including Eva Longoria, Natalie Portman, Gwen Stefani, and Kate Moss. Since its founding 19 years ago, Turk has built the company into a $40 million a year business.

Model wearing a design by Trina Turk.

RICHARD TYLER

Designer Richard Tyler.

BORN Sunshine, Australia, 1947

AWARDS Council of Fashion Designers of America
(CFDA) *Perry Ellis Award for New Fashion Talent*, 1993;
Best Designer, 1994; *Womenswear Designer of the Year*,
1994; *Perry Ellis Award for Menswear* (a tie with Edward
Pavlick and Richard Bengtsson for Richard Edwards),
1995 • Dallas Fashion Awards *Fashion Excellence Award*
(for Anne Klein), 1994

When Richard Tyler succeeded Louis
Dell'olio as designer for Anne Klein,
he was already a highly regarded fashion
name in Los Angeles, producing beautiful clothes of near-custom quality
for women and men and selling them
from his own boutique. His jackets are
particularly admired, not only for their
inventive, graceful cut, but also for their
perfectionist tailoring and finish, so flawless
they could be worn inside out. Their high
quality places the clothes firmly in the deluxe
category.

When he was eight, Tyler learned to
sew from his mother, who designed
costumes for the ballet. Her credo,
"Don't send it out

Marcia Cross attends
the 62nd annual Golden
Globe Awards wearing
Richard Tyler.

Spring/summer 1996.

unless it's perfect," has guided him ever since. In his
teen years, Tyler apprenticed with the tailor who made
suits for the Australian prime minister; at 18 he opened
his first boutique, Zippity-doo-dah, attracting clients
from the music industry.

After touring with Rod Stewart and designing for
one of his tours, Tyler landed in Los Angeles in 1978,
then spent time designing in Europe. He continued to
design for performers over the next few years. In 1987,
he established Tyler/Trafficante, a partnership with his
second wife, Lisa, and her sister Michelle to design,
manufacture, and wholesale the clothes. The first New
York showing of the women's collection was in 1993.

In 1993, Tyler also became head designer for Anne
Klein. Though his collections there were well received by
his peers and the press, traditional Anne Klein customers found them too advanced, and in 1994 the company
ended the arrangement. Tyler continues to produce his
signature line and show it in New York, with his operations based in his downtown Manhattan home studio. A
lower-priced collection, Tyler, was launched in 2002.

In 2006, Tyler designed uniforms for Delta Air Lines,
and in 2009 for workers at the Church of Scientolo-
gy's Ideal Organizations (Ideal Orgs). But many critics
found similarities between the uniforms. In 2012, trag-
edy struck when Tyler's Pasadena studio burned down.

in London. Stephens then created a lifestyle and fashion public relations firm, Concrete, and open a retail store in Soho, London selling luxury brands. The store proved to be the perfect venue to launch his first men's wear collection, Unconditional, in 2002. The name originated from the idea of unconditional love, and the collection was edgy and strong, combining street style and formal elegance. After gaining popularity, Unconditional was shown at London Fashion Week in 2005. One of Stephens's first customers was David Beckham, and his interest in the line made its popularity skyrocket. Two years later, Stephens created a small women's wear collection.

Stephens has presented his collections in New York, Amsterdam, and Shanghai. In 2008, he opened the first Unconditional flagship store in Covent Garden, London, and in 2011 he opened a store in his hometown of Manchester. Unconditional men's wear is known for its draping, while its women's wear is known for flattering the female form. Unconditional also offers basics that are androgynous with a rock and roll vibe, as well as an extremely popular cashmere line.

For spring/summer 2012, Unconditional collaborated with leather accessories designer Úna Burke to pair striking structural pieces with flowing silk dresses. Unconditional has also ventured into home goods. Stephens produces eco-fashion and gives to charity, sometimes donating his profits to the Manna Food Bank. Unconditional is one of London's best labels and has had a major impact on fashion. Kanye West, David Bowie, Will.i.am, Madonna, Patti Smith, and Gwen Stefani are among the brand's celebrity fans.

Designer Philip Stevens with a model wearing a design from the spring 2009 collection.

FOUNDED Philip Stephens; Britain, 2002

Philip Stephens is the man behind the British label Unconditional. He attended Surrey University and went into public relations, working for Lynne Franks

PATRICIA UNDERWOOD 👜

BORN Patricia Gilbert; Maidenhead, England, October 11, 1947

AWARDS Coty American Fashion Critics' Awards 1982 • Council of Fashion Designers of America (CFDA) *American Accessories Award*, 1983

Patricia Underwood worked in Paris as an au pair and at Buckingham Palace as a secretary before moving to New York City in 1968. She took an evening class at the Fashion Institute of Technology and then, with a friend, decided to go into business making hats. Underwood added scarves, shawls, and gloves to her collection in the mid-1990s. Her work is mostly ready-to-wear,

Designer Patricia Underwood.

available through department and specialty stores such as Saks Fifth Avenue and Bergdorf Goodman.

Underwood's strength is in elegantly updating classic, simple shapes from the past, such as boaters, milkmaids' hats, and nuns' coifs. Her signature hats are made of straw, felt, leather, and cashmere. Underwood's designs have often been used to complement the collections of designers such as RALPH LAUREN, MICHAEL KORS, BAND OF OUTSIDERS (SCOTT STERNBERG), Abaete and Temperley, NICOLE MILLER, and OSCAR DE LA RENTA. Her hats have also been worn in films such as *Down with Love, Cinderella, Sabrina, Six Days Seven Nights, Four Weddings and a Funeral, Austin Powers: International Man of Mystery, The Imposters, The Pallbearers, Sex and the City 2, and Return to Paradise.*

Hat designed by Patricia Underwood, 2005.

♠ EMANUEL UNGARO

BORN Aix-en-Provence, France, February 13, 1933

AWARDS *Neiman Marcus Award*, 1969

Emanuel Ungaro's (OON-gar-o) parents were Italians who fled to the south of France at the start of World War II. His early training came from his father, a tailor, who taught him how to cut, sew, and fit men's clothes. In 1955, he left Provence for Paris and took a job in a small tailoring firm. Three years later he went to work for BALENCIAGA, where he stayed until 1963, then spent two years with COURRÈGES.

Top: Designer Emanual Ungaro
Left: Autumn/winter 1995/1996

Ungaro opened his own business in 1965. His first collections were reminiscent of Courrèges—tailored coats and suits with diagonal seaming, little girl A-line dresses, and blazers with shorts. The clothes were widely copied in the youth market. Many of his special fabrics and prints were designed by Sonja Knapp, a Swiss graphic artist.

In the 1970s, Ungaro turned to softer fabrics and more flowing lines, mingling several prints in a single outfit and piling on layers. His designs became increasingly seductive, evolving into a body-conscious, sensuous look, strategically draped and shirred. Because his work was immediately and extensively copied, Ungaro moved on—but retained his penchant for mixing patterns and prints. His excellent tailoring has always been in evidence in creations as diverse as

(continued)

a men's striped jacket tossed over a slinky flowered evening dress and daytime suits with soft trousers cut on the bias. He has added ready-to-wear; a perfume, Diva; and Ungaro boutiques in Europe and America. Other projects have included furs, men's wear, bed linens, wall coverings, curtains, and knitwear.

Ungaro celebrated his 35th year in business with a New York party in September 2001; the next month he named his creative director GIAMBATTISTA VALLI as designer of ready-to-wear. Ungaro retained responsibility for haute couture. His line has since gone through three design directors, including ESTEBAN CORTÁZAR,

Above: Spring 2014.
Left: Spring 2014.

who debuted his designs in 2008 at the age of 23. In 2009, Lindsay Lohan was named artistic adviser along with head designer Estrella Archs, after Cortázar refused to work with Lohan. In 2010, GILES DEACON became creative director. In 2012, it was announced that Fausto Puglisi—best known for designing tour outfits for Madonna—would be the new creative director starting in 2013.

Designer Valentino.

BORN Valentino Garavani; Voghera, Italy, circa 1932

AWARDS *Neiman Marcus Award*, 1967 • Council of Fashion Designers of America (CFDA) *Lifetime Achievement Award*, 2000

Valentino Garavani left Italy for Paris at 17 to study at l'École de la Chambre Syndicale de la Couture Parisienne, having prepared himself by studying fashion and the French language in Milan. In 1950, he went to work for JEAN DESSÈS, stayed five years, then worked as a design assistant at GUY LAROCHE until 1958.

In 1959, Valentino opened his own couture house with a tiny atelier on Rome's Via Condotti. Within a few years, he was successful enough to move to his current headquarters. In his 1959 collection, he debuted a dress in "Valentino red"—as the shade came to be known—that appeared in every collection to follow and became symbolic of the brand. Valentino's first

major recognition came in 1962 when he showed for the first time in Florence. In 1975, he began showing ready-to-wear collections in Paris and has continued to do so, with couture showings still held in Rome. His first boutique for ready-to-wear opened in Milan in 1969, followed by one in Rome and then others around the world, including Japan. Other areas include men's wear, Valentino Più for gifts and interiors, bed linens, and curtain fabrics.

Valentino's clothes are noted for their refined simplicity, elegance, and all-out glamour, with precisely tailored coats and suits, sophisticated sportswear, and entrance-making evening dresses that are always feminine and flattering. They use beautiful fabrics and reflect exquisite workmanship, and have been worn by a diverse international clientele ranging from Jacqueline Kennedy to Elizabeth Taylor to Jennifer Lopez.

With Giancarlo Giammetti, his partner and business manager, Valentino understands the importance of the grand gesture. In 1978, he introduced his eponymous fragrance by sponsoring a ballet performance in Paris and after-theater parties at Maxim's and the Palace. In 1984, he celebrated his 25th year in business and 50th couture collection with an enormous outdoor fashion show in Rome's Piazza di Spagna. His 30th anniversary celebration was a week of lavish lunches, dinners, a ball, and two exhibits attended by an international assemblage of friends and clients. A Valentino retrospective was part of an Italian promotion at the Park Avenue Armory in 1992.

In 2008, after 45 years in fashion, Valentino retired, with an eye

(continued)

Fall 2006.

389

toward pursuing "new interests and challenges." Maria Grazia Chiuri and Pierpaolo Piccioli were named creative directors of the company, and have been lauded for blending the aesthetic values of its founder with a contemporary and sophisticated vision. In 2012, Mayhoola for Investments SPC, a private investment

Spring 2008.

vehicle backed by the royal family of Qatar, bought the Valentino brand for $903 million, with the promise that all employees would keep their positions.

Spring 2014 haute couture.

Designer Giambattista Valli with models, spring 2009.

BORN Rome, 1966

Giambattista Valli was born into a conservative Italian family and attended one of the schools of the Vatican. But an early interest in design, partly fostered by an

Fall 2013 haute couture.

♟ GIAMBATTISTA VALLI

urge to recreate drawings by YVES SAINT LAURENT, inspired the young Valli to attend the European School of Design in Germany as well as Saint Martins School of Art in London. In 1988, Valli went to work for the public relations department of Italian couturier ROBERTO CAPUCCI, where he eventually became a designer. Later he moved to FENDI, where as a senior designer he created pieces for the young and trendy Fendissime line.

In 1995, Valli became a senior designer for the Italian designer Krizia, then joined EMANUEL UNGARO in 1997. There he was promoted to art director of ready-to-wear and the Ungaro Fever youth wear line, and remained at the fashion house until 2001.

After a variety of stints in fashion design, in 2005 Valli partnered with the Italian licensee Gilmar to create his own label, Giambattista. The designs were opulent, innovative, and fluid in line. Bold colors and revealing cuts helped establish his signature. In 2008, Valli premiered his spring 2009 collection at the Royal Ontario Museum in Canada. He also collaborates with ski apparel legend Moncler and creates furs and bridal pieces. In 2010, Valli opened his first store, on Rue Boissy d'Anglais in Paris, and in 2011 he showed his first haute couture collection. Valli is highly sought after by celebrities, including Queen Rania of Jordan, Victoria Beckham, Penélope Cruz, Naomi Campbell, and Mischa Barton.

Fall 2013 haute couture.

DRIES VAN NOTEN ▲

BORN Antwerp, Belgium, May 1958

AWARDS Council of Fashion Designers of America (CFDA) *International Designer of the Year Award*, 2008 • Fashion Institute of Technology Couture Council *Artistry of Fashion Award*, 2009

Coming from three generations of tailors, Dries Van Noten (Drees van NO-tahn) took up the family trade while a student at the Royal Academy of Beaux Arts in Antwerp, working as a freelance designer for Belgian and Italian men's wear labels. His first collection under his own name was released in 1985; the next year he showed in London as part of the Antwerp Six—a group of influential avant-garde fashion designers who graduated from Antwerp's Royal Academy of Beaux Arts in 1980 and 1981. The show brought him press

Designer Dries Van Noten.

recognition and orders from adventurous retailers internationally, including Barneys New York. He opened a boutique in Antwerp in 1989, and his first Paris men's wear show was in 1991. He has since added women's wear and accessories, showrooms in Milan and Tokyo, shops in the Far East, and a men's store in Paris.

Van Noten marries opposite styles—simple with sophisticated, classic with modern—and his women's and men's collections both reflect his passion for fabrics, which are usually made exclusively for him. Although he shows in Paris and his clothes are sold around the world, he continues to live and work in Antwerp. In 2014, the Musée des Arts Décoratifs in Paris held an exhibit, *Dries Van Noten: Inspirations*, that combined his men's and women's collections with iconic pieces from the museum's fashion and textile collections. The show also included photos, videos, film clips, musical references, and renowned artworks that have nurtured the designer's creativity.

Spring 2014.

Spring 2014.

Designer John Varvatos.

BORN Dearborn, Michigan, August 8, 1954

AWARDS Council of Fashion Designers of America (CFDA) *Perry Ellis Award for Menswear*, 2000; *Menswear Designer of the Year*, 2001, 2005 • *GQ Designer of the Year*, 2007

Fall 2013.

 # JOHN VARVATOS

When John Varvatos (var-VAY-toes) presented his first collection under his own label in 1999 he was hardly a beginner, having already put in 16 years in the men's fashion industry. He attended Eastern Michigan University, studied fashion illustration and patternmaking at the Fashion Institute of Technology, and started with RALPH LAUREN in 1983.

In 1990, Varvatos was wooed away by CALVIN KLEIN to head his men's wear division and establish the cK label. In 1994, he returned to Polo RALPH LAUREN as senior vice president and head designer of men's wear, gaining further experience in marketing, production, and financing before embarking on his own in 1998. In 2001, he began designing limited edition athletic shoes for Converse (a project that continues to this day) and opened boutiques in Los Angeles, Las Vegas, San Francisco, and New York City. In 2006, he launched his first eyewear collection and John Varvatos Star USA, for younger and edgier customers.

Varvatos combines the relaxed ease of sportswear with a refined elegance of cut, luxurious materials, and meticulous craftsmanship. He believes in presenting a total wardrobe—tailored clothing, sportswear, leather accessories, and footwear.

In 2008, Varvatos opened another store in New York in the space that once housed the underground club CBGB. In 2010, he celebrated his tenth anniversary, and in the early 2010s he launched his U.S.A. fragrance and U.S.A. Boys collection. In 2012, Varvatos joined the cast of reality television show *Fashion Star*. In 2013, he launched an advertising campaign featuring musicians, including Willie Nelson and his two sons.

Spring 2014.

JOAN VASS ▲

BORN New York City, May 19, 1925
DIED New York City, January 6, 2011

AWARDS Smithsonian Institution *Extraordinary Women in Fashion Award*, 1978 • Coty American Fashion Critics' Awards *Special Award (crafted knit fashions)*, 1979 • National Cotton Council *U.S. Cotton Champion Award*, 2001

Joan Vass built her reputation on crochets and handmade or hand-loomed knits, creating imaginative, functional clothes in simple shapes and subtle colors, usually in natural fibers. Retailers and the press recognized her as a highly creative, original designer.

A graduate of the University of Wisconsin, she majored in philosophy, did graduate work in aesthetics,

Designer Joan Vass.

and worked as a curator at the New York Museum of Modern Art and as an editor at art book publisher Harry N. Abrams. Despite having no formal fashion training, she got into designing in the early 1970s when two of her concerns intersected. First, she was bothered by the plight of women with saleable skills but no outlet for them—specifically, women who could not work away from home or did not want to be contained in an office or factory. Second, she was convinced that there was a market for handmade clothing of good quality.

Vass, who had always knitted and crocheted, found a number of women with excellent craft skills, and in 1973 began designing things for them to knit and crochet, selling the articles privately. This enterprise took so much of her time that she wanted to give it up, but was dissuaded by her workers. Then came her first large order from Henri Bendel; other stores followed and she was in business. Her firm was incorporated in 1977. In 1988, Joan Vass USA for Men was introduced, and in 1992 she introduced a jewelry line, Joan Vass Spa.

In addition to Joan Vass New York—higher-priced clothes for men and women—there are Joan Vass boutiques, the moderately priced Joan Vass USA collection, and franchises in Los Angeles, Houston, and New Orleans. Michael Cunningham is the current creative director of the brand.

Spring 1996.

Designer Donatella Versace.

BORN Calabria, Italy, 1955

Donatella Versace (Verr-SAH-chay) was ten years younger than her brother, GIANNI VERSACE, but from early on served as his inspiration, even as a child wearing the clothes he designed for her. When he moved to Florence in the mid-1970s to work in knitwear design, she followed, studying Italian literature at the University of Florence and visiting him on weekends. After graduation, they shared an apartment in Milan—and when he founded his own company in 1978, she continued to serve as both muse and critic. He eventually made her responsible for her own diffusion collection, Versus.

After Gianni's murder in 1997, Donatella managed in three months to produce a creditable ready-to-wear collection. As creative director of the house she has continued to grow, with each successive ready-to-wear and couture collection showing increased confidence and a firmer grasp of her craft. Her work is very much in the Versace mode of bold prints and forthright sexiness—not for the timid but appealing strongly to entertainment figures and others for whom understatement is a foreign word.

The Versace business has always been a family affair, with oldest brother Santo as president; Donatella's husband, Paul Beck, as director of men's wear; and Gianni's one-time companion, Antonio D'Amico, in charge of Versace Sport. The company has expanded into other areas, including skincare, fragrances, table accessories, and even hotels.

(continued)

Spring 2014 haute couture.

In 2008, Donatella was made honorary chairman of London's Fashion Fringe, judging upcoming designer talent. In 2009, she hired Christopher Kane to help revive the Versus brand; he stayed through 2012. In 2011, Versace for H&M launched to huge success after Anna Dello Russo was photographed wearing a studded dress from the line. Donatella is inspired by many people, and in 2012 she made headlines by calling Lady Gaga her muse.

Above: Fall 2013 men's wear.

Left: Spring 2014.

Designer Gianni Versace.

Spring/summer haute couture, 1993.

BORN Calabria, Italy, December 2, 1946
DIED Miami, Florida, July 15, 1997

Thanks to his dressmaker mother, Gianni Versace (GEE-ahh-knee Verr-SAH-chay) was exposed 'to fashion at an early age, though he studied architecture before embarking on a fashion career. He began designing knitwear in Florence, then moved to Milan, where he designed for several prêt-à-porter firms, including Genny and Callaghan. In 1979, he showed for the first time under his own name, a collection of men's wear.

Versace became one of Europe's most popular designers, offering women many options—but always sensuous and sexy. His vivid, far-reaching imagination was fueled by an insatiable curiosity and appetite for knowledge, resulting in bold prints inspired by antiquities, Byzantine mosaics, and in the early 1980s a fabric of metal mesh so soft and pliable it could be sewn by machine. He used that fabric in beautiful, slithery evening dresses worn from California to the Riviera. As a designer he was fearless, using his mistakes to improve and grow. Like ELSA SCHIAPARELLI, he could go over the top into vulgarity, but he also produced clothes of great sophistication and elegance.

Versace also designed for the theater, including ballet costumes for La Scala and for Béjart's *Ballet of the 20th Century*. In 1992, the Fashion Institute of Technology mounted *Signatures*, a retrospective celebrating 15 years of his work.

Versace's murder snatched a vital force from the fashion world. But his business empire has survived and flourished through the efforts of the family team he formed under the creative direction of DONATELLA VERSACE. Versace boutiques around the world sell women's and men's clothes, accessories, knits, leathers, and furs, as well as fragrances for both men and women.

Autumn/winter 1995/1996.

VIKTOR & ROLF

FOUNDED Viktor Horsting and Rolf Snoeren, 1992

AWARDS Festival of Hyères *Young Designers Award*, 1993

Viktor Horsting and Rolf Snoeren studied fashion at the Academy of the Arts in Arnhem, the Netherlands, graduating in 1992. Their brand, Viktor & Rolf, first gained attention in 1993 after winning the prestigious Young Designer Award (*Salon Européen des Jeunes Stylistes*) at the Hyères International Festival of Fashion and Photography (*Hyères Festival International de Mode et de Photographie*).

Viktor & Rolf's first show, in Paris in 1998, featured an "atomic bomb" evening dress collection inspired by mushroom clouds that heralded the arrival of two

Designers Viktor Horsting and Rolf Snoeren with model.

young designers with abundant talent and a gift for attracting press attention. Subsequent shows have earned them a solid reputation for clothes that are both imaginative and wearable. After five couture collections, the designers decided to concentrate on ready-to-wear, which they began showing in March 2000.

Viktor & Rolf designs are sold in avant-garde stores, including Barneys New York, and have been featured in museum and gallery exhibits in cities such as New York, Tokyo, Groningen (the Netherlands), Yokohama (Japan), and Paris. In 2005 the pair released the perfume Flowerbomb, and in 2006 the cologne Antidote. Both were hits. In 2012, Viktor & Rolf released Spicebomb, their second men's fragrance. In 2013, they launched a bridal wear collection.

Viktor & Rolf's signature pieces were featured in a 2008 exhibit at the Barbican Art Gallery in London. The two also wrote and illustrated a book of fairy tales, *Sprookjes*, published in 2009.

Spring 2010.

Spring 2014.

⧗ MADELEINE VIONNET

BORN Aubervilliers, France, June 22, 1876
DIED Paris, March 2, 1975

AWARDS French Government *Légion d'Honneur*
(Legion of Honor), 1929

Designer Madeleine Vionnet.

The Duchess of Windsor in Vionnet dress, 1937.

A towering figure of 20th-century couture, Madeleine
Vionnet (VEE-o-nay) continues to influence fashion.
Her bias technique, cowl and halter necklines, and use
of pleating are familiar to any reputable designer.

The daughter of a police officer, Vionnet began an
apprenticeship in fashion when she was 12, and by 16
was working with a successful dressmaker called Vincent.
By 19 she had married, had a child who died, and was
divorced. At 20 she went to London, where she stayed
five years, working first in a tailor's workroom and then
for CALLOT SOEURS. She worked closely with one of
the sisters there, Madame Gerber, who was considered
even greater than PAUL POIRET and for whom she made
toiles (versions of garments used to test a pattern, usually
using cheap fabrics). In 1907, Vionnet moved to JACQUES
DOUCET, and in 1912 opened her own house, which
closed during World War I. She reopened in 1918 on
Avenue Montaigne, and closed for good in 1940.

Even while working for others, Vionnet advanced
ideas that were not always acceptable to conservative
clients. She eliminated high, boned collars from dresses
and blouses, and claimed to have eliminated corsets
before Poiret. One of couture's greatest technicians,
she invented the modern use of the bias cut, producing
dresses so supple that they eliminated the need for
fastenings. They could be slipped on over the head
and fall back into shape on the body. For even more
suppleness, seams were often stitched with fagoting—a
decorative embroidery where threads are tied together
in an hourglass.

Vionnet did not sketch, but instead draped, cut,
and pinned directly on small-scaled mannequins with
articulated joints. Designs were later translated into
full-size toiles, then into the final material. She probably
chose this method for convenience, as it would have

(continued)

399

been hard for her to achieve her effects as economically or with as little physical effort by any other means.

Vionnet introduced crêpe de Chine, a fine silk previously confined to linings, as a fabric suitable for outerwear—transforming Greek and medieval inspirations into modern, graceful, sensuous clothes. She did not allow herself to become set in her fashion ways, and in 1934 she scrapped a nearly finished collection when she realized that it was out of step with the new romantic mood. She completed an entirely new collection in just two weeks to show on the scheduled date.

Many designers trained with Vionnet. For many years her assistant was Marcelle Chaumont, who later opened her own house. Others included Mad Maltezos, of the House of Mad Carpentier, and JACQUES GRIFFE.

Bright green wool coat and purple belted sheath, 1937.

Spring 2014 haute couture.

Evening dresses, 1938.

A woman of integrity, Vionnet was the enemy of copyists and style pirates. She believed that "to copy is to steal."

Vionnet presented her final collection in 1939. In 2007, with Sophia Kokosalaki as head designer, the House of Vionnet experienced a revival. Though her first collection with the house was distributed at Barneys New York stores across America, she left to start her own line the same year. In 2008, the house hired designer Marc Audibet, who captured Vionnet's mood and art form.

Pale crêpe pajamas, 1931.

ROGER VIVIER 👜

BORN Paris, November 13, 1907
DIED Toulouse, France, October 2, 1998

AWARDS *Neiman Marcus Award*, 1961

Roger Vivier (Roe-ZHAY VIV-e-a) created shoes for over 60 years, from the 1930s—when he opened a workshop in Paris in Place Vendôme—until his death at age 90. To prepare for his métier, he studied drawing and sculpture at l'École des Beaux-Arts and apprenticed at a shoe factory owned by a relative. His shoes—lighthearted and with a spirited sense of fantasy—had a strong structural foundation that reflected his training in sculpture.

Vivier's talent was recognized by ELSA SCHIAPARELLI in 1937, when she commissioned him to design shoes for one of her collections. He soon opened his first boutique, developing a devoted celebrity following that ranged from Princess Margaret and Princess Grace to Elizabeth Taylor, Josephine Baker, and the Rothschilds. He moved to America in the late 1930s and became associated with shoe designer Herman Delman, working with him until 1955 and again from 1992

Above: Designer Roger Vivier.

Left: An evening stilletto from the Christian Dior created by Roger Vivier line, 1958.

to 1994. The shoes were sold at fine retailers such as Bergdorf Goodman and Neiman Marcus.

From 1953 to 1963, Vivier worked in Paris with CHRISTIAN DIOR, with whom he developed the first line of ready-to-wear designer shoes, Christian Dior Created by Roger Vivier. During his time with Dior, Vivier produced myriad exquisite evening shoes—always with refined, streamlined silhouettes and often exuberantly, extravagantly jeweled and embroidered. After Dior died in 1957, Vivier collaborated for many years with YVES SAINT LAURENT and other top couturiers, including BALENCIAGA, COURRÈGES, UNGARO, GRÈS, and RICCI.

In 1963, Vivier opened a boutique that Marlene Dietrich reportedly visited nearly every day and where it was not unusual for a shoe fitting to take two hours. In 1974, he left Paris for a castle in the Dordogne region of France, where he designed shoes for the Japanese market. Vivier's shoes are in the collections of the Metropolitan Museum of Art in New York and the Musée de la Mode et du Costume and Musée des Arts de la Mode in Paris.

Designer Diane von Furstenberg.

BORN Diane Simone Michelle Halfin; Brussels, Belgium, December 31, 1946

AWARDS Council of Fashion Designers of America (CFDA) *Lifetime Achievement Award*, 2005 • *Fashion Walk of Fame*, 2008

Diane von Fürstenberg has had at least three fashion careers. She started in 1971, creating moderately priced dresses of lightweight jersey, then had her own custom shop for a few years on Fifth Avenue, followed by the Diane von Fürstenberg Studio and direct sales on the QVC television network. In 1997, she returned to the mid-range dress business with an updated version of her wrap dress.

Educated in Spain, England, and Switzerland, von Fürstenberg earned a degree in economics from the University of Geneva and moved to America in 1969. She saw a need for affordable, comfortable, fashionable dresses, and decided to try designing. Her first patterns were cut on her dining table, then shipped to a friend in Italy for production. In 1971, she packed her first samples in a suitcase and started showing them to store buyers. Her signature wrap dress, with a surplice top and long sleeves, was an immediate success and made her name.

In 1976, *Newsweek* named her the most marketable designer since CHANEL. Von Fürstenberg says that the wrap dress taught her three essential F's for designing women clothes: that they be "flattering, feminine, and, above all, functional." A perfume followed, as well as a cosmetics line, a shop, home furnishings, and licenses from eyewear to luggage.

Von Fürstenberg left the moderately priced dress market in 1977, but reentered it briefly in 1985 with a collection based on her wrap dress. That was followed

(continued)

Spring 2010.

complete collection of modern, wearable, affordable clothes that appeal to active, vital women of any age.

Von Fürstenberg continues to take on new and exciting projects. In 2003, she teamed up with tennis player Venus Williams and Reebok to create a line of tennis wear. The CFDA, where she is serving her fourth term as president, awarded her its Lifetime Achievement Award in 2005. In 2008, the designer released a limited edition comic book, *Be the Wonder Woman You Can Be*, that features her life story. That same year, von Fürstenberg received a star on the Fashion Walk of Fame in New York. In 2009, a retrospective of her work titled *Diane von Fürstenberg: Journey of a Dress* was curated by ANDRÉ LEON TALLEY in Moscow and later traveled to São Paulo, Brazil, and Beijing, China.

In 2011, she introduced a home collection as well as Diane, her signature fragrance. In 2012, von Fürstenberg created a children's wear collection for GapKids. Diane von Fürstenberg celebrated the 40th anniversary of the brand's iconic wrap dress in 2014, and kicked off the year with its "Journey of a Dress" exhibition in Los Angeles.

Spring 2014.

Designer Diane von Furstenberg, 1972.

by her retailing venture design and marketing studio, and involvement with televised home shopping. In 1994, she became creative planning director for Q², QVC's weekend channel. Her 1997 reincarnation was in collaboration with her daughter-in-law, Alexandra Miller von Fürstenberg, resulting in a redesign of the famous wrap dress in silk jersey with a new body, shorter length, and subtler details. It was part of a

☐ ELLA VON UNWERTH

Photographer Ella Von Unwerth.

BORN Frankfurt, Germany, 1954

Ella Von Unwerth is known for her sexual and provocative photographs. She began her career as a model in Munich at the age of 16, and until 1986 worked under contract for Elite Modeling Agency. During a fashion shoot in Kenya in the 1990s, she took photographs of local children that were published in the French magazine *Jill*—marking the beginning of her career in photography despite her lack of formal training.

Von Unwerth gained fame when she discovered 17-year-old Claudia Schiffer and photographed her in an ad campaign for Guess Jeans that also included Anna Nicole Smith and Eva Herzigova. She has also shot campaigns for CHANEL, Miu Miu (PRADA), LOUIS VUITTON, and H&M, as well as editorials for magazines such as *Vogue* and *Vanity Fair*. Von Unwerth's photographs show her female subjects in sexy, wild, provocative, powerful poses that narrate visually arresting stories. She is one of *TIME* magazine's 100 Fashion Icons.

An accomplished filmmaker and video director, Von Unwerth has shot commercials for the television show *Sex and the City* and brands like Clinique, Revlon, and Victoria's Secret, as well as music videos for performers such as Beyoncé, Christina Aguilera, and Duran Duran. Several books of her photos have been published, including *Snaps* (1994), *Wicked* (1998), *Couples* (1999), and *Omahyra & Boyd* (2005). The publication of *Revenge* in 2003 led to exhibits of her work in New York, Paris, Moscow, and Amsterdam. She has also shot album covers for Rihanna, Janet Jackson, and Britney Spears, among others.

In 2012, a Von Unwerth exhibit titled *Do Not Disturb!* appeared at the Michael Hoppen Gallery in London, showcasing highly stylized, brightly colored images of femme fatales.

DIANA VREELAND

BORN Diana Dalziel; Paris, July 29, 1903
DIED New York City, August 22, 1989

AWARDS French Government *Chevalier of the National Order of Merit*, 1970; *Légion d'Honneur (Legion of Honor)*, 1976 • Lord & Taylor *Dorothy Shaver "Rose" Award*, 1976 • Parsons School of Design *Honorary Doctor of Fine Arts Degree*, 1977

For nearly five decades, Diana Vreeland was a powerful influence on America's fashion consciousness, first as a fashion editor and last as a museum consultant. Born in Paris to an American mother and English father, raised in a milieu saturated with fashion and the arts, she was by both nature and nurture ideally suited for her eventual vocation. As a child she was exposed to extraordinary people and events—Sergei Diaghilev, Vaslav Nijinsky, Ida Rubinstein, and Vernon and Irene Castle were all guests in her parents' apartment, and in 1911 she went to London for the coronation of George V. Her family moved to America at the outbreak of World War I.

Married in 1924 to Thomas Reed Vreeland, she accompanied her husband as his job took him to Albany, New York, then London, then back to New York City in 1937. The same year, at the invitation of CARMEL SNOW, she went to work for *Harper's Bazaar*. There she first wrote *Why Don't You?*, a column that generated suggestions such as, "Why don't you . . . turn your child into an infanta for a fancy-dress party?" After six months she became fashion editor, working closely with Snow and art director ALEXEY BRODOVITCH to make *Harper's Bazaar* an exciting, influential publication. In 1962, she joined *Vogue*, first as an associate editor, then editor-in-chief—a position she held until 1971.

After 1971, Vreeland became a consulting editor at *Vogue* and began a new career as a consultant

Editor Diana Vreeland.

to the Costume Institute of the Metropolitan Museum of Art. There she mounted a series of outstanding exhibits such as BALENCIAGA, *American Women of Style*, *The Glory of Russian Costume*, *Vanity Fair*, and *Man and the Horse*.

Vreeland, who as a child felt like an ugly duckling, reinvented herself as an elegant, completely individual woman with a strong personal style: jet black hair, heavily rouged cheeks, and bright red lips. For day and small dinners she dressed in simple uniforms—sweaters and skirts or sweaters and pants—but for big evenings she appeared in dramatic gowns.

FOUNDED 1853

Louis Vuitton (LOO-e VOO-tawn) was a carpenter's son who at the age of 16 apprenticed for luggage designer Monsieur Marechal in Paris. In 1854, he started his own business making luxury luggage for wealthy Parisian travelers. He also made luggage for aristocratic families of the court of Empress Eugenie of Paris, solidifying his company's luxury status.

In 1858, the company created the first flat trunk luggage, featuring his signature grey "Trianon" canvas. Until then, most trunks were round and difficult to stack on railroad cars. Customers found the flat trunks convenient and elegant. Vuitton won the bronze medal at the Paris Exposition Universelle in 1867 and the gold in 1889. In 1888, he introduced the "Damier" canvas, which was branded with the first Vuitton trademark logo, "Marque L. Vuitton Déposée."

After Louis Vuitton died in 1892, his son George took the company to global status. The years spanning 1893 to 1936 are considered the brand's golden age. Vuitton first displayed products in America at the 1893 World's Fair in Chicago. The bags were widely copied, so George Vuitton created the famous "Monogram" canvas with the trademark LV logo, as well as prints inspired by the Victorian era and Japonisme, a Japanese-influenced style of French art that was very popular in Paris.

In the 1930s, Vuitton began producing ladies handbags. In 1936, when George died, his son Gaston-Louis took Vuitton into a new age. In 1959, the company brought back the Monogram canvas with a new method of coating that allowed the fabric to breathe while keeping it hard and strong. The coating is still used on Vuitton bags.

By the 1970s, the Louis Vuitton brand was a symbol of luxury and refinement. A store was opened in Tokyo, and by 1980 Asia accounted for almost half of the company's revenues. In 1983, Vuitton became involved in the America's Cup, selecting challengers for the main

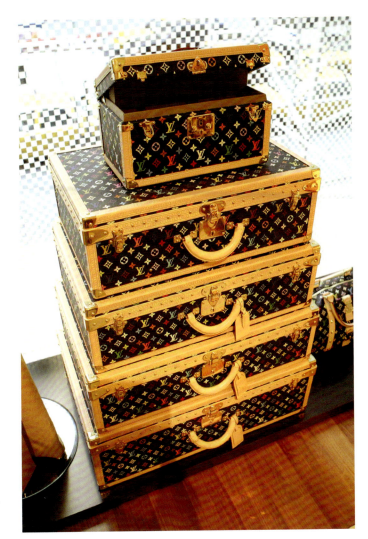

Designs by Louis Vuitton.

yachting race with the Louis Vuitton Cup. The world of Vuitton changed dramatically in 1987, when it merged with Möet Hennessy to form the LVMH conglomerate. MARC JACOBS was its creative director from 1997 to 2013, and helped make Louis Vuitton the world's largest luxury brand by using artists such as Yayoi Kusama to design its products, and celebrities such as Lil' Kim to sell them. In 2013, the company announced that NICOLAS GHESQUIÈRE would be its next creative director.

KAREN WALKER

BORN New Zealand

AWARDS *Prix de Marie Claire* Best Creative Talent, 2007

Karen Walker, New Zealand's premier fashion designer, presented her first collection in Sydney, Australia, in 1998. But it took nearly a decade before her American debut, which was at New York Fashion Week in 2006.

Walker's collections can be found at 250 stores worldwide, including three flagship boutiques in New Zealand and one in Taipei, Taiwan. Walker's designs have been featured in *Vogue*, *Teen Vogue*, *i-D*, *ELLE*, *W*, and *Nylon*, and she is known for mixing seemingly disparate styles—such as combining Victorian tailoring and ruffles with streetwear in a way that plays on

Designer Karen Walker.

conventional notions of masculinity and femininity. Walker calls her work a "celebration of the anti-It girl" and draws inspiration from, among others, Amelia Earhart, Ally Sheedy in *The Breakfast Club*, Diane Keaton in *Annie Hall*, and 1930s comic book heroines leading double lives. Her eclectic, hybrid designs radiate youthful exuberance.

In addition to her main women's wear collections, Walker designs men's wear, jewelry, eyewear, paint colors, and a footwear collaboration with Beau Coops. Through Anthropologie and Myer, in Australia, she launched a diffusion line called Hi There from Karen Walker, and in 2013 she collaborated with UNIQLO on a children's wear collection. Other recent collaborations include t-shirts with Britain's House of Holland, makeup with Boots 17, and a pop-up (temporary) concept store in New York City called The Den.

Walker appeared in the 2005 book *Sample: 100 Fashion Designers, 10 Curators*, which profiles the 100 most promising designers to emerge in the first half of the 2000s, as chosen by ten of the industry's top editors, stylists, designers, curators, and writers. She also appeared in the book *Fashion Now 2*, which presents what *i-D* considers the world's 160 most important designers. Walker's clothes have been worn by Kelly Osbourne, Björk, Claire Danes, Jennifer Lopez, Anne Hathaway, Zooey Deschanel, and Rihanna.

Left: Fall 2005.
Right: Fall 2007.

Designer Alexander Wang.

BORN San Francisco, 1984

AWARDS Ecco Domani Fashion Foundation *Emerging Designer Award*, 2008 • Council of Fashion Designers of America (CFDA) *Fashion Fund Prize*, 2008; *Swarovski Award for Accessories*, 2010; *Accessories Designer of the Year*, 2011 • *GQ Menswear Designer of the Year, 2011*

By his sophomore year at Parsons School of Design in New York, Alexander Wang was already designing out of his dormitory for the first collection of women's wear—primarily knits—on his eponymous label. To build his client base, he used to carry suitcases full of clothing samples door to door. In 2007, he launched his first complete women's collection, which he sold to more than 150 boutiques and retail stores around the world. As the 2008 recipient of the CFDA's Fashion Fund Prize, Wang received $200,000 in capital for his next project, topping off his quick ascension from dorm-room designing. Wang's milieu has always been what is known as the

Spring 2014.

⬛ ALEXANDER WANG

"model off duty" look—comfortable outfits that not only appear classic and chic but also betray a thrown-together sort of irreverence. A typical Wang outfit might comprise an oversized gray blazer with sleeves rammed up to the elbows over a white tank top and shredded cutoffs. Wang says his clothes project a sense of ease and confidence, "like you just rolled out of bed and threw something on."

In 2008, he launched a shoe collection and a lower-priced diffusion line, T, that features languid t-shirts and tanks with stretched arm and neck holes. His footwear line marks a sharp diversion from his trademark style, offering rough leather booties, heels topped with fringe, and hints of fetish fashion supplied by metal piercing rings. In 2012, Wang was named creative director of BALENCIAGA, taking over from NICOLAS GHESQUIÈRE, and in 2014 he was nominated once again for the CFDA Accessories Designer of the Year award.

Spring 2014.

VERA WANG 👗

Designer Vera Wang.

BORN New York City, June 27, 1949

AWARDS Council of Fashion Designers of America (CFDA) *Womenswear Designer of the Year*, 2005; *Geoffrey Beene Lifetime Achievement Award*, 2013

After a lifetime focused on fashion—as a child dancer, a teenage ice skating star who designed her own costumes, a *Vogue* editor for 16 years, and design director for accessories at RALPH LAUREN—Vera Wang discovered her calling. She was getting married and could find nothing to wear. So in 1990, she established her own bridal wear business. Today her name is synonymous with the words *wedding dress.*

Wang's style is sleek, modern, and sophisticated—the opposite of the sugar-puff dresses that make brides look like the figurines on top of wedding cakes. She has strong ideas about what works: weightless clothes, armholes that add grace, and enough internal support to make women feel secure while being totally comfortable. Evening clothes were a logical extension of her design philosophy; her business has also expanded into ready-to-wear, furs, shoes, china and glassware, sheets and towels, eyewear, and fragrances.

In 2005, Wang launched a playful line of clothing and accessories called the Lavender Label, and in 2007 she launched a lower-priced collection, Simply Vera, sold exclusively at Kohl's stores across America. Her lines at Kohl's now include a makeup collection and a juniors collection called Princess Vera Wang. In 2009, Wang launched Vera Wang Lavender Footwear with Brown Shoes, and in 2010 she launched a bedding collection with Revman International. The White by Vera Wang collection for David's Bridal debuted in 2011 in conjunction with a collection of engagement rings and wedding bands exclusively for Zales. In 2012, she opened her first Asian flagship store, Vera Wang Bridal Korea, and launched Black for Vera Wang, a collection of tuxedo rentals for Men's Wearhouse.

In 2001, the coffee table book *Vera Wang on Weddings* was published, providing all the information anyone would ever need about the practicalities of getting married. Wang's bridal designs have been worn by Chelsea Clinton, Alicia Keys, and Hillary Duff, and her other clothes have won a following with stylish celebrities such as Sharon Stone, Holly Hunter, Meg Ryan, and Jane Fonda.

Above: Spring 2014 bridal.

Left: Spring 2009 bridal.

BRUCE WEBER 📷

BORN Greensburg, Pennsylvania, March 29, 1946

AWARDS *CLIO Award for Recognition in Apparel*, 1986 • ICP *Infinity Award*, 2005

Bruce Weber participated in his first group photo show in 1973 and has been working steadily ever since. Scoring his first solo show just a year later, he has gone on to shoot for some of the biggest names in fashion, including Abercrombie & Fitch, CALVIN KLEIN, and RALPH LAUREN.

Weber attended a number of schools, including Denison University, New York University, and The New School for Social Research, where he studied with famed Austrian photographer Lisette Model. He is credited with giving commercial photography a previously unseen artistic bent, and his work has greatly influenced the tone of fashion photography—setting a precedent that allows photographers to interpret the work of designers and portray it in their own way.

Weber started shooting ads and commercials in the late 1970s for clients such as Lauren and Klein, and his racy work immediately created controversy. Weber is known for photographing models—often in couples or groups—in various stages of undress. One of his most famous shots is of Brazilian Olympic pole vaulter Tom Hintnaus in white Calvin Klein briefs. Weber's work is usually in black and white or sepia tones, though he has used color for some projects.

Nearly two dozen books of Weber's photographs have been published, and they are in the permanent collections of the photography division of the city of Paris as well as the Victoria and Albert Museum in London. Weber has also directed music videos,

Photographer Bruce Weber.

produced ten films, shot album covers, and had his work appear in *Vogue, Teen Vogue, Harper's Bazaar, Vanity Fair, Rolling Stone,* and *ELLE.*

In 2003, Weber put his years of fashion experience to work with Weberbilt, a line of t-shirts, board shorts, windbreakers, and other casual wear sold exclusively in London and Miami. In 2009, Weber was honored by the Gordon Parks Foundation, and the next year his photos of Miami's Haitian community were featured at the city's Museum of Contemporary Art in an exhibit called *Haiti/Little Haiti.*

Designer Stuart Weitzman.

STUART WEITZMAN

BORN Long Island, New York, July 29, 1941

AWARDS Ernst and Young *Entrepreneur of the Year*, 1999 • *Footwear News Hall of Fame*, 2001 • Footwear Plus *Designer of the Year (ladies' dress shoes)* • Footwear News *Lifetime Achievement Award*, 2012

Though he graduated from the Wharton School of the University of Pennsylvania with a degree in finance, Stuart Weitzman had shoes in his blood—his father was a shoe manufacturer—and went into the family business. As an apprentice working alongside traditional craftsmen, he learned every step of production and became a skilled patternmaker with a broad understanding of footwear engineering.

Weitzman's designs range from the highest-heeled stilettos in exotic materials—lace, silk, brocade, even platinum or 24-karat gold—to shoes made of cork, bamboo, or calfskin. Boots, moccasins, and sneakers are also part of his design vocabulary, in an unusually wide range of over 50 sizes. Each pair of his shoes goes through 80 craftsmen during production, which takes six to seven weeks. His shoes are the choice of celebrities from Calista Flockhart to Laura Bush—perhaps because he believes so strongly that "a beautiful shoe is useless unless it feels as wonderful as it looks." He has opened retail shops in selected cities across America and in Switzerland.

In 2008, Weitzman created the stunning "Retro Rose" shoe, which was adorned with $1 million worth of

Top: Iridescent shoe by Stuart Weitzman.
Bottom: Weitzman's "retro rose" shoe.

diamonds and worn by director/producer Diablo Cody at the Academy Awards. In 2013, Weitzman created the shoes for Beyoncé's *Mrs. Carter Show* world tour.

VIVIENNE WESTWOOD ⬥

Designer Vivienne Westwood.

BORN Tintwistle, England, April 8, 1941

AWARDS British Fashion Council *British Designer of the Year*, 1990, 1991; British Government *Most Excellent Order of the British Empire*, 1992; *Dame Commander of the Most Excellent Order of the British Empire*

Spring 2014.

Vivienne Westwood became involved in fashion around 1970 through her association with Malcolm McLaren, who later became the manager of the Sex Pistols. At the time she was working as a teacher, having left Harrow Art School after just one term. She went into business with McLaren, and together they owned shops in London on King's Road and in the West End.

Westwood belongs to the anti-fashion branch of design exemplified by Comme des Garçons, though her approach is totally different. Sometimes beautiful and sometimes ridiculous—but never dull—her clothes fiercely reject polite standards of dress. They are often inspired by London street life, with wild swings in influences—from the leather and rubber fetishism, punk rock, and sadomasochism of the 1970s to the New Romantic and pirate looks of the early 1980s. For fall 1994, Westwood showed bustles, placing fanny pillows under just about everything and proclaiming the rear the new erogenous zone. Despite weak finances, she has regularly shown in Paris, and her anarchic view

of dressing has had a considerable influence on other designers both in England and around the world.

Westwood was also a professor of design at the University of Berlin. Her designs, both the earliest and the most recent, were shown in the *London Fashion* exhibit at New York's Fashion Institute of Technology in 2001–02. In 2004, the National Gallery of Australia exhibited a major retrospective of her career. In 2011, she was featured in the Canadian television documentary *Vivienne Westwood's London*, and in 2013 she designed the uniforms for Virgin Atlantic.

Westwood is a strong political activist who often displays her political opinions on her clothing and in her advertisements.

Spring 2007.

414

Above: Designer Edward Wilkerson.
Right: Lafayette 148 Resort 2014.

BORN New York

Edward Wilkerson, the design director behind the bridge line Lafayette 148, became interested in fabrics and how they fit the body when he was ten. As a teenager, he attended the Art and Design High School in Manhattan, and in the summer of 1984 found a job at ANNE KLEIN, where he worked under DONNA KARAN and LOUIS DELL'OLIO. He went on to study fashion at Parsons School of Design while working for Anne Klein, and after graduation landed a three-year stint at CALVIN KLEIN. Wilkerson then accepted a position as senior designer for DONNA KARAN, where he stayed for nine years. In 1998, Wilkerson joined Lafayette 148, which had been established only two years before by company president Deirdre Quinn.

Bridge collections had never before been considered fashionable. But Wilkerson has brought Lafayette 148 solidly into fashion's middle ground. The company's main goal had been to design clothing for working women, but Wilkerson sought to enhance and celebrate women's bodies, not hide or apologize for them. Producing clothes that range in sizes from 0 to 16, he

✤ EDWARD WILKERSON

designs for petite and plus-size customers with equal attention. Lafayette 148 is the best-selling label in Salon Z, the plus-size department at Saks Fifth Avenue.

Some of Wilkerson's more extravagant designs and his forays into high-end fashion have been inspired by his travels to Africa and Indonesia. Inspired by costumes from around the world, he loves exotic textiles. Much of his palette is also defined by landscapes, and range from amber to the rich blues of the sea and sky. Wilkerson is also known for appearing at trunk shows and presenting collections in cities across America, which allows him to receive feedback directly from customers. Wilkerson's vision of fashion has attracted a celebrity clientele, including Oprah Winfrey, Diane Sawyer, Queen Latifah, and Meryl Streep.

MATTHEW WILLIAMSON

Above: Designer Matthew Williamson.
Right: Spring 2014.

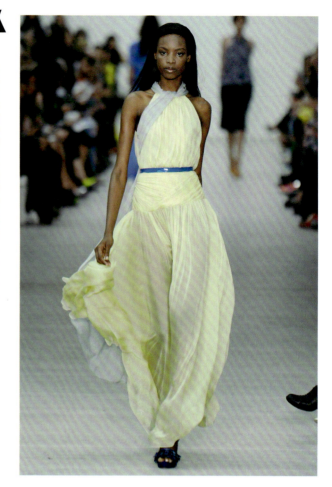

BORN Manchester, England, October 23, 1971

AWARDS *ELLE Young Designer of the Year*, 2004 • Moët & Chandon *Fashion Tribute Award*, 2005

After college in Manchester, Matthew Williamson attended London's Central Saint Martins College of Arts and Design, graduating in 1996. Between then and 1998, he worked briefly for ZANDRA RHODES and Monsoon and traveled to India to set up his business. He showed his first collection under his own label in September 1997.

His small, focused collections present modern, easy

Fall 2008.

pieces, colorful and intricately detailed, appealing to adventurous customers confident of their taste—such as Madonna and Sarah Jessica Parker. For spring 2002, Williamson introduced a small group of separates for men in the same spirit as his women's clothes, and a range of scented candles. His clothes and candles can be found at specialty stores such as Henri Bendel, Barneys, and Kirna Zabête in New York.

Williamson opened his first flagship store in London in 2004. In 2005, he was appointed creative director of PUCCI, where he stayed three years, leaving in 2008 to focus on his own label's ventures.

A self-titled book was published in 2010, and in 2012 Williamson celebrated his 15th year in business by producing the film *XV*, which stars friends of the brand. In 2013, Williamson launched shoe and bag collections.

Harry Winston designs, 2012.

BORN New York City, March 1, 1896

DIED December 28, 1978

Harry Winston grew up around jewelry—his parents owned a jewelry business in Manhattan. After Winston's mother died when he was just seven, his father relocated the family to Los Angeles. From an early age, Winston had a natural talent for finding jewelry at low cost and selling it. In 1914, the family returned to New York, and at the age of 19, Winston opened the Premier Diamond Company with $2,000 of his own money. He began using his keen eye to buy and sell on the New York Diamond Exchange.

Winston's company thrived after he discovered that precious jewelry was sold at estate sales for a fraction of its worth. He started finding true treasures, including the collection of Arabella Huntington—once the richest woman in America—which Winston was able to acquire for $2 million. Another famous find was the Baldwin Collection, which included a 39-carat

emerald-cut diamond. Its acquisition brought Winston national attention.

In 1932, he closed Premier Diamond Company and opened Harry Winston Incorporated. His legendary acquisitions included a 726-carat Jonker diamond in 1935, a 970-carat Sierra Leone diamond in 1972, and the Hope Diamond, which was purchased from the estate of Evelyn Walsh Mclean for $1 million. Winston's customers included celebrities and some of the richest people in the world. Richard Burton once bought a 69-carat diamond from Winston for Elizabeth Taylor.

Winston was a quiet, gifted man who lived in New York with his wife Edna and their two sons, Ronald and Bruce. After his death in 1978, Edna took over the business, and when she died in 1986, it was handed over to their sons. After butting heads for a decade and a half, Ronald bought out Bruce in 2000, in partnership with Fenway Partners Investment Equity. Fenway cashed out four years later, and Aber Diamond Corporation is the current owner of Harry Winston.

ANNA WINTOUR

Editor Anna Wintour.

BORN London, November 3, 1949

One of the best-known voices in media, Anna Wintour began her fashion career at the age of 15 as a shop girl at a Biba boutique in London. She never attended college, and instead entered a training program at Harrods. After toiling in retail for several years, she began her career in fashion journalism in 1970, when she became an editorial assistant at *Harper's Bazaar* and *Queen*. She moved up the editorial ladder, and in 1974 moved to New York where in1975, she was named junior fashion editor of *Harper's Bazaar*. But she left less than a year later.

Wintour then became fashion editor of the short-lived women's magazine *Viva*. She was there for two years before it folded, and in 1980 succeeded Elsa Klensch as the fashion editor at the women's magazine *Savvy*. Wintour then had a brief stint at *New York* magazine before taking the position of creative director at *Vogue* in 1983. In 1986, she returned to London to head British *Vogue*.

After two years in London, Wintour was named editor-in-chief of American *Vogue*. She has raised the magazine's profile and brought in cutting-edge photographers like ANNIE LEIBOVITZ, STEVEN MEISEL, and IRVING PENN.

A perfectionist in even her signature bob and clothing, many have called Wintour icy, rigid, and difficult to work with. In 2003, Wintour's former assistant Lauren Weisberger wrote the scathing roman à clef *The Devil Wears Prada*. Weisberger denied that the book—later made into a film—was about her former boss, but the novel nevertheless cemented Wintour's difficult reputation.

During her tenure at *Vogue*, Wintour has helped foster the careers of several major talents, including MARC JACOBS, ALEXANDER MCQUEEN, and THOM BROWNE. Committed to discovering new talent, in 2003 she partnered with the Council of Fashion Designers of America (CFDA) to create the CFDA/*Vogue* Fashion Fund, an annual celebration of up and coming designers. Honorees have included ALEXANDER WANG, Trovata, and PROENZA SCHOULER.

In 2009, *The September Issue* debuted at the Sundance Film Festival. The feature-length documentary chronicles the making of *Vogue*'s September 2007 issue. The film is not a straightforward profile of Wintour, but rather a behind the scenes look at the magazine and the world of haute couture.

In 2012, rumors swirled that President Obama was considering appointing Wintour as the U.S. ambassador to France or Britain. To retain her, CONDÉ NAST made Wintour artistic director of the company's entire portfolio of magazines in 2013. She maintains her titles at *Vogue* and *Teen Vogue*.

⚱ CHARLES FREDERICK WORTH

BORN Lincolnshire, England, October 13, 1825
DIED Paris, March 10, 1895

The founder of the house that became the world's longest-running fashion dynasty got his first job when he was 11 and worked for a number of London drapers (dealers in cloth or clothing) before moving to Paris in 1845. There Charles Frederick Worth took a job at a shop that sold fabrics, shawls, and mantles, and persuaded it to open a department of made-up dress models, which he designed. He was the first to present clothes on live models, using his young French wife as one. Worth's fashions were shown at the 1851 Great Exhibition in London and the 1855 Exposition Universelle in Paris. In 1858, Worth opened his own couture house on Rue de la Paix with his business partner Otto Bobergh, but it closed in 1870 at the outset of the Franco-Prussian War. In 1871, Worth reestablished his own couture business, Maison Worth, without his business partner, and maintained its fashion leadership for 80 years.

Worth was court dressmaker to Empress Eugénie of France

WORTH. -- Photographie Nadar.

Designer Charles Frederick Worth.

Silk dress, 1872.

and Empress Elizabeth of Austria. He also dressed the ladies of European courts and society women of Europe and America. A virtual fashion dictator, he required his customers—except for Eugénie and her court—to come to him instead of going to their homes, as had been the custom. He was an excellent businessman, was the first couturier to sell his designs to be copied in England and America, and was widely copied by others without his permission. He was the first to show a collection of clothing, and he showed them on live models. He was also the first to sell his deigns by putting on a fashion show.

Worth's designs were known for their opulence, meticulous fit, lavish use of fabrics, and elaborate ornamentation of frills, ribbons, lace, braid, and tassels. Dubbed the "Father of Haute Couture," Worth was not only the first professional designer of women's apparel, but also the first to achieve international fame as one. He was a vehement promoter of French-made textiles and is credited with inventing designs that used them, including the crinoline (a petticoat made of horsehair

(continued)

fabric) and the bustle. He also introduced a unique take on the décolleté neckline in which a courtly mantle hung from the shoulders. He innovated what is now known as the princess gown—a waistless dress that hangs straight in the front while draping in full pleats in the back—and offered the first tailored suits for women. As a craftsman, he had a formidable ability for combining different pattern pieces. Worth's designs were influenced by high art, most notably the paintings of Van Dyke, Gainsborough, and Velasquez. He enjoyed his success and lived in a grand manner.

After his death in 1895, the House of Worth continued under the leadership of his sons Jean-Philippe and Gaston, then his grandson Jean-Charles, and finally his great-grandsons Roger and Maurice. When Roger retired in 1952, Maurice took over, but in 1954 sold the house to PAQUIN. A London wholesale house continued under the Worth name until the 1970s. Parfums Worth was established in 1900 and continues today with Je Reviens, its best-known fragrance.

In 2001, a Worth court gown with train sold at auction in New York for $101,500, a world auction record. It had been worn by Elizabeth Washington Lewis, the great-great-granddaughter of George Washington's sister.

Evening dress, House of Worth, 1925.

Top: President Obama and First Lady, Michelle Obama, in Jason Wu, 2009.

Bottom: Spring 2014.

BORN Taipei, Taiwan, 1983

AWARDS Fashion Group International *Rising Star Award for Ready-to-Wear*, 2008 • Council of Fashion Designers of America (CFDA) *Swarovski Award for Womenswear*, 2010

One of the youngest successful designers in the industry, Jason Wu is considered by many to be a prodigy. Always backed by his parents, who ran an import-export business, his family moved Wu to Vancouver, Canada, at the age of nine to receive a better education. Within a year, Wu had learned to sew, pattern, and sketch, and by the time he was 14 he was studying sculpture in Tokyo. He spent his senior year of high school studying in Paris, and after that attended Parsons School of Design for three and a half years, but quit to intern at NARCISO RODRIGUEZ.

In 2006, with financial help from his parents and money he had saved since becoming a freelance designer at 16, Wu started his own label. Today he sells women's wear, resort wear, eyewear, and handbags. His clothing has been called ladylike, and features hourglass figures with nipped-in waists and floral prints. His influences include photographer RICHARD AVEDON and couturiers JACQUES FATH and CHARLES JAMES. Wu's clothes are sold at stores such as Bergdorf Goodman, Neiman Marcus, Saks Fifth Avenue, Jeffrey in Atlanta, and Ikram in Chicago. He is also creative director of Fashion Royalty, a line of high-end designer fashion dolls sold at FAO Schwarz.

In 2008, Ikram asked Wu to design a sparkly evening gown for Michelle Obama. On January 20, 2009, to Wu's surprise, Obama wore his creation to her husband's Inaugural Ball. It put Wu on the map. The white one-strap gown was decorated with tiny flowers and Swarovski crystals, and represented youth and change. It received rave reviews, and in 2010 Michelle Obama donated it to the First Ladies Collection at the Smithsonian. When Barack Obama was reelected in 2012, Michelle Obama surprised and delighted audiences at the 2013 Inaugural Ball by wearing Wu a second time. The gown was a ruby red chiffon with burnt-out cut velvet appliqués.

Wu's 2012 line for Target featured lots of pleating, bows, nipped-in waists, and other signature details, and sold out within hours. In 2013, Wu became creative director of Hugo Boss's women's wear line. He also recently collaborated with artist Nate Lowman on a limited edition t-shirt to benefit ACRIA, an organization that transforms and strengthens the lives of people with AIDS.

Designer Jason Wu.

YOHJI YAMAMOTO ⬛

BORN Yokohama, Japan, circa 1943

AWARDS *Mainichi Fashion Award*, 1986, 1994 • Japanese Government *Shiju-hosho (Medal of Honor)*, 2004 • French Government *Officier l'Order National du Merite*, 2005; *Commandeur dans l'Ordre des Arts t des Lettres*, 2011 • Council of Fashion Designers of America (CFDA) *International Award*, 1999

Yohji Yamamoto (Ya-ma-MO-toe) is a member of the Japanese avant-garde that includes REI KAWAKUBO and ISSEY MIYAKE. Although often called a "designers' designer," he is not as famous or influential as many of his contemporaries, possibly because his ideas are technically complicated and hard to copy. One of the rare true originals, Yamamoto experiments with technological fabrics such as neoprene, blending them with active sports looks in his own color palette and dimensions. Oversize clothes and a playful diversity of textures are his signature, along with asymmetrical hems and collars, holes, and torn edges. He likes surprise details: an unexpected pocket, a lapel that turns into a long, flowing shawl, and a new placement of buttons.

A graduate of Keio University, Yamamoto studied fashion at Tokyo's Bunka Fashion Institute under Chie Kolke, who had attended l'École de la Chambre Syndicale de la Couture Parisienne in Paris with YVES SAINT LAURENT. From 1966 to 1968, he followed the standard course, studying all aspects of the clothing industry; by 1972, he had his own company. He showed his first collection in Tokyo in 1976. In 1981, he established himself in France with a boutique in Paris. In 2003, his Y-3 line debuted and he

Spring 2014.

Designer Yohji Yamamoto.

incorporated it with adidas. Since then, he has shown designs for both men and women at the Paris prêt-à-porter collections.

In 2008, the Yohji Yamamoto Fund for Peace was established in conjunction with the Chinese People's Association for Friendship with Foreign Countries (CPAFFC), which each year awards an emerging Chinese designer a two-year scholarship to a fashion college in Japan or Europe.

In 2009, with more than $65 million in debt, Yamamoto's company filed for bankruptcy. But Integral Corp, a Tokyo-based firm, helped bring it out of debt by 2010. In 2010, the designer's autobiographical book *Yohji Yamamoto: My Dear Bomb,* was published, and in 2011 a retrospective of his work opened at the Victoria and Albert Museum in London.

In 2013, Yamamoto relaunched his Yohji Homme and Yohji Senses fragrances, and Y-3 and adidas celebrated ten years of the Super Position tennis shoe.

Y-3 Fall 2009 men's wear.

Designer Yeohlee.

BORN Yeohlee Teng; Penang, Malaysia, circa 1955

AWARDS Cooper-Hewitt *National Design Award (fashion)*, 2004

At the age of nine, Yeohlee (Yee-EWW-lee) convinced her mother to let her enroll in a patternmaking class. There was no ready-to-wear in Malaysia—clothes were made at home or by seamstresses and tailors—and she was dissatisfied with what her mother produced from English patterns. At 18, she went to New York to study at Parsons School of Design and two years later sold her first five-piece collection to Henri Bendel. She founded her own company in 1981.

Her work is sparse, often dramatic, and characterized by clean lines and geometric forms. The clothes are also comfortable and flattering, cut to allow the wearer to move with easy elegance. Yeohlee designs a complete collection but is most admired for her coats, long and short. Though her clothes are expensive, she feels that the timeless quality of their designs, combined with superior fabrics and workmanship, make them long-term investments. They have attracted a loyal following.

Yeohlee's designs have appeared in numerous exhibits, including at the Museum of the City of New York and

Massachusetts Institute of Technology, where they were featured with designers such as GIORGIO ARMANI, GIANFRANCO FERRÉ, CLAUDE MONTANA, and ISSEY MIYAKE. They have also been shown at the Victoria and Albert in London and at the Museum of Fashion in Paris, and are in the permanent costume collection of the Metropolitan Museum of Art in New York.

In 2001, Yeohlee had a show at the Museum at the Fashion Institute of Technology in New York called *Yeohlee: Supermodern Style*. In 2003, she published *Yeohlee: Work*, a book exploring the parallels between architecture and clothing design. In 2005, her work was included in the *New China Chic* exhibit at the Kennedy Center for the Performing Arts in Washington, D.C. The Museum at FIT featured Yeohlee's work again in its 2006 *Love and War* exhibit. In 2013, she was honored by Kent State and inducted into the school's Hall of Fame.

Resort 2014.

CHRISTINA YU 👜

BORN Hong Kong

Since 1997, Christina Yu has been creating accessories under the name Ipa-Nima that elegantly fuse unique materials, vivid color schemes, and inventive ideas. Born in Hong Kong, Yu is a style icon in Vietnam—her design home base—where her handbags are legendary. A litigator by trade, Yu started freelancing as a fashion editor for *City* magazine. She attended fashion shows in Paris and Milan, and always picked up on new trends. After moving to Vietnam, Yu was highly impressed by the workmanship of the artisans there, and learned that there were a lot of tailors but not many handbag designers.

Yu began creating private label work for designers such as Anteprima and Shanghai Toi, and decided to create her own label. She chose family-owned and -operated workshops to help make her accessories in Vietnam. A friend suggested that Yu name her company

Designer Christina Yu.

Ipa-Nima because the vibrant colors and unique embellishments of her bags are inspired by imaginative themes, ranging from a Moroccan sunset to the journey of an exiled geisha to the sensual cyber adventures of movie character *Barbarella* and beyond.

Yu's first show was held at a Christmas bazaar and was very successful. Her handbags use all types of trims, beadwork, and hardware—from brass to buffalo horn—and are unusual for Vietnamese consumers. Ipa-Nima now sells to boutiques and retail outlets all over the world, and the bags have graced the covers of *Vogue*, *Cosmopolitan*, *Harper's Bazaar*, and *TIME*.

Ipa-Nima actively supports the charities Know One, Teach One and Operation Smile. Fans of the brand's handbags include Prince Andrew (the Duke of York), Toni Braxton, Kelly Osbourne, and Hillary Clinton.

Ipa-Nima handbag by Christina Yu.

Designer David Yurman.

Top: David Yurman jewelry collection.

Bottom: David Yurman silver ID bracelet with braided details.

BORN New York City, October 12, 1942

David Yurman's career began in high school, where he sold small sculptures in the cafeteria. At 16, he was introduced to Cuban welder and sculptor Ernesto Gonzales. Sculpture became Yurman's outlet and he began apprenticing under renowned sculptors Jacques Lipshitz and Theodore Rozack. He attended New York University but left after his freshman year to hitchhike to California and make his way to a beatnik colony. In the late 1960s, he moved back to New York to work with Hans Van de Bovenkamp and met painter Sybil Kleinrock. Yurman created a sculptural piece of jewelry for her that she wore to an art opening, where the gallery owner asked if it was for sale. In 1979, Yurman and Kleinrock married, and in 1980 they launched their company David Yurman.

In 1983, Yurman created his iconic cable bracelet—a twisted silver cord with gemstones at the end. The bracelet became the foundation for all of Yurman's pieces.

The company offers jewelry for both men and women, watches, eyewear, and a fragrance. It made history when it was the first to set diamonds in sterling silver.

The business has grown to include the couple's son Evan, who is design director for the men's wear collection. He is a blacksmith and uses those skills along with a vast array of collected inspirations such as Greek coins and Japanese swords. In 2013, David Yurman men's wear created the Meteorite collection, made from 4 billion-year-old bibeon meteorite.

David Yurman continues to intrigue its clients and has a celebrity following, including Brad Pitt and Angelina Jolie. Supermodels Kate Moss, Gisele Bündchen, Jon Kortajarena, and Joan Smalls have appeared in the company's ad campaigns. In 2010, David Yurman opened a flagship two-story store in New York City called "The Townhouse," and in 2013 it debuted two special pieces in support of breast cancer research.

ZANG TOI ▲

BORN Kelantan, Malaysia, June 11, 1961

Zang Toi (Toy) left Malaysia for Canada in 1980 and moved to New York City a year later intending to study painting or interior design. But he switched to fashion, and while at Parsons School of Design went to work for Mary Jane Marcasiano. Toi graduated from Parsons in 1983 and stayed with Marcasiano for five years, concentrating on production. After doing freelance work at SHAMASK, he opened his own business in 1989.

Designing with a light touch, Toi combines Asian colors and a taste for exotic details with the forthright flair of American sportswear. The result is a fresh twist on classic looks. His clothes are young and spirited, with a sophisticated attitude, while his preference for fabrics such as cashmere and silk and his innate sense of fantasy makes them fashion of unabashed luxury.

Above: Designer Zang Toi.
Left: Spring 2014.

Toi has joined the ranks of celebrity designers, and creates apparel for headline names such as Madonna and Sharon Stone. Toi's two signature lines, Zang Toi and House of Toi, are sold at Nordstrom, Neiman Marcus, and specialty boutiques in America and around the world.

In 2011, Toi was recognized as one of the eight most influential Chinese Americans by *Vivid* magazine, and in 2013 he was conferred the honorific title *Datuk* by the king of Malaysia. He also recently launched a line of makeup with Amazing Cosmetics.

Illustrator Izak Zenou.

BORN France

Best known for his Henri Bendel girls, Izak Zenou is the most prolific illustrator in fashion. He started illustrating at 17 after attending a fashion show by France Andrevie in the late 1980s. Zenou got his start in fashion as a stylist before becoming a full-time illustrator in 1992. He has worked for high-end publications such as *Vogue*, *Essence*, and *ELLE*, and his clients have included Neiman Marcus, Nordstrom, CHANEL, and CATHERINE MALANDRINO. His vibrant, colorful drawings celebrate women, portraying them as attractive, confident, optimistic, feminine, and modern—and delight viewers by showing what is fashionable and trendy.

Zenou provides his illustrations and fashion expertise to a diverse clientele, contributing to promotional, advertising, and editorial projects for companies all over the world. Zenou's longest-running client is Henri Bendel, where he has worked for more than 15 years.

Many of his illustrations were placed on products in the store, particularly scarves, which led Zenou to start Izak, his line of accessories and bags featuring his illustrations. In 2013, Izak was expanded to include stationery, invitations, notes, and calling cards.

Zenou has created artwork for Apple accessories, including iPhone covers, and a collection for Sephora that included a lipstick coquette. Zenou also creates visuals for Frank Et Fils in Paris and Le Printemps in Tokyo. In 2012, his artwork was part of the Brooklyn Public Library's *Fashion Illustration: A Contemporary Look* exhibit. It has also appeared on several book covers, such as *New York State of Mind* by Billy Joel and *Mommy Needs a Time Out* and *Mommy Needs a Martini* by Julie Klappas, and on lifestyle and entertaining books and calendars by LILLY PULITZER. Izak products are sold at Target, Sephora, Macy's, Dillards, and specialty gift stores across America.

COUNCIL OF FASHION DESIGNERS OF AMERICA (CFDA) AWARDS

2014
Womenswear Designer of the Year, Joseph Altuzarra
Menswear Designer of the Year, Public School
Accessory Designer of the Year, Mary Kate & Ashley Olsen
Swarovski Award for Womenswear, Christopher Peters & Shane Gabier
Swarovski Award for Menswear, Tim Coppens
Swarovski Award for Accessory Design, Irene Neuwirth
Eugenia Sheppard Award, Paul Cavaco
Geoffrey Beene Lifetime Achievement Award, Tom Ford
International Award, Raf Simons, Dior
Board of Directors' Special Tribute, Ruth Finley
Eleanor Lambert Award, Bethann Hardison
Fashion Icon Award, Rihanna

2013
Womenswear Designer of the Year, Jack McCollough & Lazaro Hernandez, Proenza Schouler
Menswear Designer of the Year, Thom Browne
Accessory Designer of the Year, Phillip Lim
Swarovski Award for Womenswear, Max Osterweis & Erin Beatty, Suno
Swarovski Award for Menswear, Dao-Yi Chow & Maxwell Osborne, Public School
Swarovski Award for Accessory Design, Pamela Love
Eugenia Sheppard Award, Tim Blanks
Geoffrey Beene Lifetime Achievement Award, Vera Wang
International Award, Riccardo Tisci, Givenchy
Board of Directors' Special Tribute, Colleen Atwood, American Costume Designer
Eleanor Lambert Award, Oscar de la Renta
Fashion Icon, Lady Gaga

2012
Womenswear Designer of the Year, Reed Krakoff
Menswear Designer of the Year, Billy Reid
Accessory Designer of the Year, Reed Krakoff
Swarovski Award for Womenswear, Joseph Altuzarra
Swarovski Award for Menswear, Philip Lim
Swarovski Award for Accessory Design, Tabitha Simmons
Eugenia Sheppard Award, Garance Dore and Scott Schuman
Geoffrey Beene Lifetime Achievement Award, Tommy Hilfiger
International Award, Rei Kawakubo
Eleanor Lambert Award, Andrew Rosen
Fashion Icon, Johnny Depp

2011
Womenswear Designer of the Year, Jack McCollough & Lazaro Hernandez, Pronenza Schouler
Menswear Designer of the Year, Michael Bastain
Accessory Designer of the Year, Alexander Wang
Swarovski Award for Womenswear, Probal Gurung
Swarovski Award for Menswear, Robert Geller
Swarovski Award for Accessory Design, Eddie Borgo
Eugenia Sheppard Award, Hilary Alexander
Geoffrey Beene Lifetime Achievement Award, Marc Jacobs
International Award, Phoebe Philo for Celine
Board of Directors' Special Tribute, Arthur Elgort
Eleanor Lambert Award, Hal Rubenstein
Fashion Icon, Lady Gaga

2010
Womenswear Designer of the Year, Marc Jacobs
Menswear Designer of the Year, Marcus Wainwright & David Nevell (Rag and Bone)
Accessory Designer of the Year, Alex Bitter
Swarovski Award for Womenswear, Jason Wu
Swarovski Award for Menswear, Richard Chai
Swarovski Award for Accessory Design, Alexander Wang
Eugenia Sheppard Award, Kim Hastreiter
Geoffrey Beene Lifetime Achievement Award, Michael Kors
International Award, Christopher Bailey for Burburry
Board of Directors' Special Tribute, Alexander McQueen
Eleanor Lambert Award, Toonne Goodman
Fashion Icon, Iman

2009
Womenswear Designer of the Year, Kate & Laura Mulleavy for Rodarte
Menswear Designer of the Year, Scott Sternberg for Band of Outsiders and Italo Zucchelli for Calvin Klein (tie)
Accessory Designer of the Year, Jack McCollough & Lazaro Hernandez for Proenza Schouler
Swarovski Award for Womenswear, Alexander Wang
Swarovski Award for Menswear, Tim Hamilton
Swarovski Award for Accessory Design, Justin Giunta for Subversive Jewelry
Eugenia Sheppard Award, Edward Nardoza
Geoffrey Beene Lifetime Achievement Award, Anna Sui
International Award, Marc Jacobs for Louis Vuitton

Board of Directors' Special Tribute, First Lady
Michelle Obama
Eleanor Lambert Award, Jim Moore

2008
Womenswear Designer of the Year, Francisco Costa for
Calvin Klein
Menswear Designer of the Year, Tom Ford
Accessory Designer of the Year, Tory Burch
Swarovski Award for Womenswear, Kate & Laura Mulleavy
for Rodarte
Swarovski Award for Menswear, Scott Sternberg for
Band of Outsiders
Swarovski Award for Accessory Design, Philip Crangi
Eugenia Sheppard Award, Candy Pratts Price
Geoffrey Beene Lifetime Achievement Award, Carolina Herrera
International Award, Dries Van Noten
Board of Directors' Special Tribute, Mayor Michael
R. Bloomberg

2007
Womenswear Designer of the Year, Oscar de la Renta
and Lazaro Hernandez & Jack McCollough for
Proenza Schouler
Menswear Designer of the Year, Ralph Lauren
Accessory Designer of the Year, Derek Lam
Swarovski Award for Womenswear, Phillip Lim
Swarovski Award for Menswear, David Neville & Marcus
Wainwright for Rag & Bone
Swarovski Award for Accessory Design, Jessie Randall for
Loeffler Randall
Eugenia Sheppard Award, Robin Givhan
Geoffrey Beene Lifetime Achievement Award, Robert
Lee Morris
International Award, Pierre Cardin
American Fashion Legend Award, Ralph Lauren
Eleanor Lambert Award, Patrick Demarchelier
Board of Directors' Special Tribute, Bono & Ali Hewson

2006
Womenswear Designer of the Year, Francisco Costa for
Calvin Klein
Menswear Designer of the Year, Thom Browne
Accessory Designer of the Year, Tom Binns
Swarovski's Perry Ellis Award for Womenswear,
Doo-Ri Chung
Swarovski's Perry Ellis Award for Menswear, Jeff Halmos,
Josia Lamberto-Egan, Sam Shipley & John Whitledge
for Trovata
Swarovski's Perry Ellis Award for Accessory Design,
Devi Kroell
Eugenia Sheppard Award, Bruce Weber
International Award, Olivier Theyskens for Rochas
Lifetime Achievement Award, Stan Herman
Eleanor Lambert Award, Joan Kaner
Board of Directors' Special Tribute, Stephen Burrows

2005
Womenswear Designer of the Year, Vera Wang
Menswear Designer of the Year, John Varvatos
Accessory Designer of the Year, Marc Jacobs for Marc Jacobs
Swarovski's Perry Ellis Award for Womenswear, Derek Lam
Swarovski's Perry Ellis Award for Menswear, Alexandre
Plokhov for Cloak
Swarovski's Perry Ellis Award for Accessory Design, Nak
Armstrong & Anthony Camargo for Anthony Nak
Eugenia Sheppard Award, Gilles Bensimon
International Award, Alber Elbaz for Lanvin
Lifetime Achievement Award, Diane von Furstenberg
Fashion Icon, Kate Moss
Board of Directors' Special Tribute, Norma Kamali

2004
Womenswear Designer of the Year, Carolina Herrera
Menswear Designer of the Year, Sean Combs for Sean John
Accessory Designer of the Year, Reed Krakoff for Coach
Swarovski's Perry Ellis Award for Womenswear, Zac Posen
Swarovski's Perry Ellis Award for Accessory Design,
Eugenia Kim
Eugenia Sheppard Award, Teri Agins
International Award, Miuccia Prada
Lifetime Achievement Award, Donna Karan
Fashion Icon, Sarah Jessica Parker
Eleanor Lambert Award, Irving Penn
Board of Directors' Special Tribute, Tom Ford

2003
Womenswear Designer of the Year, Narciso Rodriguez
Menswear Designer of the Year, Michael Kors
Accessory Designer of the Year, Marc Jacobs
Swarovski's Perry Ellis Award for Ready-to-Wear, Lazaro
Hernandez & Jack McCollough for Proenza Schouler
Swarovski's Perry Ellis Award for Accessory Design,
Brian Atwood
Eugenia Sheppard Award, André Leon Talley
International Award, Alexander McQueen
Lifetime Achievement Award, Anna Wintour
Fashion Icon, Nicole Kidman
Eleanor Lambert Award, Rose Marie Bravo
Board of Directors' Special Tribute, Oleg Cassini

2002
Womenswear Designer of the Year, Narciso Rodriguez
Menswear Designer of the Year, Marc Jacobs
Accessory Designer of the Year, Tom Ford for Yves Saint Laurent
Perry Ellis Award for Womenswear, Rick Owens
Eugenia Sheppard Award, Cathy Horyn
International Award, Hedi Slimane for Dior Homme
Lifetime Achievement Award, Grace Coddington /
Karl Lagerfeld
Fashion Icon, C.Z. Guest
Creative Visionary, Stephen Gan
Eleanor Lambert Award, Kal Ruttentstein

2001

Womenswear Designer of the Year, Tom Ford
Menswear Designer of the Year, John Varvatos
Accessory Designer of the Year, Reed Krakoff for Coach
Swarovski's Perry Ellis Award for Womenswear, Daphne Gutierrez & Nicole Noselli for Bruce
Swarovski's Perry Ellis Award for Menswear, William Reid
Swarovski's Perry Ellis Award for Accessory Design, Edmundo Castillo
International Award, Nicolas Ghesquière for Balenciaga
Lifetime Achievement Award, Calvin Klein
Eugenia Sheppard Award, Bridget Foley
Humanitarian Award, Evelyn Lauder
Eleanor Lambert Award, Dawn Mello
Special Award, Bernard Arnault
Special Award, Bob Mackie
Special Award, Saks Fifth Avenue

2000

Womenswear Designer of the Year, Oscar de la Renta
Menswear Designer of the Year, Helmut Lang
Accessory Designer of the Year, Richard Lambertson & John Truex for Lambertson Truex
Perry Ellis Award for Womenswear, Miguel Adrover
Perry Ellis Award for Menswear, John Varvatos
Perry Ellis Award for Accessory Design, Dean Harris
International Award, Jean-Paul Gaultier
Lifetime Achievement Award, Valentino
Humanitarian Award, Liz Claiborne
Most Stylish Dot.com Award, PleatsPlease.com
Special Award, The Dean of American Fashion Bill Blass
Special Award, The American Regional Press
Special Award, The Academy of Motion Picture Arts & Sciences

1999/1998

Womenswear Designer of the Year, Michael Kors
Menswear Designer of the Year, Calvin Klein
Accessory Designer of the Year, Marc Jacobs
Perry Ellis Award for Womenswear, Bryan Bradley & Josh Patner for Tuleh
Perry Ellis Award for Menswear, Matt Nye
Perry Ellis Award for Accessory Design, Tony Valentine
International Award, Yohji Yamamoto
Lifetime Achievement Award, Yves Saint Laurent
Eugenia Sheppard Award, Elsa Klensch
Humanitarian Award, Liz Tilberis
Special Award, Betsey Johnson
Special Award, Simon Doonan
Special Award, InStyle Magazine
Special Award, Sophia Loren / Cher

1997

Womenswear Designer of the Year, Marc Jacobs
Menswear Designer of the Year, John Bartlett
Accessory Designer of the Year, Kate Spade
Perry Ellis Award for Womenswear, Narciso Rodriguez

Perry Ellis Award for Menswear, Sandy Dalal
International Award, John Galliano for Christian Dior
Lifetime Achievement Award, Geoffrey Beene
The Stilleto, Manolo Blahnik
Special Award, Anna Wintour
Dom Perignon Award, Ralph Lauren
Special Award, Elizabeth Taylor
Special Tributes, Gianni Versace & Princess Diana

1996

Womenswear Designer of the Year, Donna Karan
Menswear Designer of the Year, Ralph Lauren
Accessory Designer of the Year, Elsa Peretti for Tiffany & Co.
Perry Ellis Award for Womenswear, Daryl Kerrigan for Daryl K.
Perry Ellis Award for Menswear, Gene Meyer
Perry Ellis Award for Accessory Design, Miranda Morrison & Keri Sigerson for Sigerson Morrison
International Award, Helmut Lang
Lifetime Achievement Award, Arnold Scaasi
Eugenia Sheppard Award, Amy Spindler
Dom Perignon Award, Kenneth Cole
Special Award, Richard Martin & Harold Koda

1995

Womenswear Designer of the Year, Ralph Lauren
Menswear Designer of the Year, Tommy Hilfiger
Accessory Designer of the Year, Hush Puppies
Perry Ellis Award for Womenswear, Marie-Anne Oudejans
Perry Ellis Award for Menswear, Richard Tyler / Richard Bengtsson & Edward Pavlick for Richard Edwards
Perry Ellis Award for Accessory Design, Kate Spade
International Award, Tom Ford for Gucci
Lifetime Achievement Award, Hubert de Givenchy
Eugenia Sheppard Award, Suzy Menkes
Special Award, Isaac Mizrahi & Douglas Keeve for "Unzipped" / Robert Isabell / Lauren Bacall
Dom Perignon Award, Bill Blass

1994

Womenswear Designer of the Year, Richard Tyler
Accessory Designer of the Year, Robert Lee Morris, Women's / Gene Meyer, Men's
Perry Ellis Award for Womenswear, Cynthia Rowley / Victor Alfaro
Perry Ellis Award for Menswear, Robert Freda
Lifetime Achievement Award, Carrie Donovon / Nonnie Moore / Bernadine Morris
Eugenia Sheppard Award, Kevyn Aucoin / Patrick McCarthy
Special Award, Elizabeth Tilberis / The Wonderbra / Kevyn Aucoin
Special Tribute, Jacqueline Kennedy Onassis

1993

Womenswear Designer of the Year, Calvin Klein
Menswear Designer of the Year, Calvin Klein

Perry Ellis Award for Womenswear, Richard Tyler
Perry Ellis Award for Menswear, John Bartlett
Lifetime Achievement Award, Judith Leiber / Polly Allen Mellen
International Award, Prada
Eugenia Sheppard Award, Fabien Baron / Bill Cunningham
Special Awards, Fabien Baron / Adidas / Converse / Keds /
    Nike / Reebok
Industry Tribute, Eleanor Lambert

1992

Womenswear Designer of the Year, Marc Jacobs
Menswear Designer of the Year, Donna Karan
Accessory Designer of the Year, Chrome Hearts
Perry Ellis Award, Anna Sui
Eugenia Sheppard Award, Steven Meisel
International Award, Gianni Versace
Lifetime Achievement Award, Pauline Trigère
Special Award, Steven Meisel / Audrey Hepburn /
    The Ribbon Project / Visual AIDS

1991

Womenswear Designer of the Year, Isaac Mizrahi
Menswear Designer of the Year, Roger Forsythe
Accessory Designer of the Year, Karl Lagerfeld for Chanel
Perry Ellis Award, Todd Oldham
Lifetime Achievement Award, Ralph Lauren
Eugenia Sheppard Award, Marylou Luther
International Award, Karl Lagerfeld for Chanel
Special Award, Marvin Traub / Harley Davidson /
    Jessye Norman / Anjelica Huston / Judith Jamison

1990

Womenswear Designer of the Year, Donna Karan
Menswear Designer of the Year, Joseph Abboud
Accessory Designer of the Year, Manolo Blahnik
Perry Ellis Award, Christian Francis Roth
Lifetime Achievement Award, Martha Graham
Eugenia Sheppard Award, Genevieve Buck
Special Awards, Emilio Pucci / Anna Wintour
Special Tribute, Halston

1989

Womenswear Designer of the Year, Isaac Mizrahi
Menswear Designer of the Year, Joseph Abboud
Accessory Designer of the Year, Paloma Picasso
Perry Ellis Award, Gordon Henderson
Lifetime Achievement Award, Oscar de la Renta
Eugenia Sheppard Award, Carrie Donovon
Special Award, The Gap
Special Tribute, Giorgio Sant'Angelo / Diana Vreeland

1988

Menswear Designer of the Year, Bill Robinson
Perry Ellis Award, Isaac Mizrahi

Lifetime Achievement Award, Richard Avedon / Nancy Reagan
Eugenia Sheppard Award, Nina Hyde
Special Award, Geoffrey Beene / Karl Lagerfeld for House of
    Chanel / Grace Mirabella / Judith Peabody / The Wool
    Bureau Inc.

1987

Best American Collection, Calvin Klein
Menswear Designer of the Year, Ronaldus Shamask
Perry Ellis Award, Marc Jacobs
Eugenia Sheppard Award, Bernadine Morris
Lifetime Achievement, Giorgio Armani / Horst /
    Eleanor Lambert
Special Awards, Arnell / Bickford Associates and Donna
    Karan / Manolo Blahnik / Hebe Dorsey / FIT / Giorgio
    Sant'Angelo / Arnold Scaasi / *Vanity Fair*
Special Tribute, Mrs. Vincent Astor

1986

Perry Ellis Award, David Cameron
Lifetime Achievement Award, Bill Blass / Marlene Dietrich
Special Awards, Geoffrey Beene / Dalma Callado / Elle
    Magazine / Etta Froio / Donna Karan / Elsa Klench /
    Christian Lacroix / Ralph Lauren

1985

Lifetime Achievement Award, Katherine Hepburn /
    Alexander Liberman
Special Tribute, Rudy Gernreich
Special Awards, Geoffrey Beene / Liz Claiborne / Norma
    Kamali / Donna Karan / *Miami Vice* / Robert Lee Morris
    / Ray-Ban Sunglasses / "Tango Argentino"

1984

Lifetime Achievement Award, James Galanos
Special Awards, Astor Pale Hair Design / Bergdorf Goodman
    / Kitty D'Alessio / John Fairchild / Annie Flanders / Peter
    Moore NIKE / Robert Pittman MTV / Stephen Sprouse /
    Diana Vreeland / Bruce Weber

1983

Bill Cunningham / Perry Ellis / Norma Kamali / Karl
    Lagerfeld / Antonio Lopez / Issey Miyake / Patricia
    Underwood / Bruce Weber

1982

Bill Cunningham / Perry Ellis / Norma Kamali / Karl
    Lagerfeld / Antonio Lopez

1981

Jhane Barnes / Perry Ellis / Andrew Fezza / Alexander Julian
    / Barry Kieselstein-Cord / Calvin Klein / Nancy Knox /
    Ralph Lauren / Robert Lighton / Alex Mate & Lee Brooks /
    Yves Saint Laurent / Fernando Sanchez

Source: http://cfda.com/cfda-fashion-awards

BRITISH FASHION AWARDS

2013
Emerging Menswear, Agi and Sam
Emerging Womenswear, Simone Rochas
Emerging Accessories, Sophia Webster
New Establishment, J.W. Anderson
International Designer of the Year, Miuccia Prada for Prada
Model, Edie Campbell
Designer Brand, Burberry
Isabella Blow Award, Lady Amanda Harlech
Red Carpet Award, Erem
Vodafone British Style Award, Harry Styles
Menswear Designer of the Year, Christopher Bailey
Womeswear Designer of the Year, Christopher Kane
Accessory Designer, Nicholas Kirkwood
Special Recognition, Kate Moss
Special Recognition, Suzy Menkes
BFC Award for Outstanding Achievement in Fashion,
    Terry and Tricia Jones

2012
Emerging Talent Award Menswear, Jonathan Saunders
Emerging Talent Award Ready-to-Wear, J.W. Anderson
Emerging Talent Award Accessories, Sophie Hulme
New Establishment, Erdem
Model, Cara Delevingne
Designer Brand, Stella McCartney
Isabella Blow Award, Louise Wilson
Red Carpet Award, Roksanda Ilincic
Vodafone British Style Award, Alexa Chung
Menswear Designer of the Year, Kim Jones for Louis Vuitton
Designer of the Year, Stella McCartney
Accessory Designer, Nicholas Kirkwood
Special Recognition, Howard Tillman
BFC Award for Outstanding Achievement in Fashion,
    Manolo Blahnik CBE

2011
Emerging Talent Award Menswear, Christopher Raeburn
Emerging Talent Award Ready-to-Wear, Mary Katrantzou
Emerging Talent Award Accessories, Tabitha Simmons
New Establishment, Christopher Kane
Model, Stella Tennant
Designer Brand, Victoria Beckham
Isabella Blow Award, Sam Gainsbury
Red Carpet Award, Stella McCarthney
Vodafone British Style Award, Alexa Chung
Menswear Designer of the Year, Kim Jones
Designer of the Year, Sarah Burton for Alexander McQueen
Accessory Designer, Charlotte Olympia
BFC Award for Outstanding Achievement in Fashion,
    Sir Paul Smith

2010
Emerging Talent Award Ready-to-Wear, Meadham Kirchhoff
Emerging Talent Award Accessories, Husam El Odeh
Model, Lara Stone
Designer Brand, Mulberry
Isabella Blow Award, Nicola Formichetti
Digital Innovation, Burberry
British Style Award, Alexa Chung
Menswear Designer of the Year, E.Tautz
Designer of the Year, Phoebe Philo for Celine
Accessory Designer, Nicholas Kirkwood
Special Recognition, Naomi Campbell
BFC Award for Outstanding Achievement in Fashion,
    Alexander McQueen

2009
Swarovski Emerging Talent Award Ready-to-Wear,
    Peter Pilotto
Swarovski Emerging Talent Award Accessories, Holly Fulton
Model, Georgia Jagger
London 25, Kate Moss
Isabella Blow Award, Grace Coddington
BFC Collection of the Year, Christopher Kane
Menswear Designer of the Year, Kim Jones for dunhill
Designer of the Year, Christopher Bailey
Accessory Designer, Katie Hillier
Designer Brand, Burberry
BFC Award for Outstanding Achievement in Fashion,
    John Galliano

2008
Swarovski Emerging Talent Award Ready-to-Wear,
    Louise Goldin
Swarovski Emerging Talent Award Accessories,
    Nicolas Kirkwood
Model, Jourdan Dunn
Bespoke, Richard James
Isabella Blow Award, Tim Walker
Red Carpet Designer, Mathew Williamson
Menswear Designer of the Year, Christopher Bailey
Designer of the Year, Lluella Bartley
Accessory Designer, Rupert Sanderson
Designer Brand, Jimmy Choo
BFC Award for Outstanding Achievement in Fashion,
    Stephen Jones

2007
New Generation Designer, Christopher Kane
Best New Retail Concept, Marc Jacobs
Model, Agyness Deyn

Red Carpet Designer, Marchesa
Isabella Blow Award, Michael Howells
Swarovski BFC Enterprise Award, Erdem
Menswear Designer of the Year, Christopher Bailey
    for Burberry
Designer of the Year, Stella McCartney
Accessory Designer, Tom Binns
Designer Brand, Anya Hindmarch
BFC Award for Outstanding Achievement in Fashion, Dame
    Vivienne Westwood

2006
New Generation Designer, Marlos Schwab
Retailer of the Year, b Store
Model, Kate Moss
Red Carpet Designer, Vivienne Westwood
Fashion Creator, Eugene Souleiman
Swarovski BFC Enterprise Award, Jonathan Saunders
Menswear Designer of the Year, Kim Jones
Designer of the Year, Giles Deacon
Accessory Designer, Stuart Vevers for Mulberry
V & A Award for Outstanding Achievement in Fashion, Joan
    Burstein CBE

2005
New Generation Designer, Duro Olowu
Retailer of the Year, Dover Street Market
Model, Karen Elson
Red Carpet Designer, Roland Mouret
Fashion Creator, Charlotte Tilbury
Menswear Designer of the Year, Carlo Brandelli for Kilgour
Designer of the Year, Christopher Bailey
Accessory Designer, Stephen Jones
V & A Award for Outstanding Achievement in Fashion, Suzy
    Menkes OBE

2004
New Generation Designer, Giles Deacon
Retailer of the Year, Net-a-Porter.com
Model, Lily Cole
Fashion Creator, Pat McGrath
Menswear Designer of the Year, Alexander McQueen
Designer of the Year, Phoebe Philo
Accessory Designer, Mulberry
V & A Award for Outstanding Achievement in Fashion,
    David Bailey

2003
New Generation Designer, Sophia Kokosalaki
Glamour, Julien Macdonald
Most Stylish Model, Erin O'Conner
Contemporary Designer, Paul Smith
Menswear Designer of the Year, Paul Smith
Designer of the Year, Alexander McQueen
Accessory Designer, Manolo Blahnik
High Street Fashion Retailer, Reiss
Most Stylish Photographer, Mario Testino

Stylish, Katie Grand
Female Personality, Kim Cattrall
Male TV Personality, Ant & Doc
Movie Actress, Minnie Driver
Movie Actor, Ewan McGregor
Male Music Artist, Robbie Williams
Female Music Artist, Victoria Beckham
Sports Personality, David Beckham

2002
No Awards

2001
New Generation Designer, Stella McCartney
Retailer, Topshop
Model, Kate Moss
Glamour Designer, Julien Macdonald
Menswear Designer of the Year, Richard James
Designer of the Year, Alexander McQueen
Accessory Designer, Anya Hindmarch
Classic Design, Paul Smith
Contemporary Design, Burberry
Street Style, I.E. uniform
Journalist, Lisa Armstrong
Stylist, Lucinda Chambers
Rovers People's Award, Jemima Khan

2000
New Generation Designer, Tracey Boyd
Retailer, Topshop
Glamour Designer, Stella McCartney
Menswear Designer of the Year, Oswald Boateng
Designer of the Year, Hussein Chalayan
Accessory Designer, Jimmy Choo
Classic Design, Burberry
Contemporary Design, Joseph
Street Style, Maharishi
Journalist, Mimi Spencer
Stylist, Katy England
Rovers People's Award, Alexander McQueen

1999
New Generation Designer, Elspeth Gibson
Retailer, French Connection
Glamour Designer, English Eccentrics
Menswear Designer of the Year, Paul Smith
Designer of the Year, Hussein Chalayan
Accessory Designer, Manolo Blahnik
Classic Design, Burberry
Contemporary Design, Betty Jackson
Street Style, YMC
Journalist, Suzy Meekes
Stylist, Lucinda Chambers
Hall of Fame, Vidal Sassoon

1998
No Awards

COTY AMERICAN FASHION CRITICS' AWARDS

DESIGNER	AWARD	YEAR
Robin Kahn	*Special Award (belt and buckle designs for men's wear)*	1984
Donna Karan	*First Citation (women's wear with Louis Dell'Olio)*	1984
Louis Dell'Olio	*First Citation (women's wear with Donna Karan)*	1984
Jhane Barnes	*Men's Wear Return Award*	1984
Perry Ellis	*Hall of Fame (men's wear)*	1984
Perry Ellis	*Hall of Fame (women's wear)*	1984
Alexander Julian	*Second Citation*	1984
Barry Kieselstein-Cord	*Special Award (belts and jewelry)*	1984
Ralph Lauren	*Second Citation*	1984
Adrienne Vittadini	*"Winnie"*	1984
Bill Blass	*Hall of Fame Citation*	1983
Perry Ellis	*Hall of Fame Citation (women's wear)*	1983
Perry Ellis	*Men's Wear Return Award*	1983
Alexander Julian	*First Citation*	1983
Norma Kamali	*Hall of Fame*	1983
Willi Smith	*"Winnie"*	1983
Adri	*"Winnie"*	1982
Geoffrey Beene	*Hall of Fame Citation*	1982
Bill Blass	*Hall of Fame Citation*	1982
Sal Cesarani	*Men's Wear Return Award*	1982
Louis Dell'Olio	*Hall of Fame (with Donna Karan)*	1982
Norma Kamali	*Return Award*	1982
Donna Karan	*Hall of Fame (with Louis, Dell'Olio)*	1982
Geoffrey Beene	*Hall of Fame Citation*	1981
Perry Ellis	*Hall of Fame*	1981
Perry Ellis	*Men's Wear Award*	1981
Norma Kamali	*"Winnie"*	1981
Ralph Lauren	*First Citation (men's wear)*	1981
Robert Lee Morris	*Special Award (jewelry for Calvin Klein)*	1981
Ronaldus Shamask	*"Winnie"*	1981
Jhane Barnes	*Men's Wear*	1980
Perry Ellis	*Return Award*	1980
Alexander Julian	*Hall of Fame Award*	1980
Calvin Klein	*Special Award (contribution to international status of American fashion)*	1979
Geoffrey Beene	*Hall of Fame Citation*	1979
Perry Ellis	*"Winnie"*	1979
Alexander Julian	*Men's Wear Return Award*	1979
Barry Kieselstein-Cord	*Outstanding, Jewelry Design*	1979
Mary McFadden	*Hall of Fame*	1979
Joan Vass	*Special Award (crafted knit fashions)*	1979
Joan Helpern	*Special Award (footwear)*	1978
Mary McFadden	*Return Award*	1978
Geoffrey Beene	*Hall of Fame Citation*	1977

DESIGNER	AWARD	YEAR
Stephen Burrows	"Winnie"	1977
Louis Dell'Olio	"Winnie" (with Donna Karan for Anne Klein)	1977
Alexander Julian	Men's Wear Trophy	1977
Donna Karan	"Winnie" (with Louis, Dell'Olio for Anne Klein)	1977
Ralph Lauren	Hall of Fame (women's wear)	1977
John Anthony	Return Award	1976
Sal Cesarani	Special Men's Wear Award	1976
Herbert Kasper	Hall of Fame	1976
Ralph Lauren	Return Award	1976
Ralph Lauren	Hall of Fame (men's wear)	1976
Mary McFadden	"Winnie"	1976
Geoffrey Beene	Hall of Fame Citation	1975
Bill Blass	Special Award (furs for Revillon America)	1975
Carol Horn	"Winnie"	1975
Calvin Klein	Hall of Fame	1975
Calvin Klein	Special Award (fur design for Alixandre)	1975
Fernando Sanchez	Special Award (fur for Revillon)	1975
Viola Sylbert	Special Award (fur design)	1975
Monika Tilley	Special Award (swimsuits)	1975
Fernando Sanchez	Special Award (lingerie)	1974, 1977
Geoffrey Beene	Hall of Fame	1974
Stephen Burrows	Special Award (lingerie)	1974
Sal Cesarani	Special Men's Wear Award	1974
Aldo Cipullo	Special Men's Wear Award (male jewelry)	1974
Halston	Hall of Fame	1974
Calvin Klein	Return Award	1974
Ralph Lauren	"Winnie"	1974
Bill Tice	Special Award (loungewear)	1974
John Weitz	Special Men's Wear Award	1974
Oscar de la Renta	Hall of Fame	1973
Calvin Klein	"Winnie"	1973
Ralph Lauren	Return Award	1973
Judith Leiber	Special Award (handbags)	1973
John Anthony	"Winnie"	1972
Bonnie Cashin	Hall of Fame	1972
Halston	Return Award	1972
Bill Blass	Hall of Fame Citation	1971
Halston	"Winnie"	1971
Betsey Johnson	"Winnie"	1971
Anne Klein	Hall of Fame	1971
Elsa Peretti	Special Award (jewelry)	1971
Bill Blass	Hall of Fame	1970
Herbert Kasper	Return Award	1970
Ralph Lauren	Men's Wear	1970
Giorgio Sant'Angelo	"Winnie"	1970
Chester Weinberg	"Winnie"	1970
Anne Klein	Return Award	1969
Giorgio Sant'Angelo	Special Award (fantasy accessories and ethnic fashions)	1968
Bill Blass	First Coty Award for Men's Wear	1968
Bonnie Cashin	Return Award	1968
Oscar de la Renta	Return Award	1968
Oscar de la Renta	"Winnie"	1967
Rudi Gernreich	Hall of Fame	1967
Geoffrey Beene	Return Award	1966
Rudi Gernreich	Return Award	1966

DESIGNER	AWARD	YEAR
Kenneth Jay Lane	*Special Award (jewelry)*	1966
Geoffrey Beene	*"Winnie"*	1964
Sylvia Pedlar	*Return Special Award (lingerie)*	1964
Bill Blass	*Return Award*	1963
Rudi Gernreich	*"Winnie"*	1963
Halston	*Special Award (millinery)*	1962, 1969
Bill Blass	*"Winnie"*	1961
Bonnie Cashin	*Special Award (leather and fabric design)*	1961
Gustave Tassell	*"Winnie"*	1961
Rudi Gernreich	*Special Award (innovative body clothes)*	1960
James Galanos	*Hall of Fame*	1959
Pauline Trigère	*Hall of Fame*	1959
Jean Schlumberger	*Special Award (the first given for jewelry)*	1958
Claire McCardell	*Hall of Fame (posthumous)*	1958
Arnold Scaasi	*"Winnie"*	1958
Emeric Partos	*Special Award (furs)*	1957
James Galanos	*Return Award*	1956
Norman Norell	*First designer elected to Hall of Fame*	1956
Adolfo	*Special Award (millinery)*	1955, 1969
Herbert Kasper	*"Winnie"*	1955
Anne Klein	*"Winnie"*	1955
James Galanos	*"Winnie"*	1954
Charles James	*Special Award (innovative cut)*	1954
Anne Fogarty	*Special Award (dresses)*	1951
Vera Maxwell	*Special Award (coats and suits)*	1951
Norman Norell	*First Return Award*	1951
Sylvia Pedlar	*Special Award (lingerie)*	1951
Pauline Trigère	*Return Award*	1951
Bonnie Cashin	*"Winnie"*	1950
Charles James	*"Winnie"*	1950
Pauline Trigère	*"Winnie"*	1949
Adele Simpson	*"Winnie"*	1947
Tina Leser	*"Winnie"*	1945
Claire McCardell	*"Winnie"*	1944
Lilly Daché	*Special Award (millinery)*	1943
Mr. John	*Special Award*	1943
Norman Norell	*First "Winnie"*	1943

NEIMAN MARCUS AWARDS

DESIGNER	YEAR	DESIGNER	YEAR
Miuccia Prada	1995	Giuliana Camerino	1956
Emilio Pucci	1990	Pierre Balmain	1955
Arnold Scaasi	1987	Florence Eiseman	1955
Issey Miyake	1984	Vera Maxwell	1955
Karl Lagerfeld	1980	James Galanos	1954
Judith Leiber	1980	Charles James	1953
Giorgio Armani	1979	Anne Fogarty	1952
Perry Ellis	1979	Bonnie Cashin	1950
Mary McFadden	1979	Pauline Trigère	1950
Ralph Lauren	1973	Claire McCardell	1948
Rosita & Ottavio Missoni	1973	Christian Dior	1947
Hanae Mori	1973	Salvatore Ferragamo	1947
Jean Muir	1973	Norman Hartnell	1947
Bill Blass	1969	Irene	1947
Emanuel Ungaro	1969	Adele Simpson	1946
Oscar de la Renta	1968	Tina Leser	1945
Kenneth Jay Lane	1968	Adrian	1943
Valentino	1967	Norman Norell	1942
Geoffrey Beene	1964, 1965	Omar Kiam	1941
Jules-François Crahay	1962	Carmel Snow	1941
Roger Vivier	1961	Edna Woolman Chase	1940
Sylvia Pedlar	1960	Lilly Daché	1940
Anne Klein	1959, 1969	Elsa Schiaparelli	1940
Yves Saint Laurent	1958	Hattie Carnegie	1939
Gabrielle "Coco" Chanel	1957	Clare Potter	1939
Cecil Beaton	1956	Mr. John	1938

FASHION WALK OF FAME

The Fashion Walk of Fame, established in 1999 by leaders of the fashion industry, is the only permanent landmark paying tribute to the creative talents of American fashion. White bronze plaques 2^1/$_2$ feet in diameter have been embedded in granite in the sidewalk from 35th to 41st Street, on the east side of Seventh "Fashion" Avenue. Each plaque bears an original fashion sketch and the signature of the designer, with text describing his or her contribution to fashion.

DESIGNER	YEAR	DESIGNER	YEAR
Ralph Rucci	2011	Giorgio Sant'Angelo	2001
Donald Brooks	2011	James Galanos	2001
Liz Claiborne	2008	Charles James	2001
Diane von Furstenberg	2008	Donna Karan	2001
Stephen Burrows	2002	Anne Klein	2001
Lilly Daché	2002	Pauline Trigère	2001
Perry Ellis	2002	Geoffrey Beene	2000
Marc Jacobs	2002	Bill Blass	2000
Betsey Johnson	2002	Rudi Gernreich	2000
Norma Kamali	2002	Halston	2000
Mainbocher	2002	Calvin Klein	2000
Willi Smith	2002	Ralph Lauren	2000
Bonnie Cashin	2001	Claire McCardell	2000
Oscar de la Renta	2001	Norman Norell	2000

REFERENCES

A to Z Blue Jeans. http://atozbluejeans.com. (Accessed March 27, 2009.)

Abel, Ruthie. *Huffington Post*. "Behind the Seams of Avant-Garde Fashion: threeASFOUR in the Studio." September 11, 2013. http://www.huffingtonpost.com /ruthie-abel/behind-the-seams-of-avant_b_3895581 .html. (Accessed November 11, 2013.)

Admin, Anokhi. *Anokhi Media*. "Ranjana & Naeem Khan Raise $18,000 for Wishwas." September 30, 2013. http:// anokhimedia.com/blog/ranjana-naeem-khan-raise-18000 -for-wishwas. (Accessed October 15, 2013.)

Agarwal, Shradha. *The Telegraph India*. "Fashion." June 15, 2011. http://www.telegraphindia.com/1110615/jsp /entertainment/story_14114556.jsp. (Accessed November 16, 2013.)

Albo, Mike. 2008. *New York Times*. "One Size Fits Small." September 2, 2008. http://www.nytimes.com/2008/09/04 /fashion/04CRITIC.html?_r=0. (Accessed November 5, 2008.)

Aleksander, Irina. *New York Observer*. "*Marie Claire* Jumps on the Reality Show Train." September 9, 2008. http://observer.com/2008/09/imarie-clairei-jumps-on -the-reality-show-train/#axzz32D5D66i0. (Accessed November 6, 2008.)

Alexander, Hilary. *Daily Telegraph*. "Jigsaw Chic by Steven Meisel." November 11, 2008. http://telegraph.co.uk /fashion/3441013/Jigsaw-chic-by-Steven-Meisel.html. (Accessed November 11, 2008.)

Alford, Holly. Interview with Donwan Harrell. March 11, 2013.

Alpern, Sara. *Jewish Woman Archive*. "Helena Rubinstein." http://jwa.org/encyclopedia /article/rubinstein-helena. (Accessed October 2, 2013.)

Alvoni. "Marianne." http://www.alvoni.ch/index.php?p=1488. (Accessed September 20, 2013.)

Amed, Imran. *Business of Fashion*. "Fashion Means Business /Garance Dore and Scott Schuman." April 23, 2013. http://www.businessoffashion.com/2013/04/fashion -means-business-garance-dore-and-scott-schuman.html. (Accessed August 19, 2013.)

———. *Business of Fashion*. "The Business of Blogging/Garance Dore." February 21, 2013. http:// www.businessoffashion.com/2013/02/the-business-of -blogging-garance-dore.html. (Accessed September 12, 2013.)

Amies, H. *ABC of Men's Fashion*. London: Newnes, 1964.

———. *Just So Far*. St. James Place, London: Collins, 1984.

———. *Still Here*. London: Weidenfeld and Nicolson, 1984.

Anderson, Christina. *Huffington Post*. "Grace Coddington Talks About Her Memoir, Bad Manners, Balenciaga And, Of Course, Anna Wintour in Rare Interview." December 16, 2012. http://www.huffingtonpost.com/2012/12/16 /grace-coddington-memoir_n_2287674.html. (Accessed July 16, 2013.)

Anderson, Jocelyn. *WWD/ Footwear News*. "5 Questions for Walter Steiger." February 25, 2013. http://www.wwd .com/footwear-news/markets/5-questions-for-walter -steiger-6797622. (Accessed July 12, 2013.)

Anna Molonari. "Blufin History." http://blufin.it/. (Accessed November 11, 2008.)

Anne Cole. "About." http://annecole.com/index2.html. (Accessed November 17, 2008.)

Anscombe, Isabelle. *A Woman's Touch: Women in Design from 1860 to the Present Day*. London: Virago, 1984.

Answers.com. "Karl Kani." http://www.answers.com/topic /karl-kani-1.(Accessed June 20, 2011.)

———. "Katherine Hamnett." http://answers.com/topic /katharine-hamnett. (Accessed November 17, 2008.)

Armstrong, Lisa. *The Telegraph*. "Riccardo Tisi: Unmasked." October 2, 2013. http://fashion.telegraph.co.uk/columns /lisa-armstrong/TMG10348172/Riccardo-Tisci-unmasked .html. (Accessed December 12. 2013.)

Artbook.com. "Juergen Teller: Marc Jacobs Advertising 1997-2008, Volume I." http:// artbook.com/9783865217158 .html. (Accessed November 14, 2008.)

Artdaily.org. "Le Petit Palais in Paris Shows Images and Fashion by Patrick Demarchelier." http://artdaily.com /section/news/index.asp?int._sec=11&int_new=264488int _modo=1. (Accessed November 6, 2008.)

Ash, Juliet, and Elizabeth Wilson, eds. *Chic Thrills*. Berkeley, CA: University of California Press, 1993.

Ask Men.com. "Scott Schuman." http://www.askmen.com /celebs/men/business_politics/scott-schuman/. (Accessed November 6, 2013.)

Babcock, Gregory. *Complex.com*. "Peek Behind the Work of Million Dollar Man Scott Schuman." September 5, 2013. http://www.complex.com/style/2013/09/peek-behind -the-work-of-million-dollar-man-scott-schuman. (Accessed December 6, 2013.)

Baeza, Sophia Satchell. *Idol Magazine.* "Philip Stephens, Creative Director of Unconditional>Fashion Interviews." http://idolmag.co.uk/fashion-interview/philip-stephens-creative-director-unconditional. (Accessed December 12, 2013.)

Bailey, M.J. *Those Glorious, Glamour Years: The Great Hollywood Costume Designs of the 1930s.* Secaucus, NJ: Citadel Press, 1988 (reissue).

Bailey, Sarah. *Harper's Bazaar.* "Costa's Calvin Klein." April 22, 2008. http:// harpersbazaar.com/fashion/fashion-articles/francisco-costa-calvin-klein-0508. (Accessed November 6, 2008.)

Baldwin, Neil. *Man Ray: American Artist.* Cambridge: Da Capo Press, 2000.

Ballard, Bettina. *In My Fashion.* New York: David McKay, 1960.

Balmain, Pierre. *My Years and Seasons.* Translated by E. Lanchbery and G.Young. London: Cassell, 1964; New York: Doubleday, 1965.

Band of Outsiders Men. "Frank Ocean." March 12, 2013. http://band.bandofoutsiders.com. (Accessed August 12, 2013.)

Barnett, Leisa. *Vogue.com.* "A Valli Happy Occasion." June 27, 2008. http://vogue.co.uk/news/daily/080627-giambattista-valli-launches-bridal.aspx. (Accessed November 15, 2008.)

Baudot, François. *Fashion: The Twentieth Century.* New York: Universe Publishing, 1999.

BBC News. "Photographer Herb Ritts Dies." December 27, 2002. http://news.bbc.co.uk/1/hi/entertainment/showbiz/2608665.stm. (Accessed November 14, 2008.)

Beaton, Cecil. *Cecil Beaton: Memoirs of the 40s.* New York: McGraw-Hill, 1977.

———. *Cecil Beaton's Diaries—1922–1929, The Wandering Years,* 1961; *1939–1944, The Years Between,* 1965; *1948–1955, The Strenuous Years,* 1973. London: Weinfeld & Nicolson.

———. *Cecil's Beaton's New York.* London: Batsford, 1938.

———. *Fair Lady.* New York: Holt, Rinehart & Winston, 1964.

———. *Persona Grata* (with Kenneth Tynan). London: G. P. Putnam's Sons, 1954.

———. *The Book of Beauty.* London: Duckworth, 1930.

———. *The Glass of Fashion.* London: Weidenfeld & Nicolson, 1954; London: Casssell, 1989.

Bellafante, Ginia. *New York Times.* "Herb Ritts, Photographer of Celebrities, Is Dead at 50." December 27, 2002.

Bender, Marylin. *Beautiful People.* New York: Coward, McCann & Geoghegan, 1967.

Bennett, Lennie. *St. Petersburg Times.* "Back to the Drawing Board." April 4, 2003. http:// sptimes.com/2003/04/04/Floridian/Back_to_the_drawing_b.shtml. (Accessed November 15, 2008.)

Bently, Lessona, L. *Made-in-Italy.com.* "Fashion Houses: Missoni." http://www.made-in-italy.com/fashion/fashion_houses/missoni/intro.htm. (Accessed October 6, 2009.)

Bercovici, Jeff. *Media Life.* "Alexander Liberman: Major Figure in the Look of Magazines." http://medialifemagazine.com/news1999/nov99/news31122.html. (Accessed November 11, 2008.)

Bergen, Olivia. *Telegraph.* "Garance Dore's Designs on Kate Spade." August 17, 2013. http://fashion.telegraph.co.uk/news-features/tmg9482843/Garance-Dores-designs-on-Kate-Spade.html. (Accessed August 19, 2013.)

Berlinger, Max. *Esquire.* "PRPS Noir and the Case for $1,200 Jeans." May 3, 2013. http://www.esquire.com/blogs/mens-fashion/prps-1200-dollar-jeans-050313#ixzz2flijnYVD. (Accessed May 4, 2013.)

Bernard, Katherine. *Vogue.* "Belle De Jour: Paris Premier of Mademoiselle C." October 2, 2013. http://www.vogue.com/parties/the-paris-premiere-of-mademoiselle-c/. (Accessed November 12, 2013.)

Bernhard, Barbara. *Fashion in the '60s.* New York: St. Martin's Press, 1978.

Bertin, Celia. *Paris à la Mode.* London: Gollancz, 1956.

Between a Rock and a Hard Place: A History of American Sweatshops 1820–Present. http://americanhistory.si.edu/sweatshops/. (Accessed March 27, 2009.)[AU Q: Is this a physical exhibition somewhere? If so, we need to add that to the reference.]

Bianchino, Gloria, Grazietta Butazzi, Alessandra Mottola Molfino, and Arturo Carlo Quintavalle. *Italian Fashion.* New York: Rizzoli International Publications, 1988.

Bio. "Anna Wintour Biography (1949–)." http://www.biography.com/people/anna-wintour-214147#awesm=~oG8EVSYvsfQrMb (Accessed November 15, 2008.)

———. "Charles Tiffany Biography." http://www.biography.com/people/charles-tiffany-9507386. (Accessed August 10, 2013.)

———. "Estee Lauder Biography." http://www.thebiographychannel.co.uk/biographies/estee-lauder.html. (Accessed August 30, 2013.)

———. "Max Factor Biography." http://www.thebiographychannel.co.uk/biographies/max-factor.html. (Accessed September 2, 2013.)

———. "Nina Garcia. Biography." http://www.biography.com/people/nina-garcia-585954. (Accessed August 3, 2013.)

———. "Tim Gunn Biography." http://www.biography.com/people/tim-gunn-594086?page=2. Accessed August 10, 2013.)

Bissonnette, Anne (curator). *Charles Kleibacker: Master of the Bias.* http://www2.kent.edu/museum/exhibits/exhibitdetail.cfm?customel_datapageid_2203427=2274120. (Accessed November 10, 2008.)

Black, J. Anderson, and Madge Garland. *A History of Fashion.* New York: Morrow, 1980.

Blum, Stella. *Designs by Erté: Fashion Drawings & Illustrations from Harper's Bazaar*. New York: Harry N. Abrams, 1987.

BookRags. "Encyclopedia of World Biography on Annie Leibovitz." http://www.bookrags.com/biography/annie-leibovitz. (Accessed October 6, 2009.)

Bond, David. *The Guinness Guide to Twentieth Century Fashion*. Middlesex, England: Guinness Superlatives, 1989.

Borrelli, Laird. *Stylishly Drawn: Contemporary Fashion Illustration*. New York: Harry N. Abrams, 2001.

Bottega Veneta. http://www.bottegaveneta.com. (Accessed October 6, 2009.)

Boucher, François., with Yvonne Deslandres. *20,000 Years of Fashion: The History of Costume and Personal Adornment (expanded edition)*. New York: Harry N. Abrams, 1987.

Boyes, Megan. *Vogue.com UK*. "Christopher Kane Biography." May 11, 2011. http://www.vogue.co.uk/spy/biographies/christopher-kane-biography. (Accessed August 10, 2013.)

Brady, James. *Super Chic*. Boston: Little, Brown & Co., 1974.

Brandon Sun. "About." http://www.brandonsuncollection.com/about.html. (Accessed September 19, 2013.)

Broeske, Pat H. *OrangeCoast*. "Gwen Inc." March 2013. http://www.orangecoast.com/stefani/. (Accessed August 10, 2013.)

Brogden, Joanne. *Fashion Design*. London: Studio Vista, 1971.

Brooklyn Museum of Arts. *The Age of Worth*. New York, 1982.

Brooks Brothers. 2007. "Our Heritage." http://brooksbrothers.com/aboutus/heritage.tem. (Accessed October 30, 2007.)

Brown, Emma. *Interview*. "The Narrative Designer: Maki Oh." http://www.interviewmagazine.com/fashion/maki-oh-13-2013/#_. (Accessed September 2013.)

Brown, Janelle. *Salon.com*. "Liz Tilberis Harper's Bazaar Editor in Chief, a Legend in the World of Fashion, Dies of Cancer at 51." April 22, 1999. http://salon.com/people/obit/1999/04/22/tilberis/print.html. (Accessed November 14, 2008.)

Burberry. "About Burberry." http://burberry.com/AboutBurberry/History.aspx. (Accessed October 13, 2007.)

———. "Heritage." http://us.burberry.com/store/heritage/#/heritage/heritage-1800-1. (Accessed December 20, 2012.)

Burris-Meyer, Elizabeth. *This Is Fashion*. New York: Harper, 1943.

Bustler. "Cooper-Hewitt Announces Winners of the Ninth Annual National Design Awards." May 12, 2008. http://bustler.net/index.php/article/cooper_hewitt_announces_winners_of_the_ninth_annual_national_design_awards/. (Accessed November 14, 2008.)

Butterick. http://butterick.com. (Accessed March 27, 2009.)

Byers, Margaretta. *Designing Women*. New York: Simon & Schuster, 1938.

Byron Lars. "About." http://byronlarsbeautymark.com/index.php/about/. (Accessed August 10, 2013.)

Calasibetta, C.M., and Phyllis G. Tortora. *Fairchild's Dictionary of Fashion, 3rd ed*. New York: Fairchild Publications, 2003.

Carman, Rhonda Rice. "House of Creed." January 11, 2008. http://www.allthebestblog.com/2008/01/house-of-creed.html.

Carmody, Deirdre. *New York Times*. "Alexander Liberman, Conde Nast's Driving Creative Force, Is Dead at 87." November 20, 1999.

Carter, Ernestine. *Magic Names of Fashion*. New Jersey: Prentice-Hall, 1980.

———. *The Changing World of Fashion*. New York: G.P. Putnam's Sons, 1977.

———. *Twentieth Century Fashion, A Scrapbook: 1900 to Today*. London: Eyre Methuen, 1975.

Cartier. "History and Stories." http://www.cartier.us/maison/history-and-stories. (Accessed August 10, 2013.)

Cary, Christina. "Historic Dressmakers." http://www.whitebow.com/Historic_Dressmakers.html. (Accessed October 6, 2009.)

Cawthorne, Nigel. *Key Moments in Fashion: The Evolution of Style*. London: Octopus Publishing Group, 1998.

CBC News. "Leibovitz Gets O'Keeffe Accolade." http://www.cbc.ca/arts/artdesign/story/2009/10/03/leibovitz-okeeffe-honour.html. (Accessed October 6, 2009.)

Chadwick Bell. "Story: Chadwick Bell." http://chadwickbell.com/story.html. (Accessed August 13, 2013.)

Chapkis, Wendy, and Cynthia Enloe, eds. *Of Common Cloth: Women in the Global Textile Industry*. Amsterdam: Transnational Institute, 1983.

Charles-Roux, Edmonde. *Chanel: Her Life, Her World, and the Woman Behind the Legend She Herself Created*. New York: Random House, 1975.

———. *Chanel and Her World*. London: Weidenfeld & Nicolson, 1981.

Chase, Edna Woodman, and Ilka Chase. *Always in Vogue*. New York: Doubleday, 1954.

Chase, Jayne, and Jennifer Goodkind. *New York Social Diary*. "Teri Agins." http://newyorksocialdiary.com/node/2282. (Accessed November 3, 2008.)

Cheng, Andrea. *Market Watch*. "Jones to Sell Exclusive Rachel Roy Line at Macy's." April 16, 2009. http://www.marketwatch.com/story/jones-apparel-sell-exclusive-rachel. (Accessed December 3, 2013.)

Chernikoff, Leah. *Fashionista.com*." Fashion Illustrator Richard Hines On Sketching a Live Runway and His Project with Prada." December 2012. http://fashionista.com/2012/12/fashion-illustrator-richard-haines-on-sketching-the-runway-and-his-new-project-with-prada/. (Accessed October 1, 2013.)

———. *Fashionista.com*. "Prabal Gurung You Can Actually Afford: See the Designer's Collaboration for J.Crew." http://fashionista.com/2011/05/prabal-gurung-you-can-actually-afford-see-the-designers-first-collaboration-for-j-crew/. (Accessed July 14, 2013.)

Chic Report. *Fashion Week Daily.com*. "Barbie Plans to Turn the White House Pink." April 5, 2012. http://www.fashionweekdaily.com/chic-report/article/barbies-chris-benz-clad-bid-for-president. (Accessed August 13, 2013.)

Chicago Fashion Foundation. "Lana Bramlette." http://www.chicagofashionfoundation.org/index.php?option=com_content&view=article&id=6&Itemid=0. (Accessed August 15, 2013.)

Chloe. "History." http://chloe.com/version_en/. (Accessed November 11, 2008.)

Chris Benz. "Story." http://www.chris-benz.com. (Accessed August 11, 2013.)

Chrisp, Peter. *A History of Fashion and Costume Vol. 6: The Victorian Age*. New York: Facts on File, 2005.

Coleman, Elizabeth A. *Changing Fashions, 1800–1970*. New York: Brooklyn Museum, 1972.

———. *The Genius of Charles James*. Published for the exhibition at the Brooklyn Museum. New York: Holt, Rinehart and Winston, 1982.

———. *The Opulent Era: Fashions of Worth, Doucet and Pingat*. London: Thames and Hudson, 1992.

Collins, Amy Fine. *Vanity Fair*. "Toujours Couture." September 2009.

Conde Nast. "Heritage." http://www.condenast.com/about-us/heritage#/1909-conde-montrose-nast-buys-vogue-and-establishes-conde-nast-publications. (Accessed September 11, 2013.)

Conde Nast Portfolio.com. "Who Is Ungaro's New Designer Esteban Cortazar." November 30, 2007. http://portfolio.com/views/blogs/fashion-inc/2007/11/30/who-is-ungaros-new-designer-esteban-cortazar. (Accessed November 6, 2008.)

Conde Nast Russia. "History of Conde Nast." http://condenast.ru/en/about/history/. (Accessed September 11, 2013.)

Condra, Jill. *The Greenwood Encyclopedia of Clothing through World History*. Westport, CT: Greenwood Publishing, 2007.

Corbett, Rachel. *New York Magazine*. "Profile: 55DSL." http://nymag.com/listings/stores/55dsl/. (Accessed November 14, 2008.)

Cordero, Robert. *The Business of Fashion*. "First Person| Rag & Bone's Wainwright and Neville Say Focus First." September 14, 2012. http://www.businessoffashion.com/2012/09/first-person-rag-bones-wainwright-and-neville-say-focus-first.html. (Accessed October 20, 2013.)

Corrigan, J.C. *Marie Claire*. "Designer Dossier: Anna Molinari." http://marieclaire.com/hair/fashion/latest/anna-molinari-blumarine-fashion-designer. (Accessed November 11, 2008.)

Cosgrave, Bronwyn. *The Complete History of Costume & Fashion: From Ancient Egypt to the Present Day*. London: Octopus Publishing Group, 2000.

Costume Gallery. http://costumegallery.com. (Accessed March 27, 2009.)

Costume Institute, Metropolitan Museum of Art. *The World of Balenciaga*. New York, 1972.

———. *Yves Saint Laurent*. New York, 1983.

Council of Fashion Designers of America (CFDA). "CFDA Fashion Awards: Past Winners, 2009." http://www.cfda.com/index.php?option=com_cfda_content&task=fashion_awards_display&category_id=31. (Accessed October 5, 2009.)

———. "Colleen Atwood, American Costume Designer." http://cfda.com/designer/colleen-atwood. (Accessed September 10, 2013.)

———. "Marcus Wainwright & David Neville, Rag & Bone." http://cfda.com/designer/marcus-wainwright-and-david-neville-for-rag-bone. (Accessed November 20, 2013.)

———. "Tom Ford: CFDA Member Profile." http://www.cfda.com/index.php?option=com_cfda_content&task=members_display&user_name=TomFord. (Accessed October 5, 2009.)

Cowles, Charlotte. *The Cut*. "Naeem Khan's Messy Lawsuit Nipped in the Bud." http://nymag.com/thecut/2013/08/naeem-khans-messy-lawsuit-nipped-in-the-bud.html. (Accessed November 10, 2013.)

———. *New York Magazine*. "Isabel and Ruben Toledo Partner With Lane Bryant." October 8, 2013. http://nymag.com/thecut/2013/10/isabel-and-ruben-toledo-partner-with-lane-bryant.html. (Accessed October 10, 2013.)

Craig, Tina. *Bag Snob*. "The Grace of Derek Lam." April 23, 2008. http://bagsnob.com/2008/04/the_grace_of_derek_lam.html. (Accessed November 10, 2008.)

Craven, J. *Vogue.com UK*. "Mario Testino." April 20, 2008. http://vogue.co.uk/biographies/080420-mario-testino-biography.aspx. (Accessed November 14, 2008.)

Creed, C. *Made to Measure*. London: Jarrolds, 1961.

Creed Fragrances. "Official UK Website." http://www.creedfragrances.co.uk/site. (Accessed October 6, 2009.)

———. "Winner by a Nose." March 23, 2003. http://www.creedfragrances.co.uk/site/press_coverage/ios_mar_2003.

Creed Perfumes. "Official US Website." http://www.creedperfumes.us. (Accessed October 6, 2009.)

Daché, Lilly. *Lilly Dache's Glamour Book*. Philadelphia: J.B. Lippincott, 1956.

———. *Talking through My Hats*. Edited by Dorothy Roe Lewis. New York: Coward-McCann, 1946.

Damn That's Some Fine Tailoring. "Sandy Powell on Costume Design." June 21, 2013. http://dtsft.wordpress.com/2013/06/21/sandy-powell-on-costume-design/. (Accessed August 20, 2013.)

Davenport, Millia. *The Book of Costume*, Vol. 1. New York: Crown Publishers, 1976.

Daves, Jessica. *Ready-Made Miracle*. New York: G.P. Putman's Sons, 1967.

Daves, Jessica, Bryan Holme, Alexander Liberman, and Katharine Tweed, eds. *The World in Vogue*. New York: Viking Press, 1963.

Davis, Boyd. *Fashion Windows*. "Loewe by Jose Enrique Ona Selfa." March 14, 2002. http://fashionwindows.com/runway_shows/loewe/default.asp. (Accessed November 11, 2008.)

Davis, Mari. *Fashion Windows*. "Lilly Pulitzer: True American Classic." http://fashionwindows.com/fashion/lilly_pulitzer/default.asp. (Accessed November 13, 2008.)

Day, Elizabeth. *The Guardian Observer blog*. "Why Racism Stalked the London Catwalk." February 17, 2008. http://guardian.co.uk/lifeandstyle/2008/feb/17/fashion.londonfashionweek. (Accessed November 17, 2008.)

DeGraw, I.G. *25 Years, 25 Couturiers*. Denver Art Museum, Denver, CO., 1975.

Delmotta, Deanna. *Manchester Evening News*. "Unconditional Fun as Cool New Brand Hits Manchester." August 8, 2011. http://www.manchestereveningnews.co.uk/whats-on/find-things-to-do/unconditional-fun-as-cool-new-brand-867595. (Accessed October 10, 2013.)

De Marly, Diana. *Costume on the Stage 1600-1940*. Summit, PA: Rowman & Littlefield, 1982.

———. *The History of Haute Couture, 1850–1950*. New York: Holmes and Meir, 1994.

———. *Worth, Father of Haute Couture*. New York: Holmes and Meir, 1991.

Demornex, J. *Madeleine Vionnet*. Translated by Augusta Audubert. New York: Rizzoli International Publications, 1991.

DeNinno, Nadine. *International Business Times*. "New York Fashion Week: Alice + Olivia By Stacey Bendet All Grown Up For Spring 2014 [PHOTOS]." September 11 2013. http://www.ibtimes.com/new-york-fashion-week-alice-olivia-stacey-bendet-all-grown-spring-2014-photos-1404425. (Accessed November 11, 2013.)

de Osma, G. *Mariano Fortuny: His Life and Work*. New York: Rizzoli International Publications, 1994.

Derrick, R., and Robin Muir, eds. *Unseen Vogue: The Secret History of Fashion Photography*. London: Little, Brown and Company, 2002.

Deschodt, A. *Mariano Fortuny, un Magicien de Venise*. Tours, France: Editions du Regard, 2000.

Deschodt, A., and Daretta Davanzo Poli. *Fortuny*. New York: Harry N. Abrams, 2001.

Design History Mashup. "Alexey Brodovitch." April 1, 2008. http://designhistorymashup.blogspot.com/2008/04/alexey-brodovitch.html. (Accessed August 12, 2013.)

Deslandres, Y. *Poiret: Paul Poiret 1879–1944*. New York: Rizzoli International Publications, 1987.

Destination Iman. "Bio: Fashion Designer Duro Olowu." March 25, 2013. http://destinationiman.com/bio-fashion-designer-duro-olowu/. (Accessed September 11, 2013.)

Devlin, P. *Vogue Book of Fashion Photography*. London: Thames and Hudson, 1978.

Diamonstein, B. *Fashion: The Inside Story*. New York: Rizzoli International Publications, Inc., 1985.

Dior, C. *Dior by Dior*. Translated by Antonia Fraser. London: Weidenfeld & Nicolson, 1957.

———. *Christian Dior and I*. Translated by Antonia Fraser. New York: E.P. Dutton & Company, Inc., 1957.

———. *Talking about Fashion*. Translated by Eugenia Sheppard. New York: G.P. Putnam's Sons, 1954.

Dixon, H.V. *The Rag Pickers*. New York: Avon, 1971.

Dorner, J. *Fashion: The Changing Shape of Fashion through the Years*. London: Octopus Books, 1974.

———. *Fashion in the 40s and 50s*. London: Ian Allen, 1975.

Donahue, Wendy. *Chicago Tribune*. "Remarkable Woman: Lana Bramlette." Februaury 24, 2013. http://articles.chicagotribune.com/2013-02-24/features/ct-tribu-remarkable-bramlette-20130224_1_necklace-jewelry-designer-lana-jewelry. (Accessed August 15, 2013.)

Donaldson, Aurelia. *Telegraph*. "Simone Rocha Interview: Chic Off the Old Block." March 13, 2013. http://fashion.telegraph.co.uk/news-features/TMG9943293/Simone-Rocha-interview-chic-off-the-old-block.html. (Accessed October 13, 2013.)

Downey, L. "Levi Strauss: A Short Biography." 2005. http://levistrauss.com/Downloads/History-Denium.pdf. (Accessed September 23, 2007.)

Dreyfus, Hannah. *Parade.Com*. "Project Runway's Tim Gunn: 'I'm the Anti-Trend Guy.'" July 11, 2013. http://www.parade.com/52685/hannah_dreyfus/project-runways-tim-gunn-im-the-anti-trend-guy/. (Accessed August 10, 2013.)

Dudbridge, Saxony. *Catwalk Yourself*. "Unconditional." http://catwalkyourself.com/fashion-biographies/unconditional/ (Accessed October 10, 2013.)

Dumenco. Simon. *New York Magazine*. "Fashion Photographer Seeks Models/Celebrities for a Little Rough Play: Steven Klein Has Become the Fashion World's Current Superstar by Understanding How to Be Transgressive and Commercial at the Same Time." http://nymag.com/nymetro/shopping/fashion/features/n_10371/. (Accessed September 2, 2013.)

Duncan, N.H. *History of Fashion Photography*. New York: Alpine Press, 1979.

Durbin, Johnathan. *Esquire*. "Michael Bastain Has a Right to Exit." February 15, 2011. http://www.esquire.com/style/michael-bastian-0311. (Accessed August 12, 2013.)

Ecco Domani. "Fashion Foundation." http://www.eccodomani.com/fashion-foundation/award-winners/The-Blonds.asp. (Accessed August 12, 2013.)

Ehrlich, D., updated by Karen Raugust. *Fashion Encyclopedia*. "Alexander Julian." http://fashionencyclopedia.com/Ja-Kh/Julian-Alexander.html. (Accessed November 8, 2008.)

Elizabeth Arden. "Corporate Overview." http://ir.elizabetharden.com/phoenix.zhtml?c=98237&p=irol-IRHome. (Accessed August 20, 2013.)

Elizabeth Arden New York. "Her Story." http://www
.elizabetharden.com/Elizabeth-Arden-Biography/her
-story,default,pg.html. (Accessed August 20, 2013.)

Emanuel, David, and Elizabeth Emanuel. *Style for All
Seasons*. London: Pavilion: Michael Joseph, 1983.

Encyclopedia Britannica. "Alexey Brodovitch." http://www
.britannica.com/EBchecked/topic/1079780/Alexey
-Brodovitch. (Accessed August 20, 2013.)

Erté. *Erté Fashions*. New York: St. Martin's Press, 1972.

———. *Erté—Things I Remember*. London: Peter Owen
Limited, 1983.

Estee Lauder. "About Estee Lauder." http://www.esteelauder
.com/cms/about/index.tmpl. (Accessed August 30, 2013.)

Estee Lauder Companies. "Our Brands." http://www
.elcompanies.com/Pages/Our-Brands.aspx. (Accessed
August 30, 2013.)

Etherington-Smith, M. *Patou*. New York: St. Martin's
Press, 1984.

Eubank, K., and Phyllis Tortora. *Survey of Historic Costume,
2nd ed.* New York: Fairchild Publications, 1994.

Eudon Choi. "Eudon Choi Biography." http://www.eudonchoi
.com/biography.html. (Accessed September 10, 2013.)

Ewing, E., and Alice Mackrell. *History of 20th Century
Fashion, Rev. 4th ed.* New York: Quite Specific Media
Group, 2002.

EyeWitness to History. http://eyewitnesstohistory.com.
(Accessed March 27, 2009.)

Fairchild, J. *The Fashionable Savages*. New York: Doubleday,
1965.

Family Business. "The World's Oldest Family Companies."
http://www.familybusinessmagazine.com/worldsoldest
/worldsoldest4.html. (Accessed August 4, 2009).

Farber, R. *The Fashion Photographer*. New York:
Watson-Guptill, 1981.

Farrell-Beck, J., and Jean Parsons. *20th-Century Dress in the
United States*. New York: Fairchild Books, 2007.

Fashion.at. "Andrew Gn." http://fashion.at/collections
/andrewgn12-2002b.htm. (Accessed November 6, 2008.)

Fashion Blah Blah. "Interview with Richard Haines."
November 9, 2008. http://www.fashionblahblah.com/2008
/09/interview-with-richard-haines.html. (Accessed
September 20, 2013.)

Fashion Encyclopedia. http://fashionencyclopedia.com.
(Accessed March 27, 2009.)

Fashion-era. http://fashion-era.com. (Accessed March 27,
2009.)

Fashion Forum. http://fashion-forum.org. (Accessed March
27, 2009.)

Fashion Fun House Emporium. "David Blond of the Blonds:
On Betty White, High Heels, and Being Blond." May 22,
2010. http://www.fashionfunhouseemporium.com/tag
/david-blond-biography. (Accessed August 12, 2013.)

Fashion Institute of Technology. *Fortuny*. New York, 1981.

Fashion Model Directory. "Adi, Ange, Kai and Gabi As Four."
http://www.fashionmodeldirectory.com/designers/adi
-ange-kai-and-gabi-as-four/. (Accessed September 30,
2013.)

———. "Duro Olowu." http://www.fashionmodeldirectory.
com/designers/duro-olowu/. (Accessed September 11,
2013.)

———. "Florence Nightingale Graham." http://www
.fashionmodeldirectory.com/designers/florence
-nightingale-graham/. (Accessed August 20, 2013.)

———. "Justin Thornton & Thea Bregazzi." http://www
.fashionmodeldirectory.com/designers/justin-thornton
--thea-bregazzi/. (Accessed September 19, 2013.)

———. "Kevan Hall." http://www.fashionmodeldirectory
.com/designers/kevan-hall/. (Accessed July 20, 2013.)

———. "L.A.M.B." http://www.fashionmodeldirectory.com
/brands/lamb/. (Accessed September 30, 2013.)

———. "Paul Iribe." http://www.fashionmodeldirectory
.com/designers/paul-iribe/. (Accessed September 30, 2013.)

———. "Thierry Hermes." http://www.fashionmodeldirectory
.com/designers/thierry-hermes/. (Accessed September 2,
2013.)

———. "Thomas Burberry." http://www.fashion
modeldirectory.com/designers/thomas-burberry/.
(Accessed August 14, 2013.)

———. "Walter Seiger." http://www.fashionmodeldirectory.
com/designers/walter-steiger/. (Accessed October 1,
2013.)

Fashion Week Daily. "Nina Garcia to Go From Hachette to…
Hachette?" May 8, 2008. http://www.fashionweekdaily
.com/news/fullstory.sps?inewsid=2397191. (Accessed
November 6, 2008.)

———. "Project Runway Status Confirmed: Nina Garcia to
Remain as Elle Editor-at-Large through Season 5." May
15, 2008. http://fashionweekdaily.com/news/fullstory.
sps?inewsid=4354412. (Accessed November 11, 2008.)

Fashion Windows. "Ralph Ricci: Marrying the Discipline of
Art & Philosophy." http://fashionwindows.com/fashion/
chado_ralph_rucci/default.asp. (Accessed November 13,
2008.)

———. "Stuart Vevers Replaces Jose Enrique Ona Selfa at
Loewe as Creative Director." July 26, 2007. http://blog
.fashionwindows.com/?p=160. (Accessed November 11,
2008.)

Fenner, Justine. *Fashionologie*. "Break Time: Chris Benz Is
Skipping Fashion Week, and He's Not the Only One."
January 10, 2013. http://www.fashionologie.com
/Chris-Benz-Skip-Fall-2013-New-York-Fashion-Week
-Show-26725766. (Accessed August 11, 2013.)

Ferragamo, S. *Shoemaker of Dreams: The Autobiography of
Salvatore Ferragamo, 3rd ed.* Florence: Centro Di, 1985.

Fine Fashion. Philadelphia: Philadelphia Museum of Art,
1979.

Fitzpatrick, Tommye. "Turning Point| How Joseph Altuzarra Found His Signature Silhouette." August 20, 2013. http://www.businessoffashion.com/2013/08/turning-point-how-joseph-altuzarra-found-his-signature-silhouette.html. (Accessed September 25, 2013.)

Fleischner, J. *Mrs. Lincoln and Mrs. Keckley: The Remarkable Story of the Friendship Between a First Lady and a Former Slave*. New York: Broadway Books, 2003.

Fogarty, A. *Wife-Dressing*. New York: Julian Messner, 1959.

Fortini, A. *Slate*. "Defending *Vogue*'s Evil Genius: The Brilliance of Anna Wintour." February 10, 2005. http://slate.com/id/2113278/. (Accessed November 15, 2008.)

Fortuny, M. *Immagini e Materiali del Laboratorio Fortuny*. Venice: Comune di Venezia Marsilio Edition, 1978.

Fortuny nella Belle Epoque. Milan: Electa, 1984.

Foxley, D. *New York Observer*. "Calvin Klein Designer Francisco Costa Discusses Inspiration." February 8, 2008. http://observer.com/2008/calvin-klein-designer-francisco-costa-discusses-inspiration. (Accessed November 6, 2008.)

France-Presse, Agence. *Global Post*. "Hermes Creates $13,000 Basketball for Beverly Hills Store Opening" August 30, 2013. http://www.globalpost.com/dispatch/news/afp/130830/hermes-creates-13000-basketball-us-store. (Accessed September 2, 2013.)

Fraser, K. *The Fashionable Mind*. Boston: David R. Godine, 1984.

Frank, Julia. *Vogue Australia*. "Dion Lee Speaks after his NYFW Debut." September 12, 2013. http://www.vogue.com.au/fashion/news/dion+lee+speaks+after+his+nyfw+debut+,27134. (Accessed September 20, 2013.)

Funding Universe. "Lane Bryant, Inc." http://www.fundinguniverse.com/company-histories/Lane-Bryant-Inc-Company-History.html. (Accessed March 27, 2009.)

Gaines, S. *Simply Halston*. New York: Jove Publications, 1993.

Galante, P. *Mademoiselle Chanel*. Chicago: Regency, 1973.

Gallager, Jenna Gabriel. *Harpers Bazzar.com*. "Alexey Brodovitch: 1934–1958." June 1, 2007. http://www.harpersbazaar.com/magazine/140-years/bazaar-140-0607. (Accessed July 15, 2013.)

Galvin, C. *Sunday Times*. "Annie Leibovitz: Nothing Left to Hide." October 5, 2008. http://entertainment.timesonline.co.uk/tol/arts_and_entertainment/visual_arts/article4860955.ece. (Accessed November 10, 2008.)

Gap Inc. http://gapinc.com. (Accessed March 26, 2009.)

Garancedore.com. "Garance Dore." http://www.garancedore.fr/en/a-propos/. (Accessed August 19, 2013.)

Garland, M. *Fashion*. London: Penguin Books, 1962.

———. *The Changing Form of Fashion*. London: J.M. Dent & Sons, 1970.

Giambattista Valli. "Chronology." http://giambattistavalli.com/. (Accessed November 14, 2008.)

———. "Fashion Designer." http://giambattistavalli.com/. (Accessed November 15, 2008.)

Giroud, F. *Dior*. New York: Rizzoli International Publications, 1987.

Givhan, R. *Washington Post*. "Back in Fashion/In the Church of Saint Laurent, Heresy and Revival: Can Stefano Pilati Convert Reverence into Relevance?" May 27, 2007.

———. *Washington Post*. "Fashion Sense: Luxury, Pure Style, Understated Eloquence: Akris's Creations for Women of Power." May 31. 2005.

———. *Washington Post*. "Taking Off From the Runway Business: For Blass Designer, the Industry Wore Thin." June 1, 2007.

Gladwell, Malcolm. *The New Yorker*. "The Color of Money." March 28, 2011. http://www.newyorker.com/arts/critics/books/2011/03/28/110328crbo_books_gladwell. (Accessed July 20, 2013.)

Glamour. "Simone Rochas." http://www.glamourmagazine.co.uk/fashion/celebrity-fashion/2013/02/who-to-follow-at-fashion-weeks-on-twitter#!image-number=23. (Accessed October 13, 2013.)

———. "Rachel Roy." http://www.glamourmagazine.co.uk/rachel-roy. (Accessed July 20, 2013.)

Glynn, P. *In Fashion: Dress in the Twentieth Century*. New York: Oxford University Press, 1978.

———. *Skin to Skin*. New York: Oxford University Press, 1982.

Gold, A. *75 Years of Fashion*. New York: Fairchild Publications, 1975.

———. *90 Years of Fashion*. New York: Fairchild Publications, Inc., 1990.

Gorsline, D.W. *One World of Fashion, 4th ed*. New York: Fairchild Publications, 1986.

———. *What People Wore: 1,800 Illustrations from Ancient Times to the Early Twentieth Century*. New York: Dover Publications, 1994.

———. *What People Wore: A Visual History of Dress from Ancient Times to 20th Century America*. New York: Random House Value Publishing, 1987.

Greene, Walter. *New York Carib News*. "A Grand American Welcome for Designer Duro Olowu." April 10, 2013. http://www.nycaribnews.com/news.php?viewStory=3935. (Accessed September 19, 2013.)

Grundburg, Andy. *AIGA*. "Alexey Brodovitch." 1988. http://www.aiga.org/medalist-alexeybrodovitch/. (Accessed July 15, 2013.)

Gryn, Naomi. *The Guardian*. "Stitches in Time: Sandy Powell's Oscar-winning Costumes." October 17, 2012. http://www.theguardian.com/artanddesign/2012/oct/17/sandy-powell-oscar-winning-costumes. (Accessed July 30, 2013.)

Gucci Group. http://guccigroup.com. (Accessed March 27, 2009.)

Haedrich, M. *Coco Chanel: Her Life, Her Secrets*. Boston: Little, Brown & Co., 1972.

H&M. "Roberto Cavalli at H&M." http://hm.com/us /abouthm/robertocavalliathm__designercooperation .nhtml. (Accessed November 17, 2008.)

Harmin, Justine. *People Style Watch.* "Mary-Kate and Ashley's Elizabeth and James: Not Named After Little Sis." January 31, 2012. http://stylenews.peoplestylewatch .com/2012/01/31/mary-kate-and-ashley-clothing-line -elizabeth/. (Accessed July 19, 2013.)

Hart, A., and Susan North. *Seventeenth and Eighteenth Century Fashion in Detail.* New York: Rizzoli, 1998.

Hartnell, N. *Royal Courts of Fashion.* London: Cassell, 1971.

———. *Silver and Gold.* London: Evans Brothers, 1955.

Harries, Rhiannon. *The Independent.* "How We Met: Wainwright & David Neville." March 15, 2009. http:// www.independent.co.uk/news/people/profiles/how-we -met-marcus-wainwright--david-neville-1642875.html. (Accessed October 20, 2013.)

Hawes, E. *Fashion Is Spinach.* New York: Random House, 1938.

———. *It's Still Spinach.* Boston: Little, Brown and Co., 1954.

HBS Africa Business Conference. "Amaka Osakwe." http:// hbsafrica.conferenceapp.com/members/amaka-osakwe. (Accessed September 19, 2013.)

Head, E. *The Dress Doctor.* Boston: Little, Brown and Co., 1959.

Hearst Corporation. "Glenda Bailey Editor-In-Chief, *Harper's Bazaar.*" http://hearstcorp.com/biography_other .php?id=12&cat_id=6. (Accessed November 5, 2008.)

Helena Rubinstein Foundation. "About Helena Rubinstein." http://www.helenarubinsteinfdn.org/about.html. (Accessed October 2, 2013.)

Helmut Newton. "Biography." http://helmutnewton.com /helmut_newton/biography/. (Accessed Novmber 11, 2008.)

Herb Ritts. "Biography." http://herbritts.com/about/. (Accessed November 14, 2008.)

Hibbert, C., and Adam Hibbert. *A History of Costume and Fashion, Vol. 8: The Twentieth Century.* New York: Facts on File, 2005.

High, Kamau. *Adweek.* "Profile: Marc Ecco." April 7, 2008. http://www.adweek.com/news/advertising-branding /profile-marc-ecko-95439. (Accessed July 30, 2013.)

Hilgate, Mark. *Vogue.com.* "Duro Olowu Makes a Mean Dress and a Mean Coat for Spring 2014." http://www .vogue.com/vogue-daily/article/duro-olowu-makes -a-mean-dress-and-a-mean-coat-for-spring-2014/#1. (Accessed September 20, 2013.)

History Matters. "Dressmaker and Former Salve Elizabeth Keckley (ca. 1818-1907) Tells How She Gained Her Freedom, 1868." http://historymatters.gmu.edu/d/6224. (Accessed October 6, 2009.)

Holborow, Olivia. *Vogue UK.* "Who's Who: Isabel Marant." July 6, 2012. http://www.vogue.co.uk/spy/biographies /isabel-marant. (Accessed August 2, 2013.)

Holgate, Mark. *New York Magazine.* "State of Grace." August 25, 2002. http://nymag.com/nymetro/shopping/fashion /features/n7581/. (Accessed August 14, 2013.)

Holmlund, Marcus. *PAPER.*" Brandon Sun: Fur Real." http:// www.papermag.com/2012/02/brandon_sun_fur_real. php. (Accessed September 19, 2013.)

Horst. *Salute to the Thirties.* New York: Viking Press, 1971.

Horyn, C. *New York Times.* "Citizen Anna." February 1, 2007.

———. *New York Times.* "On the Runway: Reed Krakoff to Go Solo, Leaving Coach next Year." April 23, 2013. http:// runway.blogs.nytimes.com/2013/04/23/reed-krakoff -to-go-solo-leaving-coach-next-year/?_r=0. (Accessed October 3, 2013.)

———. *New York Times.* "When Is a Fashion Ad Not a Fashion Ad?" April 8, 2008.

Hot Watches. "History of Diesel." http://hotwatches.co.uk /diesel-watches/. (Accessed November 14, 2008.)

Houck, C. *The Fashion Encyclopedia.* New York: St. Martin's Press, 1982.

Howell, G. *In Vogue: Six Decades of Fashion.* New York: Viking Press, 1979.

Hubpages. "The History of Cartier." July 16. 2011. http:// jill47.hubpages.com/hub/The-History-of-Cartier. (Accessed August 14, 2013.)

Huffington Post. "Rachel Roy." http://www.huffingtonpost .com/rachel-roy/. (Accessed July 20, 2013.)

———. "Tim Gunn Reveals He Never Came Out To His Family On 'Larry King Now'" http://www.huffingtonpost .com/2013/09/18/tim-gunn-coming-out-gay-_n _3949879.html. (Accessed September 18, 2013.)

Hulanicki, B. *From A to Biba.* London: Hutchinson, 1983.

IMDb (Internet Movie Database). "Sandy Powell Awards." http://www.imdb.com/name/nm0694309/awards. (Accessed August 20, 2013.)

Industry of One. "House of the Rising Sun: Brandon Sun." http://industryofone.com/Brandon/.Uumg43ddVF8. (Accessed September 19, 2013.)

The Independent. "Herb Ritts Photographer of the Famous and Fashionable." December 30, 2002.

———. "This Man Is on Fire: Gareth Pugh—Britain's Newest Star Designer." September 15, 2008.

Informat. "Biography of Peter Som." January 18, 2007. http://infomat.com/whoswho/petersom.html. (Accessed November 17, 2008.)

———. "John Hardy Biography." http://www.infomat.com /whoswho/johnhardy.html. (Accessed July 30, 2013.)

———. "Lilly Pulitzer." http://infomat.com/whoswho /lillypulitzer.html. (Accessed November 13, 2008.)

International Center of Photography. "Steven Meisel Applied Photography." http://www.icp.org/site/c.dnJGKJNsFqG /b.2079967/k.A4A8/Steven_Meisel.htm. (Accessed September 22, 2008.)

Internet World Stats. "Usage and Population Statistics." http://internetworldstats.com. (Accessed March 27, 2009.)

Interview. "Introducing Stacey Bennett of Alice and Olivia." http://www.interviewmagazine.com/fashion /introducing-stacey-bendet-alice-and-olivia#_. (Accessed July 20, 2013.)

———. "Studio Visit: threeASFOUR Look into the Mirrors." http://www.interviewmagazine.com/fashion /threeasfour#_. (Accessed September 21, 2013.)

Investors Business Incorporated. 2007. "Charles Tiffany Found All That Glitters in Jewelry." http://money.cnn .com/news/newsfeeds/articles/newstex/IBD-0001 -20512044.htm. (November 1, 2007.)

Isabel Marant. "Bio." http://www.isabelmarant.com/en /workshop/biography/. (Accessed August 2, 2013.)

Jachimowicz, E. *Eight Chicago Women and Their Fashion, 1860–1929.* Chicago: Chicago Historical Society, 1978.

Jaeger. 2007. "About Us." http://jaeger.co.uk/index.cfm?page =1024. (Accessed October 10, 2007.)

Jed Root. "Scott Schuman." http://www.jedroot.com /photographers/scott-schuman. (Accessed August 20, 2013.)

Jewelryaccessories.com. "Paul Iribe." http://www.blog .jewelryaccessories.com/fashion-illustrators/408-paul -iribe.html. (Accessed September 30, 2013.)

John Hardy. "Our Story." http://www.johnhardy.com/spirit /our-story. (Accessed September 2, 2013.)

Johnston, L. *Nineteenth-Century Fashion in Detail.* London: V&A Publications, 2005.

Jouve, M. *Balenciaga (Universe of Fashion).* New York: Universe Books, 1998.

Judith Ripka. "Judith Ripka the Designer." http://www .judithripka.com/the-designer.html (Accessed September 29, 2013.)

Kalaw, Ana. *The Philippine Star.* "Lesley Mobo: Landing the London Dream." June, 16, 2004. http://www.philstar .com/fashion-and-beauty/254179/lesley-mobolanding -london-dream. (Accessed August 29, 2013.)

Kansas City Public Schools. "Agins, Teri: Wyandotte High School, 1971." http://kckps.org/recognition/alumni/2005 /agins.html. (Accessed November 3, 2008.)

Karan, D. *Donna Karan New York: An American Woman Observed.* New York: Donna Karan Company, 1987.

Karl Kani. "Karl Kani Legacy." http://karlkani.com/karl -kani-the-legacy/. (Accessed June 20, 2011.)

Karmali, Sarah. *Vogue.co.uk.* "River Island's Next Big Thing." July 1, 2013. http://www.vogue.co.uk/news/2013/07/01 /eudon-choi-for-river-island-design-forum---clothing -collection, (Accessed August 2, 2013.)

Keckley, E. *Behind the Scenes: Or, Thirty Years a Slave, and Four Years in the White House.* London: Penguin Books, 2005.

Keenan, B. *Dior in Vogue.* New York: Random House Value Publishing, 1988.

Kellogg, A., Amy T. Peterson, Stefani Bay, and Natalie Swindell. *In an Influential Fashion: An Encyclopedia of Nineteenth- and Twentieth-Century Fashion Designers and Retailers Who Transformed Dress.* Westport, CT: Greenwood Publishing Group, 2002.

Kennedy, S. *Pucci: A Renaissance in Fashion.* New York: Abbeville Press, 1991.

Kennett, F. *The Collector's Book of Fashion.* New York: Crown Publishers, 1983.

Kering. "Brands: Christopher Kane." http://www.kering .com/en/brands/luxury/christopher-kane. (Accessed September 19, 2013.)

Kevan Hall. "About." http://www.kevanhalldesigns.com /profile.html. (Accessed July 20, 2013.)

King, N. *J Camp Live!* "Profile: Reporter and Author Teri Agins." July 31, 2007. http://lyingisbad.com /jcamplive/?p=19. (Accessed November 3, 2008.)

Khornak, L. *Fashion 2001.* New York: Viking Press, 1982.

Koday, Dan. *Seventeen.* "Mary-Kate & Ashley Olsen Have a New Fashion Line at J.C. Penney." October 26, 2009. http://www.seventeen.com/fashion/blog/olsen-twins -launch-olsenboye-clothing-line-at-jcpenney. (Accessed August 19, 2013.)

Koenig, G. *Women's Wear Daily.* "Creed Offers a Taste of Florence." July 6, 2009.

Krupnick, Ellie. *Huffington Post.* "Tim Gunn: Fashion Seems To End At a Size 12." August 23, 2013. http://www .huffingtonpost.com/2013/08/23/tim-gunn-size _n_3799450.html. (Accessed September 1, 2013.)

Kybalova, L., Olga Herbenova, and Milena Lamorova. *The Pictorial Encyclopedia of Fashion, 2nd ed.* Translated by Claudia Rosoux. England: Hamlyn Publishers, 1968.

Lagerfeld, K. *Lagerfeld's Sketchbook: Karl Lagerfeld's Illustrated Fashion Journal of Anna Piaggi.* London: Weidenfeld & Nicolson, 1988.

Lakewood Public Library. "Women in History: Elizabeth Keckley Biography." March 9, 2009. http://www.lkwdpl .org/wihohio/keck-eli.htm. (Accessed October 6, 2009.)

Lambert, E. *World of Fashion: People, Places and Resources, 2nd ed.* New York: R.R. Bowker Company, 1979.

L.A.M.B. "L.A.M.B the Brand." http://www.l-a-m-b.com/. (Accessed August 15, 2013.)

Lana Jewelry. "Lana-Designer." http://lanajewelry.com /about-lana. (Accessed August 15, 2013.)

Langlade, E. *Rose Bertin: The Creator of Fashion at the Court of Marie-Antoinette.* Adapted from the French by Dr. Angelo S. Rappoport. New York: Charles Scribner's Sons, 1913.

Larocca, A. *New York.* "Straight Shooter." August 17, 2008.

———. *New York.* "The Dapper Mr. Browne." August 20, 2006.

Latour, A. *Kings of Fashion*. Translated by Mervyn Saville. London: Weidenfeld & Nicolson, 1958.

———. *Paris Fashion*. London: Michael Joseph, 1972.

Laver, J. *A Concise History of Costume*. New York: Oxford University Press, 1988.

———. *Fashion, Art and Beauty*. New York: Costume Institute, Metropolitan Museum of Art, 1967.

———. *Taste and Fashion*. London: George G. Harrap, 1937.

Laver, J., and others. *Costume and Fashion: A Concise History, 4th ed*. London: Thames & Hudson, 2002.

Lavine, W.R. *In a Glamorous Fashion*. New York: Charles Scribner's Sons, 1980.

Lee, S.T., ed. *American Fashion: The Life and Lines of Adrian, Mainbocher, McCardell, Norell & Trigére*. New York: Quadrangle/The New York Times Book Co., 1975.

Leese, E. *Costume Design in the Movies*. New York: Frederick Ungar Publishing, 1977.

Leung, Mariana. *Hellolamode*. "Shop and Give: Byron Lars for Fashion Fights Cancer." July 16, 2012. http://blog.hellolamode.com/2012/07/16/shop-and-give-byron-lars-for-fashion-fights-cancer/. (Accessed August 10, 2013.)

Lewis, J. *Artinfo.com*. "Artist Walk: Annie Leibovitz." October 19, 2006. http://www.artinfo.com/news/story/22798/artist-walk-annie-leibovitz. (Accessed October 6, 2009.)

Lewis, Jaquelyn. *WWD/ Footwear News*. "Walter Steiger Appoints GM, Expands Men's Retail." January 25, 2013. http://www.wwd.com/footwear-news/markets/walter-steiger-appoints-gm-expands-mens-retail-6661140. (Accessed September 29, 2013.)

Levi Strauss & Co. http://levistrauss.com. (Accessed March, 26, 2009.)

———. 2007. "Jacob Davis: His Life and Contributions." http://levistrauss.com/Downloads/History_Jacob_Davis_Biography.pdf. (Accessed October 3, 2007.)

Levin, P.L. *The Wheels of Fashion*. New York: Doubleday, 1965.

Ley, S. *Fashion for Everyone: The Story of Ready-to-Wear*. New York: Charles Scribner's Sons, 1975.

Leymarie, J. *Chanel*. New York: Rizzoli International Publications, 1989.

Lincoln Institute. "Abraham Lincoln's White House: Elizabeth Keckley (1818–1907)." http://www.mrlincolnswhitehouse.org/inside.asp?ID=60&subjectID=2. (Accessed October 6, 2009.)

Liz Claiborne Group. http://lizclaiborne.com. (Accessed March 27, 2009.)

Loughran, M. *Suite101.com*. "Elsa Peretti Jewelry Icon Designer for Tiffany & Co." October 27, 2007. http://jewelry-makers.suite101.com/article.cfm/elsa_peretti. (Accessed November 18, 2008.)

L'Oreal. "Helena Rubinstein." http://www.loreal.com/brands/loreal-luxe/helena-rubinstein.aspx. (Accessed August 4, 2013.)

LVMH Group. http://lvmh.com. (Accessed March 27, 2009.)

Lynam, R., ed. *Couture: An Illustrated History of the Great Paris Designers and Their Creations*. New York: Doubleday, 1972.

Max Factor. "The Max Factor Story." https://www.maxfactor.co.uk/heritage/the-max-factor-story. (Accessed September 18, 2013.)

Maclowe Gallery. "Jewelry Artist: Cartier." http://www.macklowegallery.com/education.asp?art+nouveau/Artist+Biographies/antiques/Jewelry+Artists/education/Cartier+/id/10. (Accessed August 14, 2013.)

Madsen, A. *Chanel: A Woman of Her Own*. New York: Henry Holt, 1990.

———. *Chanel: A Woman of Her Own (reprint)*. New York: Henry Holt, 1991.

———. *Living for Design: Yves Saint Laurent Story*. New York, Delacorte Press, 1979.

Mahoney, M., and Vladimir Dusil. *Purse Blog*. "Meet Monica Botkier." http://purseblog.com/meet-monica-botkier/. (Accessed November 13, 2008.)

Mail Online. "How a Couple of British Boarding School Boys with no Formal Training Launched New York's Coolest Fashion Label." August 15, 2013. http://www.dailymail.co.uk/femail/article-2394971/Rag--Bone-How-2-British-boys-launched-New-Yorks-coolest-fashion-label.html. (Accessed November 11, 2013.)

Maki Oh. "About." http://www.maki-oh.com/. (Accessed September 19, 2013.)

Mario Testino. "Mario Testino Bibliography." http://mariotestino.com/. (Accessed November 14, 2008.)

Marcus, Bennett. *Vanity Fair*. "Sarah Jessica Parker on Recruiting Prabal Gurung and Olivier Theyskens to Design the N.Y.C. Ballet's Costumes—and the Bespoke Dress They Made Her." September, 2013. http://www.vanityfair.com/online/daily/2013/09/nyc-ballet-costumes-prabal-gurung-olivier-theyskens. (Accessed September 21, 2013.)

Marsh, S. *The Times*. "Mario Testino: A Portrait of Celebrity." June 30, 2008. http://entertainment.timesonline.co.uk/tol/arts_and_entertainment/visual_arts/article4227229.ece. (Accessed November 14, 2008.)

Martin, J.J. *Harper's Bazaar*. "Tomas Maier: Dreamweaver." http://www.harpersbazaar.com/fashion/fashion-articles/tomas-maier-0208. (Accessed October 6, 2009.)

———. *Harper's Bazzar*. "A Fashionable Life: Isabel and Rueben Toledo." February 1, 2007. http://www.harpersbazaar.com/culture/interiors-entertaining/fashionable-life-toledo-0207. (Accessed July 30, 2013.)

Martin, R., and H. Koda. *Giorgio Armani: Images of Man*. New York: Rizzoli International Publications, 1990.

Mattingly, Kaitlin. *Start-up Fashion.* "Highlight of Kevan Hall." May 24, 2012. http://startupfashion.com/kevan-hall. (Accessed July 20, 2013.)

Mau, Dhani. *Fashionista.* "Isabel and Ruben Toledo on Fashion As Art, Skipping Fashion Week and Dressing Michelle Obama." March 7, 2012. http://fashionista.com/2012/03/isabel-and-ruben-toledo-on-fashion-as-art-skipping-fashion-week-and-dressing-michelle-obama/. (Accessed July 30, 2013.)

Maxwell, E. *R.S.V.P. Elsa Maxwell's Own Story.* Boston: Little, Brown & Co., 1954.

Maza, Erik. *Women's Wear Daily.* "Madonna, Steven Klein Foment Revolution for Art Piece." September 25, 2013. http://www.wwd.com/eye/parties/madonna-and-steven-klein-foment-revolution-for-art-piece-7186697. (Accessed October 4, 2013.)

McCall Pattern Company. "Butterick: Our History." http://butterick.com/bhc/pages/articles/histpgs/about.html. (Accessed October 20, 2007.)

McCardell, C. *What Shall I Wear?* New York: Simon & Schuster, 1956.

McConathy, D., with Diana Vreeland. *Hollywood Costume.* New York: Harry N. Abrams, 1976.

McDowell, C. *McDowell's Directory of Twentieth Century Fashion.* New Jersey: Prentice-Hall, 1985.

McQuillan, Deirdre. *The Irish Times.* "London Fashion Week: Simone Rocha Looks to Connemara for Inspiration." September 18, 2013. http://www.irishtimes.com/life-and-style/fashion/london-fashion-week-simone-rocha-looks-to-connemara-for-inspiration-1.1531013. (Accessed October 2, 2013.)

Melby, Leah. *Elle.com.* "Chadwick Bell Loves the 'Real Girls.'" February 11, 2013. http://www.elle.com/news/fashion-style/chadwick-bell-fall-2013-presentation-interview. (Accessed July 20, 2013.)

Mendes, Valerie D. *Twentieth Century Fashion: An Introduction to Women's Fashionable Dress, 1900–1980.* London: Victoria and Albert Museum, 1996.

Mendes, Valerie D., and Amy de la Haye. *20th Century Fashion.* London: Thames & Hudson, 1999.

Menkes, Suzy. *International Herald Tribune.* "Renzo Rosso Takes Control of Viktor & Rolf Label." July 21, 2008.

———.*New York Times.* "Missoni's Next Generation." September 28, 2009.

———. *New York Times.* "Simone Rochas, Family and Fashion." September 18, 2013. http://www.nytimes.com/2013/09/19/fashion/simone-rocha-family-and-fashion.html. (Accessed October 2, 2013.)

———. *International Herald Tribune.* "The High-Octane Liz Tilberis." April 27, 1999.

Michael Bastain. "Biography." http://www.michaelbastiannyc.com. (Accessed August 19, 2013.)

Micheletti, E. *All About Romance Novels.* "Charles Frederick Worth: The Father of Haute Couture." http://likesbooks.com/charlesworth.html. (Accessed September, 23, 2007.)

Milbank, C.R. *Couture: The Great Designers.* New York: Stewart, Tabori & Chang, 1997.

———. *New York Fashion: The Evolution of American Style.* New York: Harry N. Abrams, 1989.

Milinaire, C. *Cheap Chic: Update* (rev. ed.). New York: Outlet Book Company, 1978.

Miller, B.M. *Dressed for the Occasion: What Americans Wore 1620–1970.* Minneapolis, MN: Lerner Publications, 1999.

Milligan, Lauren. *Vogue.com.* "Christopher Kane's First Store." September 16, 2013. http://www.vogue.co.uk/news/2013/09/15/christopher-kane-store-london-flagship-mount-street. (Accessed September 19, 2013.)

Mirabella, G. *In and Out of Vogue.* New York: Doubleday, 1995.

Misener, Jessica. *Huffington Post.* "Carine Roitfeld: 'I'm Not Bad Looking, But I'm Not a Beauty Either.'" August 16, 2012. http://www.huffingtonpost.com/2012/08/16/carine-roitfeld-harpers-bazaar-interview-looks_n_1790920.html. (Accessed September 19, 2013.)

Missoni. http://www.missoni.com. (Accessed October 6, 2009.)

Miyake, I. *Issey Miyake Bodyworks.* Tokyo: Shokagukan Publishing, 1983.

———.*Issey Miyake Meets West.* Tokyo: Heibonsha, 1978.

Miyake, I, Kazuko Sato, Herve Chandes, Fondation Cartier, and Raymond Meier. *Issey Miyake: Making Things.* New Zurich: Scalo Verlag, 1999.

Modaitalia.net. "Roberto Cavalli Biography." http://modaitalia.net/robertocavalli/bio.htm. (Accessed November 17, 2008.)

Models.com. "Carine Roitfeld: Biography." http://models.com/models/carine-roitfeld. (Accessed September 19, 2013.)

Moffitt, P., and others. *The Rudi Gernreich Book.* New York: Taschen America, 1999.

Mohrt, F. *30 Ans d'Elegance et de Créations 1925–1955.* Paris: Jacques Damase, 1983.

Monsters and Critics. "Marc Ecko Biography." http://www.monstersandcritics.com/people/Marc-Ecko/biography/. (Accessed August 14, 2013.)

Moore, Booth. *Los Angeles Times.* "Chatting with Joseph Altuzarra About Food Trucks, Fashion." September 18, 2013. http://www.latimes.com/fashion/alltherage/la-ar-joseph-altuzarra-food-trucks-fashion-20130918,0,3992877.story. (Accessed September 25, 2013.)

———. *Los Angeles Times.* "The Obama Effect on Thakoon Panichgul." September 21, 2008.

Moral, Cheche V. *Inquirer Lifestyle.* "RTW—It's the Way to Go Global, Says Lesley Mobo." October 4, 2012. http://lifestyle.inquirer.net/69920/rtw-its-the-way-to-go-global-says-lesley-mobo. (Accessed August 29, 2013.)

Morris, B. *Lookonline.com.* "Fashion Roundtable: An Interview with Three Leading Black Fashion Journalists." November 14, 2002. http://lookonline.com/fashion-roundtable-1.html. (Accessed November 4, 2008.)

———. *The Fashion Makers: An Inside Look at America's Leading Designers.* New York: Random House, 1978.

Mugler, T. *Thierry Mugler.* New York: Rizzoli International Publications, 1988.

Muir, R. *The Independent.* "Patricia Creed: '*Vogue*' Model and Fashion Editor." April 11, 2007. http://www.independent.co.uk/news/obituaries/patricia-creed-444144.html. (Accessed October 6, 2009.)

Murphy, Robert. *Harpersbazaar.com.* "Hermes Heritage: Hermès's Pierre-Alexis Dumas Juggles Its Legacy with a New Vision for the Luxury-Goods Empire." http://www.harpersbazaar.com/magazine/feature-articles/hermes-pierre-alexis-dumas-profile-0213#slide-1. (Accessed August 19, 2013.)

Musée de la Mode et du Costume. *Élegance et Création: Paris 1945–1975.* Paris, 1977.

———. *Hommage à Schiaparelli.* Paris, 1984.

Museum of the City of New York. *The House of Worth: The Gilded Age, 1860–1918.* New York, 1982.

Naeem Khan. "The Designer." http://www.naeemkhanom/designer.html. (Accessed October 10, 2013.)

Nation Now. *Los Angeles Times.* "Tim Gunn's 29 Years of Celibacy: Yes, It's Unusual, Expert Says." January, 25, 2012. http://latimesblogs.latimes.com/nationnow/2012/01/tim-gunn-celibacy-sex.html#sthash.Jhegf2Op.dpuf. (Accessed September 18, 2013.)

National Institute of Standards and Technology Virtual Museum. http://museum.nist.gov/. (Accessed March 27, 2009.)

Naughton, J. *Women's Wear Daily.* "Halston's New Scent Formula." July 1, 2009.

Naumann, F.M. *Conversion to Modernism: The Early Work of Man Ray.* New Jersey: Rutgers University Press, 2003.

Ndekwu, Ijeoma. *Bella Naija.* "Maki Oh Autumn/Winter Debut Collection: "Everything in Proportion." March 10, 2010. http://www.bellanaija.com/2010/03/10/maki-oh-autumnwinter-debut-collection-everything-in-proportion/. (Accessed September 19, 2013.)

Neal, T. *Stylelist.* "Confirmed: Monica Botkier for Target." March 18, 2008. http://stylelist.com/blog/2008/03/18/confirmed-monica-botkier-for-target/. (Accessed November 11, 2008.)

Nemy, E. *New York Times.* "Sybil Connolly, 77, Irish Designer Who Dressed Jacqueline Kennedy." May 8, 1998.

Neo, Geo. *Illustrators Lounge.* "Fashion Fridays~Paul Iribe." January 13, 2013. http://illustratorslounge.com/fashion/fashion-fridays-paul-iribe-1883-1935. (Accessed September 2, 2013.)

Nespresso. "Scott Schuman Biography." http://www.nespresso.com/citizdotmedia/international/documents/20100113_CitiZdot_ScottSchumanBio.pdf. (Accessed August 20, 2013.)

News Online International. "Leslie Mobo: The London-based Fashion Designer Who Is Leading the Pack." March, 19 2012. http://newsonlineinternational.wordpress.com/2012/03/19/lesley-mobo-the-london-based-fashion-designer-who-is-leading-the-pack/. (Accessed August 29, 2013.)

New York Magazine, The Cut Blog. "Andrew Gn." http://nymag.com/fashion/fashionshows/designers/bios/andrewgn/. (Accessed November 8, 2008.)

———. "Bottega Veneta." http://nymag.com/fashion/fashionshows/designers/bios/bottegaveneta/. (Accessed October 6, 2009.)

———. "Chado Ralph Ricci." http://nymag.com/fashion/fashionshows/designers/bios/chadoralphrucci/. (Accessed November 13, 2008.)

———. "Celine." http://nymag.com/thecut/fashion/designers/celine/. (Accessed September 3, 2013.)

———. "Derek Lam." http://nymag.com/fashion/fashionshows/designers/bios/dereklam/. (Accessed November 8, 2008.)

———. "Derek Lam Doesn't Knock Knockoffs." March 7, 2008. http://nymag.com/daily/fashion/2008/03/derek_lam_doesnt_knock_knockof.html. (Accessed November 10, 2008.)

———. "L.A.M.B." http://nymag.com/thecut/fashion/designers/lamb/. (Accessed September 30, 2013.)

———. "Lilly Pulitzer." http://nymag.com/fashion/fashionshows/designers/bios/lillypulitzer/. (Accessed 13, 2008.)

———. "Marc Jacobs and Renzo Rosso Team Up on Menswear." November 10, 2008. http://nymag.com/daily/fashion/2008/11/marc_jacobs_and_renzo_rossi_te.html. (Accessed November 14, 2008.)

———. "Peter Som." http://nymag.com/fashion/fashionshows/designers/bios/petersom/. (Accessed November 17, 2008.)

———. "Roberto Cavalli." http://nymag.com/fashion/fashionshows/designers/bios/robertocavalli/. (Accessed November 17, 2008.)

———. "Thakoon Panichgul." http://nymag.com/fashion/fashionshows/designers/bios/thakoon/. (Accessed November 13, 2008.)

———. "Why Everyone's Watching Gareth Pugh." September 15, 2008. http://nymag.com/daily/fashion/2008/09/why_everyones_eyes_are_on_gare.html. (Accessed November 13, 2008.)

Niles, L. *Domestic Goddesses.* "Sarah Josepha Hale." http://womenwriters.net/domesticgoddess/hale1.html. (Accessed October 10, 2007.)

Nina Garcia. "Biography." http://ninagarcia.com/post/1602714022/biography/. (Accessed August 20, 2013.)

Norma Kamali. "Home: Bio." http://normakamalicollection. com/customer/bio.aspx. (Accessed November 17, 2008.)

Novellino, Teresa. "Rise of a Fashion Upstart: Brandon Sun Steals His Own Show." September 11, 2013. http:// upstart.bizjournals.com/entrepreneurs/hot-shots /2013/09/11/brandon-sun-steals-his-own-fashion-show .html?page=all. (Accessed September 19, 2013.)

NPR. "Fashion Matters in Tough Times, Says Top Designer." November 10, 2011. http://www.npr. org/2011/11/10/142211126/kevan-hall-on-why-fashion -matters-in-tough-times. (Accessed July 20, 2013.)

———. "First Black Editor-in-Chief for Condé Nast." October 1, 2012. http://www.npr.org/2012/10/01 /162088694/first-black-editor-in-chief-for-conde-nast. (Accessed July 19, 2013.)

O'Hara, G. *Dictionary of Fashion and Fashion Designers*. New York: Thames and Hudson, 1998.

———. *The Encyclopedia of Fashion*. New York: Harry N. Abrams, 1986.

Odell, A. *New York Magazine, The Cut Blog*. "Is Anna Wintour Retiring?!" November 18, 2008. http://nymag .com/daily/fashion/2008/11/is_anna_wintour_retiring .html. (Accessed November 18, 2008.)

Ogundipe, Abbas. *Fab Magazine Online*. "Nigerian Designer Amaka Osakwe Clothes Michelle Obama on Africa Tour." July 5, 2013. http://fabmagazineonline.com /nigerian-designer-amaka-osakwe-clothes-michelle -obama-on-african-tour/. (Accessed September 19, 2013.)

Olsen, K. *Chronology of Women's History*. Westport, CT: Greenwood Publishing, 1994.

O'Niel, Alanna. *Elle.com*. "Designer Profile: The Blonds— Peacock Feathers, Gold Spikes and Swarovski Crystals Infuse This Design Duo's Theatrical Style." http://www .ellecanada.com/fashion/designer-profile-the-blonds /a/40400. (Accessed August 12, 2013.)

Onyewueny, I. *My Fashion Life*. "The Gareth Pugh Aesthetic: Can You Handle It?" October 14, 2008. http:// myfashionlife.com/archives/2008/10/14/the-gareth-pugh -aesthetic-can-you-handle-it/. (Accessed November 13, 2008.)

Orecklin, M. *Time.com*. "The Power List, Women in Fashion: Anna Wintour." http://time.com/time/2004/style/020904 /power/3.html. (Accessed November 15, 2008.)

Paperpast Yearbook. http://paperpast.com/. (Accessed March 27, 2009.)

Parsons The New School for Design. "Reed Karkoff." https:// www.newschool.edu/parsons/subpage.aspx?id=56273. (Accessed September 2, 2013.)

Payne, B. *History of Costume: From the Ancient Egyptians to the Twentieth Century*. New York: Harper & Row, 1965.

Payne, B., Geitel Winakor, and Jane Farrell-Beck. *History of Costume: From Ancient Mesopotamia through the Twentieth Century, 2nd ed*. Boston: Addison-Wesley, 1992.

Pelle, M. *Valentino: Thirty Years of Magic*. New York: Abbeville Press, 1991.

Perkins, A. *Paris Couturiers & Milliners*. New York: Fairchild Publications, 1949.

Perschetz, L., ed. *W: The Designing Life*. New York: Clarkson N. Potter, 1990.

Peter Som. "About." http://petersom.com/about.html. (Accessed November 17, 2008.)

Piene, Draire. *More Magazine*. "Judith Ripka Gives Back." http://www.more.com/fashion/shoes-accessories/judith -ripka-gives-back. (Accessed October 2, 2013.)

Picken, M.B. *A Dictionary of Costume and Fashion: Historic and Modern*. New York: Dover Publications, 1998.

Platnum Guild International. *PR Newswire*. "Platinum Guild International Partners with Style Expert Nina Garcia on Campaign to Promote the Enduring Qualities of Platinum Jewelry." September 19, 2013. http://www .sacbee.com/2013/09/19/5749771/platinum-guild -international-partners.html. (Accessed August 3, 2013.)

Poiret, P. *En Habillant l'Epoque*. Paris: Grasset, 1930.

———. *King of Fashion*. Translated by Stephen Haden Guest. Philadelphia: J.B. Lippincott, 1931.

———. *Revenez-Y*. Paris: Gallimard, 1934.

Polan, B, ed. *The Fashion Year, 1938*. London: Zomba Books, 1983.

Prabhakar, H. *Forbes.com*. "Tastemakers: Fashion Design." March 14, 2007. http://forbes.com/style/2007/03/13 /tastemaker-designer-fashion-forbeslife-cx_hp _0314fashion.html. (Accessed November 5, 2008.)

Prabal Gunrung. "About." http://www.prabalgurung.com /about.php (Accessed July 14, 2013.)

Prada Group. http://pradagroup.com. (Accessed March 27, 2009.)

Preen. "Biography." http://www.preen.eu/about/. (Accessed September 19, 2013.)

Prichard, S. *Film Costume: An Annotated Bibliography*. Metuchen, NJ: Scarecrow, 1981.

Prince, D. 2007. "Louis Vuitton: The History behind the Purse." http://associatedcontent.com/pop_print .shtml?content_type=article&content_type. (Accessed November 2, 2007.)

Pruitt, Elana. *Agenda Magazine*. "Byron Lars Beauty Mark: "More About the Clothes, Less About the Hype." July 18, 2013. http://www.agendamag.com/content/2013/07 /byron-lars-beauty-mark-more-about-the-clothes-less -about-the-hype/. (Accessed August 10, 2013.)

Quant, M. *Quant by Quant*. London: Cassell, 1966.

Quant, M., and Felicity Green. *Color by Quant: Your Complete Personal Guide to Beauty and Fashion*. New York: McGraw-Hill, 1985.

Rachel Roy. "About." http://www.rachelroy.com/Biography -AboutMe/RR_BIO_ABOUT_ME,default,pg.html. (Accessed July 20, 2013.)

Rag & Bone. "About." http://www.rag-bone.com/studio
_about.html. (Accessed August 18, 2013.)

Raisbeck, Fiona. *Marie Claire*. "Hermès: History of the
Iconic Brand in Numbers." May 20, 2013. http://www
.marieclaire.co.uk/blogs/542797/hermes-history-of-the
-iconic-brand-in-numbers.html. (Accessed August 19,
2013.)

Ramos, Darkys. *BET.com*. "Rachel Roy Launches Digital
Magazine." April 8, 2013. http://www.bet.com/news
/fashion-and-beauty/2013/04/08/rachel-roy-launches
-digital-magazine.html. (Accessed July 20, 2013.)

Reed Krakoff. "Reed Krakoff." http://www.reedkrakoff.com
/online/handbags/USIndexView?storeId=16001&cat
alogId=16500&langId=-1#view=about-rk. (Accessed
September 2, 2013.)

Rhodes, Z., and Anne Knight. *The Art of Zandra Rhodes*.
London: Michael O'Mara Books, 1995.

Richard Chai. "Profile." http://www.richardchailove.com
/profile. (Accessed September 3, 2013.)

Ridley, P. *Fashion Illustration*. New York: Rizzoli
International Publications, 1980.

Rielly, Justin. *Examiner.com*. "Scorsese at 70: A Great
Designing Force Named Sandy." October 29, 2012. http://
www.examiner.com/article/scorsese-at-70-a-great
-designing-force-named-sandy. (Accessed July 20, 2013.)

Riley, R. *Givenchy: 30 Years*. New York: Fashion Institute of
Technology, 1982.

Ripka, Judith. *New York Times*. "A Designer from Day 1."
September 18, 2010. http://www.nytimes.com/2010
/09/19/jobs/19boss.html?_r=0. (Accessed September 29,
2013.)

Roberto Cavalli. "Company Profile." http://robertocavalli.
com/en/companyProfile/mission.do. (Accessed
November 17, 2008.)

Robinson, J. *Fashion in the Forties*. New York: St. Martin's
Press, 1976.

———. *Fashion in the Thirties*. New York: Oresko Books,
1978.

Rooftop. "Designer Profile: Dion Lee." May 5, 2013. http://
rooftopmelb.wordpress.com/2013/05/05/designer
-profile-dion-lee/. (Accessed September 19, 2013.)

Rochas, M. *Twenty-Five Years of Parisian Elegance, 1925–1950*.
Paris: Pierre Tisne, 1951.

Roshco, B. *The Rag Race*. New York: Funk & Wagnalls, 1963.

Ross, J. *Beaton in Vogue*. New York: Outlet Book Company,
1988.

Royal Ontario Museum. *Haute Couture: Notes on Designers
and Their Clothes in the Collection of the Royal Ontario
Museum*. Toronto, 1969.

Running with Heels. "Reaad Krakoff." http://www.running
withheels.com/index.php/2013/07/reed-krakoffbio/.
(Accessed September 2, 2013.)

Rykiel, S. *And I Would Like Her Naked*. Paris: Bernard
Grasset, 1979.

Salomon, R.K. *Fashion Design for Moderns*. New York:
Fairchild Publications, 1976.

Sanderson, L.A. *LifeinItaly.com*. "The Romantic Origins of
Missoni." November 2008. http://www.lifeinitaly.com
/fashion/missoni.asp. (Accessed October 6, 2009.)

Saunders, E. *The Age of Worth: Couturier to the Empress
Eugenie*. Bloomington, IN: Indiana University Press, 1955.

Schiaparelli, E. *Shocking Life*. New York: E.P. Dutton, 1954.

Schreier, B. *Mystique and Identity: Women's Fashions of the
1950s*. Norfolk, VA: Chrysler Museum, 1984.

Scottish Arts Council and Victoria and Albert Museum.
Fashion, 1900–1939. London, 1975.

Seckington, M. *MissGeeky.com*. "Annie Leibovitz's Disney
Dream Portrait Series." January 29, 2008. http://
missgeeky.com/2008/01/29/annie-leibovitzs-disney
-dream-portrait-series/. (Accessed November 10, 2008.)

Seebohm, C. *The Man Who Was Vogue: The Life and Times
of Condé Nast*. New York: Viking Press, 1982.

Seen Heard Known. "What I Saw Today: A Day with Famed
Illustrator Richard Haines." http://seenheardknown.com
/portfolio/what-i-saw-today-a-day-with-famed-illustrator
-richard-haines/. (Accessed October 10, 2013.)

Sevim, Nezahat. *Euronews*. "Garance Dore: From an Online
Diary to Opinion Leadership." June 17, 2013. http://www
.euronews.com/2013/06/17/garance-dore-from-an
-online-diary-to-opinion-leadership/. (Accessed August
19, 2013.)

Shoera. "Shoera Presents: Walter Steiger Shoes." May 12, 2010.
http://www.shoera.com/2010/05/12/shoera-presents
-walter-steiger-shoes/. (Accessed August 2, 2013.)

SHOWstudio. "Gareth Pugh." http://showstudio.com
/contributors/4252. (Accessed November 13, 2008.)

———. "Stefano Pilati." http://showstudio.com
/contributors/16343. (Accessed November 13, 2008.)

Sierra, Lu. *The Grio*. "Designer Byron Lars Shares Top Looks
from His Beauty Mark Collection with Lifestyle Expert
Lu Sierra." May 1, 2013. http://thegrio.com/2013/05/01
/designer-byron-lars-shares-his-vivid-beauty-mark
-collection-for-springsummer-2013/#. (Accessed August
10, 2013.)

Simone Rochas. "Bio." http://simonerocha.com/bio/.
(Accessed October 2, 2013.)

Slowey Anne. *Interview*. "The Row." http://www
.interviewmagazine.com/fashion/the-row/#_. (Accessed
October 2, 2013.)

Smith, Shannan Elinor. *Opening Ceremony*. "Back to the
Drawing Board: An Interview with Illustrator Richard
Haines." October 9, 2013. http://www.openingceremony
.us/entry.asp?pid=8636. (Accessed October 10, 2013.)

Smithsonian Institution Press. *Legacies—From Artifacts to
America*. "Gown Made by Elizabeth Keckley for Mary Todd
Lincoln, about 1864." http://www.smithsonianlegacies
.si.edu/objectdescription.cfm?ID=258. (Accessed October
6, 2009.)

Snow, C., and Mary Louise Aswell. *The World of Carmel Snow*. New York: McGraw-Hill, 1962.

SoJones. "Marc Ecco Collection." March 16, 2009. http://www.sojones.com/news/marc-ecko-collection/. (Accessed August 30, 2013.)

Somerstein, R. *American Masters*. "Annie Leibovitz: Life Through a Lens." http://pbs.org/wnet/americanmasters/episodes/annie-leibovitz/life-through-a-lens/16/. (Accessed November 10, 2008.)

Spencer, C. *Erté*. New York: Clarkson N. Potter, 1970.

Stegemeyer, A. *Who's Who in Fashion, 4th ed*. New York: Fairchild Books, 2004.

Steele, P. *A History of Fashion and Costume, Vol. 7: The Nineteenth Century*. New York: Facts on File, 2005.

Steele, V. *MSN Encarta*. "Fashion." http://encarta.msn.com/text_761585452___0/Fashion.html. (Accessed September 25, 2007.)

———. *Women of Fashion*. New York: Rizzoli Books International, 1991.

Stoll, Jamie. *W Magazine*. "Five Minutes with Ruben Toledo." October 2010. http://www.wmagazine.com/fashion/2010/10/ruben-toledo-fashion-almanac/. (Accessed July 30, 2013.)

Stone, E. *The Dynamics of Fashion, 3rd ed*. New York: Fairchild Books, 2008.

Style.com. "Quick to the Draw: A Moment with Richard Haines." June 24, 2013. http://www.style.com/stylefile/2013/06/quick-to-the-draw-a-moment-with-richard-haines-2/. (Accessed July 14, 2013.)

Stylesequel. "Celine Biography." http://www.stylesequel.com/designers/celine/biography. (Accessed September 3, 2013.)

Target. "McQ Alexander McQueen for Target (press release)." February 2009. http://pressroom.target.com/pr/news/fashion/collaborations/mcq-for-target.aspx.

Taschen. "Helmut Newton's SUMO…" http://taschen.com/pages/en/catalogue/photography/all/02601/facts.helmut_newtons_sumo.htm. (Accessed November 11, 2008.)

Teboul, D., Christine Baute, and Pierre Berge. *Yves Saint Laurent: 5 Avenue Marceau, 75116 Paris, France*. New York: Harry N. Abrams, 2002.

The Fashion Editors. *Esquire*. "Where Does Band of Outsider's Designer Go From Here?" June 14, 2011. http://www.esquire.com/blogs/mens-fashion/scott-sternberg-profile-0611. (Accessed September 18, 2013.)

The Ground Editors. *The Ground*. "How I Started…15—Marcus Wainwright and David Neville." January 26, 2013. http://www.thegroundmag.com/how-i-started-15-wainwright-and-david-neville/. (Accessed October 28, 2013.)

The Jewish Museum. "threeASFOUR: Mer Ka Ba." http://www.thejewishmuseum.org/exhibitions/three-as-four. (Accessed October 25, 2013.)

The Row. "About the Brand." http://www.therow.com/about. (Accessed August 20, 2013.)

The Satorialist. "A Conversation with Scott Sternberg, Band of Outsiders." February 16, 2012. http://www.thesartorialist.com/photos/conversations-with-scott-sternberg-band-of-outsiders/. (Accessed August 4, 2013.)

———. "Biography." http://www.thesartorialist.com/biography/. (Accessed September 2, 2013.)

The Wall Street Journal "Announcing the New Tiffany.com." October 21, 2013. http://online.wsj.com/article/PR-CO-20131021-905232.html. (Accessed October 22, 2013.)

The Washington Times. "Paris Vogue Editor to Leave after 10-year Tenure." December 18, 2010. http://www.washingtontimes.com/news/2010/dec/18/paris-vogue-editor-to-leave-after-10-year-tenure/. (Accessed July 20, 2013.)

———. "Why Bway's 'Breakfast at Tiffany's' Has No Tiaras." http://www.washingtontimes.com/news/2013/mar/19/why-bways-breakfast-at-tiffanys-has-no-tiaras/. (Accessed August 20, 2013.)

Thornton, N. *Poiret*. New York: Rizzoli International Publications, 1979.

Tiffany. "About Tiffany & Co." http://press.tiffany.com/ViewBackgrounder.aspx?backgrounderId=8. (Accessed August 10, 2013.)

Tiffany and Co. "The Tiffany Story." http://www.tiffany.com/WorldOfTiffany/TiffanyStory/Default.aspx (Accessed October 22, 2013.)

———. "Tiffany & Co. Appoints Design Director." September 10, 2013. http://press.tiffany.com/News/NewsItem.aspx?id=218. (Accessed October 22, 2013.)

Tkacik, M. *New York Magazine*. "America's Next Top Fashion Editor." August 17, 2008. http://nymag.com/fashion/08/fall/49259/index4.html. (Accessed November 6, 2008.)

Tolstoy, M. *Charlemagne to Dior: The Story of French Fashion*. New York: Michael Slains, 1967.

Tortora, P., and Keith Eubank. *Survey of Historic Costume, 4th ed*. New York: Fairchild Books, 2005.

———. *Survey of Historic Costume, 5th ed*. New York: Fairchild Books, 2010.

Toro Magazine. "PRPS: Denim with a Purpose." http://toromagazine.com/lifestyle/stylebook/20111018/prps-denim-with-a-purpose. (Accessed September 2, 2013.)

Tom Ford. "The Brand." http://www.tomford.com/#/en/thebrand/tomford. (Accessed October 5, 2009.)

Tory Burch. "About." http://toryburch.com/about.aspx. (Accessed November 5, 2008.)

Trachtenberg, J. *Ralph Lauren—Image-maker. The Man behind the Mystique*. New York: Little, Brown, 1988.

Trahey, J., ed. *Harper's Bazaar: 100 Years of the American Female*. New York: Random House, 1967.

Trina Turk. "About Us." http://www.trinaturk.com/about.aspx. (Accessed November 15, 2008.)

Tschorn, Adam. *Los Angeles Times.* "Fashion's Band of Outsiders Much in Demand: Scott Sternberg Started his Now-thriving Band of Outsiders Brand with Two Credit Cards and Moxie." October 14, 2012. http://articles.latimes.com/2012/oct/14/image/la-ig-sternberg-20121014. (Accessed September 17, 2013.)

Tsong, N. *Seattle Times.* "Fashion Designer Trina Turk Makes It Work." August 31, 2008.

Tuohy, L. *Craftstylish.com.* "We're Biased: Couture Designer Charles Kleibacker's Gowns on Exhibit in Ohio." June 7, 2008. http://craftstylish.com/item/2980/were-biased-couture-designer-charles-kleibackers-gowns-on-exhibit-in-ohio. (Accessed November 8, 2008.)

Tyrnauer, M. *Vanity Fair.* "Less is Maier." September 2008. http://www.vanityfair.com/style/features/2008/09/maier200809. (Accessed October 6, 2009.)

Ulaby, N. *NPR.* "Esteban Cortazar: Young, Veteran Fashion Designer." September 8, 2004. http://npr.org/templates/story/story.php?storyId=3894400. (Accessed November 6, 2008.)

Updike, John. *The New Yorker.* "Makeup and Make-Believe: Max Factors' Life of Beautification." September 1, 2008. http://www.newyorker.com/arts/critics/books/2008/09/01/080901crbo_books_updike?printable=true&currentPage=all. (Accessed September 18, 2013.)

Unconditional. "About." http://www.unconditional.uk.com/pages/about. (Accessed October 10, 2013.)

United Colors of Benetton. http://benettongroup.com. (Accessed March 27, 2009.)

U.S. Census Bureau. http://census.gov. (Accessed March 27, 2009.)

U.S. Department of Labor. http://bls.gov. (Accessed March 27, 2009.)

Van Meter, Jonathan. *Vogue.* "Gwen Stefani: Leader of the Pack." December 17, 2012. http://www.vogue.com/magazine/article/gwen-stefani-leader-of-the-pack/#1. (Accessed August 15, 2013.)

———. *Vogue.* "Gwen Stefani: The First Lady of Rock." April 1, 2008. http://www.vogue.com/magazine/article/gwen-stefani-the-first-lady-of-rock/#1. (Accessed August 15, 2013.)

Vecchio, W., and Robert Riley. *The Fashion Makers: A Photographic Record.* New York: Crown Publishers, 1968.

Vickers, H. *Cecil Beaton.* New York: Sterling Publishing, 2002.

Victoria and Albert Museum. "Fashion in Motion Live Catwalk Event: Missoni." http://www.vam.ac.uk/collections/fashion/fashion_motion/missoni/index.html. (Accessed October 6, 2009.)

———. "V&A: The Golden Age of Couture." http://www.vam.ac.uk/vastatic/microsites/1486_couture/. (Accessed March 27, 2009.)

Viladas, P. *New York Times Magazine.* "STYLE MATTERS: Designed For Living." April 29, 2001.

Vingan, Alyssa. *Fashionista.com.* "Mary-Kate and Asley Olsen Continue Their Fashion Industry Domination." October 7, 2013. http://fashionista.com/2013/10/mary-kate-and-ashley-olsen-continue-their-fashion-industry-domination/. (Accessed October 10, 2013.)

Vogue Australia. "Dion Lee." http://www.vogue.com.au/people/designers/dion+lee,31. (Accessed September 19, 2013.)

Vogueapedia. "Carine Roitfeld." http://www.vogue.com/voguepedia/Carine_Roitfeld. (Accessed September 20, 2013.)

———. "Celine." http://www.vogue.com/voguepedia/Celine. (Accessed September 3, 2013.)

———. "Christopher Kane." http://www.vogue.com/voguepedia/Christopher_Kane. (Accessed September 19, 2013.)

———. "Grace Coddington." http://www.vogue.com/voguepedia/Grace_Coddington. (Accessed August 12, 2013.)

———. "Isabel Marant." http://www.vogue.com/voguepedia/Isabel_Marant. (Accessed August 2, 2013.)

———. "Joseph Altuzarra." http://www.vogue.com/voguepedia/Joseph_Altuzarra#cite_note-7. (Accessed August 14, 2013.)

———. "Preen." http://www.vogue.com/voguepedia/Preen. (Accessed September 10, 2013.)

———. "Richard Chai." http://www.vogue.com/voguepedia/Richard_Chai. (Accessed September 3, 2013.)

———. "Steven Klein." http://www.vogue.com/voguepedia/Steven_Klein. (Accessed September 3, 2013.)

———. "The Row." http://www.vogue.com/voguepedia/The_Row. (Accessed October 10, 2013.)

Von Furstenberg, D. *Book of Beauty.* New York: Simon & Schuster, 1977.

Vreeland, D. *D.V.* New York: DeCapo Press, 1997.

Vreeland, D., and Christopher Hemphill. *Allure.* Boston: Bulfinch Press, 2002.

Walden, C. *Telegraph.* "Patrick Demarchelier: 'I Don't Like Exhibitionist Women…'" September 2, 2008.

Waldren, G. *The Independent.* "Thom Browne: The Long and the Short of It (An Interview)." February 25, 2008. http://www.independent.co.uk/life-style/fashion/features/thom-browne-the-long-and-the-short-of-it-786667.html. (Accessed November 5, 2008.)

Walker, Harriet. *The Independent.* "The Couple that Sews Together Grows Together." September 12, 2012. http://www.independent.co.uk/life-style/fashion/features/the-couple-that-sews-together-grows-together-8120447.html. (Accessed September 18, 2013.)

Walkley, C. *The Way to Wear 'Em: One Hundred Fifty Years of Punch on Fashion*. Chester Springs, PA: Dufour (P. Owen Ltd.), 1985.

Walter Steiger. "Biography." http://translate.google.com /translate?hl=en&sl=de&u=http://www.walter-steiger .com/walter-steiger-biographie.html&prev=/search%3Fq %3Dwalter%2Bsteiger%2Bbio%26biw%3D1787%26bih% 3D872. (Accessed October 1, 2013.)

Watkins, Greg. *AllHipHop.com*. "Karl Kani Teams With Saks for New Clothing Line." March 12, 2008. http://allhiphop .com/2008/03/12/karl-kani-teams-with-saks-for-new -clothing-line/. (Accessed September 29, 2013.)

Watson, L. *20th Century Fashion: 100 Years of Style by Decade and Designer, in Association with* Vogue. Buffalo, NY: Firefly Books, 2004.

Weitz, J. *Man in Charge*. New York: MacMillan Company, 1974.

———. *Sports Clothes for Your Sports Car*. New York: Arco Publishing, 1958.

Weston-Thomas, P. *Fashion-era*. "The Aesthetic Dress Movement: Fashion History of Aesthetics." http://www .fashion-era.com/aesthetics.htm. (Accessed September 25, 2007.)

What I Saw Today. "About." http://designerman-whatisawtoday .blogspot.com/p/about.html. (Accessed October 10, 2013.)

White, E., ed. *Fashion 85*. New York: St. Martin's Press, 1984.

White, P. *Elsa Schiaparelli: Empress of Paris Fashion*. New York: Rizzoli International Publications, 1986.

———. *Point*. New York: Clarkson N. Potter, 1973.

Whiteman, V. *Looking Back at Fashion, 1901–1939*. West Yorkshire, England: EP Publishing, 1978.

Whitley, Z. *Answers.com*. "Photography Encyclopedia: Alexander Liberman." http://answers.com/topic /alexander-liberman. (Accessed March 27, 2009.)

Wilcox, R. *The Mode in Costume, 2nd ed*. London: MacMillan, 1983.

Wilkinson, Isabel. *The Daily Beast*. "Prabal Gurung Spring Summer 2014: Electric Feel" September 7, 2013. http://www.thedailybeast.com/articles/2013/09/07 /prabal-gurung-spring-summer-2014-electric-feel.html. (Accessed September 10, 2013.)

Williams, B.E. *Fashion Is Our Business*. Philadelphia: J.B. Lippincott, 1945.

———. *Young Faces in Fashion*. Philadelphia: J.B. Lippincott, 1945.

Wilson, E. *New York Times*. "Lilly, 50, Hasn't Aged a Day." November 5, 2008.

———. *New York Times On the Runway Blog*. "Michael Bastain Carries a Torch." September 4, 2013. http:// runway.blogs.nytimes.com. (Accessed September 10, 2013.)

Wong, Byzara. *Vogue Australia*. "Breaking News: Dion Lee Acquired by Cue." June 5, 2013. http://www.vogue.com .au/fashion/news/breaking+news+dion+lee+acquired +by+cue,25569. (Accessed September 18, 2013.)

Woodson, Elizabeth. *Travel and Leisure*. "Bali's Latest Retreat: Designer John Hardy Ups the Ante on Green Style with His Plan to Reforest the World, One Island at a Time." November, 2007. http://www.travelandleisure .com/articles/stylish-traveler-bamboo-bali. (Accessed September 2, 2013.)

Woonough, Damien. *Vogue Australia*. "The Rise of Dion Lee." December 13, 2010. http://www.vogue.com.au /people/interviews/the+rise+of+dion+lee,8691. (Accessed September 19, 2013.)

Worth, J.P. *A Century of Fashion*. Translated by Ruth Scott Miller. Boston: Little, Brown & Co., 1928.

Wunderkind. "About." http://wunderkind.de/flash.htm. (Accessed October 5, 2009.)

Women's Wear Daily. "Andrew Gn RTW Spring 2009." October 1, 2008.

———. "Chloé RTW Spring 2009." October 4, 2008.

———. "Luther and Cunningham Honored by France." October 7, 2008.

Yohannon, K. *John Rawlings: 30 Years in Vogue*. Santa Fe, NM: Arena Editions, 2001.

You Tube. "Gwen Stefani Style Anecdote—Vogueapedia." http://www.youtube.com/watch?v=M4xC-NO5GIU. (Accessed August 15, 2013.)

Yoxall, H.W. *A Fashion of Life*. New York: Taplinger, 1967.

Yves Saint Laurent. "Stephano Pilati: Portrait." http://ysl.com /INT/en/index.aspx. (Accessed November 23, 2008.)

Zimbio. "100 Most Influential People in Fashion." http:// zimbio.com/100+Most+Influential+People+in+Fashion. (Accessed March 27, 2009.)

INDEX

Page numbers in bold refer to a designer's full profile page.

CREDITS

Joseph Abboud 1 (top left), Ericksen/WWD; © Conde Nast; 1 (bottom right), Ericksen/WWD; © Conde Nast; Amsale Aberra 2 (top right), Chinsee/WWD; © Conde Nast; 2 (bottom left),Iannaccone/WWD; © Conde Nast; Reem Acra 3 (top left), Iannaccone/WWD; © Conde Nast; 3 (bottom right), Aquino/WWD; © Conde Nast; Adrian 4 (top right), General Photographic Agency; 4 (bottom left), Horst P. Horst © 1948; 5, Horst P. Horst © 1932; Agnès B. 6 (top right), © Isabelle Weingarten/Sygma/Corbis; 6 (bottom left), Giannoni/WWD; © Conde Nast; Azzedine Alaïa 7 (top right), © Pierre Perrin/Sygma/Corbis; 9 (bottom left), Eichner/WWD; © Conde Nast; alice + olivia 8 (top right), Eichner/WWD; © Conde Nast; 8 (bottom left), Iannaccone/WWD; © Conde Nast; Joseph Altuzarra 9 (top right), Iannaccone/WWD; © Conde Nast; 9 (bottom left), Giannoni/WWD; © Conde Nast; 9 (bottom right), Giannoni/WWD; © Conde Nast; Marianne Alvoni 10, Marianne Alvoni; Sir Hardy Amies 11, Getty Images; Antonio 12 (top right), Antonio © 1974; 12 (bottom left), Antonio © 1974; Elizabeth Arden 13, Alan Fisher, photographer, Library of Congress Prints and Photographs Division Washington, D.C. 20540 USA; Arkadius 14 (bottom left), Giannoni/WWD; © Conde Nast; 14 (bottom right), Courtesy of Catwalking; Giorgio Armani 15 (top left), Courtesy of Fairchild Publications, Inc.; 15 (bottom right), Giannoni/WWD; © Conde Nast; 16 (top right), Time & Life Pictures/Getty Images; 16 (bottom left), Sardella/WWD; © Conde Nast; 16 (bottom right), Miranda/WWD; © Conde Nast; Laura Ashley 17 (top left), Getty Images; 17 (bottom right), Fields/WWD; © Conde Nast; 18 (top right), Photo by Jennifer Graylock/Getty Images for Swarovski; Colleen Atwood 18 (bottom left), © Presselect / Alamy; Richard Avedon 19, AP Photo/Kathy Willens

Badgley Mischka 20 (top right), Eichner/WWD; © Conde Nast; 20 (bottom left), Eichner/WWD; © Conde Nast; 20 (bottom right), Aquino/WWD; © Conde Nast; Christopher Bailey 21 (top left), Giannoni/WWD; © Conde Nast; 21 (bottom left), Giannoni/WWD; © Conde Nast; 21 (bottom right), Giannoni/WWD; © Conde Nast; Glenda Bailey 22, Courtesy of Fairchild Publications, Inc.; Cristóbal Balenciaga 23 (top right), Roger Viollet/Getty Images; 23 (bottom left), Rawlings/WWD; © Conde Nast; 23 (bottom right), Clark/WWD; © Conde Nast; 24 (top right), Time & Life Pictures/Getty Images; 24 (bottom left), Iannaccone/WWD; © Conde Nast; 24 (bottom right), Balenciaga S/S

2000, Photograph by Niall McInerney, Bloomsbury Fashion Photography Archive; Pierre Balmain 25 (top left), Getty Images; 25 (bottom right), Schatzberg/WWD; © Conde Nast; Band of Outsiders 26 (bottom left), Iannaccone/WWD; © Conde Nast; 26 (bottom right), Giannoni/WWD; © Conde Nast Jeffrey Banks 27 (top left), Time & Life Pictures/Getty Images; 27 (bottom right), Lategan/WWD; © Conde Nast; Travis Banton 28, © Bettmann/CORBIS; George Barbier; 29 (top left), Caponier/WWD; © Conde Nast; 29 (bottom right), © Stapleton Collection/Corbis; Jhane Barnes 30 (top right), Photo Courtesy of Gerardo Somoza; 30 (bottom left), Photo Courtesy of Gerardo Somoza; 30 (bottom right), Photo Courtesy of Gerardo Somoza; Neil Barrett 31 (top left), Giannoni/WWD; © Conde Nast; 31 (bottom right), Maestri+N443/WWD; © Conde Nast; Michael Bastian 32 (top right), Antonov/WWD; © Conde Nast; 32 (bottom left), Antonov/WWD; © Conde Nast; Cecil Beaton 33 (top left), Traeger/WWD; © Conde Nast; 33 (bottom right), Beaton/WWD; © Conde Nast; Geoffrey Beene 34 (top right), Ben Stern © 1968; 34 (bottom left), Horst P. Horst © 1979; 35 (bottom left), Nick/WWD; © Conde Nast; 35 (bottom right), Nick/WWD; © Conde Nast; 35 (top right), Piel/WWD; © Conde Nast; Chadwick Bell 36 (top right), Giannoni/WWD; © Conde Nast; 36 (bottom left), Boye/WWD; © Conde Nast; 36 (bottom right), Giannoni/WWD; © Conde Nast; Gilles Bensimon 37, Getty Images for IMG; Chris Benz 38 (top right), Chinsee/WWD; © Conde Nast; 38 (bottom left), Matarazzo/WWD; © Conde Nast; Christian Bérard 39 (top left), Beaton/Vogue; © Conde Nast; 39 (bottom right), Verard/Vogue; © Conde Nast; Rose Bertin 40 (bottom left), Kurt Hutton/Picture Post/IPC Magazines; 40 (bottom right), Kurt Hutton/Picture Post/IPC Magazines; Laura Biagiotti 41 (top left), © Daniel Dal Zennaro/epa/Corbis; 41 (bottom right), firstVIEW.com; Dirk Bikkembergs 42 (top left), Charles Platiau/Thomson Reuters; 42 (bottom left), Cristaldi/WWD; © Conde Nast; 42 (bottom right), Cristaldi/WWD; © Conde Nast; 42 (top right), Bikkembergs A/W 1995, Photograph by Niall McInerney, Bloomsbury Fashion Photography Archive; Manolo Blahnik 43 (top left), Courtesy of Fairchild Publications, Inc.; 43 (bottom right), Courtesy of Fairchild Publications, Inc.; 43 (bottom left), Courtesy of Fairchild Publications, Inc.; Bill Blass 44 (top right), Bert Stern © 1970; 44 (bottom left), Bert Stern/WWD; © Conde Nast; 45 (bottom right), David Bailey /WWD; © Conde Nast; 45 (top left),

Getty Images; **Kenneth Paul Block** 46 (top right), Patrick/WWD; © Conde Nast; 46 (bottom right), Courtesy of Fairchild Publications, Inc.; 46 (bottom left), Courtesy of Fairchild Publications, Inc.; **Blonds** 47 (top left), Eichner/WWD; © Conde Nast; 47 (bottom left), Chinsee/WWD; © Conde Nast; 47 (bottom right), Chinsee/WWD; © Conde Nast; **B. Michael** 48 (top left), Jamie McCarthy/WireImage; 48 (top right), Calfat/WWD; © Conde Nast; **Ozwald Boateng** 49 (top left), Dan Kitwood/Getty Images; 49 (bottom left), firstVIEW.com; 49 (bottom right), Boateng S/S 1998, Photograph by Niall McInerney, Bloomsbury Fashion Photography Archive; **Marc Bohan** 50 (top left), Picard/WWD; © Conde Nast; 50 (top right), Scavullo/WWD; © Conde Nast; 50 (bottom right), Bailey/WWD; © Conde Nast; **Monica Botkier** 51 (top right), Chinsee/WWD; © Conde Nast; 51 (bottom left), Chinsee/WWD; © Conde Nast; **Veronique Branquinho** 52 (top right), © CORBIS SYGMA; 52 (bottom left), Giannoni/WWD; © Conde Nast; **Alexey Brodovitch** 53, Time Life Pictures/Getty; **Donald Brooks** 54 (top left), Peter/WWD; © Conde Nast; 54 (bottom right), Clarke/Vogue; © Conde Nast; 54 (top right), Courtesy of Condé Nast Publications; **Thom Browne** 55 (top right), Banica/WWD; © Conde Nast; 55 (bottom left), Banica/WWD; © Conde Nast; **Barbara Bui** 56 (top left), © Lucas Dolega/epa; 56 (bottom right), Maitre/WWD; © Conde Nast; **Burberry** 57 (top left), Giannoni/WWD; © Conde Nast; 57 (bottom right), Giannoni/WWD; © Conde Nast; **Tory Burch** 58 (top right), Aquino/WWD; © Conde Nast; 58 (bottom right), Noam Galai/Getty Images; **Stephen Burrows** 59 (top left), Giannoni/WWD; © Conde Nast; 59 (bottom right), Iannaccone/WWD; © Conde Nast

Callot Souers 60, Image copyright © The Metropolitan Museum of Art. Image source: Art Resource, NY; **Ennio Capasa** 61 (top left), Vittorio Zunino Celotto/Getty Images; 61 (bottom left), Tombolini /WWD; © Conde Nast; **Roberto Capucci** 62 (top left), © Studio Patellani/CORBIS, 62 (top right), © Massimo Listri/Corbis; **Pierre Cardin** 63 (top left), Stern/WWD; © Conde Nast; 63 (top right), Maitre /WWD; © Conde Nast; 63 (bottom left), © Pierre Vauthey/Sygma/Corbis; **Hattie Carnegie** 64 (top right), George Karger/Time Life Pictures/Getty Images; 64 (bottom left), Rawling/WWD; © Conde Nast; **Cartier** 65 (top left), Eichner/WWD; © Conde Nast; 65 (bottom right), Chinsee and Iannaccone/WWD; © Conde Nast; **Bonnie Cashin** 66 (top right), Courtesy of the Stephanie Lake Foundation; 66 (bottom left), Courtesy of the Stephanie Lake Foundation; **Oleg Cassini** 67 (bottom right), Leonard McCombe/Time & Life Pictures/Getty Images; 67 (top left), AP Photo/John F. Kennedy Library and Museum; 67 (top right), Hulton Archive/Getty Images; **Consuelo Castiglioni** 68 (top right), Iannaccone/WWD; © Conde Nast; 68 (bottom right), Cristaldi/WWD; © Conde Nast; 68 (bottom left), Maestri/WWD; © Conde Nast; **Edmundo Castillo** 69

(top left), Chris Jackson/Getty Images; 69 (bottom right), Iannaccone/WWD; © Conde Nast; **Roberto Cavalli** 70 (top right), Courtesy of Fairchild Publications, Inc.; 70 (bottom left), Giannoni/WWD; © Conde Nast; **Céline** 71 (top left), Giannoni/WWD; © Conde Nast; 71 (bottom right), Giannoni/WWD; © Conde Nast; **Nino Cerruti** 72 (top right), © Sergio Gaudenti/Kipa/Corbis; 72 (bottom), TOUCHSTONE/WARNERS/THE KOBAL COLLECTION; **Richard Chai** 73 (top left), Eichner/WWD; © Conde Nast; 73 (bottom right), Iannaccone/WWD; © Conde Nast; **Hussein Chalayan** 74 (top left), Shaun Curry/AFP/Getty Images; 74 (bottom), Giannoni/WWD; © Conde Nast; 74 (top right), Chalayan A/W 2000/2001, Photograph by Niall McInerney, Bloomsbury Fashion Photography Archive; **Gabrielle "Coco" Chanel** 75 (top right), Horst P. Horst © 1937; 75 (bottom left), Edward Steichen © 1928; 76 (bottom right), Giannoni/WWD; © Conde Nast; 76 (top right), Popperfoto/Getty Images; 76 (bottom left), Giannoni/WWD; © Conde Nast; **Edna Woolman Chase** 77, Brown Brothers © 1918; **Madeline Chéruit** 78 (top), Edward Steichen © 1927; 78 (bottom), Baron Adolphe De Meyer © 1921; **Chloé** 79 (top left), Michel Dufour/WireImage; 79 (bottom right), Giannoni/WWD; © Conde Nast; **Eudon Choi** 80 (top right), Eamonn McCormach/Getty Images; 80 (bottom left), Eamonn McCormach/Getty Images; **Jimmy Choo** 81 (top left), Gareth Cattermole/Getty Images; 81 (bottom right), Giannoni/WWD; © Conde Nast; **Doo-Ri Chung** 82 (top right), Aquino/WWD; © Conde Nast; 82 (bottom right), Giannoni/WWD; © Conde Nast; 82 (bottom left), Giannoni/WWD; © Conde Nast; **Liz Claiborne** 83 (top left), Courtesy of Fairchild Publications, Inc.; 83 (bottom right), Kourken Pakchanian © 1972; **Ossie Clark** 84 (top right), Evening Standard; 84 (bottom left), Frank Barratt/Hulton Archive/Getty Images; **Clements Ribeiro** 85 (top left), Francois Guillot/AFP/Getty Images; 85 (top right), Giannoni/WWD; © Conde Nast; **Grace Coddington** 86, Eichner/WWD; © Conde Nast; **Anne Cole** 87 (top left), Courtesy of Fairchild Publications, Inc.; 87 (bottom right), Courtesy of Fairchild Publications, Inc.; **Kenneth Cole** 88 (top right), Courtesy of Fairchild Publications, Inc.; 88 (bottom right), Iannaccone/WWD; © Conde Nast; 88 (bottom left), Courtesy of Fairchild Publications, Inc.; **Esteban Cortázar** 89 (top right), Antonov/WWD; © Conde Nast; 89 (bottom right), Photo Courtesy of Jaime Rubiano; **Francisco Costa** 90 (top right), Eichner/WWD; © Conde Nast; 90 (bottom right), Aquino/WWD; © Conde Nast; 90 (bottom left), Iannaccone/WWD; © Conde Nast; **André Courrèges** 91, Courtesy of the designer/editor/photographer; 91, Courtesy of the designer/editor/photographer; 92, Courtesy of the designer/editor/photographer; 92, Courtesy of the designer/editor/photographer; **Patrick Cox** 93 (top left), Jenkins/W; © Conde Nast; 93 (top right), Courtesy of the designer/editor/photographer; 93 (bottom right), Bloomberg/Getty Images; **House of Creed** 94 (top right), Courtesy of Fairchild Publications, Inc.; 94 (bottom), Popperfoto/Getty Images; 95, © Norman Parkinson/Corbis; **Bill Cunningham** 96, Courtesy of Fairchild Publications, Inc.; **Cushnie et Ochs** 97 (top left), Mitra/WWD; © Conde Nast; 97 (top right), Mitra/WWD; © Conde Nast; 97 (bottom right), Mitra/WWD; © Conde Nast;

Lilly Daché 98 (top right), Erwin Blumenfeld © 1945; 98 (bottom left), John Rawlings © 1946; **Louise Dahl-Wolfe** 99 (bottom right), Time & Life Pictures/Getty Images; 99 (bottom left), Louise Dahl-Wolfe © 1959; **Sandy Dalal** 100 (top right), Mark Segal; 100 (bottom left), firstVIEW.com; **Daryl K** 101 (top left), Chinsee/WWD; © Conde Nast; 101 (bottom left), Rudd/WWD; © Conde Nast; 101 (bottom right), Courtesy of the designer/editor/photographer; Jessica Daves 102, © Conde Nast; **Jean-Charles de Castelbajac** 103 (top right), Giannoni/WWD; © Conde Nast; 103 (bottom right), Courtesy of Fairchild Publications, Inc.; 103 (bottom left), Giannoni/WWD; © Conde Nast; **Oscar de la Renta** 104 (top right), Iannaccone/WWD; © Conde Nast; 105 (bottom right), Giannoni/WWD; © Conde Nast; 105 (bottom left), Aquino/WWD; © Conde Nast; 104 (bottom left), Aquino/WWD; © Conde Nast; **Baron Adolf de Meyer** 106 (top right), George Hoyningen-Huene © 1934; 106 (bottom left), © Christie's Images/CORBIS; **Giles Deacon** 107 (top left), Maitre/WWD; © Conde Nast; 107 (bottom right), Giannoni/WWD; © Conde Nast; 107 (bottom left), Giannoni/WWD; © Conde Nast; **Louis Dell'Olio** 108 (top right), Randy Brooke/WireImage; 108 (bottom left), Courtesy of Fairchild Publications, Inc.; **Diego Della Valle** 109, Lalas/WWD; © Conde Nast; **Patrick Demarchelier** 110, Courtesy of Fairchild Publications, Inc.; **Ann Demeulemeester** 111 (bottom left), Giannoni/WWD; © Conde Nast; 111 (bottom right), Giannoni/WWD; © Conde Nast; 111 (top left), Giannoni/WWD; © Conde Nast; **Pamela Dennis** 112 (top right), AP Photo/Jennifer Graylock; 112 (bottom left), Aquino/WWD; © Conde Nast; **Jean Dessès** 113 (top left), Cecil Beaton © 1963; 113 (bottom left), © Bettmann/CORBIS; 113 (bottom right), Steve Granitz/WireImage; **Collette Dinnigan** 114 (top right), Maestri/WWD; © Conde Nast; 114 (bottom left), Maitre/WWD; © Conde Nast; 114 (bottom right), Cristaldi/WWD; © Conde Nast; **Christian Dior** 115 (top right), © Hulton-Deutsch Collection/CORBIS; 115 (bottom left), © Image copyright © The Metropolitan Museum of Art / Art Resource; 116 (top right), Sardella/WWD; © Conde Nast; 116 (bottom left), Giannoni/WWD; © Conde Nast; **Dolce & Gabbana** 117 (top left), AP Photo/DNR; 117 (bottom left), Giannoni/WWD; © Conde Nast; 117 (bottom right), Jones/WWD; © Conde Nast; **Carrie Donovan** 118, Jack Robinson/Getty Images; **Garance Doré** 119, Eichner/WWD; © Conde Nast; **Jacques Doucet** 120 (bottom), Mary Evans Picture Library; 120 (top right), © The Metropolitan Museum of Art. Image source: Art Resource,

NY; **Dsquared2** 121 (top left), Courtesy of the designer/editor/photographer; 121 (bottom right), Giannoni/WWD; © Conde Nast; 121 (bottom left), Giannoni/WWD; © Conde Nast; **Gilles Dufour** 122 (top right), Foc Kan/WireImage; 122 (bottom right), Iannaccone/WWD; © Conde Nast; 122 (bottom left), Iannaccone/WWD; © Conde Nast; **Randolph Duke** 123 (top left), Frazer Harrison/Getty Images for IMG; 123 (bottom left), Sardella/WWD; © Conde Nast; 123 (bottom right), Sardella/WWD; © Conde Nast; **Stephen Dweck** 124 (top left), Giannoni/WWD; © Conde Nast; 124 (top right), gorman&gorman; 124 (bottom right), gorman&gorman;

Marc Ecko 125 (top left), Iannaccone/WWD; © Conde Nast; 125 (bottom right), Ericksen/WWD; © Conde Nast; **Florence Eiseman** 126 (top right), Courtesy of the designer/editor/photographer; 126 (bottom right), Courtesy of the designer/editor/photographer; **Alber Elbaz** 127 (top right), Courtesy of Fairchild Publications, Inc.; 127 (top left), Giannoni/WWD; © Conde Nast; 127 (bottom right), Giannoni/WWD; © Conde Nast; **Perry Ellis** 128 (top right), Courtesy of Fairchild Publications, Inc.; 128 (bottom left), Courtesy of Fairchild Publications, Inc.; 129, Perry Ellis, Photograph by Niall McInerney, Bloomsbury Fashion Photography Archive; **Elizabeth Emanuel** 130 (top right), © Hulton-Deutsch Collection/CORBIS; 130 (bottom right), Courtesy of the designer; 130 (bottom left), © Bettmann/CORBIS; **Eric** 131 (top left), Courtesy of Fairchild Publications, Inc.; 131 (bottom right), Courtesy of Fairchild Publications, Inc.; **Erté** 132 (top right), Bernard Gotfryd/Getty Images; 132 (bottom right), © Bettmann/CORBIS; **Etro** 133 (top left), Tombolini/WWD; © Conde Nast; 133 (bottom right), Miranda/WWD; © Conde Nast; 133 (bottom left), Maestri/WWD; © Conde Nast

Max Factor 134 (top right), Getty Images Inc./Allure © Conde Nast; 134 (bottom right), Nelson/WWD; © Conde Nast; **John B. Fairchild** 135, Bob Peterson/Time Life Pictures/Getty Images; **Jacques Fath** 136 (top left), © Genevieve Naylor/Corbis; 136 (bottom right), Rawlingsi/WWD; © Conde Nast; **Fendi** 137 (top left), © Andreea Angelescu/Corbis; 137 (bottom left), Giannoni/WWD; © Conde Nast; 137 (top right), Fendi A/W 1998/1999, Photograph by Niall McInerney, Bloomsbury Fashion Photography Archive; **Louis Féraud** 138 (top left), © Thierry Orban/Sygma/Corbis; 138 (top right), © Pierre Vauthey/Sygma/Corbis; **Salvatore Ferragamo** 139 (top left), © David Lees/Corbis; 139 (top right), © Massimo Listri/Corbis; 139 (bottom right), Chalayan A/W 1993/1994, Photograph by Niall McInerney, Bloomsbury Fashion Photography Archive; **Gianfranco Ferré** 140 (top right), Courtesy of Fairchild Publications, Inc.; 140 (bottom left), Giannoni/WWD; © Conde Nast; 140 (bottom right), Miranda/WWD; © Conde Nast; **Alberta Ferretti** 141 (top

Nast; 192 (bottom right), Eichner/WWD; © Conde Nast; **Wolfgang Joop** 193 (top left), Courtesy of the designer; 193 (bottom left), Maitre/WWD; © Conde Nast; 193 (bottom right), Joop S/S 1996, Photograph by Niall McInerney, Bloomsbury Fashion Photography Archive

Norma Kamali 194 (top right), Iannaccone/WWD; © Conde Nast; 194 (bottom left), Iannaccone/WWD; © Conde Nast; 195 (top left), Iannaccone/WWD; © Conde Nast; 195 (bottom right), Iannaccone/WWD; © Conde Nast; **Christopher Kane** 196 (top right), Giannoni/WWD; © Conde Nast; 196 (bottom left), Giannoni/WWD; © Conde Nast; **Karl Kani** 197 (top left), Iannaccone/WWD; © Conde Nast; 197 (bottom right), Photo by Ben Rose/WireImage for BMI Nashville; **Donna Karan** 198 (top right), Centano/WWD; © Conde Nast; 199 (top left), Iannaccone/WWD; © Conde Nast; 199 (top right), Aquino/WWD; © Conde Nast; 199 (bottom right), Aquino/WWD; © Conde Nast; 198 (bottom left), Photo by Seth Sabal/Courtesy of Donna Karan; **Rei Kawakubo** 200 (top left), Courtesy of Fairchild Publications, Inc.; 200 (top right), Courtesy of Fairchild Publications, Inc.; 200 (bottom right), Giannoni/WWD; © Conde Nast; **Elizabeth Keckley** 201 (bottom left), Hulton Archive/Getty Images; 201 (top right), Library of Congress/Getty Images; **Patrick Kelly** 202 (top left), © Julio Donoso/Sygma/Corbis; 202 (bottom right), Patrick Kelly S/S 1989, Photograph by Niall McInerney, Bloomsbury Fashion Photography Archive; 202 (top right), Patrick Kelly S/S 1989, Photograph by Niall McInerney, Bloomsbury Fashion Photography Archive; **Kenzo** 203 (top left), Giannoni/WWD; © Conde Nast; 203 (top right), Giannoni/WWD; © Conde Nast; 203 (bottom left), Giannoni/WWD; © Conde Nast; **Naeem Khan** 204 (bottom left), Mitra/WWD; © Conde Nast; 204 (top right), Mitra/WWD; © Conde Nast; **Emmanuelle Khanh** 205 (top left), Foc Kan/WireImage/Getty Images; 205 (bottom left), Krausei/WWD; © Conde Nast; 205 (bottom right), © Pierre Vauthey/Sygma/Corbis; **Barry Kieselstein-Cord** 206 (top left), Courtesy of Fairchild Publications, Inc.; 206 (top right), Photo Courtesy of Kieselstein-Cord; **Charles Kleibacker** 207, Columbus Art Museum; **Anne Klein** 208 (top left), David Bailey © 1967; 209, Courtesy of Fairchild Publications, Inc.; 208 (bottom right), Ann Klein S/S 1994, Photograph by Niall McInerney, Bloomsbury Fashion Photography Archive; **Calvin Klein** 210 (top left), Courtesy of Fairchild Publications, Inc.; 210 (bottom right), Giannoni/WWD; © Conde Nast; 211 (bottom left), Courtesy of the Advertising Archive; 211 (top right), Giannoni/WWD; © Conde Nast; **Lloyd Klein** 212 (top right), © Mark Savage/Corbis; 212 (bottom left), Mark Mainz/Getty Images; **Steven Klein** 213, Eichner/WWD; © Conde Nast; **Koos** 214, Courtesy of Fairchild Publications, Inc.; 214, Courtesy of the designer/editor/photographer; **Michael Kors** 215 (top left), Aquino/WWD; © Conde Nast; 215 (bottom right), Giannoni/WWD; © Conde Nast;

215 (bottom left), Ericksen/WWD; © Conde Nast; **Reed Krakoff** 216 (bottom left), Aquino/WWD; © Conde Nast; 216 (top right), Catwalking/Getty Images; **Albert Kriemler** 217 (top left), © Eric Robert/Sygma/Corbis; 217 (bottom left), Giannoni/WWD; © Conde Nast; 217 (bottom right), Giannoni/WWD; © Conde Nast

Christian Lacroix 218 (top left), Courtesy of the designer; 218 (top right), Giannoni/WWD; © Conde Nast; 218 (bottom right), Giannoni/WWD; © Conde Nast; **Karl Lagerfeld** 219 (top left), Maitre/WWD; © Conde Nast; 219 (top right), Giannoni/WWD; © Conde Nast; 220 (top right), Giannoni/WWD; © Conde Nast; 220 (bottom), Feugere/WWD; © Conde Nast; **Derek Lam** 221 (top left), Iannaccone/WWD; © Conde Nast; 221 (top right), Iannaccone/WWD; © Conde Nast; 221 (bottom left), Iannaccone/WWD; © Conde Nast; **L.A.M.B (Gwen Stefani)** 222 (bottom left), Falk/WWD; © Conde Nast; 222 (top right), John Aquino/WWD; © Conde Nast; **Lana** 223, Photo by Jeff Schear/WireImage for Michigan Avenue; **Kenneth Jay Lane** 224 (top right), Eichner/WWD; © Conde Nast; 224 (bottom right), Courtesy of Fairchild Publications, Inc.; 224 (bottom left), Courtesy of Fairchild Publications, Inc.; **Helmut Lang** 224 (top left), Courtesy of Fairchild Publications, Inc.; 224 (bottom right), Giannoni/WWD; © Conde Nast; **Jeanne Lanvin** 226, Horst P. Horst © 1961; **Guy Laroche** 227 (top left), © James Andanson/Sygma/Corbis; 227 (bottom right), © Bettmann/CORBIS; **Byron Lars** 228 (top left), Chinsee/WWD; © Conde Nast; 228 (bottom right), Chinsee/WWD; © Conde Nast; 228 (bottom left), Chinsee/WWD; © Conde Nast; **Estée Lauder** 229 (top left), Tony/WWD; © Conde Nast; 229 (bottom right), Aquinno/WWD; © Conde Nast; **Ralph Lauren** 230 (top right), Courtesy of Fairchild Publications, Inc.; 230 (bottom left), Chinsee/WWD; © Conde Nast; 231 (top left), Giannoni/WWD; © Conde Nast; 231 (bottom left), Aquinno/WWD; © Conde Nast; 230 (bottom right), Aquinno/WWD; © Conde Nast; **Dion Lee** 232 (top right), Photo by Lisa Maree Williams/Getty Images; 232 (bottom left), Iannaccone/WWD; © Conde Nast; 232 (bottom right), Iannaccone/WWD; © Conde Nast; **Judith Leiber** 233 (top left), Antonov/WWD; © Conde Nast; 233 (top right), Mitra/WWD; © Conde Nast; 233 (bottom left), Mitra/WWD; © Conde Nast; **Annie Leibovitz** 234, Eichner/WWD; © Conde Nast; **Lucien Lelong** 235, Robert Doisneau © 1949; **Nanette Lepore** 236 (top right), Aquino/WWD; © Conde Nast; 236 (bottom left), Mitra+N1014/WWD; © Conde Nast; **Herve L. Leroux** 237 (top left), Giannoni/WWD; © Conde Nast; 237 (bottom right), Giannoni/WWD; © Conde Nast; 237 (bottom left), Courtesy of the designer/editor/photographer; **Monique Lhuillier** 238 (top right), Courtesy of Catwalking; 238 (bottom left), Chinsee/WWD; © Conde Nast; 239 (top left), Chinsee/WWD; © Conde Nast; 239 (bottom right),

Getty Images; 292 (top right), Giannoni/WWD; © Conde Nast; 292 (bottom left), Rifat Ozbeck A/W 1999/2000, Photograph by Niall McInerney, Bloomsbury Fashion Photography Archive

Thakoon Panichgul 293 (top left), Aquino/WWD; © Conde Nast; 293 (bottom left), Mitra/WWD; © Conde Nast; 293 (bottom right), Iannoccone/WWD; © Conde Nast; **Paquin** 294 (top right), Edward Steichen © 1928; 294 (bottom left), Mary Evans Picture Library; **Jean Patou** 295 (top left), Seeberger Freres/Getty Images; 295 (bottom right), Image copyright © The Metropolitan Museum of Art. Image source: Art Resource, NY; **Irving Penn** 296, John Rawlings © 1945; **Elsa Peretti** 297, Bailey/WWD; © Conde Nast; **Phoebe Philo** 298 (top right), Courtesy of Fairchild Publications, Inc.; 298 (bottom left), Giannoni/WWD; © Conde Nast; 298 (bottom right), Giannoni/WWD; © Conde Nast; **Paloma Picasso** 299, © Odile Montserrat/Sygma/Corbis; **Stefano Pilati** 300 (top right), Eichner/WWD; © Conde Nast; 300 (bottom left), Maestri/WWD; © Conde Nast; 300 (bottom right), Giannoni/WWD; © Conde Nast; **Donald Pliner** 301 (top left), Courtesy of Fairchild Publications, Inc.; 301 (bottom right), Amanda Edwards/Getty Images; **Walter Plunkett** 302 (top right), PW Design/University of Texas; 302 (bottom left), Everett Collection; **Paul Poiret** 303 (top left), Photo by Lipnitzki/Roger Viollet/Getty Images; 303 (bottom right), © Underwood & Underwood/Corbis; 304 (bottom left), V&A Images, London / Art Resource, NY. © 2014 Artists Rights Society (ARS), New York / ADAGP, Paris; 304 (top right), V&A Images, London / Art Resource, NY; **Zac Posen** 306 (top left), Iannoccone/WWD; © Conde Nast; 306 (bottom left), Chinsee/WWD; © Conde Nast; **Sandy Powell** 307 (top left), Photo by Alain BENAINOUS/Gamma-Rapho via Getty Images; 307 (bottom right), Photo by Michel Boutefeu/Getty Images; **Miuccia Prada** 308 (top right), Eichner/WWD; © Conde Nast; 308 (bottom right), Lalas/WWD; © Conde Nast; 308 (bottom left), Lalas/WWD; © Conde Nast; **Preen (Thornton Bregazzi)** 309 (top left), Giannoni/WWD; © Conde Nast; 309 (bottom right), Giannoni/WWD; © Conde Nast; **Candy Pratts Price** 310, Seckler/WWD; © Conde Nast; **Proenza Schouler** 311 (bottom right), Chinsee/WWD; © Conde Nast; 311 (top left), Giannoni/WWD; © Conde Nast; **Emilio Pucci** 312 (top right), © David Lees/Corbis; 312 (bottom left), Henry Clarke © 1966; **Gareth Pugh** 313 (top left), Eichner/WWD; © Conde Nast; 313 (bottom left), Giannoni/WWD; © Conde Nast; 313 (bottom right), Courtesy of Fairchild Publications, Inc.; **Lilly Pulitzer** 314 (top right), Nick/WWD; © Conde Nast; 314 (bottom left), © Reuters/CORBIS

Mary Quant 315, Photo by Terry Smith/Time Life Pictures/Getty Images

Paco Rabanne 316 (top right), © Eric Robert/VIP Production; 316 (top left), © Conde Nast; 316 (bottom right), Photo by Keystone/Getty Images; **Rag & Bone** 317 (top left), Iannacconei/WWD; © Conde Nast; 317 (bottom right), Giannoni/WWD; © Conde Nast; **John Rawlings** 318 (top right), © Conde Nast; 318 (bottom left), John Rawlings © 1943; **Tracy Reese** 319 (top left), Chinsee/WWD; © Conde Nast; 319 (bottom left), © Charles Dharapak/AP/Corbis; 319 (bottom right), Chinsee/WWD; © Conde Nast; **Zandra Rhodes** 320 (top left), Hill/WWD; © Conde Nast; 320 (bottom right), Hill/WWD; © Conde Nast; 321, © Danny Chan/Demotix/Corbis; **Nina Ricci** 323 (bottom left), Courtesy of Fairchild Publications, Inc.; 322, AFP/AFP/Getty Images; 323 (top right), Mitra/WWD; © Conde Nast; 323 (top left), Giannoni/WWD; © Conde Nast; **Judith Ripka** 324 (top right), Eichner/WWD; © Conde Nast; 324 (top left), Getty Images for Judith Ripka; **Herb Ritts** 325, © Beth Herzhaft; **Simone Rocha** 326 (top right), Photo by Victor Boyko/Getty Images for I.T. Limited; 326 (bottom left), Giannoni/WWD; © Conde Nast; 326 (bottom right), Giannoni/WWD; © Conde Nast; **Rodarte** 327 (top left), Chinsee/WWD; © Conde Nast; 327 (top right), Courtesy of Fairchild Publications, Inc.; 327 (bottom right), Chinsee/WWD; © Conde Nast; **Narciso Rodriguez** 328 (top right), Chinsee/WWD; © Conde Nast; 328 (bottom left), Aquino/WWD; © Conde Nast; **Carine Roitfeld** 329, Ericksen/WWD; © Conde Nast; **Lela Rose** 330 (top right), Iannaccone/WWD; © Conde Nast; 330 (bottom left), Iannaccone/WWD; © Conde Nast; 330 (bottom right), Iannaccone/WWD; © Conde Nast; **Renzo Rosso** 331 (top left), Courtesy of Fairchild Publications, Inc.; 331 (bottom right), Aquino/WWD; © Conde Nast; 331 (bottom left), Chinsee/WWD; © Conde Nast; **Maggy Rouff** 332 (top right), Photo by David E. Scherman/Time & Life Pictures/Getty Images; 332 (bottom left), © Bettmann/CORBIS; 332 (bottom right), © AP/Corbis; **The Row (Mary Kate and Ashley Olsen)** 333 (top left), Chinsee/WWD; © Conde Nast; 333 (bottom right), Giannoni/WWD; © Conde Nast; **Cynthia Rowley** 334 (top right), Aquino/WWD; © Conde Nast; 334 (bottom left), Iannaccone/WWD; © Conde Nast; **Rachel Roy** 335 (top left), Iannaccone/WWD; © Conde Nast; 335 (bottom right), Iannaccone/WWD; © Conde Nast; **Helena Rubinstein** 336, Aquino/WWD; © Conde Nast; **Chado Ralph Rucci** 337 (top left), Courtesy of Fairchild Publications, Inc.; 337 (bottom left), Iannaccone/WWD; © Conde Nast; 337 (top right), Chinsee/WWD; © Conde Nast; **Sonia Rykiel** 338, Courtesy of Fairchild Publications, Inc.

Elie Saab 339 (top left), Giannoni/WWD; © Conde Nast; 339 (bottom right), Giannoni/WWD; © Conde Nast; 340 (bottom), Giannoni/WWD; © Conde Nast; 340 (top right), Giannoni/WWD; © Conde Nast; **Yves Saint Laurent** 341 (top left), Yves Saint Laurent A/W 1991/1992, Photograph by Niall McInerney, Bloomsbury Fashion Photography Archive; 341 (bottom right), © Hulton-Deutsch Collection/CORBIS; 342 (bottom), © Fairchild Photo Service/Condé Nast/Corbis; 342 (top right), © Reuters; **Jil Sander** 343 (top left), Giannoni/WWD; © Conde Nast; 343 (bottom right), Giannoni/WWD; © Conde Nast; **Giorgio Sant'Angelo** 344 (top left), Palmieri/WWD; © Conde Nast; 344 (bottom right), Courtesy of Fairchild Publications, Inc.; **Behnaz Sarafpour** 345 (top left), Antonov/WWD; © Conde Nast; 345 (bottom right), Courtesy of Fairchild Publications, Inc.; **Jonathan Saunders** 345 (bottom left), Antonove/WWD; © Conde Nast; 346 (top right), Iannaccone/WWD; © Conde Nast; 346 (bottom left), Giannoni/WWD; © Conde Nast; 346 (bottom right), Giannoni/WWD; © Conde Nast; **Arnold Scaasi** 347 (top left), Iannaccone/WWD; © Conde Nast; 347 (bottom right), Horst P. Horst © 1966; **Elsa Schiaparelli** 348 (top right), Fredrich Baker © 1940; 348 (bottom left), © Philadelphia Museum of Art/CORBIS; 349 (top right), © Philadelphia Museum of Art/CORBIS; 349 (bottom left), Giannoni/WWD; © Conde Nast; **Scott Schuman** 350, Dabrowskii/WWD; © Conde Nast; **Jeremy Scott** 351 (top left), Chinsee/WWD; © Conde Nast; 351 (bottom left), Iannaccone/WWD; © Conde Nast; 351 (bottom right), Iannaccone/WWD; © Conde Nast; **Sean John** 352 (top right), Courtesy of Fairchild Publications, Inc.; 352 (bottom left), Eichner/WWD; © Conde Nast; **Ronaldus Shamask** 353 (top left), Iannaccone/WWD; © Conde Nast; 353 (bottom right), Chinsee/WWD; © Conde Nast; 353 (bottom left), Shamask S/S 1990, Photograph by Niall McInerney, Bloomsbury Fashion Photography Archive; **Irene Sharaff** 354 (top right), 20TH CENTURY FOX / THE KOBAL COLLECTION; 354 (bottom left), 20TH CENTURY FOX / THE KOBAL COLLECTION; **Raf Simons** 355 (top left), Dabrowski/WWD; © Conde Nast; 355 (bottom right), Giannoni/WWD; © Conde Nast; **Christian Siriano** 356 (top left), Iannaccone/WWD; © Conde Nast; 356 (bottom right), Theo Wargo/WireImage; **Martine Sitbon** 357 (top left), Giannoni/WWD; © Conde Nast; 357 (bottom left), © Frédéric Huijbregts CORBIS; 357 (bottom right), Giannoni/WWD; © Conde Nast; **Hedi Slimane** 358 (top right), Courtesy of Fairchild Publications, Inc.; 358 (bottom left), Courtesy of Fairchild Publications, Inc.; 358 (bottom right), Giannoni/WWD; © Conde Nast; **Paul Smith** 359 (top left), Dabrowski/WWD; © Conde Nast; 359 (top right), Giannoni/WWD; © Conde Nast; 359 (bottom left), Giannoni/WWD; © Conde Nast; **Willi Smith** 360 (top right), © Bettmann/CORBIS; 360 (bottom left), © Bettmann/Corbis; **Carmel Snow** 361, Photo by Walter Sanders/Time & Life Pictures/Getty Images; **Peter Som** 362 (top right), Aquino/WWD; © Conde Nast; 362 (bottom left), Mitra/WWD; © Conde Nast; **Kate Spade** 363 (top left), Eichner/WWD; © Conde Nast; 363 (bottom right), Ericksen/WWD; © Conde Nast; 363 (top right), Eichner/WWD; © Conde Nast; **Edward Steichen** 364 (top right),

Irving Penn © 1948; 364 (bottom left), Edward Steichen © 1928; **Walter Steiger** 365 (top left), Ericksen/N603WWD; © Conde Nast; 365 (bottom right), Aquino/WWD; © Conde Nast; **Jill Stuart** 366 (top right), Giannoni/WWD; © Conde Nast; 366 (bottom right), Giannoni/WWD; © Conde Nast; 366 (bottom left), Chinsee/WWD; © Conde Nast; **Anna Sui** 367 (top left), Chinsee/WWD; © Conde Nast; 368 (top right), Mitra/WWD; © Conde Nast; 368 (bottom left), Mitra/WWD; © Conde Nast; 367 (bottom right), Anna Sui A/W 1999/2000, Photograph by Niall McInerney, Bloomsbury Fashion Photography Archive; **Brandon Sun** 369 (top left), Eichner/WWD; © Conde Nast; 369 (bottom right), Eichner/WWD; © Conde Nast; 369 (bottom left), Iannaccone/WWD; © Conde Nast

Elie Tahari 370 (top right), Aquino/WWD; © Conde Nast; 370 (bottom left), Aquino/WWD; © Conde Nast; 370 (bottom right), Chinsee/WWD; © Conde Nast; **André Leon Talley** 371, Eichner/WWD; © Conde Nast), **Vivienne Tam** 372 (top right), Ericksen/WWD; © Conde Nast; 372 (bottom right), Mitra/WWD; © Conde Nast; 372 (top left), Ericksen/WWD; © Conde Nast; **Mario Testino** 373, Courtesy of Fairchild Publications, Inc.; **Olivier Theyskens** 374 (top right), Courtesy of Fairchild Publications, Inc.; 374 (bottom left), Iannaccone/WWD; © Conde Nast; **Threeasfour** 375 (top left), Aquino/WWD; © Conde Nast; 375 (bottom right), Chinsee/WWD; © Conde Nast; **Tiffany** 376, © Tiffany & Co.; **Liz Tilberis** 377, © Lynn Goldsmith/Corbis; **Riccardo Tisci** 378 (top right), Eichner/WWD; © Conde Nast; 378 (bottom left), Sardella/WWD; © Conde Nast; **Isabel and Ruben Toledo** 379 (top left), Antonov/WWD; © Conde Nast; 380, © Tannen Maury/Pool/POOL/Corbis; 379 (bottom right), Chinsee/WWD; © Conde Nast; **Philip Treacy** 381 (top left), Photo by Chris Jackson/Getty Images; 381 (bottom right), Giannoni/WWD; © Conde Nast; **Pauline Trigère** 382 (top right), © Bettmann/CORBIS; 382 (bottom left), © Bettmann/CORBIS; **Trina Turk** 383 (top left), Chinsee/WWD; © Conde Nast; 383 (bottom left), Chinsee/WWD; © Conde Nast; 383 (bottom right), Boye/WWD; © Conde Nast; **Richard Tyler** 384 (top left), © Jurgen Frank/Corbis Outline; 384 (bottom left), Sardella/WWD; © Conde Nast; 384 (top right), Richard Tyler S/S 1996, Photograph by Niall McInerney, Bloomsbury Fashion Photography Archive

Unconditional (Philip Stephens) 385, Chinsee/WWD; © Conde Nast; **Patricia Underwood** 386 (top right), K. Terrell/WireImage; 386 (bottom left), © Eric Cahan/Corbis; **Emanuel Ungaro** 387 (top right), Maitre/WWD; © Conde Nast; 388 (bottom left), Maitre/WWD; © Conde Nast; 388 (top right), Maitre/WWD; © Conde Nast; 387 (bottom left), Ungaro S/S 1995/1996, Photograph by Niall McInerney, Bloomsbury Fashion Photography Archive

Valentino 389, Courtesy of Fairchild Publications, Inc.; 390 Courtesy of Fairchild Publications, Inc.; **Giambattista Valli** 391 (top left), Archard/WWD; © Conde Nast; 391 (bottom right), Giannoni/WWD; © Conde Nast; 391 (bottom left), Giannoni/WWD; © Conde Nast; **Dries Van Noten** 392 (top right), Courtesy of Fairchild Publications, Inc.; 392 (bottom left), Giannoni/WWD; © Conde Nast; 392 (bottom right), Giannoni/WWD; © Conde Nast; **John Varvatos** 393 (top left), Aquino/WWD; © Conde Nast; 393 (bottom right), Giannoni/WWD; © Conde Nast; 393 (bottom left), Maestri/WWD; © Conde Nast; **Joan Vass** 394 (top right), Dominique Nabokov © 1987; 394 (bottom left), AP Photo/Mark Lennihan; **Donatella Versace** 395 (top left), Giannoni/WWD; © Conde Nast; 396 (top right), Giannoni/WWD; © Conde Nast; 396 (bottom left), Giannoni/WWD; © Conde Nast; 395 (bottom right), Giannoni/WWD; © Conde Nast; **Gianni Versace** 397 (top left), © Toni Thorimbert/Sygma/Corbis; 397 (top right), Versace S/S 1999, Photograph by Niall McInerney, Bloomsbury Fashion Photography Archive; 397 (bottom right), Versace A/W 1995/1996, Photograph by Niall McInerney, Bloomsbury Fashion Photography Archive; **Viktor & Rolf** 398 (top right), Blommers & Schumm/WWD; © Conde Nast; 398 (bottom left), PIERRE VERDY/AFP/Getty Images; 398 (bottom right), Giannoni/WWD; © Conde Nast; **Madeleine Vionnet** 399 (top left), Roger Viollet/Getty Images; 400 (bottom right), Image copyright © The Metropolitan Museum of Art / Art Resource; 401, Giannoni/WWD; © Conde Nast; 400 (top right), Laure Albin-Guillot/Roger Viollet/Getty Images; 399 (bottom left), Carl Oscar August Erickson © 1937; 400 (bottom left), John Rawlings © 1945; **Roger Vivier** 402 (top right), © Deborah Feingold/Corbis; 402 (bottom left), © Victoria and Albert Museum, London; **Diane Von Furstenberg** 403 (top left), Eichner/WWD; © Conde Nast; 404 (top left), Chinsee/WWD; © Conde Nast; 403 (bottom right), Chinsee/WWD; © Conde Nast; 404 (bottom right), Courtesy of the designer/editor/photographer; **Ella Von Unwerth** 405, Eichner/WWD; © Conde Nast; **Diana Vreeland** 406, Bernard Gotfryd/Getty Images; **Louis Vuitton** 407, Peter Kramer/Getty Images

Karen Walker 408 (top right), Aquino/WWD; © Conde Nast; 408 (bottom left), Giannoni/WWD; © Conde Nast; 408 (bottom right), Giannoni/WWD; © Conde Nast;

Alexander Wang 409 (top left), Courtesy of Fairchild Publications, Inc.; 409 (bottom left), Giannoni/WWD; © Conde Nast; 409 (bottom right), Giannoni/WWD; © Conde Nast; **Vera Wang** 410, Aquino/WWD; © Conde Nast; 411 (bottom left), Aquino/WWD; © Conde Nast; 411 (top right), Iannaccone/WWD; © Conde Nast; **Bruce Weber** 412, Courtesy of Fairchild Publications, Inc.; **Stuart Weitzman** 413 (top left), Mark Sullivan/WireImage; 413 (bottom right), Toby Canham/Getty; 413 (top right), Aquino/WWD; © Conde Nast; **Vivienne Westwood** 414 (top left), Courtesy of Fairchild Publications, Inc.; 414 (top right), Giannoni/WWD; © Conde Nast; 414 (bottom right), Giannoni/WWD; © Conde Nast; **Edward Wilkerson** 415 (top left), Steve Mack/FilmMagic; 415 (bottom right), Photo Courtesy of But Sou Lai; **Matthew Williamson** 416 (top left), Giannoni/WWD; © Conde Nast; 416 (top right), Giannoni/WWD; © Conde Nast; 416 (bottom left), Miranda/WWD; © Conde Nast; **Harry Winston** 417, Eichner/WWD; © Conde Nast; **Anna Wintour** 418, Mark Peterson; **Charles Frederick Worth** 419 (top right), Bibliotheque des Arts Decoratifs, Paris, France/Archives Charmet; 419 (bottom left), Image copyright © The Metropolitan Museum of Art. Image source: Art Resource, NY; 420, Image copyright © The Metropolitan Museum of Art. Image source: Art Resource, NY; **Jason Wu** 421 (bottom right, Courtesy of Fairchild Publications, Inc.; 421 (top left), Mark Wilson/Getty Images; 421 (bottom left), Chinsee/WWD; © Conde Nast;

Yohji Yamamoto 422 (top right), Seckler/WWD; © Conde Nast; 422 (bottom left), Giannoni/WWD; © Conde Nast; 422 (bottom right), Centano/WWD; © Conde Nast; **Yeohlee** 423 (top left), Seckler/WWD; © Conde Nast; 423 (bottom right), Chinsee/WWD; © Conde Nast; **Christina Yu (Ipa-Nima)** 424 (top right), Photo Courtesy of Ipa-Nima; **David Yurman** 425 (top left), Aquino/WWD; © Conde Nast; 425 (top right), Iannaccone/WWD; © Conde Nast; 425 (bottom right), Gurjian-AngeloIannaccone/Teen Vogue; © Conde Nast

Zang Toi 426 (top right), © Zack Seckler/Corbis; 426 (bottom left), Chinsee/WWD; © Conde Nast; **Izak Zenou** 427, Getty Images for Henri Bendel